Applied Economics and Policy Studies

Series Editors

Xuezheng Qin , *School of Economics, Peking University, Beijing, China*
Chunhui Yuan, *School of Economics and Management, Beijing University of Posts and Telecommunications, Beijing, China*
Xiaolong Li, *Department of Postal Management, Beijing University of Posts and Telecommunications, Beijing, China*

The Applied Economics and Policy Studies present latest theoretical and methodological discussions to bear on the scholarly works covering economic theories, econometric analyses, as well as multifaceted issues arising out of emerging concerns from different industries and debates surrounding latest policies. Situated at the forefront of the interdisciplinary fields of applied economics and policy studies, this book series seeks to bring together the scholarly insights centering on economic development, infrastructure development, macroeconomic policy, governance of welfare policy, policies and governance of emerging markets, and relevant subfields that trace to the discipline of applied economics, public policy, policy studies, and combined fields of the aforementioned. The book series of Applied Economics and Policy Studies is dedicated to the gathering of intellectual views by scholars and poli-cymakers. The publications included are relevant for scholars, policymakers, and students of economics, policy studies, and otherwise interdisciplinary programs.

Xiaolong Li · Chunhui Yuan · John Kent
Editors

Proceedings of the 7th International Conference on Economic Management and Green Development

Set 1

Editors
Xiaolong Li
Department of Postal Management
Beijing University of Posts
and Telecommunications
Beijing, China

Chunhui Yuan
School of Economics and Management
Beijing University of Posts
and Telecommunications
Beijing, China

John Kent
Supply Chain Management
University of Arkansas
Fayetteville, NC, USA

ISSN 2731-4006 ISSN 2731-4014 (electronic)
Applied Economics and Policy Studies
ISBN 978-981-97-0522-1 ISBN 978-981-97-0523-8 (eBook)
https://doi.org/10.1007/978-981-97-0523-8

© The Editor(s) (if applicable) and The Author(s), under exclusive license to Springer Nature Singapore Pte Ltd. 2024

This work is subject to copyright. All rights are solely and exclusively licensed by the Publisher, whether the whole or part of the material is concerned, specifically the rights of translation, reprinting, reuse of illustrations, recitation, broadcasting, reproduction on microfilms or in any other physical way, and transmission or information storage and retrieval, electronic adaptation, computer software, or by similar or dissimilar methodology now known or hereafter developed.
The use of general descriptive names, registered names, trademarks, service marks, etc. in this publication does not imply, even in the absence of a specific statement, that such names are exempt from the relevant protective laws and regulations and therefore free for general use.
The publisher, the authors, and the editors are safe to assume that the advice and information in this book are believed to be true and accurate at the date of publication. Neither the publisher nor the authors or the editors give a warranty, expressed or implied, with respect to the material contained herein or for any errors or omissions that may have been made. The publisher remains neutral with regard to jurisdictional claims in published maps and institutional affiliations.

This Springer imprint is published by the registered company Springer Nature Singapore Pte Ltd.
The registered company address is: 152 Beach Road, #21-01/04 Gateway East, Singapore 189721, Singapore

Paper in this product is recyclable.

Contents

International NGO Issues on Female Migrant Workers 1
   Yinwei Li

Time Lagged Effects of ESG Scores and Investor Attention on Stock Returns 9
   Jiaqi Liu

Analyzing Reasons for the Selection of Investment Objects Based on the Construction of Enterprise Ecological Value Network 18
   Caixiaoyang Ge

Analysis of the Motivation and Performance of Merger and Reorganization of Companies Under Performance Commitment--Based on the Dual Case Study of DF Company's Acquisition of Pride and Fosber 27
   Liu Yu

Monetary Policy Regulation and Macroeconomic Fluctuations—Empirical Research Based on VAR Model 41
   Xiaochen Liu

Recession Risk Prediction with Machine Learning and Big Panel Data 63
   Yunhao Yang

Investigate the Relationship Between Financial Risk and Financial Performance: An Insight of China Life Insurance Company 88
   Shikang Wang

Model Innovation and Value Creation in E-commerce Platform Ecosystems: A Case Study of Douyin 98
   Jiahang Hu and Yiming Zhong

An Investigation into the Relationship Between Transportation Network and Economic Agglomeration 108
   Chenhao Zheng

A Study of the Dual Carbon Target and Green Finance Development in Jiangxi Province 119
   Liwen Dai

Dynamic Correlation, Volatility Spillover Inside UK Capital Markets 129
Mingze Yuan and Ziqi Guo

Challenges and Opportunities of Digital Construction of Chinese
Grassroots Government in the Information Age – Taking
the Construction of "Four Platforms" in Zhejiang Province as an Example 137
Zhuofan Zong

Research on the Impact of Digitalization on Individual Investors'
Behavior from the Perspective of Behavioral Finance 146
Zhihan Zhao

A Review of ESG Research in China: From the Perspective of Chinese
Enterprises 155
Daoer Wang

PIC Planning Model and Geographic Information System Applied
on the Old District Renovation Using Intelligent Data Analysis 168
Junyuan Li, Zihao Ma, and Xiyuan Zhang

Agriculture Trade Competitiveness, and Influencing Economic Factors:
A Study on China's Agricultural Trade 180
Benjamin Kofi Tawiah Edjah

Financial Cloud Drives Digital Transformation of Enterprises:
——Taking Hisense's Application of Kingdee Financial Cloud
as an Example 188
BoYong Chen and Zhuohao Zhang

Study on the Influence of Rural Revitalization on Regional Tourism
Development: An Empirical Analysis Based on the Data of 16
Prefectures in Yunnan Province 199
Qing Wang

The Discussion of the Impact on the Stock Price After the Comments
or Recommendations from Stock Analysts–The Case Study on EV Stocks 214
Jiaxi Zhang

The Effects of Transforming the CDMO Strategy on the Business
Performance of Porton Based on Financial Statement Analysis 224
Lei Zhang

Economic Policy Uncertainty, ESG, and Corporate Performance 235
Fumian Huang

Identification and Analysis of Risk Spillover Effect of Commercial
Banks in China 247
   Moran Wang

Case Analysis of Kingfisher PLC's Operational Quality Based
on the Perspective of Financial Report 253
   Xinyi Song

Comedic Violence Advertisement and Limiting Factors 262
   Yuting Tong

The Impacts of Goal Setting on Enterprises from a Corporate Social
Responsibility Perspective 273
   Yu Chen

Behavioral Economics and Macroeconomics: Relationship Identification
by Case of Economy Crisis in 2008 280
   Haocheng Yan

The Impact of Endogenous Sentiment on US Stock Market Trading
Volume 291
   Lvqin Huang

The Factors Affecting Electric Vehicle Adoption in the United States,
2016–2021 299
   Qing Hou, Shuai Zhou, and Guangqing Chi

Assessing Endowment Effect in Different Cooperative Settings 307
   Fengyi Zhang

The Primary Performance Trait of Corporations with High Managerial
Short-Termism 314
   Yuping Wang

Research on the Factors Affecting Inequality – Evidence from China . 321
   Gengqiang Xiao

Accounting Measurement and Recognition of Digital Cryptocurrencies:
Challenges, Practices, and Recommendations 328
   Jiajun Ma

Study on the Spillover Effect of Shanghai Crude Oil Futures Price
Fluctuations on New Energy Stock Prices 338
   Zhang Xinyu

Exploring the Impact of Social Economic Status on Migrant Workers'
Sense of Social Equity from the Economic Sociology Perspective 350
   Hu Xinrui

Microeconomic Study of the Digital Economy's Importance
on Manufacturers' Management 365
   Yuyan Wang

Fintech Development and Corporate Innovation 373
   Chen Huan

Analysts' Characteristics and Forecast ability–An Empirical Study
from China's A-Share Market 382
   Mengyan Lei

Is There Salary Discrimination by Race and Nationality in the NBA?
A New Approach 391
   JiaYou Liang, ShuaiJie Zhao, and HaoYuan Zhu

Choice Overload Paradox in Online Shopping Environment 400
   Jiaxin Wang, Fang Han, Manting Ding, and Jia Zhang

The Influence of Endowment Effect on the Investment Decisions
in Hybrid Funds 414
   Huiqi Zhang

Research on Empowering Huawei's Financial Transformation
by Financial Shared Service Center 421
   Yiru Su

A Study on the Relevance of Corporate Solvency – A Case Study
of Procter & Gamble 431
   Huangzhiyi Zhang

ESG Performance Under Economic Policy Uncertainty: An Empirical
Study of Chinese Corporations 443
   Song Qiuge

Relationship Between Macroeconomy and Stock Market in the United
States 456
   Lixiang Zheng

Research on the Activated Utilization and Digital Innovation Development of Cultural Heritage Under the Concept of Sustainable Development 466
   Yuting Yu

Analysis of the Reasons for the Development of the New Energy Vehicle Industry and Prospects —Taking BYD as an Example 478
   Boyu Liu

Challenges of Stock Prediction Based on LSTM Neural Network 490
   Rufeng Chen

Explore the Impact of Natural Factors on the Use of Shared Bicycles 500
   Liu Jiamei

Economic Dynamics Analysis of Higher Education Development 511
   Tian Mo

The Impact of Fintech on Enterprise Innovation: Take Companies that Issue Fintech Concept Stocks as an Example 521
   Yuyao Sun

Resilience Assessment of the South-to-North Water Diversion Central Route Project by Using Urban Futures Method 534
   Qiaozhi Zhang

Research on Factors Influencing the Rewarding Behavior of Virtual Anchors' Fans 544
   Xinran Zhao

Analyzing the Reasons of BYD's Low-Profit Margin Through Financial Data 555
   Tianqi Ma

Analysis and Forecast of USD/EUR Exchange Rate Based on ARIMA and GARCH Models 566
   Jiatong Li, Jiawen Yin, and Rui Zhang

Forecasts on Euro-to-USD Exchange Rate Based on the ARIMA Model 576
   Qiaoyu Xie

Analysis and Forecasting of Exchange Rate Between Yuan and Dollar 588
   Sitian Yi

Forecast of China's Real Estate Industry Development Situation Based
on ARIMA Model: Taking Vanke as an Example 598
   Xiangyu Li

US Trade Balance Analysis on Imports and Exports Based on ETS
and ARIMA Models 611
   Shiqi Fan

Research on the Factors Affecting Mobility Rate Across States
in the United States 626
   Xinyu Shi

Exploring the Risks of Blockchain to the Financial Market and Its
Countermeasures 633
   Yujiang Duan, Fengfan Ge, and Zhixing Wen

To a Decentralized Future: Benefits that Blockchain Could Endow
the Financing World 642
   Yiping Li, Yuqing Liu, Ruixuan Sun, and Zihui Xu

Relevance Between ESG Scores and Annual Turnover: Evidence
from 453 Industrial Hong Kong Stocks 652
   Nanqi Liu, Changyou Qi, and Junjie Zhuge

How Does Years Since Immigration to the U.S.A. Affect Hourly Wage? 662
   Shizhe Lyu

A Controversy in Sustainable Development: How Does Gender
Diversity Affect the ESG Disclosure? 669
   Bolin Fu, Keqing Wang, and Tianxin Zhou

Controlling Shareholders' Equity Pledges, Environmental Regulations
and Corporate Green Performance—Based on Data from Listed
Companies in Highly Polluting Industries 679
   Mingfei Chen

ESG Performance's Effect on the Firm Performance the Evidence
from Chinese A-share Market 690
   Liqi Dong

The Factors Influence Purchase Intentions from the Consumer's
Perspective and the Characteristics of Green Buyers 702
   Ziyao Yang

A Study on the Motivation and Financial Performance of Haidilao's
Equity Crave-Out 716
   Tingxuan Dong

Study on the Reasons for the Failure of the Audit of Luckin Coffee
and Suggestions for Countermeasures 729
   Yufan Li

Baidu's Financial Competitiveness Research Based on DuPont Analysis
Method 738
   Yuqing Zhang

The Impact of COVID-19 on the Aviation Industry: Event Study on U.S.
Passenger Airline Stocks 752
   Yuxin Chen and Ziqing Gong

Predicting Customer Churn in a Telecommunications Company Using
Machine Learning 771
   Yinming Wu

Research on Real Estate Price Index Forecasting Based on ARIMA
Model: Taking Los Angeles as an Example 784
   Xiao Han

Research on the Reasons for Abnormal Changes in the Operation Status
of Domino's Pizza 796
   Yining Feng, Yunong Li, Jingyu Qin, and Yuankai Tao

Detect the Change Points in the Growth Rate of US Real Export Data
Based on Mean and Variance 804
   Yiwei Zhang

Forecasting the Stock Market Index with Dynamic ARIMA Model
and LSTM Model 815
   Siyuan Zhu

Public Goods Game Based on the Combination Model of Reputation
and Punishment 828
   Qing Liu

The Stylized Facts of Income Inequality in Mainland China, Korea
and Taiwan: Development and Comparison 836
   Yanshu Wang

Factors Influence Loan Default–A Credit Risk Analysis 849
  Xianya Qi

An Empirical Analysis of the Causal Relationship Between Equity
Incentives and Idiosyncratic Volatility in Chinese A-Share Listed
Companies 863
  Zhaoxuan Gan

An Empirical Analysis of the Relationship Between Chinese GDP
and Deposit Savings 873
  Yichuan Bai

FinTech Promotes the Development of Green Finance 885
  Heqing Huang and Qijie Yang

Comprehensive Analysis of China's Local Government Financing
Vehicle Debt 893
  Zihao Tang

The Relationship Between ESG Ratings and Financial Performance
of Coal Firms — the Case of China Shenhua and China Coal Energy 903
  Aimiao Zhang

Research on the Impact of Regulatory Inquiries Related to Information
Disclosure of Listed Companies – A Case Study of ANDON HEALTH 915
  Miaoxuan Ma

Research on Financial Competitiveness of a Listed Company Based
on DuPont Analysis Method 925
  Yile Kong and Xitong Zhu

Time Series Analysis in Pfizer Stock Prices in the Pre-
and Post-COVID-19 Scenarios 937
  Rixin Su

Stacking-Based Model for House Price Prediction 947
  Yiqian Zhou

A Dynamic Game Study on the "Big Data Discriminatory Pricing"
Behavior of E-commerce Platforms Under Government Regulation 959
  Zhuang Yao

Analysis on Marketing Strategy of Chinese Online Music Platform–QQ
Music 969
  Jiayi Hong

The Causality Between Executive Compensation, Equity Concentration,
and Corporate Performance: A Multiple Regression Analysis 977
   Xiao Rao

Exploring the Interplay Between Inflation, Energy Prices,
and COVID-19 Amidst the Ukraine Conflict 986
   Zeyao Li

An Empirical Analysis of Asset Pricing Models 998
   Ziqi Chen, Zhenwu Sun, and Xiaoyu Wang

The Empirical Analysis of Asset Pricing Models in the Asia-Pacific
Stock Market Under COVID-19 1008
   Hui Wang

The Impact of Technological Change on Labour Market Outcomes
and Income Inequality in China: An Empirical Analysis 1018
   Xueyao Tong

The "Strong" Development of RMB 1025
   Shengran Huang

Research on Business Value Assessment Model for New Generation Star 1035
   Ziyi Xing

Fiduciary Duty Regime of Private Fund Managers: Insights from the US
Regulatory Experience 1043
   Jia Cheng

The Impact of Capital Globalization on Green Innovation:
A Cross-Country Empirical Analysis 1054
   Yuyang Yuan

Financing Constraints, Local Government Debt, and Corporate Stock
Returns: An Empirical Analysis 1064
   Yike Lu

Sustainable Supply Chains: A Comprehensive Analyse of Drivers
and Practices 1075
   Qichao Gong, Yuxi Wang, and Yuli Zhu

Innovating Online Operational Models for Independent Hotels:
Assessing the Feasibility of a "Regional Independent Hotel Network
Alliance" in Yunnan 1083
   Qijing Li

Supply Chain Management in the Era of "Internet+": Case Analysis
of Agricultural Product Supply Chain 1094
  Huimin Liu, Yangmeng Liu, and Siyan Yi

An Empirical Study on the Causes of Default of US Dollar Debt
in the China's Property Based on Z-score Model 1102
  Yijing Wang

The Influence of Key Opinion Leaders on High-End Beauty Brands
in the Age of Self-media 1112
  Xilin Liu, Haonan Qian, and Haoyun Wen

Supply Chain Risk Management Process: Case Study of the Chinese
Aviation Industry in COVID-19 1120
  Jiangjia Xu

The Marketing Value of User-Generated Content in the Mobile Industry 1130
  Le Han, Zhuoer Wei, and Shuyan Zhang

Direct Carbon Emissions, Indirect Carbon Emissions, and International
Trade: An Analysis of OECD Member Countries 1143
  Yirong Xi

To What Extent Can We Use Google Trends to Predict Inflation
Statistically? 1156
  Minrui Huang and David Tai Li

A Literature Review on the Model of EGARCH-MIDAS, LMM, GBM
for Stock Market Prediction 1175
  Yingtong Wang

The Impact of Changes in Sales Prices of Non-durable Goods
on Consumers' Purchase Intentions When Using Online Shopping
Platforms 1185
  Zehao Xu

Analyzing Problems and Strategies of International Organizations
in Global Governance and Cooperation – Taking UNDP as an Example 1197
  Haosen Xu

Implementation of Monte-Carlo Simulations in Economy and Finance 1206
  Jintian Zhang

InstaCart Analysis: Use PCA with K-Means to Segment Grocery
Customers 1218
   Chenyu Lang

Research on the Influencing Factors of Housing Prices Based
on Multiple Regression: Taking Chongqing as an Example 1231
   Yijia Qi

Game Analysis of Cross-Border Entry of Enterprises into New Markets:
Case Study of Bytedance 1242
   Feiyue Lei and Lu Meng

Research on the Effectiveness of Clarifying Rumors by Listed
Companies in the Pharmaceutical Industry – Taking the Market
Reaction of Ling Pharmaceutical as an Example 1252
   Chuhan Wang, Beining Xu, and Qianwen Zhang

The Relationship Between ESG Performance and Financial Constraints
and Its Impact on Firm Value 1265
   Shengyang Qu

A Study on the Relationship Between ESG Performance and Stock
Returns – Take A-share Listed Company Stocks as the Example 1274
   Liqi Dong, Shifeng Deng, and Qian Gao

Digital Transformation in the New Energy Industry for Sustainable
Development: A Grounded Theory Analysis 1285
   Ming Liu

Causality Between Board Features and Corporate Innovation Level:
Empirical Evidence from Listed Companies in China 1295
   Zicheng Bu

Analysis of the Impact of Digital Inclusive Finance on Farmers' Income
Growth - An Empirical Analysis Based on 31 Provinces in China 1303
   Yuhan Sun

The Energy Consumption and Economic Growth 1315
   Yiguo Huang, Yizhen Zhang, and Heyu Cai

Research on the Merger and Acquisition Performance and Brand
Management of Cross-Border LBO—Take Qumei Home's Acquisition
of Norwegian Ekornes Company as an Example 1327
   Runbang Liu

The Impact of Investor Sentiment on Stock Returns 1361
  Xinran Fu

The Impact of Digitisation Degree on Agricultural Science
and Technology Innovation: Based on Panel Data of 31 Provinces
in China 1371
  Lanjie Huang

An Empirical Study on the Impact of Behavioural Bias on Investment
Decision-Making 1382
  Chutian Li

Matrix Factorization Model in Collaborative Filtering Algorithms
Based on Feedback Datasets 1405
  Yuqing Hu

Research on the Mall Customers Segmentation Based on K-means
and DBSCAN 1413
  Yifan Wang

Valuation and Analysis of the Canadian Banking Sector During
the COVID-19 Pandemic 1426
  Bo He

ChatGPT Concept Industry Valuation Analysis: Evidence from iFlytek
and Kunlun 1437
  Yajing Chen

Optimizing Trading Recommendations in Portfolio Trading: A Bilateral
Matching Theory Approach 1445
  Wenzheng Liu

The Impact of "Three Arrows" Policies on China's Real Estate Market:
An Event Study 1455
  Zixuan Wang, Yangjie Jin, and Jianuo Su

Corporate Social Responsibility Disclosure Quality and Stock Price
Crash Risk: Evidence from China 1474
  Minxing Zhu

An Analysis of the Effect of Social Medical Insurance on Family
Consumption 1491
  Siyun Yuan

The Influence of Impulsive Purchase on the Consumption Behaviour
in Social Media 1503
   Sirui Wang

Analysis of the Reasons of HNA Group's Bankruptcy and Future
Prevention Measures for Enterprises 1513
   Jiaheng Zhang

Cognitive Biases in Second-Hand and Pre-sale Real Estate Prices
in Nanjing 1522
   Bing Shen

How Targeted Poverty Alleviation Policy Program and Other Possible
Factors Affect the Wellbeing of Chinese Seniors 1530
   Xinru Fang

Investor Sentiment, Idiosyncratic Risk, and Stock Returns: Evidence
from Australia 1548
   Aiqi Li

Sovereign CDS Spreads and Covid-19 Pandemic 1559
   Ying Xi

Portfolio Optimization for Major Industries in American Capital Market 1570
   Xinyi Liu

The Impact of Investor Sentiment on Stock Returns Based on Machine
Learning and Deep Learning Methods 1577
   Xiangjun Chen

An Empirical Research on the Impact of ESG Performance on Chinese
Stock Market 1597
   Jiayun Yin

Research on the Application of Artificial Intelligence Technology
in Risk Management of Commercial Banks 1606
   Wensi Huang, Yiling Shi, and Wenjie Zhou

Exploring the Development Rule of GDP Based on Time-series Moran's
Index 1616
   Zhengjie Zang

An Empirical Study of U.S. Stock Market Forecasts and Trend Trading
Strategies Based on ARIMA Model 1630
   Siying Wang

Impact of 5G Commercial License Issuance on Stock Prices of Related
Listed Companies: Using Difference-in-Differences Model 1641
   Xi Zhou

Socio-Economic Determinants of National Saving in Pakistan 1649
   Munir Ahmad and Asghar Ali

Research on the Influence Mechanism of Experiential Interaction
on Consumers' Impulsive Buying 1664
   Liang Chen

A Qualitative Study on How the Covid-19 Pandemic Has Helped
in the Enablement of Entrepreneurial Ambitions Among Chinese
Entrepreneurs 1675
   Xiaodan Wang

The Application of Price-Earnings Ratio in Hong Kong Hang Seng
Index Futures Trading Strategy 1684
   Yishan Hou, Yifei Xu, and Shuye Zhou

The Effect of Governance Dimension of ESG on Corporate Performance 1694
   Huijia Zhang and Keyou Pang

Impact of Green Financing and Public Policies Towards Investment
Yield: Evidence from European and Asian Economies 1705
   Mirza Nasir Jahan Mehdi and Syed Ali Raza Hamid

The Long and Short Term Impact of COVID-19 on E-Commerce
and Retail Industries for US 1720
   Zixuan Li, Chenwen Song, and Tianrui Xiao

An Exploration of Bank Failure in Silicon Valley and the Interaction
of Failure Factors - Empirical Analysis Based on VAR Model 1746
   Tianqi Peng

Prediction of Lending Club Loan Defaulters 1765
   Xueyan Wang

Research on the CRE of China's Carbon Trading Pilot Policy 1778
   Jiayue Jiang, Meixin Wang, Mengzhen Xiao, Yuwei Yang, and Dan Wei

IEEE-CIS Fraud Detection Based on XGB 1785
   Zhijia Xiao

Unraveling the Link Between Federal Reserve Interest Rate Hikes
and the Chinese Stock Market 1797
   Jialin Li

Stock Market Volatility During and After the Covid-19 Pandemic:
Academic Perspectives 1809
   Yining Yang

Unveiling the Effects of the China-US Trade Conflict: A Comparative
Study of Stock Market Behaviors in the United States and China 1818
   Shuying Chen

Financial Analysis and Strategic Forecast of Tesla, Inc. 1831
   Xiaoke Wang

Mechanisms and Strategies of Smart Governance for Improving Urban
Resilience 1842
   Jianhang Du, Yongheng Hu, and Longzheng Du

The Impact of Low Carbon Economic Development on the Income
Gap Between Urban and Rural Residents - An Empirical Study Based
on Inter-provincial Panel Data in China 1848
   Yang Chengye

Addressing Credit Fraud Threat: Detected Through Supervised Machine
Learning Model 1863
   Yihan Yang

The Impact Caused by the COVID-19 Pandemic Re-opening on Catering
Industry in China: A Short-Term Perspective 1873
   Shiqi Pan

The Impact of the Russia-Ukraine War on Tesla: Evidence from ARIMA
Model 1882
   Jintian He

Research on the Link Between RMB Exchange Rate and Tesla's Stock
Price: A Long-Term Perspective 1893
   Jinhao Yu

Dynamic Impact of the Covid-19 on Cryptocurrency and Investment
Suggestion 1903
   Haozhe Hong

Research on the Relationship Between Chinese and American Stock
Markets: Spillover Effects of Returns and Volatility 1914
Lin Liu

Research on the Impact of China's Industrial Structure Upgrading
on the Balance of Payments Structure 1924
Yimeng Wang

The Impact of Digital Economy on Industrial Agglomeration 1933
Yuting Huang and Kaixvan Ma

Analysis of Influencing Factors of Housing Affordability Crisis
in Vancouver 1949
Jiaxuan Chen

Analysis of the Impact of Female Executives on Corporate Financial
Leverage 1960
XiangLin Cheng

Corporate Social Responsibility and Financial Performance: Evidence
from Listed Firms in China 1971
Jiali Wang

The External Shock of the Epidemic on Employees' Turnover Intention
in Central-Dominated China: The Mediating Effect of Automation
and Teleworking 1987
Xinyu Chen

Research on the Mechanism of Farmers' Interest Linkage in Agricultural
Technology Transformation 2001
Yuanyuan Chen

Analysis of Spatio-Temporal Evolution Patterns in the Green
Development of Cluster-Type Cities: A Case Study of Zibo City in China 2010
Minne Liu

Correlation Between Chinese Outbound Tourism Numbers and Chinese
Outward Foreign Direct Investment Study 2021
Peili Yu

Volatility Analysis Using High-Frequency Financial Data 2031
Junchi Wang

Can Environmental, Social and Governance Performance Alleviate Financial Dilemma? 2043
   Junyi Wang

Reinforcement Learning for E-Commerce Dynamic Pricing 2051
   Hongxi Liu

Impact of ESG Performance on Firm Value and Its Transmission Mechanism: Research Based on Industry Heterogeneity 2061
   Xingzhuo Liu

Author Index 2071

International NGO Issues on Female Migrant Workers

Yinwei Li(✉)

University of Glasgow, Glasgow G12 8QQ, Scotland
2721353L@student.gla.ac.uk

Abstract. Non-Governmental Organizations (NGOs) are confronting various global issues connected with female transient specialists. Discrimination, exploitation, and a lack of access to essential services and rights are among these issues. NGOs, however, can make a difference in the lives of female migrant workers in several different ways. This research considers possible solutions to this problem. This paper assesses approaches through different evaluation criteria, including the feasibility of the mass application, effectiveness towards beneficiaries, cost-effectiveness, and sustainability. Considering various evaluation criteria, government agencies can implement regulations to ensure social protection coverage. Studies show that NGOs not only face several pressing issues regarding female migrant workers but also have opportunities to affect their lives positively. To improve the lives of female migrant workers and reduce discrimination and exploitation, NGOs can work toward providing healthcare, education, training programs, and legal protection. NGOs can advocate for policies and programs that support female migrant workers and raise awareness about their rights and needs.

Keywords: NGOs · Discrimination · Exploitation · Mass Application · Cost-Effectiveness · Sustainability

1 Introduction

Non-Governmental Organizations (NGOs) are confronting various global issues that affect female migrant workers. These issues can be categorized as discrimination, exploitation, and a lack of access to essential services and rights, and among others. NGOs usually have financial capabilities and can make a difference in the lives of female migrant workers in several ways. NGOs have the abilities to improve the lives of female migrant workers. Women who work as migrant workers can benefit from educational and training opportunities offered by NGOs [1]. NGOs can also advocate for policies and programs that support female migrant workers and raise awareness of their rights and needs [2].

Meanwhile, female migrant workers experience many issues that affect them at workplaces compared to their male counterparts, such as lower wages, fewer opportunities, and fewer chances of advancement in their jobs or careers. Moreover, female migrant workers frequently encounter workplace sexual harassment and abuse [3]. Coupled with a lack of access to basic rights and services, domestic female migrant workers are specifically exposed to sexual harassment [3]. Rights that the workers are denied include limited access to healthcare, education, and legal protection.

Furthermore, female migrant workers need to work on the barriers that may further make them more exploited by their employees. Some of the raised issues are also caused by the worker's ignorance or naivety. Consideration of some possible approaches to solving this problem has been implemented. This paper assesses approaches through different evaluation criteria, including the feasibility of the mass application, effectiveness towards beneficiaries, cost-effectiveness, and sustainability, and can greatly help female migrant workers solve their issues, especially with the aid of NGOs.

2 Approaches to Improve Female Migrant Workers

One possible approach is to organize media campaigns to prevent misleading narratives and create a positive societal attitude toward female migrant workers. Gender campaigns can be run via traditional media channels, like television, radio, newspapers, magazines, and billboards. Also, the campaigns can be run on new digital media, such as websites, banner advertisements, and social media [4]. Media usually feature an element of providing interactivity. Such interactivity includes liking, sharing, commenting on social media content, and also downloading campaign apps. Engaging with campaigns can determine the effectiveness of a public health campaign on a broad spectrum. Although it is easy for us to implement such activities, the effectiveness of beneficiaries, cost-effectiveness and sustainability are not distinct in the short and long term. The activities can be divided into different types of campaign content, including messages, targeting, and source.

The cost-effectiveness of messages depends on the target audience, in other words, beneficiaries. Existing research indicates that messages from mass media need to consider age, sex, culture, engagement levels in targeting activity, personal characteristics, and other factors of beneficiaries [4]. However, even introducing mass media campaigns that are created algorithmically in order to target a certain audience does not assure a change of attitude on people's perspectives. Moreover, changing the attitude of the mass public has not been proven to have a significant causation in encouraging migrant women to seek higher-quality jobs. Therefore, the research eliminates this approach for the above reasons.

Another possible approach was establishing pre-departure training programs in migrants' countries of origin. Stakeholders could make strategies and design different pre-departure training programs for female migrant workers [5]. However, this approach would most likely not be mass applicable because immigrants originate from various regions across the globe, meaning their needs in these training programs would differ significantly. Hence, governments or other stakeholders would have to design different training programs and face the possibility of it not applying to migrants from other regions, making this approach rather cost-ineffective.

It is also reckoned that government agencies can implement a regulation that provides certain social protection services for female migrant workers [6]. The research investigates how the regularization affected employment and wages and the regulation's long-lasting impact in creating legal employment for migrant female workers. On a broader scale, an analogy to this would be the International Labour Standards (ILS). International labour standards lay out basic principles, articulate the rights of the workers, establish objective policies, or give guidance on the means and procedures to be implemented by the International Framework for Labour Standards (ILS). ILS is designed to promote decent work for employees of all ethnicities and nationalities [7]. Moreover, government agencies can require companies to comply with the implemented regulation and simultaneously provide them with benefits for hiring female migrant workers [8], making the process much more efficient. In addition, the output of the regulation outweighs the input in the long term, considering the benefits migrants joining the workforce can bring to the economy.

Last, beneficiaries can gain many benefits under the regulation, including equal opportunities for employment, protection of their legal rights, etc. The regulation may create long-term legal employment prospects for female migrant employees, who remain strongly attached to the formal labour market. In terms of these evaluation criteria, regulation implementation conducted by government agencies is the most effective approach. To a certain extent, many companies prefer hiring overseas employees as they are affordable and therefore, they will save a lot of money. The companies look for talent pools in those overseas countries where there is lower demand for particular skills, but also where there are also highly skilled professionals who are seeking occupations [9]. More often, it is possible to offer salaries that are competitive and which can fairly compensate their employees while they are able to save more money compared to the market rate in their local countries. At the same time, hiring female migrant workers may increase corporations' expenses. However, it may help to promote companies' images because people are likely to give business to companies with diversity. Being a diversity-positive company will also encourage a wider, more diverse pool of applicants to seek occupations.

Furthermore, government agencies should monitor the following regulations and provide insurance coverage. One of the obvious benefits is managing cash flow uncertainty. Insurance coverage provides payment-covered losses, and the uncertainty of paying for losses that may occur is greatly reduced [10]. If an unexpected event occurs, an individual or an entity can claim compensation or be reinstated to their previous financial position by the insurer. The insurance of affordable premiums compensates for the possibility of bigger losses if individuals are not insured.

3 Behaviours, Barriers, and Activities

The regulation requires stakeholders (companies and domestic employers) to provide healthcare benefits, maternity and paid family leave, and sick leave to female migrant workers. However, due to financial distress, many companies and domestic employers have difficulties complying with the regulation [11]. To overcome this barrier, governments and NGOs can provide companies under the heavy economic burden with request-based funds. A consideration is that government agencies have only so much that could be used as funds to invest in this regulation. Therefore, there will be strict factors that the stakeholders would have to meet to acquire monetary support.

Today, many countries have passed equal-opportunity laws and also adopted resolutions set by the UN on women empowerment [12]. Besides, gender budgeting is used by governments in promoting equality through the use of fiscal policy. Gender budgeting involves analysing the contradicting impacts of budgets on both men and women, allocating funds fairly, and setting some archivable targets, such as equal opportunities for school enrolment to girls and giving funds to meet the goals. Gender budgeting usually focuses on important national purse strings, and relative financial ministries are eager to note gender gaps if they understand the economic losses they can cause [13]. In some cases, domestic employers would like to avoid government monitoring which may worsen the current situation. Domestic sector unions should motivate the public that female workers are part of the financially driven forces. For instance, the latest available Sustainable Development Goal (SDG) number five emphasizes the interlinkages among all the goals, gender equality plays a pivotal role in order to drive progress in the SDGs, and women and girls also play a central role to enable them to lead the way. Meanwhile, governments and stakeholders can set up specific monitoring departments, including close surveillance and heavy fines.

From the beneficiaries' perspective, female migrant workers should seek occupations covered by the regulation. To realize this goal, they should overcome three main barriers. Firstly, most female migrant employees lack access to information about the benefits they can receive from their corporations. Setting up some gender-responsive information campaigns can help to improve this situation. At the same time, these companies can also use social media as a platform of knowledge diffusion to protect migrant female workers' legal rights. For instance, on October 19, 2020, the UN Women and FinDevCanada co-organized the "Investing in Gender Responsive Companies" event. The event was hosted by WE EMPOWER-G7 Programme and organized in support of Women Empowerment Principles (WEPs). Secondly, it is hard for female employees to balance work and maternal responsibilities. Female employees should be good career planners [14]. They should be allergic to their organizations and the reality that they must plan to have children and work simultaneously. During this period, they should set boundaries and never lose self-confidence. Thirdly, female migrant employees lack the skill sets to fulfil higher-quality jobs. To tackle this problem, they should develop their skills and cultivate their abilities through orientation and skill development programs.

4 Issues Faced by Female Migrant Workers

Migrant workers frequently experience exploitation, discrimination, and a lack of access to essential services and rights. Migrant workers do not have resources such as legal power to fight for their rights against exploitation. NGOs are equipped with resources that can help migrant workers solve the issues that affect them while at the workplace. The following are the issues that migrant workers face while at the workplace.

4.1 Discrimination at the Workplace

Discrimination against female migrant workers at work is one major issue. Compared to their male counterparts, most female migrant workers usually work in informal employment, such as domestic workers, where they are usually paid lower wages and lack access to the advancement of their positions [15]. Employers view the employees as weak, and their output is lower; therefore, they do not provide better employment contracts. Additionally, since some women work as housekeepers where regulation of work ethics has not been fully implemented, female migrant workers frequently experience workplace sexual harassment and abuse. This discrimination may significantly impact the lives of female migrant workers and their families. The effect can be physiological and health wise.

4.2 Lack of Access to Basic Rights

Female migrant workers also lack access to basic rights and services. Since female employees work in companies or jobs that have not abided by government regulations, the employees are vulnerable to exploitation. Employees should have access to healthcare, education, and legal protection [2]. When a basic service such as access to healthcare services is denied, people become weak or have mental detrimental. Therefore, their output declines which might also lead to further denial or rights since they might be denied quality or enough food necessary for our growth. However, since they do not have human recourses to fight for their rights legally, female employees who lack access to their basic rights end up being denied their rights.

4.3 Exploitation

Employers and recruiters frequently exploit female migrant workers. Most female migrant workers are usually recruited online. Afterward, most of them are employed in the domestic sector. Their employers decide the amount of money to pay them and also dictate the terms of employment. Most of them are paid less than the minimum wage or are forced to work in hazardous conditions [2]. Female migrant workers' lives can be significantly impacted as they are verbally abused and forced to work more than what they were told before they departed their countries. Their employees can force them to work for more hours with the minimum wages they get paid.

5 Solutions for the Issues Facing Female Migrant Workers

5.1 Education and Training Programs

Women who work as migrant workers can benefit from educational and training opportunities offered by NGOs. NGOs can plan for education and training programs that will help better the lives of migrant workers in the following ways.

Firstly, the rights and requirements of female migrant workers can be the subject of advocacy work by NGOs [2]. Female migrant workers will learn about their rights and how to get services from education and training programs. Gender equality at workplaces is one right that female migrant employees need to enjoy. The workers should not be mistreated or exploited just because they are women. All employees should be subjected to equal rights and terms of employment if they belong to the same employment category. In the training programs, the right to better healthcare services can also be taught. NGOs should teach the workers what their employers need to do in case their employees fall sick. If employers do not provide healthcare privileges which might be expensive or they are denied the right to healthcare services, NGOs can take the employees who do not have access to a hospital or take legal action against the employers who deny the workers such services. Also, NGOs can provide mental or primary healthcare services [16].

Secondly, female migrant workers' chances of finding better-paying jobs can be improved through education and training programs [2]. Helping female migrant workers find work is another essential solution that international NGOs can provide. Most female migrant workers usually have fewer skills which make them work in the agricultural sector, hospitality, and other jobs that do not require high skills. However, NGOs can sponsor the workers to learn skills that can help the workers get employment in industries that require highly skilled labour. The workers can be employed in the technology industries s where they will be subjected to better employment contracts. After training, NGOs can Support female migrant workers by linking them to employers who create employment opportunities for female migrant workers or providing services for job placement [17].

Finally, NGOs can assist female migrant workers in preparing resumes, improving their interview skills, and learning about job opportunities and requirements. There are the basic needs that employers look for in employees. If shown such necessities, female migrant employees get a better chance of getting good jobs.

5.2 Supporting Female Migrant Workers in Navigating Complex Legal Systems

Navigating legal systems frequently present difficulties for female migrant workers. The workers must understand immigration laws and regulations to navigate the legal system in cases of discrimination or abuse [18]. By providing information and assistance, NGOs can assist female migrant workers in navigating these complicated legal systems. The aid could mean helping female migrant workers get the legal help they need by giving them advice or collaborating with legal representatives. Similarly, NGOs will help female migrant workers file complaints or provide legal representation.

5.3 Collaborating with Other Organizations and Stakeholders

By collaborating with other organizations and stakeholders, NGOs can play a crucial role in addressing the challenges faced by female migrant workers [19]. For example, NGOs can work with governments, the private sector, and community groups. These organizations can collaborate to share resources and expertise and develop more efficient solutions to the problems faced by female migrant workers. The resources are owned by NGOs and collaborating with these organizations can help advocate for policies that support female migrant workers. These policies include implementing measures that help employers abide by the employment policies and also the requirements of migration requirements [13]. Similarly, NGOs and stakeholders can champion the increment of Female migrant workers in the unions and associations that fight for the rights of international employees [13].

NGOs and other stakeholders can collaborate to help female migrant workers obtain affordable housing. Under international laws, affordable housing can be defined in form of access to secured housing conditions [20]. Affordable housing should also ensure the workers are not subjected to eviction and there is also security in the region. However, access to affordable housing has been difficult for female migrant workers who live independently or support their families [20]. By providing female migrant workers with safe and affordable housing, NGOs and stakeholders can play a crucial role in addressing this issue. Their roles may entail developing long-term housing solutions or providing temporary housing. Also, they can ensure that the housing is safe and meets the needs of female migrant workers.

Programs that specifically address the requirements to employ female migrant workers can also be developed by NGOs [21]. Governments have the power to implement minimum wage requirements at job levels. NGOs can collaborate with governments to ensure all employees meet such requirements. Similarly, creating programs that offer female migrant workers financial assistance or establishing support groups for these workers who are financially stranded.

6 Conclusion

Female migrant employees are exploited due to several reasons. It might result from social media platforms, traveling, or workplaces. They encounter several barriers that decrease their efficiency at the workplace. Several approaches can be taken to reduce exploitation. If better considerations are implemented, the barriers that prevent them from exploitation or fathering their studies and getting better job opportunities can be overcome. Despite even dozens of countries implementing laws that govern employment contracts, female migrant workers still undergo several workplace challenges. However, governments are not better placed to handle the needs of migrant workers as they have many projects to handle. Therefore, the challenges faced by female migrant workers are crucially addressed by international NGOs.

Discrimination, exploitation, and lack of access to fundamental rights and services, and difficulties locating employment opportunities and affordable housing are among the most notable issues faced by female migrant workers. The solutions to issues of this great magnitude need practical solutions like education and training programs, legal assistance, healthcare services, job placement services, and safe and affordable housing. Due to the financial requirements of these issues, it is recommended that solutions be provided by international NGOs with the help of other stakeholders.

NGOs can also develop programs that cater to the particular requirements of female migrant workers and assist them in navigating intricate legal systems. To fully meet the needs of female migrant workers, collaboration with other organizations and stakeholders is also essential. Education and training programs can assist female migrant workers in developing new skills and increasing their chances of finding better-paying jobs and avoiding exploitation. Finally, NGOs can advocate for policies and programs that support the rights and requirements of female migrant workers.

References

1. Healy, L.M., Thomas, R.L.: International Social Work: Professional Action in an Interdependent World. Oxford University Press (2020)

2. Bettio, F., Simonazzi, A., Villa, P.: Change in care regimes and female migration: the 'care drain' in the Mediterranean. J. Eur. Soc. Policy **16**(3), 271–285 (2006). https://doi.org/10.1177/0958928706065598
3. Tayah: Protecting migrant domestic workers: the international legal framework. International Labour Organization (2016)
4. Woods Waller, G.: Media campaigns. Encyclopaedia of Social Work (2013). https://doi.org/10.1093/acrefore/9780199975839.013.236
5. Ma, H., Loke, A.Y.: A qualitative study into female sex workers' experience of stigma in the health care setting in Hong Kong. Int. J. Equity Health **18**(1), 1–14 (2019)
6. Mayer, T., Tran, T.: Displacement, Belonging, and Migrant Agency in the Face of Power, pp. 1–37 (2022). https://doi.org/10.4324/9781003170686-1
7. The International Framework for Labour Standards: Labour Standards in International Supply Chains, pp. 42–58. https://doi.org/10.4337/9781783470372.00009
8. Hung, S.L., Fung, K.K.: Working with female migrant workers in Hong Kong. Community Organising Against Racism (2017). https://doi.org/10.1332/policypress/9781447333746.003.0018
9. Al Ariss, A., Koall, I., Özbilgin, M., Suutari, V.: Careers of skilled migrants: towards a theoretical and methodological expansion. J. Manage. Dev. **31**, 92–101 (2012)
10. Weiss, M.A., Meier, K.: The political economy of regulation: the case of insurance. J. Risk Insur. **56**, 368 (1989)
11. Hall, B.J., Garabiles, M.R., Latkin, C.A.: Work-life, relationship, and policy determinants of health and well-being among Filipino domestic workers in China: a qualitative study. BMC Public Health **19**(1), 1–14 (2019)
12. Weatherspoon, F.D.: Equal employment opportunity. Equal Employment Opportunity and Affirmative Action, pp. 3–202 (2018). https://doi.org/10.4324/9780429398049-2
13. Panday, P.K., Chowdhury, S.: Participatory budgeting and gender-responsive budgeting. Gender Responsive Budgeting in South Asia, pp. 50–64 (2021). https://doi.org/10.4324/9781003148661-4
14. Mapp, S., McPherson, J., Androff, D., Gatenio Gabel, S.: Social work is a human rights profession. Soc. Work **64**(3), 259–269 (2019)
15. Fouskas, T., Gikopoulou, P., Ioannidi, E., Koulierakis, G.: Gender, transnational female migration and domestic work in Greece. Collectivus Revista de Ciencias Sociales **6**(1), 99–134 (2019)
16. Ma, H., Loke, A.Y.: Nurses' attitudes towards and willingness to care for sex workers questionnaire. PsycTESTS Dataset (2020)
17. Aras, B., Duman, Y.: I/NGOs' assistance to Syrian refugees in Turkey: opportunities and challenges. J. Balkan Near East Stud. **21**(4), 478–491 (2019)
18. Williams, F.: Care: intersections of scales, inequalities, and crises. Curr. Sociol. **66**(4), 547–561 (2018)
19. Miles, L., Lewis, S., Teng, L.W., Yasin, S.M.: Advocacy for women migrant workers in Malaysia through an intersectionality lens. J. Ind. Relat. **61**(5), 682–703 (2019)
20. Regmi, P.R., Aryal, N., van Teijlingen, E., Simkhada, P., Adhikary, P.: Nepali migrant workers and the need for pre-departure training on mental health: a qualitative study. J. Immigr. Minor. Health **22**(5), 973–981 (2020)
21. Cao, A., Li, P.: We are not machines: the identity construction of Chinese female migrant workers in online chat groups. Chin. J. Commun. **11**(3), 289–305 (2018)

Time Lagged Effects of ESG Scores and Investor Attention on Stock Returns

Jiaqi Liu(✉)

Hunan University, 2 Yuelu South Road, Yuelu District, Changsha, Hunan, China
823594377@qq.com

Abstract. This paper explores whether the effects of environmental, social, and governance (ESG) and investor attention on stock returns have time lags. We hypothesize that the effect of ESG score on stock returns is time-lagged, and the effect of investor attention on stock returns is time-lagged. We conducted a panel analysis of ESG scores, Baidu index separately regarding annual excess stock returns, and added control variables such as size, sales and leverage. Considering that the impact of ESG score and Baidu index is long-term, we introduced time lag. We find that both hypotheses hold, and ESG scores four years ago had the greatest impact on the stock returns of the year, investor attention two years ago had the greatest impact on the stock returns of the year. The contribution of this thesis is to introduce time lags when analyzing the impact of ESG scores or investor attention on stock returns.

Keywords: ESG · Investor Attention · Stock Returns · Panel Analysis · Time Lag

1 Introduction

First introduced by the United Nations Environment Programme in 2004, the ESG concept refers to environmental, social and governance and is an investing philosophy and corporate rating standard that concerns itself with the environmental, social and corporate governance performance of companies rather than their traditional financial performance. Originally, many scholars viewed the only social responsibility of business as the increase in production [1]. As people become more aware of environmental responsibility, so the understanding of ESG by investors and companies is changing. Lioui argues that ESG risks are ubiquitous and can hardly be avoided by investors [2]. One study concluded that the applied of ESG has transformed "responsible investing" from a normative attempt of improving investment ethics to an exploratory practice of valuation [3]. Hubel and Scholz [4] construct a group of ESG-based investments for the Euro market during the duration 2003–2016. Using their ESG-enhanced asset price-setting model, they find more risk in the portfolios with more ESG risk [4]. These studies in which scholars have increasingly focused on the effect of ESG on stock returns. Many researchers believe that ESG investments are beneficial in increasing company value. Bénabou et al. [5], explained that "doing well by doing good" holds because Corporate Social Responsibility strengthens the firm's strategic market position and attracts socially responsible stakeholders that are willing to exchange money for moral value [5]. However, Kvam, E et al. [6] investigate the link between stock returns and ESG and got the opposite result. They found that higher ESG scores are associated with lower stock returns on average [6].

Ignoring ESG factors may have negative effects on portfolio performance. Investors use non financial data such as ESG factors to decide whether to invest in a firm ESG investments are based on an assessment of a company's non-financial market data with the aim of informing investors about the company's social and environmental commitments. It represents opportunities and risks facing the firm [7]. In addition, Dorfleitner et al. find that ESG risk cannot be eliminated by asset portfolio diversification [8]. This means that investors need to pay extra attention to ESG risks.

Many researchers have devoted themselves to exploring the impact of ESG rating differences on stock returns. Several of them found that stock returns were correlated positively with ESG rating disagreement, showing that a risk premium is present for companies with more divergent ESG ratings. The relationship is mainly driven by environmental-level disagreement [9]. Consolandi et al. find that not only do changes in ESG ratings (ESG dynamics) have a uniform effect on stock performance, but also that the market appears to reward greater rewards for companies that operate in industries with a high concentration of ESG material [10]. Avramov et al. show that the only stocks in which the average ESG rating is negatively correlated with future stock performance are stocks with less ESG divergence [11].

Both ESG and investor focus can reflect company reputation issues. Reputational capital is an important intangible asset through which firms communicate their key characteristics to the firm's stakeholders [12]. A good reputation allows firms to charge premium prices [13]. Some studies have found that ESG investments can yield superior yields and avoid risk, especially downside risk [14, 15]. On the other hand, poorer ESG events can cause unquantifiable damage to reputation [16].

Publicity can play a role in promoting ESG investments. Corporate environmental social responsibility is a "perceived corporate social responsibility" [17]. And investors are non-perfectly rational people with limited cognition [18]. With limited attention span investors having only partial access to stock information, they are more inclined to purchase stocks that they know or that they care about [19]. Investors can obtain relevant information from the media. In markets where information frictions exist, media coverage increases the amount and speed of information dissemination, effectively reducing information costs and correcting information asymmetries, thereby increasing stock returns [20]. However, by selectively disseminating public knowledge and directing public attention to topics of interest, the media attracts the public's attention and becomes a "proxy" for public opinion. [21].

The creativity of this paper is to consider the time lag of the effect of ESG score and investor attention on stock returns. We hypothesized that the effect of ESG score on stock returns is time-lagged, the effect of investor attention on stock returns is time-lagged. To avoid the interference of different years and stocks. We normalize the ESG scores in the sample data, and introduce size, leverage, and gsales to reduce the error. Panel analysis is conducted separately for the impact of ESG score and investor attention on stock returns. We found that the impact of ESG score and investor focus both have time lags on stock returns. ESG score four years ago has the largest impact on stock returns in the current year. However, Investor focus two years ago had the largest impact on stock returns in that year.

This paper proceeds in the following order. Section 2 presents the sources and processing of data, and the ideology of data analysis. Considering the characteristics of the data, this paper finally screens the sample including 1450 stocks from 2011 to 2020. Panel analysis is conducted separately for the impact of ESG score and investor attention on stock returns. Section 3 presents the results of the study and discusses them. Section 3 derives the results of the panel analysis and analyzes the results to discuss the mechanism of the effect of ESG score and investor attention on stock returns. Section 4 makes conclusions and summarizes the results, contributions and shortcomings of this paper.

2 Research Design and Methodology

2.1 Data and Sample

Due to the late start of ESG in China, there is less data available in the early stage. Our sample period is from January 1, 2011 to December 31, 2020. ESG scores are retrieved from the Hexun database, which is a local ESG rating agency in China. According to the description provided by Hexun.com, the ESD score is a comprehensive evaluation of social responsibility in five parts: shareholder responsibility, employee responsibility, environmental responsibility, social responsibility, and supplier-customer responsibility for consumer rights. Combine them with industry characteristics to give the appropriate weight. We selected stocks with more than ten years of data and removed the financial sector, special treatment stock. Finally, we screened a total of 1450 stocks for this paper sample and found the annual stock returns from investing.com. To avoid macroeconomic effects, we got Shibor from investing.com to get stock excess returns. Considering the slight variation in scoring criteria from year to year, we normalized the ESG scores. Since Baidu is the largest Chinese search engine, we chose Baidu Index to evaluate the attention of investors. Taking into account the different companies, we obtained the year-over-year growth rates of total assets, total liabilities, and operating income from the company's annual reports.

2.2 Methodology

ESG Score. The purpose of this part of the analysis is to assess whether there is a time lag in the impact of ESG scores on equity excess returns. We choose company size, financial leverage, and gsales to represent the differences between companies.

The panel consists of 1450 stock in China. The annual observations start in 2011 and end in 2020. The panel is balanced. We first performed a Grand causality test for 0 to 8 to select the most appropriate lag order and performed a panel regression. We constructed the following model:

$$ER_{j,t} = \alpha + \beta_{t-i,j} ESG_{t-i,j} + \gamma_1 SIZE_{j,t} + \gamma_2 LEV_{j,t} + \gamma_3 GSALES_{j,t} + \varepsilon_{j,t} \qquad (1)$$

where ER is the stock yearly excess return, in stock return minus Shior. ESG is the standardized ESG score, SIZE is the logarithm of total assets, LEV is calculated by dividing the total liabilities by the total assets, GSALES is the year-on-year growth rate of operating income. $\varepsilon_{j,t}$ is the residual of the regression. $\beta_{t-i,j}$ describes the sensitivity of the stock yearly excess return to the standardized ESG score.

Attention of Investors. The purpose of this part of the analysis is to assess whether there is a time lag in the impact of attention of investors on equity excess returns. We chose Baidu Index for the attention of investors. We chose company size, financial leverage, and gsales to represent the differences between companies. The panel consists of 1450 stock in China. The annual observations start in 2011 and end in 2020. The panel is balanced. We first performed a Grand causality test for 0 to 8 to select the most appropriate lag order and performed a panel regression. We constructed the following model:

$$ER_{j,t} = \alpha + \beta_{t-i,j}LGB_{t-i,j} + \gamma_1 SIZE_{j,t} + \gamma_2 LEV_{j,t} + \gamma_3 GSALES_{j,t} + \varepsilon_{j,t} \quad (2)$$

where ER is the stock yearly excess return, in stock return minus Shior. IGB is the logarithm of Baidu Index, SIZE is the logarithm of total assets, LEV is calculated by dividing the total liabilities by the total assets, GSALES is the year-on-year growth rate of operating income. $\varepsilon_{j,t}$ is the residual of the regression. $\beta_{t-i,j}$ describes the sensitivity of the stock yearly excess return to the logarithm of Baidu Index.

3 Results and Discussion

Table 1. Descriptive statistics of the calculated indices.

	ER	ESG	LGB	SIZE	GSALES	LEV
Mean	8.201201	0.597282	12.08092	9.63105	11.9933	0.432509
Median	−4.27	0.395656	12.08659	9.554024	6.802609	0.413423
Maximum	1371.1	4.79605	20.10189	12.92228	472.788	13.39692
Minimum	−287.09	−2.482154	4.043051	6.489072	−92.63646	−0.194698
Std. Dev	53.41414	1.44629	1.225518	0.60148	49.41153	0.3201
Skewness	4.634018	0.444509	−2.044909	0.966135	5.063555	14.73097
Kurtosis	62.39916	2.730471	16.22701	5.84367	42.98832	458.596
Jarque-Bera	2183402	7.946776	109585.4	7141.325	15669.12	1.26E + 08
Sum Sq. Dev	41363809	460.1861	20605.98	5245.428	537129.8	1485.623
Observations	14499	221	13721	14500	221	14500

Table 2. Correlations.

	ER	ESG	LGB	SIZE	GSALES	LEV
ER	1					
ESG	−0.032491	1				
LGB	−0.12185	0.368008	1			
SIZE	−0.032785	0.643871	0.588128	1		
GSALES	−0.080968	0.031745	0.154015	0.095677	1	
LEV	0.03303	−0.046218	−0.234438	0.003635	−0.039996	1

ESG Score. Within the sample, we ran panel regressions of stock returns on ESG score, attention of investors. Descriptive statistics of the variables used in our analysis are presented in Table 1. Table 2 shows the correlations between the explanatory variables. The correlation coefficients are all within an acceptable range. In the ESG score sample, we obtained the optimal lag order of 4 on the Granger causality test. The panel regression results are shown in Table 3. The impact of the ESG score four years ago is greater, with coefficients of 2.83 with t-statistic of 1.4068. It is significant at 5%. In addition, the impact of the ESG score two years ago is second only to the four years ago, with the coefficient of −2.77. The results of the statistical analysis of the model are shown in Table 4. The adjusted R-squared is 0.1653. Given the associated F-statistic of 4.4243, this difference is significant at the 1% level.

Table 3. Panel regression results.

Variable	Coefficient	Std. Error	t-Statistic	Prob
C	−66.40209	39.59149	−1.677181	*0.096
ESG	−1.629334	1.992083	−0.817905	0.415
ESG(-1)	2.330674	1.359983	1.713753	*0.0891
ESG(-2)	−2.773905	1.262426	−2.197282	**0.0299
ESG(-3)	0.608803	2.096404	0.290403	0.772
ESG(-4)	2.828118	2.0103	1.406814	0.162
SIZE	5.880918	3.916013	1.501762	0.1357
GSALES	−0.053055	0.018041	−2.94084	***0.0039
LEV	−3.210364	8.574002	−0.37443	0.7087

Attention of Investors. In the attention of investors sample, we obtained the optimal lag order of 4 in the Granger causality test. The panel regression results are shown in Table 5. The impact of the logarithm of Baidu Index two years ago is greater, with coefficients of 8.85 with t-statistic of 6.434. It is significant at 5%. In addition, the impact of the

Table 4. Statistical analysis results of the model.

Weighted Statistics	
R-squared	0.216269
Adjusted R-squared	0.165294
S.E. of regression	22.66551
F-statistic	4.242689
Prob(F-statistic)	***0.00016
Mean dependent var	−9.687964
S.D. dependent var	25.4699
Sum squared resid	63188.23
Durbin-Watson stat	2.31174

Note: * $p \leq 0.1$, ** $p \leq 0.05$, *** $p \leq 0.01$

logarithm of Baidu Index one year ago is second only to the two years ago, with the coefficient of −6.74. The results of the statistical analysis of the model are shown in Table 6. The adjusted R-squared is 0.1948. Given the associated F-statistic of 4.4772, this difference is significant at the 1% level.

Table 5. Panel regression results.

Variable	Coefficient	Std. Error	t-Statistic	Prob
C	−91.56883	30.56715	−2.995661	***0.0034
LGB	0.373635	1.215415	0.307414	0.7591
LGB(-1)	−6.742222	1.718897	−3.922411	***0.0002
LGB(-2)	8.850063	1.375511	6.434017	***0
LGB(-3)	−1.013524	1.733676	−0.58461	0.56
LGB(-4)	−1.414145	1.257059	−1.124963	0.2631
SIZE	8.327074	2.289601	3.63691	***0.0004
GSALES	−0.043133	0.022706	−1.899645	*0.0602
LEV	−1.424169	13.51109	−0.105407	0.9162

Table 6. Statistical analysis results of the mode.

Weighted Statistics	
R-squared	0.250794
Adjusted R-squared	0.194778
S.E. of regression	22.60194
F-statistic	4.477229
Prob(F-statistic)	***0.000104
Mean dependent var	−9.482213
S.D. dependent var	25.76354
Sum squared resid	54660.68
Durbin-Watson stat	2.485257

Note: * $p \leq 0.1$, ** $p \leq 0.05$, *** $p \leq 0.01$

4 Conclusions

This paper explores whether the effects of environmental, social, and governance (ESG) and investor attention on stock returns have time lags. The creativity of this paper is to consider the time lag of the effect of ESG score and investor attention on stock returns. We hypothesize that the effect of ESG score on stock returns is time-lagged, and the effect of investor attention on stock returns is time-lagged.

Considering the short history of ESG development in China and the lack of early data, we selected data for the decade from 2011 to 2020 and screened 1450 stocks as a sample. After panel analysis, our results provide evidence that the effect of ESG score on stock returns is time-lagged, ESG scores four years ago had the greatest positive impact on the stock returns of the year, but ESG score two years ago had a great negative impact on stock returns. The effect of investor attention on stock returns is time-lagged. Investor attention two years ago had the greatest positive impact on the stock returns of the year, but investor attention one year ago had a great negative impact on stock returns.

From this we can see that the medium-term impact of ESG on stock returns is superior to the short-term impact. For the medium term, an increase in ESG score increases stock returns and, conversely, for the short term stock return effect, an increase in ESG score is detrimental to stock returns. We conjecture that the impact of ESG has a lag, with investment in ESG playing a role in the medium term, while for the short term, investment in ESG ties up firm resources. We can see that investors' attention affects the change of stock returns with a lag. We find. The Baidu index in the first two years of, has the greatest impact on stock returns. We speculate that investors' attention does not act directly on the change in stock returns, and most individual investors pay attention to a stock for a long time before investing, thus there is a time lag between investors' attention and the change in stock returns. The results from the data analysis show a time lag of 1 to 2 years for this component.

Based on the above analysis, we make the following recommendations. First, companies should make reasonable ESG investments that seek to promote stock growth in the long term, but do not take too much of the company's short-term growth capital. Second, appropriate publicity for the company, attention of investors can affect stock returns in the short term, but be aware that excessive attention is not enough. Companies can invest in order to increase investor attention and maintain a certain level, which will help improve stock returns and create a virtuous cycle.

In conclusion, our empirical results help firm and investors to better understand ESG and investor attention to stocks. By allocating the company's share of investments in different parts of the company, the company can achieve a reasonable allocation of long-term and short-term development resources to ensure the long-term sustainable and balanced development of the company. Investors can analyze the stock's next move based on the strength of the relevant company's publicity, public opinion, and ESG scores, and thereby realize profits.

I view this thesis as one that can be further studied in the following areas: 1. Whether the impact of each component of the ESG score on stock returns has a time lag. 2. The impact of investors' attention to good or bad events on stock returns. 3. Analyze the impact of ESG scores and the attention of investors on stock returns with quarterly or even monthly data.

References

1. Friedman, M.: The social responsibility of business is to increase its profits. In: Corporate Ethics and Corporate Governance, pp. 173–178. Springer, Heidelberg (2007). https://doi.org/10.1007/978-3-540-70818-6_14
2. Lioui, A.: Is ESG risk priced? SSRN 3285091 (2018)
3. Leins, S.: 'Responsible investment': ESG and the post-crisis ethical order. Econ. Soc. **49**(1), 71–91 (2020)
4. Hübel, B., Scholz, H.: Integrating sustainability risks in asset management: the role of ESG exposures and ESG ratings. J. Asset Manag. **21**(1), 52–69 (2020)
5. Bénabou, R., Tirole, J.: Individual and corporate social responsibility. Economica **77**(305), 1–19 (2010)
6. Kvam, E., Molnár, P., Wankel, I., Ødegaard, B.A.: Do sustainable company stock prices increase with ESG scrutiny? Evidence using social media, 15 March 2022
7. Coleman, L., Maheswaran, K., Pinder, S.: Narratives in managers' corporate finance decisions. Account. Financ. **50**(3), 605–633 (2010)
8. Dorfleitner, G., Halbritter, G., Nguyen, M.: The risk of social responsibility–is it systematic? J. Sustain. Financ. Invest. **6**(1), 1–14 (2016)
9. Gibson Brandon, R., Krueger, P., Schmidt, P.S.: ESG rating disagreement and stock returns. Financ. Anal. J. **77**(4), 104–127 (2021)
10. Consolandi, C., Eccles, R.G., Gabbi, G.: How material is a material issue? Stock returns and the financial relevance and financial intensity of ESG materiality. J. Sustain. Financ. Invest. 1–24 (2020)
11. Avramov, D., Cheng, S., Lioui, A., Tarelli, A.: Sustainable investing with ESG rating uncertainty. J. Financ. Econ. **145**(2), 642–664 (2022)
12. Fombrun, C., Shanley, M.: What's in a name? Reputation building and corporate strategy. Acad. Manag. J. **33**(2), 233–258 (1990)
13. Klein, B., Leffler, K.B.: The role of market forces in assuring contractual performance. J. Polit. Econ. **89**(4), 615–641 (1981)

14. Dunn, J., Fitzgibbons, S., Pomorski, L.: Assessing risk through environmental, social and governance exposures. J. Invest. Manag. **16**(1), 4–17 (2018)
15. Hoepner, A.G., Oikonomou, I., Sautner, Z., Starks, L.T., Zhou, X.: ESG shareholder engagement and downside risk (2018)
16. Glossner, S.: ESG risks and the cross-section of stock returns. In: Paris December 2017 Finance Meeting EUROFIDAI-AFFI, June 2017
17. Lichtenstein, D.R., Drumwright, M.E., Braig, B.M.: The effect of corporate social responsibility on customer donations to corporate-supported nonprofits. J. Mark. **68**(4), 16–32 (2004)
18. Eyster, E., Rabin, M., Vayanos, D.: Financial markets where traders neglect the informational content of prices. J. Financ. **74**(1), 371–399 (2019)
19. Liu, F., Ye, Q., Li, Y.J.: The interaction between media attention and investor attention on stock returns: an empirical study based on Chinese financial stocks. J. Manage. Sci. **17**(1), 72–85 (2014)
20. Dyck, A., Zingales, L.: Private benefits of control: an international comparison. J. Financ. **59**(2), 537–600 (2004)
21. Rogers, E.M., Dearing, J.W., Bregman, D.: The anatomy of agenda-setting research. J. Commun. **43**(2), 68–84 (1993)
22. Khan, M.: Corporate governance, ESG, and stock returns around the world. Financ. Anal. J. **75**(4), 103–123 (2019)
23. Amel-Zadeh, A., Serafeim, G.: Why and how investors use ESG information: evidence from a global survey. Financ. Anal. J. **74**(3), 87–103 (2018)

Analyzing Reasons for the Selection of Investment Objects Based on the Construction of Enterprise Ecological Value Network

Caixiaoyang Ge[✉]

Department of Business, XinJiang University, Urumqi 830000, XinJiang, China
107552102752@stu.xju.edu.cn

Abstract. In the context of the internet era, the enterprise value creation model has changed from a value chain to a value network. Ecological value networks are a form of enterprise network organization that can achieve resource allocation, which refers to the cooperation of different enterprises to gather their competitive advantages on an invisible value platform, forming a greater advantage and synergy, in order to better survive in the competitive market environment. However, most of the existing research on ecological value networks has been conducted in the field of management, and less research has been conducted in cross-disciplinary fields. The purpose of this paper was to apply a case study to explore why Mihoyo chose Soul to improve its ecological value network, combining organizational ecology and resource-based theory. This article concluded that Mihoyo chose Soul to build its ecological value network because of Soul's ability to meet Mihoyo's needs for enterprise niche width expansion, improve competitiveness, and comply with corporate strategy and resources. This paper suggested that Mihoyo can also better meet the needs of the enterprise by realizing enterprise niche management, innovating and opening up a "new track" timely adjusting the company's strategy, and establishing strategic alliances.

Keywords: Ecological value network · Enterprise niche · Corporate strategy · Mihoyo

1 Introduction

1.1 Research Background

At a time when the internet economy is expanding rapidly, intangible assets like traffic and product content have become important strategic resources. This is especially true for internet companies, where the importance of this resource is very clear. To be able to enjoy more traffic and resources to enhance their competitiveness, enterprises in the internet era have started to build their ecological value networks. The ecological value network theory requires enterprises to focus not only on their own development but also on the value creation system of the entire network to realize the hive effect. Building an enterprise ecological value network is more in line with the needs of today's enterprises to cope with the new competitive landscape and is gradually becoming one of the most important strategies for enterprises to adapt to the new competitive landscape. And corporate venture capital (CVC) is an important means for internet enterprises to build and improve their ecological value network. Because internet enterprises are not only a major subject of CVC but also have a good foundation for building an ecological value network [1]. Therefore, more and more internet enterprises choose to use CVC instead of costly enterprise acquisitions to improve their ecological value network; for example, Alibaba invested in Sina Weibo and Tencent invested in Bilibili.

In the context of this development, Mihoyo, a Chinese online game company, is also using CVC to enhance its ecological value network. In 2021, Mihoyo used CVC to invest in China's hottest social software, Soul, so that it entered the sector of social software for the first time and filled its gap in the ecological value network.

In the field of value networks, researchers have done in-depth studies on how to propose and define the idea, as well as on how value networks form, how they work, and what their competitive advantages are [2–8]. In 2006, Yan and Liu wrote about why enterprise value networks were made. They said that in today's rapidly changing information technology and network economy, businesses have a rigidity problem because they can't keep their core competitiveness in all parts of creating value. Enterprises must grow, improve, and keep their core competencies, and they can solve the problem of core rigidity by putting together a value network [4]. A corporate ecological value network is built on top of value networks. In 2022, Cai et al. say that corporate ecological value networks are built gradually during the process of implementing strategically-oriented CVC with a unique structure and layout that meets the strategic development needs of enterprises [5]. In 2000, Verna points out that an ecological value network is a form of enterprise network organization that can achieve resource allocation, referring to the cooperation of different enterprises to gather their respective competitive advantages in an invisible value platform, forming greater advantages and synergies to better survive in the competitive market environment [6].

1.2 Research Gap

The current existing research has studied value networks in sufficient depth, but there are still certain research deficiencies. To begin with, despite the fact that the perspective of ecology can often bring a broader vision to the study of management phenomena, few papers discuss the reasons why enterprises build ecological value networks from the perspective of organizational ecology [9]. Secondly, the existing studies do not combine resource-based theory and value network theory to explain the reasons for the selection of objects for the construction of ecological value networks by enterprises. Finally, although the emergence of value networks has strong characteristics of the internet era, few scholars have taken internet enterprises as the research object of value networks [10].

To fill the above research gap, this paper will examine why Mihoyo chose Soul to improve its ecological value network from the perspective of the needs of internet companies, combined with organizational ecology and resource-based theory. In the internet era, the competition of enterprises has changed from single-player competition in the past to the competition of enterprise networks, and the demand of enterprises for building value networks is increasing. How enterprises choose to build their ecological value networks is not only related to their future competitiveness and enterprise development strategies, but also to their current investment choices and value creation. The exploration of this issue has strong theoretical and practical significance.

1.3 Structure of This Paper

This article is divided into three parts: first, the case description, where the current situation of Mihoyo and Soul will be briefly introduced, as well as the background that motivated Mihoyo to invest in Soul. The second is the case study. From the perspective of Mihoyo's construction of an ecological value network, this paper will analyze why Mihoyo chose Soul from three perspectives: the requirement to expand the width of the enterprise niche, improve competitiveness, and avoid vicious competition, driven by enterprise strategy and resource demand. Thirdly, based on the above analysis, this paper will give suggestions for Mihoyo to better expand its ecological value network, improve competitiveness, and meet strategic resource needs. Finally, this paper concludes with a summary of the full paper and an outlook for the future.

2 Case Description

Mihoyo Technology Co Ltd. was established in 2014 in Shanghai, China, the company's scope of business includes the development of technologies in the field of network technology, computer technology, communication equipment technology, and electronic technology. Nowadays, Mihoyo has become one of the world's most popular mobile game companies with its product "Genshin Impact". Throughout its development, Mihoyo can be seen to have been trying to cooperate with companies in different fields to improve its ecological value network (see Fig. 1). However, before Mihoyo's investment in Soul, there had been a gap in the layout of the social software sector. Social software now serves as an important tool for companies to advertise, explore potential market customers, and maintain their corporate image, and many companies have realized its importance, such as Musk's acquisition of Twitter. Thus, Mihoyo's inability to satisfy the need in the social software industry is a critical weakness in its attempt to create an ecological value network.

Founded in 2016, Soul has become the hottest social platform in China today. It has made Generation Z the core of its user, based on its unique positioning and features in the social software industry as well as its immersive experience. At the same time, Soul was founded to build a "Youth Meta-verse" and Mihoyo has been building its own "Meta-verse", which makes the development concepts of the two coincide. Therefore, on 19 June 2021, Mihoyo used CVC to invest in Soul in Series D-4, with an investment amount of approximately RMB 9.33 million and a shareholding ratio of 5.47% [11].

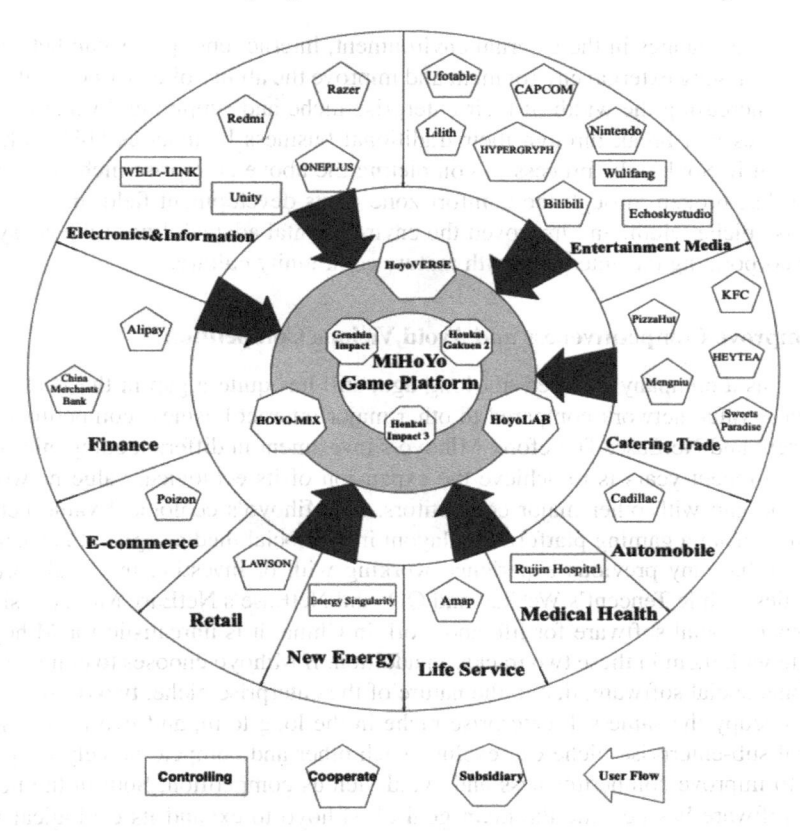

Fig. 1. The layout of the Mihoyo ecological value network (Photo credit: Original).

3 Analysis of the Problems

3.1 The Requirement to Expand the Width of the Enterprise Niche

In terms of organizational ecology theory, the reason for Mihoyo to improve its ecological value network is to gain access to the expansion of its enterprise niche. The concept of the enterprise niche evolved from the biological niche and refers to the multidimensional resource space that a company occupies in its strategic environment [12]. The width of the enterprise niche of an organizational ecosystem represents the ability of the ecosystem to obtain resources from the environment and maintain its survival, and its ability to match the environment in which the ecosystem is located largely influences the survival and development of that ecosystem [13].

As a company in the internet industry, Mihoyo has faced many challenges in recent years brought about by the changing external environment. The development of technologies such as big data and artificial intelligence, as well as the popularity of technologies such as live streaming and block chain, have brought pressure for change to internet companies, while the gradual exhaustion of the netizen dividend and the changing market demand have put higher demands on the growth models of internet companies. In the face of these changes in the external environment, internet enterprises can better cope with the changing external environment and improve the ability of ecosystem value creation by increasing the width of their enterprise niche and supplying diverse products and services that break through their traditional business boundaries [14]. Mihoyo's investment in Soul is the process of completing the above enterprise niche expansion. Mihoyo has broken through the comfort zone of its development field, increased the enterprise niche width, and improved the environmental adaptability of the ecosystem after incorporating the enterprise with mature community culture.

3.2 Improve Competitiveness and Avoid Vicious Competition

Mihoyo, as a company founded not long ago, still has quite a gap in the width of its ecological value network compared to other major internet business competitors, such as Tencent and NetEase. Therefore, Mihoyo's investment in different companies in the market in recent years is to achieve the expansion of its ecological value network to bridge the gap with other major competitors. As Mihoyo's ecological value network has grown from a gaming platform, its layout in the social media segment is weak and it has not had any previous experience working with or investing in social software companies. While Tencent's WeChat and QQ, and NetEase's NetEase Mail, consists of the basis of social software for life and work in China, it is unrealistic for Mihoyo to compete with them in these two tracks. In addition, if Mihoyo chooses to compete with traditional social software, due to the nature of the enterprise niche, two or more firms cannot occupy the same sub-enterprise niche in the long term, and two firms with an identical sub-enterprise niche can exclude each other and compete fiercely [15]. As a result, to improve competitiveness and avoid vicious competition, Soul in the field of dating software has become the main goal of Mihoyo to expand its ecological value network.

Today in China, dating software has developed a community culture with a large number of highly sticky quality users and a content marketing atmosphere, which is an important source of data and traffic. And more importantly, there is no single competitor in the market. In today's social environment where people are facing increasing mental and physical pressure, the demand for dating software in the market is also rising. The unique functions of Soul can be distinguished from traditional social software, and can better meet the social needs of contemporary young people, which has become a new trend in the field of social software. Therefore, by investing in Soul, Mihoyo has made its first attempt to lay out the social software segment, better filled the gap of the ecological value network in the field of social software layout, and narrowed the gap with its main competitors in this field. At the same time, it avoids vicious competition, expands the development space of the entire ecosystem, and improves the competitiveness of its ecological value network.

3.3 Driven by Enterprise Strategy and Resource Demand

According to resource-based theory, an enterprise is a collection of resources that are difficult to imitate, and the differentiated combination of resources it possesses can form its competitive advantage [16]. At different stages of development, the external environment and the capacity of its resources are constantly changing dynamically, which determines the differentiated corporate strategy and resource needs of the enterprise at different development periods [17].

Soul is a perfect fit for Mihoyo's current corporate strategy and resource requirements. Firstly, from the perspective of a "Market expansion strategy", Mihoyo's ecosystem needs a high-paying audience group. According to Soul Prospectus, 74.9% of Soul's monthly active users are Gen Z in 2021. Quest Mobile's 2021 Mobile Game Crowd Insight Report, the main source of customers for mobile games are millennials and Gen Z, accounting for approximately 47.4% [18]. In addition, according to Mihoyo's CEO Wei Liu, the core user age group for Mihoyo's products is between 18–29 years old. Therefore, Soul and Mihoyo's audience groups have a high degree of overlap. Not only that, but the huge user traffic accumulated by Soul also contains a huge consumption capacity. In 2019–2021, the average monthly number of paying users of Soul are 0.27 million, 0.93 million, and 1.7 million respectively, while the average monthly revenue per paying user is RMB21.9, 43.5, and 60.5 respectively, with a paying ratio of 2.3%, 4.5% and 5.2% [11]. This shows that a large number of the same audience group also provides Mihoyo with a rich pool of potential paying users, allowing it to fully exploit the commercial value of its products. Therefore, Mihoyo has chosen to invest in Soul to meet its strategic need to expand its market share and tap into its potential user base.

Secondly, the "Drainage development strategy" requires high-quality and high-viscosity market flows for Mihoyo's ecosystem. After several years, Soul has developed a rather full content operation and community structure. Soul Prospectus says Soul is China's second most active daily dating software user. In 2021, Soul had 31.6 million monthly active users, up 51.6%, and 9.3 million daily active users, up 55.8% [19]. A high-quality weekly retained gamer costs $10 to acquire, and Soul has tens of millions of monthly active users. Mihoyo's RMB 9.33 million Soul investment yielded a significant return. After some time, Soul has acquired the strategic resources needed by the Mihoyo ecosystem and can deliver large market traffic to its core profitability platform. Mihoyo chose Soul to address its strategic demand for high-quality market traffic.

In summary, Soul not only meet Mihoyo's corporate strategy of "Market expansion strategy" and "Drainage development strategy", but it also meets Mihoyo's resource requirements, which is why Mihoyo has chosen Soul to build its ecological value network.

4 Suggestions

4.1 Extending Ecological Value Networks Based on the Concept of Enterprise Niche Management

When multiple companies enter the same ecological value network, if the resource needs of the companies entering the network overlap, and if the value creation and market positioning are the same, the enterprise niche will be completely or partially overlapped, resulting in competition between each other, and the function of the ecological value network will not be maximized [15]. To maximize the hive effect of the ecological value network, Mihoyo should adopt the concept of enterprise niche management to avoid the negative effects of overlapping enterprise niches in space and time.

First, Mihoyo should establish the management concept of "Spatial enterprise niche". When Mihoyo expands its ecological value network in the future, it should choose areas where there is less overlap with existing companies in the value network, especially the weakest areas. And where companies in the same area can complement each other's strengths. This is a significant way to avoid internal friction in the ecological value network, maximize the use of valuable network resources and achieve win-win cooperation.

Second, Mihoyo needs to establish a "Time enterprise niche" management concept. Before Mihoyo enters a new sector or enterprise to expand its ecological value network, it needs to identify a portfolio of resources with greater potential for value creation in its ecosystem, and invest in that portfolio when it is more empowering and exit when it is less empowering. In this way, Mihoyo can maximize the number of times the same enterprise niche changes over the timeline, ensure that the enterprise niche provides the maximum amount of resource empowerment, while developing along the innovative ecological dimension to optimize the allocation of resources and enjoy the highest level of resource empowerment with the least amount of investment.

4.2 Enhancing Competitiveness Through Innovation and Opening Up "New Track"

In today's world, in the face of new trends and opportunities for technological innovation, companies have made innovation the core of their corporate strategy and the most important means of enhancing their core competitiveness. In this context, Mihoyo is not only constructing an ecological value network to enhance its competitiveness, but also creating a "New track" in existing areas through its innovation to fundamentally improve its competitiveness.

By using a differentiation strategy to innovate and create a "New track", Mihoyo can build on its unique platform to expand into existing areas. Compared to its main competitors, Mihoyo's dominant platform is "Quadratic element" products. Nowadays, as the impact of "Quadratic element" culture and audience groups continue to expand, Mihoyo, as one of the leaders in the "quadratic element" sector today, can build platforms dedicated to serving various areas of the "Quadratic element" community with its own accumulated large group of high quality "Quadratic element" users, to achieve the opening of new tracks in different areas. By establishing its unique core competencies through innovation, Mihoyo can gain a long-term competitive advantage by occupying a different enterprise niche from its competitors in the market competition.

4.3 Timely Adjust Development Strategies and Build Strategic Alliances to Meet Resource Needs

For enterprises, their strategy and resource requirements are different at different stages of development. This requires Mihoyo to accurately identify its core resource needs and adjust its strategy on time to match its strategy with its resource needs. At the same time, Mihoyo may choose to form strategic alliances with companies to gain access to more strategic resources and to enjoy long-term, efficient access to the resources it needs [20].

Firstly, in the future, with Mihoyo's long-term business development, the company has gradually accumulated enough loyal users and the high viscosity of traffic has become the company's advantageous resource, so the core resources need to be transformed into a mature profit model. Therefore, Mihoyo's development strategy should be changed from "Market expansion strategy" to "Profit transformation strategy", to build its ecological value network with companies that have mature sales channels, enhance its profitability and expand its profit scale. In addition, once Mihoyo has a large number of highly sticky users, its core needs have been transformed into basic resources such as content products. Strategic positioning should also be changed from "Drainage development strategy" to "Diversion development strategy", by investing in the content production side of the ecological value network, combining its traffic advantages with the advantages of high-quality content products of the invested companies to maximize the commercial value of the enterprise.

Secondly, Mihoyo has the option of forming strategic alliances with other companies to meet core resource requirements. In strategic alliances, Mihoyo can identify, possess and learn from strategic resources more effectively, and long-term alliance cooperation can facilitate the establishment of trust mechanisms between member companies, which in turn creates a sense of trust in the sharing of resources to obtain real core technologies and valuable information to occupy or maintain a competitive advantage in the market.

5 Conclusion

In the internet era, the pattern of competition has changed from competition between individual enterprises to competition between enterprise networks. Ecological value networks are more conducive to the new competitive landscape than value chains, so there is an urgent need for companies to build ecological value networks. Against this background, this paper examines the case of Mihoyo's investment in Soul to build its ecological value network. This paper explored the question of why Mihoyo chose Soul to build its ecological value network by analyzing three aspects: the width of the enterprise niche, competitiveness, and corporate strategy and resource requirements. And ultimately concluded that, firstly, Soul meets Mihoyo's need to expand the width of its enterprise niche in response to changes in the macro environment. Secondly, Soul meets Mihoyo's need to improve its competitiveness against its main competitors and to avoid vicious competition. Finally, the core resources provided by Soul are in line with Mihoyo's current corporate strategy and resource requirements.

The research contributions and innovations of this paper are as follows: First, in terms of theoretical significance, this paper innovatively chooses to analyze the reasons for the object selection of enterprises to build an ecological value network from the perspective of organizational ecology theory and resource-based theory, which can be a more unique and in-depth analysis of the reasons and enrich and supplement the relevant theories in the field of the value network. Secondly, in terms of practical significance, this paper analyzes and gives suggestions on the aspects of Mihoyo's enterprise niche width, competitiveness, enterprise strategy, and resource demand, which can provide a reference for Mihoyo's future development. In addition, the case study of Mihoyo also has certain reference significance for other internet companies with similar positioning.

There are some problems with this paper. First, when looking at why Mihoyo chose Soul to build the ecological value network, there may be other important reasons that haven't been looked at yet because of the influence of personal subjectivity. These other possible reasons need to be looked at from different angles in the future. Second, this paper is mostly based on qualitative analysis. It needs some quantitative analysis to make the demonstration stronger, and the demonstration process needs to be improved in the future by adding relevant quantitative analysis.

References

1. Li, F., Whalley, J.: Deconstruction of the telecommunications industry: from value chains to value networks. Telecommun. Policy **26**(9), 451–472 (2002)
2. Khknen, A.K., Virolainen, V.M.: Sources of structural power in the context of value nets. J. Purch. Supply Manag. **17**(2), 109–120 (2011)
3. Zhang, X., Chen, L.R.: Research on the mechanism of value network formation in multinational corporations: an extension of value chain theory. Econ. Manag. **22**, 12–17 (2004)
4. Yan, Z.F., Liu, D.: A modular network of core competencies. Sci. Technol. Manag. **5**, 75–78 (2006)
5. Cai, W.J., Jiang, Y.C., Su, J.L., Zhu, J.G.: Research on the timing of corporate venture capital based on the framework of ecological value network: case study of Alibaba and Tencent investing in Bilibili. Account. Res. **5**, 105–117 (2022)
6. Verna, A.: Reconfiguring the value network. J. Bus. Strateg. **21**(4), 36–39 (2000)
7. Yu, D.H., Rui, M.J.: Value flow and innovation based on modular network organization. China Ind. Econ. **12**, 48–59 (2008)
8. Zhou, X.: Endogenous interpretation of competitive advantage of enterprise value network: knowledge management. Bus. Econ. Manag. **2**, 28–31 (2006)
9. Moore, J.F.: The Death of Competition: Leadership and Strategy in the Age of Business Ecosystems. Harper Business New York (1996)
10. Bovet, D., Kramer, J.: Value Nets: Breaking the Supply Chain to Unlock Hidden Profits. Wiley, New York (2000)
11. HKMEx Homepage. http://www.hkex.com.hk/. Accessed 3 Oct 2023
12. Hannan, M.T., Freeman, J.H.: The population ecology of organizations. Am. J. Sociol. **82**(5), 929–964 (1977)
13. Sorenson, O., McEvily, S., Ren, C.R.: Niche width revisited: organizational scope, behavior, and performance. Strateg. Manag. J. **27**(10), 915–936 (2006)
14. Hannan, M.T., Freeman, J.H.: Organizational ecology. Ann. Rev. Sociol. **10**(1), 71–93 (1984)
15. Xu, F., Li, J.H.: Research on the principles and models of enterprise niche. China Soft Sci. **5**, 130–139 (2005)
16. Wernerfelt, B.: A resource-based view of the firm. Strateg. Manag. J. **5**(2), (1984)
17. Eisenhardt, K.M., Schoonhoven, C.B.: Resource-based view of strategic alliance formation: strategic and social effects in entrepreneurial firms. Organ. Sci. **7**(2), 136–150 (1996)
18. Quest Mobile Homepage. https://www.questmobile.com.cn/. Accessed 3 Nov 2023
19. BaiJiaHao Homepage. https://baijiahao.baidu.com/. Accessed 3 Nov 2023
20. Das, T.K., Teng, B.S.: A resource-based theory of strategic alliances. J. Manag. **26**(1), 31–61 (2000)

Analysis of the Motivation and Performance of Merger and Reorganization of Companies Under Performance Commitment--Based on the Dual Case Study of DF Company's Acquisition of Pride and Fosber

Liu Yu[✉]

International College of Zhengzhou University, Zhengzhou 450000, Henan, China
liuyu1101144305@163.com

Abstract. In order to explore how performance commitment affects the performance of corporate merger and reorganization, this paper analyzes performance through financial index method based on double case analysis. There are many case studies on DF Company's acquisition of Pride Company, but this paper focuses on the analysis of the differences between Fosber and Pride at the time of acquisition, so as to explore the motivation of merger and reorganization under the performance commitment and the performance after merger. Reorganization is a favorable means to improve the competitiveness of enterprises, and it is also a "credit enhancement commitment" made in the case of information asymmetry. However, performance commitment does not mean once and for all, and the motivation of merger and reorganization is also an important factor to be considered when making performance commitment. There are many case studies on the failure of DF Company's merger of Pride Company, but on why DF Company acquired many companies, only Pride Company got into interest disputes, while other acquired companies fulfilled their performance commitments well. On this basis, this paper analyzes the differences between Fosber and Pride at the time of acquisition, in order to explore the motivation of merger and reorganization under the performance commitment and the performance after merger.

Keywords: merger and reorganization · performance commitment · merger motivation

1 Introduction

Merger and reorganization is a favorable means to improve the competitiveness of enterprises. And in its process there are often risks brought by information asymmetry. Therefore, in order to avoid losses and improve the efficiency of the transaction, enterprises usually sign performance commitments to bind the subsequent business cooperation. In fact, the performance commitment made by the merger and reorganization party in the case of information asymmetry is a 'credit enhancement commitment' to the listed company, which increases the valuation of the merger and reorganization assets and increases the revenue of the asset seller through the performance commitment [1]. However, signing a performance promise does not mean that it is once and for all, and many problems such as over-valuation and unclear business strategic planning can lead to invalidation of the performance promise. In order to avoid benefit disputes or corporate losses due to the lapse of performance commitments, before signing performance commitments, merger and reorganization parties should target the selection of targets, develop contracts and integration finishing based on relevant information [2], and prudently develop performance commitments based on the actual operating conditions and future development prospects of the company. Otherwise, the strong pressure from performance commitments is likely to cause management to take inappropriate measures to implement the bets [3].

At the same time, the motivation of merger and reorganization is an important factor to be referred to when formulating performance commitments. The motives for merger and reorganization of Chinese enterprises are diverse. While adjusting the unreasonable shareholding structure is the fundamental motive for the high proportion of property rights of most listed companies, purchasing the assets of the acquirer at a low price and eliminating loss-making enterprises are also common motives for merger and reorganization [4]. The motives for domestic enterprises' merger and reorganization mainly include market expansion and shell listing, while the motives for cross-border merger and reorganization are mainly manifested as seeking cross-border resources, acquiring advanced technology of multinational enterprises and using nationalized brand and market resources [5]. In essence, the purpose of the existence of performance commitments is to assess the value of the underlying assets reasonably and accurately, and to reduce the huge risks that the acquirer may bear through performance commitments for a certain period of time [6]. However, it is clear that many merger and reorganization restructuring cases in recent years have not exerted the efficacy of performance promises, and many performance promises have ended in failure. After analyzing the merger and reorganization performance based on various methods, it can be found that the explanatory power of comprehensive indicators, etc. On merger and reorganization performance is not significant [7], while financial indicators, such as profitability and operating capacity, can better measure the merger and reorganization performance [8].

Therefore, in order to investigate how performance commitments affect the merger and reorganization performance of companies and why performance commitments mostly end in failure, this paper selects the cases of merger and reorganization of Pride and Fosber by DF company and analyzes the merger and reorganization performance by analyzing financial indicators. There are many studies on the failed cases of merger and reorganization of Pride by DF company, but there are few studies on why DF company acquired several companies, while Pride was caught in the interest dispute, the other acquired companies completed their performance commitments well? Based on this, this paper analyzes the differences between Fosber and Pride when they were acquired, in order to explore the motivation of merger and reorganization under performance commitment and post-merger performance.

2 Case Review

2.1 Introduction of Tripartite Companies

Guangdong Dongfang Precision Science and Technology Co., Ltd. It (hereinafter referred to as DF company) was established in 1996 and listed in 2011. Mainly engaged in corrugated printing and packaging, it is a provider of corrugated box printing and packaging equipment integrating design, research and development capability, production and sales. Prior to its IPO, DF company's main assets and business scope were limited to the domestic market. Since 2014, DF company has been gradually entering the international market.

Fosber S.p.A. Fosber S.p.A. (hereinafter referred to as Fosber) is an Italian corrugated box manufacturer, founded in Florence, Italy in 1978. Its main business is high-end corrugated cardboard production lines. In 2014 and 2019, DF company acquired 60% and 40% of Fosber Group's shares respectively. Fosber Group has now become a wholly-owned subsidiary of DF company.

In 2014, DF company established a subsidiary in the Netherlands, which acquired 60% of Fosber's shares. The acquisition took the form of cash payment. DF company used its own cash and applied for a loan from a bank to pay for the acquisition amount of 40.8 million euros and used over-issued funds of about 66.5 million yuan to pay for the deposit of the bank loan. In order to reduce the risk brought by the acquisition, DF company signed a three-year performance commitment with Fosber and agreed to pay performance compensation in cash.

Beijing Pride Power System Technology Limited. It (hereinafter referred to as Pride) was established in 2010, jointly funded by several companies and not listed. Mainly engaged in the research and development of new energy vehicle power battery materials, focusing on the research and development of passenger car power system, belongs to the high salary technology enterprise.

In 2016, DF company took a hybrid Merger and reorganization approach to acquire 100% of Pride's equity for 4.75 billion yuan. The Merger and reorganization issued 320 million shares and paid 1.8 billion yuan in cash to pay for the acquisition consideration, generating a high goodwill of 4.14 billion yuan. At the same time, in order to reduce the risk caused by information asymmetry, DF company signed a performance commitment with Pride for a commitment period of four years, and the profit commitment period is four fiscal years from 2016–2019. And it is agreed that the performance compensation for the first three years will be paid in priority equity, followed by cash payment, and the fourth year will be paid in pure cash (Tables 1 and 2).

2.2 Performance Commitments and Degree of Completion of the Two Acquisition Agreements

Fosber

Table 1. Fosber's performance commitments and degree of completion

	2014	2015	2016	Total amount
Performance commitment/10 thousand Euros	700	750	750	2200
Actual completion /10 thousand euros	700.27	583.98	1200.88	2485.13
Completion degree /%	100.04	77.86	160.12	112.96

Pride

Table 2. Pride's performance commitments and degree of completion

	2016	2017	2018	2019	Total amount
Performance commitment/100 million yuan	2.50	3.25	4.23	5.00	9.98
Actual completion/100 million yuan	3.33	2.61	−2.17	3.77	7.54
Completion degree /%	133.20	80.31	−51.77	37.78	75.55

3 Case Analysis

3.1 The Intention of DF Company to Make Two Acquisitions

Acquisition of Fosber: Get a Win-Win Situation and Enter the International Market Fosber is the world's second largest manufacturer of corrugated boxes, with a large share of the international market. In 2014, Fosber's sales exceeded 1 billion yuan, but at this point, Fosber was facing two problems: no one to take over and a gap in the Asian market. Therefore, Fosber intends to find a buyer to take over the company in order to enhance the development of the company and its research and development capability. And DF company has been actively seeking to enter the international market since it went public in 2011. After the acquisition of Fosber, DF company can directly take over the market share of Fosber in Europe and America. After the acquisition of Fosber, DF company acquired 60% of Fosber's shares, and Fosber also filled the vacant Asian market.

Acquisition of Pride:

DF Company Needs to Diversify. In 2014, DF company acquired 60% of Fosber and set performance commitments. Although Fosber is extremely profitable, it is still only a corrugated box manufacturer in the same industry as DF company. In the past decade, national policies have tilted more toward environmental protection and green development. Since it went public in 2011, DF company has been actively pursuing technological transformation in the face of policy restrictions and the extremely low percentage of intelligent corrugated paper plants. At the same time, the new energy industry is being strongly supported by the state, and Pride is one of the leading players. Therefore, DF company expects to continue to acquire Pride in order to diversify its business.

The Development Prospect of Pride is Worthy of Expectation. DF company is a traditional manufacturer with slow profit growth. In contrast, Pride has been focusing on the research and development of new energy batteries since its establishment in 2010, and has become the leader in China's lithium battery industry in just a few years. in 2015, Pride turned its losses into profits and achieved a net profit of 100 million yuan, and reached 113 million yuan in 2016. Therefore, DF company, as a traditional enterprise with abundant cash flow, is very eager to merge and acquire Pride, a leader in the emerging industry.

3.2 Changes in Financial Indicators of DF Company Before and After the Merger

Four aspects are considered: Profitability, Operating capacity, Solvency, and Development capacity.

Profitability. Profitability is a judgment of an enterprise's ability to generate profits and an indicator of its operating results over a certain period of time. The following chart shows the trend of profitability indicators of DF company during the period of 2011–2019. (Table 3)

Table 3. DF company's Profitability Indicators

	2011	2012	2013	2014	2015	2016	2017	2018	2019
Return on equity (%)	21.00	19.21	15.36	10.07	7.20	6.90	8.85	−67.71	36.87
Net profit on sales (%)	34.93	35.57	35.78	9.20	6.51	8.37	11.12	−58.43	18.44
Gross profit margin on sales (%)	22.11	8.68	7.20	27.21	24.94	26.25	22.34	17.31	16.92

As can be seen from Fig. 1, DF company's acquisition of Fosber did not result in improved profitability. Fosber and DF company are both leading international corrugated carton manufacturers with a large degree of overlap in business content, so that DF

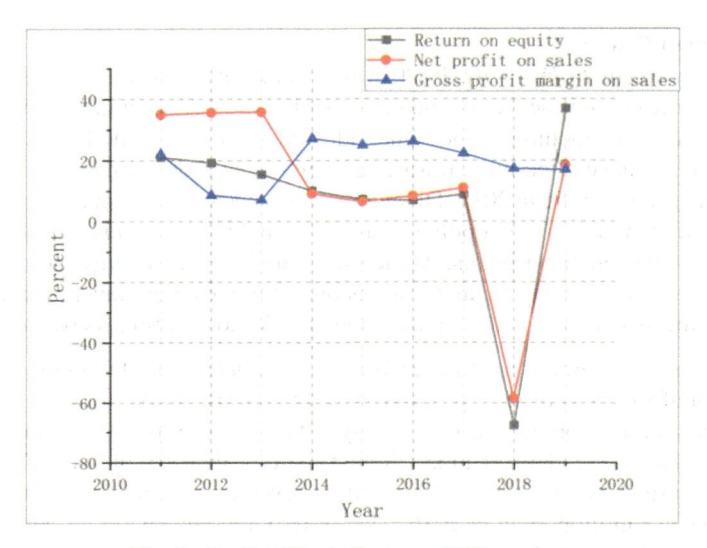

Fig. 1. Profitability indicators of DF company

company's gross and net profit margins on asset sales have remained relatively stable for several years after the acquisition. Therefore, the expectation of improving profitability was probably one of the main reasons for DF company's acquisition of Pride. However, the acquisition of Pride only brought a small increase initially, and in 2018, DF company made an impairment provision for goodwill and the return on net assets hit the bottom. After the sale of Pride in 2019, the indicators of DF company returned to normal.

Operating Capacity. Operating capacity reflects the efficiency of a company's operation. This paper selects some financial indicators of DF company from 2011 to 2019 as the basis for measuring operating capacity (Table 4).

Table 4. DF company's Operating Capacity Indicators

	2011	2012	2013	2014	2015	2016	2017	2018	2019
Inventory turnover (times)	2.55	2.03	2.06	4.25	2.96	2.96	5.17	5.64	10.31
Days of accounts receivable turnover (days)	23.41	31.79	42.90	41.03	69.03	66.76	59.94	175.20	63.16
Days of inventory turnover (days)	141.25	177.00	174.98	84.70	121.50	121.61	69.57	63.81	34.91

From Fig. 2 and Fig. 3, it can be seen that the merger and acquisition of Fosber is a big test for DF company, as the volume of Fosber is much larger than DF company,

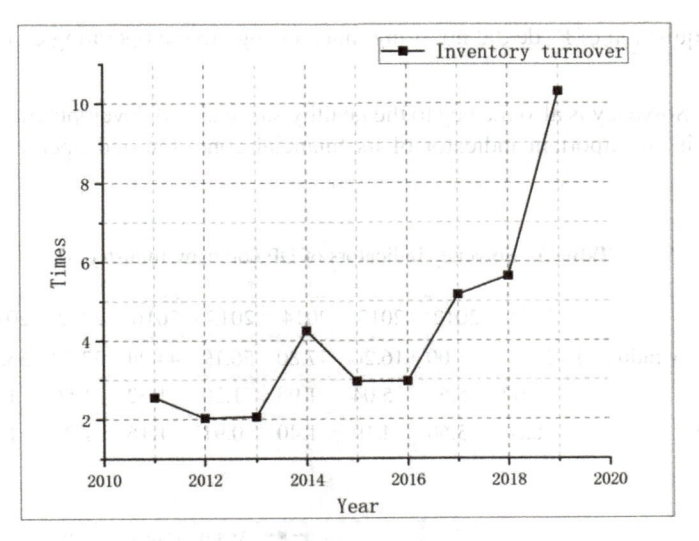

Fig. 2. Change in the number of inventory turnover

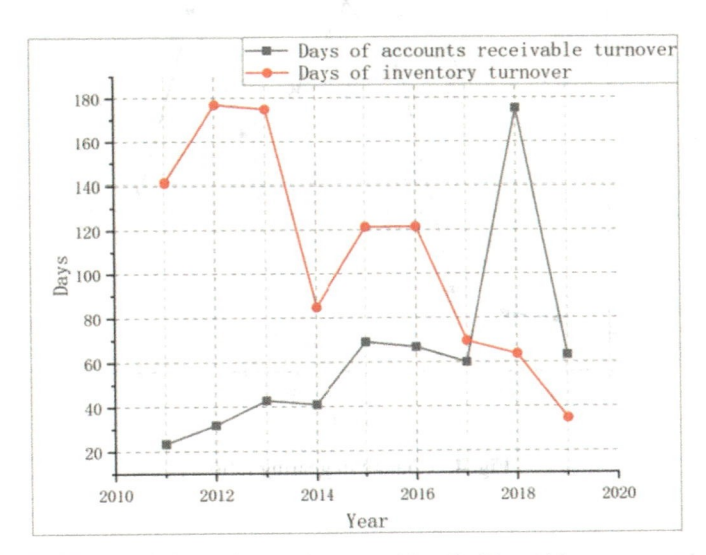

Fig. 3. Change in turnover days of accounts receivable and inventory turnover

and its business development scope and production base are located in Europe and America. After the merger, DF company needs to pay time to inventory and investigate Fosber's production equipment and production lines, and further plan the development of their respective blank areas. Therefore, the inventory turnover days and accounts receivable turnover days have increased slightly after the merger. After the acquisition of Pride, the inventory turnover days started to decline gradually, but the number of accounts receivable and inventory turnover both increased significantly, which shows that the acquisition of Pride did not bring much change to the operating capacity of DF company.

Solvency. Solvency is also the key to the healthy survival and development of an enterprise, and is an important indicator of its financial condition and operating capacity (Table 5).

Table 5. Solvency indicators of DF company Industry

	2011	2012	2013	2014	2015	2016	2017	2018	2019
Asset-liability ratio (%)	12.13	13.00	16.26	47.80	56.19	44.24	37.99	55.13	29.83
Current ratio	7.02	6.60	5.04	1.95	1.30	1.52	1.56	1.80	3.27
Quick ratio	6.04	5.60	4.19	1.40	0.91	1.16	1.32	1.56	2.83

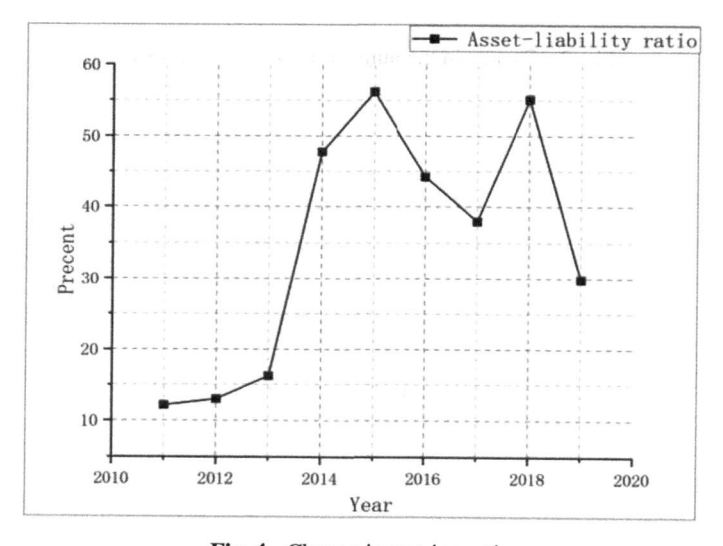

Fig. 4. Change in gearing ratio

As can be seen from Fig. 4, the high gearing ratio of DF company in the early period is greatly linked to the cash acquisition method it chose. After the acquisition of Fosber, the gearing ratio of DF company increased extremely rapidly and reached the peak in 2015. Since then, it has been decreasing year by year, and since 2016, with the completion of the merger and reorganization business, DF company's gearing ratio has reached a new low. However, with the failure of Pride's performance commitment in 2018, DF company's gearing ratio rose sharply again until it was sold for billions yuan in 2019 and then decreased. The quick ratio and current ratio in Fig. 5 likewise reflect changes in Eastern Precision's solvency in addition to its debt service. After the acquisition of Fosber, whose annual sales were more than three times its own, DF

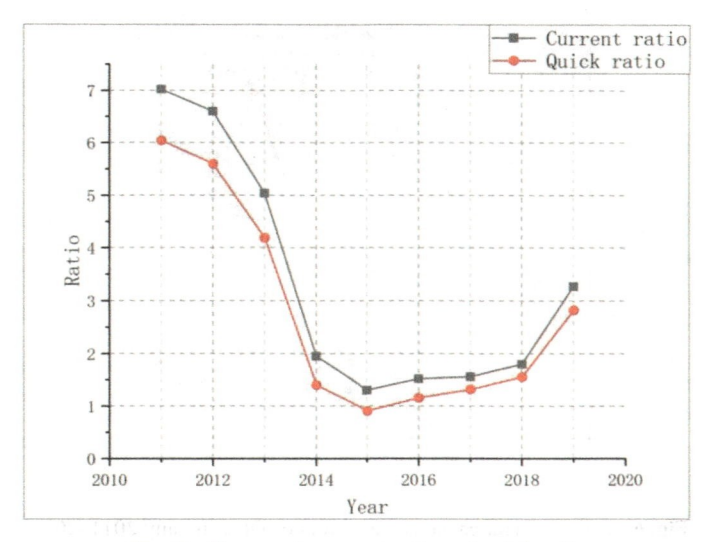

Fig. 5. Changes in current ratio and quick ratio

company's quick ratio and current ratio dropped sharply until the acquisition of Pride, when they gradually rebounded. This shows that the way DF company set up the merger and reorganization and the size of the merger and reorganization company affected its subsequent debt servicing ability.

Development Capacity. Development capability can, to a certain extent, infer the future development prospect of an enterprise, therefore, this paper selects development capability as a financial indicator to measure the performance of DF company (Table 6).

Table 6. DF company Development Capability Indicators

	2011	2012	2013	2014	2015	2016	2017	2018	2019
Deduct of non-net profit growth rate (%)	63.02	−9.51	4.41	29.83	−35.30	−9.07	623.24	−1205.98	111.23
Revenue growth rate (%)	32.78	−8.26	10.26	225.78	8.78	18.43	205.52	41.34	50.63
Net profit growth rate (%)	78.17	−16.28	−12.17	49.84	−22.91	47.53	412.76	−890.22	147.42

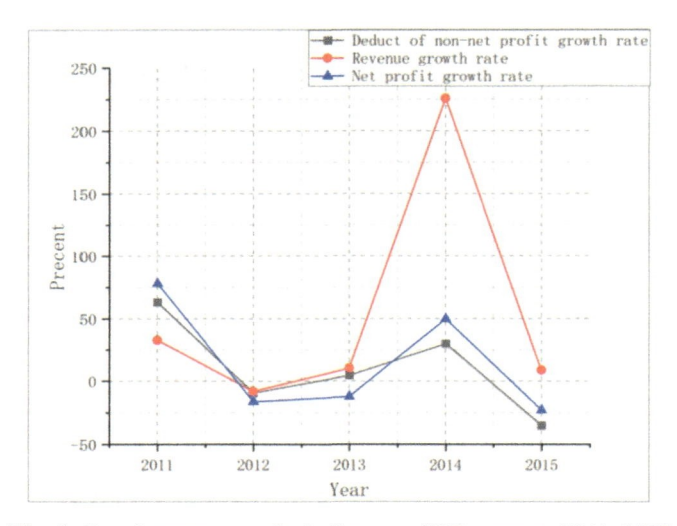

Fig. 6. Development capacity indicators of DF company 2011–2015

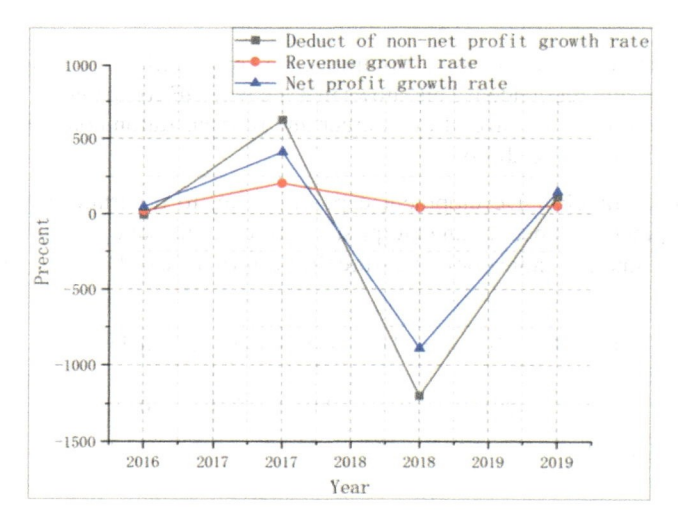

Fig. 7. Development capacity indicators of DF company 2016–2019

As shown in Fig. 6 and Fig. 7, after the acquisition of Fosber, the net profit growth rate and operating income growth rate of DF company have increased significantly, and the net profit growth rate has turned negative to positive. In order to judge the profitability of Fosber, DF company and Fosber agreed to an observation period in 2013, and Fosber promised that the net profit of the year would not be less than 6.5 million Euros. 2014, DF company released the announcement of merger and reorganization restructuring and announced that the actual net profit of Fosber in 2013 was 709.33 million Euros. This shows that Fosber's net profit, etc. is in a stable development state. However, in 2015,

Fosber failed to complete the set performance commitment, and the indicators of that year ushered in another decline. The addition of Pride, a new industry, has greatly boosted DF company's development capacity, and the new energy batteries it operates are highly profitable and rapidly developing, opening up a new development path for DF company. However, the same dispute generated by Pride in 2018 caused the bottom of the level of various indicators of DF company, which was sold the following year and returned to normal.

3.3 Analysis of the Reasons for the Failure of the Merger and Reorganization Pride Case

Lack of Effective Control by the Acquirer. DF company acquired 100% of the equity of Pride in 2016. However, after the completion of the merger and reorganization restructuring, DF company gave Pride greater autonomy in various aspects such as production, operation and management, and did not intervene in Pride's original corporate business strategy and corporate staffing. The majority of the board of directors and senior management of Pride are held by Pride's original employees. The lack of control over Pride by DF company also led to its inability to detect Pride's actual operating conditions and corporate strategy in a timely manner. Since the merger and reorganization, Pride's management personnel have been re-elected and handed over their jobs several times, and there have been several changes of important position members within three years. With the loss of actual control by DF company, the confusion within the management of Pride greatly hindered the internal management of the company.

Excessive Merger and Reorganization Premiums. When DF company acquired Pride in 2016, Pride's net assets were only 227 million yuan, but the appraisal company eventually assessed an appraised value of 4.75 billion yuan, with an appraisal appreciation rate of nearly two thousand times. This move generated extremely high goodwill in order to make Pride nearly unprofitable after the $3.8 billion goodwill accrual by DF company in 2018. Although Pride began to gradually return to profitability in 2019, the previously caused interest disputes and failed performance commitments have doomed the end of DF company's sale of Pride.

Pride does not Receive Sufficient Financial Support. Pride is mainly engaged in new energy vehicle power battery. Since 2016, China's subsidies for the new energy vehicle battery industry have been reduced year by year, and problems such as imperfect support for new energy vehicles and short deliverable mileage have also restricted the development of the whole industry. Without a large amount of capital investment, it would be difficult for Pride to face such a difficult situation when it has just turned a loss into profit. Therefore, at the beginning of the merger, DF company promised to crowdfund one billion yuan to invest in the development of the new factory site in Liyang city and the subsequent research and development capability work. However, in the follow-up process, Pride did not get the fund although it applied for it. The new plant in Liyang city is the key development project of Pride, and from the depreciation of Pride's machines, the depreciation rate of Pride's equipment is high, which requires great investment to keep its high capacity. Therefore, in the state of technology research and development and capital chain obstruction, it is really difficult to maintain high output level.

Cross-Border Merger and Reorganization. Pride focuses on new energy automotive power batteries, while DF company has been deeply involved in the corrugated box production and sales industry and outboard power equipment for many years. Although DF company's production lines became intelligent and integrated after the acquisition of Fosber, its industry was ultimately far from new energy batteries. DF company's top management's lack of understanding of the new energy battery industry also led to its eventual loss of control and its inability to plan ahead or correct Pride's development path in a timely manner.

3.4 What are the Differences Between Fosber and Pride in the Process of Fulfilling Performance Commitments?

Clear Management of Fosber Subsidiaries. In terms of personnel arrangement, the two sides established a joint venture subsidiary after the merger, which is responsible for production and sales, so all the movements of the subsidiary can be informed by DF company at the first time. Meanwhile, in the shareholders' meeting held on March 26, 2014, Fosber accepted the resignation of three original directors and appointed five new directors, three of whom were nominated by DF company. Except for the change of board members, there was no change of Fosber's core technical staff and core management. In terms of business handling, Fosber has been operating for many years and its production lines are sufficient and complete, and all matters are in order. The merger and acquisition did not affect Fosber's original production process.

The Performance Commitment Set by Fosber is Objective and Feasible. Fosber's performance commitment is objective and feasible, and there is no extremely high premium. In 2013, DF company and Fosber agreed on a one-year observation period, and Fosber committed to a net profit of €6.5 million for that year. The subsequent audit confirmed that Fosber's actual net profit in 2013 was €709.33 million. Therefore, DF company set up the performance commitment for the acquisition of Fosber based on this value, which required Fosber to complete the net profit income of 7million, 7.5 million and 7.5 million Euros in three fiscal years from 2014 to 2016, respectively. According to the audit announcement issued by DF company in 2017, Fosber exceeded the three-year performance commitment.

Both Acquiring Parties are Familiar with the Business. Fosber has been established for many years, and its production lines and equipment are extremely well established, so there is no need for additional investment in research and development capability, etc. Fosber and DF company are both corrugated box manufacturers. The merger will only expand market share for DF company, and does not involve planning or integration into new industries.

4 Conclusion and Insights

Through the above analysis, the motivation of DF company's merger and reorganization of Pride and Fosber is clearly shown. The purpose of DF company's acquisition of Fosber is to enter the international market and expand its market share, while the acquisition of Pride is to promote the diversification of the company and open up a new track. However, when setting performance commitments on both occasions, DF company did not manage to exercise the same objective caution: (1) The high valuation premium of Pride was high. Before the merger and acquisition, DF company valued Pride at 4.75 billion yuan, generating extremely high goodwill. This behavior made investors worry and also sowed hidden dangers for the subsequent development of Pride. (2) The performance commitment of Pride is not objective and reasonable. The high valuation and high premium at the time of the merger and acquisition caused DF company to set extremely high and unreasonable performance promises. In order to avoid the failure of the performance promise, Pride frequently changed the top management and changed the development route, which eventually led to the disorder of Pride's internal operation.

Therefore, before proceeding with merger and reorganization restructuring, enterprises should conduct thorough planning and detailed investigation. Firstly, merger and reorganization is a powerful means to improve the competitiveness of an enterprise, but when conducting merger and reorganization restructuring, attention should be focused on the motivation of the enterprise for merger and reorganization. If the enterprise is in the position of diversification and development intending to conduct cross-industry merger, it should cautiously evaluate the development prospect of the merged company, and at the same time deeply understand the cross-industry so as not to lose control and be unable to plan or amend the development route. Second, when setting performance commitments, it is also important to objectively evaluate the actual profitability and future development trend of the merger and reorganization company to avoid setting too high a target that may lead to disputes if it cannot be completed. It is also important to set appropriate payment methods for acquisition payments and performance compensation to avoid causing cash flow shortages in the company or the management of the merger and reorganization company doing whatever it can to complete the performance commitment.

References

1. Jingda, W., Qingquan, F.: Research on performance commitment and policy impact in Merger and reorganization restructuring of listed companies. Acc. Res. **10**, 71–77+97 (2017)
2. Yi, S., Changqi, W.: Risk control in corporate mergers and acquisitions: the role of professional consulting organizations. Nankai Manage. Rev. **15**(04):4–14+65 (2012)
3. Xianlu, W., Yifeng, W.: Exploration of performance commitment and risk prevention–an example of DF company Jingong's merger and acquisition of pride. Friends Acc. **19**, 95–100 (2020)
4. Wenmei, W.: An analysis of the motivation of mergers and acquisitions of listed companies in China. Theory Pract. Finan. Econ. **S1**, 87–89 (2001)
5. Wenjia, Z.: Analysis of the motives of cross-border mergers and acquisitions of Chinese enterprises. Finan. Dev. Res. **03**, 3–9 (2015)

6. Wei, D., Hua, S., Ying, H.: "High premium" or "high quality"? –research on the reliability of performance commitment of Merger and reorganization restructuring of listed companies in China. Econ. Manage. **41**(02), 156–171 (2019)
7. Fang, C., Shimin, J.: Analysis of corporate financial indicators and Merger and reorganization performance. Econ. Issues **06**, 117–119 (2007)
8. Yimei, L.: The construction of financial evaluation index system for small and medium-sized enterprises. Bus. Modernization **29**, 324 (2006)

Monetary Policy Regulation and Macroeconomic Fluctuations—Empirical Research Based on VAR Model

Xiaochen Liu[✉]

Zhengzhou University, Zhengzhou 450001, Henan, People's Republic of China
liuxiaochen0210@163.com

Abstract. The objective of this study is to investigate the effect of changes in the money supply and interest rates on the gross domestic product (GDP) and the consumer price index (CPI), respectively. The Taylor Rule and the VAR model will be utilized, along with least squares estimation and impulse response functions. As a consequence of this study's findings, various instruments of monetary policy will be compared in order to evaluate the efficacy of the policy effect that macroeconomic fluctuations have on monetary policy. After analysis, it is concluded that the interest rate, a price-based monetary policy tool, is more sensitive to macroeconomic fluctuations and has a more significant adjustment to macroeconomic fluctuations. In the future, according to this paper, It is crucial that the central bank focus more on interest rate-based price management.

Keywords: Monetary Policy · Economic Fluctuation · Taylor Rule · Impulse Response

1 Introduction

Positive developments in the global economic situation have occurred in recent decades, but there has also been turbulence, particularly in recent years. For example, the overall picture of the US economy in 2022 can be summed up as "contractionary monetary policy, slack credit policy." Its primary policy goal is to use government financial subsidies to improve household balance sheets and stimulate subsequent end demand. In the United States, the rate of inflation has repeatedly reached new highs, driven by both the demand and supply sides of the consumption end demand. High inflation, written into the history of U.S. inflation, prompted the Federal Reserve to embark on an unprecedented cycle of aggressive rate hikes. Since the second quarter of 2021, U.S. monetary policy has lagged far behind the rapidly rising inflation curve. To combat inflation, the Fed began an aggressive cycle of rate hikes in March 2022. By November 2022, the Fed would have raised 375 BP. As a result of China's and the United States' dissimilar monetary policies as well as the aggressive interest rate raise policy of the United States, China's financial markets have fluctuated frequently in recent years. Exchange rates have been affected, and cross-border capital flows have been hit. In addition, because Russia and Ukraine occupy an important position in the supply side of the global commodity market, the outbreak of the Russia-Ukraine war also has a negative impact on the commodity flow. For example, in terms of energy, affected by the Russia-Ukraine war and European policies, the supply of crude oil, gas, and other energy products in Europe was severely hindered, which aggravated the energy crisis in Europe. In terms of crops, Ukraine, as a major exporter of grain, abandoned a large amount of farmland due to the outbreak of war, resulting in a sharp decline in grain output and sharp fluctuations in the prices of related products. Furthermore, the imposition of sanctions against Russia by Western countries has impacted global macroeconomic operations. For China, due to the influence of the Russia-Ukraine war, the geopolitical uncertainty is intensified, and the economic risks faced by enterprises are still unknown. Meanwhile, the COVID-19 situation is not encouraging. As a whole, the epidemic situation in China presents a multi-point outbreak situation, and with the relaxation of the policy, the disease will spread more widely, which is going to affect the economy of China.

The central bank is one of the important players in the financial market. Numerous methods used by the central bank to control the amount of money available for circulation to fulfill the nation's economic goals. Monetary policy is a common name for this. It is a synthesis of a country's monetary policy trends at various stages of development. As the financial market in China has developed, the market has played a more and more significant role in the allocation of China's financial resources as a result of the development of the market, and the space for monetary policy regulation also increases. Monetary policy needs to serve the needs of different stages of development. However, following China's numerous "exchange rate reforms," how monetary policy is implemented is augmented by the increased flexibility of the two-way floating RMB exchange rate. Focusing on monetary policy also helps China respond to new changes in the global economy, and monetary policy is increasingly important.

Monetary policy mainly includes four aspects: policy target, monetary policy tool, transmission mechanism, and policy effect. The policy target refers to the goal that the policy maker expects to achieve by making monetary policy. Policy objectives can be subdivided into four categories: the international balance of payments, price stability, economic expansion, and full employment. Monetary policy instruments refer to the means of regulation. The People's Bank of China divides monetary policy tools into nine types, including open market operations, deposit reserves, central bank loans, interest rate policies, standing lending facilities, medium-term lending facilities, supplementary mortgage loans, targeted medium-term lending facilities, and structural monetary policy, the last five of which are new policy tools. Monetary policy instruments can be further divided into price and numerical types. At present, the analysis believes that in China's monetary policy control tools, price tools are gradually taking the dominant position. The transmission mechanism refers to the logical chain between the introduction of monetary policy and how it actually affects the economy. More specifically, it can be defined as what types of channels and processes have the greatest impact on the economy. Common channels include the interest rate, exchange rate, Tobin's Q, and some channels based on financial markets (stocks, real estate), etc. The effect of a policy is the degree of its ultimate impact on the economy. As can be seen from the policy objectives of monetary policy, monetary policy is actually different counter-cyclical adjustment measures taken by the central bank at different stages to smooth out the impact of economic cycle fluctuations and achieve economic objectives.

There is a strong correlation between monetary policy regulation and business cycle changes. It is the main government measure to control the macroeconomy. According to the Law of the People's Bank of China, China's monetary policy's overarching objective is "to safeguard the stability of the currency value and promote economic growth," which shows the strong correlation between monetary policy and macroeconomic fluctuations. Appropriate monetary policy can maintain price stability and provide financial support for economic development. The more complete the market system is, the more significant monetary policy is in the regulation of economic fluctuations. For China, monetary policy is becoming increasingly important in the process of developing a high-quality economy. As the world economic situation changes and the post-pandemic economic situation becomes increasingly complex, traditional economic regulation methods are no longer in line with the new development trend. More effective and sensitive monetary policy tools are needed to respond to and regulate macroeconomic fluctuations. We here discuss the interest rate monetary policy tool as well as the quantity monetary policy tool in this paper. We present a study that examines the impact of various monetary policy tools on China's economic fluctuations through the analysis of actual data, as well as provide references and recommendations for the monetary policy tools that will be used to regulate macroeconomic fluctuations in the future in China based on the analysis of actual data.

2 Literature Review

2.1 Monetary Policy

Twinoburyo and Odhiambo examined the connection between macroeconomics and monetary policy and argued that monetary policy can have a positive impact on economic growth and that its importance is reflected in both short-term and long-term economic growth [1]. Xu Xiaoguang et al. [2]. Analyzed the effects of mixed monetary policies under different financial conditions through the time-varying parameter state-space model and smooth transfer regression model, and the results showed that monetary policies can support the bottom economy when external impacts on the economy occur. Xie Ping analyzed the problems encountered in the implementation of monetary policies in China and believed that the main reasons for the new problems in the implementation were that China's market was not as sound as that of developed countries [3], the room for policy choices was limited, and China's system was special. However, with the development of globalization, the monetary policy implemented by China also needs to be coordinated with the international community, and the importance of monetary policy also increases. Chen et al. [4]. Used Qual VAR to investigate how macroeconomic fluctuations are affected by the People's Bank of China's monetary policies. The analysis's findings demonstrate that the People's Bank of China has used a number of policy instruments to implement and manage China's macroeconomic growth in order to preserve China's overall macroeconomic stability. Koivu analyzed the connection between asset prices and China's monetary policy by using the structural vector autoregression method [5]. He finds that rising asset prices in China do correlate with the easing of monetary policy. Zhuang Ziguan et al. [6]. Examined quantitative and price-based monetary policy rules in depth and used Bayesian methods to estimate the new Keynesian dynamic stochastic general equilibrium model with expected and unexpected monetary policy shocks. As a result, how monetary policy affects investment is greater than those of inflation, according to him. In addition, for China's macroeconomic fluctuations, quantitative monetary policy has a longer duration and greater degree of influence, while the regulating effect of price monetary policy is more obvious in consumption and inflation. Money supply and interest rate are common quantitative and price monetary policy tools, respectively.

During the course of the reform of China's financial system, Wang Jie has made clear that Interest rate liberalization reform and financial system reform in China are closely related [7]. In order to facilitate the effective allocation of capital and the establishment of a financial system, interest rate liberalization reform is conducive to the effective allocation of capital, which strengthens the links between China's economy and the global economy as well. Yi Gang believes that China's market-oriented interest rate system has been relatively complete and that the formation and transmission mechanism of market-oriented interest rates have been basically formed [8]. It uses monetary policy tools to regulate the financial system's liquidity. In the event of the release of the policy interest rate control signal, the interest rate corridor is assisted to guide the operation of prevailing market-benchmark interest rates with the policy interest rate at the center of the operation. Simultaneously, we adjust resource allocation through the banking system and loan interest rates in order to achieve monetary policy objectives. Chen Langnan and Tian Lei argued that imposing shocks on interest rates would cause prices to fall [9]. This process is more durable than raising reserve requirements and more powerful in explaining the variance of long-run price forecasts. Yao Xuesong et al. [10]. Believe that market interest rates have a profoundly favorable effect on short-term economic growth but no significant long-term impact. Short-term performance of the economy tends to have a favorable impact on the market interest rate, while long-term performance does not tend to have such a positive impact. Market interest rates and money supply have little effect on each other.

Sheng Songcheng and Wu Peixin pointed out that the money supply [11], M2, is an important indicator of monetary policy. It is more sensitive to economic variables than other monetary scalars and can respond systematically to the CPI. M2 as a monetary policy only plays a stage role. Considering the long-term development, they believe that after the market-oriented reform of interest rates and exchange rates, interest rates will be a better choice for monetary policy. In an article published in Xin Zhao et al. [12], the authors developed an autoregressive model with three variables and a vector error correction model, which they used to assess the impacts of currency shocks on real output and prices by using a test for Granger causality and an impulsive response capability. The results show that shocks to the money supply's impact on price levels is more persistent than that of real output, and monetary shocks in China's impact on real output takes 2–3 years to fully show up. Time-lag factors restrict the macro-controlling impact of Chinese monetary policy. Ma Yihua analyzed the changes in the money supply itself and the relationships among the money supply [13], economic growth, and price level, respectively, through the GHRCH and VEC models. He argues that the effects of money supply and price levels on monetary expansion are uneven in the near future. Yao Xuesong et al. [10]. Believe that economic growth in China is significantly boosted by the country's money supply. Short-term economic expansion significantly reduces the money supply, but this effect is not long-lasting.

2.2 Taylor Rule

Using historical analysis and response analysis, Xie Ping and Rochon first tested the applicability of Taylor Rule to China's monetary policy and concluded that Taylor Rule could provide a reference for the use of China's monetary policy [14]. Lu Jun and Zhong Dan believe that the Taylor Rule has practicality for China's interbank offered rate [15]. It can provide guidance for the implementation of monetary policy. They also point out that the "Taylor-type rule," a forward-looking Taylor rule, introduces the previous Fed funds rate on the basis of the original Taylor rule to take into account the smoothing of interest rate movements when monetary policy is implemented. Tan Xiaofen believes that the Taylor Rule can reflect the essential logic of monetary policy implementation in developed economies and is suitable for China to use as a reference when implementing monetary policies [16]. Taylor Rule has a distinct advantage in that it can provide optimal monetary policy advice for the balance of various macroeconomic conditions and guide monetary policy implementation. With the improvement of China's interest rate liberalization, Taylor Rule will be more suitable for China's economic regulation mechanism.

2.3 VAR Model

In 1980, Christopher Sims proposed the vector autoregressive model, also known as the VAR model. Orden and Fackler pointed out in their analysis of the VAR model that the prominent feature of the model is that it assumes mutually orthogonal behavioral shocks and does not restrict the hysteresis relation [17]. The effect of the VAR model in policy analysis mainly depends on whether reasonable identification limits can be proposed. Philippe Jorion introduced the VAR model, including its basis [18], calculation method, application range, and other aspects, in his works. Liu Yufei believed that the VAR model has special significance for financial regulation and provides a more practical indicator for measuring market risks [19], which is convenient for financial institutions to carry out market risk management and supervision by regulatory authorities. The data given in the distribution of key words in CNKI show that the VAR model is mainly applied in finance, macroeconomic and sustainable development, economic system reform, investment, securities, and other fields. Now VAR model has been widely used to analyze and forecast a number of related economic indicators. Fung employed the VAR model to assess the impacts of monetary policies in seven East Asian economies [20]. The results show that the results obtained by the impulse response function of the VAR model in most economies are consistent with expectations. Based on Chinese data, Geng Qiang and Fan Jingjing conducted a statistical evaluation of the practical effects of various monetary policy tools using the VAR test [21]. They analyzed the policy effects of benchmark interest rate, deposit reserve ratio, rediscount rate, credit quota, and exchange rate change, respectively, and found that benchmark interest rate and rediscount rate are better fine-tuning tools for macroeconomics. Enterprises with a higher degree of marketization are more sensitive to monetary policy, and there should be some explanation for the inefficiency of monetary policy to some extent because of the peculiarities of the system in which it operates. Xu Xiaoguang et al. [2]. Believe that the interest rate, as a policy tool, plays a more significant role than the money supply when external impacts on the economy occur.

Previous investigations have examined the effects of monetary policy tools from different perspectives, but at present there is no research literature using VAR model to compare and evaluate the effects of tools for quantitative monetary policy money flow and price monetary policy tools interest rate on macroeconomic fluctuations. Therefore, this paper aims to supplement the analysis of the application and results of interest rate monetary policy tools and money supply in China's macroeconomic background, and answer the question of which one is more sensitive to macroeconomic fluctuations and has more significant regulation effects as the two are respectively Price-based and quantitative instruments for monetary policy. By utilizing the least squares estimation of Taylor Rule, this paper uses the macroeconomic data of China to analyze the sensitivity of the two monetary policy tools to macroeconomic fluctuations. Meanwhile, VAR models of the two monetary policy tools are established respectively. The impulse response function is used to compare and analyze the magnitude of quantitative monetary policy instrument money supply and price monetary policy instrument interest rate on macroeconomic fluctuations when they are affected separately, which provides valuable analysis results and policy suggestions for the monetary policy model of China's macroeconomic regulation in the future under the new economic situation.

3 Establishment and Analysis of Empirical Model

3.1 Variable Selection and Data Preprocessing

In this paper, the weighted average inter-bank lending rate (seven days) (INT) is selected as the measure of interest rate, wide money supply growth rate (M2) as the indicator of the money supply, the gross domestic product (GDP) as the measure of economic growth, and the consumer price index (CPI) and inflation rate (PI) as a measure of the price level. This paper selected 76 quarterly data sets from the first quarter of 2000 through the fourth quarter of 2018 as research samples. All data are from the National Bureau of Statistics, the China Economic Net statistical database, and the CSMAR series research database of Guotai'an.

In terms of data preprocessing, in order to unify the research caliber, quarterly data were uniformly adopted, the natural logarithm of GDP was taken to eliminate heteroscedasticity, and LNGDP was obtained, as shown in Fig. 1. Since both LNGDP data and CPI data have seasonal characteristics, we made seasonal adjustments for them to obtain LNGDP_SA and CPI_SA, and the results are shown in Figs. 2 and 3. We used HP filtering to generate the CYCLE_GDP sequence for GDP data, and the results are shown in Figs. 4 and 5. We processed PI and set the inflation target at 0.02, generating the inflation gap (PI_GAP) sequence as shown in Fig. 6 (PI_GAP = pi-0.02).

LNGDP

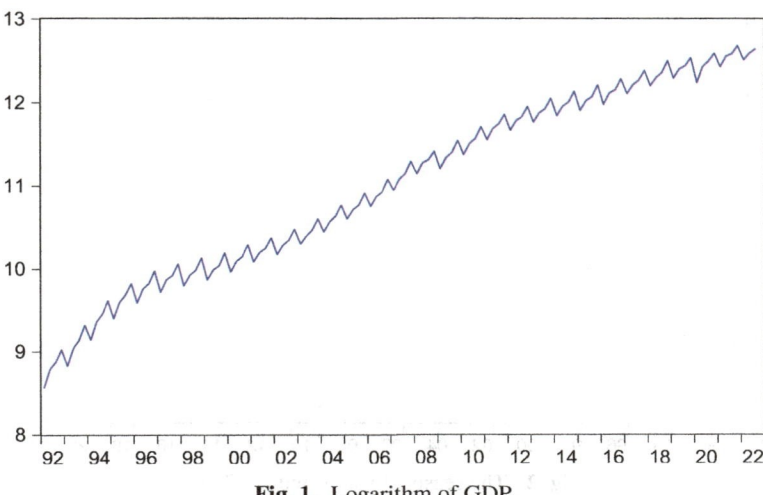

Fig. 1. Logarithm of GDP.

As shown in Fig. 1, after taking the logarithm of GDP, the series as a whole presents an increasing trend. At the same time, the quarterly data showed a cyclical feature in different years, accompanied by seasonal factors. Its seasonal performance is such that the four quarters of each year generally show an increasing trend and peak in the fourth quarter. Between the fourth quarter of the previous year and the first quarter of the following year, there was a substantial decrease. The reason for such data characteristics is that many items must be closed at the end of the year, so data from the fourth quarter is typically larger than data from other quarters. Because the analysis is required to be a pure economic change trend and the impact of seasonal factors will cover up its short-term change trend, thus affecting the accuracy and comparability of data, it is necessary to carry out seasonal adjustment on the data with seasonal characteristics. Since both LNGDP and CPI data have seasonal characteristics, LNGDP_SA and CPI_SA are obtained through seasonal adjustment, and the results are shown in Figs. 2 and 3.

Figures 2, 3, 4, 5 and 6 is analyzed based on the actual situation and the economic data obtained. In 1994, under the background of market economy reform, commodity prices and investment overheated due to the full opening, and severe inflation occurred. China's domestic inflation rate in 1993 was 13.2%. In 1994, China's domestic inflation rate was 21.7%, the peak of inflation. From 1992 to 1994, the annual inflation rate was 13.2%, 21.7%, and 14.8%, respectively. Cost-push inflation occurred in the first half of 1992–1993; structural inflation emerged in 1994–1995. In 1992 and 1993, China carried out market-economy reform. Commodities can be freely priced according to market supply and demand instead of being limited by tickets, national statistical pricing, and so on. Local government real estate development has reached a boiling point. The rapid expansion of social financing and bank funds led to a sharp rise in investment, industry, money issuance, and prices. The original industrial structure is out of whack, and inflation occurs. To combat inflation, the government adopted a "moderately contractionary"

LNGDP_SA

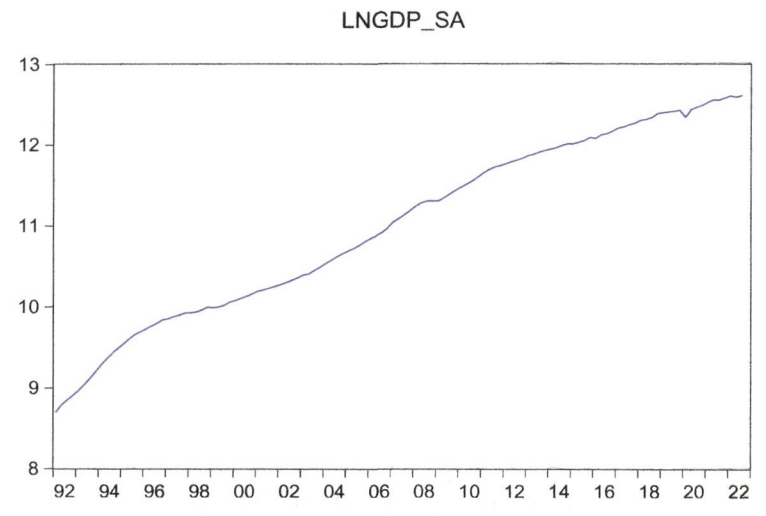

Fig. 2. The seasonally adjusted LNGDP.

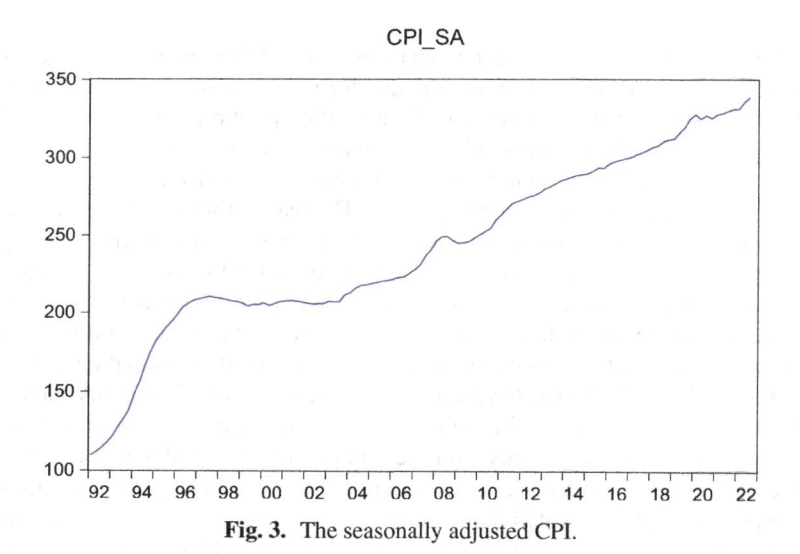

CPI_SA

Fig. 3. The seasonally adjusted CPI.

monetary policy. As we can see from the inflation gap chart, it peaked in 1994, which is also consistent with reality. In 1996, the bank accumulated a large number of bad debts, and non-performing loans reached a very serious state. The government began to take measures to guard against bank risks. Bank loans are not as readily available to businesses as before. Due to the difficulties in obtaining loans, enterprises have to sell their products at lower prices to maintain their businesses, which leads to the decline of commodity prices in the market. From 1994 to 1998, the overall market experienced economic expansion, which was consistent with the analysis result of HP filter greater

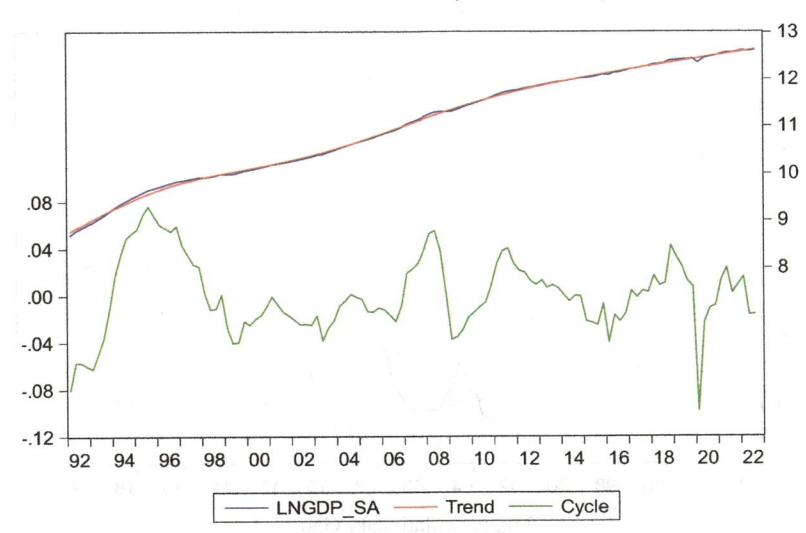

Fig. 4. HP filter.

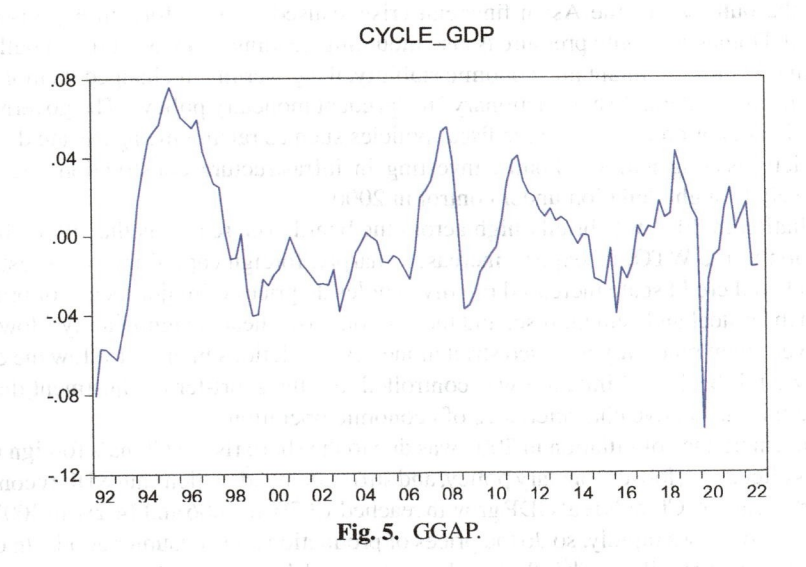

Fig. 5. GGAP.

than 0, as well as the trend of rapid rise in CPI. During this period, GDP growth was also relatively fast.

Deflation in 1999 was caused by banks' reluctance to lend and a decline in peripheral demand in the context of commercial banking reform and the East Asian financial crisis. At this node, the CPI image flattens out or even drops slightly, the HP filtering efficiency is zero, presenting an economic recession situation, and GDP growth slows down. In

Fig. 6. Inflationary Gap.

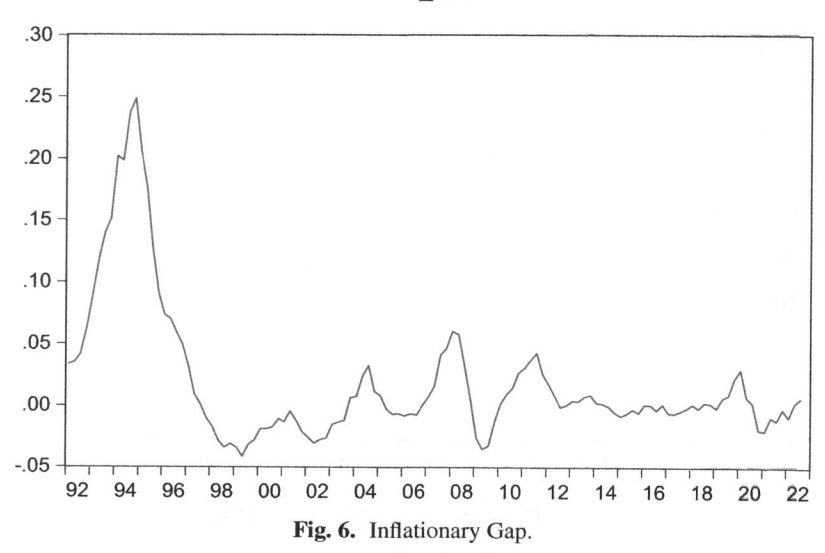

1997, the outbreak of the Asian financial crisis caused China's foreign exports to be blocked. Domestic supply pressure is also mounting, leading to a worsening of deflation in China. In order to maintain economic stability, the government changed its monetary policy from "moderately contractionary" to "prudent monetary policy." The government controlled deflation through active fiscal policies such as raising the aggregate demand of society, issuing national bonds, investing in infrastructure construction, etc., and effectively brought deflation under control in 2000.

Inflation in 2004 was briefly high across the board. The reason is that after China's accession to the WTO, its exports increased sharply, foreign capital inflow, investment demand, and credit scale increased rapidly, wholesale prices of major means of production such as steel and cement rose, and the economy overheated significantly. However, the government randomly imposed strict monetary restrictions in order to slow the economy, M1 fell back, and inflation was controlled, but the short-term adjustment did not change the substantive characteristics of economic operation.

The emergence of inflation in 2007 was due to the sharp rise in China's foreign trade surplus after 2004, loose monetary policy, and strong demand, which caused the economy to overheat again. China's real GDP growth reached 12.7% in 2006 and 14.2% in 2007. As the economy grows rapidly, so do the prices of production and consumer goods. In order to guard against possible high inflation, the central bank has repeatedly adopted monetary policy to ease. In 2007, it raised the deposit reserve rate 10 times and the benchmark deposit and lending rates six times. But with the onset of the global economic crisis in 2008, China's monetary policy turned loose. Due to both the bankruptcy of small and medium-sized enterprises in China and the rapid fall in external demand caused by the United States' subprime mortgage crisis led to the development of the global financial crisis, the deflation in 2009 was mainly the result of the bankruptcy of small and medium-sized enterprises in China. At this node, the HP filter is less than 0, there is a significant decrease in the CPI, and GDP growth slows down.

A subprime mortgage crisis that erupted in the United States in the second half of 2007 has gradually spread to other parts of the world, causing the global financial crisis to worsen. China is also affected by the financial crisis; the M2 growth rate of the money supply declined, the export growth rate was negative, and the CPI was negative for months. In order to cope with deflation, the government adopted loose monetary policies to stabilize the economic situation and launched the "4 trillion-yuan investment plan" for infrastructure investment during this period so that the economic situation gradually stabilized and recovered. The inflation in 2011 was mainly due to the aftereffects of the earlier stimulus policies and imported inflationary pressure. Monetary policy gradually shifted from loose to normal at the end of 2009, but the effects of the previous loose policy are still lingering. There is excess RMB liquidity in the market, the price level is gradually rising, and there is a tendency to overheat the economy. Meanwhile, since 2010, overseas economies have gradually recovered from the financial crisis, and the global economy has entered a state of recovery.

In 2011, an armed conflict broke out in Libya. The Libyan war broke out, and the price of international crude oil soared. China is heavily dependent on imports of commodities such as crude oil and iron ore. This exposed China to imported inflationary pressures during this period. The domestic economy is inflating due to a combination of factors. The HP filter is less than 0. After 2012, GDP and CPI growth slowed down, which is also consistent with reality.

In 2020, the COVID-19 outbreak had a negative impact on the economy. HP filter less than 0, CPI, and GDP have all decreased significantly. After the outbreak of the epidemic, the service industry and tourism industry were greatly affected by the restrictions of epidemic prevention measures, and foreign trade was also affected by the shutdown of production and the lack of transport capacity, resulting in a sharp decline in output. However, with the continuous upgrading of epidemic prevention measures, the popularization of vaccines in recent years, and the resumption of work and production accompanied by precise epidemic prevention, the Chinese government has maintained a more active economic policy. Accompanied by the implementation of a strong fiscal policy, China's macroeconomic recovery continues. The reality is also consistent with the results of the data graph.

3.2 Least-Squares Estimation and Empirical Analysis Based on Taylor Rule

The Taylor Rule is an equation, proposed in 1993 by economist John Taylor, that links the Federal Reserve's benchmark interest rate to the level of inflation and economic growth. Taylor believes that the equilibrium interest rate is an economic factor that has a stable correlation with prices and economic growth. Therefore, the equilibrium interest rate should be used as the main tool of the government's monetary policy adjustment to stabilize economic fluctuations. The inflation gap—the distinction between the actual and target rates of inflation—is mathematically connected to the gap between the actual and prospective levels of gross domestic product using the Taylor formula (the output gap). Adjust the equilibrium interest rate to account for output gaps and inflation. Interest rates are higher when inflation is above the inflation target; otherwise, interest rates are lower. Similarly, interest rates are higher when actual GDP is higher than potential GDP; below, interest rates are lower.

The standard Taylor rule model is generally expressed as follows:

$$i_t = \pi_t + r_t^* + \alpha_\pi (\pi_t - \pi_t^*) + \alpha_y (y_t - \bar{y}_t) \tag{1}$$

In this formula, t means that the data comes from different years; i_t is the short-term equilibrium interest rate; π_t is for the real inflation rate; r_t^* is the equilibrium real interest rate; π_t^* stands for the target inflation rate. The target is often set by the central bank, and since different targets may be set each year, the figure is fluid. y_t is for real gross domestic product; $\bar{y}_t$ stands for potential GDP. Because it reflects an equilibrium state of output, or what you might call a long-term output, it is not observable. α_π And α_y are policy parameters, and both of them are greater than 0. In Taylor Rule, since both α_π and α_y are greater than 0, when the real inflation rate rises by 1% point, The central bank needs to increase nominal interest rates by more than 1% point ($1 + \alpha_\pi$ percentage points) to smooth out economic fluctuations. The reason why the central bank's interest rate adjustment will be transmitted to the real economy is that, for example, if the interest rate is lowered by the central bank, it will make it less economical to deposit money in the bank and reduce the loan cost, which will lead to an increase in consumption and investment. Utilizing the transmission mechanism, the regulation of monetary policy affects the real economy in a negative way. This is how central banks regulate fluctuations in the economy.

In a series of articles on the Taylor Rule, they raised more questions about the rule, analyzed it, studied it, and expanded it to form a series of rules called the "Taylor analogue rule". Jun Jun and Zhong Dan (2003) believed that some of the "Taylor analogue rule" were different from the original Taylor rules in that the "Taylor analogue rule" would consider the smoothing of interest rates by the Federal Reserve. That is, because the Federal Reserve has the tendency to smooth interest rates, the monetary policy's time to act in reaction to inflation and output shortfalls would be longer, and it would be completed in several quarters instead of one. This "Taylor analogue rule" would therefore take into account the prior benchmark Fed rate and the output and inflation gaps. In the Taylor rule correlation analysis of Chinese data, this interest rate is the equilibrium interest rate of the previous period. Therefore, the formula is based on Taylor Rule and further adds the lag term of the interest rate to get:

$$i_t = C + \beta i_{t-1} + \alpha_\pi (\pi_t - \pi_t^*) + \alpha_y (y_t - \bar{y}_t) \tag{2}$$

In this formula, the C constant term and $\bar{y}_t$ potential GDP cannot be observed; π_t^* the target inflation rate can be considered artificially set; α_π and α_y policy parameters can be artificially set; and i_{t-1} the equilibrium interest rate in the last period is given. On the basis of this formula, when the monetary policy instruments used are INT and M2, the least squares estimation of the Taylor rule is carried out, and Table 1 and 2 respectively display the outcomes:

Table 1. Results of least squares estimation of monetary policy instrument INT.

Variable	Coefficient	Std. Error	t-Statistic	Prob.
C	0.007664	0.002016	3.801238	0.0003
INT(-1)	0.732104	0.068955	10.61716	0.0000
PI_GAP	0.007694	0.041807	0.184044	0.8545
CYCLE_GDP	0.080938	0.041536	1.948595	0.0552
R-squared	0.765161	Mean dependent var		0.027732
Adjusted R-squared	0.755376	S.D. dependent var		0.008379
S.E. of regression	0.004144	Akaike info criterion		−8.083062
Sum squared resid	0.001237	Schwarz criterion		−7.960392
Log likelihood	311.1563	Hannan-Quinn criter		−8.034037
F-statistic	78.19758	Durbin-Watson stat		1.963353
Prob(F-statistic)	0.000000			

In terms of the statistical significance test, it can be obtained from the data in Table 1: $R^2 = 0.765516$; the modified coefficient of determination $\overline{R^2} = 0.755376$. This demonstrates that the model successfully fits the sample. The F test is significant at a significance level of $\alpha = 0.1$. This indicates significant regression equation, that is, the "one period lag of interest rate," the "inflation gap," the "output gap," and other variables combined do have a big effect on "nominal interest rate." The t statistics corresponding to INT (−1) and CYCLE_GDP are significant; the t statistic corresponding to PI_GAP is not significant. This indicates that the explanatory variables "one period lag of interest rate" and "output gap" have significant effects on the explained variable "nominal interest rate," respectively, when other explanatory variables remain unchanged. The "inflation gap" has no significant effect on the explained variable, "nominal interest rate." In terms of the evaluation of economic significance, the estimates from the model indicate that, assuming other variables stay constant, the nominal interest rate should rise by 0.732104% on average for every 1% increase in interest rates with a lag period. Whenever the inflation gap widens by 1%, the nominal interest rate should increase by 0.007694% on average; every 1% increase in the output gap should, on average, increase the nominal interest rate by 0.080938%. In the estimation results, the coefficients of PI_GAP and CYCLE_GAP are both greater than 0, which corresponds to their practical economic significance. This estimate suggests that when inflation is higher than expected, the central bank should raise interest rates. When the actual GDP is higher than the potential GDP, the central bank should raise interest rates to increase the cost of investment, which in turn reduces investment and output in order to control inflation. This is consistent with the Taylor Rule.

As shown by the analytical findings in Table 2, $R^2 = 0.853465$ and $\overline{R^2} = 0.847359$. The model clearly fits the sample well, as evidenced by this. The F test is significant at a significance level of $= 0.1$. This indicates that the regression equation is significant, that is, the combination of variables such as "one lag of money supply growth," "inflation gap," and "output gap" does have a significant impact on the "nominal interest rate." The

Table 2. The monetary policy instrument is the least squares estimate result of M2.

Variable	Coefficient	Std. Error	t-Statistic	Prob.
C	0.010559	0.007668	1.377137	0.1727
M2(-1)	0.929051	0.049229	18.87211	0.0000
PI_GAP	−0.257688	0.180695	−1.426091	0.1582
CYCLE_GDP	−0.028872	0.168360	−0.171489	0.8643
R-squared	0.853465	Mean dependent var		0.154101
Adjusted R-squared	0.847359	S.D. dependent var		0.043873
S.E. of regression	0.017141	Akaike info criterion		−5.243526
Sum squared resid	0.021154	Schwarz criterion		−5.120856
Log likelihood	203.2540	Hannan-Quinn criter		−5.194501
F-statistic	139.7829	Durbin-Watson stat		1.497045
Prob(F-statistic)	0.000000			

t statistics corresponding to M2(-1), CYCLE_GDP, and PI_GAP were not significant. This indicates that when other explanatory variables remain unchanged, the explanatory variable "one period lag of interest rate" has a significant impact on the explained variable "nominal interest rate," while "inflation gap" and "output gap" have no significant impact on the explained variable "nominal interest rate," respectively. In terms of the economic significance test, the model estimates show that, assuming other variables remain unchanged, the nominal interest rate should increase by 0.929051% on average for every 1% increase in the growth rate of the money supply lagging one period. Every 1% increase in the inflation gap should reduce nominal interest rates by 0.257688% on average; every 1% increase in the output gap should, on average, reduce nominal interest rates by 0.028872%. The coefficients of PI_GAP and CYCLE_GAP in the estimation results are both greater than 0, which conforms to Taylor's rule. In the estimation results in Table 2, the coefficients of PI_GAP and CYCLE_GDP are both less than 0, that is, the policy parameters are negative, corresponding to their practical economic significance. The results of this estimate suggest that the central bank should reduce the money supply when Contrary to expectations, inflation is higher than it should be. When actual GDP is higher than potential GDP, central banks should reduce the money supply. It is harder for businesses to get credit, leading to less investment, resulting in decreased productivity and keeping inflation under control. This is similar to the conclusion reached by the Taylor Rule. Its conclusion is also consistent with the characteristics of the money supply itself. When the economy is in recession or overheating, the money supply should move in the opposite direction from interest rates.

By comparing the analysis results of the Taylor Rule least-square estimation of two different monetary policy tools, it can be seen that the interest rate, as a monetary policy tool, is more sensitive to macroeconomic fluctuations, while the money supply is relatively insensitive.

3.3 Establishment of the VAR Model

The VAR model was proposed by Sims in 1980. This model can be used to estimate the dynamic relationship among all endogenous variables in the model. The VAR model is used to estimate the INT and M2 of monetary policy instruments, respectively. Before we can build the VAR model, we must first determine the best lag order k. Table 3 and Table 4 are obtained using the lag length criteria, and the results of the judgment criteria for each optimal lag order can be obtained. The number with an asterisk (*) is the optimal lag order under a certain judgment standard.

Table 3. The optimal lag order of the VAR model of INT is selected as a monetary policy tool.

Lag	LogL	LR	FPE	AIC	SC	HQ
0	−55.30738	NA	0.000931	1.534405	1.626407	1.571174
1	424.1988	908.5381	3.91e-09	−10.84734	−10.47933	−10.70026
2	452.8712	52.06297*	2.33e-09*	−11.36503*	−10.72101*	−11.10765*
3	455.3477	4.301365	2.78e-09	−11.19336	−10.27334	−10.82567
4	459.3625	6.656046	3.18e-09	−11.06217	−9.866137	−10.58418
5	465.0210	8.934446	3.51e-09	−10.97424	−9.502194	−10.38594
6	474.1041	13.62464	3.55e-09	−10.97642	−9.228373	−10.27782
7	480.8232	9.548200	3.84e-09	−10.91640	−8.892341	−10.10749
8	487.7237	9.261292	4.16e-09	−10.86115	−8.561085	−9.941934

* indicates lag order selected by the criterion
LR: sequential modified LR test statistic (each test at 5% level)
FPE: Final prediction error
AIC: Akaike information criterion
SC: Schwarz information criterion

Table 4. The monetary policy tool is the optimal lag order of the M2 VAR model.

Lag	LogL	LR	FPE	AIC	SC	HQ
0	−159.7497	NA	0.014542	4.282886	4.374889	4.319655
1	316.6551	902.6616	6.62e-08	−8.017239	−7.649229	−7.870165
2	344.2260	50.06292	4.07e-08*	−8.505947*	−7.861928*	−8.248566*
3	350.0824	10.17175	4.43e-08	−8.423222	−7.503196	−8.055535
4	356.2329	10.19685	4.80e-08	−8.348235	−7.152201	−7.870242
5	367.9090	18.43585	4.52e-08	−8.418657	−6.946615	−7.830358
6	379.2238	16.97222*	4.31e-08	−8.479573	−6.731523	−7.780968
7	386.0110	9.645061	4.65e-08	−8.421343	−6.397285	−7.612432
8	390.8367	6.476575	5.32e-08	−8.311493	−6.011427	−7.392275

* indicates lag order selected by the criterion
LR: sequential modified LR test statistic (each test at 5% level)
FPE: Final prediction error
AIC: Akaike information criterion
SC: Schwarz information criterion
HQ: Hannan-Quinn information criterion

According to Akaike information criterion (AIC), a lag order of 2 is selected, and the VAR model between INT, LNGDP_SA, and CPI_SA and the VAR model between M2, LNGDP_SA, and CPI_SA are established, respectively. The estimation results of the VAR models for the two are shown in Table 5 and Table 6.

Table 5. The monetary policy instrument is the estimated result of the VAR model of INT.

	INT	LNGDP_SA	CPI_SA
INT(−1)	0.692986	−0.245169	44.28045
	(0.11507)	(0.29393)	(33.9545)
	[6.02244]	[−0.83410]	[1.30411]
INT(−2)	0.048944	−0.547158	−24.72828
	(0.11266)	(0.28778)	(33.2441)
	[0.43444]	[−1.90129]	[−0.74384]
LNGDP_SA(−1)	0.099079	0.792230	32.20458
	(0.04492)	(0.11474)	(13.2548)
	[2.20573]	[6.90445]	[2.42966]
LNGDP_SA(−2)	−0.103261	0.237472	−29.16048
	(0.04605)	(0.11762)	(13.5878)
	[−2.24250]	[2.01890]	[−2.14608]
CPI_SA(−1)	0.000873	0.005214	1.203953
	(0.00043)	(0.00110)	(0.12661)
	[2.03403]	[4.75690]	[9.50881]
CPI_SA(−2)	−0.000750	−0.005902	−0.259239
	(0.00041)	(0.00105)	(0.12181)
	[−1.81608]	[−5.59686]	[−2.12816]
C	0.019336	−0.110836	−20.85455
	(0.02583)	(0.06597)	(7.62061)
	[0.74871]	[−1.68013]	[−2.73660]
R-squared	0.794762	0.999820	0.999032
Adj. R-squared	0.776915	0.999804	0.998948
Sum sq. Resids	0.001081	0.007051	94.09637
S.E. equation	0.003957	0.010109	1.167782
F-statistic	44.53250	63752.08	11870.60

(*continued*)

Table 5. (continued)

	INT	LNGDP_SA	CPI_SA
Log likelihood	316.2761	245.0008	−115.9556
Akaike AIC	−8.138845	−6.263180	3.235674
Schwarz SC	−7.924172	−6.048507	3.450347
Mean dependent	0.027732	11.30598	252.0790
S.D. dependent	0.008379	0.722010	36.00422
Determinant resid covariance (dof adj.)	1.79E-09		
Determinant resid covariance	1.34E-09		
Log likelihood	452.8712		
Akaike information criterion	−11.36503		
Schwarz criterion	−10.72101		

Table 6. Monetary policy tools are estimated by the VAR model of M2.

	M2	LNGDP_SA	CPI_SA
M2(-1)	0.920730	0.082425	0.086448
	(0.10955)	(0.08380)	(8.88616)
	[8.40444]	[0.98362]	[0.00973]
M2(-2)	−0.205002	−0.058258	−1.554389
	(0.10796)	(0.08258)	(8.75675)
	[−1.89891]	[−0.70550]	[−0.17751]
LNGDP_SA(-1)	−0.283646	0.919392	31.81302
	(0.16637)	(0.12726)	(13.4951)
	[−1.70486]	[7.22448]	[2.35737]
LNGDP_SA(-2)	0.366778	0.115120	−28.73307
	(0.17194)	(0.13152)	(13.9470)
	[2.13311]	[0.87530]	[−2.06017]
CPI_SA(-1)	−0.005279	0.003895	1.265666
	(0.00149)	(0.00114)	(0.12082)
	[−3.54437]	[3.41834]	[10.4760]
CPI_SA(-2)	0.003408	−0.004740	−0.320402
	(0.00142)	(0.00109)	(0.11518)
	[2.40020]	[−4.36423]	[−2.78174]

(continued)

Table 6. (*continued*)

	M2	LNGDP_SA	CPI_SA
C	−0.409063	−0.153262	−20.69818
	(0.11556)	(0.08839)	(9.37333)
	[−3.53986]	[−1.73389]	[−2.20820]
R-squared	0.898392	0.999780	0.999007
Adj. R-squared	0.889557	0.999761	0.998921
Sum sq. Resids	0.014668	0.008582	96.50620
S.E. equation	0.014580	0.011152	1.182641
F-statistic	101.6801	52379.59	11573.89
Log likelihood	217.1675	237.5359	−116.9165
Akaike AIC	−5.530724	−6.066734	3.260961
Schwarz SC	−5.316052	−5.852061	3.475634
Mean dependent	0.154101	11.30598	252.0790
S.D. dependent	0.043873	0.722010	36.00422
Determinant resid covariance (dof adj.)		3.12E-08	
Determinant resid covariance		2.34E-08	
Log likelihood		344.2260	
Akaike information criterion		−8.505947	
Schwarz criterion		−7.861928	

3.4 Impulse Response Function and Empirical Analysis

Following the establishment of the VAR model, impulse response function analysis is performed on the two VAR models to determine the outcomes of monetary policy instruments on GDP and the consumer price index, respectively. When the monetary policy instrument is INT, the result of the impulse response is shown in Fig. 7. When the monetary policy instrument is M2, the result of the impulse response function is shown in Fig. 8.

As can be seen from the impulse response function in Fig. 7, an impact on INT in the period 0 has a significant impact on GDP after the period 6, and the impact is negative. From period 6 to period 11, the trend increases and becomes stable after period 11. The effect on CPI is not significant. An impact on GDP in the period 0 has a significant impact on INT from the period 2 to the period 5, and the impact is positive. From the period 2 to the period 4, the trend is stable and the growth reaches the maximum value of 0.0014, and from the period 4 to the period 5, the trend is decreasing. It had a significant influence on the CPI during the 10 periods analyzed, and the influence was positive. The influence trend increases from the first period to the fourth period and decreases after the sixth period. The trend from the fourth period to the sixth period is stable and reaches a maximum of 1.1. An impact on CPI in the zero period has a significant impact on INT from the third to the fourth period, and the impact is positive. The impact reaches its maximum in the third period, increasing by 0.0015, and then decreases. It has a significant impact on GDP from the second to the third period, reaches a maximum increase of 0.006 in the third period, and then decreases. As can be seen from the role of the impulse response in Fig. 8, when a shock is exerted on M2 in phase 0, the impact on GDP and CPI is not significant. When an impact is exerted on GDP in the 0 period, M2 has a significant impact from the 2nd to the 5th period, and the impact is negative. From the 2nd to the 3rd period, the decrease of M2 shows an increasing trend; from the 3rd to the 4th period, the trend is stable and the decrease reaches the maximum value of 0.007; from the 4th to the 5th period, there is a decreasing trend. It had a significant influence on CPI in the 10 periods analyzed, and the influence was positive. The influence trend is increasing from the first period to the fourth period, and the trend is stable after the fourth period. The maximum increase is 1. An impact on CPI in the period 0 has a significant impact on INT in the period 2–8, and the impact is negative. The impact increases from the second to the fourth period, reaches its maximum in the fourth period, decreases by 0.011, and then decreases. It has a significant impact on GDP in the second period, which is 0.004.

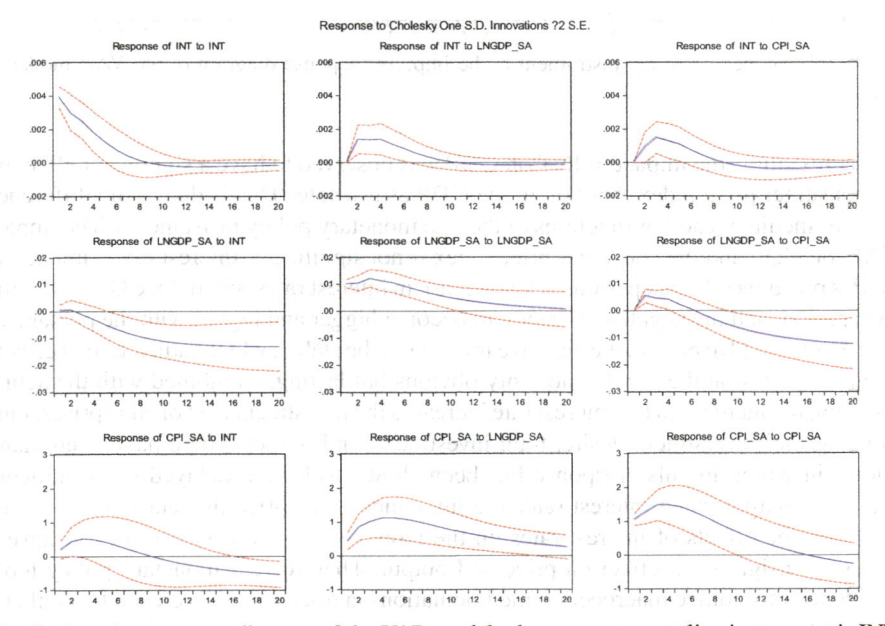

Fig. 7. Impulse response diagram of the VAR model whose monetary policy instrument is INT.

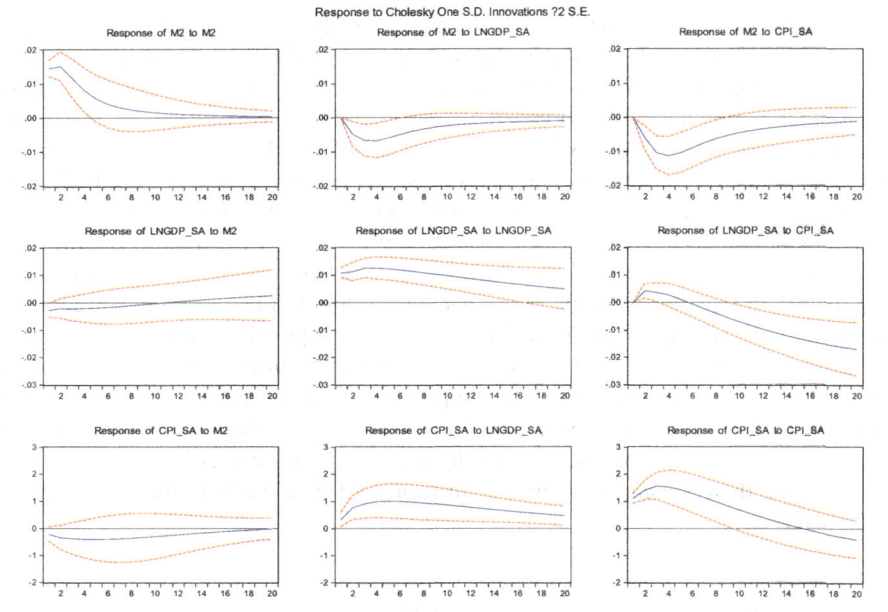

Fig. 8. The monetary policy instrument is the impulse response diagram of the VAR model of M2.

In this study, the impact of INT on GDP was observed to have a significant effect on the consumer price index, but not on the GDP as a whole. This is due to the difference in the immediate reaction functions of the two monetary policy instruments. The impact of M2 on GDP and the consumer price index is not significant. Interest rates' impact on GDP is postponed for six periods. The increase in interest rates will reduce GDP after the sixth period, and the negative impact will become bigger and bigger with the passage of time. Until the 11th period, the negative impact will be stable, which indicates that effects of interest rates on the GDP is not only obvious but lasting. Combined with the actual situation, the increase in the interest rate increases the investment cost of enterprises, thus reducing their investment desire, total investment, and output. There have been many studies in which impulse response has been shown to have a delayed but significant impact on output when interest rates are implemented as price monetary policy tools. However, the effects of interest rates on the money supply has been shown to have a relatively insignificant effect on price and output. Therefore, if monetary policy tools are needed to stabilize macroeconomic fluctuations, a price-based interest rate would be a more effective choice.

4 Conclusion

In this paper, the money supply is a quantitative monetary policy tool and the monetary policy instrument interest rate will have what impact on output and price, respectively, under the framework of the Taylor rule and VAR model, using least squares estimation and impulse response function analysis.

By comparing the least square estimation results of Taylor Rule and the empirical results of impulse response function, the effect of interest rate as monetary policy is more sensitive. However, money supply is relatively insensitive to macroeconomic fluctuations, so among the two monetary instruments, interest rate, a price-based tool for monetary policy, is more useful in regulating and controlling macroeconomic fluctuations.

As a monetary policy tool, the money supply has no significant influence on GDP or the consumer price index. The possible reasons are as follows: M2 is not a very accurate tool that can reflect the actual money supply in reality, and many influencing factors are not included in the statistical scope of M2, such as some off-balance sheet assets of commercial banks or some things outside the scope of official statistics. The actual money supply is different from the disclosed M2. Due to the existence of financial disintermediation, financial disintermediation is essentially the disintermediation of capital financing, such as deposits and loans. Therefore, a lot of money supply may not operate in the financial system, so M2 cannot reflect the actual money supply. Compared with M2, total social financing can more accurately reflect the real money supply.

China's Law on the People's Bank of China defines the goal of monetary policy as "maintaining the stability of the value of the currency and thereby promoting economic growth." Therefore, this paper believes that compared with quantitative policy tools like money supply regulation, price regulation based on interest rates is more sensitive to market economic fluctuations and has a more significant impact on macroeconomic fluctuations. The central bank should pay more attention to price-based regulation and control based on interest rates in the future macroeconomic regulation and control, and gradually increase the proportion of interest rate regulation and control measures in monetary regulation and control, as this will be a better choice to promote the development trend of macroeconomic stability and improvement. At the moment, macroeconomic control measures based on the quantitative monetary policy tool money supply can gradually be replaced by a price monetary policy tool interest rate or an emerging monetary policy tool. This gradual adjustment of the composition of monetary policy instruments can better adapt to the development of China's macro-economy in the new era and effectively improve the effect of China's monetary policy instruments on the regulation of China's macro-economic fluctuations.

References

1. Twinoburyo, E.N., Odhiambo, N.M.: Monetary policy and economic growth: a review of international literature. J. Cent. Banking Theory Pract. **7**(2), 123–137 (2018)
2. Xiaoguang, X., Danna, Z., Zunxin, Z.: The choice of monetary policy tools for economic recovery under the influence of the novel coronavirus outbreak: based on the effect analysis of mixed monetary policy. Quant. Econ. Res. **04**, 1–24 (2020)
3. Ping, X.: The challenge of chinese monetary policy in the new century. J. Finan. Res. **01**, 1–10 (2000)
4. Chen, H., Chow, K., Tillmann, P.: The effectiveness of monetary policy in China: evidence from a Qual VAR. China Econ. Rev. **43**, 216–231 (2017)
5. Koivu, T.: Monetary policy, asset prices and consumption in China. Econ. Syst. **36**(2), 307–325 (2012)

6. Ziguan, Z., Hongjing, J., Dingming, L.: Macroeconomic effects of monetary policy: perspectives on expected and unexpected shocks. China Ind. Econ. **07**, 80–97 (2018)
7. Jie, W.: Interest rate marketization is critical to the reform of our country's financial system. Manage. World **01**, 196–197 (2001)
8. Gang, Y.: Interest rate system and interest rate liberalization reform in China. J. Finan. Res. **09**, 1–11 (2021)
9. Langnan, C., Lei, T.: Based on the perspective of policy tools, conduct research on the impact of Chinese monetary policy. Econ. (Q.) **01**, 285–304 (2015)
10. Xuesong, Y., Xin, L., Linlin, X., Zhiyong, W.: Money supply, market interest rate, and Chinese economic growth: an empirical study using the mediation effect and the VAR model. Tech. Econ. Manage. Res. **04**, 80–85 (2022)
11. Songcheng, S., Peixin, W.: The dual transmission mechanism of china's monetary policy: "two intermediate targets, two regulatory objects" mode of research. Econ. Res. J. **10**, 37–51 (2008)
12. Xin, Z., Yufeng, L.: A reexamination of the relationship between money supply, GDP and price level in China. Statistics Decis. **03**, 121–125 (2013)
13. Yihua, M.: An empirical analysis of the relationship between money supply, economic growth and price level. Statistics Decis. **19**, 155–158 (2019)
14. Ping, X., Xiong, L.: Taylor rule and its test in Chinese monetary policy. Econ. Res. J. **03**, 3–12+92 (2002)
15. Jun, L., Dan, Z.: Cointegration test of Taylor rule in China. Econ. Res. J. **08** (2003)
16. Xiaofen, T.: Taylor Rule and its adaptation to Chinese monetary policy. J. Cent. Univ. Finan. Econ. **07**, 20–25 (2006)
17. Orden, D., Fackler, P.L.: Identifying Monetary Impacts on Agricultural Prices in VAR Models. Am. J. Agr. Econ. **71**(2), 495 (1989)
18. Philippe, J.: Value at risk: the new benchmark for controlling market risk. McGraw – Hill, New York (1997)
19. Yufei, L.: VAR model and its application in financial supervision. Econ. Sci. **01** (1999)
20. Fung, B. S. C.: A VAR analysis of the effects of monetary policy in East Asia. SSRN Electronic Journal (2002)
21. Qiang, G., Jingjing, F.: Empirical analysis of implementation effects of different monetary policy instruments: VAR test based on Chinese data. Contemp. Finan. Econ. **03**, 55–61 (2009)

Recession Risk Prediction with Machine Learning and Big Panel Data

Yunhao Yang[✉]

University of California, Davis, Davis, CA 92507, USA
yyang523@ucr.edu

Abstract. The machine learning models have been considered a good choice for forecast recession, especially with multiple variables. In this paper, we compare the forecast ability of the machine learning models and traditional methods in the recent 5 years and focus on the recession forecast in two situations, the 2008 financial crisis for the U.S. and the 2011 Italy sovereign crisis. We find that some machine learning models perform well in the forecast of the trend of the GDP growth rate. For the recession forecast, the best models are different for different situations maybe because of the different reasons causing the recessions. In the recent 5 years, the recession-related to COVID-19 reflects some special and unprecedented. We may need to research the impact of it in some specific fields.

Keywords: Machine Learning Model · Recession Forecast · COVID-19 · Big Panel Data

1 Introduction

An economic recession always occurs with some special shocks and its impact will last for a long time. The impact of the recession always not only reflects the dilemma and problems for the current time but also would affect the development of the economy in the future, so the forecast of the recession is important for the policymakers. The forecast can help the policymakers realize the crisis of recession earlier and adjust the policies timely to reduce the impact of the recession and to end the recession as soon as possible. For another hand, the forecast of the recession may help the policymakers find the reasons for the recession and then can avoid the happening of the recession as much as possible. In this paper, we mainly discuss the ability of recession forecast of the machine learning models and compare them to the traditional methods. Some previous research shows that traditional methods can not give an accurate recession forecast, especially when considering more variables in a long historical period. We compare the traditional VAR method with the machine learning methods in recession forecast and find that some machine learning models indeed perform better than the traditional method in the regression forecast, but for different situations, the performance of the models is also different.

We focus on the U.S and Italy data and choose 7 variables including stock price, M2, the difference between 3-month and 10-year treasury bill rate, unemployment rate, debt ratio, import ratio, and investment ratio to evaluate real GDP in different models including VAR, MIDAS, KNN, random forest, SVM, and gradient boosting. And we focus on the 2008 financial crisis for the U.S., the 2011 sovereign crisis for Italy, and the recent 5 years for both two countries to compare the recession forecast abilities of different models. The 2008 financial crisis is a serious crisis over the world but not only for the U.S. The cause of this crisis is the cheap credit and lax lending standards that fueled a housing bubble, then the burst of the bubble cause the collapse of the banking system. The Great Recession came to follow is the most serious recession after the Great Depression. This recession has had a profound impact on the global economy and even lasted until now. And for the 2011 Italy sovereign crisis, the crisis began in Greece. Greece needed a great number of aid funds to pay the sovereign debt, then the crisis spread to other EU members soon, including Italy. The incomplete structure of the Eurozone has been considered the cause of this crisis. To this day, the impact of the crisis still lasts. And in the recent 5 years, COVID-19 is the main shock for the whole world. Different from the previous two crises, the shock of COVID-19 is unprecedented and totally out of the blue. Both the 2008 financial crisis and Italy's sovereign crisis are caused by problems in the economic system and some triggers induced the recession, but COVID-19 is a shock totally exogenous but affects the economy comprehensively.

For the 2008 financial crisis in the U.S., SVR model gives the related accurate recession forecast, and for the 2011 sovereign crisis in Italy, the KNN regression model gives the accurate recession forecast. For the recent 5 years, the impact of COVID-19 is significant and unprecedented, no models including the traditional methods and machine learning models can reflect the strong fluctuation caused by COVID-19. To better realize the impact of COVID-19, we introduce Google mobility data in the U.S to analyze how COVID-19 affects the social economic life as much previous research points out, the impact of COVID-19 can not be evaluated by the traditional macroeconomic indicators, like GDP and industrial production, but need to be analyzed by some specific fields in social life.

The rest of the paper proceeds as follows: Sect. 2 gives the literature review to conclude some points in the previous research. Section 3 gives the basic description of the models used in the paper. Sections 4 and 5 show the results for the U.S. and Italy. Section 6 discusses COVID-19. Section 7 is the conclusion part.

2 Literature Review

For the traditional method in econometrics, the vector auto-regression model is the most usual one. A structural var model of the Australian economy [1] employs the structure VAR model to study the Australian economy. Covid-19 and the macroeconomic effects of costly disasters [2] uses data of the costly and deadly disasters in recent US history to construct the VAR model to evaluate and forecast the economic impact caused by COVID-19 shock. Macroeconomic forecasting in the time of covid-19. Manuscript [3] build a VAR model to estimate 6 key macroeconomic indicators. And for the recession forecast, some previous research focuses more on the recession trend. Dynamic probit models and financial variables in recession forecasting [4] examines various financial variables as the predictive variables in the dynamic probit models to conduct recession forecasting. This paper researches the probability of a recession in the United States and Germany. The paper shows that the domestic term spread, defined as the difference between the long-term interest rate and short-term interest rate, has great power in recession forecasting. Moreover, the lagged values of the stock returns and the foreign term spread are also statistically significant as predictive variables.

However, as many researchers point out, the traditional methods might not be proper for the big data and the machine learning methods may be the good choices in recession forecast. New tricks for econometrics [5] synthesizes several machine learning methods which can be potentially used in the economic forecast and gives the examples in many different fields including regression methods and classification methods. For the regression method, Predicting economic recessions using machine learning algorithms [6] shows that random forest can give an early warning for the recession. The paper focuses on the forecast of short-term GDP growth rate using the variables from the financial market and finds that although the machine learning model improves outcomes compared with the traditional model, it is more sensitive to recession than the traditional models. And for the classification machine learning method, Yield curve and recession forecasting in a machine learning framework [7] researches the recession predictive ability of yield curve, defined as the difference between short-term treasury bill rates and long-term treasury bill rates, employing support vector machine as the classification to forecast the recession. Comparing the regression methods and classification methods for recession forecasting, the regression machine learning models can evaluate not only the trend but also the degree of the recession, but the classification models might be more sensitive.

For the traditional models or the machine learning models, an important potential problem is the frequencies of the economic indicators. Some research gives us some reference about the mixing-frequencies analysis. On the economic sources of stock market volatility [8] employs a new class of component volatility models based on GARCH process and mixed data sampling (MIDAS), called the GARCH - MIDAS to study the relation between stock market volatility and macroeconomic activity. This new class of models can distinguish different frequency variables in economic activities and link them to stock market volatility. However, for our research, this type of model might be too complicated and not really proper since our research focuses more on the recession performance of the macroeconomic data, like GDP. The stock data would be considered the independent variable in our research. Forecasting us output growth using leading indicators: An appraisal using midas models [9] gives an example of using the MIDAS model in forecasting the real GDP growth rate of the United States with 10 leading indicators including term spread, stock price index, consumer confidence, real money supply (M2) and others. This paper introduces the auto-regressive MIDAS model which can combine different frequency variables with lags. Now-casting and the real-time data flow [10] gives more details about the now- casting problem in Handbook of economic forecasting and show the basic principle of combining the higher and lower frequency data. Comparing the dsge model with the factor model: an out-of-sample forecasting experiment [11] compares the performance in the forecasting of the DSGE model with the factor model and shows that the factor model can provide a good forecast for the growth rate but the predictive ability depends on the number of factors. These mixing-frequencies methods are good supplements for the methods we use in the paper.

Another problem we should notice is the impact of COVID-19. Much previous research focuses on it and gives many evaluations and forecasts of the impact of COVID-19 on the economy. Covid-19 and the macroeconomic effects of costly disasters [2] points out that there will be steep declines in economic activity caused by COVID-19 shock, with the longer the duration of the shock, the larger the cumulative losses. Covid-induced economic uncertainty [12] discusses three indicators, stock market volatility, newspaper-based economic uncertainty, and subjective uncertainty in business expectation surveys and summarize that the COVID-19 has already created uncertainty shock larger than the financial crisis of 2008–2009 and much similar to the Great Depression. The economic impacts of covid-19: Evidence from a new public database built using private sector data [13] uses several sources of private sector data to construct a new database that can be used to evaluate the economic impact of COVID-19 and focus on the heterogeneity by some important gradients, like income, different sectors, COVID incidence, different areas, and different wage rates. Macroeconomic forecasting in the time of covid-19. Manuscript [3] try to forecast the evolution of the economy following the outbreak of COVID-19. This paper builds a VAR model to estimate 6 key macroeconomic indicators. As much research mentioned, there is no example in history similar to COVID-19, so the economic status of it might be very special which would influence the effect of the forecast.

3 Models

In the paper, we use the traditional models and machine learning models to forecast the GDP growth rate for the U.S. and Italy, including the VAR model, MIADS model, random forest, KNN regression, support vector regression model (SVM), and gradient boosting model. In this section, we will introduce how we use the data to fit these models and give the forecast outcome. In Table 1, we conclude the descriptions of the models we use in the paper.

The general frame of our work is fitting different models with our independent variables to get the estimation of our dependent variable, the GDP growth rate. Here we will give the basic linear form of our model.

$$GDP_t = \beta_0 + \beta_1 Stock_t + \beta_3 M2_t + \beta_4 yield_t + \beta_5 unemployment_t \\ + \beta_6 dept_t + \beta_7 import_t + \beta_8 investment_t + \varepsilon_t$$

where the debt is the debt ratio, import is the import ratio, and investment is the investment ratio. In this linear form, we only consider the panel data at the same time, here is the same quarter, but actually, the lag data have an effect on the GDP growth rate and the current variables are the performance as same as the GDP growth rate, so we will introduce the lag data of all the variables in our model. To fit the models, we need to adjust the frequencies of some variables. In the machine learning models, since the frequency of the response variable, the GDP growth rate, is quarterly, we need to transform all other variables to quarterly. Because most of the data is monthly, here we choose a simple way

Table 1. Models.

Model	Description
VAR	The traditional vector auto-regression model
MIDAS	The regression with mixed data sampling
KNN regression	The simple regression based on the K-nearest-neighbor with weak learning ability
Random Forest regression	The regression based on the random forest with CART regression tree
Support Vector Regression	The regression based on the support vector machine
Gradient Boosting	The boosting method using negative gradient to estimate the residual

to adjust the frequencies of the variables. We just use the mean value of the variables in one quarter to stand for the level of the variables in that quarter. As the description in Table 1, most of the variables is the successive growth rate calculated by the difference of log to make them stationary, and the mean values also keep stationary. Similarly, in the traditional VAR model, we also need the variables with the same frequencies, so we adjust the variables in the same way as in machine learning models. For the traditional VAR model, the lag for all variables would be the same and for the machine learning models and the MIDAS model, we can choose different lags for different variables. For the MIDAS model, due to the mixed data sampling method, we can use the data with different frequencies. The basic method we introduce the lag data into the machine learning models is to generate the lags of the variables as the new variables to expand the panel data. Then we will delete the first several observation rows of the data because these rows contain missing values due to the lag. Here, we give the linear form with lag data based on the U.S. case.

$$GDP_t = \beta_0 + \sum_{i=1}^{2} \beta_i GDP_{t-1} + \beta_3 Stock_{t-i} + \sum_{i=1}^{5} \beta_{3+i} M2_{t-i} + \sum_{i=1}^{3} \beta_{8+i} yield_{t-i} + \sum_{i=1}^{8} \beta_{11-i} unemployment_{t-i}$$
$$+ \beta_{20} dept_{t-1} + \beta_{21} import_{t-1} + \sum_{i=1}^{2} \beta_{21} investment_{t-i} + \varepsilon_t$$

where the lag orders can be decided by the auto-regression orders calculated by the AIC.

In general, as the benchmark of all models, we only use the GDP growth rate to fit the basic AR model. And for the traditional VAR model, we use the quarterly-mean data to fit the model with first-order lag. And for the machine learning models and the MIDAS model, we choose different lags for different variables according to AIC.

4 Data

Our basic data set is based on the macroeconomic data of the U.S. To make sure all the variables are stationary and have clear economical meanings, we would do some transformations to the data. Specifically, we use the difference of the log to calculate the successive change rate of all the variables except yield. For the response variable, we focus on the GDP growth rate to evaluate the recession. As much previous research mentioned, the yield curve, defined as the difference between the short-term and long-term treasury bill rate, has a good ability in recession forecast, so we also introduce this variable in our models. As for the stock market, we choose the daily price of the S&P 500 index to stand for the stock market level. For the monetary and international trade factors which are related to the GDP, we consider M2, real total export goods and services, real import goods and services, and foreign exchange reserves. As an important part of the combination of GDP, real investment is also a part of our data. For the time period, we collect the data from Jan 1980 to Dec 2021 and we choose the data before 2017 as the fitting or training part of our data set, the rest as the forecast part. The GDP growth rate in history (can be seen in Fig. 1), generally fluctuated between 0 to 0.02, and there are only several quarters with a negative GDP growth rate, which stands for a recession. Among them, the most obvious recession is about 2008, which is the period of the subprime mortgage crisis. And for other times, although the GDP growth rate fluctuates to some degree, it generally keeps stable. For the statistical properties, the GDP growth rate is stationary with a 0.0069 mean value and 0.000039 variances. And the descriptive statistics of all variables can be seen in Table 2.

Table 2. Descriptive Statistics.

Variable	Description	Mean	Variance
GDP	Real GDP	0.006364766	0.0001367958
stock	S&P 500 Index	0.023182776	0.0061977960
M2	M2	0.015924624	0.0001375592
yield	Difference between 3-month and 10-year treasury bill rate	−1.776447106	1.3028219729
unemployment	Unemployment rate	−0.002380598	0.0127984845
debt	Gross government debt/Total export	0.010445816	0.0014930802
Ratio importration	Total import/Foreign exchange reserves	−0.008173234	0.0022729144
investment ratio	Real investment/GDP per capital	0.004497685	0.0009718374

Except for the yield, we use the difference of log to calculate the successive change rate of the variables.

For variables in quarterly-mean form, we calculate the correlation matrix using Pearson correlation and find that except for the yield curve, all other variables are significantly correlated to the GDP growth rate. To be specific, M2 (−0.43), unemployment (−0.85), and debt ratio (−0.74) are negatively correlated to the GDP growth rate. S\&P index (0.25), import ratio (0.55), and investment ratio (0.6) are positively correlated to the GDP growth rate. Generally, this outcome is consistent with the basic theory of macroeconomics. For the yield curve, it seems inconsistent with the conclusion in the previous research that it has a good ability to recession forecast, but this is only from the viewpoint of correlation. The complete correlation matrix can be seen in Fig. 1.

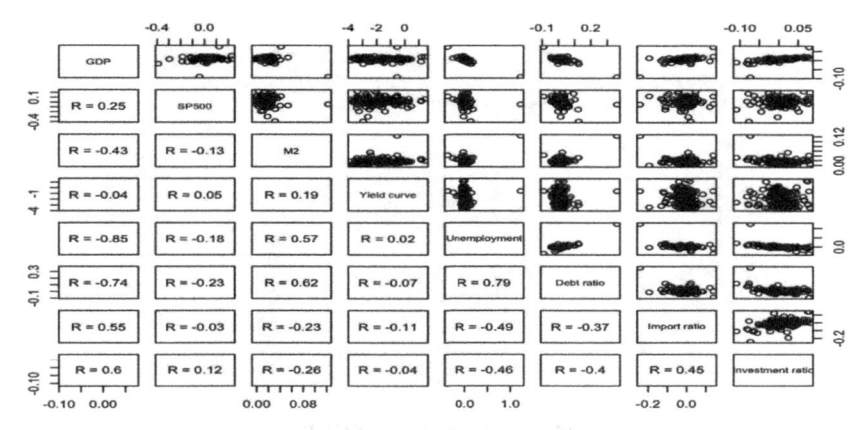

Fig. 1. Variables Correlation Matrix for the U.S.

We collect the data for Italy from 2000, which is a shorter period compared to the data for the U.S. Due to the different statistical methods and different calculations, the investment ratio for Italy is totally different from the investment ratio for the U.S., but we still include it in our models. And for other variables, the comparison with the same variables for the U.S. can be seen in Table 3. To make the comparison more reasonable, we compare the variables except the investment ratio in the same period, from 2000 to 2022. And part of visualization of the comparison can be seen in Fig. 2, 3 and 4. For the change rate of GDP, the U.S. has the higher mean value and higher variance, but general trends for the U.S. and Italy are similar. The main difference occurs between 2010 and 2016. After the financial crisis in 2008, the recession in the economy lasted for several years for Italy and in this period, the change rate of the GDP for Italy is generally lower than for the U.S. In the period after 2020, the fluctuation caused by the COVID-19 seems to be stronger for Italy than for the U.S, but the trend of the fluctuation is as same as the trend for the U.S. And for the independent variables in the model, the results of the comparison for them are similar, having the generally similar trend and the main differences occurring between 2010 and 2016.

For the Italy data, the statistical method of some variables are different to the data for the U.S, but we can still change them to the similar form. And for the stock market data, we choose the Italy FTSE data to stand for the stock market level. Moreover, due to different data source and statistical facilities, the time range of the data for Italy is different to the time range of the data for the U.S.The descriptive statistics of the variables for Italy can be seen in Table 3.

5 Results

For the U.S. case, we first forecast the GDP growth rate in the recent 5 years as the general forecast in the paper to check the difference in performances of the models. For the model fitting, we fit the machine learning models using cross-validation and calculate the sum of mean square error (MSE) of them as the evaluation indicator. The MSE of the cross-validation can be seen in Table 4. KNN regression model has the

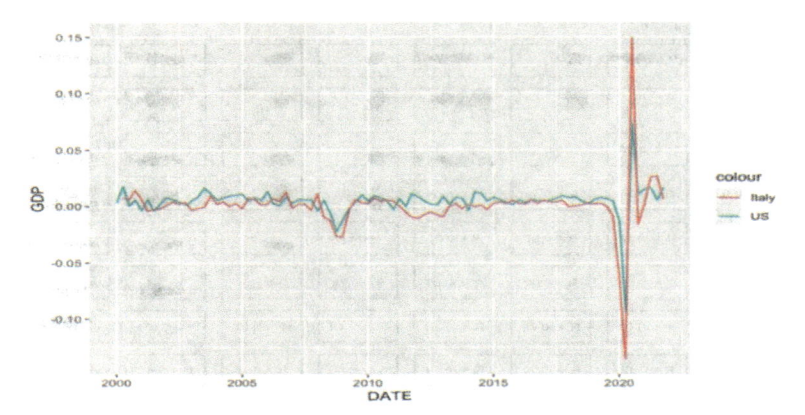

Fig. 2. Comparison of GDP

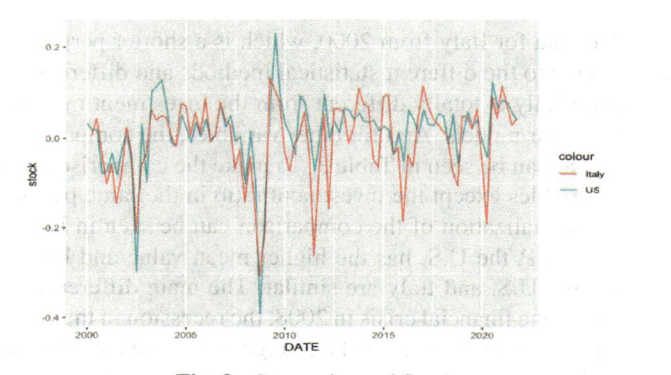

Fig. 3. Comparison of Stock

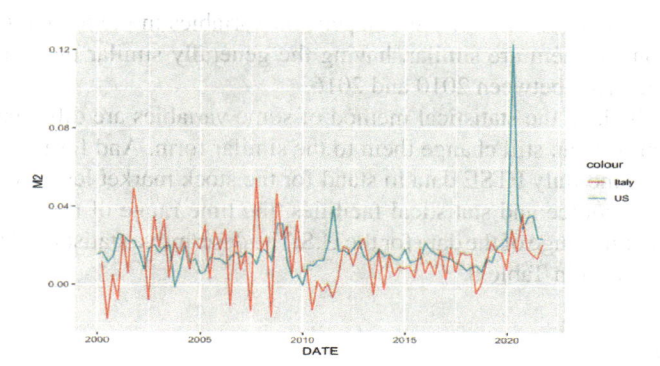

Fig. 4. Comparison of M2

smallest MSE (0.0000385) among all the machine learning models, but generally, the MSE of the machine learning models is very close. For the forecast, we can see the

Table 3. Descriptive Statistics for Italy

Variable	Mean	Variance
GDP	0.0005208938	0.0005772163
stock	−0.0059506361	0.0079439624
M2	0.01357689	0.0001948100
yield	−2.1199927969	1.6215014386
unemployment	−0.0018021029	0.0013924101
debt ratio	−0.0027730473	0.0057721812
import ratio	0.0003418337	0.0051455733

forecast value and the real value in Table 5 and the forecast MSE for all models can be seen in Table 6. Figure 5 gives us a visualization of the forecast. For the MSE for the cross-validation of the machine learning models or the MSE for the forecast outcome, most of the models perform very similarly. The support vector regression model (SVR) has the smallest MSE in the forecast. For the specific forecast performance, all models give a relatively stable forecast before the first quarter of 2020 as same as the actual GDP growth rate compared to the later period. However, from the first quarter of 2020, the actual GDP growth rate fluctuates strongly, but only the random forest model, SVR model, and MIDAS model show the fluctuation in the forecast and the trend of SVR seems to be mostly close to the real value. To check the difference between the advanced models and the benchmark AR model, we conduct the Diebold-Mariano test (DM test). The outcome of the test can be seen in Table 7. For the whole forecast period, only the MIDAS model shows significant differences (p-value smaller than 0.05) compared to the benchmark AR model.

Table 4. MSE for Cross-Validation

Model	MSE
KNN	0.0000385
Random Forest	0.0000338
Support Vector Regression	0.0000477
Gradient Boosting	0.0000393

Although the DM test tells us most of the models do not show significant differences compared to the AR model, we still notice that the performance of the models may be different in different periods. Due to the too strong fluctuation after 2020, we cut the forecast outcome into two parts, the period before 2020 and the period after 2020. We first compare the MSE of all models in two different periods. The MSE can be seen in Table 8 and Table 9. The forecast MSE before 2020 for all models is obviously smaller than the forecast MSE after 2020. And compared to the MSE of the whole period, the

Table 5. Forecast Outcomes for the U.S.

	actual	AR	VAR	MIDAS	KNN	RandomForest	SVR	GradientBoosting
2017/1/1	0.00471	0.00576	0.00684	0.00746	0.00705	0.00812	0.00546	0.01078
2017/4/1	0.00558	0.00592	0.00638	0.00887	0.00569	0.00540	0.00740	0.00407
2017/7/1	0.00717	0.00609	0.00613	0.00880	0.00660	0.00515	0.00683	0.00210
2017/10/1	0.00936	0.00617	0.00585	0.00559	0.00697	0.00643	0.00575	0.00537
2018/1/1	0.00760	0.00622	0.00558	0.00752	0.00785	0.00744	0.00660	0.00820
2018/4/1	0.00830	0.00626	0.00532	0.00536	0.00810	0.00777	0.00607	0.00896
2018/7/1	0.00481	0.00627	0.00508	0.01005	0.00811	0.00788	0.00636	0.00933
2018/10/1	0.00223	0.00628	0.00485	0.00766	0.00794	0.00810	0.00509	0.00899
2019/1/1	0.00596	0.00629	0.00464	0.00543	0.00785	0.00610	0.00194	0.00313
2019/4/1	0.00790	0.00629	0.00445	0.00651	0.00839	0.00577	0.00412	0.00785
2019/7/1	0.00683	0.00630	0.00426	0.00874	0.00710	0.00565	0.00421	0.00616
2019/10/1	0.00468	0.00630	0.00408	0.00644	0.00546	0.00487	0.00520	0.00595
2020/1/1	0.01312	0.00630	0.00392	0.00625	0.00575	0.00502	0.00524	0.00470
2020/4/1	0.09362	0.00630	0.00376	0.00264	0.00575	0.00124	0.00023	0.00782
2020/7/1	0.07276	0.00630	0.00360	−0.02440	0.00599	-0.00340	0.04216	0.00001
2020/10/1	0.01109	0.00630	0.00346	−0.00664	0.00629	0.00772	−0.01693	0.00751
2021/1/1	0.01522	0.00630	0.00332	0.01316	0.00692	0.01147	0.02405	0.01059
2021/4/1	0.01627	0.00630	0.00318	0.01214	0.00730	0.01149	0.02908	0.01223
2021/7/1	0.00569	0.00630	0.00306	0.02176	0.00703	0.00968	0.02790	0.01515
2021/10/1	0.01667	0.00630 3	0.0029	0.01670	0.00735	0.00936	−0.00726	0.01477

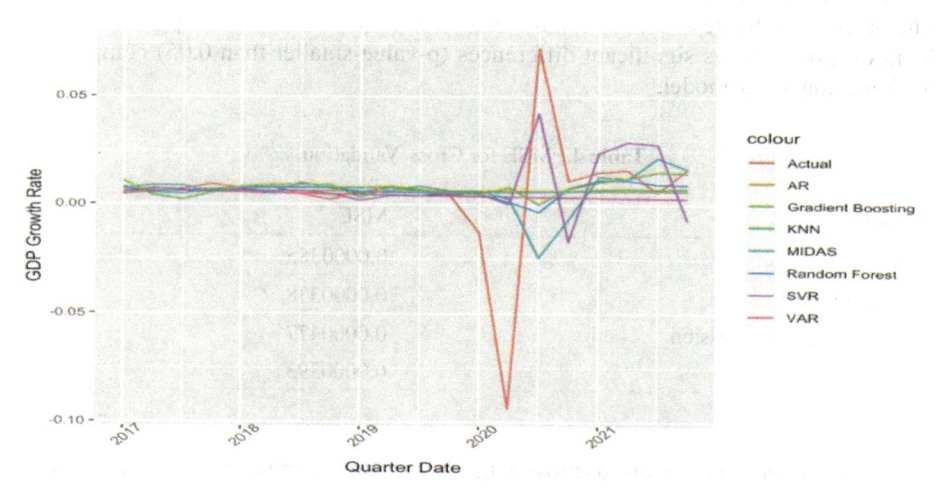

Fig. 5. Actual and forecast value.

MSE in the first quarter is also much smaller and the MSE in the second period is much closer to the MSE in the whole period. Therefore, in these two periods, the performances of the models are different. All models perform worse in the period after 2020 and the

Table 6. Forecast MSE.

Model	MSE
AR	0.000756
VAR	0.000759
KNN	0.000750
Random Forest	0.000765
Gradient Boosting	0.000810
SVR	0.000612
MIDAS	0.000989

Table 7. Diebold-mariano test.

Model	Statistic	p-Value
VAR	−1.6705	0.0948
KNN	1.5574	0.1194
Random Forest	0.8808	0.3784
Gradient Boosting	−0.9585	0.3378
SVR	−1.2059	0.2278
MIDAS	−12.4941	0.0000

performance after 2020 affects the MSE in the whole forecast period. In the period before 2020, the range of the fluctuation of the GDP growth is similar to the historical data, from 0 to 0.01. Although all models give the forecast in the same range, the degrees of fluctuation is different. The AR and VAR models give smooth forecast curves in this period, but the MIDAS model show fluctuation in this period. For the machine learning models, all the models show fluctuations, but the trend of the SVR model is the most similar to the actual value, which is consistent with the outcome of MSE that SVR has the smallest MSE. For the period after 2020, there exists a huge fluctuation in the GDP growth rate. The smallest (-0.0936) and largest (0.0727) GDP growth rate in the whole period including the history data occur in two successive quarters. This fluctuation is so large that we even can not see other fluctuations in the same figure and almost non of the models give the closed forecast except the SVR model. For the differences between the advanced models and benchmark AR model, the outcome of the DM test in two periods can be seen in Table 10. In the period before 2020, except KNN model, other models show significant differences compared to the AR model, and after 2020, the gradient boosting model and SVR model do not show significant differences compared to AR. Therefore, for the forecast error, the models are different from the AR model in general.

For the machine learning models, random forest, SVM, and gradient boosting (GBM), the feature importance and predictive contribution calculated in shapely value

Table 8. Forecast MSE before 2020.

Model	MSE
AR	0.00000357
VAR	0.00000493
KNN	0.00000497
Random Forest	0.00000621
Gradient Boosting	0.00001315
SVR	0.00000594
MIDAS	0.00000916

Table 9. Forecast MSE after 2020.

Model	MSE
AR	0.00188607
VAR	0.001890327
KNN	0.001868879
Random Forest	0.001905635
Gradient Boosting	0.002005474
SVR	0.001521757
MIDAS	0.002459429

Table 10. Diebold-mariano comparison.

Model	Statistic before 2020	p-Value before 2020	Statistic after 2020	p-Value after 2020
VAR	−2.0528	0.0401	−2.0917	0.0365
KNN	0.3318	0.7401	3.3958	0.0007
Random Forest	−2.5957	0.0094	10.1356	0
Gradient Boosting	−5.9910	0.000	0.7988	0.4244
SVR	−2.0654	0.0389	−0.9158	0.3598
MIDAS	−10.0280	0.0000	−40.4363	0.0000

for the variables can be seen in Fig. 6, 7, 8, 9, 10 and 11. For the random forest model, GDP with first-order lag, unemployment rate with first-order lag, GDP with second-order lag, and import ratio with first-order lag are the first four important variables of the model and for the predictive part, the import ratio is the feature has the largest contribution and the contribution is positive. The M2 with first-order lag is the most important feature of the SVM model, and the root means a square error of it is larger than all other features. For the predictive contribution, the first four largest contribution features have a negative contribution and the import ratio with the first order is the feature that has the largest positive contribution to the SVM model. For the gradient boosting model, the stock price with first-order lag is the most important feature and in the predictive part, the import ratio with first-order lag has the largest contribution and the contribution is positive. In the case of the U.S., for the different models, the feature importance and predictive contribution are different. And for each model, the feature importance and predictive contribution for the same feature are also different. The import ratio with first-order lag is the feature with a related large predictive contribution for all models. And compared to the features with larger order lag, the features with smaller order lag tend to be more important and have larger contributions.

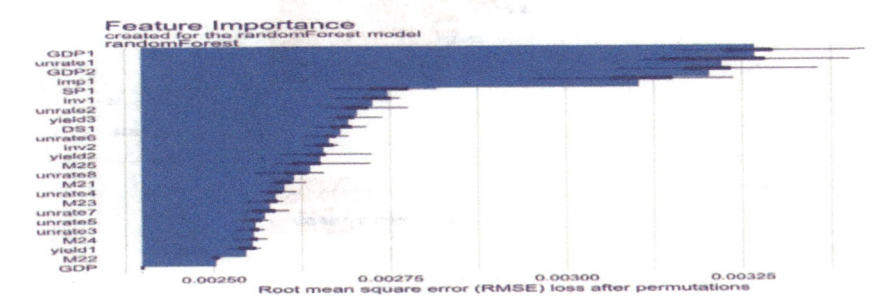

Fig. 6. Feature importance of random forest for the U.S.

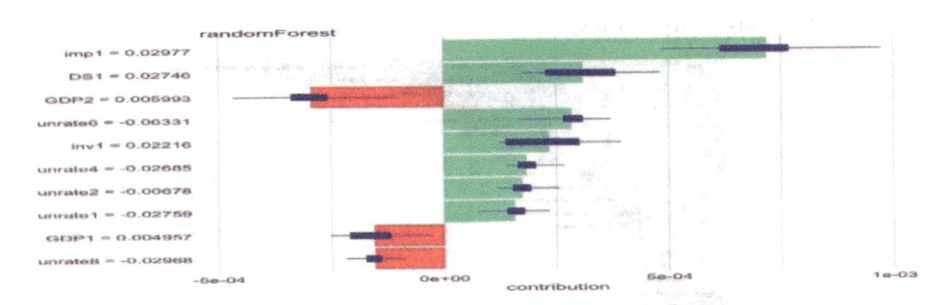

Fig. 7. Feature contribution of random forest for the U.S.

Besides the forecast for the GDP growth rate in the recent 5 years, we also focus on the recession forecast in a specific period. For the U.S. case, we focus on the period of the financial crisis in 2008. In this period, GDP decreased in four successive quarters from the third quarter of 2008 to the second quarter of 2009. Such successive decreases fit the definition of economic recession. We use our models to forecast the GDP growth rate in this period to check whether these models can give the forecast of the recession.

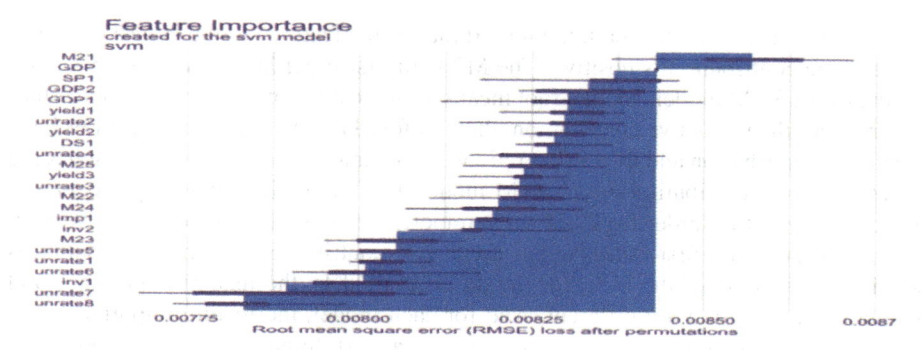

Fig. 8. Feature importance of SVM for the U.S.

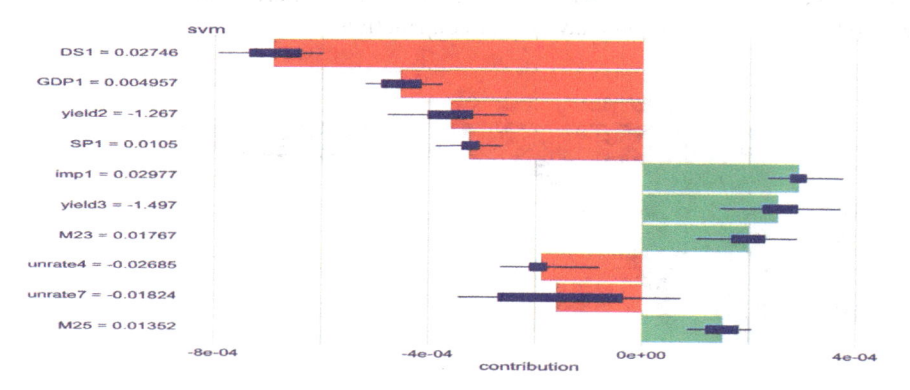

Fig. 9. Feature contribution of SVM for the U.S.

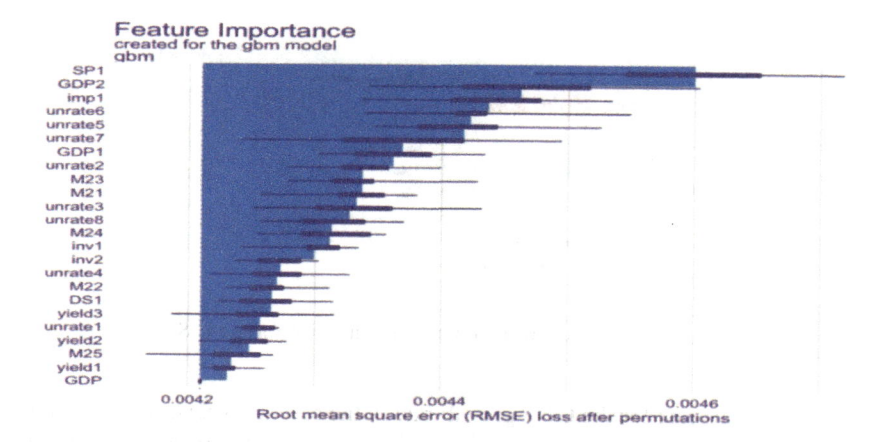

Fig. 10. Feature importance of gradient boosting for the U.S.

Compared to the general forecast, the forecast of the recession not only focuses on the

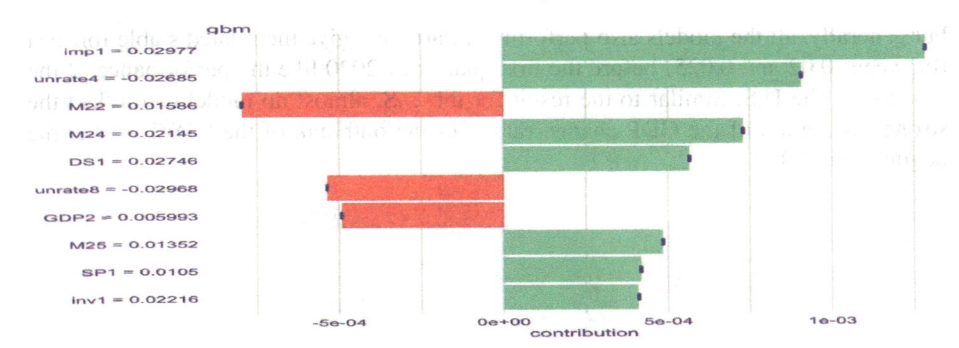

```
              gbm
imp1 = 0.02977
unrate4 = -0.02685
M22 = 0.01586
M24 = 0.02145
DS1 = 0.02746
unrate8 = -0.02968
GDP2 = 0.005993
M25 = 0.01352
SP1 = 0.0105
inv1 = 0.02216
              -5e-04    0e+00    5e-04    1e-03
                       contribution
```

Fig. 11. Feature contribution of gradient boosting for the U.S.

error but also focus on the negative direction of the GDP growth rate. The forecast outcome can be seen in Table 11. Among the machine learning models, only the SVR model gives the successive negative forecast in this period, but the forecast recession occurs from the first quarter of 2009, when the real recession has already occurred two quarters before, and last to the third quarter of 2009 when the real recession has ended for two quarters. The recession forecast of SVR model shows significant hysteresis.

Table 11. Recession forecast for the U.S.

period	actual	VAR	KNN	Random Forest	SVR	Gradient Boosting	MIDAS
2008/1/1	−0.00408	0.00721	0.00670	0.00516	0.00560	0.00448	0.00628
2008/4/1	0.00571	0.00294	0.00697	0.00348	0.00416	0.00175	0.01794
2008/7/1	−0.00528	−0.00017	0.00834	0.00429	0.00587	0.00784	0.01319
2008/10/1	−0.02207	0.00093	0.00896	0.00538	0.00788	0.00510	0.01398
2009/1/1	−0.01173	0.00704	0.00968	0.00572	−0.00393	0.00834	−0.00428
2009/4/1	−0.00169	0.00327	0.00983	0.00443	−0.01504	0.00462	0.00749
2009/7/1	0.00361	0.00418	0.00940	0.00624	−0.01542	0.00848	0.00187
2009/10/1	0.01062	−0.00012	0.00965	0.00698	−0.00059	0.00693	0.00766

In the case of the U.S., we discuss the performance of different models in general GDP growth rate forecast and recession forecast and find that the machine learning models may perform better than the traditional methods. For the Italy case, we repeat our work can try to find whether there exist some similarities between these two countries.

For the results for Italy, we can say that it is generally similar to the results for the U.S. The forecast results for Italy can be seen in Table 12 and the curves of the results can be seen in Fig. 12. The forecast MSE for different periods can be seen in Tables 13, 14 and 15. The forecast curves also show the similarity of the results for the two countries. Compared to the results for the U.S, the forecast results for Italy shows more fluctuations, but generally, all the models also perform similarly and give the related stable forecast (between -0.02 and 0.025) before the first quarter of 2020 like the performance of the models for the U.S. Similar to the result for the U.S, almost no model can reflect the strong fluctuation of the GDP change rate after the outbreak of the COVID-19 at the beginning of 2020.

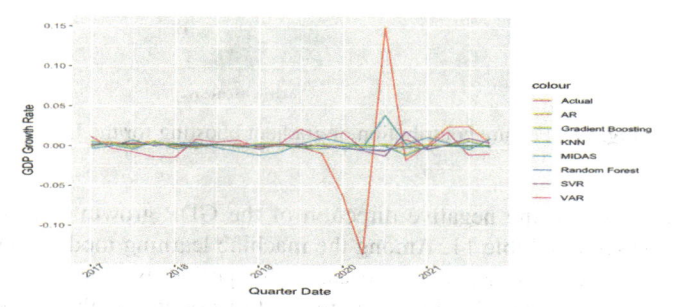

Fig. 12. Forecast outcome for Italy.

Table 12. Forecast outcomes for Italy.

period	actual	AR	VAR	MIDAS	KNN	RF	SVR	GB
2017/1/1	0.00548	0.00216	0.01191	−0.00269	0.00591	0.00251	0.00009	−0.00086
2017/4/1	0.00399	0.00180	−0.00287	0.00038	0.00185	0.00313	0.00309	0.00392
2017/7/1	0.00381	0.00161	−0.00724	0.00803	−0.00362	0.00236	0.00331	−0.00128
2017/10/1	0.00535	0.00152	−0.01337	0.00039	0.00597	0.00275	0.00125	0.00301
2018/1/1	−0.00035	0.00147	−0.01404	0.00401	−0.00274	0.00232	0.00206	0.00171
2018/4/1	0.00024	0.00144	0.00879	0.00536	0.00185	0.00280	0.00033	−0.00222
2018/7/1	0.00119	0.00143	0.00524	−0.00126	0.00338	0.00295	0.00191	0.00167
2018/10/1	0.00296	0.00143	0.00798	−0.00604	−0.00072	0.00149	0.00214	−0.00042
2019/1/1	0.00197	0.00142	−0.00099	−0.01058	0.00396	0.00116	−0.00320	−0.00148
2019/4/1	0.00279	0.00142	0.00367	−0.00651	0.00396	0.00087	0.00316	0.00146
2019/7/1	0.00009	0.00142	0.02265	0.00424	−0.00117	0.00136	0.00348	−0.00106
2019/10/1	−0.00812	0.00142	0.01083	0.01202	−0.00132	0.00168	0.00110	0.00348
2020/1/1	−0.06093	0.00142	0.01837	0.00526	0.00100	−0.00227	−0.00011	−0.00004
2020/4/1	−0.13528	0.00142	−0.00285	0.00152	0.00214	−0.00320	−0.00447	−0.00174
2020/7/1	0.14923	0.00142	−0.00526	0.03982	0.00100	−0.00385	−0.01143	0.00280
2020/10/1	−0.01585	0.00142	0.00969	0.00345	−0.01016	0.00158	0.02002	−0.00145
2021/1/1	0.00211	0.00142	−0.00036	0.01264	0.00228	−0.00265	−0.00183	0.00276
2021/4/1	0.02608	0.00142	0.01961	0.00557	0.00204	0.00323	0.00372	0.00159
2021/7/1	0.02692	0.00142	−0.00893	−0.00228	0.00100	0.00317	0.01214	0.00795
2021/10/1	0.00649	0.00142	−0.00750	0.01153	0.00205	0.00304	0.00615	0.00026

For the MSE of the models, the MIDAS model has the smallest MSE among all the models, but generally, the MSE of all models is very closed, which is similar to the result for the U.S. For the model evaluation, MIDAS is the model with the smallest MSE for Italy, but in the first period, the benchmark AR model has the smallest MSE. And after 2020, MIDAS has the smallest MSE, which is consistent with the whole period. Comparing the MSE value, the forecast MSE for all models for the U.S. are smaller than the MSE for all models for Italy. Actually, the mean value of the real GDP change rate for Italy (0.000907) is smaller than the mean value of the real GDP change rate for the U.S (0.0053), and the variance of the real GDP change rate (0.00242) is larger than the variance of the real GDP change rate for the U.S (0.00079) in the forecast period, so the difference between two economies may be caused differences in the forecast. For two different periods, the MSE before 2020 is obviously smaller than the MSE after 2020, which is similar to the result for the U.S. All models perform worse after 2020 similar to the situation for the U.S, which may imply that the impact of the COVID-19 on Italy is similar to the impact on the U.S. Generally, as the evaluation indicator of the model performance, the results of MSE for Italy and the U.S are similar, including the similar performance for the whole period and the similar difference in two different periods. The MSE can be seen in Tables 14, 15 and 16.

Table 13. Forecast MSE for Italy.

Model	MSE
AR	0.00230
VAR	0.00258
KNN	0.00230
Random Forest	0.00229
Gradient Boosting	0.00222
SVR	0.00244
MIDAS	0.00188

The result of DM test for Italy can be seen in Table 16. For the whole period, the forecast error of VAR and SVR models show a significant difference compared to the benchmark AR model. Similar to the result of the U.S, most of the models do not show significant difference compared with the benchmark AR model in the whole forecast period, but specifically, for the U.S case, the MIDAS model is the only one significantly different from the AR model and for the Italy case, there are two models, VAR and SVR significantly different to the AR model. In general, the results for Italy are similar to the results for the U.S. Few models perform really well to forecast the GDP change rate from 2017 to 2021, and COVID-19 caused a special and obvious shock for both these two countries and no model can forecast the fluctuation caused by it. Some specific details show the difference due to the difference between the economy of the two countries.

The feature importance and predictive contribution calculated in shapely value for the variables of the machine learning models can be seen in Fig. 13, 14, 15, 16, 17 and

Table 14. Forecast MSE for Italy before 2020.

Model	MSE
AR	1.146450e−05
VAR	1.450445e−048
KNN	1.168287e−05
Random Forest	1.162839e−05
Gradient Boosting	2.025775e−05
SVR	1.477870e−05
MIDAS	7.677647e−05

Table 15. Forecast MSE for Italy after 2020.

Model	MSE
AR	0.00575
VAR	0.00623
KNN	0.00574
Random Forest	0.00571
Gradient Boosting	0.00552
SVR	0.00608
MIDAS	0.00460

Table 16. Diebold-mariano test for Italy.

Model	Statistic	P-value
VAR	−10.944	7.067392e−28
KNN	0.6849637	0.4933
Random Forest	1.486	0.13704
Gradient Boosting	0.270	0.7866
SVR	−6.7316735	1.677227e−11
MIDAS	−0.9310306	0.3518

18. For the random forest model, the GDP with first-order lag is the most important feature and the feature that has the largest predictive contribution the features with large importanceare also the features that have a large contribution. The debt ratio with 8-order lag is the most important feature of SVM model and the GDP with first-order lag is the second most important feature. For the predictive contribution, most of the features that have large contrition have a negative contribution and the GDP with first-order lag is

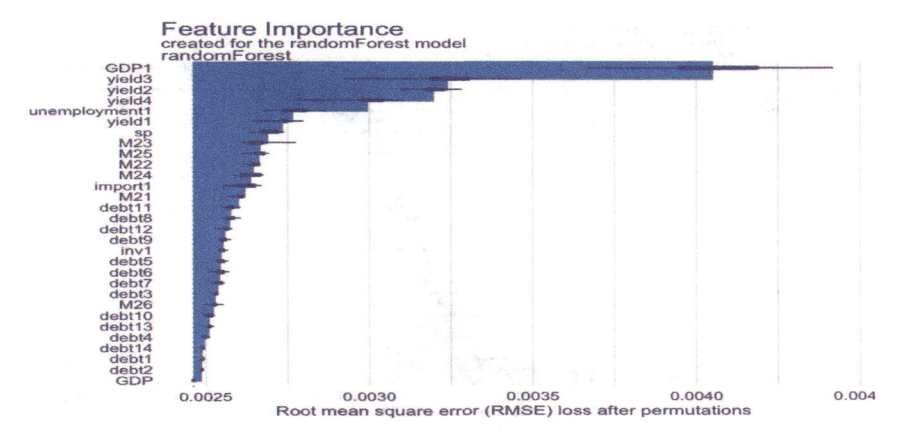

Fig. 13. Feature importance of random forest for the Italy.

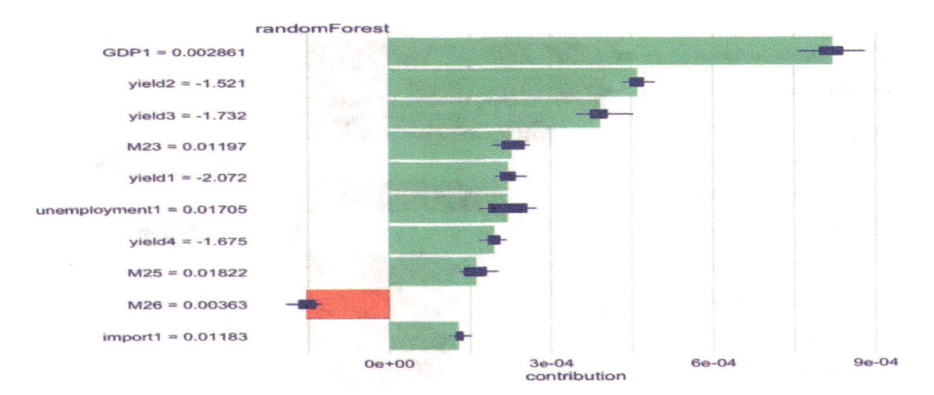

Fig. 14. Feature contribution of random forest for the Italy.

the feature that has the largest positive contribution. For the gradient boosting model, the GDP with first-order lag is the most important feature and the unemployment rate with first-order lag is the feature that has the largest contribution and its contribution is negative. For the case of Italy, the random forest model shows consistency in feature importance and predictive contribution and for all models, the GDP with first-order lag seems to play a more important role than in the case of the U.S.

The recession forecast for Italy focuses on the period of the 2011 sovereign crisis. In this period, the GDP decreased 7 successive quarters from the third quarter of 2011 to the first quarter of 2013, which is a really long recession period even compared to the 2008 financial crisis. The recession forecast can be seen in Table 17. Among all the models, the KNN model gives the negative GDP growth rate forecast in the corresponding period. Different from the recession forecast for the U.S., the machine KNN model performs much better than other models, which gives the related accurate and time-efficient recession forecast. In general machine learning models performs better

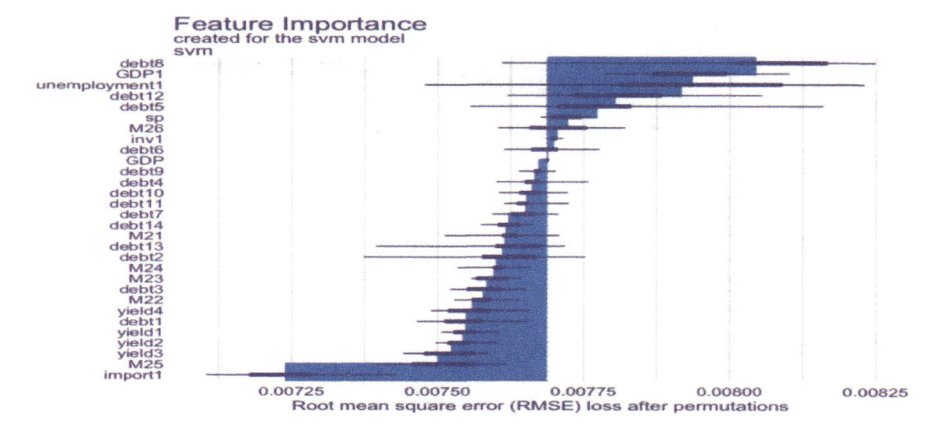

Fig. 15. Feature importance of SVM for the Italy.

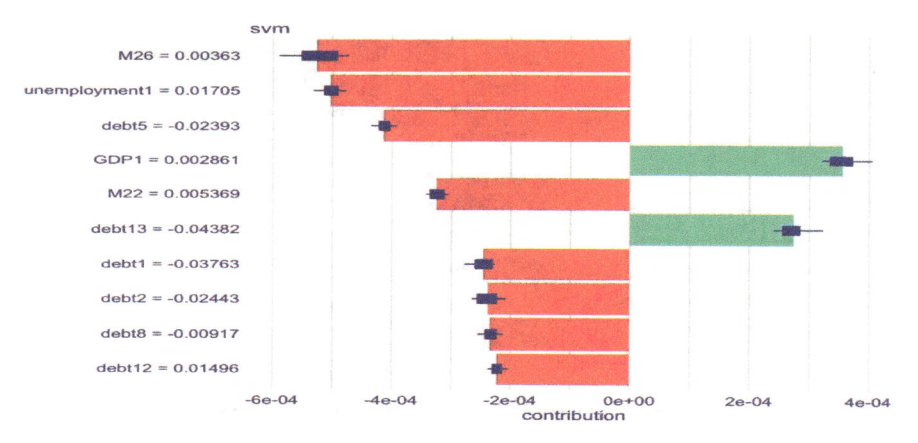

Fig. 16. Feature contribution of SVM for the Italy.

than the traditional methods, but for different countries, the champion model is different. And we also notice that the sensitivities of the forecast for different periods are different for both of these two countries. This might be caused by the fact that the causes of different recessions are different. As we discussed before, the reasons for the 2008 financial crisis and the 2011 Italy sovereign crisis are mainly endogenous, but the shock of COVID-19 is totally exogenous. This might cause the special economic status of the impact of COVID-19.

6   Viewpoint for COVID-19 in the U.S.

Considering that the U.S. is the country with the most serious epidemic(having the most accumulated cases and most accumulated deaths) and the economy of Italy is still affected by the terrible economic situation of the Eurozone, we focus on analyzing the

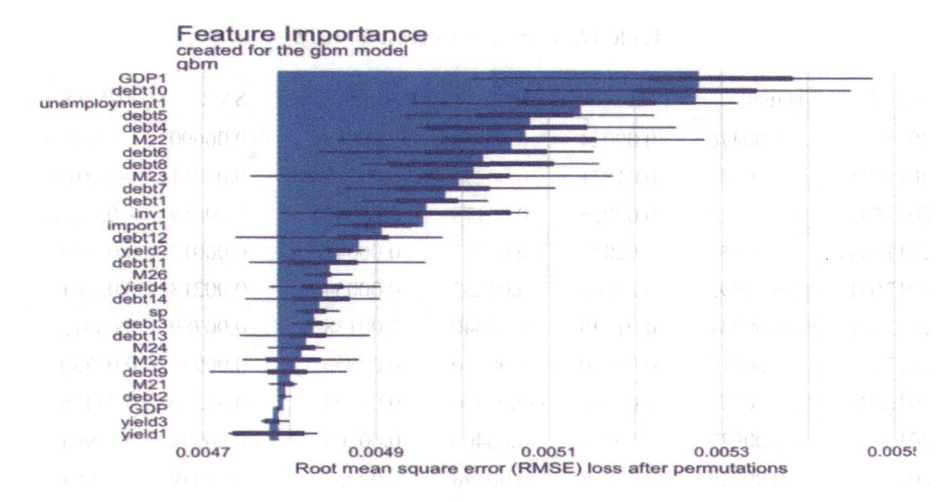

Fig. 17. Feature importance of gradient boosting for the Italy.

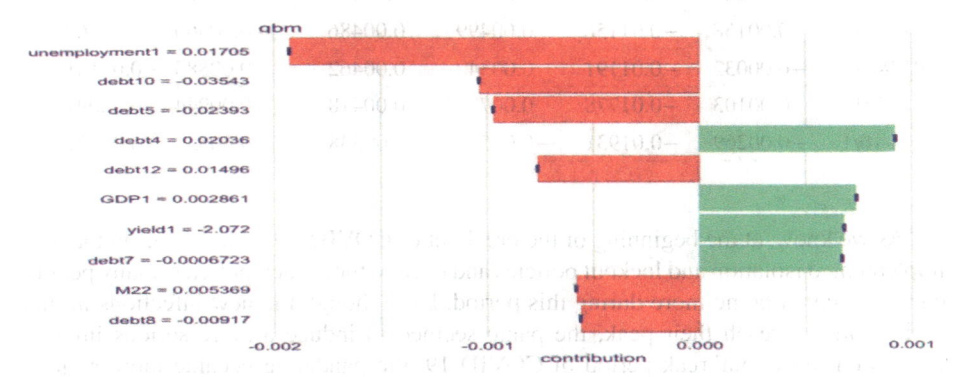

Fig. 18. Feature contribution of gradient boosting for the Italy.

impact of COVID-19 on the U.S. As the description mentioned before, the GDP growth rate fluctuate strongly from the first quarter of 2020, which is the time that COVID-19 began to spread in the U.S. This fact may imply the special economical status of COVID-19. As previous research points out, there is no example similar to COVID-19 in history, so we may consider that the impact of COVID-19 on the economy also can not be evaluated by the traditional methods with the macroeconomic indicators. This guess is consistent with the forecast outcome. Most of the models, especially the traditional AR and VAR models do not show any significant fluctuations in this period. And some other models, like the SVR, random forest, and MIDAS show fluctuations to some extent, but the fluctuations show obvious hysteresis, which means that these models can not give an accurate forecast outcome base on the long historical data. Therefore, we may need to treat COVID-19 as a very special case to evaluate its impact.

Table 17. Recession forecast for Italy.

period	actual	VAR	KNN	RandomForest	SVR	MIDAS
2011/1/1	0.00476	0.00024	0.00464	0.00318	0.00690	−0.00877
2011/4/1	0.00045	0.01971	0.00291	0.00375	0.01011	−0.00196
2011/7/1	−0.00524	0.00925	0.00178	0.00346	0.00659	−0.00344
2011/10/1	−0.00953	0.02017	−0.01252	0.00042	0.00012	0.01359
2012/1/1	−0.01092	0.01109	−0.01252	0.00054	0.00213	0.03861
2012/4/1	−0.00741	0.01045	−0.00540	0.00138	0.00789	0.05912
2012/7/1	−0.00519	0.00540	−0.00626	−0.00060	0.00931	0.03730
2012/10/1	−0.00755	0.00041	−0.00406	0.00493	0.01346	0.03476
2013/1/1	−0.00937	−0.00790	−0.00406	0.00265	0.00904	0.02964
2013/4/1	0.00020	−0.00878	0.00148	0.00258	0.01039	0.02961
2013/7/1	0.00230	−0.00880	0.00499	0.00428	0.01013	0.02669
2013/10/1	−0.00222	−0.00636	0.00479	0.00400	0.00888	0.01741
2014/1/1	0.00158	−0.01156	0.00499	0.00486	0.00960	0.02168
2014/4/1	−0.00032	−0.01191	0.00340	0.00462	0.00885	0.02101
2014/7/1	0.00103	−0.01778	0.00726	0.00418	0.00944	0.02091
2014/10/1	−0.00269	−0.01931	−0.00582	0.00338	0.00551	0.02077

As we know, at the beginning of the breakout of COVID-19, many states in the U.S. implemented isolation and lockout policies and even without such policies, many people chose to stay at home more during this period. Even though the new infections in this period did not reach their peak, the panic seemed to induce a more serious impact. Compared to the outbreak period of COVID-19, the pandemic became more serious at the beginning of 2021 and the end of 2021, but the GDP growth rate only decrease sharply at the beginning of 2020, which is the time of the outbreak of the COVID-19 and recover to a stable level in the subsequent quarters. This fact shows an interesting point of COVID-19. Although the epidemic was becoming more and more serious after 2020, people and society still recover to normal mode. Therefore, we can not simply analyze the impact of COVID-19 on the economy based on its severity of it, like the new infections or the accumulated deaths. Actually, the response to COVID-19 is the main reason which would affect the economy. To better realize the public reflection to COVID-19, we refer COVID-19 Community Mobility Report generated by Google. This report charted movement trends over time by geography, across different categories of places such as retail and recreation, groceries and pharmacies, parks, transit stations, workplaces, and residential. We believe that this report can give us a very special insight to realize how COVID-19 affect people's life.

As the report says, "as global communities responded to COVID-19, we heard from public health officials that the same type of aggregated, anonymized insights we use in products such as Google Maps would be helpful as they made critical decisions to combat COVID-19". This data is not generated by the original basic visiting data, like the number of people visiting different places, but shows how visitors to (or time spent in) categorized places change compared to the baseline days. A baseline day represents a normal value for that day of the week. The baseline day is the median value from the 5-week period Jan 3 – Feb 6, 2020.

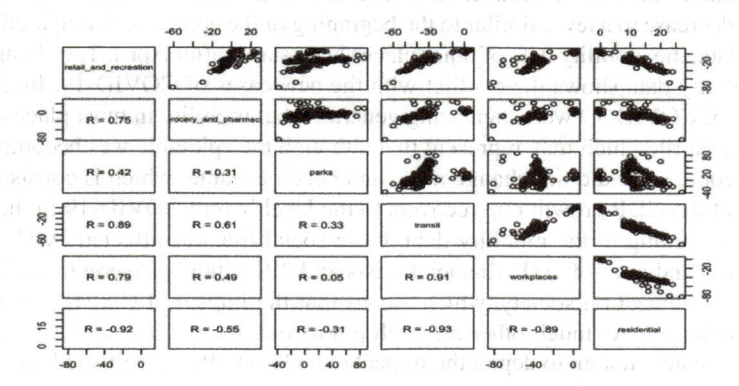

Fig. 19. Correlation matrix for mobility data.

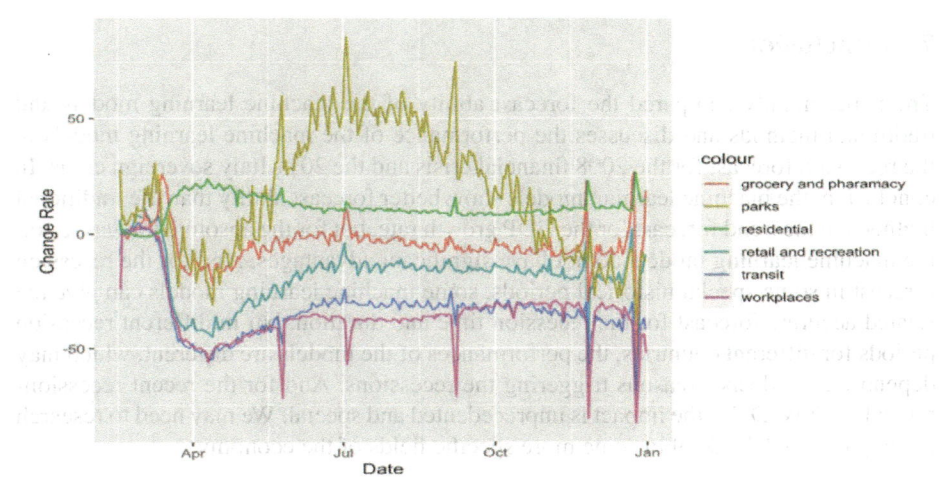

Fig. 20. Mobility curve.

This report provides the mobility data of the U.S. in the whole of 2020, which is the time COVID-19 outbroke and spread in the U.S. The original data shows obvious periodic and this periodic is caused by the difference between the working days and holidays, so we are just concerned about the weekdays of the mobility data and we still find that the mobility in different places shows a significant correlation. Some of them are positive correlative, like the workplaces and transit, and some of them are negative correlative, like the workplaces and the residential. The correlation matrix and the curve of the mobility data can be seen in Fig. 19 and Fig. 20. At beginning of the outbreak, the first quarter of 2020, the percentage changes compared to the baseline in all places except the residential decreased sharply, which is consistent with the fact that the lockdown policies made people stay at home more. Then as time passed, the mobility data of all places recover, but most of them are still lower than the baseline. The most interesting part is the mobility data of the park. It recovers to a level higher than the baseline in the middle of 2020, but decrease to a level similar to the beginning of the epidemic. Compared to other mobility data, the mobility data of other places keep stable after April. The change curve of the mobility data shows the conflict with the new cases of COVID-19. In 2020, the new cases of COVID-19 were increasing generally, but mobility in most places became stable after April, which may represent that although the epidemic was becoming more serious, people's life did not change more and become stable, which is consistent with the fact that the GDP growth rate recovers to the level before COVID-19 in the middle of 2020. According to the mobility data, basic social life was affected by COVID-19 significantly, and both of 2008 financial crisis and 2011 Italy's sovereign crisis do not have such an impact on society, which means that the impact of COVID-19 might be more complicated. As much other research points out, the traditional macroeconomic indicators are not enough to depict the impact of COVID-19. We still need more details in the specific fields of the social economic life like the labor market, education, social welfare, and other fields to research the impact of COVID-19.

7 Conclusion

The paper mainly compared the forecast ability of the machine learning models and traditional methods and discusses the performance of the machine learning models in the recession forecast for the 2008 financial crisis and the 2011 Italy sovereign crisis. In conclusion, the machine learning models show better forecast ability than the traditional methods in the trend forecast for the GDP growth rate, but for the absolute forecast error, the machine learning models do not have significant advantages. And for the recession forecast in some special historical periods, some machine learning models can give the related accurate forecast for the recession time and duration, but in different recession periods for different countries, the performances of the models are different, which may depend on the deeper reasons triggering the recessions. And for the recent recession-related to COVID-19, the impact is unprecedented and special. We may need to research the impact of COVID-19 in some more specific fields of the economy.

References

1. Dungey, M., Pagan, A.: A structural var model of the Australian economy. Econ. Rec. **76**(235), 321–342 (2000)
2. Ludvigson, S.C., Ma, S., Ng, S.: Covid-19 and the macroeconomic effects of costly disasters. Technical report, National Bureau of Economic Research (2020)
3. Primiceri, G.E., Tambalotti, A.: Macroeconomic forecasting in the time of covid-19. Manuscript, Northwestern University, pp. 1–23 (2020)
4. Nyberg, H.: Dynamic probit models and financial variables in recession forecasting. J. Forecast. **29**(1–2), 215–230 (2010)

5. Varian, H.R.: Big data: new tricks for econometrics. J. Econ. Perspect. **28**(2), 3–28 (2014)
6. Nyman, R., Ormerod, P.: Predicting economic recessions using machine learning algorithms. arXiv preprint arXiv:1701.01428 (2017)
7. Gogas, P., Papadimitriou, T., Matthaiou, M., Chrysanthidou, E.: Yield curve and recession forecasting in a machine learning framework. Comput. Econ. **45**(4), 635–645 (2015)
8. Engle, R.F., Ghysels, E., Sohn, B.: On the economic sources of stock market volatility. In: AFA 2008 New Orleans Meetings Paper (2008)
9. Clements, M.P., Galvão, A.B.: Forecasting US output growth using leading indicators: an appraisal using MIDAS models. J. Appl. Econ. **24**(7), 1187–1206 (2009)
10. BaÅLnbura, M., Giannone, D., Modugno, M., Reichlin, L.: Now- casting and the real-time data flow. Handb. Econ. Forecast. **2**, 195–237 (2013)
11. Wang, M.-C.: Comparing the dsge model with the factor model: an out-of-sample forecasting experiment. J. Forecast. **28**(2), 167–182 (2009)
12. Baker, S.R., Bloom, N., Davis, S.J., Terry, S.J.: Covid-induced economic uncertainty. Technical report, National Bureau of Economic Research (2020)
13. Chetty, R., Friedman, J.N., Hendren, N., Stepner, M., et al.: The economic impacts of COVID-19: evidence from a new public database built using private sector data. Technical report, national Bureau of economic research (2020)

Investigate the Relationship Between Financial Risk and Financial Performance: An Insight of China Life Insurance Company

Shikang Wang(✉)

Guangzhou Huashang College, Guangzhou 511300, Guangdong, China
author1920522982@qq.com

Abstract. The largest state-owned financial and insurance business in China, China Life Insurance Company is a significant institutional investor in the Chinese capital market. Since financial risk and financial performance are closely correlated, and insurance companies must strike a balance between the two in order to increase their performance capacity. Therefore, this paper selects the financial ratios of the Chinese life insurance company sector from 2011 to 2021 and uses quantitative and multiple regression equation models to look into the connection between Chinese life insurance businesses' financial risk and performance.

Keywords: China Life Insurance Company · Financial Risk · Insurance · Regression Equation Models

1 Introduction

The largest state-owned financial and insurance group in China is China Life Insurance Company, which also plays a significant institutional role in the country's capital market. The scope of the business includes everything from life insurance to property insurance to business and occupational annuities to banking, funds, asset management, wealth management, industrial investment, international trade, and other things. In addition, insurance is a kind of financial arrangement for apportioning accident losses.

As one of the important characteristics of the insurance industry, the risk of this industry is greater than that of other industries. Financial risk and financial performance are closely related. Based on the previous study, in the insurance industry, there is a significant correlation between financial risk and financial performance. For example, the financial performance of Indian life insurance firms is negatively impacted by their financial risk. Ethiopia company's financial performance has been affected by some financial risks. Therefore, it is crucial to look into the connection between financial risk and performance in order to improve an insurance company's financial performance through effective financial risk management. The previous study about the relationship between financial risk and financial performance focused on Indian, Jordanian, Ethiopia, Kenya, and Ghana. The research literature on the Insurance field in China is limited. Therefore, this paper selects the Chinese insurance field for research, and verifies the relationship between China Life's financial risk and financial performance by using quantitative and multiple regression equation models.

In addition, China Life's financial assets face the risks of unreasonable asset structure, low return on assets, and low asset utilization efficiency. Losses caused by financial risks such as vacancies in paid-in capital, excessive proportion of liabilities and assets, and occupation of life insurance liability reserves will reduce the company's repayment level and affect the company's reputation. Some serious situations may lead to bankruptcy.

Therefore, this paper selects the Chinese insurance field for research, and examines the connection between financial risk and the success of Chinese life insurance companies financially by employing quantitative and multiple regression equation models. This article can fill the gaps in China's insurance-related research and provide guidance for companies' financial risk management, helping companies better manage financial risks, and further maximize shareholder benefits.

2 Literature Review

Based on the previous study, In the insurance industry, financial risk and financial performance are significantly correlated. Morara and Sibindi have thoroughly investigated the connection between Kenya's insurance industry's financial risk and financial performance [1]. They choose several variables in order to measure financial risk. In detail, they utilized the solvency ratio to estimate the solvency risk and the loss ratio to measure the underwriting risk. Their result demonstrated that both the underwriting risk and the solvency risk have a detrimental effect on the company's financial performance.

Likewise, Wani and Dar have been examined the impact of the Indian Insurance industry's financial risk and its financial performance. They selected 24 currently operating insurance companies to represent the whole industry and collected data from 2005 to 2012. Also, they applied return on asset (ROA) to evaluate the financial performance of the business, and they selected the following risk to measure the financial risk, which is the capital management risk calculated by the ratio of capital and reserves to total assets for insurance company, the solvency risk that measured by the solvency ratio and the loss ration as a proxy variable for underwriting risk. What is more, they also considered the company capital volume and company size which using the natural logarithms of the book value of equity and the total assets of the company, respectively, because these two variables have been proven that they have some effect on the financial performance. In addition, they conducted the multiple regression equation models by SPSS. The result proved that the Indian insurance company's financial performance has been negatively affected by solvency risk and capital management risk. They also found out that the company size and the company capital volume also have a major favorable effect on the financial success of the organization. However, their result supported that Underwriting risk and financial performance have no correlation.

Similarly, Zelie studied the impact of Ethiopia's insurance company's financial risk on its financial performance [3]. Zelie utilized the return on capital employed to represent the company's profitability, and the current ratio and the debt ratio as proxy variables of liquidity and leverage ratio separately. They also included a variable for firm size, which is determined by the natural logarithm of a company's total assets, in their model.

Based on the previous literature findings, this paper has selected the following variables to measure the Chinese insurance company's financial risk and financial performance. Their result demonstrated that the debt ratio and the current ratio both have a significant negative impact on its profitability, and the size of the business and its profitability are not significantly correlated.

3 The Research Variable of Chinese Insurance Company Financial Risk

3.1 Leverage Risk

Leverage Risk and ROA have a favorable relationship. Kiio assessed the impact on insurer liquidity for 41 insurers operating in Kenya from 2009 to 2013 using four variables: quick ratio, leverage ratio, log net premium, and loss ratio [4]. And found that the link between profitability, as defined by return on assets, versus the log of the quick ratio and net premium is valid and favorable. Poorer financial performance is linked to more leverage. Leverage ratios measure how well a company uses its debt to finance its assets. Leverage ratios can also reflect a company's long-term solvency. The level of leverage of insurers, as measured by gearing ratios, has a statistically significant negative impact on the financial performance of Ethiopian insurers.

Therefore, this paper proposed the following hypothesis:

H1a: There is no significant relationship between Chinese insurance company leverage risk and its financial performance;

H1b: There is a significant relationship between Chinese insurance company leverage risk and its financial performance.

3.2 Solvency Risk

One might get the conclusion that the financial success of Ethiopian insurance companies was significantly influenced by the solvency ratio. The smaller the Solvency risk, the better the performance. Hence, The Solvency Risk affects a company's financial performance negatively.

Therefore, this paper proposed the following hypothesis:

H2a: There is no significant relationship between Chinese insurance company solvency risk and its financial performance;

H2b: There is a significant relationship between Chinese insurance company solvency risk and its financial performance.

Generally speaking, a company's solvency is a gauge of its long-term financial health. Refers to the business's capacity to promptly meet its long-term financial obligations. The phrase "solvency ratio" refers to a company's capacity to pay for its long-term fixed costs as well as accomplish long-term expansion and growth. A solvency ratio of more than 20% is regarded as sound from a financial standpoint. The ability of the corporation to repay its obligations and endure for a long period increases with the ratio [5]. Morara did a research, the study's findings showed a strong correlation between insurance businesses' solvency and their financial performance in Kenya [1]. However, out of all the independent criteria, the solvency ratio and firm size had the least significant impacts on the financial success of the Ethiopian insurance company [6].

3.3 Underwriting Risk (Loss Ratio)

The effectiveness—or lack thereof—of insurers' underwriting performance is reflected in underwriting risk. The metric is the Benefits Paid to Net Premium Ratio., For instance, Risk-taking businesses are more prone to have changing cash flows than are those with less risk-averse management [8]. Therefore, the financial performance of an insurance company and the risk it underwrites are significantly inversely correlated.

Therefore, this paper proposed the following hypothesis:

H3a: There is no significant relationship between Chinese insurance company underwriting risk and its financial performance;
H3b: There is a significant relationship between Chinese insurance company underwriting risk and its financial performance.

3.4 Volume of Capital

The quantity of capital is the difference between all assets and all liabilities. It can sometimes be calculated using the equity capital to total assets ratio. As it reveals the financial disadvantage of the business, capital volume is frequently utilized as one of the factors affecting insurance businesses' profitability. A study conducted by the United Arab Emirates found profitability has a strong and positive relationship with capital. Therefore, this paper proposed the following hypothesis:

H4a: The company's volume of capital does not have an impact on the Chinese life insurance company's financial performance.

H4b: The company's volume of capital does have an impact on the Chinese life insurance company's financial performance (Fig. 1).

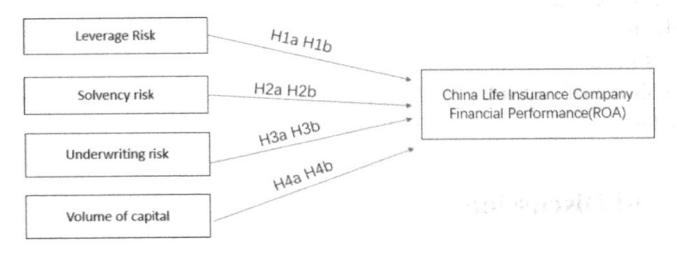

Fig. 1. Theoretical framework.

4 Methodology

With data from the WIND database from 2011 to 2021, this study will use a quantitative approach and multiple regression equation model analysis to examine the relationship between financial risk and the financial performance of China Life Insurance Company.

The dependent variable in this study is ROA, which serves as a proxy for China Life Insurance Company's financial performance. The financial performance of the company, as determined by ROA, is therefore the dependent variable (y) in our research model. Leverage ratio, log of book value of total equity, loss ratio, and solvency ratio are the explanatory variables (X).

4.1 Dependent Variable

The dependent variable is China Life Insurance Company's financial performance. A measurement that is based on accounting, called ROA, is used to quantify financial performance. The formula of ROA is as follows:

$$\text{Return on assets (ROA)} = \frac{EAT}{Total\ Assets} \times 100\%$$

4.2 Independent Variables (Explanatory Variables)

$$\text{Leverage ratio} = \frac{Total\ debt}{Total\ equity} \times 100\%$$

$$\text{Underwriting Risk} = \frac{Benefits\ Paid}{Net\ Premium}$$

$$\text{Solvency ratio} = \frac{Actual\ Solvency\ Margin}{Required\ Solvency\ Margin} \times 100\%$$

Volume of capital:

$$ROA = \alpha + \beta_1 LevR + \beta_2 SR + \beta_3 LR + \beta_4 VOC + \epsilon$$

Levr = Leverage ratio
SR = solvency ratio
LR = Loss ratio
VOC = volume of capital
ϵ = error term

5 Result and Discussion

5.1 Descriptive Statistics

It can be seen from the above table that the maximum Mean is the Solvency ratio and the minimum Mean is ROA. The biggest Standard Deviation is the Solvency ratio and the minimum Standard Deviation is the Volume of capita (Table 1).

Table 1. Descriptive statistics (Created by Author).

	N	Mean	Standard Deviation	Minimum	Maximum
ROA	44	0.291	0.034	−0.263	0.828
Leverage ratio	44	88.430	0.150	85.779	90.066
Solvency ratio	44	798.144	11.464	619.093	948.596
Loss ration	44	34.075	1.892	12.272	75.961
Volume of capital	44	11.482	0.018	11.250	11.687

5.2 Diagnostics for Regression Analysis

It is critical to conduct the diagnostics test before performing the regression model to ensure the model result is BLUE (Best Linear Unbiased Estimator).

Heteroscedasticity Test. Since it is necessary to ensure the accuracy of asymptotic covariance and standard error, the linear regression model needs the assumption of homomorphic statistics. Besides, the results of regression estimation and hypothesis testing are also unreliable since the regression model estimator is not blue (the best linear unbiased estimator). Therefore, the alternate method to examine this premise is the Breusch-Pagan Test. The hypotheses of this test are as follows.

H0: The error variances are all equal, demonstrating homoscedasticity;
H1: The error variances are not equal, demonstrating heteroscedasticity.
The decision rule of the Breusch pagan Test is as follows:

(1) Reject the null hypothesis if the P-value < level of significance ($\alpha = 0.1$);
(2) Do not reject the null hypothesis if the P-value > level of significance ($\alpha = 0.1$) (Table 2).

Table 2. Result of the heteroscedasticity test (Created by Author).

Dependent variables	F-statistic	P value	Decision
ROA	1.131	0.356	Homoscedasticity

The outcome indicated that, while the P-value of 0.356 is higher than the 0.1 threshold of 90% significance, the null hypothesis should not be rejected. Thus, this model is homoscedasticity and do not exist the heteroscedasticity problem.

Autocorrelation Test. There is no autocorrelation between the error terms, as shown by the covariance between them being equal to zero. The standard error will be overestimated as a result of the error term's autocorrelation. To establish whether the residual has an autocorrelation issue, James Durbin and Geoffrey Watson's Durbin-Watson test is used [7].

The hypothesis of Durbin-Watson is as below.

Ho: $\rho = 0$ (There is no first - order autocorrelation exist in residuals);

Hi: $\rho > 0$ (There is a first - order autocorrelation exist in residuals).

The Durbin Watson test's decision rule states that the residual does not exhibit first-order autocorrelation at a 90% significance level if the outcome of the Durbin Watson statistic is close to or equal to 2 [8, 9] (Table 3).

Table 3. Durbin Watson test results (Created by Author).

Dependent Variable	D-W Statistics
ROA	1.956

The D-W test result proved that there is no autocorrelation problem exists in this model as the D-W Statistics value is close to two, thus accepting the null hypothesis at a 90% significance level.

Residual Normal Distribution Test. Shapiro Wilk and Kolmogorov Smirnov tests are mainly used to detect whether the residues are normally distributed [10, 11, 12]. However, Kolmogorov Smirnov test is better suited for bigger sample sizes, whereas Shapira Wilk test is more frequently employed for lower sample sizes (n < 50). The Shapira Wilk test is used in this study depend on the limited sample size, and the outcomes are as follows (Table 4).

Table 4. Results of Kolmogorov Smirnov test (Created by Author).

Model	N	T-test Statistic	P-value
ROA	44	0.950	0.055

The hypothesis of the Kolmogorov-Smirnov test is that:

Ho: The residual followed the normal distribution (ur ~ N $(0, \sigma^2)$).

H1: The residual did not follow the normal distribution.

The statistic result suggested this model residual followed a normal distribution test as the P-value at 0.055 is smaller than 0.1 at a 90% significance level.

Multi-collinearity Test. The independent variable (explanatory variable) in the regression model should not change with other independent variables to ensure that there is no multicollinearity problem in the model [13]. Multi collinearity means that the change of one explanatory variable will change the other [14]. If the regression model has multiple collinearity problems, the results will be invalid, because the model will not be able to test the relationship between independent variables and dependent variables. Therefore, the estimated regression parameters are invalid. In addition, the P value will also be inaccurate, and the confidence interval of the regression coefficient will become wider, which makes it more difficult to reject the null hypothesis. The multicollinearity problem can be caused by insufficient research data or improper use of dummy variables [15]. Variance inflation factor (VIF) is widely used to detect whether there is multicollinearity in regression models. When the VIF value is greater than 10, there is collinearity between the independent variables of the regression model [16, 17] (Table 5).

Table 5. Result of VIF (Created by Author).

Variable	Tolerance(1/vif)	VIF
LevR	1	1
SR	1	1
LR	0.963	1.038
VOC	0.611	1.636

The regression model's VIF values are all less than 10. This demonstrates that the model's multicollinearity is not a concern.

Stationary Test. As a statistical test, Extended Dickey Fuller (ADF) is widely used to test whether data is stable or non-stationary by checking whether data contains unit root. The assumptions of ADF test are as follows (Table 6):

$$ROA = \alpha + \beta_1 LevR + \beta_2 SR + \beta_3 LR + \beta_4 VOC + \epsilon$$

Ho: The data is non-stationary, implying the data contains unit roots.
Hi: The data is stationary

Table 6. Results of the ADF test (Created by Author).

Variables	T-Statistic	Prob.**
ROA	−6.97	0.0000
LevR	−6.46	0.0000
SR	−6.94	0.0000
LR	−13.50	0.0000
VOC	−6.33	0.0000

According to the results above, all data are stationary because their P-Values are less than 0.1, rejecting the null hypothesis at a 90% level of significance (Fig. 2).

$$ROA = -52.684 + 0.594 * LevR - 0.009 * SR - 0.007 * LR + 0.701 * VOC$$

Variable	Coefficien	T Stat	P-value
Intercept	-52.684	-2.075	0.045
Lev R	0.594	1.866	0.7
SR	-0.009	-2.177	0.036
Loss Ratio	-0.007	-2.99	0.005
VOC	0.701	2.211	0.033
No.of Observation	44		
Multiple R	0.58504		
R-Square	0.34227		
Adjusted R Square	0.25573		
Standard Error	0.19404		

Fig. 2. General Ols regression model result (Created by Author).

The financial success of the Chinese life insurance company and the leverage ratio are significantly positively correlated, as shown in the above table, as the P-value at 0.07 is less than 0.1, thus rejecting the H1a at a 90% significance level.

The financial performance of Chinese life insurance businesses and solvency risk are strongly inversely correlated, as the P-value at 0.036 is less than 0.1, thus rejecting the H2a at a 90% significance level.

Underwriting risk significantly negatively affects the financial performance of Chinese life insurance firms, as the P-value at 0.05 is less than 0.1, thus rejecting the H3a at a 90% significance level.

There is a significant positive relation between underwriting risk and Chinese life insurance companies' financial performance, as the P-value at 0.033 is less than 0.1, thus rejecting the H4a at a 90% significance level.

6 Conclusion

This paper studies the relationship between the financial risk and financial performance of China Life Insurance Company. This paper selects the financial ratios from 2011 to 2021. Through the multiple regression equation models, the author found that if China Life Insurance Company wants to improve its financial performance, it needs to reduce the solvency risk and unwritten risk through effective risk management, because these two risks have a detrimental effect on the company's financial success. At the same time, China Life Insurance Company can improve its financial performance by increasing the volume of capital. At the same time, the results of the model prove that an appropriate leverage ratio is helpful to enhance the insurance firms' financial performance.

Since China Life Insurance has not classified its assets into liquid and non-liquid assets, this paper does not consider liquidity risk. Therefore, future researchers can choose to consider liquidity risk under the condition of sufficient data. At the same time, the variables studied in this paper belong to internal factors that affect the risk of the insurance industry, but this industry is also affected by other macro factors, such as GDP, inflation, etc. Therefore, future scholars can consider these macro effects in the model of future research.

References

1. Morara, K., Sibindi, A.B.: Assessing the Solvency, Underwriting Risk and Profitability of the Kenyan Insurance Sector. Acta Universitatis Danubius. Œconomica, **17**(5) (2021)
2. Wani, A.A., Ahmad, S.: Relationship between financial risk and financial performance: an insight of Indian insurance industry. Wani, AA, & Dar, SA (2015). relationship between financial risk and financial performance: an insight of Indian insurance industry. Int. J. Sci. Res. **4**(11), 1424–1433 (2015)
3. Zelie, E.M.: Determinants of financial distress in case of insurance companies in Ethiopia. Res. J. Finan. Acc. **10**(15), 27–32 (2019)
4. Kiio, P. N.: The relationship between liquidity and profitability of insurance companies in Kenya (Doctoral dissertation, University of Nairobi) (2014)
5. Bawa, S.K., Chattha, S.: Financial performance of life insurers in Indian insurance industry. Pac. Bus. Rev. Int. **6**(5), 44–52 (2013)
6. Deyganto, K.O., Alemu, A.A.: Factors affecting financial performance of insurance companies operating in Hawassa city administration, Ethiopia. Universal J. Acc. Finan. **7**(1), 1–10 (2019)
7. Durbin, J., Watson, G.S.: Testing for serial correlation in least squares regression. I. In: Kotz, S., Johnson, N.L. (eds.) Breakthroughs in Statistics, pp. 237–259. Springer, New York (1992). https://doi.org/10.1007/978-1-4612-4380-9_20
8. Stimson, J.A.: Regression in space and time: a statistical essay. Am. J. Polit. Sci. 914–947 (1985)
9. Chen, Y.: Spatial autocorrelation approaches to testing residuals from least squares regression. PLoS ONE **11**(1), e0146865 (2016)
10. Mishra, P., Pandey, C.M., Singh, U., Gupta, A., Sahu, C., Keshri, A.: Descriptive statistics and normality tests for statistical data. Ann. Card. Anaesth. **22**(1), 67 (2019)
11. Kim, N.H.: A modification of the shapiro-wilk test for exponentiality based on censored data. Korean J. Appl. Stat. **21**(2), 265–273 (2008)
12. Metz, J. A., Haccou, P., Meelis, E.: On the Shapiro-Wilk test and Darling's test for exponentiality. Biometrics, 527–530 (1994)
13. Alin, A.: Multicollinearity. Wiley Interdisc. Rev. Comput. Stat. **2**(3), 370-374 (2010)
14. Farrar, D.E., Glauber, R.R.: Multicollinearity in regression analysis: the problem revisited. Rev. Econ. Stat. 92–107 (1967)
15. Graham, M.H.: Confronting multicollinearity in ecological multiple regression. Ecology **84**(11), 2809–2815 (2003)
16. Jeremy, M.: Tolerance and variance inflation factor. Wiley statsref: statistics reference online (2014)
17. Premkumar, G., Ramamurthy, K., Liu, H.N.: Internet messaging: an examination of the impact of attitudinal, normative, and control belief systems. Inf. Manage. **45**(7), 451–457 (2008)

Model Innovation and Value Creation in E-commerce Platform Ecosystems: A Case Study of Douyin

Jiahang Hu[1(✉)] and Yiming Zhong[2]

[1] Hangzhou Dianzi University Information Engineering College, Hangzhou 311305, China
`229380433@hziee.edu.cn`
[2] Rangsit University, Paholyothin 87, Muang Pathumthani 12000, Thailand

Abstract. With the rapid development of Internet technology, an increasing number of companies have begun to focus on the development of ecological models. These models are designed to achieve the goals of multi-party cooperation, resource sharing and value co-creation through the creation of an ecosystem. By continuously innovating their business models based on this ecosystem, enterprises can achieve resource integration and improve efficiency, expand the scale and influence of their ecosystem, enhance user experience, and promote business growth. This study aims to explore the operational cases of ecological platforms to uncover the "black box" of their new model architecture, value configuration combination and value creation mechanism. Through the analysis of typical ecological platforms and various operational cases within the ecosystem, this study aims to provide insights into ecological model innovation and value creation for more enterprises to practice in the future.

Keywords: Model Innovation · Value Creation · E-commerce Platform Ecosystems · Douyin E-commerce

1 Introduction

With the rapid development of mobile internet and the direct impact of the COVID-19, consumer habits have shifted from offline to online. This has led to continuous innovation of e-commerce models, with many enterprises seeking to adapt to the digitization trend through business model innovation. In this context, Douyin E-commerce, which is based on an ecosystem, is undoubtedly the most personalized and disruptive e-commerce model. This paper focuses on the rapidly developing ecological e-commerce platform - Douyin E-commerce - based on existing research on business models, business model innovation, the value brought by business model innovation, and the basic theory of network effects. By examining the development process of Douyin E-commerce and its macro environment, this study explore how it innovates its business model by reorganizing existing functional modules and businesses, and analyze the various values brought by such innovation. This paper covers a detailed analysis of platform attributes, operational model innovation, C2M model innovation, intelligent algorithm innovation, and other aspects. Through case study and demonstration, this research aim to answer the following questions: Firstly, what business model innovation do successful ecological platforms adopt? Secondly, how can innovative business models configure value? And thirdly, where does the value brought by innovative business models manifest? Our aim is to enrich knowledge related to business model design and value theory of ecological e-commerce platforms and to strengthen understanding of the logic of enterprise value creation in the internet era.

2 Literature Review on Business Models

Research on business models began in the 1990s, and Drucker referred to it as enterprise management theory [1]. As the goal of a business is to create value, scholars have studied the business model and its components from the perspective of value creation, combined with the profit model. Stewart defined the business model as a logical summary of how a company generates profits and sustains its development [2]. Afuah viewed it as the comprehensive embodiment of an enterprise's current profit model, long-term profit strategy, and methods to maintain competitive advantages [3]. Chesbrough believed that the business model represents an enterprise's behavior to create market value [4]. However, equating business models solely with profitability is not accurate. Therefore, Tang proposed that a business model is a unique operating system with core competitiveness formed by an enterprise's organic combination of internal and external elements [5]. In Osterwalder's business model component model, nine components are included: value proposition, value configuration, customer definition, cost structure, competitiveness, sales channels, revenue model, business partners, and customer relationships. This model emphasizes that a business model is a logical combination of different components that creates value for customers and achieves commercial purposes based on profits [6].

In contrast, research on business model innovation focuses on how companies can capture market changes and quickly switch business models to gain a competitive advantage. Scholars have explored the factors that affect business model innovation from internal and external perspectives. External research suggests that technological advances in communication technology, data analysis, or changes in customer consumption habits can affect the innovation of business models [7, 8]. From an internal perspective, an enterprise's technology can guide business model innovation. To explore the value contained in the technology better, the enterprise should combine the innovation mode with its technology [9]. Besides technology, some scholars believe that business model innovation results from changes in the enterprise's internal structure. The change and reorganization of various business model components can lead to innovative changes [10].

Regarding the value of business model innovation, scholars have conducted research based on profitability and development perspectives. Weng found that most successful companies rely on business model innovation to achieve leapfrog development and increase commercial value [11]. Bucherer also found that although the value brought by business model innovation is subtle, it is continuous and determines the company's long-term development to some extent [12]. At the same time, another group of scholars combined the value co-creation theory with the basic idea of network effects to explore:

Li et al. believe that after completing the transition from a "value exchange" business model to a "value co-creation" model, companies can alleviate resource constraints and advantage selection problems, thereby gaining a competitive advantage to help with development [13]. Zhong et al. also argue that the subjects of bilateral markets are more likely to interact and co-create value through the internet - this new model drives platform development by stimulating network effects [14].

3 Case Study

3.1 Case Description

Douyin e-commerce ecosystem has undergone three development stages, each in a different environment. The nascent stage began in 2014 when ByteDance's app "Today's Headlines" first attempted e-commerce. However, due to Taobao's overwhelming competitive advantage in the market, which occupied 60.40% of the market share (according to Huachuang Securities), ByteDance focused on developing and operating mobile applications. In 2017, Douyin was launched, focusing on the short video social field. With the maturity of its short video business, Douyin launched the "Douyin Shopping" module in November of the same year to establish a "social + e-commerce" ecosystem. In 2020, with the comprehensive outbreak of COVID-19, the demand for online shopping surged. Douyin quickly joined forces with many celebrities and fully engaged in live-streaming e-commerce, officially entering the stage of ecological development.

The ecological development stage began in April 2021 when Douyin clarified the new positioning of the "interest-based e-commerce" platform at the e-commerce ecosystem conference. By using users' historical data to push products, Douyin e-commerce became more innovative. In the same year, its GMV reached about 700–880 billion yuan, a growth of 320% compared to 2020, and the number of purchasing users increased by 69%. This marked Douyin's ecosystem as a new choice for merchants and consumers. The Douyin e-commerce ecosystem includes the short video social sector, live-streaming, and e-commerce sector, forming an in-site closed loop.

During the Ecological Expansion Stage, in May 2022, Douyin made a significant announcement at the "Second Ecological Conference". The platform stated that it would enhance "interest-based e-commerce" to "pan-interest-based e-commerce", which would encompass the entire spectrum of shopping requirements across all scenarios. This development represents the latest addition to Douyin's expanding e-commerce ecosystem, "Douyin Life Service", which now encompasses the food delivery and travel sectors.

3.2 Business Model Innovation and Value Expression of Douyin E-commerce Ecosystem

Efficient operation alone cannot guarantee an enterprise's sustained success. The key to a competitive strategy is to establish differentiation, which involves identifying a unique value proposition through a forward-thinking selection of innovative operational activities [15]. In the ever-evolving realm of the internet, the selection of the right innovative models and value propositions can often be a decisive factor in achieving success.

Dual-Wheel Driven Business Model That Leverages Network Effects to Create Business Value. The Douyin e-commerce ecosystem possesses transactional and social attributes, which fosters closer connections and more frequent interactions between different types of users on the platform. This characteristic provides better opportunities for triggering network effects for brand activities compared to traditional e-commerce platforms. Douyin e-commerce leverages an innovative "dual-wheel driven model" that combines user private traffic and ecosystem public traffic for activity promotion, enabling better value creation and establishment of business barriers. In this process, network effects play a crucial role. Eisenmann and Hinz's research indicates that platform-based business models' value creation and business barrier establishment rely on network effects, including network same-side effects and cross-side effects [16, 17]. Douyin e-commerce stimulates network effects through "dual-wheel" promotion. Users' real-time updates, such as shopping or activity sharing, trigger notifications to their friends and family in their private domain, making it more likely for them to participate in the activity.

Moreover, video content posted by fellow consumers in the public domain can also inform strangers about brand activities, lending more credibility compared to self-promotion by the brand. This, coupled with the concurrent promotion of public and private domain traffic, increases participation in the activity through the "herd effect." Such collective participation stimulates network same-side effects, resulting in successful brand activities and enhanced social value for consumers. The partnership between Douyin's e-commerce ecosystem and "Milk Tea Ice City" (MiXue) resulted in a revenue doubling, underscoring the significance of network effects in driving business value within the Douyin e-commerce ecosystem.

In June 2021, MiXue launched a campaign called "Sing the Theme Song and Make a Short Video on Douyin to Win Discounts at the Store," accompanied by a catchy theme song. As a result, the campaign quickly gained traction on social media. Users found that they could view others' activity videos in the recommended section and saw their friends and family members participating in the campaign, further increasing its network effect. With the "dual-wheel" driving force, each participant connected through the social attribute, gaining social value and discounts. The campaign continuously enticed non-participants to join in, further promoting the activity. According to a survey, during the campaign, the "MiXue theme song" tag received a total of 4.37 billion views on different platforms, with 120 million views on Kuaishou topic alone.

The significant traffic generated during the campaign quickly translated into commercial value. According to data, MiXue's revenue was 2.566 billion yuan, 4.68 billion yuan, and 10.351 billion yuan from 2019 to 2021, respectively. Though the company's revenue grew steadily before 2021, the growth rate remained flat. However, after the launch of the campaign in 2021, the revenue surpassed the 10 billion yuan mark, reaching 2.86 times the average of the previous two years. This exceptional growth highlights the innovative "dual-wheel driving model" of Douyin, which stimulated the network effect of brand activities and rapidly created commercial value.

Smart Algorithm + UGC Model: Implementation of Operational and Marketing Value. The Douyin (TikTok) ecosystem has introduced an "overlay recommendation mechanism" (information flow funnel algorithm) based on the traditional UGC model.

This mechanism benefits the platform and the merchants within the ecosystem, especially in merchant marketing. Now, all reviewed works will be quantified by Douyin through the "overlay recommendation mechanism" based on the number of likes, comments, and saves obtained by the results within a certain period after uploading and assigned a "work weight index". Only works that meet the "work weight index" and enter the next level of flow pool standards will be re-recommended by the platform, thereby obtaining new traffic injection.

From the perspective of platform operation, Douyin's innovative model is an efficient means of content acquisition and filtering. Due to the decentralized nature of the UGC model, users can freely create content, bringing a steady stream of traffic and benefits to the platform. In addition, the winner-takes-all mechanism of the "overlay recommendation mechanism" filters out low-quality content to some extent, reducing traffic and workforce waste in the operation process. Combining the UGC model and intelligent algorithms also has value in merchant marketing. From the model's perspective, video creators can use ready-made resources provided by other creators, such as music and monologues, under its unique UGC model to complete video creation. Suppose users use the marketing content of merchants as material for their work. In that case, they indirectly help the brand or product information spread, thereby achieving the purpose of "zero-cost viral spread".

Regarding the marketing value of this dissemination method, Yao believes that viral dissemination can ensure the effectiveness of information while considering the speed of dissemination, enabling information to achieve maximum impact and marketing value in the shortest possible time [18]. Looking at the impact of Douyin's ecosystem algorithm on marketing value, Jiang found in their research on Douyin's flow distribution model that Douyin's recommendation algorithm shows a "Matthew effect" trend, that is, 3% of videos occupy 80% of traffic, and the retention time of high-quality content is as long as 90 days, increasing the possibility of achieving exponential growth [19]. Therefore, the combination of Douyin's ecosystem with the model and algorithm means that high-quality works at the top of the flow pool will form the "Matthew effect" through algorithm mechanisms, thereby attracting user attention for a long time and increasing the probability of user materialization or secondary creation of content, synchronously increasing the probability of "viral spread". This can also be illustrated by the marketing case of "T97 Coffee" in Douyin's e-commerce ecosystem.

Based on the innovative model of Douyin's e-commerce ecosystem, "T97 Coffee", a Douyin e-commerce partner, became popular online due to its unique appearance and humorous live broadcast slogans of "T97 Big Mouth Sister" during in-store broadcasts. Many secondary creators edited her live clips and made them into short video materials and collaborative templates. After being followed by millions of fans, the content related to "Big Mouth Sister" began to spread virally within Douyin's e-commerce ecosystem, bringing huge exposure at zero cost to both the "Big Mouth Sister" and the "T97" coffee brand. According to data, videos tagged with "T97 Big Mouth Sister" have been exposed over 720 million times on Douyin and 290 million times on Kuaishou, with a total of over 2 billion views of videos tagged with "T97 Big Mouth Sister" across the entire internet. Through a live broadcast and an innovative e-commerce model based on viral marketing, "T97 Coffee" has become a phenomenon in the online celebrity product industry. The store's fan base has increased by millions, and its sales have exceeded 1 billion yuan within less than a year of its launch. This phenomenon fully demonstrates the marketing value of viral marketing based on the Douyin e-commerce ecosystem innovation model.

C2M + KOL Value Co-creation Model Facilitates Rural Revitalization and Achieves Social Value. Through the continuous injection of resources from the "New Farmer Program", the Douyin e-commerce ecosystem has achieved comprehensive value co-creation with KOLs. Through the drive of KOLs, the C2M model of short videos and live streaming has been perfectly applied in the agricultural, rural, and farmer fields. This model allows consumers to communicate directly with producers to meet personalized product customization needs. For agricultural producers at the village or household level, this model will enable them to directly sell their agricultural products to consumers through the flow brought by KOLs, avoiding sales losses due to information asymmetry and increasing farmers' income.

Additionally, this model can realize order-based production and a direct connection between production and sales, reducing inventory costs and production risks on the production side and speeding up the flow of funds. He proposed the poverty alleviation method of "short videos + live streaming", which achieves the goal of poverty alleviation by selling agricultural products through information assistance and ensuring the assisted people's dignity [20]. Based on this model, Dan pointed out that the C2M model can help agricultural product producers reduce inventory costs and production risks and accelerate the flow of funds [21]. Therefore, Douyin e-commerce proposed the "New Farmer Program" in 2020, aiming to promote value co-creation with agricultural KOLs comprehensively, promote the dissemination of information on agriculture, rural areas, and farmers, and help alleviate poverty and rural areas revitalization. In recent years, with the emergence of some top agricultural KOLs, this model has been proven to help sales and poverty alleviation, promote employment, and have significant social value.

In poverty-stricken and economically underdeveloped Wangqing County, farmer Bingqiang Wu faced uncertainty in agricultural product circulation and price pressure from distributors, leading to meager income and a vicious cycle of disengagement. However, since joining the "New Farmer Program", Wu has used the UGC model to connect production and sales directly, meeting consumers' demands for high-quality, safe, and inexpensive organic food while bringing positive changes. After over a year of operation, Wu has gained popularity in agriculture and rural areas and sold over 100 tons of rice, generating more significant profits. For instance, pears that once sold for 0.5 yuan per kilogram to distributors can now sell for more than 6 yuan per kilogram thanks to the UGC model shortening the price difference. This short-circuit profit has driven income increases for thousands of rural residents and employed over 1,500 locals. This success is not an isolated case, as the Douyin e-commerce rural development report shows that 2.83 billion orders of agricultural specialties were directly connected to the market through Douyin e-commerce in 2022, achieving the goal of "going from the village to the city." Additionally, the "Douyin New Farmer" project has led to a 252% increase in agricultural e-commerce KOLs and a 152% increase in small and micro agricultural commodity merchants. It has expanded to 146 agricultural counties and cities, supporting the industrialization development of 69 landmark agricultural products. The Douyin e-commerce ecosystem has become an essential link between high-quality agricultural products and consumers nationwide, generating significant social value in poverty alleviation and employment protection.

4 Negative Impacts and Suggestions Brought by Innovation and Development

4.1 Copyright Infringement Issues in UGC Model

In the UGC model, many merchants often add BGM or other clips of derivative works when publishing their results with commercial links to enrich the content of their careers. However, according to relevant laws and regulations, using others' works for creation should obtain the original copyright owner's permission. Otherwise, these actions will constitute an infringement of the right of adaptation. This also means that most merchants on Douyin e-commerce have already formed copyright infringement when adding BGM or clip segments to their works. Since the results published on Douyin e-commerce often have a profit-making nature, the original copyright owner has the right to file a copyright infringement lawsuit. To avoid this issue as much as possible, when using others' works for creation, one should obtain the copyright owner's authorization and pay the corresponding remuneration. Suppose the copyright owner cannot be contacted, or the copyright owner needs to be clarified. In that case, the work's name and source should be indicated, and avoid using it for commercial purposes to comply with the "fair use" provisions of relevant laws and regulations as much as possible. Suppose creators do not want their works to be casually reproduced and edited. In that case, it is suggested to declare "no forwarding" when uploading their copyrighted works and use watermarks or other tangible and recognizable ways to maintain their legitimate rights and interests.

4.2 Issues with False Advertising Brought by UGC Model

To attract traffic, some Douyin e-commerce merchants add false product information to attract consumers to buy goods or services. This behavior can cause considerable losses to the platform and consumers. For example, in July 2019, a "100 Yuan Whitening Mask" product appeared on the Douyin e-commerce platform. The product claimed to make the skin white and smooth and was priced at only 100 yuan. However,Consumers purchasing this product find that the product quality may not be as advertised, and it did not even have a whitening effect. Subsequently, consumers sought justice, and after an investigation by relevant authorities, it was confirmed that the Douyin e-commerce platform indeed had false advertising behavior and was punished accordingly. This case shows that Douyin's review of merchant-posted information needs to be stronger, allowing incorrect information to spread at will and causing losses to customers and the platform. Douyin e-commerce should strengthen its review of advertising information to change this situation and promptly discover and deal with fraudulent advertising behavior. At the same time, Douyin e-commerce should also enhance users' awareness of anti-fraud, let users understand the forms and harm of false advertising, avoid being misled, and actively establish a 24-h reporting hotline to receive users' feedback and investigate problematic products promptly and take appropriate measures.

4.3 Commission Issues in the Emerging Business of Life Services

The core logic of the Douyin e-commerce ecosystem is its content creation platform, meaning merchants in the life services sector also need to engage in a large amount of continuous content production to promote their services and brands on the forum. This cost can be avoided for merchants with strong content production capabilities and large-scale private traffic, such as Starbucks. However, small and medium-sized merchants often need more ability to create high-quality content. Due to the existence of the information flow funnel algorithm, low-quality and homogeneous works cannot serve the purpose of promotion. Therefore, in the short term, they can only rely on KOLs to promote their services, directly resulting in them paying commissions that typically include both platform and KOL promotion fees. While Douyin's platform fee is lower than that of its competitors, if the KOL commission is added up, its general commission is higher than that of Meituan, which is undoubtedly very detrimental to the development of this new business. Therefore, Douyin urgently needs to learn from the successful experiences of significant merchants in the live-streaming e-commerce sector and provide guidance to small and medium-sized merchants on in-site operation, content production, and personalized positioning to reduce the commission rates. The average commission rates of Douyin and Meituan are shown in Table 1.

Table 1. Commission rates of Douyin and Meituan (source: Meituan and Douyin official websites).

Type	Douyin (Average)	Meituan (Average)
Food	3.5%	2.5%
Accommodations	7%	4.5%
Play	3%–5%	2%
Relaxation	5%–8%	3.5%
Beautify	5%–6%	3.5%
Wedding	10%	8%
Parents-child campaign	4%–5%	4.5%
Education	4%–5%	4.5%

5 Conclusion and Future Prospects

Based on the analysis, we can effectively address the three questions posed at the beginning of this article. Firstly, the Douyin ecosystem adopts a "dual-drive business model" that combines e-commerce and social values, stimulating network effects and attracting users from different traffic domains to participate in activities. Its innovation lies in creating business value for the platform and merchants. Secondly, the platform adopts an "intelligent algorithm + UGC" operational model, combining algorithms and UGC models to ensure high-quality content remains popular and increases the likelihood of viral spread under the UGC model. This innovative model has brought marketing value to businesses on the platform. Finally, Douyin e-commerce utilizes a "C2M + KOL value co-creation" model, which combines C2M and KOL to promote agricultural sales, increase income, and reduce poverty, achieving its social value.

Looking forward to the future, the Douyin e-commerce ecosystem launched its nationwide takeaway business on March 1, 2023. As other companies within the ecosystem mature, it will undoubtedly have a significant impact on the current "takeaway" business giant "Meituan." If the issues mentioned above are corrected promptly, the superior business models of other businesses within the ecosystem can be replicated, creating continuous competitive advantages until the "miracle of development" of Douyin live-streaming e-commerce is reproduced. Douyin e-commerce will become a true super-giant, covering all areas, with the ability to compete with the world's most prominent players in the e-commerce industry.

References

1. Drucker, P.F.: The theory of the business. Alfred P. Sloan: Critical Eval. Bus. Manage. **2**, 258–282 (1994)
2. Stewart, D.W., Zhao, Q.: Internet marketing, business models, and public policy. J. Public Policy Mark. **19**(2), 287–296 (2000)
3. Afuah, A., Tucci, C.L.: Internet Business models and Strategies: Text and Cases, vol. 2, p. 384. McGraw-Hill, New York (2003)
4. Chesbrough, H., Rosenbloom, R.S.: The role of the business model in capturing value from innovation: evidence from Xerox corporation's technology spin-off companies. Ind. Corp. Chang. **11**(3), 529–555 (2002)
5. Tang, D., Rang, B.: Business model: the highest form of enterprise competition. Bus. Admin. **11**, 20–21 (2009)
6. Osterwalder, A., Pigneur, Y., Tucci, C.L.: Clarifying business models: origins, present, and future of the concept. Commun. Assoc. Inf. Syst. **16**(1), 1 (2005)
7. Spieth, P., Schneckenberg, D., Ricart, J.E.: Business model innovation–state of the art and future challenges for the field. R&d Manage. **44**(3), 237–247 (2014)
8. Wirtz, B.W., Pistoia, A., Ullrich, S., Göttel, V.: Business models: origin, development and future research perspectives. Long Range Plan. **49**(1), 36–54 (2016)
9. Chesbrough, H.: Business model innovation: opportunities and barriers. Long Range Plan. **43**(2–3), 354–363 (2010)
10. Demil, B., Lecocq, X.: Business model evolution: In search of dynamic consistency. Long Range Plan. **43**(2–3), 227–246 (2010)
11. Massa, L., Tucci, C.L.: Business model innovation. Oxford Handb. Innovation Manage. **20**(18), 420–441 (2013)
12. Bucherer, E., Eisert, U., Gassmann, O.: Towards systematic business model innovation: lessons from product innovation management. Creativity Innovation Manage. **21**(2), 183–198 (2012)
13. Li, S., Luo, J., Hu, W.: From value transaction to value co-creation - Research on the value transformation process of innovation-oriented enterprises. Manage. World **38**(03), 125–145 (2022)
14. Zhong, Z., Tang, S., Pierre, V.: Research on value co-creation based on service-oriented logic. Soft Sci. **1**(28), 31–35 (2014)

15. Liu, B.: Research on the differentiation strategy of vivo products under the background of COVID-19. Mod. Commer. **33**, 19–22 (2022)
16. Eisenmann, R., Parker, G.: Strategies for two sided markets. Harv. Bus. Rev. **84**(10), 92–101 (2006)
17. Hinz, O., Otter, T., Skiera, B.: Estimating network effects in two-sided markets. J. Manag. Inf. Syst. **37**(1), 12–38 (2020)
18. Yao, R.: Talking about the viral spread of short videos - Take Jieyin celebrity Li Jiaqi as an example. Press Commun. **14**, 145–147 (2019)
19. Wang, Q., Jiang, J.: How does the Internet short video business model achieve value creation? - a double case study of Jitterbug and Racer. Foreign Econ. Manage. **43**(02), 3–19 (2021)
20. He, S.: a preliminary study on short video + poverty alleviation based on racer platform. New Media Res. **5**(07), 35–36+40 (2019)
21. Huang, D.: Research on Pricing and Service Decision of C2M agricultural products supply chain considering user demand preference. South China Univ. Technol. (2019)

An Investigation into the Relationship Between Transportation Network and Economic Agglomeration

Chenhao Zheng(✉)

Xianjiaotong University, Xian Shaan 710000, China
1776223420@qq.com

Abstract. This paper mainly studies the influence of the transportation network on economic agglomeration. This paper first discusses the mechanism of inter-regional accessibility's influence on labor mobility and regional economic potential and further analyses its heterogeneity. Several factors have contributed to the improvement of inter-regional access in the study, according to the research, as a result of the development of transportation networks. As a result of the enhanced access to the transportation network, the trends of labor mobility from underdeveloped western and central regions to developed eastern regions are understandable. Meanwhile, it also improves the regional economic potential and promotes the process of regional urbanization. It is well known that over the last two to three decades, China has developed a rapidly growing network of transportation, and the interregional connectivity has improved significantly. Consequently, some labor-intensive industries have been transferred from the developed eastern regions to the less developed western and central regions in order for those regions to upgrade their own industrial structure. At the same time, undertaking industrial transfer will also help underdeveloped areas in central and western China evolve from agricultural peripheries to manufacturing centers. This paper provides a basis for effective economic development across the country by coordination regional economic development and promoting high-quality development of the Chinese economy, as it provides a basis for efficient economic development in the Chinese region.

Keywords: Transportation Network · Economic Agglomeration · Labor Mobility

1 Introduction

According to the Central Committee of the Communist Party of China (CPC), the development pattern of the Chinese economy will be accelerated in the course of 2020, characterized by the domestic cycle being the main engine and the domestic and international cycles adding strength to each other, which will have significant and far-reaching implications for China's high-quality economic development as well as world prosperity. At the same time, the Belt and Road Initiative led by China aims to create a pattern of interconnectivity between land and sea and a two-way opening up between east and west, which is in line with the double circular system. The construction of the "Belt and Road Initiative" has led to the creation of a series of transportation infrastructure, including the China-Laos Railway and Bin-Nan Expressway. As a result of the "Belt and Road Initiative," a large transportation network has been established throughout the countries and regions along the route, which has effectively contributed to the economic agglomeration of these countries and regions, which has then driven their economic development and agglomeration. With China's economy continuing to grow at a rapid pace, the level of development differs greatly from region to region. There is no doubt that transport networks and economic agglomerations are closely related. Research on regional economic development is also becoming increasingly important. This paper focuses on the relationship between transportation networks and economic agglomeration, analyses the development of China's transportation network and regional economy, and draws meaningful conclusions and suggestions.

2 The Influence of Transportation Network on Economic Agglomeration

The transportation network is the cornerstone of inter-regional trade, and its influence on economic agglomeration is direct and effective. A transportation network contributes to the flow of economic resources across different regions by influencing transportation costs. This promotes the agglomeration of different economic factors in the development process of different regions. In order to fully exploit the spillover effect of economic agglomeration space, the transportation network is crucial [1]. Since the beginning of this century, China has entered a transportation network construction boom, represented by the high-speed rail network. High-speed rail is a new engine for urban development. By reducing the spatial barriers to the flow of production factors, the high-speed rail network facilitates the optimal allocation of labor, capital, and other production factors in a wider range of regions, and thus supports and promotes economic agglomeration. The positive impact of economic agglomeration on the economy can in turn increase the government's investment in transportation network construction, thus forming a favorable cycle for regional economic development. Following sections discuss the mechanisms of how a transport network impacts the formation of economic agglomerations and the heterogeneity of different regions in terms of agglomeration (Fig. 1).

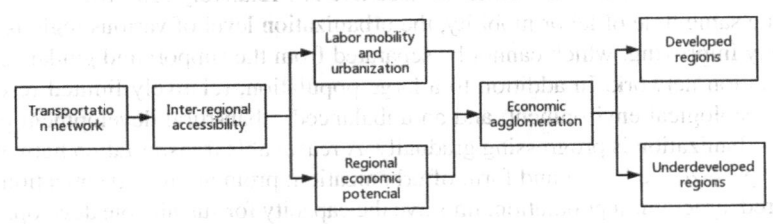

Fig. 1. The logic diagram of the influence of transportation network on economic agglomeration.

2.1 Mechanism Analysis

Inter-regional Accessibility. Transport networks can improve inter-regional accessibility by reducing travel times. Inter-regional accessibility refers to the ease of travel between regions, and a fully developed transportation network can reduce the timeliness of cargo transportation and reduce transportation costs, thus narrowing the actual distance between different regions and accelerating industrial cooperation between different regions. But at the same time, we should also note that, on the one hand, the high accessibility between regions is good for the less developed western and central regions, so that they can more easily obtain the spillover resources and technologies of the developed eastern regions and integrate into the industrial system of the developed eastern regions. On the other hand, a result of this may be an excessive flow of capital from underdeveloped central and western regions to developed eastern regions, resulting in a reduction in per capita resource ownership in the underdeveloped central and western regions. This is incompatible with the healthy operation of existing industries and the development of future economic growth in the underdeveloped western and central regions. In a nutshell, transportation network development has effectively improved inter-regional accessibility, allowing the underdeveloped western and central regions to exchange the developed eastern regions' spillover resources and technologies at the cost of resources and factors and integrate them into the regional industrial system. In the long run, this has more advantages than disadvantages.

Labor Mobility and Urbanization. Transport networks promote economic exchanges between regions, thus facilitating labor mobility and speeding up urbanization. The transportation network makes labor flow from rural to urban, from small cities to big cities, and from underdeveloped western and central regions to developed eastern regions. From a spatial perspective, there is heterogeneity in the direction of labor flow in different regions. For the eastern region, the construction of the transport network represented by the high-speed rail network can increase its attractiveness to the labor force by improving the convenience of urban life. But for the western and central regions, the developed transportation network will promote the outflow of local labor. Furthermore, the marginal effect limits the increase in labor remuneration brought about by urban scale. Too large an urban scale will significantly increase the cost of living, so that the increase of labor remuneration cannot offset the increased cost of living. Therefore, for some high-end workers, it is most economical to live in medium-sized cities near first-tier cities that have already opened high-speed trains. In this way, we can not only have high-quality resources provided by first-tier cities but also live at a relatively low cost [2].

At the same time of labor mobility, the urbanization level of various regions is also constantly improving, which cannot be separated from the support and guidance of the transportation network. In addition to a large population, relatively limited resources, a fragile ecological environment, and an unbalanced urban-rural development pattern, China's urbanization is progressing gradually. A reasonable transportation network layout can optimize the layout and form of urbanization, promote the citizenization of the transferred agricultural population, improve the capacity for sustainable development of cities, and ensure that urban and rural areas are developed in an integrated manner. As a result, the necessary human capital for economic agglomeration is provided [3].

Regional Economic Potential. The transportation network has a positive effect on the improvement of regional economic potential. As can be seen from the above, the construction of a transport network can improve the level of local economic agglomeration, including manufacturing and service industries. For the manufacturing industry, agglomeration can generate economies of scale, thus reducing production costs and improving production efficiency. The economic potential of a region can be significantly enhanced by manufacturing agglomerations, resulting in increased domestic demand, optimizing and upgrading local manufacturing structures, and supporting the development of the service sector. At the same time, improving the overall competitiveness and structural level of the service industry will obviously promote its agglomeration. Therefore, the development of a transportation network can promote the agglomeration of manufacturing and service industries at the same time and improve the regional economic potential [5].

2.2 Analysis of Heterogeneity

As previously stated, the influence of the transportation network on economic agglomeration is heterogeneous, with the developed eastern region having a greater influence than the less developed central and western regions. Transport infrastructure development is advantageous for the development of the developed areas in the east as it facilitates the agglomeration of labor and increases the efficiency of the industrial structures. For the less developed areas in western and central China, the development of the transportation network may lead to the loss of production factors, but it is also conducive to the initial economic agglomeration.

Economic Agglomeration of Developed Regions in Eastern China. Most developed regions have relatively prosperous, innovative high-tech sectors with huge agglomeration benefits, whose enormous agglomeration benefits are caused by the precise division of labor, the rapid formation of new companies, and a small degree of local forward and backward linkages [6]. In the developed eastern regions, the industrial driving force of economic growth has gradually changed from the manufacturing industry to the "two-wheel drive" of manufacturing and service industries, and this trend is more obvious in the high-grade central cities. After analyzing the relationship between manufacturing and service industries, it can be found that the agglomeration of producer services promotes the growth of urban total factor productivity by improving technical efficiency, especially the total factor productivity of the manufacturing industry. The growth of the total factor productivity within central cities has not been impacted by manufacturing agglomeration a great deal with respect to the growth of the total factor productivity within central cities as a whole. However, manufacturing agglomeration in high-level central cities can have a positive effect on the growth of urban total factor productivity by promoting technological progress [7].

Economic Agglomeration of Underdeveloped Regions in Central and Western China. At present, the economic development of the less developed areas in the western and central regions is mainly restricted by technology and capital, and the laying of a transportation network can alleviate such constraints so as to realize the enhancement of economic agglomeration. During the early stages of economic agglomeration, less developed regions in the central and western regions primarily transferred industries from developed regions, such as labor-intensive enterprises, energy-consuming enterprises, and high-polluting enterprises with the aim of achieving a shift from agriculture to manufacturing as well as the transition from a periphery region to an industrial center [8]. In spite of that, there is a tendency for the industrial configuration of the less developed regions of the western and central regions to be too unrealistic at the present time. The primary processing industry still dominates, and the lack of high-tech, high-grade, and high-value-added industries leads to their being locked in the low end of the industrial value chain. The development of a transportation network will help the less developed regions in the western and central regions to overcome the initial stage of economic agglomeration, continuously boost their development, and gradually complete their industrial chain, improve their industrial level, and form industrial clusters [9].

3 The Development of Transportation Networks

Figures 2, 3 and 4 show the development status of the provincial transportation network in 2000, 2010, and 2020. Among them, depending on the province, the road network density is calculated by dividing the total mileage of rail, highway, and inland waterways, as well as the urban and rural areas of the province by the total mileage of roads, according to the data from the China Statistical Yearbook[Due to data limitations, the data for road network density were used for 2000, 2010, and 2018.]. First of all, the development of the provincial transportation network shows a trend of substantial growth. Among them, the length of roads and the density of the network increased the fastest from 2000 to 2010, while the length of the railway increased the most from 2010 to 2020. Second, Shanghai, Chongqing, Henan, Shandong, and Jiangsu have the highest road network density in China, while Heilongjiang, Gansu, Inner Mongolia, Qinghai, Xinjiang, and Tibet have the lowest. Shanghai's road network density, for example, was 1.0469 km/sq

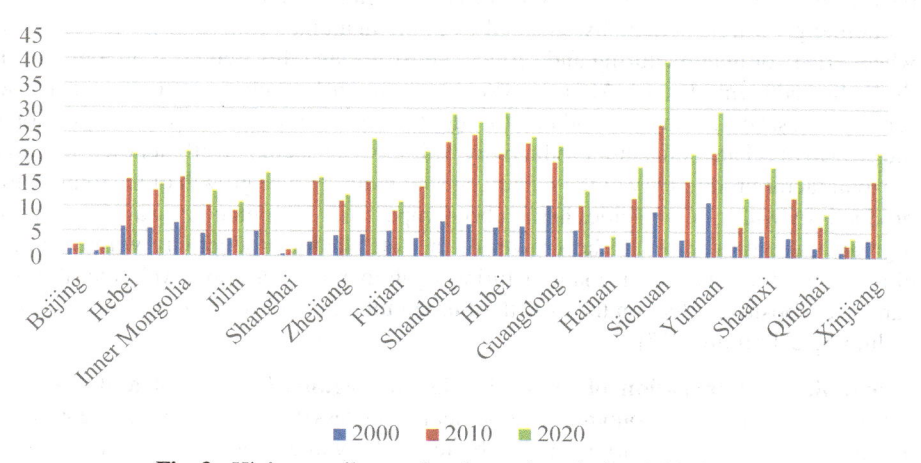

Fig. 2. Highway mileage of each province (unit: 10,000 km).

km in 2000, 2.2813 km/sq km in 2010, and 2.4531 km/sq km in 2018. In contrast, the road network density in Heilongjiang, Gansu, Inner Mongolia, Qinghai, Xinjiang, and Tibet is generally lower than 0.4 km/sq km. Finally, the density of road networks in Guizhou, Xinjiang, Chongqing, Xizang, Hubei, Anhui, Qinghai, and Henan all increased by more than 300 percent between 2000 and 2018, while those in Fujian, Hainan, Guangdong, Tianjin, and Beijing grew by less than 110 percent. In general, the density of the road network in the eastern region has been found to be greater than 1 km/sq km, though the rate of growth has been relatively slow throughout the years. In the western and central regions, there are provinces with high road network densities, such as Chongqing and Henan, as well as many provinces with road network densities lower than 1 km/sq km, but the overall growth rate is still significantly higher than that in the eastern region.

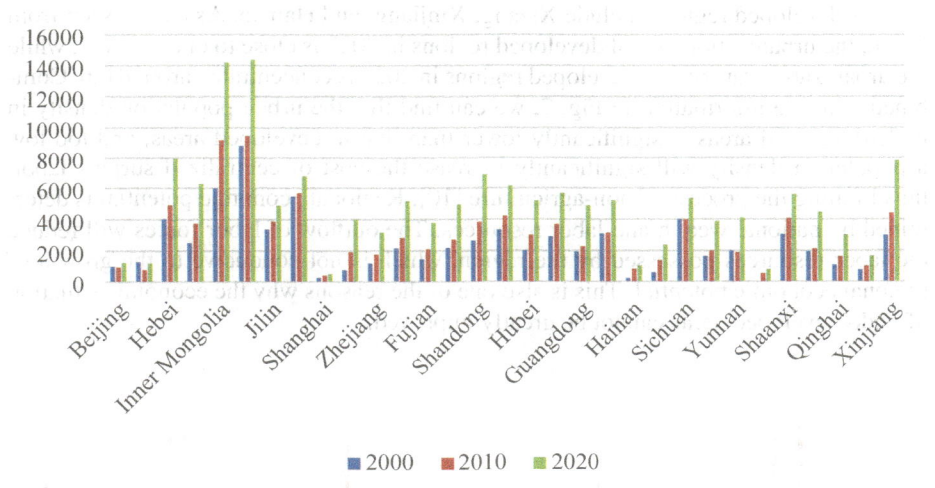

Fig. 3. Railway mileage of each province (unit: km).

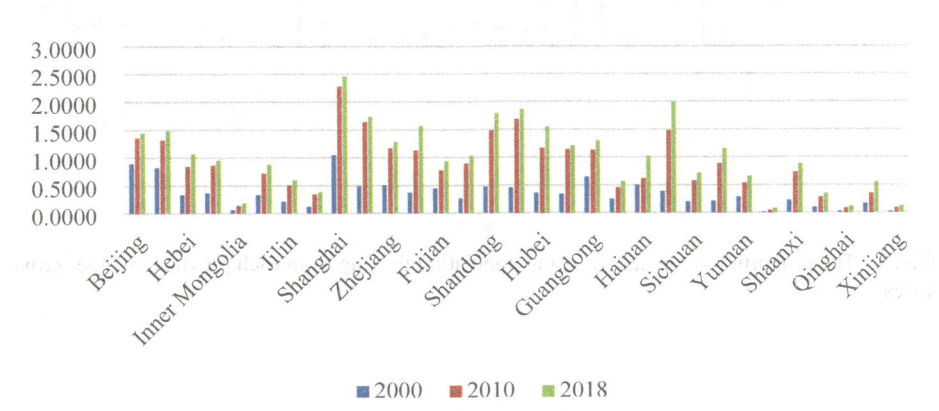

Fig. 4. Provincial road network density (unit: km/km2).

4 The Agglomeration of Regional Economies

4.1 Economic Potential

Figures 5, 6 and 7 show the development of the indicators of economic potential in our provinces. As can be seen from Fig. 5, in Beijing, Tianjin, Shanghai, Jiangsu, Zhejiang, Fujian, Guangdong, Hainan, Xizang, Xinjiang, and the other 10 provinces, the proportion of out-of-province flowing population in the total floating population increased significantly in 2010 compared with 2000 and reached its peak, and then declined somewhat in 2020 but remained above 30%. In this section, the ten provinces are divided into developed regions and less developed regions. Beijing, Tianjin, Shanghai, Jiangsu, Zhejiang, Fujian, and Guangdong are some of the developed regions in China, while the less developed regions include Xizang, Xinjiang, and Hainan. As can be seen from Fig. 6, the urbanization rate of developed regions in 2020 is close to or above 0.7, while the urbanization rate of less developed regions in 2020 is concentrated around 0.6. Combined with the information in Fig. 7, we can find that the urban population density in underdeveloped areas is significantly lower than that in developed areas, and too low a population density will significantly increase the cost of centralized surplus labor, thus limiting the process of non-agriculture [10]. Regional economic potential is determined by national wealth and labor resources. The outflow of labor forces will reduce the labor resources possessed by the region, which is not conducive to the growth of regional economic potential. This is also one of the reasons why the economic situation of underdeveloped areas cannot be greatly improved.

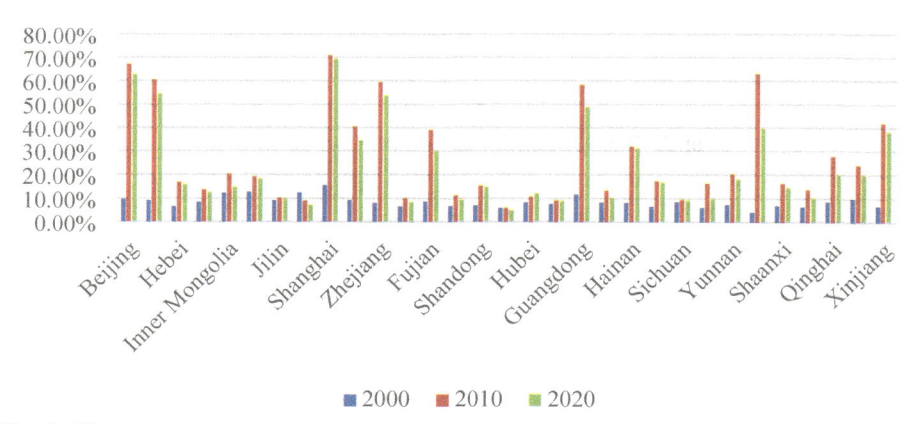

Fig. 5. The proportion of the total floating population flowing from each province to other provinces.

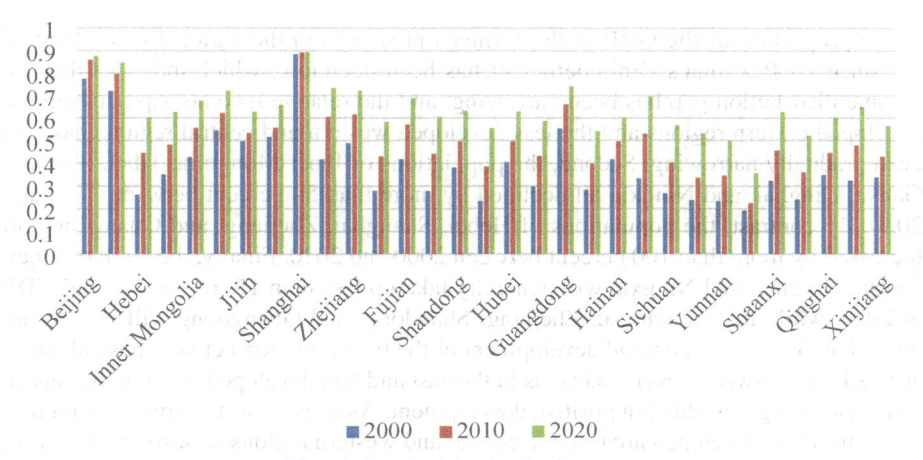

Fig. 6. Provincial urbanization rate.

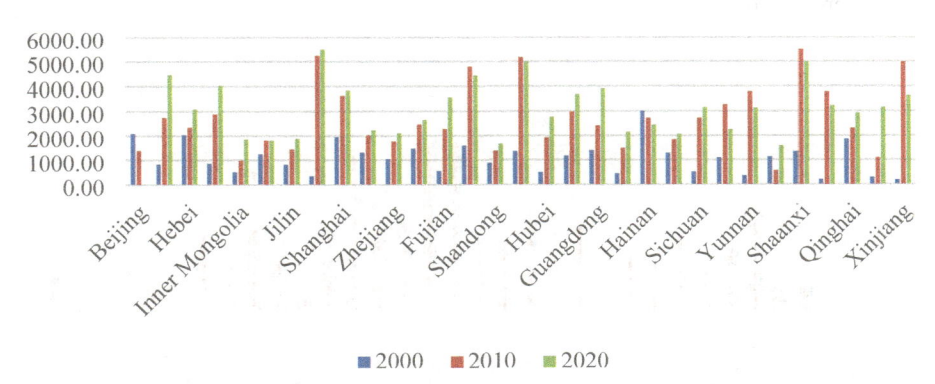

Fig. 7. Urban Population Density of each Province (unit: person/km2).

4.2 The Development of Economic Agglomeration

Economic agglomeration is inseparable from labor agglomeration, and the degree of labor agglomeration can be reflected by the Gini coefficient. Gini coefficients are a measure of how labor agglomeration is distributed in a particular region, and as such their height is a measure of how economic agglomeration is distributed in the region [11]. Figures 8 and 9 show the development of indicators related to economic agglomeration in each province. This paper calculates the national Gini coefficients of 0.27, 0.23, and 0.20 in 2000, 2010, and 2020, respectively, based on the population share and GDP share of each province. The formula chosen is as follows:

$$G = 1 - \sum_{i=1}^{n}(X_i - X_{i-1})(Y_i + Y_{i-1})$$

G represents the Gini coefficient, represents the sum of the proportion of the population of the former i provinces in the national population, and represents the sum of the proportion of the GDP of the former i provinces in the national GDP. First of all, since 2000, China's Gini coefficient has been declining, which indicates that the income distribution gap has been narrowing, and the relative income gap between the developed eastern regions and the less developed western and central regions has also been gradually narrowing. Second, the populations of Inner Mongolia, Tibet, Shaanxi, Gansu, Qinghai, and Ningxia all declined by more than 50 percent between 2000 and 2020. By contrast, the populations of Hebei, Shanghai, Zhejiang, and Guangdong all increased by more than 100 percent between 2000 and 2020. Finally, the GDP of Tibet, Gansu, Qinghai, and Ningxia will generally take up less than 1% of the national GDP in 2020, while that of Jiangsu, Zhejiang, Shandong, and Guangdong will all take up more than 6%. Since the rapid development of the transportation network has enhanced accessibility between developed areas in the east and less developed areas in the central and western regions, this is a positive development. As a result of the rapid migration of labor from less developed areas in the central and western regions to developed areas in the east, economic agglomeration and economic development of developed areas in the east are promoted.

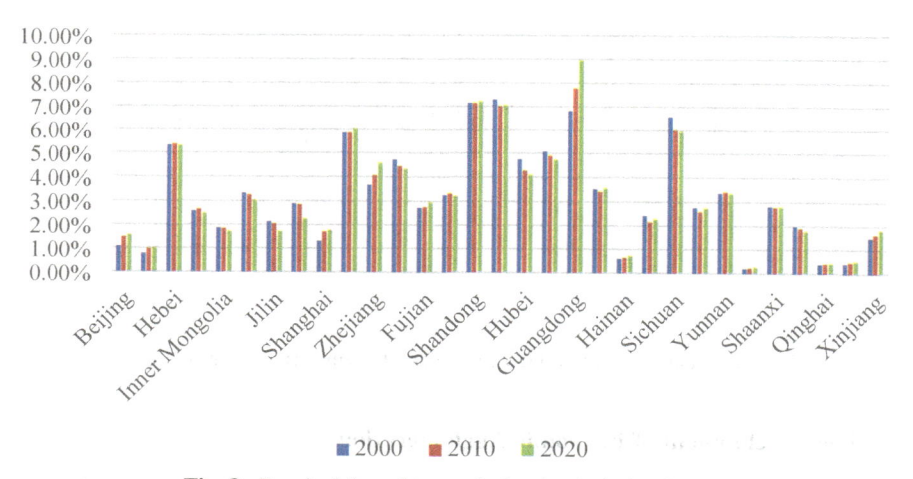

Fig. 8. Provincial road network density (unit: km/km2).

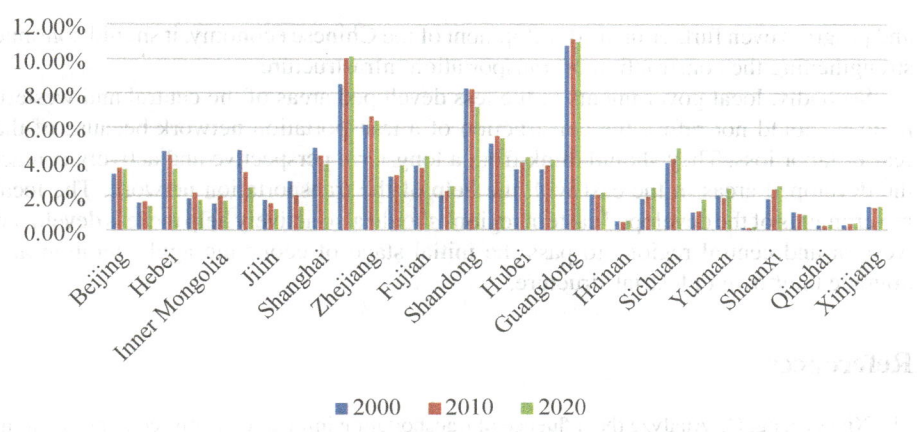

Fig. 9. The proportion of provincial GDP to national GDP.

5 Conclusions and Recommendations

This paper reviews and arranges the views on the relationship between transportation networks and economic agglomeration and draws some meaningful findings and conclusions by analyzing related indicators. The study found the following:

Firstly, the development of the transportation network has effectively improved regional accessibility and promoted regional economic exchanges, allowing labor to flow from less developed areas in the central and western regions to developed areas in the east and continuously improving each region's urbanization level and economic potential.

Secondly, the influence of the transport network on economic agglomeration is heterogeneous. Developing the transportation network is beneficial for the agglomeration of labor and the upgrading of industrial structures in the developed areas of the east because of the benefits associated with the development of the transportation network. For the less developed regions in western and central China, the development of the transportation network may bring about the loss of production factors, mainly labor, but it can also ease the constraints on technology and capital. At the same time, the transportation network also helps the less developed areas in the western and central regions better undertake the industrial transfer of the developed areas and survive the initial stage of economic agglomeration.

Thirdly, With the development of transportation infrastructure, China attaches a great deal of importance to the construction of transportation infrastructure. In the last two decades, the transportation network has been dramatically developed and improved. The growth rate of the road network density in some parts of central and western China has even exceeded 300%, which greatly improves the economic potential and the degree of economic agglomeration in all regions.

Taking into account the above findings, the following recommendations are made in this paper:

Firstly, as China continues to construct transportation infrastructure and to develop a transportation network in order to promote the agglomeration of its economic sectors and progress even further in the development of the Chinese economy, it should continue strengthening the construction of transportation infrastructure.

Secondly, local governments in the less developed areas of the central and western regions should not refuse the construction of a transportation network because of the fear of labor loss. They should think from a long-term perspective and actively contact the developed areas in the east with the help of the transportation network. The local governments of the developed eastern regions should also actively help the less developed western and central regions to pass the initial stage of economic agglomeration and upgrade their own industrial structure.

References

1. Xiangzheng, G.: Analyze the influence of transportation infrastructure on economic agglomeration. chinaqking.com
2. Xu, X., Feng, Y., Linnan, Y., et al.: How does high-speed rail affect labor mobility: new perspectives and new evidence. Modern Econ. Sci. **44**(4), 12 (2022)
3. Xianping, X.: Accelerating the improvement of the comprehensive transport network to promote urbanization. Integr. Transp. **1**, 5 (2013)
4. Xiaojing, L.: Market potential, agglomeration economy and service industry development. Nanjing University (2013)
5. Chunhua, X.: Provincial differences in market potential and producer services agglomeration: evidence from China. Ind. Econ. Rev. **6**, 14 (2016)
6. Agglomeration economy in high-tech firms in developed production areas: A case study of Denver (Boulder) cnki.net
7. Jun, L., Zhennan, C.: An empirical study on industrial agglomeration and total factor productivity growth in central cities-as well as on the influence of urban level differentiation. Urban Dev. Res. **25**(12), 9 (2018)
8. Tingfang, J.: A study on the development path of economic agglomeration in underdeveloped regions: a case study of Qingyuan city in Guangdong province. China's Collective Econ. **3X**, 2 (2011)
9. Jianbao, L., Qi, L.: Game of agglomeration and transfer of manufacturing industry and evolution of industrial spatial structure in Guangdong: a case study of ceramic industry transfer (Nanzhuang-Qingyuantan, Foshan)]. Guangdong Sci. Technol. **4**, 6 (2012)
10. Lin, Y.: Breaking through the bottleneck and accelerating the development of urbanization in western China according to local conditions. China Econ. Trade Herald **000**(027), 33–36 (2013)
11. Qi, Z., Wei, S.: Industrial agglomeration and regional economic development: An empirical analysis based on location entropy and Gini coefficient. J. Chizhou Univ. (2019)

A Study of the Dual Carbon Target and Green Finance Development in Jiangxi Province

Liwen Dai(✉)

Henan University of Economics and Law, 180 Jinshui Dong Lu, Zhengzhou, Henan, China
979095428@qq.com

Abstract. China is in a historical period of continuous transformation between old and new growth drivers, and traditional extensive industries are incapable of meeting the dual carbon target energy conservation and emission reduction requirements, which not only requires rural revitalization but also presents new challenges to green financial innovation. As part of the strategy for rural revitalization, the transformation of rural economic growth mode and the optimization and upgrading of the industrial structure cannot be separated from the support of low-carbon green financing. Rural green finance is currently hindered by many difficulties associated with rural economic transformation. According to the premise of "carbon neutrality and carbon peak," developing green and low-carbon finance is an essential component of rural revitalization and an important means of solving problems associated with agriculture, rural areas, and farmers. As one of the major agricultural provinces in China, the implementation of rural revitalization in Jiangxi Province is particularly important. Taking Jiangxi Province as an example and combining with the current situation of rural revitalization development in Jiangxi Province, this paper analyzes the existing problems of green finance in helping rural revitalization in Jiangxi Province, explains the obstacles of green finance in helping rural revitalization, and puts forward suggestions such as perfecting the supporting mechanism of green finance in supporting rural revitalization, improving the supply system of green finance in rural revitalization, and introducing talents to popularize green finance.

Keywords: Green Finance · Rural Revitalization · Carbon Peak · Carbon Neutrality

1 Introduction

Higher requirements for green investment and financing have been put forward to achieve dual carbon, but profound changes have also been forced on the green financial system [1]. As one of China's typical resource-based economic provinces, Jiangxi is currently in a period of green economic recovery with accelerated industrialization and urbanization, transformation and upgrading of traditional industries, and continuous cultivation and growth of strategic emerging industries.

A major objective of China's "14th Five-Year Plan" is to promote a green, low-carbon, and circular approach to agriculture. In order to improve the environment and cope with climate change, green finance provides strong financial support for the development of green agriculture. In addition to emitting a large amount of carbon dioxide, agricultural production also acts as a large carbon sink [2]. The key to achieving the dual carbon goal is to take full advantage of agricultural advantages, develop green agriculture, reduce agricultural emissions, and sequester carbon. Green finance plays an important role in the coordinated development of the economy, ecology and environment, supports green agriculture, promotes carbon sequestration and emission reduction in agriculture, and green investment activities promote the development of the rural economy.

2 Literature Review

The financial industry is able to provide rural revitalization services using a new financial instrument, green and low-carbon finance, at a historic time. It has been argued that rural revitalization provides a good opportunity for rural green development, and rural green finance is essential to the realization of green and sustainable development. At a historic time, the financial industry is able to provide rural revitalization services using a new financial instrument, green and low-carbon finance. It has been argued that rural revitalization provides a good opportunity for rural green development, and rural green finance is essential to the realization of green and sustainable development. This new financial instrument has the potential to help rural areas become more sustainable and resilient in the face of changing economic and environmental conditions. By investing in green and low-carbon finance, rural areas can benefit from increased economic growth, improved access to essential services, and increased environmental protection. The use of green and low-carbon finance is a positive step towards achieving sustainable development in rural areas. An and Liu believed that rural revitalization provides a good opportunity for rural green development. In addition to effectively promoting rural supply-side structural reform, rural revitalization was stimulated by sustainable development and improved the rural ecological environment [3]; Wang and Xu argued that green finance contributes to the development of ecological agriculture. And new agricultural forms such as smart agriculture and low-carbon agriculture develop rapidly, which is conducive to embedding the concept of green development into the agricultural industry chain, promoting the upgrading of the agricultural industry, and achieving industrial prosperity [4].

With the continuous development of the economy and society, rural financial subjects show a trend of diversification, rural cooperative credit cooperatives have begun to take shape, the Agricultural Bank of China and private lending institutions have developed in parallel mode, etc. As the economy and society continue to develop, rural financial subjects have become increasingly diversified. Rural cooperative credit cooperatives have been established, and the Agricultural Bank of China and private lending institutions have been developing in a parallel manner. These changes have had a significant impact on the rural financial sector, and have opened up new opportunities for rural residents to access financial services.

The traditional financial model needs continuous iteration to escort the rural revitalization strategy, which brings more demand for rural green finance practices. In the rural revitalization strategy, the transformation of rural economic growth mode and the optimization and upgrading of industrial structure cannot be separated from the support of low-carbon green finance. As for the path of green finance helping rural revitalization, Yang and Zou argued that green finance helps agricultural production to link smallholder production with modern agriculture, promotes the comprehensive management of the rural ecological environment, and improves the rural financial environment [5]. At present, China is in the process of promoting socialist modernization, in this context, green finance can effectively help the implementation of a rural revitalization strategy. Starting from the agricultural industry chain, Wang and Li believed that the integration of the agricultural industry chain and the comprehensive improvement of the rural supply chain would help to improve the allocation of green financial resources and bring new impetus to the activation of the rural economy. As a new financial product and service mode, green finance is an important measure to solve the problems of agriculture, rural areas, and farmers and boost the effective implementation of the rural revitalization strategy [6]. Green finance is a new financial product and service mode that is becoming increasingly important for tackling the issues of agriculture, rural areas, and farmers. It is seen as an effective way to implement the rural revitalization strategy, as it provides a means of financing and investment that can help to promote sustainable development in rural areas. Green finance can help to reduce poverty and promote economic growth, while also protecting the environment. It can also help to provide access to financial services for rural populations, which can in turn help to improve living standards. Green finance is therefore an essential part of the rural revitalization strategy, and its use should be encouraged to ensure that the goals of the strategy are achieved. Zuo explained that green financial innovation has an impact on the implementation of the rural revitalization strategy: it promotes the prosperity of rural industries, strengthens rural governance, breeds civilized rural customs, and finally guides rural areas to achieve common prosperity. Therefore, it is necessary to promote the innovation of green finance with the concept of collaborative development. From the perspective of coordinated development, the deep integration of the new development concept into the financial system will certainly promote the high-quality development of China's financial system [7]. At present, China has made some progress in the field of green finance, but it still faces some problems. Inclusive finance, green finance, and smart finance in all provinces and cities show an overall growth trend, and the three have synergistic effects. Among them, the promotion of green finance should introduce the idea of supporting economic development.

However, green finance also faces some difficult problems. Green and low-carbon finance require the integrated development of urban and rural areas, but the urban-rural dual economic structure cannot be broken in a short period. As for the development of green finance to help rural revitalization, Zuo Zhenglong believes that the support of green finance to rural revitalization is in the preliminary exploration stage, the development of rural green finance is still in its infancy, the concept of green development of financial institutions needs to be strengthened, and the main means of developing green finance are disconnected from the actual needs of agriculture, rural areas and farmers [8]. Yang Shiwei pointed out that there are many difficulties and constraints in supporting rural revitalization in China's green finance, such as insufficient talent introduction, weak supply capacity, and imperfect system policies [9]. Du and Zhou argued that the current green financial instruments are relatively single, the green and low-carbon financial market is not innovative enough, its liquidity is not strong, its price mechanism has not been fully formed, and the synergistic effect is poor [10]. Therefore, the quality of green finance to boost rural revitalization can optimize the path of financial services in many aspects, such as improving rural financial legislation, innovating rural green finance theory, improving the comprehensive service system of rural finance, and strengthening the prevention of fin-tech risks.

To sum up, the availability of rural green finance in China urgently needs to be improved, and the green finance market is still not perfect. Therefore, exploring how green finance helps rural revitalization under the "dual carbon" goal is of theoretical value and practical significance. The exploration of how green finance can help rural revitalization under the "dual carbon" goal is of both theoretical and practical value. This is due to the fact that green finance can provide a way to support the transition to a low-carbon economy, while also helping to improve the living standards of rural communities. By understanding how green finance can be used to achieve both of these goals, it can provide a valuable insight into how rural revitalization can be achieved in a sustainable manner. Furthermore, by understanding the potential benefits of green finance, it can help to inform policy decisions that can help to ensure that rural communities are able to benefit from the transition to a low-carbon economy.

3 Analysis on the Development Status of Green Finance in Jiangxi Province

3.1 Status Quo of Rural Revitalization and Development in Jiangxi Province

In terms of agricultural development, according to the Strategic Plan for Rural Revitalization of Jiangxi Province (2018–2022) and the data of Jiangxi Provincial People's Government, in 2021, the grain output of Jiangxi province reached 43.85 billion catties, an increase of 5.16% compared with 2012. The scale of high-standard farmland reached 23.057 million mu, an increase of 300.3% compared with 2012, making a great contribution to ensuring the country's food stability; The progress rate of agricultural science and technology is 61.5%, an increase of 9% compared with 2012. Science and technology have gradually become the main driving force of agricultural growth in Jiangxi Province. Agricultural development is an important part of rural revitalization. Science and technology have become increasingly important to the agricultural growth of Jiangxi Province. This growth has been driven by advances in technology, such as the use of modern agricultural machinery and the introduction of new crop varieties. As a result, agricultural development has become a key part of rural revitalization in the province. Improved agricultural production has helped to improve the living standards of rural residents, and has also provided a boost to the local economy. With continued investment in science and technology, Jiangxi Province is well-positioned to continue to develop its agricultural sector and contribute to the overall growth of the region.

Data from the Jiangxi Provincial People's Government shows that the penetration rate of tap water in rural areas of Jiangxi Province is expected to reach 85.8% in 2021. Furthermore, the penetration rate of harmless sanitary toilets in rural areas has reached 92.16%. Additionally, more than 25 natural villages have been connected to cement roads, indicating the great strides being made towards modernizing the rural environment. This improvement of the rural environment symbolizes the gradual realization of the goal of building a "clean, comfortable, beautiful and livable" new countryside in Jiangxi Province (Table 1).

Table 1. Development status of rural revitalization in Jiangxi Province.

Indicators		Units	In 2012	In 2021	Growth (%)
Development of agriculture	Output of grain	Hundred million catties	416.97	438.5	5.16
	High-standard farmland scale	Ten thousand mu	576	2305.7	300.3
	Rate of progress in Agricultural science and technology	%	52.5	61.5	9
The rural environment	Rural tap water penetration rate	%	—	85.8	—
	The penetration rate of harmless sanitary toilets in rural areas	%	58.9	92.16	33.26
	Proportion of natural villages with more than 25 households having access to cement (oil) roads	%	47.5	—	—

3.2 The Status Quo of Green Finance in Assisting Rural Revitalization and Development in Jiangxi Province

In terms of macro policy support, the Nanchang Central Sub-branch of the People's Bank of China and relevant departments have jointly issued several documents, including the Implementation Opinions on Financial Services for Rural Revitalization in Jiangxi to Support the Priority Development of Agriculture and Rural Areas, the Work Plan for the Establishment of Financial Services for Rural Revitalization Demonstration Zone, and the Implementation Opinions on Carrying out the Pilot Work of Mortgage Loan for the Use Right of State-owned Agricultural Land in Agricultural Reclamation. In September 2021, together with Jiangxi Banking and Insurance Regulatory Bureau and other relevant departments, it issued Several Measures for Financial Support to Consolidate and Expand the Achievements of Poverty Alleviation and Comprehensively Promote Rural Revitalization in Jiangxi. These documents support green financial services for rural revitalization in terms of policy and point out the direction for financial services for rural revitalization in Jiangxi Province.

In terms of capital supply support, from 2018 to 2020, Jiangxi Rural Commercial Bank issued more than 300 billion yuan of credit funds for rural revitalization, helping rural revitalization in Jiangxi Province. A total of 20.21 billion yuan in loans for urban-rural integration helped narrow the urban-rural gap; In 2021, the Finance Department of Jiangxi Province allocated 300 million yuan to support the promotion of double cropping rice planting and rice tanker farming, enhance land utilization, create basic conditions for improving grain output, and timely provide one-time subsidies of 645 million yuan to actual grain farmers. By the end of November 2021, the loan balance of the green food industry chain of the Agricultural Bank of China Jiangxi Branch is 15.5 billion yuan, promoting the development of the green food industry chain in the province.

In terms of green financial product support, the premium income of agricultural insurance in Jiangxi Province reached 2.729 billion yuan in 2021, covering three major food crops, including rice, wheat, and corn, to ensure that grain farmers "harvest protection from drought and flood" and optimize the environment for agricultural production and development. In the first three quarters of 2021, the provincial Rural Commercial Bank issued a total of 128.31 billion yuan of loans to support the development of modern agriculture; 63,000 loans totaling 17.25 billion yuan were issued to support the construction of beautiful villages, escorting Jiangxi province to build beautiful villages with Jiangxi characteristics.

4 Difficulties in Assisting Rural Revitalization and Development of Green Finance in Jiangxi Province Under the Dual Carbon Target

4.1 The Supporting Policy Mechanism is not yet Sound

In order to support a certain issue or cause, a policy mechanism has not yet been fully developed or established. As a result, the policy is not yet sound or reliable enough to achieve the desired results. In the absence of a sound policy mechanism, the issue or cause may not be effectively addressed. The policy mechanism should be solid before it is implemented in order to ensure that it will be successful in achieving the desired result. Several basic institutions are not yet in a sound state. An effective implementation of environmental economic policies requires an effective legal system to support its development, but the current relevant legal system is not perfect, and cannot support the development of green finance in a sound manner. The basic systems related to carbon emission rights, energy use rights, and pollution emission rights are not perfect, which restricts the development of green businesses. The support of green finance for rural revitalization still lacks operational rules, the existing mechanism still stays at the macro guidance level, the actual binding force is insufficient, and the credit personnel still have difficulties in operation. To achieve the dual carbon goal, the industrial structure in rural revitalization will be greatly adjusted, but it is faced with a series of problems such as a long investment cycle, unstable returns, and high risks, while the cost of agricultural production will rise sharply. At present, the government's support for inclusive subsidies for green industries is insufficient, which cannot provide effective incentives for financial institutions and agricultural enterprises.

4.2 The Supply System is not Perfect

The rural green financial service organization is not perfect yet. Postal savings banks and other financial institutions are weak in providing credit services to townships. The problem of rural banks and other small rural financial institutions is very serious, and the funds needed to support rural revitalization projects are limited; As the main force serving agriculture, rural areas, and farmers, rural commercial banks started the green credit business late, with a lack of relevant credit products and a small total investment. At present, the main body of green finance is credit bonds, funds, insurance, and other green finance business scale and coverage are small, and mainly for large projects, large enterprises, green industry in rural areas as the object, farmers as the main body of green financial products are few. It is difficult to adapt to the requirements of rural revitalization for ecological protection, green agriculture, and other key areas of diversification. Green projects are characterized by long investment cycles, low yields, and the high risk of the agricultural industry, so they urgently need support from risk compensation mechanisms.

4.3 It is Difficult to Innovate and Develop Green Financial Products

Lack of integration of green financial products. Although various financial institutions continue to increase green financial products, there are problems such as product dispersion and weak synergistic effects. This is highlighted in the weak coordination and integration of green credit, bonds and development funds, insurance, and other financial instruments. The use effect of green financial instruments is not significant. The source of green funds in the financial market is single, and there are significant defects in the use of policy-based finance, green bonds, green fund APP, and other financial instruments. There is a shortage of green finance professionals, and green finance puts forward higher requirements for practitioners, requiring professional knowledge background.

5 Path Thinking of Promoting Green Financial Services for Rural Revitalization in Jiangxi Province

Through the analysis of the above problems, it can be seen that although Jiangxi Province has implemented the method of assisting rural revitalization through green finance for many years, there are still problems in all aspects.

5.1 Improve the Supporting Mechanism for Green Finance to Support Rural Revitalization

First, we need to improve fiscal and tax support policies. In order to generate operating income for green credit businesses and provide tax exemption support, it is necessary to stimulate the enthusiasm of rural financial institutions and personnel for green credit development. To do this, we need to improve the risk compensation mechanism for green finance. This could include the introduction of incentives such as tax breaks or subsidies for green credit businesses, as well as the development of new risk management tools and strategies. Additionally, it is important to create a supportive regulatory environment that encourages the development of green finance and provides incentives for rural financial institutions to adopt green credit practices. Some green credit projects in rural revitalization have great risks, so local governments can establish green guarantee funds to reduce credit risks, encourage and leverage the development of more financial institutions, and have more social capital to participate in rural green credit projects. We will improve regulatory policies. In combination with the goal of "dual carbon" construction and the current development of green finance in the context of rural revitalization, financial regulatory authorities should issue more standardized documents to encourage the expansion of the areas supported by green finance. For agriculture-related financial institutions that have achieved remarkable results in supporting rural revitalization, we can start from the deposit reserve ratio, institutional setting, and other aspects, and give appropriate preference in business approval.

5.2 Improving the Supply System of Green Finance in Rural Revitalization

First, we should improve the organizational system of green financial services. We will further improve the organizational system of green finance, support rural revitalization, and increase the positioning of service functions for rural green industries in terms of traditional support for agriculture and small objects. Second, innovation of green financial products. We will continue to develop existing green credit products and gradually expand our service areas. Emission right mortgage, patent right pledge, and usufruct pledge are the tools of financing mortgage guarantee. Financial institutions are encouraged to strive to develop green bonds, funds, and insurance products, support rural revitalization projects, and promote the green transformation and development of rural industries. Foster a good environment for green finance and financing. We will improve the environment for green finance and give key support to targeted RRR cuts and capital replenishment; We will improve risk prevention measures for green finance, and reduce and prevent the non-performing rate of green finance related to agriculture and rural areas.

5.3 Strengthen the Introduction of Financial Talents and Popularize Green Finance

Although green finance has the word "green," its essence is still closely related to finance. Finance is a professional field that requires certain professional knowledge, and most farmers, who are the main body of "agriculture, rural areas, and farmers", lack financial knowledge. In this case, to carry out green finance smoothly, it is necessary to have relevant professional talents to popularize the knowledge of green finance to farmers. In recent years, there is a serious brain drain in Jiangxi Province, and Beijing, Shanghai, Guangzhou, and other places have launched talent introduction policies to grab high-quality talents. Therefore, relevant departments need to introduce some talent introduction policies, such as giving a certain number of subsidies and bonuses and getting certain preferential treatment for buying houses and cars in the province, to attract non-local talents to employment in Jiangxi as much as possible without losing local talents. In the case of ensuring talent, the government can cooperate with relevant local financial institutions to enter towns and villages to popularize green financial knowledge for farmers, encourage farmers to pay attention to ecological protection in the process of production, and build a beautiful countryside.

6 Conclusion

In conclusion, my study has explored the dual carbon target and green finance development in Jiangxi Province. I have analyzed the current situation and challenges faced by Jiangxi in achieving the dual carbon target and promoting green finance. Through empirical analysis and case studies, I have identified several policy recommendations and strategies to promote the development of green finance and reduce carbon emissions in Jiangxi Province. Firstly, it is important to improve the regulatory framework for green finance, including the establishment of a green finance regulatory system and the development of green finance standards. Secondly, promoting the development of green industries and green supply chains can help to reduce carbon emissions and achieve sustainable economic growth. Thirdly, incentivizing the adoption of renewable energy technologies and the implementation of energy-saving measures can further reduce carbon emissions and promote the development of green finance. Overall, my study provides valuable insights into the dual carbon target and green finance development in Jiangxi Province, and offers practical recommendations for policymakers, financial institutions, and businesses. By implementing these recommendations, Jiangxi can achieve its dual carbon targets, promote sustainable economic development, and contribute to the global effort to combat climate change.

References

1. Zhou, M., Chuang, F.: Research on the effective connection between financial assistance in poverty alleviation and rural revitalization: based on the perspective of carbon peak and carbon neutral. Modern Auditing and Acc. **393**(12), 24–25(2021)
2. Shi, Q.: Empirical research on green finance supporting rural revitalization and promoting common prosperity. Jilin Finan. Res. **484**(05), 42–45(2022)
3. An, G., Liu, K.: The role of green finance in rural revitalization. China Finan. **880**(10), 63–65 (2018)
4. Wang, S., Xu, X.: Promoting green finance to help rural revitalization. People's Forum **662**(8), 106–107 (2020)
5. Yang, L., Liu, J.: Irrigating the "flowers" of rural revitalization with heart and feeling [N]. Guang 'an Daily, 2022–05–10(002)
6. Wang, X., Li, H.: Improving the financial service capacity of rural revitalization. China Finan. **950**(08), 34–36 (2021)
7. Zuo, Z.: Green financial innovation helps rural revitalization: mechanism, dilemma, and path. Acad. Exchange **330**(09), 83–95 (2021)
8. Zuo, Z.: Mechanism, Dilemma and path choice of green and low-carbon financial services for rural revitalization: based on the perspective of urban-rural integration development. Contemporary Econ. Manage. **44**(01), 81–89 (2022)

9. Yang, S.W.: Organic connection between poverty alleviation and rural revitalization: significance, internal logic and realization path. Future Dev. **43**(12), 12–15 (2019)
10. Du, L., Zhou, L.: Research on the synergistic effect of inclusive finance, green finance, and intelligent finance. New Finan. **391**(08), 49–57 (2021)
11. Rasoulinezhad, E., Taghizadeh-Hesary, F.: Role of green finance in improving energy efficiency and renewable energy development. Energ. Effi. **15**(2), 14 (2022). https://doi.org/10.1007/S12053-022-10021-4
12. Arif, A., Vu, H.M., Cong, M., Wei, L.H., Islam, M.M., Niedbała, G.: Natural resources commodity prices volatility and economic performance: evaluating the role of green finance. Res. Policy **76**, 102557 (2022). https://doi.org/10.1016/J.RESOURPOL.2022.102557
13. Gholipour, H.F., Arjomandi, A., Yam, S.: Green property finance and CO2 emissions in the building industry. Global Finan. J. **51**, 100696 (2022). https://doi.org/10.1016/J.GFJ.2021.100696
14. Moxey, A., Smyth, M.A., Taylor, E., Williams, A.P.: Barriers and opportunities facing the UK Peatland code: a case-study of blended green finance. Land Use Policy **108**, 105594 (2021). https://doi.org/10.1016/J.LANDUSEPOL.2021.105594

Dynamic Correlation, Volatility Spillover Inside UK Capital Markets

Mingze Yuan[1](✉) and Ziqi Guo[2]

[1] Faculty of Science and Engineering, University of Liverpool, Liverpool L69 7ZX, UK
sgmyuan4@liverpool.ac.uk
[2] School of Management, University of Liverpool, Liverpool L69 7ZX, UK
hszguo12@liverpool.ac.uk

Abstract. By evaluating spot and futures markets, we quantify the dynamic correlation and volatility spillovers in the UK internal capital markets. Our results fill in the investigation of intra-capital market conditions during the epidemic period. Firstly, we calculate their dynamic correlation coefficients using VAR-DCC. Secondly, we figure out the hedging ratio using VAR-BEKK. The results show that the UK equity index is highly correlated with the futures index and has a significant volatility spillover effect, that the hedge ratio for the UK internal capital market is approximately 0.91202 and that the UK equity futures market is a good hedge against equity market risk. Finally, we further discuss the results of the analysis, the results of which are beneficial to relevant investors in the financial markets, and plan for further in-depth research.

Keywords: UK · VAR-DCC · VAR-BEKK · Hedging

1 Introduction

With the outbreak of COVID-19 in 2019, global financial markets are experiencing the turbulence of varying degrees [1]. Economic growth slowed by 3.5% in 2020 as a result of the pandemic, the worst recession since the 1930s and far more dangerous than the 2008 global financial crisis [2]. Hedging is usually one of the important means for people to reduce risk losses, especially during the epidemic, some stock futures and other markets have seen greater volatility than before if people do not make good allocation of these assets. This is unacceptable for people living in a declining global economy at a time of the pandemic. Therefore, taking reasonable risk-hedging measures at the moment is what people must do.

At present, there have been some relevant studies, such as the research on the jump dynamic lead lag relationship between Chinese stock index and futures index during the epidemic period [1], Tang and Argua using DCC-MGARCH to study the hedges between fossil fuels and clean-energy stocks, gold and bitcoin [3], Muhammad et al. approach to study the safe-haven nature of bitcoin against major Australian stock indexes during

---

M. Yuan and Z. Guo—These authors contributed equally.

the first and second waves of the epidemic [4], Jiang et al. have used cryptocurrencies to hedge EPU and stock market volatility [5], walid et al. have analyzed the hedging relationship between oil and precious metals from the Asian crisis to the epidemic [6], Haq et al. studies the possibility of green bonds to hedge against economic policy uncertainty during the epidemic in China and the United States [7], Salisu et al. have accomplished the spillover and hedging effects of volatility in health stocks and travel stocks based on US research [8], but there are few studies on the risk hedging of UK stock index and futures, so we study this aspect to supplement the blank in the current research field.

This paper examines the dynamic correlation and volatility spillover analysis of the UK internal capital markets in Covid-19. We choose the UK capital market because, Ricard mentioned that as a major global financial centre, the UK has the deepest financial markets in the world [9]. We, therefore, draw on a context for our analysis, for example, a study of the impact of risk hedging on UK capital markets and risk aversion in a Covid-19 environment. Moreover, Karan argued as the epidemic is importantly distinct from the 2008–2009 trade crash, and as relatively few investigations have focused on equity internal capital markets during Covid-19 to date [10], this study seeks to fill this gap. We contribute to the literature on the impact of Covid-19 on global financial markets by analysing the volatility spillovers and dynamic correlations of internal capital markets in the context of non-traditional financial crises. To the best of our knowledge, this paper makes the following contributions to the literature. Firstly, we apply the VAR-DCC model to calculate their dynamic correlations. Through data collection, collation and analysis, we conclude that futures and spots within the UK capital market are closely related. Second, we also apply the VAR-BEKK model to obtain its volatility spillover effects and conclude that there is a volatility spillover between the futures and spot markets in the UK internal capital market. Third, we calculate the hedging effectiveness based on the estimation results of the VAR-BEKK model. The results show that the hedging efficiency is 0.9304, which shows that futures can better hedge the risk of the spot.

The rest of this paper is organized as follows. Section 2 shows the data. Section 3 depicts the methods and Sect. 4 presents the results and Sect. 5 is the conclusion.

2 Methodology

2.1 DCC-GARCH

The DCC model is widely used to describe the dynamic correlation coefficient between assets. Sabri Burak and Caner stated that the idea of the DCC model is that the covariance H_t model can be decomposed into the conditional standard deviation D_t and the correlation matrix and that both D_t and R_t are time-dependent in the DCC model and is shown below [11]. Detailed information on the DCC model is shown in the following equations.

$$H_t = D_t R_t D_t \qquad (1)$$

In Eq. (1), H_t is the 2 × 2 conditional covariance matrix, R_t is the conditional correlation matrix, and D_t is the diagonal matrix of time, with the standard deviation on the diagonal.

$$D_t = diag(h_{11t}^{\frac{1}{2}}, \ldots h_{33t}^{\frac{1}{2}}) \tag{2}$$

$$R_t = diag(q_{11t}^{-\frac{1}{2}}, \ldots q_{33t}^{-\frac{1}{2}}) Q_t diag(q_{11t}^{-\frac{1}{2}}, \ldots q_{33t}^{-\frac{1}{2}}) \tag{3}$$

$$Q_t = (1 - \theta_1 - \theta_2)\overline{Q} + \theta_1 \xi_{t-1} \xi_{t-1}' + \theta_2 Q_{t-1} \tag{4}$$

Q_t is a symmetric positive definite matrix. $\overline{Q}$ is the 2×2 unconditional correlation matrix with respect to the normalized residual ξ_{it}. The parameters θ_1 and θ_2 are non-negative and the sum of the two arguments is less than unity. Based on the above equations, the correlation estimator Is shown below,

$$\rho_{i,j,t} = \frac{q_{i,j,t}}{\sqrt{q_{i,i,t} q_{j,j,t}}} \tag{5}$$

2.2 BEKK

As for the BEKK model, the formula is shown below,

$$H_t = CC' + A\varepsilon_{t-1}\varepsilon_{t-1}'\varepsilon'A' + BH_{t-1}B' \tag{6}$$

In Eq. (6), the conditional variance-covariance matrix is specifically represented by H_t, the lower triangular matrix is specifically represented by C, and A and B are square matrices of order n.

2.3 VAR

In the traditional multi-variable GARCH model, we usually identify the return equation as a constant plus a residual term, but this may not be very appropriate for most financial time series. However, VAR models can be used to show contemporary relationships between variables [12]. In this paper, we replace the mean equation of the traditional multi-variable GARCH model with the VAR model to form the VAR-DCC and VAR-BEKK GARCH models. The following is an explanation of the VAR model.

$$y_t = A_1 y_{t-1} + \cdots + A_p y_{t-p} + Bx_t + \varepsilon_t \tag{7}$$

In Eq. (7), y_t is a k-dimensional endogenous variable, and x_t is a D-dimensional exogenous variable. A_1, ..., A_p and B are coefficient matrices to be estimated, and ε_t is disturbance vector. They can be correlated with each other synchronously, but not with their own lag value or with the variables on the right side of the equation.

3 Data

The data for this article is from InvestingFinance (https://cn.investing.com/). We select the UK FT100 and UK Futures 100 index, from march, 2019, to 31 Mach, 2022. In order to facilitate further research, we sorted out the data to match the actual situation. Finally, we obtain 525 data. The reason we chose this period is that we believe that the UK's spot and futures markets during this period can well represent their hedging relationship in the event of an outbreak. Some basic information of the selected data is shown below (Table 1).

Table 1. Descriptive statistics of the selected date.

	spot	future
Mean	0.0003	0.0003
Variance	0.0002	0.0002
Max	0.0905	0.0864
Min	−0.1087	−0.0959

By visualizing the data, we can find the average, maximum and minimum value of the spot during this period is the highest between them. Futures and spot have roughly the same mean and variance, but futures have larger mean and variance overall.

4 Empirical Results and Discussion

4.1 VAR-DCC and VAR-BEKK

The data statistical analysis found that the British capital markets within the dynamic correlation coefficient always maintain the ups and downs, but in June 2, 2020, on March 18, 2021 and June 17, 2021, a big drop in account changes in the international economic situation, the capital market will also receive the serious influence, The average remained at about 0.958, and the variance remained at about 0.00068 (Table 2).

As shown in Fig. 1, there is a strong correlation between spot and futures in the UK capital market. The correlation coefficient was greater than 0.9 in almost the whole sample period. And found that the extreme values occurred in June 2020 and mid-June 2021. These abnormal phenomena can be summarized into the following reasons. It is in June 2020, the world is common to be hit new crown outbreak, the outbreak of disaster has a serious impact on the world economy, Britain is no exception, plus just completed British prime minister election in early may, the new prime minister in office will be carried out in a series of economic improvement measures, the futures price of the new policy may caused this time compared with the ordinary moment fluctuation. This may have contributed to the anomaly in early June 2020. Second, the UK consumer price Index rose in mid-June 2021 due to the impact of the global COVID-19 pandemic, and consumer price inflation rose sharply in various areas: this may be the reason for the outlier in mid-June 2021. Dealerships open up after the UK lockdown, demand increases, prices rise, global semiconductor shortage affecting new car production; Higher housing costs for owner-occupiers and higher gas and electricity prices; The price of daily necessities have generally risen. This may have contributed to the anomaly in mid-June 2021.

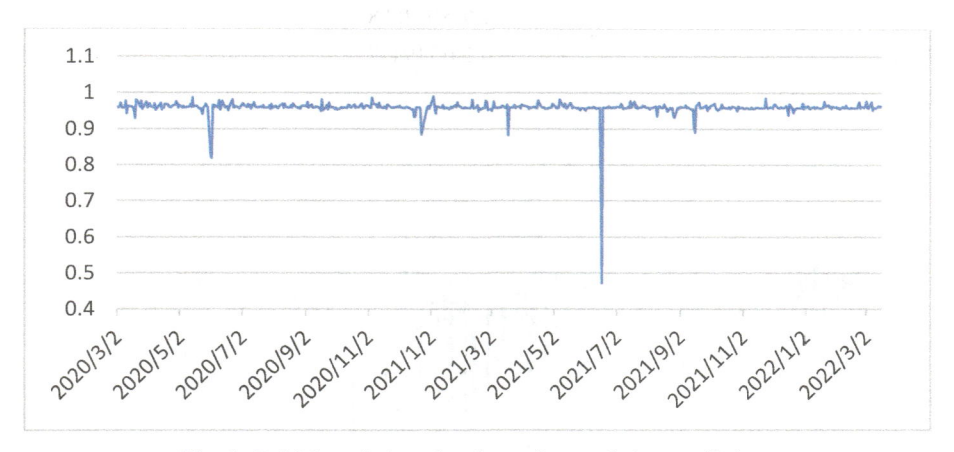

Fig. 1. British capital market dynamic correlation coefficient.

For the Bekk model (Fig. 2), the figure shows that the dataset is affected by dense up and down fluctuations, with many large drops and a rapid return to the average level. Also on June 17, 2021, the VAR-BEKK value experienced the largest drop, which is similar to the magnitude of the change in VAR-DCC. The average value of hedging ratio is about 0.912, among which the maximum value of this data set is about 1.088, and the minimum value is about 0.202. It can be seen from the variance of 0.0084 that this value is relatively stable (Table 3).

Table 2. VAR-DCC dynamic correlation coefficient.

	Correlation
Mean	0.958125056
Variance	0.000675136
Max	0.989271558
Min	0.470938676

4.2 Hedging

Johnson proposed a minimum variance hedge ratio model in which the risk of a given portfolio is minimized [13]. The model assumes that asset a can be used as a hedge for

Table 3. VAR-BEKK hedging ratio.

	Hedge ratio
Mean	0.912023473
Variance	0.008350502
Max	1.088013598
Min	0.201719447

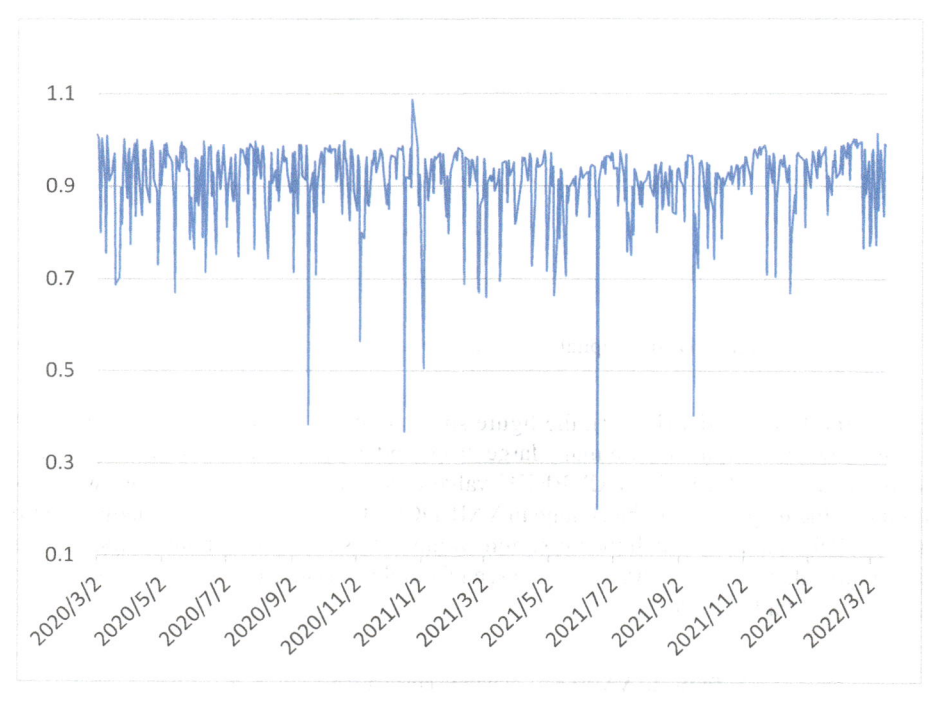

Fig. 2. VAR-BEKK hedging ratio.

asset b, then their hedged portfolio returns are calculated as in Eq. (8).

$$R_{H,t} = R_{s,t} - \gamma_{f,t} R_{f,t} \qquad (8)$$

$R_{H,t}$ stands for hedge portfolio yield, $\gamma_{f,t}$ represents for hedge ratio, $R_{s,t}$ and $R_{f,t}$ stand for spot yield and futures yield respectively.

To further ensure the effectiveness of the constructed hedging strategy, we additionally calculate the value of hedge effectiveness to make the hedging strategy more convincing. The formula for calculating HE is as follows.

$$HE = \frac{var_{unhedged} - var_{hedged}}{var_{unhedged}} \qquad (9)$$

The variance of the unhedged portfolio($\text{var}_{\text{unhedged}}$) is the variance of the spot return index. The variance of the hedged portfolio($\text{var}_{\text{hedged}}$) is the variance of the yield($R_{H,t}$). The closer the HE is to 1, the better the hedging efficiency and the lower the risk. Some results about the above formula are displayed in Table 4.

Table 4. Optimal hedging ratio and hedging efficiency for UK spot and futures.

Hedge Characteristic	Optimal Hedge Ratio	Hedging Effectiveness
Value	1.088	0.9304

Table 4 shows that the optimal hedge ratio for futures is 1.088, which indicates that spots can be hedged by shorting futures by 1.088 on average. In addition, the HE value of 0.9304 indicates that shorting carbon futures in the portfolio can effectively hedge about 93% of the carbon spot price return variance.

5 Conclusions

In this paper, we collect our data set of 525 data on the UK stock index and futures from March 2019 to March 2022 to analyze the dynamic correlation and volatility spillover of the two markets. The novelty of our paper is that we fill a gap in the research on the hedging risk of UK stock indices and futures indices during the epidemic. In our paper, the results of the VAR-DCC model demonstrate a high correlation between the UK stock index and the futures index, while the VAR-BEKK model demonstrates a significant two-way volatility spillover effect between the UK stock index and the futures index. In addition, we have constructed a hedging strategy based on VAR-BEKK-GARCH, which has proven to be an effective hedge for investors in the UK futures market against the UK equity market. Our results will enable investors to further understand the hedging relationship between the futures and equity markets. In addition, our results will facilitate investors who invest in both futures and equities to hedge their risks more effectively and maximize their profits in the face of risk.

Meanwhile, there are still other methods to calculate the dynamic correlation coefficients between futures and stocks or more, such as Copula-DCC-GARCH [14], DCC-MIDAS [15], etc. In this paper, we only use the VAR-DCC-GARCH model to discover the relationship between stocks and futures, and some of the alternatives mentioned above will be carefully evaluated and used in our subsequent studies. Furthermore, we have only used futures and equity assets for hedging in this part of hedging, and we will try more asset combinations such as commodity assets, energy assets, financial assets, virtual currency assets, precious metal assets, etc. in the following research.

References

1. Liu, W., Gui, Y., Qiao, G.: Dynamics lead-lag relationship of jumps among Chinese stock index and futures market during the Covid-19 epidemic. Res. Int. Bus. Financ. **61**, 101669 (2022)

2. International Monetary Fund. World Economic Outlook Update, January 2021: Policy Support and Vaccines Expected to Lift Activity. [online] IMF (2021)
3. Tang, C., Aruga, K.: Relationships among the fossil fuel and financial markets during the COVID-19 pandemic: evidence from Bayesian DCC-MGARCH Models. Sustainability **14**(1), 51 (2021)
4. Kamran, M., Butt, P., Abdel-Razzaq, A., Djajadikerta, H.G.: Is Bitcoin a safe haven? Application of FinTech to safeguard Australian stock markets. Studies in Economics and Finance, ahead-of-print(ahead-of-print) (2021)
5. Jiang, Y., Wu, L., Tian, G., Nie, H.: Do cryptocurrencies hedge against EPU and the equity market volatility during COVID-19? – new evidence from quantile coherency analysis. J. Int. Finan. Markets. Inst. Money **72**, 101324 (2021)
6. Mensi, W., Nekhili, R., Vo, X.V., Kang, S.H.: Oil and precious metals: volatility transmission, hedging, and safe haven analysis from the Asian crisis to the COVID-19 crisis. Econ. Anal. Policy **71**, 73–96 (2021)
7. Haq, I.U., Chupradit, S., Huo, C.: Do green bonds act as a hedge or a safe haven against economic policy uncertainty? Evidence from the USA and China. Int. J. Financ. Stud. **9**(3), 40 (2021)
8. Salisu, A.A., Akanni, L.O., Vo, X.V.: Volatility spillovers and hedging effectiveness between health and tourism stocks: empirical evidence from the US. Int. Rev. Econ. Financ. **74**, 150–159 (2021)
9. Baldwin, R., Tomiura, E.: Thinking ahead about the trade impact of COVID-19. In: Economics in the Time of COVID-19, pp. 59–71 (2020)
10. Rai, K., Garg, B.: Dynamic correlations and volatility spillovers between stock price and exchange rate in BRIICS economies: evidence from the COVID-19 outbreak period (2021)
11. Arzova, S.B., Özdurak, C.: Dynamic linkages between germany trade trends and export of turkey: evidence from DCC-GARCH model and news impact curves. Efil J. Econ. Res. **4**(4), 19–37, 19 p. (2021)
12. Ueda, R.M., Souza, A.M., Menezes, R.M.C.P.: How macroeconomic variables affect admission and dismissal in the Brazilian electro-electronic sector: a VAR-based model and cluster analysis. Physica A **557**, 124872 (2020)
13. Johnson, L.L.: The theory of hedging and speculation in commodity futures. In: The Economics of Futures Trading, pp. 83–99. Palgrave Macmillan, London (1976)
14. Chen, Y., Qu, F.: Leverage effect and dynamics correlation between international crude oil and China's precious metals. Physica A: Stat. Mech. Appl. **534**, 122319 (2019)
15. Yaya, O.S., Ogbonna, A.E., Adesina, O.A., Alobaloke, K.A., Vo, X.V.: Time-variation between metal commodities and oil, and the impact of oil shocks: GARCH-MIDAS and DCC-MIDAS analyses. Resour. Policy **79**, 103036 (2022)

Challenges and Opportunities of Digital Construction of Chinese Grassroots Government in the Information Age – Taking the Construction of "Four Platforms" in Zhejiang Province as an Example

Zhuofan Zong(✉)

Jiangxi University of Science and Technology, Ganzhou 341000, Jiangxi, China
sierrazong@163.com

Abstract. With the continuous development of digital technology, the governance of grassroots governments has ushered in new challenges and opportunities in the era of data. Whether grassroots government governance can get rid of the shackles of traditional governance concepts and rectify the pain points of grassroots government governance depends on the innovation effect of grassroots government governance in the era of data. This paper mainly analyzes the necessity of grassroots government governance innovation in the digital era, the research and analysis of the creation of Zhejiang's "four platforms", and the specific innovation model of grass-roots government, so as to summarize the choice of ways and means of grass-roots government governance innovation. The suggestions put forward in the paper can enable the grass-roots government to further play its role in serving the public, constantly benefit the people and create a happy and comfortable living environment for the people.

Keywords: Digitalization · Grassroots Government · Information Sharing · Four Platforms

1 Introduction

With the concept of digitalization and informatization such as "digital city" and "digital earth" proposed, governments at all levels continue to promote the construction of "digital government". With the continuous optimization of the top-level design and the implementation of governments at all levels, despite the great achievements made by the State Council and provincial and municipal governments, there are still obvious weaknesses in the governance capacity building of grassroots governments. In the context of the era of data, it is particularly important and of practical significance to discuss how grass-roots government governance should be innovative.

This paper specifically expounds the shortcomings in the process of grass-roots government digitalization. Through analyzing the results of "four platforms construction" in

Zhejiang Province, it summarizes the experience of grass-roots government digitalization, and puts forward measures and suggestions for grass-roots government to further improve, so that the grass-roots government can continue to improve and enhance its own level on the basis of existing digitalization in combination with the actual situation.

2 Analysis of Digital Construction of Chinese Grassroots Government in the Information Age

2.1 The Necessity of Grass Roots Government Governance Innovation in the Digital Age

Government digital transformation is an important part of China's comprehensive deepening of reform and opening up and promoting government governance. Among them, the grassroots government governance has a direct impact on the people's concept of the central government, and the effect of grassroots governance has the most direct and rapid impact on the people. With the arrival of the digital era and the deepening of reform, grassroots government governance has emerged problems that need to be solved urgently.

The Sharing Level of Digital Government Information Resources is Low, and the Development of Information Resources is Insufficient. Information resources are strategic resources for the development of modern society and an important way for the government to master the dynamics and needs of urban residents. The inadequate development of information resources by grassroots governments in the digital era has led to the government's inability to timely accept the demands of urban residents for government governance, and has not been able to achieve the effect of significantly improving administrative efficiency. The delay in solving citizens' demands has greatly reduced the happiness index of citizens' lives and the credibility of the government in the hearts of citizens.

At the same time, there is a lack of unified rules and standards among the grassroots governments, which makes the functional departments of the grassroots governments work independently, creating "islands of information" [1]. There is a disadvantage of "fragmented" management in the government. The segmentation between government departments and between local governments at all levels leads to business segmentation, which leads to the segmentation of events and business processes. The low information circulation between departments greatly limits the improvement of the overall service efficiency of the government [2]. It greatly weakens the links between grassroots governments, making it difficult to connect with each other and bring into full play the overall benefits. The lack of unified standards easily leads to a large number of data duplications, data conflicts and other problems in information resources such as databases developed by grassroots governments themselves.

The Digital Transformation Progress of Grassroots Government Does Not Match the Resources. Since the concept of digital government was put forward, government digitalization, especially the construction of digital transformation of grassroots governments, has been widely spread throughout the country, and governments at all levels have paid high attention to it. However, many cities and counties have affected the progress and quality of digital government reform due to the mismatch of regional resources.

On the one hand, affected by the technological foundation and economic development among regions, the municipal governments in different regions have different investments in the construction of government digital infrastructure, and the transformation progress and development quality in different regions are uneven. Taking the Pearl River Delta region and the east and northwest regions of Guangdong Province as examples, the development of government affairs informatization in Guangzhou and Shenzhen, two super large cities, has been in the forefront of the country, and other cities in the Pearl River Delta also have a relatively high level of development. However, the less developed regions in the east and northwest of Guangdong Province, in terms of digital infrastructure, service platforms, resource integration and sharing, the development and utilization of data resources, and the improvement of people's awareness of informatization. There is an obvious gap with the Pearl River Delta [3]. The construction of government online services has a certain effect, with high penetration in some areas; online service is convenient, but the process efficiency is not high, and feedback perception still needs to be strengthened [4].

On the other hand, township grassroots governments are generally subject to greater constraints in terms of talents and funds. Although the provincial government has formulated the policy of "one game for the whole province", emphasizing the investment in the construction of relevant infrastructure under the framework system uniformly formulated by the whole province, the grassroots lacks the personnel and funds for operation and maintenance. In addition, there is a certain difficulty in converting the digital working mode to the traditional working mode at the grassroots level.

Superimposition of Old and New Problems in Grass-Roots Governance. In 2018, the year-end blockbuster work 2018, Top Ten Targets for Grassroots Governance, of the Half Moon Talk magazine, extracted ten pain points strongly reflected by grassroots cadres from a series of research results throughout the year, namely: frequent supervision and inspection, abuse of accountability, pressure "shaking the pot", leaving traces everywhere, heroes of material theory, lazy cadres, typical quick success, policy fights, rising "ceiling", and lack happiness [5].

From the current form of grass-roots government governance, grass-roots government pain points still exist. At the same time, due to the impatience of digital transformation, a series of problems, such as lack of technology, capital and human resources, have arisen, greatly increasing the burden of grass-roots governance. The superposition of old and new problems has brought a huge burden to the governance of grassroots governments, which is not conducive to the transformation of governance of grassroots governments, and is likely to lose more than gain.

The Problem of Digital Security Needs to be Solved Urgently. In the digital era, information security has aroused extensive concern from all walks of life. As a grass-roots government, most of the data types involved in the process of grassroots social governance are relatively private issues such as the basic information and personal appeals of the people. In the process of using a digital platform to build, data loss or theft is very likely to occur. The founder of 360 found that the National Security Bureau of a major country has carried out cyber attacks on China for more than 10 years, which has threatened China's national security. This year, the network has become the front of a new type of war, and major enterprises and important government departments are at risk of data leakage. In this age of big data, data has become a new target of attack [6]. Nowadays, there are more than 200,000 hacker websites in the world. Whenever a new attack method is generated, it can spread all over the world within a week [7].

In this case, how to use the digital platform to build a digital government safely has become a major challenge in the governance process of grassroots governments.

3 Exploration of Grass Roots Government Governance in the Age of Data

The arrival of the digital era has promoted local governments to actively explore the governance model of grassroots governments. In the process of exploration, Zhejiang's research and construction of the governance model of grassroots governments are in the leading position in China. "Four Platforms for Grass roots Governance" is its key project. It is an important carrier for Zhejiang to carry out grass-roots governance work and promote the implementation of "one run at most" reform at the grass-roots level [8].

3.1 Creation of "Four Platforms"

For a long time, "seeing, not managing" has become a major difficulty for grass-roots governments in the process of social governance. The reason is that the grass-roots government is lack of resource allocation and human resources in the process of social governance. The functional coordination capacity among various departments of the grass-roots government is insufficient. In order to solve most problems in the process of grass-roots government governance, Zhejiang proposed the concept of building "four platforms". "Four platforms" are the abbreviation of four functional working platforms for comprehensive governance, market supervision, comprehensive law enforcement and convenient services (see Table 1 for details). The creation of "four platforms" in Zhejiang Province is a major innovation in technology and a typical successful case since the concept of digital government was proposed. In the process of governance, it introduces big data technology, integrates relevant resources, integrates its services and achieves full coverage of information, realizing the seamless connection between villages and towns [9].

The establishment of "four platforms" is to integrate the daily management of grass-roots government departments, reallocate and adjust the allocation of resources to make governance more effective. With the help of platform public application system, new technologies such as the Internet of Things and cloud computing, the integration of information software and the opening of information islands are the technical support for promoting the rapid operation of the "four platforms" [10]. Based on this concept, the grass-roots government has adjusted, streamlined its institutions, made it efficient and convenient for the people, and greatly improved its administrative efficiency.

Table 1. Functions of "Four Platforms".

Modular	Work focus	Organization of work
Comprehensive treatment work platform	Strengthen the construction of letter and visit criticism, rectification, national security, anti drug propaganda and public security flow management	Matters requiring cooperation from multiple platforms shall be coordinated and arranged by specialized personnel. Deepen grid management, endow grid management with more social functions, and achieve multi member integration and multi use
Market supervision platform	Strengthen supervision over food and drug safety, market supervision, safe production, fire safety, environmental protection, forest management, and livestock and poultry breeding	
Comprehensive law enforcement platform	Standardized management of illegal land use, investigation of dilapidated buildings, municipal greening, city appearance, traffic safety, rural environment, market town environment, waste recycling, and sanitation facilities	
Convenient service platform	Strengthen the construction of convenient services for trade union work, Youth League Committee work, women's federations and families, Party building publicity, weak support, culture, education and sports, family planning, rural health, elderly funeral, labor supervision, and people's livelihood services	

3.2 Implementation of "Four Platforms"

How to effectively achieve unified command, rapid response, coordination and order during the implementation of the "four platforms" is a problem that needs to be considered during the implementation of the "four platforms". Grassroots governments should actively combine local administrative policies and formulate relevant operating mechanisms to enable the "four platforms" to operate orderly and achieve efficient management.

Through the implementation of the "four platforms", the grassroots government has broken the vertical and horizontal gap, and the information has been circulated, truly achieving the effect of vertical connectivity and horizontal linkage. Through the establishment of the "four platforms", Zhejiang Province, taking them as the carrier, has constantly improved the grass-roots governance management system, improved the level of grassroots social management and service to the masses, played the role of information technology in grassroots governance, actively connected with the people's livelihood demands, and promoted social harmony and stability based on the practical solution of the people's interests [11].

According to the data provided by Hangzhou City, Zhejiang Province, in 2016, the "four platforms" in X Town, Zhejiang Province, accepted and completed 79675 items of approval services, further expanded the service content, extended the service scope, and made it easier for the surrounding enterprises to handle affairs. The decentralization of pension medical insurance, unemployment assistance, marriage and real estate archives certification of the Archives Bureau and other livelihood services has achieved remarkable results. Only the social security window handled 15695 items of livelihood services throughout the year, achieved the goal of "running at most once". By the end of 2021, the "four platforms for grassroots governance" had accepted 80.46 million items of various kinds, and 77.97 million items had been completed, with a completion rate of 96.9%; from January to August 2021, a total of 8.29 million items were accepted and settled, 99.6% of which were properly settled at the township and village levels.

4 Measures to Improve Grass Roots Government Governance in the Digital Age

4.1 Improve the Development of Information Resources

Information resources play an important role in the government's understanding of people's livelihood dynamics and information. In order to enable grassroots governments to suit the remedy to the case and achieve good governance results in the process of social governance, improving the development of information resources, breaking information islands, and making information available for effective circulation are effective measures for grassroots governments to improve social governance efficiency in the digital era. By building a digital platform and speeding up the flow of information, the grassroots government can be guaranteed to master the dynamics of people's livelihood. The full development of information resources will enable grassroots governments to better understand the interests of the people, better meet the needs of the people's lives, and improve public happiness.

In the information age, the government organizational structure is objectively required to change in the direction of flattening. The introduction of intelligent technology in government governance enables data and information to converge, integrate, open and share, and interconnect. Effectively solve the problems of information islands, data barriers and fragmentation, and break through the narrow view of interests and political achievements [12].

4.2 Improve Resource Matching

As a key component of the "Digital Earth", "Digital City" is undoubtedly the inevitable trend of China's development in order to achieve universal modernization. It is an important means for China to achieve the goal of building a moderately prosperous society in an all-around way, and it is the only way for China to take the road of socialism with Chinese characteristics [13].

Through the measures of driving low-level development areas by high-level development areas, the technical level and digital transformation progress of each region should be unified as far as possible. Actively support the construction of digital platforms and service platforms in underdeveloped regions, improve the matching between their digital transformation progress and resources, and reduce regional development and transformation differences. At the same time, grass-roots governments should actively formulate policies to attract and retain talents, introduce relevant technologies, attract high-tech talents, and promote the improvement and development of grass-roots government governance in multiple ways and angles.

4.3 Establish a Supervision System for Grassroots Cadres

In view of the top ten pain points of grassroots governance, the government should actively formulate a post-supervision system for grassroots governance, combine post-supervision with self-management, rectify the style of grassroots cadres, rectify the unhealthy atmosphere, and make grassroots cadres truly trustworthy in the hearts of the people. When formulating the digital government transformation strategy, the grass-roots government should combine its own situation and not be eager for quick success. It should guard against arrogance and rashness, be down-to-earth, steadily build the digital transformation strategy of the grassroots government, and carry out reform and innovation in an orderly manner.

4.4 Use Digital Security Technology

In order to maintain people's trust, grassroots governments should actively use digital confidentiality technology, cooperate with trustworthy technology companies, and build a digital platform with excellent confidentiality, so that people's interests and basic information can be well protected. At the same time, the use of digital confidentiality technology has improved the status of grassroots governments in the hearts of the people, and better maintained the national status and stability of the country and society, made people's lives run orderly.

5 Conclusion

According to the current practice of grassroots governments, the digitalization of grassroots governments is still facing great challenges. The unsmooth information exchange of grassroots governments has led to the government's "fragmented" management. During the digital transformation, the inconsistent development speed and quality of provinces have impacted the digital transformation of grassroots governments due to the low efficiency of the government's online services, the superposition of traditional problems of grassroots governments, and the existence of digital security risks. Under this kind of impact, the grass-roots government should suit the remedy to the case and constantly strengthen the development and utilization of information resources. The provinces should support each other and speed up the transformation, establish relevant grassroots cadre management system and adopt a series of digital confidentiality technologies to speed up their own transformation.

The capacity building of grassroots governments in the digital era is the trend of the times. They still have shortcomings such as isolated information islands, data leakage risks, etc. As grassroots governments, they should correctly understand their own problems, actively adjust their own policies, improve and improve in an orderly manner, deepen the construction of grassroots digital governments into practice, solve problems at the source, and realize the people's appeal of "running once", In the current era of digital government, only when the grass-roots government continues to improve its own functions, deepen its understanding of digital government, expand the scope of application of digital governance, actively build and share databases, reduce data redundancy, can people's quality of life be improved, people's happiness index can be improved, and the grass-roots government can truly play its role in serving the public, can it continue to benefit the people, create a happy and comfortable living environment for the people.

References

1. Xu, X.: Digital City Government Management. Science Press, Beijing (2006)
2. Tao, C., Gao, A.: Research on optimizing the business environment driven by the digital transformation of the government – taking Dongguan city as an example. E-government (2021)
3. Wen, H.: Trends and challenges of digital transformation of grass roots government. Natl. Gov. (38), 11–14 (2020)
4. Li, Y.: The effect of e-information technology on improving government governance is significant - the special report on "improving digital government service and governance capabilities and new technologies, new applications and network security" was released. China Qual. Wanlihang (2022)
5. Xinhua News Agency. The Top Ten Targets for Grass-roots Governance. Qiushi, vol. 2, pp. 69–75 (2019)
6. Sun, B., Zhou, H.: Member of the National Committee of the Chinese People's Political Consultative Conference and founder of 360: national hackers are entering the arena, and digital security requires top-level design. China Econ. Weekly (05), 80–81 (2022)
7. Deng, W.: Digital security: a new dimension of national security. Qiu Suo (02), 85-87 (2004)
8. Hu, C.: Is it possible that "the government is the platform"—a case study of collaborative governance digital practice. Gov. Res. (2020)
9. Zheng, Y., Xin, Y.: "Technological empowerment" of rural governance: operation logic, action dilemma and path optimization – take the "four platforms" of F Town in Zhejiang Province as an example. J. Hunan Agric. Univ. Soc. Sci. Ed. (03), 60–68 (2021)
10. Qiu, H.: Discussion on problems and countermeasures in the construction of "Four Platforms" of grass roots governance system – based on the investigation and analysis of the pilot project of Yangxunqiao town in Northern Zhejiang. J. Shandong Univ. Sci. Technol. (Soc. Sci. Ed.) (2018)
11. Li, X.: Innovation path of integrated governance at the grassroots level driven by system and technology – take the construction of "four platforms" for grass-roots governance in Zhejiang Province as an example. J. Party School CPC Tianjin Municipal Committee (01), 79-85 (2021)

12. Lei, H., Wang, Q.: Technology enabling, user driven and innovation practice: innovation of government governance model in the intelligent age. J. Southwest Univ. Nationalities (Hum. Soc. Sci. Ed.) **42**(02) (2021)
13. O'Neill, R.: The transformative impact of e-Government on public governance in New Zealand. Public Manag. Rev. **11**(06) (2009)

Research on the Impact of Digitalization on Individual Investors' Behavior from the Perspective of Behavioral Finance

Zhihan Zhao(✉)

Tianjin University, Tianjin 300354, China
zhaozhihan@tju.edu.cn

Abstract. As the world enters an irreversible digital transformation, massive information penetrates into all aspects of people's lives, especially the financial field based on information utilization and information management. Under the guidance of digital social networks, the investment behavior of individual investors who are relatively unprofessional has been affected by a non-negligible impact. Based on the division of investors' investment steps and the analysis of the influencing factors of specific steps from the perspective of behavioral finance, it is found that the impact of digitalization on individual investor behavior is quite complex and promotes investors to the ideal investment path from both positive and negative directions. The complex impacts of digital transformation on individual investors require investors to strengthen their own information collecting and processing capabilities, taking advantage of the positive effects of digitalization, and abandoning its negative effects. It also requires the vigorous supervision and prevention of financial market regulators to jointly build a stable market order.

Keywords: Digitization · Individual Investors · Irrational Behavior · Behavioral Finance

1 Introduction

The digital transformation of the era is a slow but firm developing process, transforming from traditional offline interactions to online related transactions based on the Internet. In the context of global digitalization, massive amounts of information flood our senses, improving the accuracy of people's impressions, the delicacy of descriptions, and the comprehensiveness of decision-making processes [1]. Compared with other traditional industries, the financial industry, as the main audience of data information, reflects an above-average degree of digitization. The financial industry consists of businesses such as accounting, auditing, financing, and risk measurement, and its essence is the acquisition, utilization, and management of credit [2]. The choice of enterprises to carry out digital transformation meets the needs of the times, and at the same time brings opportunities and challenges to active individual investors in the market. Digital transformation has provided individual investors with more comprehensive corporate financial information, but the massive information brought by the Internet does not match the relatively poor information collecting, information screening, and information processing capabilities of individual investors [3]. Insufficient correspondence will be fully reflected in the irrational investment behavior of individual investors.

Compared with more professional institutional investors, individual investors often play an unpredictable variable role in the investment market. After Fama put forward the efficient market hypothesis and the Capital Asset Pricing Model, the market researches based on the Capital Asset Pricing Model are generally carried out internationally, but it is found that the behavior of individual investors deviates from the "perfectly rational" assumption [4]. Facing the continuous emergence of irrational individual investor behavior, behavioral finance theory emerged as the times require. Scholars in the past analyzed the heterogeneous preferences of individual investors through the different cognitive biases involved in behavioral finance theory, including the bounded rationality of individual investors due to the difficulty in obtaining information [5]; the overconfidence that they firmly believe that they can find excellent investment opportunities [6]; and characteristics such as disposition effect, geographical preference and industry preference trying to describe the reasons for investors' irrational behavior [7]. However, there are many theories in behavioral finance, and scholars have different explanations for the irrational behaviors of individual investors, and the analysis of investor behaviors is relatively simple and general.

In the academic field, in order to understand the behavior of individual investors in the process of investing in securities more fully and in detail, the complete investment process is divided into five steps: formulating investment policies, conducting securities analysis, constructing investment portfolios, revising investment portfolios, and evaluating investment performance. Based on the investment knowledge in the academic field and the understanding of different cognitive biases, this paper uses the connections between digital transformation and investors' psychological expectations, starting from the theories of behavioral finance, and combining the characteristics of the era of "digitalization of globe, digitalization of all people, and digitalization of everything" to answer the following question: Under the premise that investors are known to have irrational behaviors, what kind of psychological biases are affecting each investment step of individual investors? How do different behavioral finance theories explain the irrational characters of each investment step? In the current era of digital transformation, does the innovative transformation and creative expansion of big data, artificial intelligence, financial technology and other information affect the different investment steps of individual investors? How should individual investors conduct rational investment planning in the digital age?

2 Literature Review

2.1 Digital Development and Dissemination

In the current situation where the world is gradually shifting from "manufacturing" to "creating", various industries, enterprises, and departments of enterprises are gradually transforming from tangible materialization to visible digitalization.

The digital economy is the foundation and premise of digitalization. Li believes that one of the most important goals of the current world is to promote the digital economy to go out, so that its emerging peak innovation capabilities can be quantified and developed to the greatest extent in different segments [8], while Qi emphasized that enterprises should vigorously develop and transform under the leadership of the digital economy, and build an organizational structure that is precise, modular, and maximized efficiency [9].

In terms of the digital transformation of enterprises, Wu first proposed that digital mergers and acquisitions is an important way for enterprises to rapidly increase the degree of digital transformation, which can significantly promote enterprise innovation [10]; Legner et al. believed that one of the important tasks of enterprise digital transformation is to understand IT, adapt to IT, and use IT [11]; Hu et al. analyzed in detail the intermediary and regulatory effects of corporate digitalization on corporate performance, and established a mature and stereotyped corporate digital transformation framework policy [12].

2.2 Research on Individual Investor Behavior Deviation

Research on Irrational Behavior of Individual Investors. In traditional financial theory, scholars often conduct analysis on the basis of "investors are completely rational", but the complete rationality of investors only exists in assumptions. Simon proposed in the literature that the rationality contained in people's behavior is limited and is constrained by the behavioral environment, and then put forward the related theory of bounded rationality [13]; Hasan et al. proposed that due to the market that is not completely transparent, the ambiguity brings greater information needs to individual investors, which makes irrational behaviors more likely to occur [14]; Fang pointed out that the psychological states of individual investors in the investment process will be greatly increased and they are partially reflected in the irrational behaviors of investors' investment activities. Because individual investors generally lack mature consumption investment concepts, it is difficult to grasp the correct investment goals and investment opportunities [15]; Feng analyzed investment through questionnaires to point out how factors such as age, gender, and individual work experience of investors promote or restrict investors' irrational behaviors [16].

Research on Behavioral Finance Theory. Simon proposed and defined bounded rationality for the first time in the literature, overturning the CAPM model's assumption of complete rationality for investors [13]; Larwood proposed that with the increase of corporate managers' knowledge and the expansion of information, it is easy to overestimate one's own knowledge and acuity, forming the embryonic form of overconfidence [17]; Kahneman first proposed representativeness bias, calling on investors to pay attention to the essence of things so as to avoid being confined to a certain representative feature[18]; Lin proposed that the herd effect will lead to irrational behavior among investors and strengthen related links, and the following effect of many individual investors on a certain irrational behavior is very likely to lead to market bubbles or even collapse [19]; Finally, Wang explored the causes of corporate M&A premium phenomenon—in order to avoid the failure of M&A, managers often choose to spend a lot of money—to explain the influence of investors' endowment effect and pseudo-endowment effect on investment behavior [20]. Researches on different theories of behavioral finance at home and abroad showed that behavioral finance has gradually occupied the high ground of observing investor behavior and has become an important ideological basis for market research. The existing research field of behavioral finance proposes and applies relevant theories based on the different psychological characteristics of individual investors, but generally discusses investor behavior as a whole. This paper takes a different approach, trying to divide the investor's investment process into steps and find the most prominent influencing factors, so as to more fully explore the interpretation of digitization on individual investor behavior from the perspective of behavioral finance.

3 Behavioral Finance Explanation of the Impact of Digitization on the Behavioral Steps of Individual Investors

3.1 Impact of Behavioral Finance Interpretations on the Process of Making Investment Policies

Based on bounded rationality, worldwide digital transformation permeates all aspects of decision-making when individual investors formulate investment policies. In the traditional efficient market hypothesis, individual investors in the market have the absolutely rational characteristics based on the complete symmetry and transparency of market information, which allows individual investors to make completely reasonable investment decisions. However, factors such as investors' professional skills, personality traits, and experience in the industry have challenged this theory. Formulation of investment policies is the beginning of individual investors' investment behavior, including the choice of investment goals and the determination of the amount of investment wealth. However, investors are often trapped in different information islands, making it difficult to make optimal decisions. Nowadays, the digital transformation is being promoted worldwide, and the previously obscure and incomplete information has been greatly transformed into an easy-to-understand form of expression. The completeness, authenticity and reliability of the information are guaranteed through data presentation and network links, which has broken the limitations of investors to the greatest extent. The digital transformation allows investors to make more rational judgments based on comprehensive information from various sources, and formulate investment policies that are in line with their own financial status, investment goals and financial strength.

Based on overconfidence, various information and materials brought by digital transformation can become a "catalyst" or "sedative" for individual investors' overconfidence, which is determined by investors' own information collecting and understanding capabilities. Overconfidence generally exists in the psychological expectations of individual investors, and is more or less reflected in their investment activities according to the characteristics of investors such as age, gender, education and work experience. Due to the internal and external expressions of overconfidence, investors will inevitably have the "complacency" and the "fluke mentality" when formulating investment policies, which may make its investment policies subjective and one-sided. The digital transformation of the big era affects investors' overconfidence and the formulation of investment policies in both positive and negative aspects. Digital transformation has a strong amplification effect on information and the ability to filter and push relevant information according to investors' psychological preferences, which allows investors to immerse themselves in the ocean of information they prefer for a long time, greatly enhancing their confidence, and it is difficult to make objective and calm investment choices; big data can also enable investors to obtain more comprehensive information and experience resources when looking for information, and realize the shortcomings and limitations of their own investment policies based on previous investment experience and lessons. Risks should be considered in the selection of the final investment target and the decision on the amount of investment.

3.2 Impact of Behavioral Financial Interpretations on the Process of Conducting Security Analysis

Based on representativeness bias, the massive information brought by the digital age can enable investors to more comprehensively understand and analyze individual securities or securities groups in financial assets. Psychological theory believes that human's attention is a limited resource, and it is difficult to be equally distributed to all aspects of things. In the process of securities analysis, investors often pay too much attention to a certain representative aspect of securities, forming overly subjective or even wrong rules when analyzing historical data and information, which in turn leads to misjudgment of future trends. Digital transformation has broadened the sources of information for investors, allowing them not only to obtain financial information on securities, but also to understand relevant industry trends and leading macroeconomic conditions, enabling investors to increase their understanding of all aspects of securities when conducting securities analysis. For example, the rise in a company's stock price in recent years may not entirely represent its excellent business capabilities, but may also be due to the guidance of national policies and the growth of related industries. These comprehensive considerations will increase the feasibility and reliability of investors' securities analysis.

Based on the herd effect, digital transformation has aggravated the "blind obedience" psychology of individual investors, and also increased the possibility of securities prices deviating from their intrinsic value. One of the most important purposes of security analysis is to determine whether a certain security deviates from its intrinsic value, and the root of the deviation from the intrinsic value lies in the expectations of most investors in the market on the security. Digital transformation has expanded the influence of the "leaders" in the herd effect, inciting through information, and made most investors in the market who lack investment professionalism and investment ideas expect to move closer to a few "leaders" and respond to securities market trends. For individual investors who generally lack professional knowledge and investment experience, this abnormal and unhealthy price trend may create obstacles to their security analysis process.

3.3 Impact of Behavioral Finance Interpretations on the Portfolio Construction Process

As one of the most important theories of behavioral finance, herding effect and its characteristics mainly play a role in the selection of investment securities by individual investors and the construction of investment portfolios. The construction of investment portfolio mainly includes the selection of investment securities and the grasp of investment opportunities, and these two aspects are extremely susceptible to the influence and restriction of various factors. To choose the correct and suitable securities, investors need to obtain a full understanding of all aspects of the securities. To grasp the right investment opportunity, investors also need to make reasonable predictions about the market trend. For individual investors who lack professional knowledge, these two aspects are costly and risky. Therefore, more individual investors tend to follow others to determine their investment portfolios, and the transformation of the digital age has further deepened the behavioral characteristics of individual investors. In a more idealized capital market, investors don't know much about other people's investment methods, and they have different considerations for different securities' expectations. Long-short games occur frequently, which controls the dynamic balance of the market. However, the massive amount of information brought by digital transformation has brought great impetus to individual investors in the market, making investors more willing to choose the low-cost, convenient and quick "following" investment method, which has aggravated their "all gain or all loss" The gambler's mentality of gaining or losing money is not conducive to investors' objective and independent construction of investment portfolios.

Take the "GameStop" incident in the US stock market that has caused heated discussions as an example. In order to compete with investment institutions, a group of retail investors gathered in the USB forum, led by financial analysts and the first batch of retail investors who bought GameStop stocks, almost frantically longed for the stocks of GameStop and caused the US stock market to break 17 times. In the end, the regulatory agencies forcibly intervened to maintain the stability of the market. What is the impetus behind this madness? The role of herding effect cannot be ignored. For the retail investors in USB, the big data network communication platform promoted the statement that "GameStop's stock price continued to rise, and institutions lost to retail investors" praised them. All the declarations made them ecstatic, and made them follow the footsteps of the "leader" without hesitation to drive up the stock price of GameStop. However, if they calm down, they will find that under the constant long-short game, the stock price of GameStop has greatly deviated from the actual value, and the fall of stock price is irreversible. Regrettably, at the moment when digital information strengthens the herd effect, they have lost the ability to independently and calmly choose their own investment portfolios, and finally ended dismal when the stock price fell back to $51.09.

3.4 Impact of Behavioral Finance Interpretations on the Portfolio Modification Process

Based on the endowment effect, digital transformation can increase the determination and efficiency of investors to revise their portfolios. In psychological theory, the endowment effect is often expressed as people's high attention and optimistic evaluation of what they have, which can also be expressed as aversion to the unknown and complacency in the investment process. The existence of the endowment effect makes investors unwilling to make timely corrections when facing a decline in the income of holding securities, and investors are more inclined to continue to hold stocks, looking forward to the day when the stock price rises again, which may result in a decline in the overall return of individual investors' portfolios. The information and materials brought by digital transformation have broadened the investment channels of investors and brought more choices for investors. Investors can make adjustments to their investment portfolios through a variety of better securities evaluated by big data, and reduce the negative impact of the endowment effect on portfolio returns.

3.5 Impact of Behavioral Finance Interpretations on the Process of Assessing Investment Performance

Digital transformation can enable individual investors to make a more comprehensive evaluation of investment performance based on outcome bias. The outcome bias theory holds that a satisfactory outcome does not necessarily mean a satisfactory process. When evaluating investment performance, due to the lack of professional knowledge and relevant information, individual investors are more inclined to compare the performance of the investment portfolio with the benchmark level to judge whether the investment is successful. However, investment performance exceeding the benchmark level does not mean that the investment decision is completely correct; investment performance not reaching the benchmark level does not indicate that there are major problems in this investment decision. The national macroeconomic situation, the bottleneck of industry development and the inevitable risk deviation in the market are all important factors that lead to fluctuations in investment performance. Through the information and resources brought by digital transformation, investors can more comprehensively evaluate the results of this investment, pointing out the advantages and disadvantages of each step in the investment process, and they can better understand the influencing directions and weights of various factors that lead to the investment results to lay a good foundation for the next investment.

4 Conclusion

4.1 Analysis Conclusion

The article concludes: from the perspective of behavioral finance, according to the perspective of different investment steps, the information resources and massive experience brought by digitalization have had an indelible impact on the investment behavior of individual investors in both positive and negative aspects. Among these two, the positive impact is mainly reflected in increasing the degree of rationality in the process of formulating investment policies; obtaining more comprehensive data on corporate characteristics when analyzing securities; making timely investment behaviors of buying or selling related securities in revising the investment portfolio; and evaluating investment performance. At the same time, investors will pay attention to avoiding the judgment bias of "satisfactory result means satisfactory process". The negative impacts focus on overconfidence and complacency when formulating investment policies; the herd effect shortens investment visions and weakens individual investors' independent decision-making abilities when analyzing securities and building securities portfolios. Therefore, facing the digital age that has entered an irreversible trend, investors should fully integrate various information resources, strengthen their ability to collect and digest information, and keep a clear mind at all times to make the most reasonable investment behavior decisions based on their own investment situations. At the same time, various regulatory departments in the financial market must always be alert to the expansion of digitalization on investor irrational behavior, promptly discovering and killing the seedlings of irrational behavior, in order to maintain market order and avoid market failure.

4.2 Research Significance and Prospect

Based on previous scholars' analysis of the overall impact of digitalization on individual investor behavior from different perspectives of behavioral finance, this article subdivides investor behavior into five modules and gradually analyzes the impact of digitalization on its behavior from the perspective of investor psychology, overcoming the weaken that overall research is too arbitrary and general, making up for the lack of research in the academic field on "how digitalization improves or worsens investor behavior in various aspects or steps of the investment process from the perspective of behavioral finance", which is beneficial for future investors to analyze digitalization from various aspects and perspectives, which is of great significance to maintain the stability of the financial market by effectively improving the irrational behavior brought about by the digital economy. However, due to the author's limited time, energy, and ability to obtain information, there is a lack of effective data to quantify investor investment behavior in the article research, which leads to the lack of reliability and persuasiveness comparing with the research articles with relatively detailed data. To improve the deficiencies of the article: obtain first-hand information on the psychological conditions of individual investors through questionnaires; broaden the research perspectives and introduce institutional investors as research controls to enhance intuitiveness and professionalism.

References

1. Wang, D., Liu, C.: Individual sensation changes and meaning resonance in the digital age. Nanjing Soc. Sci. **2022**(03), 118–126 (2022)
2. Zhao, J., Li, J.: The "Digital Revolution" of the global financial market: transaction structure, investment behavior and risk characteristics. Explor. Controversy **2021**(08), 25–36+177 (2021)
3. Wang, Y., Feng, X., Hou, D.: Can enterprise digital transformation improve analysts' forecasting accuracy? – based on the dual perspective of information disclosure and information mining. J. Zhongnan Univ. Econ. Law 1–14 (2023)
4. Meng, J.: A literature review of individual investors' trading behavior research. China Price **346**(02), 78–81 (2018)
5. Wang, M., Sun, X.: Traders bounded rationality, information noise relationship and financial market information efficiency. Oper. Res. Manag. 1–8 (2023)
6. Bender, S., Choi, J., Dyson, D., Robertson, A.: Millionaires speak: what drives their personal investment decisions? J. Financ. Econ. **146**(1), 305–330 (2022)
7. Yan, Y., Xiong, X., Lei, L., et al.: From "looking at leopards in the pipeline" to "building a strategic view": individual investor behavior in the background of big data. Chin. Manag. Sci. 1–12 (2023)
8. Li, X.: New features of digital economy and formation mechanism of new momentum of digital economy. Reform **309**(11), 40–51 (2019)

9. Qi, Y., Xiao, X.: Enterprise management reform in the digital economy era. Manag. World **36**(06), 135–152+250 (2020)
10. Wu, C., Zhang, F.: Digital M&A, digital transformation and enterprise innovation. Mod. Financ. Econ. (J. Tianjin Univ. Financ. Econ.) **2023**(03), 21–38 (2023)
11. Legner, C., Eymann, T., Hess, T., Matt, C., et al.: Digitalization: opportunity and challenge for the business and information systems engineering community. Bus. Inf. Syst. Eng. **59**(4), 301–308 (2017)
12. Hu, Y., Zhuang, Y.: The influencing factors and performance research progress of enterprise digital transformation. J. Kunming Univ. Sci. Technol. (Nat. Sci. Ed.) 1–10 (2023)
13. Simon, H.: On the possibility of accurate public prediction. J. Socio-Econ. **26**(2), 127–132 (1997)
14. Hasan, R., Kumas, A., van der Laan Smith, J.: Market ambiguity and individual investor information demand. J. Contemp. Account. Econ. (1), 126–141 (2018)
15. Fang, Q.: Research on the irrational behavior of individual investors in the securities market. China Market **931**(12), 110+114 (2017)
16. Feng, X.: Research on Individual Investors' Stock Investment Behavior. Southwestern University of Finance and Economics (2019)
17. Kahneman, D., Tversky, A.: On the interpretation of intuitive probability: a reply to Jonathan Cohen. Cognition **7**(4), 409–411 (1979)
18. Larwood, L., Whittaker, W.: Managerial myopia: self-serving biases in organizational planning. J. Appl. Psychol. **62**(2), 194–198 (1977)
19. Lin, J.: Investor Behavior contagion and its enlightenment in the social media era—a case study of game station. Financ. Dev. **11**(8), 74–79 (2021)
20. Wang, X., Jia, Y., Ma, Z.: Avoiding "cooked ducks flying away": CEO family attributes, pseudo-endowment effect and M&A premium. Foreign Econ. Manag. **43**(06), 74–89 (2021)

A Review of ESG Research in China: From the Perspective of Chinese Enterprises

Daoer Wang(✉)

Southwest University of Finance and Economics, Liulin Campus, Wenjiang District, Chengdu, Sichuan Province, China
wdaoer@qq.com

Abstract. With the continuous advancement of China's action plan for peak carbon dioxide emissions and carbon neutral standardization improvement, China's ESG system has also made great progress. ESG research based on the perspective of Chinese enterprises is also gradually enriched. Among them, the research results of the ESG rating system and disclosure mechanism in China are becoming more and more perfect. The important role of ESG in enterprise value, financial performance, and financing costs has been further demonstrated. Research on ESG investment has broad prospects. This paper is a summary of the relevant literature in China. It not only pulls out and summarizes the main research views, but it also analyzes and summarizes the existing research areas so that future academic research can be pointed in the right direction.

Keywords: ESG · Chinese Enterprises · Information Disclosure · Enterprise Value · Investment

1 Introduction

In recent years, the excessive emission of carbon dioxide has led to the enhancement of the greenhouse effect, which has a continuous adverse impact on the global climate. Global carbon dioxide emissions rebounded strongly in 2021, rising 6% from 2020 to 36.3 billion tons, the highest annual level on record. Controlling carbon emissions to slow down global warming and promote the healthy development of human society has once again become an important global issue. China's economy has grown rapidly in the past few decades. In 2021, China's GDP reached 114.40 trillion-yuan, accounting for 18 percent of the global GDP, making it the world's second largest economy. But at the same time, in 2021, China's carbon emissions reached 11.9 billion tons, accounting for 33% of global carbon emissions. This is the world's largest annual carbon emissions of any country. In this context, China's climate action has attracted international attention. Specify the carbon neutral and carbon peak targets for China to achieve in the face of climate change. China's policy development deployment is to reduce energy consumption, reduce carbon emission intensity, control coal consumption scale, and develop clean energy during the period 2021–2030 to achieve the goal of rapid carbon emission reduction in the period 2031–2045. We should focus on renewable energy, replace traditional energy consumption in a large area, and reduce emissions in the secondary industry. From 2046 to 2060, deep decarbonization will be achieved and negative emission technologies such as carbon capture, utilization, and storage will be implemented. The setting of this goal will bring about systemic changes in Chinese society, which are both an opportunity and a challenge to economic growth. Under such conditions, ESG has become the focus of attention of the Chinese government and enterprises based on its positioning as a "quality-enhancing" emerging economy.

ESG is the abbreviation of "Environment, Social, and Corporate Governance." It is a value concept, an investment strategy and an evaluation tool that focuses on environmental, social and corporate governance performance instead of just financial performance. It is an important index used to evaluate the financial value of sustainable development of enterprises. In 2015, the Chinese government issued "the Guidelines on the Classification of Social Responsibility Performance," "the Guidelines on the Compilation of Social Responsibility Reports" and other standard documents, initially establishing the norms for corporate social responsibility reports. In August 2017, the government reviewed and approved "the Guidelines on Accelerating the Construction of a Green Financial System," which explicitly further promotes environmental disclosure by listed companies. In September 2018, the China Securities Regulatory Commission added chapters on stakeholders, environmental protection, and social responsibility to the "Standards on the Governance of Listed Companies," which stipulated that listed companies should disclose environmental information and fulfill social responsibilities such as poverty alleviation and corporate governance information in accordance with laws and regulations and the requirements of relevant departments. With the deepening of China's emphasis on ESG, the overall trend of ESG development continues to go up. According to the China Responsible Investment Forum, as of 2020, China's ESG market size is about 13.71 trillion yuan, a statistical increase of about 22.9% over 2019, among which the scale of green loans accounts for more than 80%. In 2021, the ESG market size will have doubled from that of 2020. The faster building of China's ESG system and the better ESG performance of businesses can not only help society grow in a sustainable way, but they can also lower businesses' financing costs and operational risks and raise their operating income.

Academic research in the ESG field has become increasingly rich with the gradual maturation of the global ESG system and the rapid development of ESG in China. China's national conditions and markets are not exactly the same as those of other countries. With the further deepening of the dual carbon policy, the development of the ESG system in China has also seen new changes. Many scholars also come to many new conclusions in further research. The purpose of this paper is to focus on many existing ESG-related studies in China, organize and integrate China's green and dual carbon policies based on the perspective of Chinese enterprises, and build a relatively complete existing research context of the ESG system. From different ESG research perspectives, a relatively clear existing ESG research framework system will be divided and its views will be elaborated. To sum up the results of a lot of academic research and find the gaps in ESG research in China so that new ideas can be used to help ESG research grow in the future.

The following parts of this paper are as follows: The second part will start from the existing ESG system, sort out the existing research on ESG disclosure policies and ESG evaluation systems, and then sort out the current development situation of ESG in China by comparing it with the international ESG development system and studying ESG performance from unique perspectives such as finance, staff, and green index. The third part is based on the influence of ESG performance on enterprises, from three aspects such as enterprise value, enterprise performance, and enterprise financing cost. The fourth part is the review of the existing research on ESG investment, from the aspects of investor decision-making, stock selection preference, institutional investment strategy, and investment outlook. The fifth part is for the future ESG system construction of some unique views and thinking.

2 Research on ESG Rating System and Information Disclosure Mechanism in China

Many scholars have done relevant research on the development of the ESG system in China and put forward unique views on the improvement of the ESG evaluation system. Based on the background of COVID-19, Sun Na et al. argued that the goal of corporate governance should be changed from "maximizing the interests of shareholders" to "taking into account stakeholders" by discussing the lack of corporate social responsibility. In the process of deepening the market economy, enterprises should actively assume the relevant responsibilities and pay attention to product quality, production safety, and environmental protection. They suggest that companies should be guided to balance profit orientation and social responsibility by reinforcing correct corporate values [1]. Qiu Huan and Li Xia concluded that social, economic, and environmental factors are the basic elements of sustainable development evaluation and enterprise sustainable development index by comparing and analyzing the application of enterprise sustainable development index in China and the world. They believe that the sustainable development evaluation system with Chinese enterprise characteristics should still be based on the reference of the existing indicator systems at home and abroad [2]. Wang Pangjiang and Huang Jianhua used hierarchical analysis, the Delphi method, and the Satty scale method to embed the contribution indicators formed by ESG represented by environmental protection, social responsibility, and corporate governance into the BSC improvement framework through recursive hierarchical construction, judgment matrix construction, standardized treatment of evaluation indicators, and weight calculation. Construct an ESG system based on BSC. They suggested that, under the guidance of the ESG rating system, enterprises should conduct a comprehensive analysis of financial and non-financial indicators; long-term goals and short-term goals; outcome indicators and driving indicators; leading indicators and lagging indicators; and finally make a judgment on the sustainable development of enterprises [3]. Jing Ru Ru proved the important role of ESG data completeness, consistency, and timeliness through multi-dimensional evaluation of multi-period data of a number of A-share listed companies and bond issuers, as well as horizontal and horizontal comparison within the industry. She believes that ESG rating agencies should establish a more comprehensive and systematic ESG data platform and unify the content of ESG information disclosure. At the same time, since listed companies are the source of the ESG rating system, they should gather ESG data in a standard way [4].

The sound development of the ESG information disclosure system has also been the focus of scholars' research. Ma Xianfeng et al. studied the international ESG information disclosure method and found that the current voluntary disclosure system of listed companies in China has the problems of selective disclosure of information that is difficult to verify and concealment of negative information. They stressed the need to establish a mandatory ESG disclosure system for listed companies and recommended that state-owned, large, and highly polluting enterprises take the lead [5]. Ma Xianfeng and Wang Junxian compared the current situation of Chinese and international ESG disclosure and found that although there are differences between the development of the Chinese market and international ESG standards, ESG information disclosure has a good practical basis. They suggested the formulation of standardized ESG information disclosure guidelines for listed companies and selected listed companies, such as Shanghai and Shenzhen 300, as pilots to promote by sector [6]. Zhang Yimeng et al. summarized the influence of ESG information disclosure elements on the sustainable development of enterprises and proposed that, influenced by values and market atmosphere, China's ESG disclosure should be adjusted to include special indicators such as "poverty alleviation" and "sharing" and play the macro-control role of the Chinese government. Preferential policies such as tax reduction, green credit, and IPO will be given to enterprises to mobilize their enthusiasm for independent ESG disclosure [7]. Du Yonghong analyzed that there are serious environmental risks in China's listed companies, and it is the trend of The Times to change from voluntary to mandatory information disclosure. He suggested strengthening the ESG audit system, building a reasonable index evaluation system in line with China's national conditions, extensively promoting big data and collaborative audit mechanisms, and enhancing the ability of enterprises to cope with the crisis [8]. The research group of the Beijing Securities Regulatory Bureau reviewed the development process of ESG information disclosure rules in the A-share market and found that the regulatory requirements of the Chinese government have become the main driving force for ESG disclosure of enterprises. Most enterprises still have the problem that the disclosure is in form and the lack of investment demand guidance. They think that ESG information disclosure guidelines should be made available with both mandatory and voluntary requirements. They also want to work with ESG investments to help listed companies learn more about ESG information disclosure and get better at it [9].

At present, China's ESG system construction is still in the exploratory stage. The comparison with international experience and mainstream standards is of great significance to the development of China's ESG system. Li Tianxing analyzed the world's representative sustainable development indicator systems at different scales since the 1990s, from world organizations to different countries to important prefecture-level cities in China, and believed that the research on sustainable development indicator systems had made important contributions to the sustainable development of mankind. He suggested that in the process of promoting the construction of the general index system, more attention should be paid to the unique culture of the vast minority areas in China and the corresponding humanistic management mode for sustainable development [10]. Feng Jialing et al. compared ESG disclosure in the United States, the European Union, and Hong Kong, China, as well as typical ESG information disclosure principles and guidelines, and concluded that China's ESG information disclosure still has significant problems, such as "no standard, no clear guidance, no perfect policy system, and no regulatory service department." They believe that "dual guidance of government and market" should be implemented to build an ESG social service ecological network, strengthen ESG service organizations, and promote the further implementation of ESG. On the basis of reviewing the development history of the ESG system and conducting in-depth research on the development of ESG in the 21st century [11]. Huang Shizhong summarized the representative framework of ESG reports and the outstanding problems existing in them. He believes that ESG and sustainability reporting for Chinese companies will gradually converge with international reporting standards [12]. Wang Kai and Zhang Zhiwei sorted out the situations of 14 famous Chinese and international ESG rating agencies and made a comparative analysis of their ESG evaluation systems. They found that China's existing ESG evaluation system still has core problems such as poor quality of information disclosure, inconsistent rating results, and an imperfect ecosystem. They suggested that Chinese enterprises should strengthen the awareness of ESG among market players, combine it with the overall situation of China's social and economic development, establish and improve third-party institutions, and develop an ESG ecosystem with Chinese characteristics [13]. Chen Ning and Sun Fei, by comparing the Chinese and international ESG development present situation, pointed out that the development of the ESG system at present in China still lags behind foreign countries in many aspects of the environment and the data system research of social awareness and market influence is limited. Because the ESG system also has not reached a consensus in the world and the rating process is still opaque and not separate, this results in a large deviation. They said that to make the ESG system work better, the Chinese government should strengthen the institutional framework, speed up the building of databases, and encourage collaboration between industry and regulatory authorities [14].

Some scholars have also explored the development of China's ESG system from some unique perspectives. Xing Xiaoliu designed the evaluation index of corporate social responsibility from the perspective of employees based on the content of corporate social responsibility for employees and established the evaluation model of corporate social responsibility from the perspective of employees by using the fuzzy comprehensive evaluation method. He suggested that businesses do dynamic vertical and industry-horizontal evaluations of themselves to figure out where their social responsibility practices stand from a scientific point of view [15]. Cao Qun and Xu Qian compared the exploration and practice of the international financial ESG system through case analysis, proposed the connotation of China's financial ESG system, and constructed the corresponding financial ESG index system. They suggested that, on the basis of accurately defining the concept of financial ESG, the Chinese government should improve relevant laws, increase the adoption rate of financial ESG, improve the governance of financial ESG, and related disclosure standards. Based on the experience of international rating agencies, domestic green credit and risk identification practices, and according to China's national conditions and enterprise characteristics [16]. Zhang Hongli et al. combined Industrial and Commercial Bank of China's internal customer data with third-party authoritative data to construct the ESG green evaluation system and form the Green development index and Green investment index. He said that support for green businesses and projects should be increased, that a group of qualified, responsible investors should be cultivated, and that the growth of green and sustainable investment should be guided [17].

3 Research on the Impact of ESG on Chinese Enterprises

With the continuous development of the ESG system, driven by the continuous supervision of the Chinese government, more and more enterprises are embarking on a sustainable development path, improving their environmental performance, shouldering social responsibility, and strengthening corporate governance. However, when ESG is integrated into the corporate system and enterprises are transforming for sustainable development, it is inevitable to pay higher costs. Although the government can impose mandatory constraints on enterprise behavior as a profit-making organization, if the transformation does not bring value growth for the enterprise, the enterprise will lack the power of transformation, and the ESG concept will not be embedded in the operation process of the enterprise for a long time. On the contrary, if better ESG performance can bring about the improvement of market value and the reduction of financing costs, it will become the independent choice of enterprises to increase sustainable development and construction. Because of this, some scholars focus their research on how ESG behavior affects non-financial indicators of businesses. This gives Chinese businesses an internal reason to use ESG behavior.

The influence of ESG behavior on firm value is the focus of many scholars. Wu Mengyun and Zhang Linrong, through the signal transmission theory, higher order theory, and the senior management team embeddedness perspective, will be in the ESG environmental responsibility index (E) as an independent variable. A regression model was established to study the effect of corporate environmental responsibility (CER) on enterprise value. This model is supported by the proxy index of the content analysis method to establish corporate environmental responsibility (CER). At the same time, they considered the influence of top management team characteristics on corporate environmental responsibility, discussed its moderating effect, and found that the implementation of corporate environmental responsibility conveys a signal of good performance and responsibility to society and positively affects corporate value [18]. Yu Xiaohong and Wu Wenjing took A-share listed companies in Shanghai and Shenzhen as research samples, and on the basis of removing incomplete data from financial listed companies and various indicators, Winsorize the variables and control variables of TobinQ and related CSR indicators. They used the RESSET and CSMAR databases to build a fixed-effect model. After Stata12.0 analysis of the data, they found that the implementation of social responsibility (S) in the ESG index has a negative impact on current enterprise value, but long-term enterprise value is significantly positive [19]. Liu Yiguo and Zhu Long found that good corporate governance (G) in the ESG index will make the company have higher financial security in the future, which is conducive to the improvement of the company's profitability, and investors are willing to pay a higher premium [20]. Zhang Lin and Zhao Haitao selected the data of Wind Green A-share listed companies, introduced six control variables, such as company size, asset-liability ratio, and company growth, and adopted the lag method for micro variables, adding the annual dummy variable ydum to estimate the two-way fixed effect model. They investigated the moderating effect of firm heterogeneity on ESG and firm value, and found that ESG performance has a significant positive impact on firm value, especially for non-state-owned enterprises, small enterprises, and enterprises in non-polluting industries [21]. Zhang Fen selected representative indicators of listed companies, established multiple regression and quantile regression models, used statistics to test the data descriptiveness and correlation, and used Q-Q plots to verify their practicability. She was verified through the analysis of empirical testing and robustness ESG three dimensions of social responsibility information disclosure and the relationship between green innovation and enterprise value, and found that environmental information disclosure can significantly improve the low level of enterprise value, and the social aspects of the information disclosure of enterprise value are the stronger the influence on the improvement of enterprise value function [22]. Gu Jiaying, based on sustainable development theory, resource dependence theory, stakeholder theory, and so on, sampled stocks as samples and fixed effects models and found that corporate governance positively promotes the environmental performance and social responsibility of the role of enterprise value, unrestricted selection, non-state or cross-listing class enterprises, The effect of ESG on firm value is more obvious [23].

As for the impact of ESG performance on financial performance, the research finds that there is an interactive intertemporal impact between CSR and financial performance. In the long run, there is an obvious two-way promotion relationship between social responsibility performance and corporate financial performance, with a positive change (Zhang Zhaoguo et al. [24], Yang Huo [25]). Li Gang made use of panel data of stocks in the CSI 300 Index and selected earnings volatility, the number of institutional investors, and inefficient investment as alternative variables of business risk, institutional investor participation, and inefficient investment to empirically test the unilateral impact of ESG performance on financial performance and the mediating channel of the impact. It is found that better ESG performance can improve the financial performance of enterprises. ESG performance will affect its financial performance through the intermediary channels such as business risk and investor participation [26]. Li Yiyuan compared 2,693 listed companies in Shanghai and Shenzhen A-share markets, selected three indicators such as environmental protection expenditure, poverty alleviation expenditure, and the largest shareholder's shareholding as core variables, and used two-way fixed effects and a systematic GMM model to study the influence of ESG behavior on the current and lag periods of different aspects of enterprise growth. He found that for listed companies with ESG behavior, environmental protection behavior can significantly improve the market, innovation, and financial growth of enterprises, and targeted poverty alleviation behavior can directly promote the growth of enterprises in the current period, but the concentration of equity will have a negative impact on the financial performance of enterprises in the party flag [27]. Li Jinglin et al. took 11,700 data samples of A-share main board listed companies with an asset-liability ratio of over 1 as samples to capture the relevant data for financial index analysis and governance structure index in the GTA database. They used Stata11 and multiple linear to conduct multivariate regression analysis, and found that under different levels of corporate performance and property rights, ESG performance and its three dimensions have different effects on corporate financial performance. ESG performance has a bigger effect on promoting businesses that do poorly, are not owned by the government, and care a lot about the environment [28].

In addition, many studies have found that good ESG performance can help companies reduce financing costs. Qiu Muyuan and Yin Hong selected information from 1762 listed enterprises in the past six years, analyzed and studied financial data in the Wind database and ESG performance data in IPE, and used fixed effects and random effects of static panel and GMM estimation under dynamic panel to respectively build indicators of corporate environment, social responsibility, and corporate governance. In particular, by introducing macro-control variables such as the economic cycle and monetary policy, it is found that enhancing ESG performance can reduce financing costs and increase enterprise valuation. From the perspective of three specific dimensions, environmental factors and corporate governance have a greater impact on corporate financing costs, especially with high quality environmental disclosure performance, which can reduce the adverse impact of negative environmental behaviors on corporate financing [29]. Tong Jia adopted a two-way fixed effect model and a causal stepwise regression test method and found that many listed companies generally have high financing constraints and there are large differences among different enterprises. ESG performance can significantly positively affect firm value, among which financing constraints play an important mediating role. That is, ESG performance can further improve firm value by alleviating financing constraints [30]. Zhao Xueyan used CSI 300 and had 500 companies as the research object. On the basis of the samples, descriptive statistics, correlation analysis, and multiple grouping regression on the basis of the model based on PEG, we compared the cost of equity financing and debt financing of enterprises, finding that enterprises' promotion of ESG performance can improve enterprise debt financing costs. In terms of enterprises with different ownership natures, ESG performance has a greater impact on equity financing costs of non-state-owned enterprises than on debt financing costs of state-owned enterprises. He thinks that the growth of ESG bond financing in China isn't enough right now, and the market's response isn't very good, so we should work to deepen ESG bond financing [31].

4 Research on ESG Investment

With the development of the ESG investment concept being gradually and widely paid attention to, ESG investment has opened a new direction and road for the development of Chinese enterprises. ESG investment is favored by more and more investors. The new generation of investors pays more and more attention to the investment concept of ESG instead of purely pursuing financial performance and investment return. Yin Hong proposed that although there are still some problems in the Chinese market, such as a lack of abundant ESG-themed investment products, poor understanding of ESG investment by investors and inadequate supervision of financial institutions, ESG investment in China has a broad development prospect and relevant policies are being gradually established. ESG investment has become an important tool to promote the high-quality development of the Chinese economy [32]. Positive ESG behavior of enterprises can not only win a good reputation for themselves, improve the value of enterprises, but also facilitate investors' ability to effectively identify risks and opportunities that cannot be identified by traditional standards, and more accurately evaluate the financial return potential of enterprises. In view of this, many scholars focus their research on the field of ESG investment.

The ESG index has a guiding role for investors in choosing investment strategies. Chen Xiaodan selected representative indicators in ESG, combined with the Smart Beta factor, established a stock selection model, and used an analytic hierarchy process (AHP) and fuzzy comprehensive evaluation method to evaluate the ESG performance of A-share listed companies. She used the dynamic clustering method to screen sample stocks and assign weights to them to construct the ESG30 index and establish investment strategies. She found that the application of the ESG investment concept can help market investors choose stocks according to ESG indicators and reduce the risk of uncertainty brought by investment [33]. Wang Chaoqun et al. statistically analyzed the ESG evaluation system and results of the China Bond Valuation Center and nearly 5,000 issuers of public credit bonds in the whole market and found that the issuance of ESG theme bonds such as Chinese green bonds has increased strongly in recent years, which has become a long-term and stable income investment strategy in the field of fixed income investment. The ESG factor has also been deeply applied to portfolio investment and index tracking by investment institutions and has been explored and applied to credit rating [34]. Yan Yiming et al. found that there is a positive correlation between ESG strategy and investment performance. After institutional investors integrate ESG evaluation into investment decisions, they can significantly improve the risk control ability of their investment portfolio, reduce its volatility, and improve their long-term income ability. Through ESG screening and ESG index investments, investors can choose between active and passive investments, and they can trade long-term returns for risk assessment [35].

Investors are also increasingly paying attention to ESG metrics in their decision-making process. Zhou Fangzhao et al. took A-share listed companies in Shanghai and Shenzhen as research samples, divided them into institutional investors' independence and investment behavior characteristics, and found that the overall shareholding ratio of institutional investors in China was low, and the shareholding level of institutional investors differed greatly among listed companies [36]. Compared with non-independent institutional investors and short-term trading institutional investors, independent institutional investors and long-term stable institutional investors have an obvious preference for shareholding, especially for state-owned enterprises. However, investment in companies with better ESG performance will have higher excess returns. In the post-epidemic context, companies with good ESG performance will have greater anti-risk ability, and the cumulative excess returns will be much higher than those with poor ESG performance. The Sharpe ratio and maximum retracement were both higher for the ESG portfolio than for the CSI 800 at all levels. However, in the ESG index, the excess return of the index under the theme of social and corporate governance is higher and the risk is smaller. The secondary and tertiary indexes have outstanding excess return performance. She suggested that investors should pay more attention to the quantitative indicators at the second and third levels of the ESG evaluation system [37]. Zhang Qiaoliang and Sun Ruijuan used an experiment to look at how investors decided to "anchor" on different levels of performance and information disclosure. They found that in a good financial performance with bad ESG performance, under the condition that the independent report users to the company's valuation and user levels are the same, and in a bad situation, financial performance and good ESG performance have a strong anchoring effect on the value judgment of investors [38].

5 The Literature Review

The research on the ESG evaluation system in China is gradually enriching. Various characteristic indexes, evaluation methods, and index settings proposed by scholars have reference significance for the development of ESG. However, there is still a lack of relevant research in some areas. For example, although some scholars have mentioned the construction and improvement of an ESG rating system adapted to China's national conditions, there is still a lack of corresponding literature proposing a complete enterprise ESG rating system with Chinese characteristics. Some ESG index systems put more emphasis on E or S, and some indexes give more weight to G. However, most ESG rating agencies usually combine the scores of the three categories of indicators together to give comprehensive scores. As a result, some enterprises with outstanding contributions in certain fields have mediocre comprehensive ESG scores. Further research is needed to rationally allocate the weight of each indicator in the ESG system. Although scholars have paid attention to the different effects of the ESG evaluation system on enterprises in different industries, little literature mentions the construction of ESG evaluation systems and indicators with industrial characteristics, and this direction needs to be further studied. The existing ESG disclosure reports have various disclosure methods, but there is still a lack of research on unified disclosure content and standards. Many studies have mentioned speeding up the improvement of ESG laws and regulations, but there is still a lack of research on how to construct specific ESG laws. China has made some progress in the certification of ESG disclosure information of enterprises by third parties, but the principles, standards, procedures of inspection and professional third-party data verification methods are still lacking corresponding supplements. At the same time, the indicators of the different dimensions in the ESG evaluation system don't exist on their own, and there aren't many studies on how these three dimensions relate to each other and work together in China. This is something that scholars will need to look into more in the future.

With the in-depth study of ESG data, scholars have found that China's ESG data still has problems such as inaccurate basic data, unclear standards and an insufficient degree of refinement. It is also becoming increasingly important to assess data quality. How to study the data system with wider coverage and a longer time span still needs further study. Some scholars have mentioned the construction of ESG data similar to financial indicators, but there is still a lack of demonstration on how to collect ESG data statistics with integrity, accuracy, and timeliness and build a complete ESG database. Many scholars are also conducting research on ESG data collation methods, but it is rarely mentioned how to make ESG original data structured and high-frequency to improve the timeliness and accuracy of evaluation. At present, some ESG data evaluation results are far from the information demand frequency of the securities and financial industries. It merits further investigation. Some scholars suggest that ESG data disclosure can still be based on qualitative description, supplemented by quantitative data display, and the introduction of AI-related intelligent technology. However, issues such as a lack of quantitative indicators, a lack of dynamic data, and a lack of good methods still require more attention.

ESG investment is an important part of the in-depth implementation of the ESG system. Some scholars have studied the current ESG investment strategies and structures in China, but there is still a lack of research on the combination of investment strategies such as mixed class, negative screening, and positive screening. How to strengthen the construction of S and G as the focus of funds and themes still needs to be in-depth. At the same time, most of the investment entities and indexes studied by scholars have adopted the internationally accepted ESG hybrid indicators, and there is still a lack of research on improving the relatively single ESG investment style in China by applying them to the theme of China's national strategic development direction and characteristic indicators. Many studies have proposed the importance of the ESG investment concept, but there are few studies on how to effectively guide investors and institutional investors to establish common and in-depth ESG investment habits and strengthen the market orientation of ESG. How to improve the effectiveness of verification indicators and data products, reduce the dependence on financial indicators in the formulation of evaluation methods, and build an independent investment system can also become the field of future research.

References

1. Sun, N., Hao, R., Wang, B.: Reflections on corporate governance and corporate social responsibility in the context of the epidemic. Financ. Manag. Stud. (12), 103–106 (2020)
2. Qiu, H., Li, X.: A review of theories and methods of enterprise sustainable development index evaluation. Petrol. Petrochemical Today **25**(06), 39–43 (2017)
3. Wang, B., Huang, J.: Construction of enterprise sustainable development evaluation system – based on environmental, social and governance factors. Financ. Manag. Stud. (09), 109–118 (2020). https://doi.org/10.19641/j.cnki.42-1290/f.2020.09.020
4. Jing, R.: ESG Data Quality Assessment and Its Application. Shandong University (2021). https://doi.org/10.27272/d.cnki.gshdu.2021.001079
5. Ma, X., Wang, J., Qin, E.: ESG information disclosure system of listed companies. China's Financ. (16), 33–34 (2016)
6. Ma, X., Wang, J.: Consideration on ESG information disclosure system of listed companies. China's Financ. (20), 69–70 (2021)
7. Zhang, Y., Xu, G., Zhang, J., Zhuo, Y.: Review and prospect of ESG information disclosure research. Manag. Technol. Small Medium-Sized Enterprises (Mid-Month Issue), (12), 121–124 (2021)
8. Du, Y.: Research on ESG audit under the constraint of carbon neutral carbon peak target. J. Harbin Inst. Technol. (Soc. Sci. Ed.) **24**(02), 154–160 (2022). https://doi.org/10.16822/j.cnki.hitskb.2022.02.019
9. Research Group of Beijing Securities Regulatory Bureau. Research on Environmental, Social responsibility and Corporate Governance (ESG) information disclosure of listed companies. Financ. Account. (11), 25–28 (2021)
10. Li, T.: Research progress of sustainable development index system at home and abroad. Ecol. Environ. Sci. **22**(06), 1085–1092 (2013). https://doi.org/10.16258/j.cnki.1674-5906.2013.06.019

11. Feng, J., Li, H., Sun, Z.: Comparison of ESG information disclosure standards at home and abroad and its enlightenment to China. Contemp. Mag. (03), 57–64 (2020)
12. Huang, S.: ESG philosophy and corporate reporting reconfiguration. Account. Issue (17), 3–10 (2021). https://doi.org/10.19641/j.cnki.42-1290/f.2021.17.001
13. Wang, K., Zhang, Z.: Current situation, comparison and prospect of ESG rating at home and abroad. Account. Issue (02), 137–143 (2022). https://doi.org/10.19641/j.cnki.42-1290/f.2022.02.019
14. Chen, N., Sun, F.: Comparison of ESG system development at home and abroad and suggestion on the construction of ESG system in China. Dev. Res. (03), 59–64 (2019)
15. Xing, X.: Research on the evaluation system of corporate social responsibility from the perspective of employees. Technol. Innov. Manag. 34(06), 573–576 (2013). https://doi.org/10.14090/j.cnki.jscx.2013.06.017
16. Cao, Q., Xu, Q.: Research on the construction of financial 'Environmental, Social and Governance' (ESG) system. Res. Financ. Regul. (04), 95–111 (2019). https://doi.org/10.13490/j.cnki.frr.2019.04.007
17. Industrial and Commercial Bank of China Green Finance Research Group, et al.: ESG green rating and green index research. Financ. Forum 22(09), 3–14 (2017). https://doi.org/10.16529/j.cnki.11-4613/f.2017.09.002
18. Wu, M., Zhang, L.: Research on the characteristics of executive team, environmental responsibility and enterprise value. East China Econ. Manag. 32(02), 122–129 (2018). https://doi.org/10.19629/j.cnki.34-1014/f.170604011
19. Yu, X., Wu, W.: Corporate governance, social responsibility and enterprise value. Contemp. Econ. Res. (05), 74–78 (2014)
20. Liu, Y., Zhu, L.: An empirical study on corporate governance and firm value. Manag. Rev. 23(02), 45–52 (2011). https://doi.org/10.14120/j.cnki.cn11-5057/f.2011.02.006
21. Zhang, L., Zhao, H.: Does corporate Environmental, Social and Corporate Governance (ESG) Performance affect corporate value? – an empirical study based on A-share listed companies. Wuhan Financ. (10), 36–43 (2019)
22. Zhang, F.: ESG information disclosure, Green Innovation and Enterprise value. Shandong Normal University (2021). https://doi.org/10.27280/d.cnki.gsdsu.2021.000082
23. Gu, J.: The impact of environmental, Social responsibility and Corporate Governance (ESG) on corporate value. Academy of International Trade and Economic Cooperation, Ministry of Commerce (2022). https://doi.org/10.27054/d.cnki.ggjms.2022.000106
24. Zhang, Z., Jin, X., Li, G.: An empirical study on the intertemporal interaction between corporate social responsibility and financial performance. Account. Res. (08), 32–39+96 (2013)
25. Huo, Y.: Research on the correlation between corporate governance, social responsibility and financial performance. Beijing Jiaotong University (2016)
26. Li, G.: Corporate ESG Performance and Financial performance. Southwestern University of Finance and Economics (2020). https://doi.org/10.27412/d.cnki.gxncu.2020.002059
27. Li, Y.: Research on the influence of ESG behavior on enterprise growth. Harbin Institute of Technology (2021). https://doi.org/10.27061/d.cnki.ghgdu.2021.003184
28. Li, J., Yang, Z., Chen, J., Cui, W.: Research on the mechanism of ESG promoting enterprise performance – based on the perspective of enterprise innovation. Sci. Manag. Sci. Technol. 42(09), 71–89 (2021)
29. Qiu, M., Yin, H.: ESG performance and financing cost of enterprises in the context of ecological civilization construction. Quant. Tech. Econ. 36(03), 108–123 (2019). https://doi.org/10.13653/j.cnki.jqte.2019.03.007
30. Tong, J.: ESG performance, financing constraints and firm value analysis. Happening (29), 89–91 (2021)

31. Zhao, X.: The impact of corporate ESG performance on its financing cost. Beijing Foreign Studies University (2021). https://doi.org/10.26962/d.cnki.gbjwu.2021.000383
32. Yin, H.: China's ESG investment prospects are promising. Financial Expo (01), 44–45 (2021)
33. Chen, X.: Research on index investment Strategy based on ESG Evaluation System. South China University of Technology (2020). https://doi.org/10.27151/d.cnki.ghnlu.2020.001578
34. Wang, C., Zhang, C., Cao, J.: Research on the application of ESG in fixed income investment. Financ. Aspect (11), 27–33 (2020)
35. Research Group on Business Environment and Strategy of Financial investment Institutions, Yan, Y., Su, J., Yan, Z., Tian, X.: ESG investment concept and application prospect. China Econ. Rep. (01), 68–76 (2020)
36. Zhou, F., Pan, W., Fu, H.: ESG responsibility performance of listed companies and institutional investors' shareholding preference: empirical evidence from Chinese A-share listed companies. Sci. Decis.-Mak. (11), 15–41 (2020)
37. Huang, L.: ESG investing - what works for investors. Shandong University (2021). https://doi.org/10.27272/d.cnki.gshdu.2021.000839
38. Zhang, Q., Sun, R.: ESG information disclosure model and anchoring effect in investors' decision making. Account. Commun. (29), 26–28+129 (2015). https://doi.org/10.16144/j.cnki.issn1002-8072.2015.29.009

PIC Planning Model and Geographic Information System Applied on the Old District Renovation Using Intelligent Data Analysis

Junyuan Li[1(✉)], Zihao Ma[2], and Xiyuan Zhang[3]

[1] Hainan University, Haikou, China
junyuan1@asu.edu
[2] Hebei University of Technology, Tianjin, China
[3] Northeast Normal University, Changchun, China
zhangxy528@nenu.edu.cn

Abstract. Nowadays, urbanisation in China has evolved from incremental expansion to stock improvement, and the organic renewal of old cities is one of the key objectives of the new phase of urban transformation and development, where quality is the focus. Residents are the most crucial group to be concerned about in the renovation process of old neighborhoods, along with other important stakeholders such as the government, property companies and social capital. In the renovation process, the residents' power is neglected and their needs are often not met, making it difficult to achieve sustainable development in the renovation of old districts. Taking the Shiwangping neighbourhood in Shijingshan District, Beijing as an example. This study uses a combination of qualitative research and questionnaires to get the case information and analysis it. The old neighborhood renovation problem in terms of participatory, progressive and cooperative are solved by Participatory& Incremental& Collaborative (PIC) model.

Keywords: Older neighbourhoods · PIC planning models · Community governance

1 Introduction

With the development of the city, many neighbourhoods are gradually obsolete, with lack of elderly care facilities, lagging safety management, and no establishment of their own community culture. The quality and even the security of life of the residents are seriously threatened owing to the longtime of completion and the high number of missing public services, which at the same time restricts the development of the city. In order to enhance the quality of residents' life in the neighbourhood and facilitate urban development, the renovation of these regions has become an essential way of urban renewal. On 1 December 2017, Ministry of Housing and Urban-Rural Development of the People's Republic of China proposed to carry out pilot renovation of old communities in some

J. Li, Z. Ma and X. Zhang—These authors contributed equally.

cities, comprehensively carry out actions to build a better environment and a harmonious society together and explore new models for the renovation of old neighbourhoods. On 27 August 2021, Beijing government released the "Beijing Municipal Plan for the Renovation of Old Neighbourhoods", which sets out a new model for the renovation of old neighbourhoods. The Plan sets a new direction for the renovation of old communities in Beijing, and really puts matters into practice to improve people's life quality.

This study is dedicated to the use of the Participatory& Incremental& Collaborative (PIC) model for innovation in the renovation of old neighbourhoods through the investigation of the situation and data analysis of the case neighbourhoods. For example, innovative management models to cultivate the main community forces; to address the follow-up maintenance and orderly management of old neighbourhood renovation to achieve organic development. From the urban area and the continuity of life of the community residents, this paper will explore how the renovation of old neighbourhoods can be a "community cure" in a progressive way with active participation of the residents in the renewal process, and continuously enhance the residents' awareness of community creation.

2 Literature Review

As an important part of urban regeneration, the transformation of old neighborhoods is both a systematic regeneration practice and a comprehensive urban governance exercise. In recent years, the old neighborhoods transformation has become many scholars' focus. Some scholars have conducted studies on the problems of original district renovation, for example, Zhou et al. proposed that there are problems in the renovation of old districts in terms of cultivating the capacity of comprehensive consulting services for enterprises and improving the standard system [1]. Zhou Jinyuan and others found that the transformation of old neighborhoods has problems such as the lack of relevant laws and regulations, the insufficient unified planning and coordination, the relative lag of property reform, and the low level of participation of residents [2]. Yu Xiaoyan studied that the aging of housing buildings and infrastructure in old neighborhoods is serious, and the haphazard construction, dirty and disorderly conditions exist to varying degrees; modern property management services are severely lacking, and the governance pattern of multiple subjects participating in the work of old neighborhoods has not yet been formed; all sectors of society are concerned about the governance of old neighborhoods. This has led to a relative lag in government policy guidance, insufficient financial investment in hardware upgrading and soft environment management, and a relative lack of humanistic care [3]. Song Yang Yang analyzed the problems of old neighborhood renovation and proposed that residents hinder the renovation of old neighborhoods, the government's poor macro-control role, the lack of allocation of relevant social organizations, and the difficulty of financing renovation [4].

By analyzing the existing problems of old neighborhood renovation, some scholars propose governance solutions for those problems. More and more scholars focus on the analysis of community governance and social management aspects of the transformation of old neighborhoods, such as Zhao Chunfei, proposes that the difficulties of residents' participation are as follows: many difficult demands of the transformation of old neighborhoods, the imperfect system of residents' participation mechanism, fund-raising mechanism and the unmature long-term management mechanism [5]. It is proposed that the government should guide the renovation of old districts, emphasize public participation in exploring autonomous co-management, actively launch residents' funding to encourage social capital participation, and improve the property management mechanism to consolidate the renovation results. By analyzing the dilemmas that exist in the practical work of renovation of old districts in China, other scholars put forward suggestions on policy systems, working mechanisms, and operational models. Xu Xuanguo and others scholars found, through reflecting on the experience of the "three communities" in Shenzhen's H community in recent years, that "community" as a key element has reshaped the relationship pattern between the local state and grassroots society, and in practice has facilitated the transformation of the relationship between the state and society from a dichotomy to a dichotomous and symbiotic relationship; the integrated construction of social work in grassroots social governance is indispensable [6]. Fang Yaqin et al. suggest that the current dilemma of "weak participation" in urban community governance provides an integrated and inclusive solution to the problem of community social capital, which is the cultivation of social capital by identifying residents' specific community interaction needs and creating the corresponding structural conditions for them to form a continuous interactive system in the community [7].

Some scholars put forward principles and priorities for the transformation of old neighborhoods, and others based on the perspective of urban planning and management and sustainable development, by analyzing the urban problems brought by largely closed neighborhoods, and concluding that opening up largely closed neighborhoods in urban planning management and sustainable development [8]. Chen Jie et al. summarize the significance of the transformation of old neighborhoods and propose principles for promoting sustainable development to implement the transformation of old neighborhoods [9]. Wang Bo et al. summarize the status of sustainable development research in residential communities, explaining the urgency and necessity of sustainable development research in residential neighbours. Based on existing situation, he puts forward the current point in sustainable development among residential communities, improving the spatial environmental quality of residential communities, maintaining ecological balance, and facilitating the natural energy and conservation [10]. On the basis of sustainable community development, the definition of sustainable development in residential communities is also proposed.

3 Method

3.1 Background of the Case Study

In this paper the case selected is Shiwanping Community, Shijingshan District, Beijing. As early as 2008, the property in the community released the news of the upcoming demolition of the district to residents and attracting some of the demolition investment, while more than ten years later, no news of the demolition but the renovation followed. At the end of October 2020, the old city building in the former city community of Shiwanping Street was officially launched to improve the original district. The top-to-bottom renovation costs were funded by the government, and the upgrade changed the problems of ageing buildings, dilapidated appearance, congested roads and inadequate public services, as well as renewing the new drainage pipes to solve the drainage problems that had plagued the residents for years, and insulating the staircases of all the units, Although the hardware has been completely upgraded, the human dimension is still lacking. In this case, the participatory development component of the PIC model was particularly inadequate, failing to take into account the aspirations and needs of the residents of the old neighbourhood, and there was little contribution from the grassroots. There is a lack of participation by residents of the neighbourhoods. In terms of the progressive development component, there is a lack of monitoring of the neighbourhood improvement process, a lack of flexibility in identifying problems and responding to them accordingly. In the collaborative development component, there is a lack of communication between the various sectors, and the renovation process is inefficient in terms of cooperation and unsatisfactory results.

More specifically, there are many elderly people, disadvantaged groups, low in calibre residents and their personal interests are paramount, so it occurs frequently, like piling up, throwing and dumping, illegal occupation the public space and then planting vegetables. At the same time, there are some problems with the living habits of the elderly and vulnerable groups in particular. Tricky issues with the disposal of personal belongings and rubbish are more prominent, over time, have led to the formation of disorderly piles and disposals.

The housing development in community emphasis on construction and light management, which led to a disconnect between construction and management, developers became lax.

The property management of the district is extensive and difficult to achieve full coverage. At present, the task of property work in the Shiwanping Community is arduous, and there is a serious shortage of staff. Although property have clarified the leaders in charge and set up corresponding institutions to take charge of property management and supervision, they lack full-time staff and office funding, and some of them are only formal and do not play a substantive role. There is the problem of low fees and insufficient management costs. The current property charge for a Shiwanping Community is 0.50 RMB per square meter per month, a rate that makes it difficult to invest in services and hardware in Beijing.

3.2 Questionnaire Survey

The questionnaire survey was mainly targeted at the permanent residents of the Shiwanping community, and the age of those surveyed was between 20 and 70 years old. There are mainly company employees, retirees, laid-off workers, returnees and leaseholders. In the questionnaire, the questions can be divided into several groups. Respondents submitted their basic information (gender, age, education level) at first. Then it goes to their current identification and occupation in the community and the ownership of their house. After that respondents are required to answer questions about their understanding and satisfaction with community service as well as the desire to deal the community work. We also investigate the method that the residents use to receive and feedback the community issues. For the community staffs, they are asked to express whether they confirm the selection process or not and some of them give their suggestions about the future improvement of the community service in the final part.

3.3 The PIC Planning Model

Timothy and Tosun propose a three-part framework for systematic and sustainable planning in tourism destinations, namely the PIC planning model as shown in Fig. 1 [11–13]. They suggest that this approach is applicable to heritage sites as the need for the involvement of members of the community, the preservation of resident sites and a collaborative approach to destination.

The model is equally applicable to the study of the transformation of old neighborhoods, to achieve continuity of life in old neighborhoods, to promote the healing of old neighborhoods through the active participation of residents, and to nurture and reinforce the strength of the main body of old neighborhood.

The theoretical connotations of PIC modeling are described as following:

Participatory core elements: community voice; community control; all stakeholders; economic opportunity; public awareness and education.
Incremental core elements: careful selection of development options; gradual implementation; continuous monitoring and evaluation.
Collaborative core elements: public agencies; administrative levels; private sector services; private and public sectors; same-level politics across political boundaries.

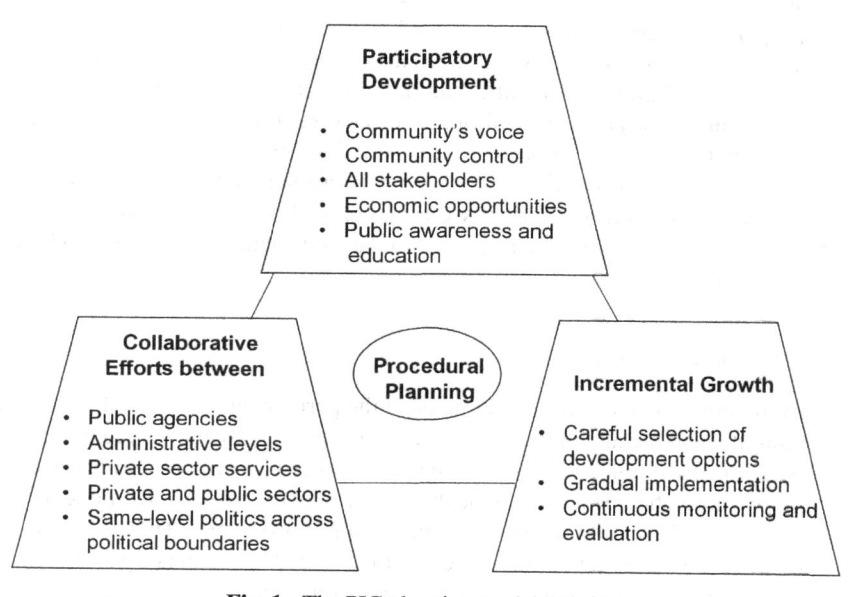

Fig. 1. The PIC planning model [11–13].

4 Result

4.1 Results of Questionnaire Investigation

The survey selected six age groups of residents, namely 20–10 years old, 31–40 years old, 41–50 years old, 51–60 years old, 61–70 years old and 71 years old or above, in which two age groups, 31–40 years old and 61–70 years old, were dominant, with a male to female ratio close to 1:1, in line with the demographic background of the community in this survey. From the analysis of the questionnaire results, more than 70% of the residents could not clarify the functions of the community service centre, and most of them had an optional attitude towards community services and management, and had a lukewarm attitude towards participation in community management services, while 56.1% of the residents did not recognise the community management workers. By combining the questionnaires, we understand that the following problems exist in the existing community service centres. Community workers have limited professionalism, poor work awareness and poor service attitudes. There is no clear unified and complete way for the community to communicate information, and all residents in the community cannot be informed in a timely manner. The absence of a systematic and scientific work protection system leads to inefficient work services. The lack of feedback channels prevents residents from communicating their opinions in a timely manner, with 76.31% of residents choosing to gossip and chat when problems are identified in the community. The range of services is small and narrow, and 60.98% of residents would like to see an increase in the range of services available. In this regard, we could provide vocational training for community service centre staff and set up feedback channels, such as dedicated phones and mailboxes, to monitor community services and staff and collect good advice. We could also standardize and diversify the channels of information and communication, and increase the number of service categories.

In this paper, principal component analysis is used to analyze the results of the 29 representative questionnaires, as shown in Table 1. Principal component analysis is a statistical analysis method that converts multiple variables into a few principal components through dimensionality reduction technology, and these principal components can reflect most of the information of the original variables. Data processing using software, The data were first subjected to KMO and Bartlett's test, the KMO value of $0.876 > 0.7$, close to 1, indicates that our data can be factor analysed; and the Bartlett's spherical test of significance $p = 0.001$ indicates that the variables are highly correlated.

We have numbered the 8 factors to facilitate the presentation of the results that follow.

Table 1. KMO and Bartlett's test.

KMO Number of sampling tangibles		0.876
Bartlett Sphericity Test	Approximate cardinality	38.759
	Degree of freedom	28
	Significance level	0.001

Among the questions in the questionnaires, eight most important ones are deeply analyzed, and these questions can be seen in Table 2.

In Table 3, a starting eigenvalue greater than 1 indicates that the general criteria for a useful factor are met. The cumulative percentage, used to illustrate the contribution of the factors, is higher indicating that the factors explain more of the overall picture. Generally, a cumulative percentage above 70% indicates a more satisfactory score. The principal component analysis extraction method used to analyze four principal components has a total post-rotation loadings contribution of 85.515%.

The scores for each sample on each factor are summarized in Table 4. After processing, the 8 questions with the highest scores and the most significant ones in the above picture are selected. In the following, therefore, we address each of these eight main issues.

Table 2. Eight most important questions in the questionnaires.

Question No.	Composition
7	Do you understand the basic functions of the current CSCs?
8	How satisfied are you with the attitude of the community workers?
9	If your community needs your support or participation in governance
13	You are aware of and have participated in the selection of managers within the community
14	Do you think the way your community selects its officers is reasonable?
15	How satisfied are you with the property management in your community?
16	What do you think of the service attitude of the property management staff?
18	Does your community select managers?

4.2 Existing Problems of Shiwanping Community Released by Data and Background Question

Management Confusion. Complexing living groups and inefficient management lack collaboration. Residents of old neighbourhoods include unit workers, retirees, laid-off workers, relocated households, foreign home buyers and leaseholders. As the previous grassroots managers were mostly from the neighbourhoods in the area, they did not strictly manage the situation for reasons of human kindness, and the upper management ignored the phenomenon and did not communicate with the grassroots managers. It lacked economic attractiveness of the community and operated the ineffective introduction of social capital; the intertwined problems of the community, involving several governmental parts, of which the scope of management is vague, causes the government to neglect the governance of the community management and the guidance of the community residents' body.

Table 3. Explanation of total variance.

	Initial Eigenvalue		
No.	Total	Variance%	Cumulative%
7	1.380	17.244	17.244
8	1.296	16.202	33.446
9	1.155	14.440	47.886
13	1.012	12.651	60.537
14	0.958	11.980	72.516
15	0.775	9.693	82.209
16	0.752	9.395	91.604
18	0.672	8.396	100.000
	Extraction of sum of squares of loads		
No.	Total	Variance%	Cumulative%
7	1.380	25.745	25.745
8	1.296	22.746	22.746
9	1.155	19.477	19.477
13	1.012	17.546	17.546
	Sum of squared rotating loads		
No.	Total	Variance%	Cumulative%
7	1.289	25.698	25.608
8	1.208	22.517	48.126
9	1.180	19.601	67.727
13	1.165	17.788	85.515

Extraction method: Principal component analysis

Insufficient Participatory Development. The management of the district was under marketization through the formation of an industry committee, which gradually led to the loss of management in the district. However, due to the complex composition of the main body of the old district, the poor enthusiasm for participation and the cumbersome process of organization, the number of industrial committees formed is now small, difficult to run and immature in development. The enthusiasm of the masses to participate is quite low, and the current weak sense of management ownership inhabiting the old district instead a great resistance to the transformation and management of the original district; at the same time, the community's consciousness of the residents' body is so slight that it is hard to guide their behavior.

Property Management: Lack of Progressive. There is also the problem that some property managers do not regulate their own behaviour. Some property companies have

Table 4. Explanation of total variance.

	Composition			
	1	2	3	4
7	0.932	0.15	0.018	0.279
8	0.862	0.389	0.132	0.088
9	0.809	−0.133	−0.043	0.425
13	0.794	0.366	−0.146	−0.138
14	0.497	0.812	0.062	0.05
15	−0.016	−0.725	0.619	−0.024
16	−0.005	−0.1	0.974	−0.028
18	0.187	0.049	−0.03	0.95

Extraction method: Principal component analysis
Rotation method: Kaiser normalised maximum variance method

not set up the correct business concept, and only pay attention to fees but not to services, failing to provide services to owners in accordance with property contract requirements, service standards and service levels. Poor communication with property owners under various circumstances led to a weak trust between owners and properties. The property owners do not fulfil their intelligence and there is a serious lack of public participation in the management process. The management plans for the community are not scientifically planned and are not subsequently monitored and implemented to collect suggestions from the residents and make adjustments to the management.

4.3 The PIC Model in Dealing with Renovation of Aged Neighbourhoods

Collaborative development aspects, up and down collaboration to ensure equity and efficiency. The implementation of integrated property management, under the premise of safeguarding the collective interests of property owners, focuses on social benefits and organically combines economic and environmental benefits to promote community management in many aspects. Establish a combination of public and private, top-down external management system and bottom-up internal management system. A top-down form of line management is adopted to strengthen the links between the various levels, improve efficiency and meet practical needs. A bottom-up internal management mechanism to keep abreast of the needs of the residents' body and respond to their concerns. The government and residents discuss the transformation decisions, share the transformation risks and share the results in the transformation of the district, so as to achieve the overall development goals of the old city transformation in a collaborative development approach. The residents, an important participant in the transformation, be given full consideration after the completion of the hardware aspects of the 100,000 sq. ft. district and should be people-oriented. Residents' committees should be set up in the district to manage the renovation affairs and put forward renovation opinions, and to give them the opportunity to collaborate with the local government in the renovation, so that they can explore their potential and integrate their growth, and ultimately achieve the goal of promoting the overall development of the district through joint renovation by the government and residents. It also introduces social capital to participate in collaborative efforts to improve the main body of old district renovation and further improve the management level and quality of old district renovation. The development reflects a process that emphasises respect for differences, equal consultation and coming from the masses to the masses, i.e. with the assistance of the goverence.

5 Discussion

5.1 Application of PIC Modeling in this Case

Analysis of the applicability of the PIC planning model to the renovation of old neighborhoods as shown in Table 5.

Collaborative development. Effective collaborative retrofitting combines government-led, social public agency participation, social capital construction services, and cooperation between government departments to improve retrofitting efficiency and reduce impediments such as retrofitting systems.

Participatory development. Effective participatory retrofitting combines the core elements of the participatory approach, for responding to the concerns of community members, allowing community residents to increase their sense of ownership, bringing in social capital through community retrofitting, while providing economic benefits such as jobs for community residents, leading to public participation and raising awareness among residents.

Progressive development: flexibility. The monitoring and implementation of renovation projects in older neighbourhoods takes into account the actual situation, bringing up unreasonable renovation points and making timely adjustments to the renovation plan. Increase the community residents as a supervisory group to better realize the vital interests of the residents of the old community.

The PIC planning model is closely related to the renewal of old habitat. The old communities can be treated with a developmental perspective, and the end of any renewal work is not the end of community renewal. It is a people-oriented, participatory, progressive and cooperative approach to the transformation of old neighbourhoods and to the internal development of the city, stimulating the motivation and endogenous impetus of the various interest groups to cultivate the responsibility and obligation of the main forces for the transformation of old neighbourhoods.

5.2 Utilization Possibility of PIC Model on Renovation of Older Nerghborhoods

This study attempts to draw on the existing experience of PIC in the field of tourism by studying the well-established PIC planning model in the field of tourism and applying it to the community management aspects of the renovation of older neighborhoods. It provides a new perspective to understand, analyze and solve the community management problems of old neighborhoods. Based on the PIC planning model, this paper offers suggestions for management in the renovation of the Shiwanping district in Shijingshan

Table 5. PIC model applied in old neigborhoods' renewal management.

Resident	Roles	Collaboration; Participatory; Incremental;
	Actions	Participation in community management; Promote community Information;
	Influences	Inspire residents to take responsibility; Increase motivation and participation in community management; Nurturing the main force;
Developer	Roles	Collaboration; Participatory; Incremental;
	Actions	Investment; Assistance with property management; Bringing in other capital investment;
	Influences	Bringing in capital to improve management and enrich the range of community services;
Property	Roles	Collaboration; Participatory; Incremental;
	Actions	Management Training; Always follow up on resident feedback; Addressing the lives of Residents;
	Influences	Improve management, address issues such as the community environment and provide more humanistic care and other services;
Government	Roles	Collaboration; Participatory; Incremental;
	Actions	Supervision; Master planning; Regulation;
	Influences	Holding the overall direction and regulating the balance of interests of all parties;

District. Through questionnaires, research interviews and other means, more realistic and reliable information about the case is obtained. The analysis of the reality of the Shiwanping district reveals that the management problems that arise in the transformation of the district are complex, involving multiple interests, and the complex backgrounds of the members of the various interest groups, the confusion of property rights, the lack of cultivation of the main forces of the district, the lack of community awareness, and the financial problems. This has led to a series of environmental problems in the community, land use problems such as the arbitrary occupation of public space in the community and the lack of separation between public and private management personnel and therefore the lack of binding and effective management regulations for some community members.

The PIC old district renovation model is proposed to analyze the coordinated management of district residents, property managers, government-assigned district managers and internal district managers from the perspective of the core interest groups of the district management system. The main interest groups will be linked internally to each other to check and supervise each other's functions; the strengths of each body will be brought into play to promote the healing of old districts.

6 Conclusion

In this paper, the renovation of old neighborhoods was analyzed through case studies and propose a theoretical framework for the renovation of PIC old neighborhoods based on the PIC planning model. Due to the current epidemic, national policies and other factors, one case has been selected for research in this article. In the future, more cases can be selected to verify the applicability of the PIC model in community management, and the PIC old neighbourhood renovation model can be applied to more cases for promotion. However, this is a new attempt to apply the PIC theory in the field of tourism to the community management aspect. The results proves that the PIC planning model is important for the study of old community renovation problems, and its applicability needs to be further analyzed and explored through empirical evidence in China.

References

1. Zhou, G., Zhang, J., Zhang, C.: A discussion on the characteristics of old neighborhood transformation and the opportunities and problems it brings. Chongqing Architect. **20**(03), 33–35 (2021)
2. Zhou, J.: Research on community governance in the context of transformation of old neighborhoods. Huazhong Normal University (2018)
3. Yu, X., Zhang, Y., Zhao, Y.: An empirical study on the problems and countermeasures of comprehensive governance in urban old neighborhoods. J. Chang'an Univ. (Soc. Sci. Ed.) **22**(03), 68–77 (2020)
4. Song, Y.Y.: Research on the transformation of urban old neighborhoods and its path. J. North China Univ. Technol. (Soc. Sci. Ed.) **21**(06), 44–47 (2021)
5. National Development and Reform Commission, Social Survey Group, Zhao, C.: Promoting the transformation of old neighborhoods with "public participation. China Econ. Trade J. (18), 32–35 (2021)
6. Xu, X., Xu, Y.: The "three communities linkage" in grassroots social governance: connotation, mechanism and its practical logic: an exploration based on Shenzhen H community. Soc. Sci. (07), 87–96 (2016)
7. Fang, Y., Xia, J.: Social capital cultivation in community governance. China Soc. Sci. (07), 64–84 & 205–206 (2019)
8. Zhang, Y., Wang, R.: A study on the necessity of opening up large gated communities - based on the perspective of urban planning management and sustainable development. Value Eng. **38**(19), 16–18 (2019)
9. Chen, J.: Promoting sustainable development of urban renewal and old neighborhood transformation. China Real Estate (22), 62–64 (2021)
10. Wang, B., Rao, J.: Overview of research on sustainable development of residential communities in China. Sichuan Build. Sci. Res. (02), 74–76 (2001)
11. Porterfield, G.A., Hall, K.B.: A Concise Handbook of Community Planning. Xiaojun, Z., Fang, P. (translation). China Construction Industry Press, Beijing (2003)
12. Tosun, C., Timothy, D.J.: Arguments for community participation in the tourism development process. J. Tourism Stud. **14**(2), 2–15 (2003)
13. Tosun, C., Timothy, D.J., Öztürk, Y.: Tourism growth, national development and regional inequality in Turkey. J. Sustain. Tourism **11**(2–3), 133–161 (2003)

Agriculture Trade Competitiveness, and Influencing Economic Factors: A Study on China's Agricultural Trade

Benjamin Kofi Tawiah Edjah[✉]

Economics and Management School, Wuhan University, Wuhan 430072, China
benjaminedjah6@163.com

Abstract. This study examined the agricultural competitiveness of China with Ghana and Myanmar and economic influencing factors in relations to China's agricultural competitiveness with Ghana and Myanmar. RCA and RSCA indexes were employed to measure the trend of China's Competitiveness using twenty-two representative agricultural products. The study further uses four economic export determinant factors to study the influencing factors of agricultural export trade competitiveness of China with Myanmar and Ghana from 2011 to 2020 period. Using the Panel data analysis, the random effect regression model was employed to measure the influencing factors. The determinant studied were FDI, GDP, real exchange rate, and inflation. The result of the study shows that, (1) From the trend of competitiveness, China has strong agriculture competitiveness with Ghana and Myanmar, but has stronger competitiveness with Myanmar than with Ghana (2) and due to China's win-win cooperation with Myanmar and Ghana through "the Belt and Road Initiative" (BRI) and the Sino-Africa relations respectively, the GDP, and real exchange rate of Ghana and Myanmar have a positive and significant impact on China's agriculture competitiveness. The result of the study indicate that competitiveness is revealed in economic growth and the share of agriculture in included to this growth.

Keywords: Agriculture Trade · Competitiveness · Economic Growth · Economic Factors

1 Introduction

The competitiveness of agricultural trade has recently drawn significant attention. Particularly with China and other countries. In light of China's rapid economic expansion and rising economic influence on the world economy. The competitiveness of China's agricultural exports [1] are empirically examined in this article. The purpose of this article is to provide an understanding of the competitiveness of Chinese agricultural products in the market for developing nations through the analysis of a number of economic determinants, including exchange rates, FDI, GDP, and inflation, using Myanmar and Ghana by employing the panel data regression method.

A country's export is a measure of its competitiveness, and the ability of the nation's agricultural products to continue to turn a profit on the global market. Also the competitive advantage of expanding international trade, particularly agricultural export trade, is referred to lead to the competitiveness of the agricultural products trade.

The worldwide market has now become a vital support for guaranteeing the effective supply of agricultural products in China [2]. Several scholars indicated that competitiveness of China's agriculture sector is primarily driven by core factors such as the availability of agricultural resources, the adoption of modern agricultural technologies, access to reliable infrastructure, and an efficient supply chain for the main crop as well as livestock [3]. Findings from several scholars reveal considerable disparities in agricultural product trade competitiveness between China and the areas and countries along the Belt and Road route, [2, 4]. In Asia, Myanmar is China's long-lusting diplomatic trade partner since 1954, and agricultural trade has become a significant component of the two countries economic relations. In recent years, Chinese businesses have invested heavily in agriculture-related projects in Myanmar, such as tea plantations, and fruit production [5]. The Chinese government also boosts bilateral Agricultural Cooperation through various initiatives including agricultural research and development, import and export facilitation. Furthermore, several China-Myanmar agriculture cooperation have established to promote food security through joint investments in agricultural infrastructure.

China and Ghana on the other hand have also increased their agricultural trade cooperation significantly in recent years [6]. Chinese investment in Africa's agricultural sector has helped develop rural infrastructure, facilitate technology transfer, and boost production efficiency [7] particularly with Ghana. China is also helping to promote mechanization in Ghana's farming sector by way of providing materials and equipment along with offering agricultural technical assistance and Educational support. As a result of this collaboration between the two nations, there has been positive impact in terms of food security, and agricultural sustainability. China's trade and cooperation pattern has shown a successful win-win cooperation for both countries.

This paper measures China's competitiveness of the agricultural products trade with Ghana and Myanmar based on current Agricultural trade cooperation and further uses the panel data analysis to study the economic factors of Ghana and Myanmar affecting the competitiveness of agricultural product trade of China with them.

2 Method and Materials

2.1 Method and Materials of Agriculture Competitiveness

To get the overview trend of the agriculture competitiveness of China with its trading partners Ghana and Myanmar, the research used the RCA index and RSCA as a method to measure China's agriculture competitiveness.

The revealed comparative advantage (RCA) is an index commonly used in international economics to calculate a country's relative advantage or disadvantage in a specific country class of goods [8]. The significant aspect of the RCA index is how it demonstrates the extent of agricultural competitiveness by analysing the trade performance of agricultural products. Mathematically the RCA model is represented as:

$$RCA = \frac{X_{ij}^k / X_{ij}^t}{X_{iw}^k / X_{iw}^t} \quad (1)$$

Here, X_{ij}^k represents the trade volume of product k exported from country i to country j, and X_{ij}^t represents the total export volume from country i to country j. X_{iw}^k represents the export volume of product k from country i to the world, and X_{iw}^t represents the total export volume from country i to the world. If RCA > 1, it indicates that the export of product k from country i to country j has a strong competitiveness, and vice versa.

The Revealed Symmetric Comparative Advantage (RSCA) is a tool used to measure the relative efficiency of agriculture production between two countries in a bilateral trade setting. This index will help us gain insight into the agriculture trade patterns of China with Ghana and Myanmar and to evaluate the potential for trade cooperation. The RSCA is mathematically represented as:

$$RSCA = \frac{RCA - 1}{RCA + 1} \quad (2)$$

This index varies from −1 to +1. The closer the value is to +1, the higher the competitiveness of a country in the commodity of interest.

See Table 1 for the selected agriculture product. The agricultural product was selected based on the WTO definition of agricultural product, and data was retrieved from the UN comtrade data base.

2.2 Regression Variable Selection and Data Collection

To measure the influencing factors of China's agricultural competitiveness with Ghana and Myanmar, considering the availability of data the variables studied include inflation, exchange rate, Gross Domestic Product (GDP), and Foreign Direct Investment (FDI). These data were retrieved from the world bank database for Ghana and Myanmar, from 2011 to 2020 as the selected period. For our short-term analyses.

Model Analysis and Variables. Panel analysis regression was employed to assess the suitable model for our study. Panel data analysis takes into account the individual variable heterogeneity that arises from changes over time. This method approach enabled the study to explore the relationship between the predictors and outcome variables within the countries. Panel data analysis is the ideal choice for this particular study, given different countries with different economic variables that change over time were studied. To provide the most representative analysis of the factors influencing China's competitiveness with Ghana and Myanmar, three models regression were evaluated: the Ordinary Least Squares model (OLS), the Fixed Effects (FE) Model, and Random Effects (RE) Model. Again, to select a consistent model, statistical tests such as the F-test, and Hausman's test was used.

Hausman Test and F-Test. To determine whether to use fixed or random effects, the Hausman test was conducted. The size of the Probability greater than the chi-square (Prob

Table 1. Agricultural Product Categorization.

Section of SITC	code	Division of SITC
0 Food and Live Animals	00	Live animals
	01	Meat and meat products
	02	Milk products and birds
	03	Fish and fish products
	04	Cereals
	05	Vegetables and fruits
	06	Sugar, molasses and honey
	07	Coffee, Tea, Cocoa and spices
	08	Feeding stuff for animals
	09	Compound and oleaginous fruits
1 Beverages and Tobacco	11	Beverages
	12	Tobacco and tobacco products
2 Crude Materials inedible, except fuel	21	Hides and skins
	22	Oil seeds and oleaginous fruits
	23	Natural rubber
	24	Cork and wood
	25	Pulp and waste paper
	26	Textile fibre
	29	Crude animal materials
4. Animals and Vegetable Oils. Fat and Waxes	41	Animals oil and Fat
	42	Fixed Vegetable Fats and Oils
	43	Animal or Vegetable oils fats processed

Source: Organized from UN Comtrade Database

> chi2) value through the Hausman test determines which regression is accepted. The criterion of the Hausman test is: when Prob > chi2 is greater than 0.05, the panel random effect model should be selected; and vice versa. Taking RCA, as the dependent variable, the Prob > chi2 results of the Hausman test was 0.9388. Therefore, the random effect should be chosen for the model. The Rho for the RE was equalled to zero, which shows that the estimated result is near OLS estimates. To determine this and find other suitable models, ordinary least square regression was conducted and proven to be significant model with the Prob > F to be 0.0011, which is less than 0.05. F-test was made and shows that all model parameters are zero. Showing that the OLS model is also the best fit and also confirms the RE model is a stable model for the regression. The RE model was selected because the RE allows generalizing the inferences beyond the sample used in the model. And we believe that differences across the selected countries have some

influence on the dependent variable. This confirmed reliability and stability of the our result estimates.

The model used in this study is:

$$RCAit = \beta 0 + \beta * GDPit + \beta * FDIit + \beta * RERit + \beta * INFLATIONit + \alpha + uit + \varepsilon it \tag{3}$$

Dependant and Independent Variables. RCAit, the dependent variable is the revealed comparative advantage (competitiveness) of China.

For the 4 independent variables, the Gross Domestic Product of Ghana and Myanmar was considered in current US dollars, and FDI uses the net inflows in current US dollars. Inflation was the annual percentage of their consumer prices and the exchange rate was measured as their local currency per US dollars period average.

3 Result Analysis and Discussion

3.1 Result and Discussion of China's Agriculture Competitiveness with Ghana and Myanmar

Table 2 and Fig. 1 highlights the Revealed Comparative Advantage (RCA) and Revealed Symmetric Comparative Advantage (RSCA) of China's agriculture products with Myanmar and Ghana from 2011 to 2020. Regarding China's agriculture products with Myanmar, the RCA index had a general upward trend from 2011 to 2020, except for a drop in 2012 and 2015. This indicates that China's agricultural products have become increasingly competitive in the Myanmar market from 2011 to 2020. The RSCA index also generally increased from 2011 to 2020, except for a drop in 2015. This suggests that China's agriculture products have become increasingly balanced in the Myanmar market from 2011 to 2020. On the other hand, China's agriculture products with Ghana have a slightly different trend. The RCA index had a general upward trend from 2011 to 2020, and also made a drop in 2015.

The trend further shows that China has strong agricultural competitiveness with both Myanmar and Ghana. It can be seen that China has a stronger competitiveness with Myanmar than Ghana. Myanmar shows an overall increase in competitiveness and Ghana shows a fluctuating trend of competitiveness. In 2020 China recorded its highest competitiveness with Myanmar at 2.1, and its highest with Ghana was 1.2 in 2013. It can be seen from Fig. 1 that the difference in the competitiveness of agricultural products export between the two countries became larger from the selected period. But China still maintains its comparative advantage over the selected period for both countries.

3.2 Data Regression Result and Discussion

According to the model regression results in Table 3 which shows the whole regression results of the whole sample. We found that Ghana and Myanmar GDP and exchange rate significantly and positively affect the RCA index of China. To sum up this indicate that with the GDP, the expansion of Ghana and Myanmar's economy and their economic growth has a significant impact on China's agriculture competitiveness with them. The

Table 2. Calculated RCA index of China's Export with Myanmar and Ghana.

year	Myanmar		Ghana	
	RCA	RSCA	RCA	RSCA
2011	1.0	0.00	0.8	−0.11
2012	0.8	−0.11	1.0	0.00
2013	1.1	0.05	1.2	0.09
2014	1.4	0.17	1.1	0.05
2015	0.9	−0.05	0.9	−0.05
2016	1.4	0.17	1.0	0.00
2017	1.6	0.23	1.1	0.05
2018	1.7	0.26	1.1	0.05
2019	1.8	0.29	1.1	0.05
2020	2.1	0.35	1.0	0.00

Source: Calculated by the author based on the data from the UN comtrade database

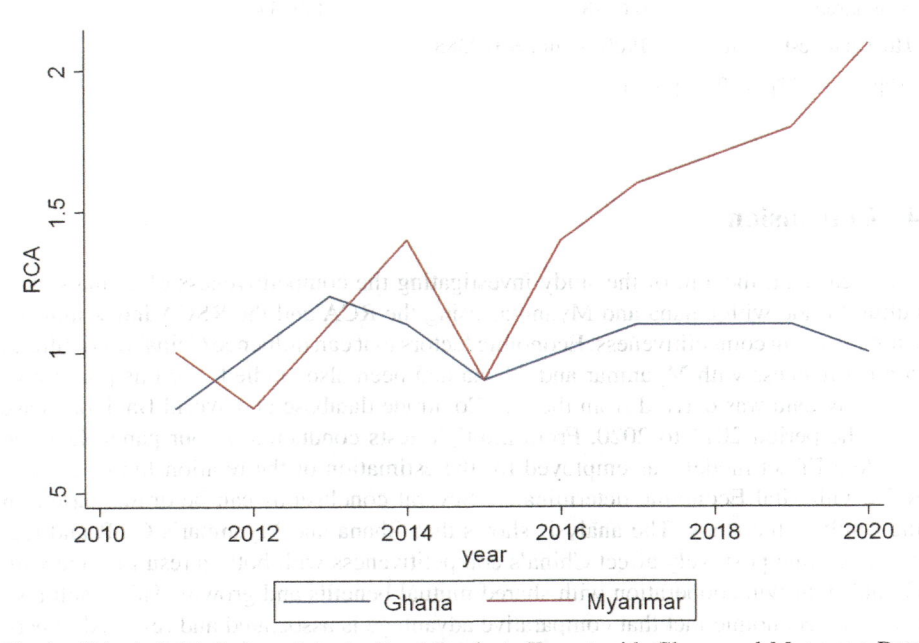

Fig. 1. China's RCA Index of Agricultural Products Export with Ghana and Myanmar. Data Source: U.N Comtrade Database.

relation between economic growth and competitiveness and principle of China's win-win cooperation through BRI and Sino-Africa cooperation are the argument in supports of the result. The principles of China's win-win cooperation through their bilateral trade are centred around shared progress and affluence rather than self-propagation. It emphasize on mutual benefits. The effect of the real exchange rate is positive and significant, indicating Ghana and Myanmar real depreciation and appreciation of their domestic currency affect China's competitiveness of agricultural trade to both countries.

FDI was negative and insignificant, indicating a week relations to China's competitiveness, likewise their inflation, which was insignificant but positive.

Table 3. Result of RE and FE model regression.

Variables	Random effect		Fixed effect	
	Coefficient	t value	Coefficients	t value
GDP	.0138**	2.16	.0122*	1.83
FDI	.0184	−0.30	−.0325	−0.50
INFLATION	.0188	1.31	.0092	0.52
RER	.0004***	3.55	.0005**	2.65
_cons	.0608	0.13	.2063	0.42
R-squared	0.6818		0.6534	
Huasman test result	Prob > chi2 = 0.9388			

***$p < .01$, **$p < .05$, *$p < .1$.

4 Conclusion

It is clear that, the aim of the study investigating the competitiveness of China's agricultural trade with Ghana and Myanmar using the RCA and the RSCA index indicate China's strong competitiveness. Economic factors that can influence China's agricultural competitiveness with Myanmar and Ghana had been also studied. For this purpose of the study data was derived from the UN Comtrade database and World Bank database from the period 2011 to 2020. From multiple tests conducted on our panel data, the Random Effect model was employed for the estimation of the relationship of China's RCA with vital Economic determinants. Several conclusions can be drawn based on the result of the study. The analysis shows that Ghana and Myanmar's GDP, and real exchange rate positively affect China's competitiveness with both, a result in line with China's win-win cooperation with shared mutual benefits and growth. This result also prove the economic fact that comparative advantage is associated and revealed in economic economic growth. And the result of the study prove to the extent that comparative advantage that is competitiveness is a determinant of economic performance, moreover it has been proved that competitiveness is revealed in economic growth and the share of agriculture in included to this growth.

References

1. Lenka, F.: China's trade competitiveness in the area of agricultural products after the implementation of the World Trade Organization commitments. Agric. Econ. (Zemědělská ekonomika) **64**(9), 379–388 (2018). https://doi.org/10.17221/163/2017-agricecon
2. Zhou, L., Tong, G.: Research on the competitiveness and influencing factors of agricultural products trade between China and the countries along the 'Belt and Road.' Alex. Eng. J. **61**(11), 8919–8931 (2022). https://doi.org/10.1016/j.aej.2022.02.030
3. Peng, J., Zhao, Z., Liu, D.: Impact of agricultural mechanization on agricultural production, income, and mechanism: evidence from Hubei province, China. Front. Environ. Sci. (2022). https://doi.org/10.3389/fenvs.2022.838686
4. Zhang, D., Sun, Z.: Comparative advantage of agricultural trade in countries along the belt and road and China and its dynamic evolution characteristics. Foods **11**(21), 3401 (2022). https://doi.org/10.3390/foods11213401
5. Hua, X., Zhang, L., Kono, Y.: Fruit booms and investor mobility along the China-Myanmar and China-Laos borders. Ecol. Soc. **27**(3) (2022). https://doi.org/10.5751/es-13380-270335
6. Amanor, K.S., Chichava, S.: South-South cooperation, Agribusiness, and African agricultural development: Brazil and China in Ghana and Mozambique. World Dev. **81**, 13–23 (2016)
7. Siméon, N., Li, X., Xiao, S.: China's agricultural assistance efficiency to Africa: two decades of Forum for China-Africa Cooperation creation. J. Agric. Food Res. **9**, 100329 (2022). https://doi.org/10.1016/j.jafr.2022.100329
8. Edjah, B.K.T., Wu, J., Tian, J.: Research on the comparative advantage and complementarity of China-Ghana agricultural product trade. Sustainability **14**(20), 13136 (2022). https://doi.org/10.3390/su142013136

Financial Cloud Drives Digital Transformation of Enterprises
——Taking Hisense's Application of Kingdee Financial Cloud as an Example

BoYong Chen[1] and Zhuohao Zhang[2(✉)]

[1] Institute for International Educational Cooperation, Tianjin University of Commerce, Tianjin 300400, China
[2] School of Business Administration, Zhongnan University of Economics and Law, Wuhan 430073, China
202021060258@stu.zuel.edu.cn

Abstract. Financial Cloud is the new engine that drives digital transformation. In recent years, more and more enterprises have started to develop information systems using the cloud computing model. Traditional enterprises urgently need to apply the Cloud to achieve digital transformation, and awareness and ability to apply the Cloud are increasing. However, in the process of Financial Cloud construction, enterprises still face the problems of infrastructure construction, Cloud platform management, and applying SaaS. Besides, enterprises need to handle management challenges caused by the change in the business model, operation mode, and service content in the process of Financial Cloud construction. This paper will take the application of Kingdee Financial Cloud in Hisense Group as an example to explore the broad application scenarios of Financial Cloud in a modern intelligent enterprise, the potential problems of applying the Financial Cloud, the changes that enterprises need to make, and the digital transformation which Financial Cloud brings to enterprises to help them realize value.

Keywords: Financial Cloud · Digital Transformation · Hisense Group · Kingdee Cloud

1 Introduction

1.1 Research Background

In the era of the digital economy, new technologies are emerging in the present and foreseeable future, and a new wave of technological revolution and industrial transformation is coming. The digital transformation of enterprises is extremely urgent. On the one hand, the business ecology is being upended, and the consumption pattern is transforming digitally. The people-oriented business concept is becoming increasingly

---

B. Chen and Z. Zhang—These authors contributed equally.

prominent, so enterprises must provide customized and personalized service according to customers' requests. On the other hand, the business model needs to be digitally reconstructed. Enterprises need process reengineering and need to adjust vision and culture, management structure, and so on, all aspects. In the face of the new business environment, enterprises should use digital technology to facilitate digital transformation.

1.2 Research Significance

As the core part of enterprise management function, financial management needs to process a mass of data generated at any time, so digital financial transformation is very important for realizing enterprise digital intelligence. Financial Cloud can first processize and standardize decentralized mass data as a shared service platform to support business management and strategic decision-making. Secondly, introducing the Financial Cloud provides an application environment for other emerging technology and promotes the innovative application of information technology in enterprises. Financial Cloud helps companies better cope with uncertain and fast-changing business environments and helps them move towards an intelligent age.

2 Financial Cloud

2.1 Financial Cloud Concept

Financial Cloud is a financial system based on a financial shared service mode that integrates emerging technologies such as Big Data, Artificial Intelligence, Robotic process automation, and the Internet of Things to provide an experience of financial services whenever and wherever possible and facilitate the integration between financial and business sectors, which can centralize financial capabilities, and realize digital financial transformation [1]. It can cover the strategic, tactical, and operational layers of finance functions and process transactions covering accounting, report, fund, tax, auditing, and so on in a standardized and streamlined manner and finally consolidate resources, reduce costs, improve efficiency, and improve customer satisfaction.

2.2 Financial Cloud Features

As a financial shared service platform based on the integration of business and finance in the financial management field, Financial Cloud has the characteristics of a shared platform, business, finance, and tax integration, human-computer synergy, and real-time data, which drives the formation of integrated management and promote the digital upgrading of enterprises as shown in Fig. 1.

2.3 Overview of Financial Cloud Development

Financial Cloud is the innovation and revolution of management mode driven by information network technology. It focuses on customer demand and pays more attention to enterprise core business to realize value creation. Ford pioneered the use of financial

Shared service	Integartion of business,fiannce and tax	Human-computer synergy	Real-time data
• A shared platform integrating business,finance and manegement • Sharing data sources, storage and calculations	• Data interchange • Alignment of policys • Connection of various processes	• Efficient automation of the entire financial management process • Release human creativity and engage officers in high-value work such as strategic decision-making	• Sharing data between all departments • Integration of information technology and financial management

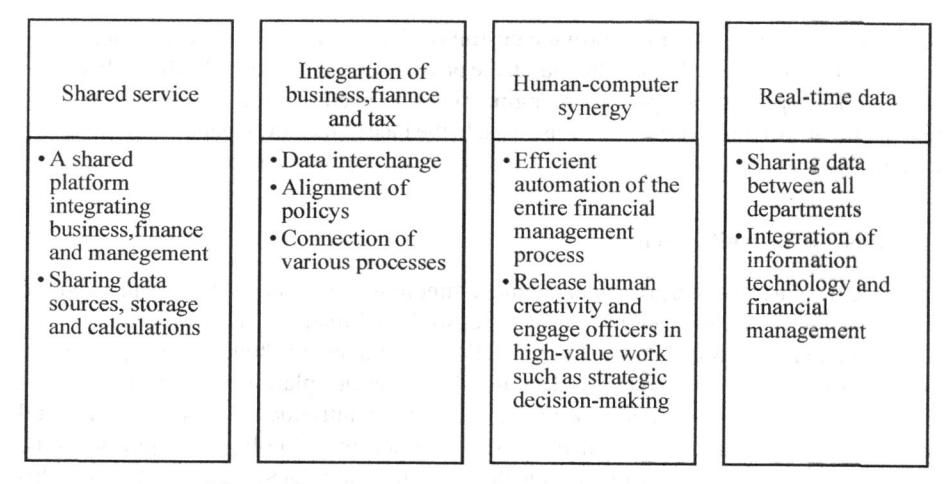

Fig. 1. Financial Cloud Features. Photo credit: Original

shared services in the 1980s. DuPont, Hewlett-Packard, IBM, and other giants have since set up financial shared centers. In China, ZTE set up a financial shared service center in 2005, the first one in the country. In 2011, ZTE Cloud formally introduced the concept of Financial Cloud. Since then, a growing number of Chinese companies, including some large state-owned enterprises, have started setting up financial shared centers [2]. So far, China's Financial Cloud market has reached 300 billion RMB.

2.4 Financial Cloud Application Scenario

As a new technology that can drive enterprises to realize digitization and intelligence, the Financial Cloud has various application values in financial management. It can realize the great value of financial digitization transformation and enhance enterprises' competitiveness, innovation, control, risk resistance, and financial management. Here's a look at the financial cloud application scenario:

Cost Management. Based on invoice identification technology, Financial Cloud can provide intelligent reimbursement for employees in all cases and realize the integration of business, finance, and taxation. Whole process management of public cost can be achieved in multi-scenario of project, contract, and installment payment. Financial Cloud helps the enterprise control the marketing and management cost efficiently and effectively by setting cost budgets, cost standards, cost limits, etc. [3].

Financial Accounting. From a global perspective, Financial Cloud integrates various smart technologies to help companies digitally transform their finances. Based on a multi-accounting system, multi-accounting book, and multi-accounting standard, it integrates intelligent RPA technology to provide enterprises with detailed financial accounting and management accounting, including general ledger, transaction, assets, and inventory [4]. Financial Cloud provides enterprises with paperless electronic accounting files and standard audit file-export services to realize digital accounting.

Financial Sharing. Based on AI robots using machine learning algorithms, Financial Cloud realizes the digital employee concept. The financial shared service middle office, combined with business, accounting, taxation, and capital, helps enterprises promote efficiency, lower risks, and dig deep management value of data.

Tax Administration. Financial Cloud breaks down the data barriers against business, finance, and taxation and realizes the integration. The Financial Cloud platform achieves real-time online updates of tax law policies and preset risk indicators and enables policy compliance. Intelligent tax calculation and automated tax declaration for all types of taxes can also be realized. Financial Cloud will raise the tax administration level in all aspects.

Finance Middle Office. Financial Cloud is driven by the middle office, which helps enterprises realize management innovation. The middle finance office is the next stage of shared finance. Based on the financial capability engine and digital employee technology, Financial Cloud can quickly construct the enterprise's personalized middle office and build the enterprise's differentiated competitiveness [5]. Financial Cloud constructs the integrated data center according to the accounting event to record the business and realize the financial intelligence.

Treasury Management. Depending on innovative technology and scene driving, with business and finance integration as its core, Financial Cloud assists enterprise's capital management, thus supporting more efficient business synergy, creative business innovation and comprehensive value creation.

3 Hisense's Application of Kingdee Cloud to Achieve Digital Transformation

3.1 Application Background

With over 80,000 employees, 31 industrial parks, and 23 research and development centers covering the entire value chain of R&D, production, sales, and service, Hisense faces great management challenges. As digitization improves, Hisense needs to raise operational efficiency with upstream and downstream industry chains. At the same time, in the face of the new channels, there is the islanding phenomenon in the channel warehouse and the high cost of the entire chain. Besides, logistics pressure has also increased with the emphasis on timeliness and convenience in retailing. In order to achieve digital transformation, Hisense needs to make the following changes [6], as shown in Fig. 2.

3.2 Application Status and Impacts

In order to cope with the digital transformation dilemma, Hisense Group has adopted Kingdee Cloud-Hub and Kingdee Cloud Constellation to build the Hisense Hichat Platform and Hisense Marketing system shared-warehouse jointly to realize business connectivity and intelligent collaboration.

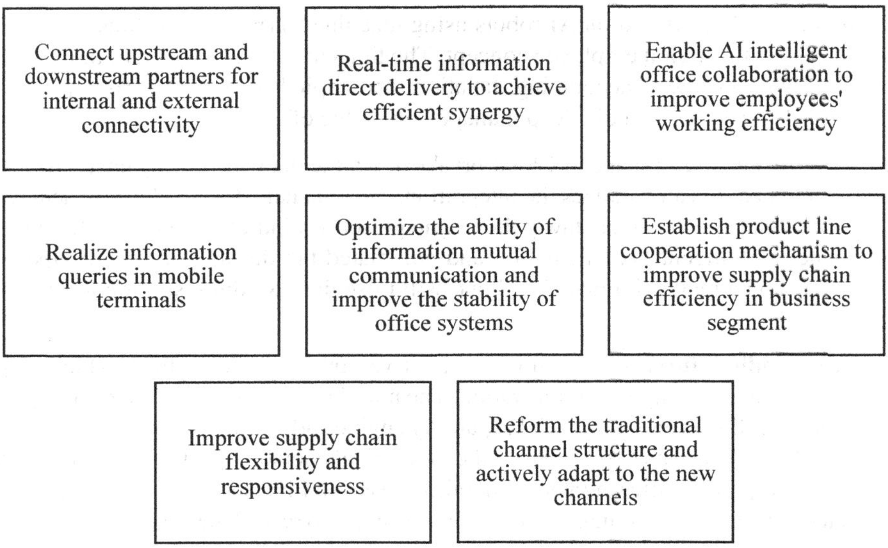

```
┌─────────────────────┐  ┌─────────────────────┐  ┌─────────────────────┐
│ Connect upstream and│  │ Real-time information│ │ Enable AI intelligent│
│ downstream partners │  │ direct delivery to  │  │ office collaboration │
│ for internal and    │  │ achieve efficient   │  │ to improve employees'│
│ external connectivity│ │ synergy             │  │ working efficiency  │
└─────────────────────┘  └─────────────────────┘  └─────────────────────┘

┌─────────────────────┐  ┌─────────────────────┐  ┌─────────────────────┐
│                     │  │ Optimize the ability│  │ Establish product   │
│ Realize information │  │ of information mutual│ │ line cooperation    │
│ queries in mobile   │  │ communication and   │  │ mechanism to improve│
│ terminals           │  │ improve the stability│ │ supply chain        │
│                     │  │ of office systems   │  │ efficiency in       │
│                     │  │                     │  │ business segment    │
└─────────────────────┘  └─────────────────────┘  └─────────────────────┘

              ┌─────────────────────┐  ┌─────────────────────┐
              │ Improve supply chain│  │ Reform the traditional│
              │ flexibility and     │  │ channel structure and │
              │ responsiveness      │  │ actively adapt to the │
              │                     │  │ new channels          │
              └─────────────────────┘  └─────────────────────┘
```

Fig. 2. Changes that Hisense Needs to Make. https://www.kingdee.com/success-stories/1460446580862685185.html

Hichat Platform

Hisense Group built the Hichat platform based on the Kingdee Cloud [7], as shown in Fig. 3. Centring on business ecology, advertising, corporate culture, and so on, the Hichat platform realizes smart offices, real-time decision-making, connectivity with business partners, and employee care. The specific capabilities of the Hichat platform are as follows:

First, build a platform for intra-group information aggregation. Hichat platform can realize message sharing, loading, and precise message search, improving efficiency and user experience. Employees raise their working ability in a professional environment, and a platform has been successfully built for employees to share and interact with each other.

Second, build an interactive business ecosystem and break down barriers to communication between upstream and downstream enterprises. Hichat has successfully built a business ecology platform that connects upstream and downstream, enabling information mutual communication and business synergy between internal and external users and helping partners' developments.

Third, establish the consolidated entry for decision-making of Hisense Group. The entry for mobile types of equipment has been built, and Hisense uses the platform to deliver information more timely and greatly increases the efficiency of decision-making.

Fourth, improve office efficiency and enhance the office experience. Hichat platform builds Hisense AI capabilities to help it achieve a smart office, and smart scenarios such as voice recognition, voice file finding, voice creating calendars, and so on to improve office efficiency.

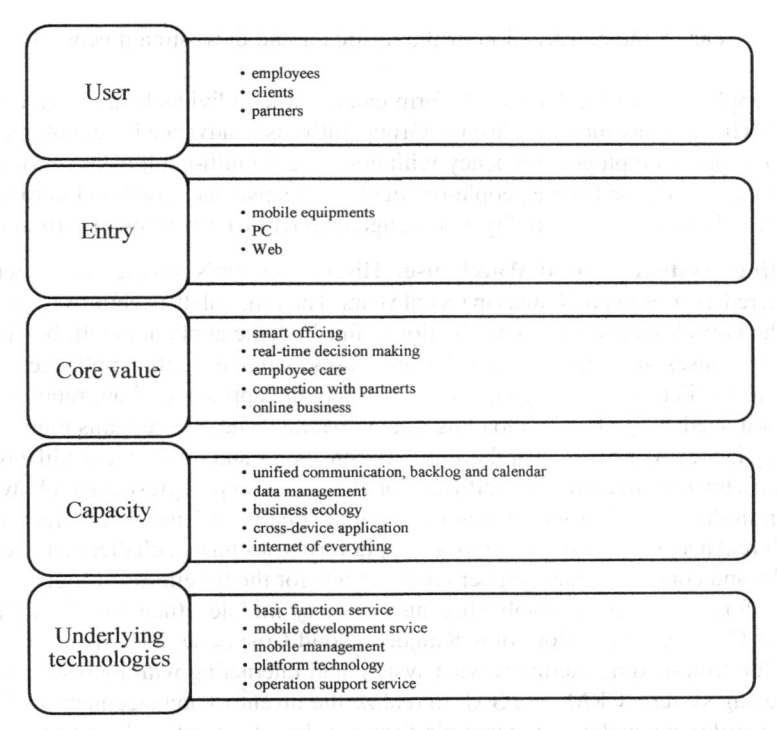

User	• employees • clients • partners
Entry	• mobile equipments • PC • Web
Core value	• smart officing • real-time decision making • employee care • connection with partnerts • online business
Capacity	• unified communication, backlog and calendar • data management • business ecology • cross-device application • internet of everything
Underlying technologies	• basic function service • mobile development srvice • mobile management • platform technology • operation support service

Fig. 3. The structure of Hichat platform. https://www.kingdee.com/success-stories/146044658 0862685185.html

Fifth, construct an internal multimedia interactive channel for Hisense. By reconstructing the audio and video modules, Hichat builds the ability for online collaboration, training, and meeting.

Finally, enrich mobile human resources management functions and set up various office scene applications. Hichat platform enables sign-in modules and develops payroll applications for production-line workers, improving user experience and reducing human resources costs. Applications such as scheduling management and work reporting can provide intra-group office services.

The collaborative officing platform set up by Hisense Group strongly supports employees in their daily office work. Launching the Hichat platform helps Hisense employees move into mobile officing mode. The platform integrates applications in various fields such as marketing, finance, supply chain, human resources, and so on. It has become the basic platform for daily mobile officing, business collaboration, and communication among Hisense employees.

Secondly, the Hichat platform assists Hisense in building an interactive ecosystem of the upstream and downstream value chain and provides a platform for interaction and mutual information communication. Dealers can complete information interaction and handle some businesses with Hisense Group through the Hichat platform. Hisense will continue to enrich the construction of the upstream and downstream ecosystem in the future.

The application of the Hichat platform can activate individuals and organizations. Through Hichat construction, Hisense Group fully uses advanced technologies such as AI to improve employee efficiency with convenient multi-equipment services. The platform helps Hisense from a people-oriented perspective and based on Internet users' thinking, activate individual vitality and strengthen internal unity through various means.

Marketing System Shared-Warehouse. Hisense Group's marketing system has encountered a series of challenges in recent years. The original distribution chain is long. When the household appliances production is finished, the appliances will be placed in CDC warehouses and then in agents' warehouses. After that, the appliances will be transfer to retailers, and finally customers can buy the appliances from retailers. Each circulation needs to go through loading and unloading. The cost remains high, and the efficiency is low. As a result, warehouses between agents and retailers exist like isolated islands. As the manufacturer, it is difficult for Hisense Group to grasp the real inventory situation in the channel. Such a situation is not conducive to Hisense's insight into the market's real needs. The rise of e-commerce platforms has further challenged traditional channels, and consumers have higher requirements for the timeliness of logistics.

Therefore, Hisense has established an inventory middle office based on Kingdee Financial Cloud Constellation, plus Kingdee Cloud Cosmic as the core service, connecting the front-end marketing service system and interacting with logistics platform, warehousing system, CRM, and SAP to realize the inventory management of Hisense, agents, distributors, and e-commerce platforms in the whole value chain and inventory query, sharing, and sourcing [8], as shown in Fig. 4.

marketing service	inventory service	logistics and warehousing service
• B2B platform • performs data management • after-sales protection	• global inventory • perform inventory management	• LMS and WMS • Hisense's large logistics platform

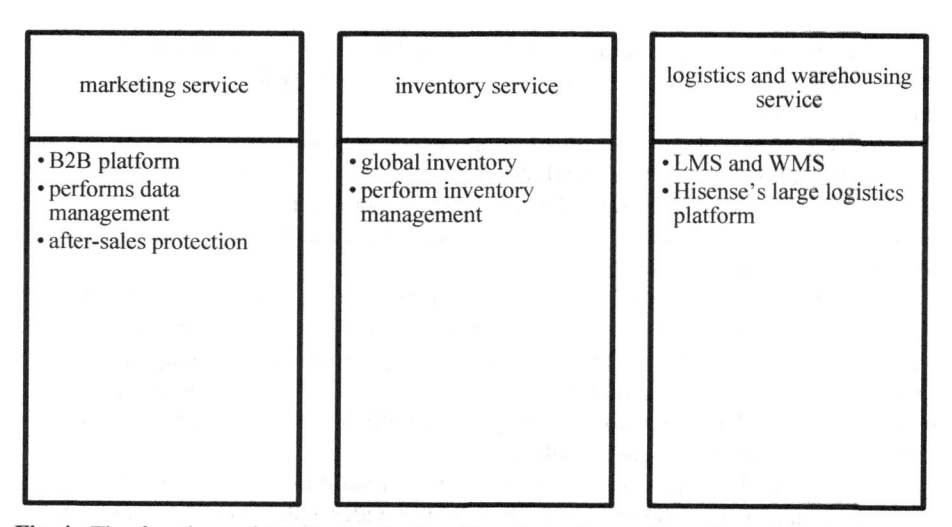

Fig. 4. The functions of Marketing System Shared-warehouse. https://www.kingdee.com/success-stories/1460446580862685185.html

(1) *Marketing Service.* The shared-warehouse creates a B2B platform for Hisense, realizing the management of merchants' procurement, sales, and inventory, establishing sales, e-commerce, and service systems, and performing data management, order processing, and after-sales protection.
(2) *Inventory Service.* The marketing system shared-warehouse can provide global inventory services, realizing inventory data mutual communication and real-time updating and performing inventory management.
(3) *Logistics and Warehousing Services.* Hisense's logistics platform has been successfully built, providing waybills, scheduling, and order management. At the same time, LMS and WMS have been established to strictly manage transportation and input and output of warehouses.

The marketing system shared-warehouse built by Hisense gradually eliminated the constraints of the traditional ERP model, allowing the company to achieve comprehensive links with suppliers, agents, etc., empowering management, and realizing data insight, forecasting, analysis, and risk control.

4 Enlightenment of Financial Cloud Application

4.1 Hisense's Financial Cloud Application Enlightenment

Financial Cloud is the foundation of enterprise digital transformation and an innovative service model. In applying Kingdee Financial Cloud, Hisense's business is undergoing diversification. The application of the Financial Cloud requires the support of relevant talents and the reengineering of corporate process and culture. The corporate management has become more complex. Hisense is facing a series of challenges in management. As a network platform that provides shared services, the Financial Cloud will naturally face network risks, such as data leakage and network viruses, which also requires Hisense to make corresponding preparations. All in all, High return often co-exists with high risk. Not only Hisense Group but any enterprise applying Financial Cloud, is bound to face the risks. The Financial Cloud application can create huge value for enterprises, but it requires enterprises to make comprehensive changes.

4.2 Application of Financial Cloud in Digital Enterprises

With the active innovation in the global cloud computing field and popularization of Cloud among enterprises, the Financial Cloud has become the key to promoting the transformation of traditional enterprises. The size of the enterprise is different, so the focus of the Financial Cloud is also different. Large enterprises that cover the whole country's businesses and even the world have massive users and data and have high requirements for real-time updating and availability of data. The Financial Cloud can reduce costs and increase efficiency for their operations, respond well to business emergency problems, and reduce system risk. For small and medium-sized enterprises with weak technical capabilities and prominent industrial structure contradictions, Cloud solves the time, cost, security, and technical risks encountered in the traditional IT model. It is an important weapon for the transformation and breakthrough of small and medium-sized enterprises.

The application of the Financial Cloud enables enterprises to realize the integration of business and finance, thereby abstracting the financial capabilities of enterprises and building a financial engine that can be quickly assembled with other systems. For example, the accounting engine fully uses intelligent technology to realize standardized and efficient business and financial integration processing, support agile business innovation, and promote digital transformation of enterprises.

Financial Cloud will also promote the application of new technologies in enterprises. Enterprises will use new technologies such as VR, RPA, OCR, NLP, and physical robots to support financial and management accounting, improve accounting efficiency and quality, develop decision-making by detecting risk, analyzing data and forecasting, and provide the digital intelligence experience for enterprises.

Regarding intra-group collaboration, the Financial Cloud builds a multi-legal person, multi-business department dynamic accounting model from multiple perspectives, such as organization and business processes, to adapt to the enterprise management structure.

From the perspective of precise decision-making, the Financial Cloud builds a management system of capital business visualization, real-time capital risk management and control, overall planning of financial resources, and data-driven decision-making, which helps enterprises manage funds.

Finally, in terms of industry ecology, through the connection with business partners, taxation authority, banks, and so on, the integration of business, finance, and taxation is realized so that finance can manage and drive business and promote the digital transformation of enterprises.

4.3 Existing Shortcomings and Challenges of Financial Cloud Applications

(1) The Business Complexity Is High and the Management Is Out of Order. The Financial Cloud application time in Chinese enterprises is very short at this stage. Hence, most enterprises are still in the preliminary stage. Enterprises lack practical experience and professional talents in the application process. The enterprise's management is becoming more complicated, and enterprise management will be confused in the short term. At the same time, the enterprise has many internal business departments. Suppose the enterprise fails to understand its own business completely. In that case, it will inevitably increase the degree of chaos in the internal management of the enterprise, resulting in various unnecessary management problems [9].

(2) The Risks of Network Security Are Relatively Large, and the Cost of Technical Operation Is High. All financial software must be attached to network technology to realize their value. However, network security risks still need to be carefully controlled. Suppose an enterprise wants to apply the Financial Cloud successfully. In that case, the first problem to be solved is to ensure network security and avoid internal information leakage and loss. During application, the enterprise needs to carry on the real-time monitoring to the network security to avoid attacks of viruses and hackers and stealing of the enterprise's confidential information, which needs a lot of investments from the enterprise.

(3) **Enterprise Resource Allocation Lacks Rationality, Resulting in a Waste of Resources.** Most enterprises' applications of the Financial Cloud stay in the initial stage and various resources have not been invested, so the problem of resource waste is not obvious at this stage. If the application enters the stage of optimization and upgrading, enterprises will use the Financial Cloud more widely. Most of the business activities will require the enterprise to introduce a large number of hardware equipment and professional talents, which will increase the operating cost of the enterprise, and will inevitably lead to a waste of resources [1].

4.4 Financial Cloud Application Suggestions

Advice for Managing Disorder. The enterprise should make good application plans and arrange the scope of the application reasonably. The application of the Financial Cloud needs to be based on strategic level, take into account all aspects of an enterprise's business activities, building a good environment for the actual application. If the Financial Cloud is directly applied without regard to business environment, it will have a certain degree of blindness, making enterprise management more difficult. The enterprise can organize a discussion among the project leaders or the department managers, using Brainstorming or the ANFIELD method, Determine the scope of Financial Cloud applications within the enterprise, and make preliminary planning and deployment so as to ensure the application specificity of each stage.

Advice for Resource Allocation. The enterprise should rationally plan departments and optimize their corporate governance structures. In promoting and applying the Financial Cloud in the enterprise, it is necessary to introduce new departments and professional talents. The unreasonable post-setting will inevitably increase the degree of chaos in the internal management of the enterprise. Therefore, when an enterprise sets up Financial Cloud related departments, it should ensure its reasonableness, clearly divide job responsibilities, and reduce unnecessary jobs.

Advice for Cybersecurity. Manage and control network risks to avoid information leakage. With the rapid development of various information technologies, network security is in the spotlight. For enterprises to apply Financial Cloud, the confidentiality of internal information is extremely important. Once the confidential information is leaked, it will definitely cause enormous economic damage to the enterprise. Therefore, the enterprise should strength the network security training for employees, ensure account and password security of all departments and employees, make timely backups of data information, and clearly divide the authority of managers and employees. Besides, good communication should be established with the Financial Cloud provider. The enterprise needs to make timely feedback on application problems to the provider and actively adopt the network risk prevention measures given by the provider to ensure the effective application of the Financial Cloud [10].

5 Conclusion

5.1 Findings

With the advent of the digital economy era, the financial sharing model is maturing rapidly, and the integration of business, finance, and management is an important symbol of the digital transformation of enterprises. As the key to realizing the digital transformation, the Financial Cloud can improve the standard and process level in accounting, tax declaration, employee management, and inventory management and help enterprises control risk. Digitalization is the general direction of the future development of enterprises, but the Cloud transformation of enterprises is by no means an easy task. Enterprises will need to clarify strategies, make good application planning, and realize changes in corporate culture, structure, and management models.

5.2 Limitations and Future Study

The paper focuses on the benefits of Financial Cloud for enterprise digital transformation and provides suggestions for application from a macro perspective. Future study can pay more attention to the basic structure of Financial Cloud platform and explore the different functions of IaaS, SaaS, and PaaS. Besides, it is advisable to get some first-hand data from employees to see how they feel about the Financial Cloud application in the enterprise, so the study can better understand the Cloud application status and provide suggestions for its next development.

References

1. Yang, J.Q.: Problems and countermeasures in enterprise finance cloud application. China SMEs **319**(06), 138–139 (2022)
2. Sun, Y.C.: Financial cloud: from shared services to financial digitization. Financ. Account. (09), 20–25 (2022)
3. Du, W., Zhong, F.Y.: Enterprise group financial cloud construction research. Age Wisdom (06), 37 (2018)
4. Zhai, Z.Q.: Financial cloud propels companies to the next level. China Account. J. (013), 10 (2022)
5. Meng, C.H.: Financial cloud applications in small and medium enterprises in the digital age. Int. Bus. Account. (16), 76–79+83 (2022)
6. Xing, X.L.: Digital transformation drives financial transformation. Chin. Account. Gen. (01), 162–164 (2021)
7. Hisense group: intelligent coordination, mobile office. https://www.kingdee.com/success-stories/1460446580862685185.html. Accessed 1 Mar 2023
8. Kingdee Cloud Constellation. https://www.kingdee.com/download/56741. Accessed 1 Mar 2023
9. Han, B.L.: Problems and countermeasures in enterprise finance cloud application. Account. Stud. (34), 26–27 (2020)
10. Xie, W.X.: Construction and application of financial cloud sharing model. China Mark. (22), 147–148 (2020)

Study on the Influence of Rural Revitalization on Regional Tourism Development: An Empirical Analysis Based on the Data of 16 Prefectures in Yunnan Province

Qing Wang[✉]

Lijiang Culture and Tourism College, Yunnan 674100, China
sodalight@163.com

Abstract. In October 2017, the Chinese government put forward the "rural revitalization strategy" to promote the development of the rural economy, among which the promotion of the rural tourism industry is one of the important measures of industrial revitalization in the strategy. Based on the panel data of 16 prefectures and prefectures in Yunnan Province, this paper conducts an empirical study on the impact of rural revitalization on regional tourism development by constructing an econometric regression model. The regression results show that the increase in the proportion of agricultural land and the disposable income of rural residents in the four rural vitalization strategies has a significant impact on the development of regional tourism. The influence of per capita agricultural output value on regional tourism development is U-shaped. The improvement of rural infrastructure is negatively related to the development of regional tourism. Furthermore, this paper finds that the proposal of a rural revitalization strategy can strengthen the promoting effect of the agricultural land proportion factor on regional tourism. This paper provides an empirical basis for the positive impact of China's rural revitalization strategy on regional tourism development and also provides corresponding suggestions for further promoting the strategy and developing the regional tourism industry.

Keywords: Rural Revitalization · Rural Tourism · Tourist Economy · Fixed Effect · Panel Data Regressive Analysis

1 Introduction

Rural revitalization is one of the development strategies that China is currently emphasizing and vigorously implementing. Implementing the rural revitalization strategy was a major decision and plan made at the 19th National Congress of the Communist Party of China. It is a historic task to achieve a decisive victory in building a modern, moderately prosperous socialist country in all respects, and a major focus of work related to agriculture, rural areas, and farmers in the new era ["Opinions of the CPC Central Committee and the State Council on Implementing the Rural Revitalization Strategy"]. Following China's victory in the fight against poverty, the comprehensive implementation of the rural revitalization strategy can help to solve the problem of development in the poorest areas. From the five aspects of industrial revitalization—talent revitalization, cultural revitalization, ecological revitalization, and organizational revitalization—a comprehensive view puts forward very Chinese characteristics of modern rural development ["Rural Revitalization and Promotion Law of the People's Republic of China"].

The COVID-19 pandemic has greatly affected the global tourism industry, especially in cities with a high proportion of tourism-based economies. Due to the impact of the novel coronavirus pneumonia, the number of tourists in China in 2020 was 2.879 billion, down 52.1% from 2019 ["Annual Report on China's Domestic Tourism Development 2021"], and the per capita GDP of Yunnan Province in 2020 was 16% lower than that in 2019 ["Yunnan Statistical Yearbook"]. However, with the overall shrinking of tourism revenue, we can still notice that the structure of China's tourism market is undergoing obvious changes. (1) The main structure of tourism is sinking, and the travelling rate of the rural population has increased. Data from the Annual Report on China's Domestic Tourism Development 2021 shows that the urban and rural tourism markets present a dual structure. Urban residents are the main source of tourists, but the rural tourism market has huge potential ["China Tourism News"]. In 2021, rural residents' outbound tourist and military spending increased by 15.66% year-on-year. (2) The development speed of some tourist destinations is changing, and new forms of tourism, such as ecotourism and cultural tourism, have become tourism hot spots. In 2019, cultural tourism projects accounted for 30.36% of the total PPP tourism projects, with a total investment of 249.478 billion yuan; the total investment in eco-tourism was 19.9245 billion yuan [China Ministry of Finance Comprehensive Information Platform]. (3) The proposal of a rural revitalization strategy has driven the development of rural tourism to a certain extent. Rural tourism is a combination of rural revitalization and tourism. After the release of the 13th Five-Year Tourism Development Plan and the Guiding Opinions of the State Council on Promoting the Revitalization of Rural Industries, various regions have actively started to apply for rural tourism model villages and green tourism routes. On the one hand, rural tourism can guide local governments to promote rural economic development and environmental improvement. On the other hand, it can also guide tourism subjects' interest in and cognition of rural areas, promote the flow of talents, and achieve urban-rural integration. A series of problems have emerged as a result of the implementation of the rural revitalization strategy and the structural adjustment and transformation of the tourism industry: can rural revitalization promote regional tourism economies; how to promote regional tourism economies; what is the mechanism of action; and how to improve tourism product design based on the mechanism of action. The study of these issues is very practical in terms of the synergy mechanism between rural revitalization and overall economic development, as well as promoting the development of the tourism economy.

The relationship between rural revitalization and tourism development has also aroused extensive attention and discussion in the academic community. Some scholars believe that tourism development is an important way to implement the rural revitalization strategy. According to Lu Lin et al., the development of rural tourism can not only increase rural residents' income, digest rural surplus labor force, improve rural residents' living environment, but also improve their pride and quality of life and change their traditional views [1]. Some scholars further argue that the implementation of a rural revitalization strategy can promote the development of tourism. Nong Fengfang et al. believe that the integration of red culture and tourism can promote the development of the tourism economy by enriching the people through tourism, integrating industries, and expanding the popularity of tourism [2]. Yang Dongwei et al. believe that rural revitalization can promote the development of tourism resources, environment, facilities, and management and promote the development of rural tourism [3]. Taking Hainan Province as an example, Geng Songtao et al. advocated that, under the background of rural revitalization, cultural and tourism integration should be adopted to promote rural revitalization and enrich the people through tourism by creating cultural symbols combined with local characteristics. Another group of scholars did empirical research on the impact of rural revitalization on tourism [4]. According to the study of Du Yan et al., the coordinated development level of rural revitalization and rural tourism is low based on the empirical results. Rural tourism is significantly affected by comprehensive income, urbanization rate, per capita GDP, and other indicators [5]. According to Xie Yanlin et al., rural residents' per capita tourism expenditure has a significant and positive impact on domestic tourism income [6].

Yunnan Province has diversified ecological resources, a profound folk culture, and a high contribution rate of tourism to its economy. At the same time, the proportion of rural population is nearly 48.95%, the proportion of mountainous areas is 84%, and the cultivated land of 80,933,200 mu is suitable for the sample data set. Based on the data of 16 prefectures in Yunnan Province from 2008 to 2020, this study selected 4 factors related to rural vitalization as rural vitalization endowment factors. Through panel regression analysis, this study studied the influence of the trend and fluctuation of rural endowment factors on regional tourism revenue in the past 13 years. The findings are as follows: Rural vitalization endowment factors have a significant impact on the number of tourist arrivals. The cross term between the dummy variable of the time when rural vitalization was proposed and the endowment factor of rural vitalization was added into the extension study. The study found that the influence of cultivated land area on tourist arrivals was strengthened after the rural vitalization strategy was proposed.

The innovations and contributions of this paper are as follows: (1) According to the strategic direction of China's rural vitalization, appropriate indicators are selected as rural vitalization endowment factors, and the basic conditions of rural vitalization in various regions are quantified. (2) The positive impact of China's rural revitalization strategy on the development of the local tourism industry has been empirically verified. (3) Based on the empirical results, it puts forward specific measures to promote the implementation of a rural revitalization strategy and the development of the tourism economy.

The structure of this paper is as follows: the first part is the introduction; the second part is the data selection and model design; the third part is the analysis of experimental results and conclusions; and the fourth part is the conclusion and policy recommendations.

2 Data Selection and Model Design

2.1 Sample Selection and Data Sources

This paper takes the economic data of Yunnan Province and its 16 prefectures from 2008 to 2020 as samples. The index names and calculation methods are shown in Table 1. Each variable involves 208 observed values. All data were collected from the China Statistical Yearbook and the Yunnan Statistical Yearbook from 2009 to 2021 (Table 2).

Table 1. Variable symbols and meanings.

	Variable symbols	Variable name	Variable meanings
explained variables	ln_TP	Tourism demand of each prefecture in Yunnan	Logarithm of tourist arrivals
explanatory variables	ln_R	Disposable income of rural residents in tourist destination	Logarithm of per capita disposable income of rural residents
	At_AoptRurp	Per capita agricultural output	Agriculture, forestry, husbandry, and fishery value/rural population
	At2	Per capita agricultural output value of the second item	At_AoptRurp quadratic term
	Ra_pct	Agricultural land ratio percent	Agricultural land area/survey area
	Rur_Infra	Rural infrastructure	Numbers of villages called through the network/numbers of village committees investigated
control variables	Pc_GDP	Per capita GDP of each prefecture in Yunnan	Economic development level of tourist destination
	Tr	Highway traffic density in Yunnan Province	Density of expressway
	Tr2	Traffic density quadratic term	The square of the density of the freeway
	Tr_GDP	Share of revenue from tourism	Proportion of tourism revenue in national economy

(*continued*)

Table 1. (*continued*)

	Variable symbols	Variable name	Variable meanings
	Invrmt	The proportion of wetland area	Wetland area/survey area
	3A	Numbers of scenic spots	Numbers of 3A scenic spots and above
	HtlCtr	Employment level in tourism	Employment in accommodation and catering/Total employment
	C_dummy	dummy variable	1 after the proposal for rural vitalization in 2017
interaction terms	At*C_Dummy	interaction term	Interaction term between At_AoptRurp and Dummy C
	Ra*C_Dummy	interaction term	Interaction term between Ra_pct and Dummy C
	Infra*C_Dummy	interaction term	Interaction term between Rur_Infra and Dummy C

Table 2. Descriptive statistics of variables.

Variable	Mean	Std. dev.	Min	Max
ln_TP	7.26	0.97	4.80	9.83
ln_R	9.20	0.41	8.47	9.75
At_AoptRurp	1.08	0.63	0.21	3.33
At2	1.55	2.10	0.04	11.12
Ra_pct	0.85	0.05	0.75	0.94
Rur_Internet	1.58	2.62	0.33	16.97
Rur2	9.33	38.47	0.11	287.90
Pc_GDP	10.03	0.60	8.55	11.45

(*continued*)

Table 2. (*continued*)

Variable	Mean	Std. dev.	Min	Max
Tr	0.62	0.24	0.18	1.16
Tr2	0.45	0.33	0.03	1.35
Tr_GDP	0.35	0.38	0.00	2.11
Envrmt	1.13	0.78	0.03	3.10
GDPgrt	1.14	0.07	0.86	1.38
3A	7.26	5.58	0.00	22.00
HtlCtr	0.02	0.01	0.00	0.07

2.2 Explained Variable

Tourism demand is generally measured by tourism income or tourist receptions [7]. This paper selected tourist receptions ln_TP as the explained variable.

2.3 Explanatory Variables

Based on the previous literature on the factors affecting rural vitalization policies, rural tourism, and tourism demand, this paper selects the per capita disposable income of rural residents, the per capita agricultural output value, the agricultural land ratio, and the rural Internet access rate as the core explanatory variables. These variables are the driving force behind rural vitalization, so the basic conditions of rural vitalization in various regions are measured to a certain extent. That is, the rural revitalization endowment factor.

In the study of influencing factors of tourism demand, the income level of the tourist source is one of the important influencing factors of tourist destination reception (Stabler) [8]. Per capita disposable income of tourist origin usually has a positive and significant impact on regional tourism demand [9]. Stabler divided the research methods for influencing factors of tourism demand into equations and a single equation [8]. The system of equations can distinguish tourist sources, which is widely used in the research of cross-border entry-exit tourism in Europe [10]. The rule of a single equation directly regards the tourist source of tourism demand as a whole [11, 12]. Limited by data availability, the single equation method is used in this paper. The indicators describing the income level of tourism subjects include the per capita disposable income of national residents, the per capita disposable income of national urban residents, and the per capita disposable income of national rural residents. The main purpose of this paper is to study the impact of rural revitalization on regional tourism demand, so the per capita disposable income of rural residents in China is selected. Endowment factor 1 for rural vitalization in this paper is the ln_R of disposable income of rural residents in the destination.

Due to the sharing of production factors and the overexploitation of natural resources, the per capita agricultural output may inhibit the development of regional tourism, but on the other hand, the economic benefits it brings and the construction of agricultural and forestry landscapes can promote the development of regional tourism. In order to study the specific influencing mechanism between rural production development and regional tourism demand, this paper referred to the study of Chen Xi et al. [13], calculated the ratio of agricultural productivity At_AoptRurp equal to the total agricultural, forestry, husbandry, and fishery production and rural population, and set it as the endowment factor of rural revitalization 2.

The ratio of agricultural land area can directly reflect regional primary industry development as well as land resource utilization and distribution. Wang Zhaofeng et al. showed that the area of agricultural land can have a significant impact on rural tourism [14]. In this paper, the ratio of agricultural land Ra_pct is calculated to be equal to the area of agricultural land divided by the area of the statistical survey, and it is set as the endowment factor of rural revitalization 3.

The rate of rural access reflects the convenience of rural life and tourism. In this paper, the degree of rural infrastructure improvement calculated by Rur_Internet is the number of villages connected to the Internet by telephone divided by the number of village committees investigated, which is set as the endowment factor of rural revitalization 4.

2.4 Control Variables

In addition to the above core explanatory variables, this paper selects six control variables by referring to previous studies, including per capita GDP of tourist destinations, tourism income ratio, highway traffic density, wetland area ratio, number of 3A scenic spots, and tourism employment level.

In the research on the relationship between the economic level of tourist destination and local tourism income, some views hold that the original ecological landscape in less developed areas is more able to attract tourists, while others hold that big cities are more able to create higher tourism income due to their huge population size and capacity and high-quality capital resources. Ma Lijun showed that the economic level of destination and destination were positively correlated with tourism demand in a statistical sense [15]. This paper selects per capita GDP as control variable 1.

The proportion of tourism revenue in regional GDP is reflected by the proportion of tourism revenue in regional GDP, which mainly reflects the industrial structure of a city and the importance of tourism industry in the region. Although Yunnan Province is not dominant in absolute terms, it is truly a big tourism province in terms of the proportion of tourism income. Zhang Man controlled the variables reflecting the proportion of tourism industry income in the study of tourism income [12]. In this paper, the proportion of tourism revenue Tr_GDP is selected as control variable 2.

Highway traffic density reflects the transportation convenience of tourist destinations and the improvement of local infrastructure construction. Many scholars choose this variable when studying factors related to tourism demand [8, 9, 11]. In this paper, highway traffic density Tr is selected as control variable 3.

Wetland area ratio and the number of 3A or above scenic spots reflect the proportion of wetland area and the number of 3A scenic spots in a region. Zou Jianqin used environmental factors and the number of A-level scenic spots as control variables in the research on the distribution of natural scenic spots endowment [15]. In this paper, Envrmt, the proportion of wetland area, and the number of 3A scenic spots were selected as control variables 4 and 5.

The employment level of tourism industry is the ability of a regional tourism industry to absorb employment, which reflects the scale and degree of development of tourism industry. Both Lin Yuxia [11] and Zhang Man [12] controlled indicators reflecting the development of the tourism industry, such as the number of travel agencies, travel agency income, etc. Based on data availability, this paper selects tourism employment level HtlCtr as the control variable 5.

2.5 Model Design

The logical diagram of the influence of rural revitalization strategy on regional tourism demand can be drawn as Fig. 1.

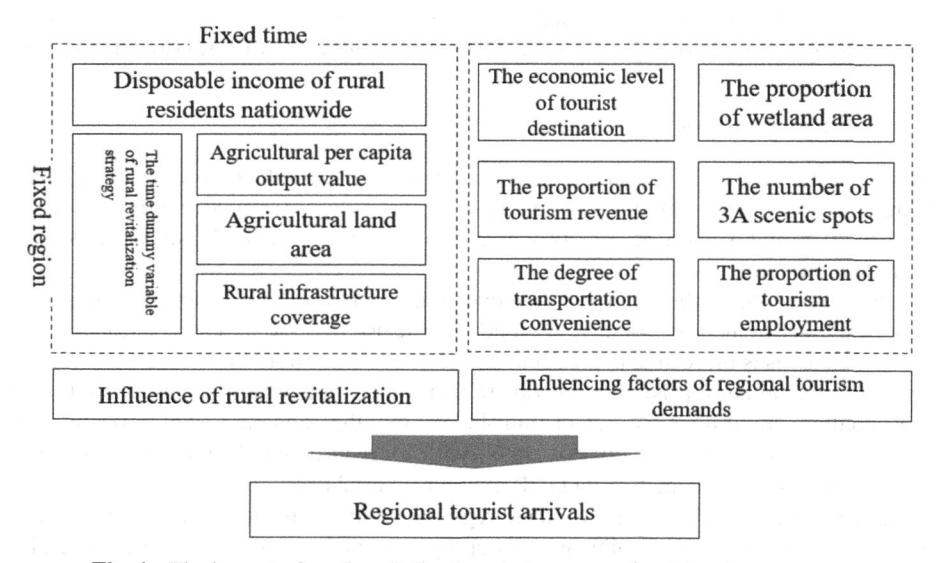

Fig. 1. The impact of rural revitalization strategy on regional tourism revenue.

The basic regression model of this paper is as follows:

$$F.\ln TP_{t,j} = \alpha_0 + \beta_1 \ln\_R_t + \beta_2 At\_AoptRurp_{t,j} + \beta_3 At2_{t,j} + \beta_4 Ra\_pct_{t,j} + \beta_5 Rur\_Infra_{t,j} + \beta_6 Pc\_GDP_{t,j} + \beta_7 Controls_{t,j}$$

t is the time Angle. T = 1, 2, ... 13, 13 years in total. j is the Angle symbol of the region. J = 1, 2, ... 16, a total of 16 states. ln_TPt,j is logarithm of tourist reception. ln_Rt is the national per capita disposable income in rural areas, and time fixed effect is used here. At_AoptRurp is per capita agricultural output value. At2 is the quadratic term of per capita agricultural output value. Ra_Pct is the ratio of rural land area. Rur_Infra is the rural telephone network access rate. Controls is the control variable.

In order to mitigate the influence of heteroscedasticity, the robust standard error was used in regression. In order to mitigate the endogenous effects, the data of the dependent variable was set to F.ntp one phase in advance.

3 Analysis of Experimental Results and Conclusions

3.1 Core Explanatory Variable Analysis

Table 3. Experimental result.

	F.ln_TP FE	F.ln_TP MLE
ln_R	0.368*	0.372*
	(0.173)	(0.178)
At_AoptRurp	−1.380311**	−1.190**
	(0.402)	(0.357)
At2	0.239*	0.214*
	(0.107)	(0.090)
Ra_pct	3.704**	3.587***
	(1.216)	(0.709)
Rur_Infra	−0.061***	−.064***
	(0.011)	(0.008)
Pc_GDP	1.640***	1.490***
	(0.190)	(0.210)
Tr	−5.953**	−3.073
	(1.201)	(1.715)
Tr2	3.886**	2.217*
	(1.207)	(1.082)
Tr_GDP	0.318*	0.218
	(0.131)	(0.113)
Invrmt	−0.062	−0.084
	(0.062)	(0.068)
3A	0.005	0.010
	(0.007)	(0.006)
HtlCtr	5.012	4.114
	(5.810)	(3.856)
Cons	−12.533***	−12.115***
	(1.429)	(1.428)
R^2	0.915	0.915

*, **, ***respectively represent a significant increase in the level of 10%, 5%, 1%.

The first column of Table 3 reports the regression results of the basic model between the influence of rural revitalization strategies and tourism demand. The regression results show that the disposable income of rural residents, the per capita agricultural output value, the per capita secondary agricultural output value, the ratio of agricultural land area, and the improvement of rural infrastructure are statistically significantly correlated with the number of tourist receptions. Specifically, when the disposable income of rural residents increases by 1%, the number of tourist receptions increases by 0.36%; when the ratio of agricultural land area increases by 1%, the number of tourist arrivals increases by 3.70%. When the rural access rate increases by 1%, the number of tourist arrivals decreases by 0.06. In addition, the relationship between agricultural productivity and tourist arrivals is U-shaped, that is, with the increase in agricultural productivity, the number of tourist arrivals decreases first and then increases.

Accelerating the increase of rural residents' income, expanding the middle-income group, and improving income distribution in the process of rural revitalization are key to achieving substantial progress in promoting common prosperity. The results of this study show that the income level of rural residents in China has a positive impact on regional tourist arrivals. It shows that the current stock and increment of rural residents' income can not only meet the daily needs of life but also promote the formation of their travel demand. It shows that the further implementation of the rural revitalization strategy can continue to drive the development of Yunnan's tourism economy.

The ratio of agricultural land area is positively correlated with the number of tourist arrivals, and the influence factor is the highest among the four factors. Mountainous areas account for two-thirds of China's total area, and most rural areas are distributed in mountainous areas. The characteristics of agricultural land are lower per capita occupancy, more suitable forest land, and less suitable land resources. China sticks to the "red line" of 1.8 billion mu of arable land to ensure food security. This study proves that adhering to the protection of agricultural land can not only ensure national food security but also promote the growth of regional tourism revenue. First of all, the protection and rational use of agricultural land can increase farmers' income, improve farmers' living standards, and stimulate the formation of rural tourism demand. Second, the rural revitalization strategy advocates the integrated development of the primary, secondary, and tertiary industries in rural areas. In this process, it emphasizes the rational utilization and protection of agricultural land, which can maintain the stability and sustainability of the rural ecological environment. Third, properly developed agricultural land is the most beautiful rural tourism scenery. Yunnan's characteristic folk villages, Hani terrace landscape, spring rapeseed flower sea, and other cultural and natural landscapes cannot be separated from the protection of agricultural land.

The U-shaped relationship between agricultural productivity and tourist arrivals indicates that rural tourism strategies should have different priorities in areas with different levels of rural economic development. In the case of limited rural development resources in the initial accumulation period, one-sided emphasis on per capita agricultural output value will indeed negatively affect tourism income. In view of the region where per capita agricultural output value is low and in the accumulation period, on the one hand, the improvement of industrial structure and the exploration of new development modes should be emphasized; on the other hand, certain special "cultivation periods" should be given to the development of agricultural production or tourism. In the developed areas of the rural economy, the development of rural productive forces can promote the development of the tourism industry. This is because economic benefits and resource surpluses can provide blood and nutrition for tourism development. In such areas, the promotion of rural production efficiency should be vigorously advocated so as to create synergy and a win-win situation between agriculture and tourism.

The coverage degree of rural network facilities has a negative correlation with the number of tourist receptivity, which reflects that the number of tourist receptivity is low in areas with high coverage degrees of rural network facilities to a certain extent. This result is reasonable to some extent. Because the focus of rural tourism is on experiencing idyllic rural scenery, some primitive villages may be more appealing to tourists. Of course, the development of rural infrastructure not only serves the development of tourism but also needs to balance the convenience of local residents. On the other hand, the results show the importance of striking a balance between rural modernization and the protection of original ecological characteristics.

3.2 Analysis of Control Variables

Among the six control variables, the economic level of tourist destination Pc_GDP, highway traffic density Tr, secondary term Tr2 of highway traffic density, and the proportion of tourism revenue Tr_GDP are significantly correlated with regional tourist arrivals.

Among them, the economic level of the tourist destination is positively and significantly correlated with the number of tourist arrivals, which is consistent with the conclusion of Ma Lijun [15]. Economically developed regions have sufficient sources of tourism investment and development funds, can accommodate a large number of tourists, can carry more large-scale tourism projects, have convenient public transportation and infrastructure, and can form resource sharing partnerships with other sectors. The benefits listed above have a mutually beneficial effect on the regional economy and tourism revenue.

In addition, the research shows that the higher the proportion of tourism income, the higher the tourism income, which is consistent with the conclusions of Zhang Man [12]: the more a region is dominated by tourism, the more it can obtain tourism income, which also indicates that the tourism input and output stage of Yunnan Province is still in the growth stage and belongs to economies of scale.

The relationship between transportation convenience and tourism income is prone to divergence in various studies [8]. Some scholars' research results show that transportation is positively promoting the tourism economy [9, 16], and other scholars' research results show a negative correlation between transportation and the tourism economy [15]. In this study, the relationship between highway density and tourist arrivals is U-shaped, indicating that remote cities and well-trafficked cities are favored by tourists as the two ends of transportation convenience, while cities in the middle of traffic development are not dominant. Remote cities benefit from the attraction of undeveloped natural landscapes to attract some tourists, while cities with developed transportation can organize large-scale, high-turnover tourism activities. Using the different modes of cities at both ends as a model, cities in the middle must develop their own original ecological tourism reserve resources on the one hand while increasing traffic construction on the other.

3.3 Robustness Test

This paper further established a random effects model and used MLE method for estimation as robustness test. The results obtained (the second column of Table 3) were consistent with the basic regression, that is, the change of regression method had very little change in factor coefficient and factor significance, indicating that the results of basic regression were relatively robust.

3.4 Further Analysis

In 2017, China put forward the rural revitalization and development strategy. According to the strategic direction of China's rural vitalization, appropriate indicators are selected as the rural vitalization endowment factor, and the basic conditions of rural vitalization are quantified. In the further analysis, this paper introduces the interaction term between the time dummy variable of rural vitalization and the rural vitalization endowment factor into the regression, and constructs a dual fixed model through the application of event analysis method. This paper studies whether the proposal of rural revitalization strategy can strengthen the effect of endowment factors on tourism.

Table 4 Regression results show that the disposable income of rural residents, per capita agricultural output value, secondary terms of per capita agricultural output value and agricultural land area are still significant after the interaction item is added. In addition, the interaction term Ra*Dummy_C regression coefficient between the ratio of agricultural land area and the dummy variable is statistically significantly positive, which proves that the proposal of the rural revitalization strategy strengthens the promoting effect of the ratio of agricultural land area on tourist arrivals, that is, the rural revitalization strategy can indirectly promote the development of regional tourism by promoting the protection of rural land.

For the other three endowment factors, the research results do not show significant interaction terms, which may be related to the short time period after the proposal of the rural vitalization strategy (only 4 years by the time of the completion of the study). The rural vitalization strategy is still in the stage of improvement and implementation, and its impact needs to be considered again after the policy implementation is relatively mature and a certain amount of data is accumulated.

Table 4. Analysis results of interaction terms.

	F.ln_TP fixed effect
ln_R	0.459*
	(0.185)
At_AoptRurp	−1.220**
	(0.367)

(*continued*)

Table 4. (*continued*)

	F.ln_TP fixed effect
At2	0.205*
	(0.101)
Ra_pct	3.408***
	(0.711)
Rur_Infra	−.121
	(0.143)
Pc_GDP	1.454***
	(0.215)
Tr	−5.965***
	(1.594)
Tr2	3.890***
	(1.004)
Tr_GDP	−0.010
	(0.127)
Invrmt	0.036
	(0.071)
3A	−.007
	(0.007)
HtlCtr	2.997
	(4.030)
C_dummy	−1.258
	(0.667)
InterAt	−.087
	(0.117)
InterRa	1.890*
	(0.854)
InterInfra	0.056
	(0.144)
Cons	−11.270***
	(1.474)
R^2	= 0.927

*, **, ***respectively represent a significant increase in the level of 10%, 5%, 1%.

4 Conclusions and Policy Recommendations

This paper makes a quantitative analysis of the influence of rural revitalization on regional tourism development through the method of econometric regression. This paper firstly selects four "endowment factors" of rural revitalization according to the focus of rural revitalization and finds that, among the four factors, the proportion of agricultural land and the increase of rural residents' disposable income have a positive and significant impact on regional tourism development. The influence of per capita agricultural output value on regional tourism development is U-shaped. The improvement of rural infrastructure is negatively related to the development of regional tourism. Furthermore, this paper finds that the proposal of a rural revitalization strategy can strengthen the promoting effect of the agricultural land proportion factor on regional tourism. According to the above research conclusions, this paper puts forward the following four suggestions:

Firstly, we will continue to advance the rural revitalization strategy and deepen rural reform. This study shows that the growth of the three rural vitalization endowment factors can significantly promote the growth of regional tourist arrivals. In addition, the promotion of rural vitalization has been able to promote regional tourism development through the factor of rural arable land area. Therefore, from the perspective of the development of the regional tourism industry, China should reach consensus on helping and benefiting farmers and developing rural areas, support the implementation of a rural revitalization strategy from the perspective of action, and cooperate with the government to develop the rural economy. The rural revitalization strategy not only revitalizes the rural economy, but also forms a promoting relationship with regional tourism development, according to the conclusion of this paper.

Secondly, regional tourism should be developed according to local conditions and characteristics. The U-shaped influence of per capita agricultural output value and transportation convenience on tourism indicates that regional tourism should be developed according to the specific local conditions. The topography and climate of Yunnan's high-altitude region are not suitable for the cultivation of large areas of cash crops, but its special snow landscape of mountains and rivers can attract tourists who love the ecological scenery of the plateau. When designing tourism products in such areas, they should not follow the trend and emphasize the creation of agricultural landscapes. Instead, they should combine their own advantages and pay more attention to the display of natural landscape (such as the Nujiang River Grand Canyon), the original appearance of local folk culture (such as Lijiang Dongba culture), and local rare crops (such as matsutake, saffron, plateau blueberry, etc.). It is intended to give tourists a great contrast with city life and a sense of shock. The low-latitude areas of Yunnan have a pleasant climate, fertile soil, and high coverage of wetlands. In the tourism design of such areas, they can combine their own ecological advantages and focus on leisure and health tourism (such as the natural wetland park in Kunming and the ecological corridor around the lake in Dali). Landscapes for agricultural production (such as Dali wheat fields and Honghe Hani terraces) should also be developed in response to the rural revitalization policy. It is intended to bring a comfortable leisure experience to tourists while showing the natural beauty of farmland, crops, and wetland ecology.

Thirdly, further strengthen the protection of agricultural land. The results of this study show that the ratio of agricultural land area can promote the number of tourist arrivals, and the results of further analysis show that the promoting effect is further strengthened after the proposal of a rural revitalization strategy. The research results show that the strategic significance of agricultural land protection is not limited to food security and other fields but can directly or indirectly promote tourism development. Agricultural land resources are essential for agricultural development and serve as a link between the primary, secondary, and tertiary industries. They can play a key role in the integration of the three rural industries. Therefore, attention should be paid to the protection of agricultural land.

Fourthly, ecological protection should be taken into account while developing the economy, especially the original ecological landscape. It is found in this paper that the increase in the number of villages through the local network will negatively affect the development of the regional tourism industry, which may be caused by the failure to coordinate the construction of infrastructure and the protection of the original ecological landscape. Therefore, we should pay more attention to the protection of the local ecological environment and natural landscape while developing the regional economy, especially in the tourism areas with folk culture and original ecological landforms. To achieve coordinated development and organic integration, we must strike a balance between the maintenance of ecological landscapes and the construction of infrastructure.

References

1. Lu, L., et al.: Research framework and prospect of rural tourism guiding rural revitalization. Geogr. Res. **1**(38), (2019)
2. Nong, F., et al.: Study on the coupling mechanism of Red culture and tourism to enrich people under the background of rural revitalization. Modern Bus. Trade Ind. **43**(19), (2022)
3. Yang, D., et al.: A study on the coupling and coordinated development of rural revitalization and rural tourism – a case study of Bohou Village, Sanya City. J. Anhui Agric. Sci. **50**(15), 253–255 (2022)
4. Geng, S., et al.: Research on the coordinated development of rural tourism and cultural industry under the background of rural revitalization. J. Nanjing Agric. Univ. (Soc. Sci. Ed.) **1**(2), (2021)
5. Du, Y., et al.: Study on the coupling and coordinated development of high quality rural tourism and rural revitalization in Shandong Province. J. Nat. Sci. Hunan Normal Univ. **45**(03), (2022)
6. Xie, Y., et al.: An empirical analysis of the main influencing factors of domestic tourism revenue – based on multiple linear regression model. J. Beijing Inst. Print. **28**(01), (2020)
7. Jiao, X., et al.: Forecasting international tourism demand: a local spatiotemporal model. Ann. Tour. Res. **83**, 102937 (2020)
8. Zhang, H., et al.: Analysis of influencing factors and countermeasures of domestic tourism demand of urban residents. Resour. Dev. Mark. **30**(6), (2014)
9. Stabler, M.J., et al.: Economics of Tourism. The Commercial Press (2017)
10. Li, G., Song, H., Witt, S.: Modelling UK Outbound Tourism Demand Using EC-LAIDS Models (2017)
11. Lin, Y., et al.: Domestic tourism demand based on panel quantile method. Appl. Stat. Manag. **37**(9), (2018)
12. Zhang, M., et al.: The impact of negative Internet attention on tourism development: based on spatial correlation analysis of tourism demand. Tour. Trib. **36**(7), (2021)
13. Chen, X., et al.: Empirical test of the effect of the integration of agriculture and tourism on agricultural labor productivity: a case study of leisure agriculture and rural tourism demonstration counties in China. Modern Agric. 6 (2022)
14. Wang, Z., et al.: Coupling study of highway traffic network and rural tourism development – a case study of Daxiangxi. J. Central South Univ. For. Technol. (Soc. Sci. Ed.) **3**(16), (2022)
15. Ma, L., et al.: The promoting effect of "The Belt and Road" on the tourism demand of the countries along the routes: an analysis and evaluation based on the network attention. World Reg. Stud. **31**(01), 41–52 (2022)
16. Ruan, W., et al.: Spatial and temporal variation of China's tourism demand to Thailand and its influencing factors. Tour. Trib. **34**(5), (2019)

The Discussion of the Impact on the Stock Price After the Comments or Recommendations from Stock Analysts–The Case Study on EV Stocks

Jiaxi Zhang(✉)

University of Manchester, Manchester M50 3AT, UK
zjzjxxi@163.com

Abstract. Comments or suggestions from credible experts will give the stock greater momentum, with a big number of positive comments providing the stock a stronger upward momentum over time and a large number of negative comments giving the stock a stronger downward momentum. Therefore, it is necessary to investigate the link between the stock price movement after analyst recommendations and analyst remarks, as well as the length of analyst comments. The report utilizes electric vehicle (EV) firms Tesla and Nio as a case study for significant comment date and subsequent share price fluctuations. There is a positive correlation between comments and share price, and the longer the length, the greater the impact.

Keywords: Investment Value · Recommendation · Comments from Analysts · EV Industry · Behavioral Finance

1 Introduction

The efficiency of the market determines that the information could be embedded and reflected in the share price, and there may become information could be omitted or hidden from the public, where only a few insiders or professional analysts could know, where giving them advantages over individual investors in the market [1]. Therefore, individual investors, most of them are not equipped with professional investment skills, may blindly or intentionally follow the opinion of the experts, who claimed to be able to successfully predict the stock price. Though the analysts' predictions are more like guidance or a single opinion in the market, they could still spread substantial effects on the stock price and can affect the future direction vastly [2]. It can be explained by the behavioral finance of momentum and herding effects, where individual investors would be driven to follow the opinions of the analysts, and become an even larger power to drive the price of the stock. This paper intends to introduce the effect of the analysts' comments and recommendations on certain stocks, and how and why the stock price would be shifted by scholars and reviews. Then the paper will conduct a case study to testify to the effect by selecting two leading players in the electric vehicle (EV) industry, which are Nio and Tesla, and see how the analysts can affect its share price within certain time frames. The results will be carefully analyzed based on the theories and framework of behavioral finance, and all data will be retrieved from Yahoo Finance.

2 Literature Review

2.1 The Investment Value of the Analyst Words

The research was conducted by Womack in 1996 trying to indicate the value of the brokerage analysts over stocks. The author demonstrated that stock forecasting firms invest massively themselves, and build credibility on this solid ground [3]. Investors tend to be influenced by the recommendations of the analysts, yet their attitudes toward buying and selling signals were different [3]. Womack discovered that when the firm published a buying signal, the recommendation would bring a drift to mean for the certain stock for a 2.4% increase in stock price, however, the selling signal would display a much larger movement, where the stock price can be drifted as much as 9.1% down in average [3]. The author also testified to the duration of the effect and concluded that the buying signal created a much shorter-lived reaction to investors, with only a few weeks long, and the selling signals can last much longer, with approximately 6 months [3]. The reasons investors follow the voice of the analysts can be attributed that the information collection and analysis can be surprisingly costly [3]. Individual investors usually have less capability in acquiring in-depth data from the company and market and lack the necessary tools and knowledge in interpreting the information [4]. Therefore, a conclusive, easy-to-understand signal provided by professional investment firms could be the optimized solution in seeking guidance from the market. On top of that, the prominent companies must maintain certain regulatory rules set by the government, and a good reputation in the industry, thus, the investors believed that it would be less likely the investment firms will intentionally misguide or misinform the public.

As the stock price can reflect a certain degree of market, industry, and firm-level information, there are various movements and deviations of the market price to what public information presents [5]. There are three major informed participants in this game, insiders, institutional investors, and financial analysts [5]. All of them have the advantages of collecting data and making a more analytical and well-supported investment decision compared to normal individual investors [5]. Therefore, their movements are closely monitored and processed, and the investment direction and selection can also be copied or followed by individual investors. Therefore, when unified opinions are claimed by those players, they can have massive influence over the market price, and some of the opinions can even break the regulation of the SEC. The SEC filed against Elon Musk after his open tweets saying that he could take Tesla, private, at a certain price per share, which the price offered was significantly higher than the public trading price. However, the movement was not proved by the shareholder's meeting, and that information was not valid or legal to openly claim. However, Elon Musk, one of the key figures in Tesla, can be seen as a form of insider, and when he speaks, the weight of his voice can be influential, and the fact was, many investors believed the speech, and the price of the Tesla share price skyrocketed [6]. The reason for the disruption was that the public believed the credibility of Elon Musk as a public representative, and an active entrepreneur with fame in the country, and his public claim must be thoroughly processed and testified before voicing out. However, it turned out that Elon Musk did not obtain any credential permit from the company and shareholder's meeting, and it was more like a joke or unintended speech.

The researchers discovered that the analysts' activities are highly correlated to the price change of the shares, and when the analyst's made judgment or recommendation over certain stock, the fluctuation of the stock price tend to be significant [5]. That was based on the assumption that the "experts" can win over the market, and have the "magic" tool or insider information, that others cannot easily acquire [2]. However, this myth was broken by scholars saying that the analysts did not have an abnormal return on the portfolio, and it indicated that the analysts cannot win over or ignore the power of the market and external influential factors like politics, global crisis, and market change [2]. Surprisingly, when it comes to the sell pieces of advice, the analysts indeed demonstrated an overperformed result, that the strategies recommended made certain values to the investors, as the over-valued stock would be phased out in the early stage sometimes [2].

2.2 The Forecast Adjustments and Biased Recommendation

The research from Michaely and Womack displayed that the recommendation from the sell-side analysts and underwriters can be biased, as the interest has conflicted with the other investors [2]. It is understandable as the analysts usually work for sell-side companies, or financial institutes, where they are themselves the major players in the stock market. Therefore, the recommendations and strategies released can be intentionally biased to misguide and misinform the investors and clients to make a profit from the reverse operation. It may sabotage the reputation of the company; however, the recommendations can sometimes be well-backed by the data and soldi persuasion, therefore, it may also not easy to detect such a move [2]. Research indicated that analysts can be overacting on certain signals or indicators, and can bring emotional influence over the followers and public [7]. There were plenty of reasons behind it, to begin with, the analysts may weigh the occurrence of the matters more seriously than it should be [7]. The analysts have their own analytical or forecasting tools and formula for determining the trend and fluctuation of the stock market, and they prefer to explain the change of the stock price based on the information acquired at the present, therefore, the emerging new information, or the matter that may or may not affect the stock can be exaggerating on commenting the price change of the stock. Secondly, the analysts may gain fame and reputation by bringing emotions and surprising news to the market, where the opinions of the analysts may easily obtain attention from the peer, media, and normal investors. The publicity of the analysts is vital for their career, as it determines the influences and credibility of the analysis made. Therefore, they tend to voice up and overact to make a scene and draw attention from others [7]. The institutional players and analysts were also found intertwined when it comes to the firm that was held significantly by the institutions [8]. The other key factor influencing the biased of the stock can be the number of the stock held by the institutions, as when a particular stock was vastly held by investment companies, the analysts tend to focus more on the price changes and provide more pieces of advice over this stock. Then the price change of the stock can be quite sensitive and will be interpreted massively [8]. When the behavior of the analysts and institutional players are highly correlated, then the comments or recommendations over the stock can be questionable.

2.3 The Revision of the Analysis

When the company reveals the earning statement, and the directors or the C suites revealed a series of vital information or native that may influence the future revenue and share prices, the analysts would revise the analytical report regarding the expectation of the share price to buy [9]. According to a traditional framework, the public information would have already been fully reflected in the share price, and it has merely any opportunities for arbitration, as the mispricing would not exist. Yet, the common movement that the analysts would is that they would release revised recommendations over certain stocks, and suggest further operations of the investors [9]. The research found that around 25% of the analysts' reports were released within three days of the earning announcement, and it indicated that the earning announcement can vastly alter the attitude or the perspectives of the analysts, and the reasons can be vital enough to understand the motive and logics of analysts recommending or commenting stock to the investors, and why investors follow [9]. What's more, the research further stated that there were plenty of key perspectives that how analysts can gather and process information acquired from earnings announcements. First, the weights would be altered and influenced to forecast the earning expectations, as the real figure came out from the publication so that the key numbers will be switched from the calculated one to the real one. Then, the earning announcement also allowed the analysts to revise their previous forecast, and they can calibrate the prediction so that in the future, the overall performance of the precision of the anticipation will be improved [9]. And for the confirmation bias hypothesis, the research also raised that analysts would act strongly to the signals [9].

2.4 The Positive Impact

It was believed that the analysts' activities, including the judgment and recommendations, can help the stock to have more synchronization with the information derived from the intra-industry, and they contributed much more transparent and fair information to the public, where the price of the stock can be more realistic and fairer in long term [5]. The analysts can also raise the "Glamour Stocks", where they are highly appraised and recommended by general analysts, and the stock price is maximized to lower the cost of financing so that they could be better discovered, and developed with sufficient funding and recognition [1]. It was also suggested that the analysts' comments can contribute to market efficiency, as the recommendations derived from the latest earning announcements can have substantially better earning response coefficients [9].

3 Methodology

The essay will be conducted through a case study of the analysts' predictions on electric vehicle stocks that are currently listed on the US stock market. There are seven leading companies' stocks in the EV industry, and they are Tesla (TSLA, NASDAQ), Lucid

(LCID, NASDAQ), Rivian (RIVN, NASDAQ), General Motors (GM, NYSE), Ford (F, NYSE), Nio (NIO, NYSE), and XPeng (XPEV, NYSE). And the research will select 2 brands from them, which are Tesla, and Nio. The analysts' comments and recommendations will be sought from Yahoo Finance, where the analysts report on those companies with recommendations of buy or sell. The share price will be analyzed according to the time the comments of the analysts had been published, and the fluctuation over the comments will be retrieved according to the measurement of 3 days, 15 days, and 1 month, either suggesting for short or long for the stock. The fluctuation and changes will be recorded to see how the share price of those EV companies can be influenced by the analysis, and other factors will be removed like the market shock that can influence the whole market.

3.1 Why EV Industry?

The EV industry is a newly emerged market, where many players are rushing into the equity market, and expanding their business worldwide, there are only a few types of research on the factors that can influence share price change of the EV companies, and the gap of the research for this topic is also clear, that the EV market receives rather large and frequent attention from the analysts and media. The share price model and valuation model of the EV companies are rather premature, and the investors are unsure of the investment strategies of the EV companies, which would result in huge fluctuation of the price change that can be related to the emotional or informational guidance. Many analysts are also watching the EV industry closely, especially since there are two rising topics, Tesla and its founder Elon Musk, and the Chinese EV brands [10]. Overall, the EV industry then becomes a fine target to analyze the effect of the comments from analysts on stock price, and the analysis created by the experts can be easily found.

3.2 Why These Two Companies?

Tesla is either a good investment or a potential grower for many research companies and investors, and it can be easily testified by many kinds of measurements. It is impossible to leave Tesla out of the list of any EV stocks. Tesla is indeed the dominating and leading player in electric vehicles. It began the revolution. Moreover, with the hot trending topic of CEO Elon Musk, TSLA stock overcome unimaginable challenges. A few years ago, it came near bankruptcy on a financial level, but it is still alive and well [11]. The Tesla team's achievement stunned Wall Street, and it has valuable meaning to understand this company from the perspective of the analysts.

NIO Inc. is a China-based holding company involved primarily in the research, development, and production of premium smart electric cars. The company's primary focus is on the design, development, production, and marketing of premium smart electric cars. The majority of the company's products include ES8, ES6, EC6, and ET7. The company develops solutions for battery switching and autonomous driving [12]. It is a representing company for Chinese-made EV manufacturers and can fit the US stock trading regulations, which indicated that this brand aims to develop globally, and can be seen as a flagship of the EV market (Tables 1 and 2).

4 Data Analysis

Table 1. Tesla correlation of the recommendation and stock price change.

Date of the Suggestions	Recommended Movement	3 Days Stock Change	15 Days Stock Change	30 Days Stock Change	Effect
2021.9.10	Buy	+0.91%	+5.18%	+7.56%	Positive
2021.11.5	Buy	−4.83%	−6.96%	−17.43%	Negative
2022.1.7	Buy	+3.04%	−9.44%	−11.65%	Negative
2022.3.4	Buy	−4.02%	+9.88%	+36.64%	Positive
2022.7.1	Buy	+2.56%	+5.64%	+30.81%	Positive

Table 2. No correlation between the recommendation and stock price change.

Date of the Suggestions	Recommended Movement	3 Days Stock Change	15 Days Stock Change	30 Days Stock Change	Effect
2021.10.1	Buy	−5.6%	+6.59%	+14.43%	Positive
2021.12.3	Buy	+0.59%	−12.41%	+4.11%	Negative
2022.3.4	Buy	−2.74%	+8.75%	+28.02%	Positive
2022.5.6	Buy	−9.18%	+7.24%	+28.55%	Positive
2022.8.5	Buy	−0.25%	−6.28%	−15.38%	Negative

Notes: The designed date of the stock price would sometimes can not be retrieved due to the non-trading days, therefore, the price will be picked from the nearest trading day

There are other variables like the emerging news related to the companies and industries, which cannot be separated from the fluctuation, yet in long-term forecasting, the effect of those variables can be insignificant, as those companies are relatively stable in production and operation.

When the positive and negative are present at the same time, then the final effect will be decided by adding up the negative and positive to have the final value, to determine which side has a stronger effect.

4.1 The Discussion of the Analysis

The abnormal aspect of the analysis would be all buy suggestions from the analysts. Therefore, a certain number of the hold or sell advice from few analysts, but the number of analysts against the buy is insignificant so the analysis only takes the advice from the overwhelming side of the opinion. It is peculiar that all recommendations towards EV industries are positive, and it was explained with the following possibilities. To begin with, the EV industry is new to the market, and the valuation model is not yet accepted or generalized so most analysts hold a positive view the EV companies, and they believed that once the valuation model for EV companies is matured, the share price of the EV companies will be increased, as currently most of them are undervalued [11]. The other reason would be the unfinished sophistication of this business model, as the EV industries bring out many surrounding technologies, research, and investments, such as the innovation of batteries, the smart city project, the switching stations, and the EV rental business. Therefore, analysts believed that there is still plenty of room for EV companies to demonstrate their business model and increase their value to the market. Although the all-buy suggestion did not allow us to testify to the comments and suggestions of the sell side, the data still is sufficient to testify to the relationship between the recommendation and the effect of the share price.

The effect for both Tesla and Nio is similar, with 3 out of 5 being positive, and the rest is negative. It indicated that the analysts influence the share price, but it does not always work out, as there are days that the analysts' predictions are opposite to the trend of the share price. Therefore, it is concluded that the influence is presented, but the power of the influence is insignificant to direct the overall trend of the business share price. And we could say that the effect of the analyst's comments on the share price is not significant in the EV industry.

From the time perspective, it is apparent that the longer the time, the better positively correlated to the analyst's comments. This phenomenon is especially obvious in Nio, as for the three-day effect, four out of five demonstrate a reverse trend to the analysis prediction, yet when it comes to 15 days, three out of five demonstrate a positive relation, and the overall percentage keeps enlarging in 30 days. Tesla can also be spotted with the same pattern, indicating that the effect will spread over time, and the longer the time, the stronger the effect of the analyst's prediction in EV industries. Since no longer tests were being done, it is unsure that the trend will continue for a much longer period.

5 Theoretical Analysis

This positive relationship between the analyst's prediction and stock price can be found in the theory of behavioral biases in the financial markets. It was believed that the momentum of behavioral finance has been triggered by this phenomenon. The word refers to the effect that the price of the stock will be leveled higher or pushed lower than its original power, where an external or internal power will deliver a force of momentum to the stock, making the stock overacts itself [13]. In this case, the analysts act like the external power, that can push the stock price either higher or lower than it ought to be, as the investors would be convinced by the tendency of the stock price changes. This effect gets more obvious when the timeline is longer, as when the tendency is set, the force of driving high or low can be stronger day by day. From the research, the initial change of the trend was rather small, and when the trend started to move large, more investors would be convinced and joined the rise or the fall of the share price, and when 30 days passed, the share price has already changed much, possibly than it should be. The momentum could also be explained by the disposition effect, which refers to the willingness to sell the potential winning stock quickly, and holds the losing stocks for too long [14].

The other available theory within the study of behavioral finance would be the herding effect. Herding is a phrase often used in the context of the stock exchanges to describe the conduct of a trader who, rather than pursuing individual thought and knowledge, copies the activities they see other investors doing or the movements of the market itself. People are almost always in complete agreement with each other about these two things. Herding, which is among the foundational framework in the recently created field of behavioral asset pricing, is one factor that contributes to the explanation of economic abnormalities [15]. In this case, analysts act with herding effects, and spread that influence over other investors, making the overall market pursue the same direction.

5.1 Other Factors and the Accuracy of the Fluctuation

The development of the media, the popularity of the stock selection application, and easy access to the stock information can also be contributing factors to the analysis. All of them can ease the entry barrier of the stock exchange and can bring more opinions from analysts to the public, where the investors would have more opportunities and less cost to retrieve professional opinions [16]. However, it also indicated that individual investors could be much easier to get affected by the voice of the analysts and become more panicky than before, as they receive conflicting and various types of messages and information daily. The herding effect could be more obvious in this case when the individual investors can easily get access to the other investors on the same paper. Therefore, the voice of the analysts could be vital and significant to the investors who rely on much over these channels in acquiring guidance and information. Some other factors and forces may disturb the intention of the analysis from retrieving data that only was affected by the comments from analysts. The factors include the operation and business performance of the company, the technology-related news impacting the industry, the change in market demand, and governmental policies. Those can not be separated from the observed price change, and it will not have a substantial impact on the result, therefore, those factors are not discussed in this research, yet they may impact the accuracy of the research.

6 Conclusion

This research has discussed the effect of the analysts' comments and recommendations on the share price of the EV industry, conducted by the case study of the reaction of the stock market to the analyst's prediction reports. The result demonstrated that the positive correlation between the comments and recommendations, and the share price can be spotted in both Tesla and Nio, which represent the leading roles of the EV industries, the relationship can be regarded as insignificant. That was not compatible with the literature reviews and hypothesis made in the beginning, however, it can also be interpreted by various possibilities, including the EV industry traits, as it is a rather new and emerging industry, with vast undetected space to grow, therefore, it is not possible to fully reconstruct the business model or valuation mode for this industry. On the other hand, the EV industry can also be seen as a sensitive industry that can be overreacting to external market changes, like the effect of Covid-19, or the Ukraine war at present.

Therefore, the effect of the comments and recommendations on the share price of the EV industry must be carefully examined under a more prudent model of experiments. What's more, this paper also found out that the longer the time, the more correlated to the analysts' prediction, where 30 days are more accurate than 15 days, and 3 days effect was the minimum. All in all, there is further research required on the behavioral finance framework study to examine the phenomenon of the effect released from the experts' comments and recommendations in other industries.

7 Limitation

Due to the invalid information collection and restricted analysis factors, the result of the research can not fully and completely reflect the influence of analysts' comments and may be affected by other influencers like governmental policies, news, business performance, and market changes. Those factors were challenging to determine, and difficult to observe from the price change, therefore, the result of the research may not accurately reflect the price change to the analysts' comments.

References

1. Dechow, P.M., Hutton, A.P., Sloan, R.G.: The relation between analysts' forecasts of long-term earnings growth and stock price performance following equity offerings. Contemp. Account. Res. **17**(1), 1–32 (2000)
2. Michaely, R., Womack, K.: Brokerage recommendations: stylized characteristics, market responses, and biases. Adv. Behav. Finan. II, 389–422 (2005)
3. Womack, K.: Do brokerage analysts' recommendations have investment value? J. Finan. **51**, 137–167 (1996)
4. Adams, M.E., George, S., Dougherty, D.: Enhancing new product development performance: an organizational learning perspective. J. Prod. Innov. Manage.: Int. Publ. Prod. Dev. Manage. Assoc. **15**, 403–422 (1998)
5. Piotroski, J., Roulstone, D.: The influence of analysts, institutional investors, and insiders on the incorporation of market, industry, and firm-specific information into stock prices. Account. Rev. **79**, 1119–1151 (2004)
6. US SEC. Elon Musk Settles SEC Fraud Charges; Tesla Charged With and Re-solves Securities Law Charge. http://www.sec.gov/news/press-release/2018-226. Accessed 16 Aug 2022
7. De Bondt, W., Thaler, R.: Do security analysts overreact?. Am. Econ. Rev., 52–57 (1990)
8. Ackert, L., Athanassakos, G.: A simultaneous equations analysis of analysts' forecast bias, analyst following, and institutional ownership. J. Bus. Finan. Account. **30**, 1017–1042 (2003)
9. Yezegel, A.: Why do analysts revise their stock recommendations after earnings announcements? J. Account. Econ. **59**, 163–181 (2015)
10. Thomas, V.J., Maine, E.: Market entry strategies for electric vehicle start-ups in the automotive industry–lessons from Tesla motors. J. Clean. Prod. **235**, 653–663 (2019)
11. Electric Vehicle Stocks With 'Buy' Analyst Ratings. https://hk.finance.yahoo.com/news/7-electric-vehicle-stocks-buy-094551360.html. Accessed 16 Aug 2022
12. Nio Official Website. https://finance.yahoo.com/quote/NIO/profile?p=NIO. Accessed 16 Aug 2022
13. Du, D.: Momentum and behavioral finance. Managerial Finance (2012)

14. do Nascimento Pitthan, F.: Can momentum be explained by fund flows or disposition effect? The impact of behavioral biases and capital flows in Brazilian market movements. Int. J. Trade Econ. Finan. **12,** 1–8 (2021)
15. Kudryavtsev, C., Hon-Snir, S.: Rational'or'Intuitive': are behavioral biases correlated across stock market investors? Contemp. Econ. **7,** 31–53 (2013)
16. Tetlock, P.: Giving content to investor sentiment: The role of media in the stock market. J. Finan. **63,** 1139–1168 (2007)

The Effects of Transforming the CDMO Strategy on the Business Performance of Porton Based on Financial Statement Analysis

Lei Zhang(✉)

Department of Business, Xinjiang University, Urumqi 830000, Xinjiang, China
107552003632@stu.xju.edu.cn

Abstract. Contract Development and Manufacturing Organization (CDMO) refers to customization, development, and production in the medical field and is a newly emerging research and development (R&D) outsourcing model in the medical field. The target of this paper was to explore how the CDMO strategy transformation of Porton Fine Chemicals Ltd. (Porton) will affect the company's business performance. This paper employed the method of financial statement analysis to investigate the operating performance of Porton. In order to better utilize the CDMO strategy to improve business performance, this paper concluded that enterprises should vigorously develop their Contract Research Organization (CRO) businesses, strive to increase production capacity, and improve their credit policies so as to control the proportion of accounts receivable. The contribution of this paper was to analyze the impact of Porton's CDMO transformation strategy on the business performance of the company and provide ideas for the development of other companies, especially those in the pharmaceutical industry, to accomplish CDMO transformation and improve business performance.

Keywords: Porton · CDMO · CRO

1 Introduction

1.1 Research Background

Due to the increasing innovation capacity of small companies and the growing market share of the innovative drugs they generate, the structure of the global pharmaceutical industry has changed significantly over the last decade. However, the inherent drawbacks of R&D and production of innovative drugs, such as high capital investment and time-consuming and unstable results, place high demands on the overall capabilities of small companies. Therefore, to improve the efficiency of R&D production and return on investment, more and more companies choose to cooperate with third-party companies that provide CDMO services, and this behavior has also led to the rising heat of the global CDMO market.

CDMO refers to customization, development, and production in the medical field and is a newly emerging R&D outsourcing model in the medical field. CDMO can help more R&D-oriented companies complete practical technology transformation and provide innovative process development and large-scale production services for pharmaceutical companies. At first, the CDMO market in Europe and the United States occupied a large market share. However, in the later period, due to the restrictions of strict environmental protection policies, high R&D and production costs, and insufficient capacity allocation, the market center gradually shifted to China, India, and other countries. Since 2015, China has also introduced a series of policies to support the CDMO industry. In June 2016, the General Office of the State Council issued the "Pilot Program of the Drug Listing License System," which separates the management of the drug's listing license from the manufacturing license, and this policy has driven the development of the drug manufacturing outsourcing service industry. In 2017, Porton's two core customers, Gilead and Johnson & Johnson, sold fewer products, leading to the company's first decline in operating revenue and parent profit in nearly a decade, with operating revenue down 11% and parent profit down 37% [1]. To solve the problem of declining sales performance, Porton no longer implemented the development strategy of "big customer + big product". In terms of clients, adopt a strategy of "3 + 5 + N", that is, no longer only depend on the three major customers but choose to cooperate with more companies at the same time. In terms of business, through the acquisition of J-STAR, the Contract Manufacture Organization (CMO) and CRO businesses were combined to realize the transformation to the CDMO business.

Founded in July 2005, Porton is a leading pharmaceutical R&D and manufacturing outsourcing organization in China. In 2022, Porton ranked third among the top 20 CDMO companies in China. Porton has realized the transformation to CDMO through the combination of CMO and CRO. In addition to providing traditional production services, the company pays more attention to R&D and innovation in the production process.

In the pharmaceutical field, there are many papers and studies related to CMO and CRO, such as Cheng's, which applied Wuxi AppTec, a CRO company, as the research object to explore the relationship between equity incentives and corporate performance by interpreting the equity incentive policy of the company in the past years [2]. Ye exploited Tigermed, the first listed CRO company in China, as the research object to explore the rationality of equity incentive programs in CRO companies from two levels of motivation and implementation effect [3]. Cao took the global biopharmaceutical CDMO and CMO market as the object of research and studied the future development space and investment strategy of this market [4]. Focusing on the CRO and CMO markets, Gu analyzed the key factors driving the rapid development of the industry [5].

1.2 Research Gap

Although there is a large amount of research on the CRO, CMO, and CDMO markets, the decline in the company's operating results was generated by the decrease in products sold by two of its core customers in 2017. This event made the company realize that a single CMO business type could hardly support the sustainable development of the company, so it combined CMO and CRO through the acquisition of J-STAR in 2017 to accomplish the transformation to CDMO. Few scholars have studied the behavior of the strategic transition from CMO to CDMO, so to fill this part of the research gap, this article is going to explore whether the strategic transition of the company from CMO to

CDMO can solve the decline in business performance. This paper hopes to provide ideas for the development of other companies through analyzing the strategic transformation of Porton, especially for other companies in the pharmaceutical industry to accomplish the transformation of CDMO.

1.3 Structure of This Paper

This paper will take Porton as the main research object and collect the relevant information from the company's financial statements, such as operating income, net profit, current assets, and current liabilities, to analyze the company's profitability, operating ability, and solvency. In the process of case analysis, this paper will analyze the main reasons for the decline in the company's operating performance and demonstrate how these reasons have led to the decline in the company's operating performance. At the same time, this paper will give reasonable opinions and suggestions based on the problems that have arisen in the company's operation.

2 Literature Review

The balance sheet, income statement, statement of changes in owners' equity, cash flow statement, and notes are all examples of financial statements. They show how a business is performing financially at a certain point in time and how it is performing during a certain time period. The process of processing, calculating, and comparing the information in the above statements is called "financial statement analysis". Financial statement analysis refers to the process of processing, calculating, and comparing the data in the above statements. Yang argued that financial statement analysis is an essential process for an enterprise to understand its financial situation and business performance more comprehensively and deeply, to forecast the future development trend based on historical data, and finally to formulate a reasonable and effective development strategy [6]. The data in the financial statements are the basic data for the implementation of financial management in enterprises. Tang concluded that by processing these data, it can provide scientific and effective data for the formulation and implementation of financial management decisions of enterprises, thus improving the reliability and effectiveness of financial management [7]. In addition, the analysis of financial statements can also identify the problems and risks in the financial management and operation management of enterprises, such as whether the operating income is declining or the current liabilities are too high, and then take measures to solve them. Jin argues that it can also reduce financial and operational risks for businesses while promoting the steady and sustainable development of enterprises [8].

In accounting practice, the most common methods of financial statement analysis include the comparative method, ratio method, and factor analysis. This paper mainly adopts the comparative method and ratio method to analyze the financial statements and understand the profitability, solvency, and operating capacity of enterprises by calculating comparative profitability indicators, solvency indicators, and operating capacity indicators. The profitability of an enterprise refers to its ability to obtain profits from its business activities, which is the key to measuring the overall strength of the enterprise.

Net sales margin, return on net assets, and net margin on total assets are important indicators for evaluation and analysis. The short-term solvency of an enterprise refers to its ability to repay current liabilities with current assets, which can generally be measured by the current ratio and quick ratio. This ratio can measure its ability to repay its daily maturing debts. Operating capacity reflects the ability of the enterprise's daily operations, and the general financial staff adopts indicators such as inventory turnover ratio, accounts receivable turnover ratio, and the current asset turnover ratio to measure the efficiency of the enterprise's asset utilization. The analysis of the above financial indicators can dig deeper into the opportunities and challenges behind the financial statement data, turn the financial statement data into useful information, and help information users make better decisions.

3 Case Description

Porton (see Fig. 1) was established in 2005 and listed on the Shenzhen Stock Exchange in 2014. Porton's main partners are global pharmaceutical companies and new drug R&D institutions, providing them with chemical APIs, chemical formulations, and biologics from pre-clinical to clinical trials and through to market. At the beginning of its establishment, the main business of the company was CMO. That is, accept the commissions of pharmaceutical companies and provide all the services required to generate products. CMO does not involve substantial R&D work and is mainly applied in post-clinical and commercial projects. After acquiring J-STAR in 2017, Porton began to expand into CRO, providing professional services for the R&D processes of various institutions through contracts, including pre-clinical and clinical R&D. Before 2017, the company adopted the development strategy of "big product + big customer".

Fig. 1. Brand of Porton [9].

As can be seen from Table 1, in 2016, the revenue from anti-virus and anti-diabetes products accounted for 74.11% of the total revenue in that year. As can also be seen from the financial reports prior to 2017, the company's products were mainly focused on anti-diabetes, anti-AIDS, and anti-hepatitis C types.

As can be seen from Table 2, in 2016, the revenue from the top 2 customers accounted for 56.44%, and the revenue from the top 5 customers accounted for 71.36%. In terms of customers, it implements the strategy of "big customer" and establishes long-term strategic cooperative relations with major customers such as Johnson & Johnson and Gilead. Before 2017, the top five customers accounted for more than 70% of the revenue.

In 2017, Proton's operating revenue and parent profit decreased by 11% and 37%, respectively, as a result of a decrease in end-use demand for anti-hepatitis C type products

Table 1. Proportion of Operating Revenue by Product in 2016 [10].

Type of product	Proportion of operating revenue
Anti-virus	57.32%
Anti-diabetes	16.79%
Hypolipidemic	6.99%
Anti-cancer	4.51%
Else	14.39%

Table 2. Proportion of Total Sales of The Company's Top 5 Customers in 2016 [10].

Name	Proportion of total sales
Customer 1	36.19%
Customer 2	20.25%
Customer 3	6.7%
Customer 4	4.88%
Customer 5	3.35%
Total	71.36%

from Proton's primary customer Gilead and the adjustment of stocking strategies by customers of anti-diabetic products [1]. This was the only year in the company's history in which both revenue and profit fell. In order to no longer rely only on large customers and reduce business risks, Porton transformed its strategy into "3 + 5 + N" to expand customer groups and establish CDMO capabilities. Among them, three are the traditional large customers: Johnson & Johnson, Gilead, and GSK; five are Pfizer, Novartis, Roche, Boehringer Ingelheim, and Allergan; and N refers to small customers. In 2021, after years of strategic transformation, four of the top ten customers of the company are small companies, accounting for about 20% of the revenue, which has become a new driving force in the company's development [1]. The impact of large customers on the company is also gradually diminishing, and the revenue fluctuations generated by large customers continue to decrease. In terms of business, the 2017 acquisition of J-STAR has become a crucial component of CDMO's expansion. J-STAR has rich and extensive experience in chemical synthesis, process analysis, crystallization technology, etc. The acquisition of J-STAR's customer resources, R&D equipment, and technical personnel, which is conducive to increasing CRO capabilities, and the combination of CMO and CRO to establish CDMO skills, enabled Porton to expand its company to the front end of early business. Since its strategic transformation in 2017, Porton has shown accelerated growth in operating revenue and net income. As for the expense ratio, it is relatively stable overall, with the company's selling expense ratio and financial expense ratio remaining at a low level. The administrative expense ratio decreases year by year with the realization of the scale effect, from 12.67% in 2017 to 7.55% in the third quarter of 2022 [1]. However, with the transformation of the company's strategy, the company continues to increase its investment in R&D, resulting in an increase in the R&D expense ratio from 6.33% in 2017 to 8.64% in the third quarter of 2022 [1]. Porton's gross margin level has been increasing since 2017, but it is still lower than that of other companies in the CDMO industry, such as Asymchem Laboratories (Tianjin) Co., Ltd. And Pharma Block Sciences (Nanjing), Inc. In addition, Porton's fixed asset utilization and current asset quality need to be further improved.

4 Analysis on the Problems

4.1 The CRO Business is not Mature Enough, Resulting in a Low Gross Profit Margin

As can be seen from Fig. 2, since the strategic transformation of Porton in 2017, the gross profit margin of the company has shown an overall upward trend. However, before the third quarter of 2022, the gross profit margin was still lower than that of Asymchem, the benchmark enterprise in the CDMO industry. The CRO business at Porton is not mature enough, resulting in a low gross profit margin.

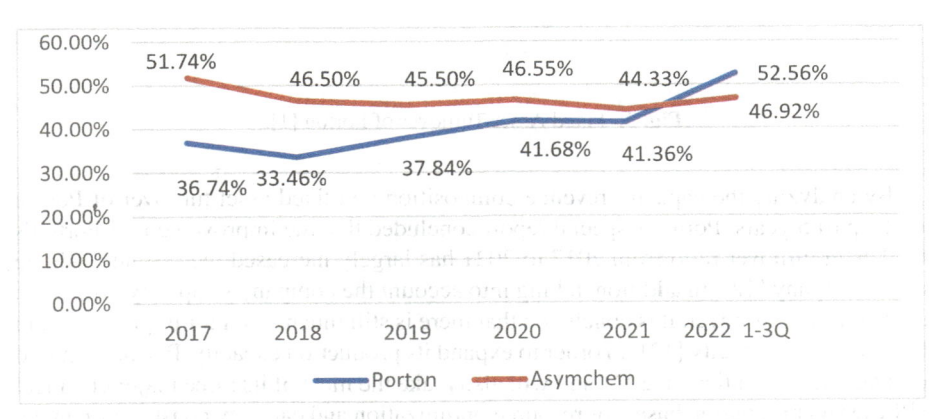

Fig. 2. Porton and Asymchem Gross Profit Margin Comparison [1].

Huang concluded that through the M&A behavior, Proton started to develop its CRO business vigorously by making the most of R&D technology synergy, and the business started to extend to the early stage of drug development, which was able to increase the order volume and optimize the operational efficiency [11]. Porton has only started to vigorously develop its CRO business and transition to its CDMO business since 2017. The implementation of Po's CRO business has improved the gross margin of the company to a certain extent, but the level of CRO is not mature enough compared to Asymchem, a benchmark company in the industry, so it leads to a lower gross margin than the company.

4.2 Insufficient Production Capacity Leads to Low Fixed Asset Turnover

As can be seen from Fig. 3, since the strategic transformation in 2017, Porton's fixed asset turnover has been increasing, but the overall level is low. The lack of production capacity leads to low fixed asset turnover.

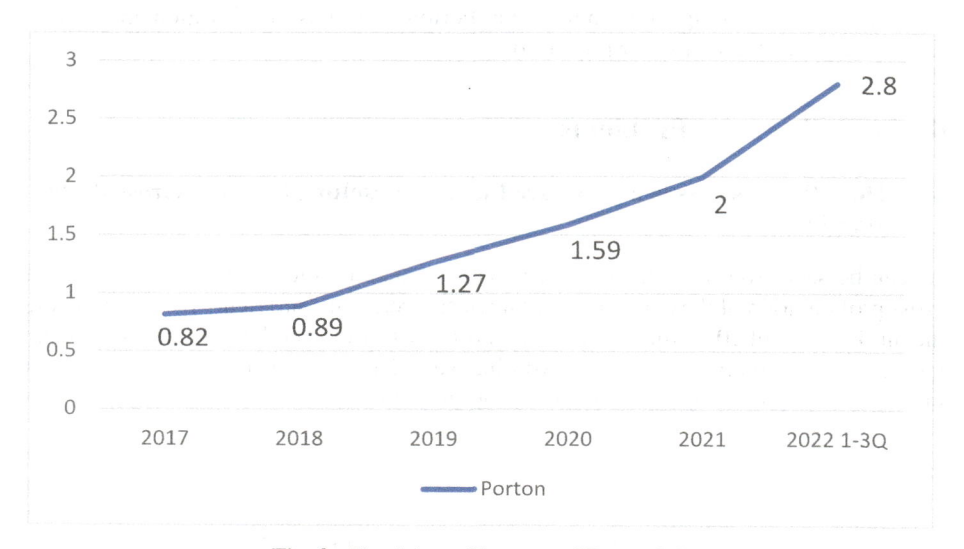

Fig. 3. Fixed Asset Turnover of Porton [1].

By analyzing the capacity-revenue composition and fixed asset turnover of Porton for the past 5 years, Porton's special report concluded that the improvement of Porton's fixed asset turnover ratio from 2017 to 2021 has largely increased the revenue volume of the company [12]. In addition, taking into account the company's capacity utilization and fixed asset turnover, it is concluded that there is still much room for improvement in the company's capacity [12]. In order to expand its production capacity, Porton acquired Yuyang Pharmaceutical in 2021 and will also make the most of its three major chemical API CDMO production bases for resource optimization and capacity construction in the future. This acquisition has boosted the company's production capacity and increased its fixed asset turnover. Increasing production capacity can accelerate fixed asset turnover, but the current production capacity still has more room for development. Therefore, although the asset turnover ratio is increasing year over year, the overall level is still relatively low.

4.3 Management Reasons Yield a Large Proportion of Accounts Receivable

As can be seen from Fig. 4, the proportion of accounts receivable in current assets and total assets of Porton has gradually increased since 2018. The proportion of accounts receivable gradually increases, which will bring greater financial pressure to enterprises. The inadequate management of accounts receivable due to management reasons is one of the reasons for this phenomenon.

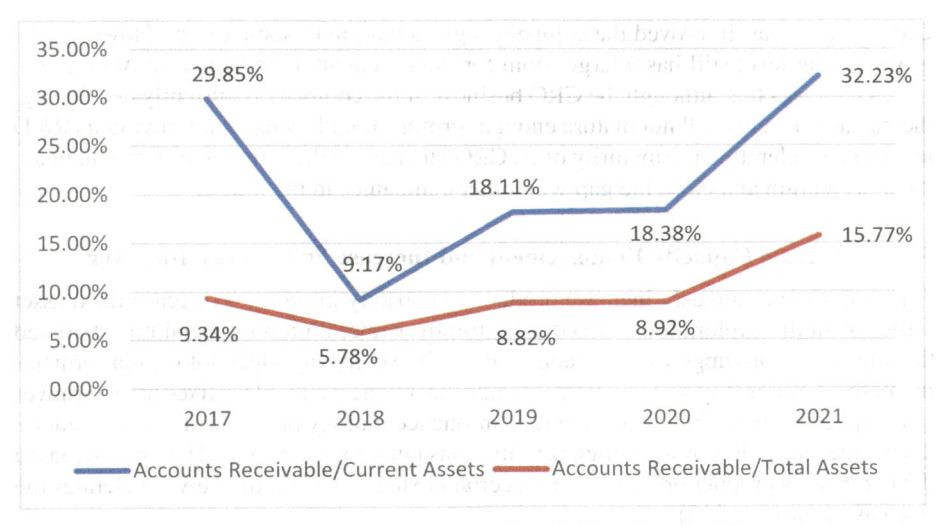

Fig. 4. Proportion of Accounts Receivable of Porton [1].

Fu examines the problems in accounts receivable management of Chinese pharmaceutical manufacturing companies and proposes targeted solutions [13]. Through her analysis, she concludes that management reasons are one of the reasons for the large proportion of accounts receivable in pharmaceutical manufacturing companies [13]. The management ignores the consequences that a large proportion of accounts receivable will bring a large capital pressure to the company while deliberately extending the credit period in order to maintain the relationship with large customers and prevent customer loss [13]. Proton's customers are all fully qualified large pharmaceutical companies such as Johnson & Johnson, Gilead, and Pfizer, and with huge contracts, these large orders are crucial to the company's performance. In addition, the CDMO market in China is also very competitive, with companies of the same type as Proton, such as Asymchem and Zhejiang Jiuzhou Pharmaceuticals. Therefore, in order to maintain the relationship with large customers and prevent the loss of customers, the management generally relaxes the credit policy for large customers, resulting in slow collection of accounts receivable and a large and increasing proportion.

5 Suggestions

5.1 Accelerate the Development of the CRO Business to Improve Gross Margin

Porton must improve their R&D level and accelerate the development of their CRO business in order to increase their gross profit margin. Through exploring the CRO and CMO markets, Gu found that CRO can quickly organize a team with high specialization and rich experience in new drug R&D, reduce the R&D and management costs of enterprises through the scale effect, improve the gross margin of enterprises, and ultimately help enterprises to develop better [5]. Since Porton launched its CRO business in 2017, the overall gross margin has shown an upward trend, indicating that the development of the

CRO business has improved the company's gross margin to some extent. However, the gross margin level still has a large room for improvement, comparable to Asymchem, which indicates that although the CRO business of the company is currently developing, the business level is still not mature enough. Proton should focus on improving its R&D level and accelerating the maturity of its CRO business in the future in order to maintain its gross margin and close the gap with other companies in the industry.

5.2 Accelerate Capacity Enhancement and Increase Fixed Asset Turnover

Porton must continuously increase production capacity in order to increase fixed asset turnover. In the exploration of fixed asset turnover rate, Porton's special report argued that the continuous upgrading and application of the company's technology platform has increased the company's production capacity and thus accelerated the fixed asset turnover rate, especially from 2020 when the four-in-one technology platform of "crystallization + enzyme catalysis + fluid + high activity" was put into operation [12]. It has increased the company's production capacity to a certain extent, which ultimately accelerates the fixed asset turnover [12].

Pharmaceutical R&D companies like WuXi Biologics, which bought Pfizer's manufacturing site in Hangzhou in 2021, and Zhejiang Jiuzhou Pharmaceuticals, which bought Sandoz's pharmaceutical plant in Zhongshan in 2022, have built or bought production sites to quickly increase their capacity. Proton also plans to build and develop a Slovenian manufacturing location. New sites could boost manufacturing capacity, operational efficiency, and fixed asset turnover.

5.3 Improve Credit Policy and Control the Percentage of Accounts Receivable

Enterprise management needs to improve the customer credit policy in order to keep the amount of accounts receivable within a reasonable range. Fu concluded that the enterprise's accounts receivable management can be improved by making the credit policy better [13]. Accounts receivable management can also call for different reasons for accounts receivable default, and it can set customer credit conditions according to the enterprise's internal financial situation and external economic environment, such as extending customer repayment periods when capital is loose and competition is fierce [13]. The credit policy of an enterprise's accounts receivable includes three aspects: credit criteria, credit terms, and collection policy. Porton can start with these three aspects and adjust the credit policy according to the different situations of accounts receivable. For some accounts receivable that often exceed the credit period and have a long overtime as well as enterprises with a poor industry outlook, Porton can appropriately tighten the credit policy so that it can speed up the collection of accounts receivable, reduce the percentage of accounts receivable, and at the same time relieve the financial pressure of the enterprise.

6 Conclusion

The global CDMO market is growing, and China's CDMO market is growing quickly and has a large market space. This is because the center of the market has moved to China and the Chinese government is helping. With China's CDMO market growing all the time, this paper looks at how pharmaceutical companies can improve their business performance by changing their CDMO strategies. Porton is used as a case study. Through the analysis of the profitability of Potton, it was found that the CRO business level of the company is not mature enough. As a result, the gross profit margin of the company has been rising since the strategic transformation, but it is still lower than that of Asymchem, the benchmark enterprise in the CDMO industry. By looking at Porton's operating capacity, it was found that the company didn't have enough production capacity, which led to a low turnover of fixed assets. In the exploration of corporate accounts receivable, it is found that corporate management considers the proportion of accounts receivable to be too large. Based on the problems, this paper later gave two suggestions. In summary, this paper argues that the CDMO strategy transformation at Porton can improve the decline of enterprise business performance. In order to better utilize the CDMO strategy to improve business performance, it is suggested that enterprises vigorously develop CRO businesses, strive to increase production capacity, and improve credit policies so as to control the proportion of accounts receivable and relieve the financial pressure on enterprises.

The main contribution of this paper is that it looks at how Proton improved its business performance by changing its CDMO strategy. This can help other businesses, especially those in the pharmaceutical industry, improve their business performance by changing their CDMO strategies.

The limitation of this paper is that the financial indicators analyzed are limited. This paper only analyzes the operating ability and profitability of enterprises but does not analyze the solvency of enterprises. In the analysis of enterprise operating capacity and profitability, only fixed asset turnover and gross profit margin indicators are applied. In addition, the analysis of the improvement in business performance due to the CDMO strategy is based on the authors' own summary analysis, which is subjective. As also recommended above, future investigations should exploit more financial indicators in order to better understand the improvement of the CDMO strategy on enterprise operating performance.

References

1. Porton's financial data. https://xueqiu.com/S/SZ300363. Accessed 03 Mar 2023
2. Cheng, S.M.: Research on the relationship between equity incentive and corporate performance of CRO companies: a case study of Wuxi AppTec. Mod. Bus. **21**(2), 66–68 (2022)
3. Ye, X.J.: Research on the motivation and implementation effect of equity incentive in CRO enterprises: a case study of Tigermed. Mon. J. Finan. Account. **18**(1), 24–33 (2020)
4. Cao, F.: Outlook and investment strategy analysis of CDMO/CMO of Chinese Biopharmaceutical. Zhang Jiang Sci. Technol. Rev. **5**(9), 56–60 (2019)
5. Gu, Y.: CRO, CMO crack research and development difficult, new drug research and development ushered in the best era. China Strat. Emerg. Ind. **33**(2), 46–48 (2017)
6. Yang, Q.Q.: The role of financial statement analysis in financial management and optimization measures. Invest. Entrepreneurship **33**(15), 81–83 (2022)
7. Tang, H.Y.: Financial statement analysis of small and medium-sized manufacturing enterprises: the case of Company A. Finan. Life **8**(5), 31–33 (2022)

8. Jin, X.H.: A study on the value of financial statement analysis application in enterprises. China Collective Econ. **3**(12), 156–158 (2022)
9. Official website of Porton. http://www.porton.cn. Accessed 03 Mar 2023
10. 2016 Annual Report. https://xueqiu.com/S/SZ300363. Accessed 03 Mar 2023
11. Huang, H.B.: Research on the performance of cross-border M&A guided by technology synergy: based on the case study of the Cross-border M&A J-STAR of Porton. Friends Account. **20**(2), 79–85 (2022)
12. Special report. https://max.book118.com/html/2022/0308/8104106012004062.shtm. Accessed 03 Mar 2023
13. Fu, X.F.: Analysis of problems and countermeasures of accounts receivable management in pharmaceutical manufacturing enterprises. Bus. News **18**(8), 99–101 (2021)

Economic Policy Uncertainty, ESG, and Corporate Performance

Fumian Huang[✉]

Queen's Business School, Queen's University Belfast, Belfast BT9 5EE, UK
fhuang04@qub.ac.uk

Abstract. Based on a sample of Chinese A-share non-financial listed firms from 2009–2020, this paper investigates the effect of economic policy uncertainty on corporate financial performance and the moderating effect of ESG ratings. The paper finds that economic policy uncertainty has a negative impact on corporate performance and finds that ESG rating performance is able to mitigate the negative impact of economic policy uncertainty on corporate financial performance when considering the ESG ratings of the firms in the sample. It enriches the research on the economic consequences of economic policy uncertainty and supplements to the literature of corporate performance and ESG practices. This paper suggests that incorporating ESG practices facilitates firms risk management.

Keywords: Economic Policy Uncertainty · ESG · Corporate Performance

1 Introduction

As a systematic risk, economic policy uncertainty raises numerous issues, particularly in recent years with pandemics, international instability etc., which impact on the economic environment and lead generating expectations of potential policy changes by governors in the affected countries. This is then ultimately transmitted to the various market participants. Therefore, the economic consequences of economic policy uncertainty are gaining more attention, especially in countries where economic policy implementation is more robust, i.e., China, and are of particular value for research. In addition, ESG ratings as an emerging indicator are being widely practiced by listed corporations. It is also worthwhile to consider whether the insurance mechanisms of ESG practices can enable corporates to mitigate risk in the midst of economic policy uncertainty.

The impact of economic policy uncertainty on corporate performance has been explored in previous literature. The main argument is that the change in the extent of economic policy uncertainty triggers firms to take the necessary actions, including inventory management, reducing investment and financing activities, adjusting surplus management, etc., to defend possible external shocks but that the implementation of these actions will be transmitted to the corporate performance [1–3]. Yet, few papers have evaluated the moderating effect of ESG factors on corporate performance shocks caused by economic policy uncertainty. Thus, this paper provides an essential supplement by investigates the impact of the economic uncertainty on corporate performance and evaluate the role of ESG in mitigating the impact of economic policy uncertainty on corporate performance.

This paper uses Chinese A-share listed firms as observations in the period of 2009 to 2020 and concludes that economic policy uncertainty has a negative impact on corporate performance. Further research demonstrates that the performance of corporate ESG practices mitigates the negative impact on corporate performance arising from economic policy uncertainty. The results hold after a series of robustness check, including alterative measure of main variables.

The contributions of this paper include: (1) As a new area of research, this paper enriches the literature on the economic consequences of economic policy uncertainty. (2) Enriching the literature on the factors affecting firm performance, this paper explores the effect of exogenous factors on corporate performance through the perspective of economic policy uncertainty. (3) This paper introduces the moderating role of ESG on the impact of economic policy uncertainty, providing new perspectives on ESG practices of corporations.

Remainder of the paper. The paper can be organized as follow. Section 2 is literature review and hypothesis development. Following that is Sect. 3 which is research design. After that is empirical result, conclusion, and reference list in the end.

2 Literature Review and Hypothesis Development

2.1 Literature on Economic Policy Uncertainty

Economic policy uncertainty is the uncertainty that results from political subjects not being explicit about the economic policy expectations, the implementation of the policy, the uncertainty resulting from the direction and intensity of changes in policy stance [1, 4]. China, the subject of this paper, has a higher level of economic policy uncertainty than other countries, which is reflected in the high degree of intervention and involvement of the Chinese government in economic activities. Hence, the Chinese sample has the significant research value.

Previous research on the effect of economic policy uncertainty have mainly distinguished between macro and micro perspectives. In the macro perspective, studies on the impact of economic policy uncertainty have focused on the impact and relevance of economic indicators such as the exchange rate, investment, consumption, and a country's money supply etc. At the micro level, scholars have focused on the impact of economic policy uncertainty on the behavior of firms in economic activity. Although changes in firm behavior can be indirectly transmitted to firm performance, there is limited literature directly exploring the impact of economic policy uncertainty on firm performance. Notably, the Economic Policy Uncertainty Index (EPU) published by Baker et al. [4] expands the scope of scholarly research on the relevance of the effects caused by economic policy uncertainty.

Specifically, most studies in the macro perspective argue that rising economic policy uncertainty has a negative shock on macroeconomic stability. Moreover, the literature by Liu et al. [5], which focuses on China, mentions that economic policy uncertainty has the largest impact on some key economic indicators particularly in investment and consumption. Similarly, the literature by Xu and Wang [6] confirms that elevated uncertainty has a negative impact on consumption and demand. In Addition, scholars in the micro perspective focus more on the impact of economic policy uncertainty on firms in economic activities. In particular, increased economic policy uncertainty leads firms to take proactive actions in terms of governance and financial management. In governance, firms will adjust their internal controls and risk management strategy to reduce operational risk and thereby mitigate the impact of uncertainty. In financial management, firms will adapt their operating, financing and investment activities. In operational activities, the increase in the level of economic policy uncertainty will lead to higher operational risk and liquidity risk, which will result in inventory adjustments and production reductions [2], by reducing the level of inventory holdings to minimize the impact of economic policy uncertainty on product costs and sales. In the financing activities, increased uncertainty in economic policies will raise the cost of financing for firms as the supply side is more inclined to tighten credit at this time, which will lead firms to reduce their financing needs while increasing their incentive to hold cash to prevent liquidity risk [3]. As a result, firms in times of uncertainty will engage in surplus management to reduce cash outflows. In terms of investment activities, firms reduce the level of investment in fixed assets and reduce the frequency of investment in M&A activities [7, 8]. In addition, Tabash et al. [9] find that firms choose to reduce debt financing and go for more equity financing at this time. Conversely, Deng [1] argues that economic policy uncertainty leads firms to increase their investment in technology to improve their business resilience. Li et al. [10] find that Chinese manufacturing firms try to increase their position in financial assets to regulate and hedge their Revenue from main business, but this often entails exposure to certain risks as a result.

2.2 Literature on ESG

The concept of ESG was first introduced by the United Nations Environment Program in 2004 and has evolved into a new type of corporate governance indicator. Currently, ESG is mainly scored and published by third-party rating agencies, similar to credit rating indicators for firms, but ESG is more inclined to non-financial indicators of firms, which focus on the environmental, social and corporate governance dimensions of a corporation's performance to generate a ranking based on certain criteria. As a complement to financial disclosure, ESG ratings are becoming an important basis for investment decisions.

After the introduction of ESG concept, scholars' research on ESG focused more on the feasibility analysis of ESG implementation and the impact of ESG implementation on enterprises with the majority of literature on the relation between ESG and corporate performance. Although the impact of ESG practices on corporations is controversial, more scholars have concluded that ESG practices have a non-negative impact on corporate performance and related performance.

With the rapid growth in the involvement of ESG rated firms, research has shifted to focus on the subsequent performance of firms participating in ESG ratings, as well as the return performance of investments based on ESG ratings. In recent years, there has been a booming trend of research on ESG ratings. Wang et al. [11] argue that the value discovery and risk mitigation functions of ESG ratings improve the valuation level of firms. Raimo et al. [12] found that an increase in the level of ESG ratings reduces the external financing costs of firms. Luo and Wu [13] argued that ESG ratings reduce the level of information asymmetry between firms and investors and management's operational risk, t improving analysts' forecasting accuracy. Wang et al. [14] mention that corporates with excellent ESG performance have lower financial risk and higher investment efficiency. Xiao et al. [15] mentioned in their study that ESG ratings enable firms to reduce their internal uncertainty and thus have a negative impact on audit fees. Xu et al. [11] state that firms accounting surplus information is more transparent when their have better ESG performance.

However, scholars continue to question ESG practices. Li and Xu [16] mention that there are firms that engage in tokenistic behavior merely to improve their ESG scores, which not only distorts internal corporate disclosure but also misleads investors and the market in a serious way. Similarly, Liu et al. [17] argue that ESG rating activities can lead firms to focus on the quantity of ESG practices rather than the quality in order to gain rankings, which will also lead to additional costs for firms. Likewise, Li and Zheng [18] debate that ESG practices can lead to higher costs for firms, which is detrimental to the growth of firms in their formative years.

Although there are research discussing the correlation between ESG ratings and firm performance, there is limited literature on whether ESG ratings enable firms to maintain stability in performance amidst economic policy uncertainty. Specifically, whether firms with high ESG ratings perform better in periods of rising or unstable of economic policy uncertainty compared with firms with low ESG ratings is a question that needs to be answered. It is worth noting that the literature by Vural-Yavaş [19] points out that firms' ESG performance becomes better when economic policy uncertainty rises because firms use ESG activities as an insurance to reduce their potential risks.

2.3 Research Hypotheses

Whilst there is limited research on the relationship between economic policy uncertainty and firm performance, the existing literature concurs that changes in the level of uncertainty will cause firms to adjust their behavior in response to possible situations, which in turn will have an influence on firm performance [1]. Under the shareholder interest maximization theory, firms will take appropriate corporate governance and financial management actions to minimize losses and ensure that shareholders' interests are maximized even in times of economic policy uncertainty.

Nevertheless, there are costs associated with corporate actions. In the case of corporate governance, improving the level of internal controls and the ability to monitor risk will increase the cost of governance. Equally, defensive financial management actions in the midst of economic policy uncertainty may reduce a corporate's revenue, reducing foreign investment, lowering inventories, increasing cash holdings and lowering the level of future production plans, etc. All of actions will have a negative impact on corporate performance. In short, economic policy uncertainty affects firms' risk-taking appetite, which will trigger firms to spread risk. Ultimately, these actions arising from uncertainty are transmitted to corporate performance [3].

Based on the above analyses, this study proposes the following hypothesis.

Hypothesis 1: Economic Policy Uncertainty is Negatively Associated with Corporate Performance. In the perspective of stakeholder theory, a better ESG rating enables a corporation to build a great reputation and transmit it to its internal and external stakeholders, thus gaining a positive response from them. Furthermore, as an extension of reputation theory, ESG ratings can generate reputational insurance for the firm ensuring that the firm has the support from stakeholders in times of economic policy uncertainty [19, 20].

Additionally, information asymmetry theory suggests that ESG ratings is able to reduce the level of information asymmetry between firms and market participants. The value of information disclosure on ESG practices, as an important complement to corporate financial disclosure, is also significant. Higher ESG ratings imply higher quality levels of disclosure and greater information transparency [21], which can also remarkably reduce the risk of information asymmetry for information recipients. The suppression of corporate information risk is crucial in times of economic policy uncertainty for investors and markets.

Moreover, the public ranking of ESG ratings drives positive action by firms. To achieve a higher ESG rating, managers have an incentive to improve corporate governance, take on more social responsibility and improve disclosure, which in turn leads to an improvement in the overall level of the firm's performance. Thus, a virtuous circle between ESG ratings and corporate actions will cause an increase in the degree of protection against uncertainty risks.

Based on the above analyses, this study proposes the following hypothesis.

Hypothesis 2: ESG Weakens the Negative Effect of Economic Policy Uncertainty on Corporate Performance.

3 Research Design

3.1 Sample and Data

Considering the point of implementation of the new accounting standards in 2007 in China and the wind ESG Index measurement started in 2009, this paper will take a sample of Chinese A-share listed corporations from 2009–2020 to explore the impact of economic policy uncertainty on corporate performance and the extent to which ESG ratings mitigate this impact. EPU data is retrieved from Baker's official website (www.policyuncertainty.com), ESG data is retrieved from the Wind database, and financial, governance and other data are retrieved from the CSMAR database.

Based on the practice of existing studies, this essay excludes financial firms, firms that are specially treated by the China Securities Regulatory Commission (ST, and *ST firms), the sample of firms listed in the current year and the sample of firms with serious data deficiencies. Finally, a total of 31161 observations were obtained.

3.2 Empirical Model

In this paper, the model (1) is constructed with corporate financial performance, i.e., ROA, as the dependent variable and EPU as the independent variable. Subsequently, the

ESG variable will be introduced to form an interaction term between EPU and ESG to replace the original explanatory variables to construct model (2).

$$ROA = \alpha_0 + \alpha_1 * EPU + \alpha_2 Controls + Firm\,FE + Year\,FE + \varepsilon \quad (1)$$

$$ROA = \alpha_0 + \alpha_1 * EPU * ESG + \alpha_2 Controls + Firm\,FE + Year\,FE + \varepsilon \quad (2)$$

3.3 Variables

Independent variable: EPU Index is derived from the proportion and frequency of policy-related economic uncertainty articles in a country's news [4]. Specifically, the study counts each news publication in the target country by using a composite text filter to counts the frequency statistics of economic uncertainty when specified words I. e. uncertainty, policy, regulation etc. appear. In this paper, the results of EPU data are selected with the one of style of observation mode by Baker et al., which is the South China Morning Post (SCMP), a major English language newspaper in Hong Kong, as the main subject of observation with the measurement interval starting from January 1995 on a monthly basis to the present. Based on the needs of the study, this paper will convert the monthly based EPU data into annual data by means of calculating the annual average.

Dependent variable: Following the approach from Deng [1], this paper uses ROA and ROE to measure corporate performance.

Moderating variable: The ESG ratings from the Wind database are used in this paper. Compared to other rating standards, Wind ESG ratings have a broader coverage and are locally adapted to Chinese firms based on international standards. The Wind ratings are categorized into nine levels: AAA, AA, A, BBB, BB, B, CCC, CC and C, from highest to lowest. Based on the above rating distribution, the ESG is assigned a value of 9 for AAA, 8 for AA and the following, and 1 for C.

Control variables: Following previous studies [1, 13], this paper controls for firm size (the natural logarithm of total assets), PPE (the proportion of fixed assets to total assets), Cfo (net cash flow from operation activity scaled by total assets), Firm fixed effect, Year fixed effect, Indep (independent director ratio board number), Leverage, Board, HHI and Dual (Table 1).

Table 1. Variable Definitions.

Variables	Definition
Independent variables	
EPU	Economic Policy Uncertainty Index
Dependent variables	
ROA	Net profit/average total asset
ROE	Net profit/average net asset

(*continued*)

Table 1. (*continued*)

Variables	Definition
Mediation variable	
ESG	ESG performance score
Control variables	
Size	The natural logarithm of total assets
PPE	Fixed assets/Total assets
Cfo	Net cash flow from operation activity scaled by total assets
Indep	Independent director ratio board number
Leverage	Total debt/total asset
Board	Natural logarithm of the number of board members
HHI	Herfindahl-Hirschman Index
Dual	Dummy variable to measuring the level of corporate governance
Firm FE	Firm-fixed effect
Year FE	Year-fixed effect

4 Empirical Results

4.1 Summary Statistics

Table 2 illustrates the results of descriptive statistics for all variables in the study sample. The maximum value of economic policy uncertainty as a dependent variable over the time horizon included in the sample is 791.874, the minimum value is 98.888 and the standard deviation is 246.957, which indicates that the volatility of economic policy changes in China during the examined interval is high and has significant research value.

For the dependent variable, ROA has a maximum value of 0.210, a minimum value of −0.339 and a mean value of 0.034. Similarly, ROE has a maximum value of 0.350, a minimum value of −0.988 and a mean value of 0.050, indicating a wide variation in the profitability of the sample of corporations. For the moderating variables, the mean value of the ESG score performance of the firms in the sample was 6.48, indicating that the overall performance of firms listed in China that participated in the ESG rating was preferable.

4.2 Baseline Regression Results

Table 3 demonstrates the results of the regression of the empirical model, where columns (1) and (2) are used to explain hypothesis 1. Following this, columns (3) and (4) are used to explain hypothesis 2. All models control for Firm FE and Year FE.

Initially the regression model in column (1) without the control variables results in a statistically significant negative at the 1% level with a t-value of −12.06, which indicates that EPU has a negative impact on ROA. Subsequently, the inclusion of control variables

Table 2. Descriptive Statistics.

Variable	N	Mean	SD	Min	p25	p50	p75	Max
ROA	31161	0.034	0.067	−0.339	0.012	0.034	0.064	0.210
ROE	31161	0.050	0.162	−0.988	0.027	0.067	0.113	0.350
EPU	31161	369.932	246.957	98.888	127.624	363.874	460.470	791.874
ESG	31161	6.480	1.132	1.000	6.000	6.000	7.000	9.000
Size	31161	22.212	1.430	19.296	21.219	21.996	22.944	27.104
PPE	31161	0.212	0.166	0.001	0.082	0.179	0.307	0.706
Cfo	31161	0.044	0.074	−0.203	0.005	0.044	0.086	0.256
Leverage	31161	0.444	0.215	0.049	0.272	0.436	0.604	0.977
Indep	31161	0.380	0.071	0.250	0.333	0.364	0.429	0.600
Board	31161	2.294	0.258	1.609	2.197	2.303	2.485	2.944
HHI	31161	0.284	0.118	0.202	0.218	0.253	0.298	0.827
Dual	31161	0.257	0.437	0.000	0.000	0.000	1.000	1.000

including firm size, PPE, Cfo, Leverage, Ind, Board, HHI and Dual in column (2) results in a significant negative at the 1% statistical level with a t-value of −16.58, indicating that the coefficients of the explanatory variables remain significantly negative after the inclusion of the control variables, which confirms that economic policy uncertainty has a negative impact on the financial performance of firms. This confirms that economic policy uncertainty has a negative impact on the financial performance of firms. Thus, this result supports hypothesis 1.

In addition, the regression model in column (3) introduces an interaction to EPU × ESG to calculate the moderating effect of ESG ratings in the negative effect of EPU on ROA.

The result is significantly positive at the 1% statistical level with a t-value of 8.14, indicating a positive moderating effect after the insertion of ESG. Subsequently, after adding the same control variables in column (4) as in column (2), the result is significantly positive at the 1% statistical level with a t-value of 6.41, implying that the coefficients of the explanatory variables are still significantly positive after the inclusion of the control variables, which confirms that ESG performance can weaken the impact of economic policy uncertainty on corporate financial performance. Hence, this result supports hypothesis 2.

4.3 Robustness Tests

In the regression analysis, the return on total assets (ROA) was chosen as the dependent variable for setting the financial performance indicators of the firm. ROA is a key indicator of corporate profitability that assesses the revenue generated per unit of total assets. Furthermore, return on equity (ROE) is also an essential indicator that is influenced by net profit margin, asset turnover and multiple of equity, which means that the results of

Table 3. Baseline Results.

	(1) ROA	(2) ROA	(3) ROA	(4) ROA
EPU	−0.000*** (−12.06)	−0.000*** (−16.58)	−0.000*** (−10.76)	−0.000*** (−11.57)
EPU × ESG			0.000*** (8.14)	0.000*** (6.41)
ESG			0.001 (1.09)	−0.001 (−0.67)
Size		0.019*** (15.59)		0.017*** (14.62)
PPE		−0.067*** (−9.80)		−0.068*** (−10.12)
Cfo		0.171*** (20.91)		0.171*** (20.98)
Lev		−0.164*** (−30.22)		−0.159*** (−29.67)
Indep		0.018*** (2.98)		0.018*** (3.01)
Board		−0.013*** (−6.13)		−0.012*** (−5.75)
HHI		0.055*** (4.45)		0.052*** (4.31)
Dual		0.001 (0.95)		0.001 (0.87)
Constant	0.047*** (25.22)	−0.261*** (−10.19)	0.043*** (7.39)	−0.235*** (−9.22)
Firm FE	Yes	Yes	Yes	Yes
Year FE	Yes	Yes	Yes	Yes
N	31161	31161	31161	31161
Adj R2	0.039	0.190	0.053	0.195

Note: *, **, and *** indicate significance at the 10%, 5%, and 1% levels, respectively

the sample ROA and ROE are varied to some extent by the three aforementioned factors of the firm itself. Therefore, this paper replaces the ROA in the regression model with ROE by replacing the key variables, keeping the rest of the parameters the same, for robustness testing, and the regression results are shown in Table 4. In the table, it is observed that before and after the inclusion of the control variables and the interaction variable, the directionality and significance remain consistent with the results of the main regression, which implies that the previous findings are still robust to the substitution of key variables.

Table 4. Robustness tests.

	(1) ROE	(2) ROE	(3) ROE	(4) ROE
EPU	−0.000*** (−9.56)	−0.000*** (−15.51)	−0.000*** (−9.38)	−0.000*** (−10.75)
EPU × ESG			0.000*** (7.51)	0.000*** (6.07)
ESG			0.002 (1.04)	−0.001 (−0.66)
Size		0.054*** (16.03)		0.051*** (15.25)
PPE		−0.145*** (−7.69)		−0.148*** (−7.96)
Cfo		0.350*** (16.43)		0.350*** (16.50)
Lev		−0.398*** (−23.12)		−0.385*** (−22.92)
Indep		0.046*** (2.82)		0.046*** (2.85)
Board		−0.038*** (−6.29)		−0.035*** (−5.92)
HHI		0.081*** (2.69)		0.074** (2.51)
Dual		0.002 (0.40)		0.001 (0.32)
Constant	0.078*** (15.05)	−0.842*** (−11.65)	0.067*** (4.28)	−0.773*** (−10.85)
Firm FE	Yes	Yes	Yes	Yes
Year FE	Yes	Yes	Yes	Yes
N	31161	31161	31161	31161
Adj R2	0.026	0.148	0.040	0.154

Note: *, **, and *** indicate significance at the 10%, 5%, and 1% levels, respectively

5 Conclusion

This article uses a sample of A-share listed firms in China from 2009 to 2020 and confirms through empirical research that economic policy uncertainty has a negative impact on corporate performance. Further analysis demonstrates that the performance of corporate ESG ratings moderates the negative impact of economic policy uncertainty, i.e., corporate ESG performance is able to positively mitigate the impact of economic policy uncertainty on corporate financial performance.

In summary, this essay complements the study of the economic consequences of economic policy uncertainty on the one hand, and the study of the effect of exogenous factors on corporate financial performance as well, which provides a new complement to the impact of economic policy uncertainty on firms from a micro perspective. On the other hand, this paper also provides a new positive perspective on the discussion of the pros and cons of corporate ESG practices, which implies that corporations could revisit the potential benefits of ESG practices in terms of mitigating the impact of the external uncertainties they may face. That is, firms could use ESG practices as a strategy to counteract uncertainty in order to ensure a stable level of corporate financial performance in an uncertain environment.

Nevertheless, this paper focuses on a sample of Chinese listed companies, as non-listed companies are not considered due to the limitations of the sample, which means that the impact of economic policy uncertainty on non-listed companies and the moderating effect of ESG practices are not considered. Future research could therefore expand the data on unlisted companies to consider whether their performance is consistent with the current results.

References

1. Deng, M.: The impact of economic policy uncertainty on firm performance - empirical evidence from non-financial listed firms in China. Ind. Technol. Econ. **02**, 97–106 (2019). (In Chinese)
2. Huang, X.: Macroeconomic policy uncertainty, inventory adjustment, and firm performance. Soft Sci. (12), 47–51+67 (2020).https://doi.org/10.13956/j.ss.1001-8409.2020.12.08. (In Chinese)
3. Peng, T., Huang, F.G., Sun, L.X.: Economic policy uncertainty and risk-taking: evidence based on venture capital. J. Manage. Sci. **03**, 98–114 (2021). https://doi.org/10.19920/j.cnki.jmsc.2021.03.007. (In Chinese)
4. Baker, S.R., Bloom, N., Davis, S.J.: Measuring economic policy uncertainty. Q. J. Econ. **131**(4), 1593–1636 (2016)
5. Liu, S., Wang, X., Wang, H.: An empirical analysis of the impact of economic policy uncertainty on macroeconomics. Stat. Decis. Making **06**, 115–117 (2020). https://doi.org/10.13546/j.cnki.tjyjc.2020.06.026. (In Chinese)
6. Xu, C.-W., Wang, W.-F.: The impact of economic policy uncertainty on macroeconomics - An empirical and theory-based dynamic analysis. Econ. (Q.) **01**, 23–50 (2019). https://doi.org/10.13821/j.cnki.ceq.2018.02.02. (In Chinese)
7. Li, W., Su, Y., Wang, K.: How does economic policy uncertainty affect cross-border M&A: evidence from Chinese firms. Emerg. Mark. Rev. **52**, 100908 (2022). (In Chinese)
8. Song Ke, X., Lei, L.Z., Fang, W.: Can ESG investment facilitate bank liquidity creation? –An examination of the moderating effects of economic policy uncertainty. Financial Studies **02**, 61–79 (2022). (In Chinese)
9. Tabash, M.I., Farooq, U., Ashfaq, K., Tiwari, A.K.: Economic policy uncertainty and financing structure: A new panel data evidence from selected Asian economies. Res. Int. Bus. Financ. **60**, 101574 (2022)
10. Li, S., Liu, C., Tan, X.: Does economic policy uncertainty drive manufacturing firms' "de-realization" - Based on the identification of mediating and moderating effects. Econ. Theory Econ. Manage. **04**, 40–55 (2022). (In Chinese)

11. Wang, H., Chen, B., He, Y.: Does ESG responsibility fulfillment improve corporate valuation? --A quasi-natural experiment from MSCI ratings. J. Econ. (2022). https://doi.org/10.16513/j.cnki.cje.20220921.001. (In Chinese)
12. Raimo, N., Caragnano, A., Zito, M., Vitolla, F., Mariani, M.: Extending the benefits of ESG disclosure: the effect on the cost of debt financing. Corp. Soc. Responsib. Environ. Manag. **28**(4), 1412–1421 (2021)
13. Luo, K., Wu, S.: Corporate sustainability and analysts' earnings forecast accuracy: evidence from environmental, social and governance ratings. Corp. Soc. Responsib. Environ. Manage. **29**, 1465–1481 (2022)
14. Wang, L., Lian, Y., Dong, J.: A study on the mechanism of ESG performance on corporate value. Secur. Mark. Herald (05), 23–34 (2022). (In Chinese)
15. Xiaofang, L.F., Wen, S., Hao, X., Huayu, S.: Do ESG ratings of listed firms affect audit fees? – A quasi-natural experiment based on ESG rating events. Audit Res. **03**, 41–50 (2021). (In Chinese)
16. Xu, X., Qiao, P., Huang, Q.: Can ESG responsibility performance convey more transparent information? Ind. Econ. Rev. https://doi.org/10.19313/j.cnki.cn10-1223/f.20220719.001. (In Chinese)
17. Li, S.R., Xu, T.C.: Advances in environmental-social responsibility-corporate governance research. Dyn. Econ. **08**, 133–146 (2022). (In Chinese)
18. Liu, B., Lu, J.R., Ju, T.: Formalism or substantiveism: a study of green innovation under soft regulation of ESG ratings. Nankai Manage. Rev. (2022). (In Chinese)
19. Li, S.H., Zheng, S.L.: Does the implementation of ESG inhibit firm growth? Econ. Issues **12**, 81–89 (2022). https://doi.org/10.16011/j.cnki.jjwt.2022.12.015. (InChinese)
20. Vural-Yavaş, Ç.: Economic policy uncertainty, stakeholder engagement, and environmental, social, and governance practices: the moderating effect of competition. Corp. Soc. Responsib. Environ. Manag. **28**(1), 82–102 (2021)
21. Zhang, D., Liu, L.: Does ESG performance enhance financial flexibility? Evid. China Sustain. **14**(18), 11324 (2022). https://doi.org/10.3390/su141811324
22. DeLisle, R.J., Grant, A., Mao, R.: Does ESG decrease information asymmetry? evidence from earnings conference call tones and subsequent returns. (Working Paper) (2021). https://www.efmaefm.org/0EFMAMEETINGS/EFMA%20ANNUAL%20MEETINGS/2021-Leeds/papers/EFMA%202021_stage-2049_question-Full%20Paper_id-330.pdf

Identification and Analysis of Risk Spillover Effect of Commercial Banks in China

Moran Wang[✉]

Beijing Jiaotong University, Beijing 100044, China
22125362@bjtu.edu.cn

Abstract. This paper constructs the Delta Conditional Value at Risk (ΔCoVaR) model based on the traditional Value at Risk (VaR) model to measure the systematic risk and spillover effect of the stock price of China's commercial banks. According to the data of listed commercial banks in China from 2006 to 2021, this paper finds that the ΔCoVaR index is a good description of the risk spillover effect of the banking system in China, and the ΔCoVaR index is in good agreement with the actual economic performance in different stages in China, which has good practical significance.

Keywords: China's Commercial Banks · Systematic Risk · ΔCoVaR Model

1 Introduction

Commercial banks have a significant impancy in China's economy and financial system. Different from the central bank, commercial banks cannot directly participate in the macro-control of China's economy, but they are direct economic signal transmitters and control targets. Commercial banks are important hubs for communication between financial markets and the real economy and are also important transmission channels for macro-policy control. Commercial banks now play a more significant role as financial intermediaries due to the consistent growth of China and rising financial liberalization, and they are always affecting the stability of the financial system. Therefore, the risk status of the commercial banking system is very important to the macroeconomic stability of our country and it of great significance to calculate the risk spillover effect of commercial banks on the whole financial system.

This paper builds a Delta Conditional Value at Risk (ΔCoVaR) model based on the traditional Value at Risk (VaR) model, and then measures the systematic risk and risk spillover effect of the stock prices of commercial banks in China. The traditional VaR model measures the maximum possible loss of a financial institution or investment portfolio over a given time period in the future under normal market conditions and a certain level of confidence. However, the VaR model itself also has certain limitations. For example, it cannot measure the spillover effect of stock price risk well. Therefore, Adrian and Brunnermeier put forward a ΔCoVaR model based on the VaR model [1]. ΔCoVaR equals the difference between the VaR of a financial institution to the financial system during a crisis and that under normal circumstances. The model can well measure the contribution and spillover effects of individual financial institutions to the whole financial system when they are in crisis.

2 Literature Review

Due to the importance of systematic risk, many domestic and foreign scholars have carried out in-depth analysis. In the existing literature, there are various methods for measuring systematic risk, including contingent claims, ΔCoVaR, systemic expected shortfall (SES), etc. Contingent claims mainly analyze different types of assets of financial institutions and their possible future earnings, and then measures the impact of future earnings and default rate of assets on systematic risk. The representative pieces of literature are Lehar and Gray et al. [2, 3]. Acharya et al. used SES to find out how much value the financial institutions had contributed to systematic risk and found that SES components could predict systematic risk during the 2007–2009 financial crisis [4]. Adrian and Brunnermeier proposed the ΔCoVaR model based on a large number of transaction data in financial markets to build the corresponding model [1], and uses tail risk to measure the dynamic change of risk spillovers between financial institutions. This method is simple and practical, and has been widely used, such as Girardi and Ergün, Reboredo and Ugolini, and Sun et al. [5–7]. Therefore, this paper uses the ΔCoVaR model to measure the systematic risk status and spillover effect of China's listed banks.

3 Empirical Model and Data Source

3.1 ΔCoVaR Model

First, VaR_q^i is the q-quantile of the return of a commercial bank, namely:

$$P(R^i \leq \text{VaR}_q^i) = q \tag{1}$$

Then, $\text{CoVaR}_q^{s|R^i=\text{VaR}_q^i}$ is the impact on the entire financial system when a commercial bank is in trouble, namely:

$$P(R^s \leq \text{CoVaR}_q^{s|R^i=\text{VaR}_q^i} | R^i = \text{VaR}_q^i) = q \tag{2}$$

Among them, R^s is the rate of return for the entire financial system. The relative contribution value of a commercial bank to the risk of the entire financial system ΔCoVaR is:

$$\Delta\text{CoVaR}_q^{s|i} = \text{CoVaR}_q^{s|R^i=\text{VaR}_q^i} - \text{CoVaR}_q^{s|R^i=M^i} \tag{3}$$

where, $\text{CoVaR}_q^{s|R^i=M^i}$ is the value at risk at 50%-quantile.

Finally, according to the setting of Adrian and Brunnermeier [1], considering the time change, the aforementioned model of ΔCoVaR can be defined as:

$$R_t^i = \alpha^i + \gamma^i F_{t-1} + \varepsilon_t^i \tag{4}$$

$$R_t^s = \alpha^{s|i} + \beta^{s|i}R_t^i + \gamma^{s|i}F_{t-1} + \varepsilon_t^{s|i} \tag{5}$$

Among them, the variable subscript t represents the value of the variable at time t. F_{t-1} is other control variables at time t-1. α^i and $\alpha^{s|i}$ are constant terms in the corresponding regression equation. $\beta^{s|i}$ is the influence degree of a certain commercial bank on the whole financial system γ^i and $\gamma^{s|i}$ are the influence degree of other control variables on a certain commercial bank and the whole financial system respectively.

At the quantizing point q, Eqs. (4) and (5) can be written:

$$\text{VaR}_t^i(q) = \hat{\alpha}_q^i + \hat{\gamma}_q^i F_{t-1} \tag{6}$$

$$\text{CoVaR}_t^q(q) = \hat{\alpha}_q^{s|i} + \hat{\beta}_q^{s|i}\text{VaR}_t^i(q) + \hat{\gamma}_q^{s|i}F_{t-1} \tag{7}$$

Therefore, relative to the 50%-quantile, the spillover effect $\Delta\text{CoVaR}_q^{s|i}(q)$ of a commercial bank on the entire financial system at quantile q is:

$$\Delta\text{CoVaR}_q^{s|i}(q) = \text{CoVaR}_t^q(q) - \text{CoVaR}_t^q(50\%) = \hat{\beta}_q^{s|i}(\text{VaR}_t^i(q) - \text{VaR}_t^i(50\%)) \tag{8}$$

3.2 Data Source

The sample used in this paper is the Bank of Shanghai listed in the PRC, and the sample range is from November 2006 to December 2021. The sample length of each commercial bank is required to be more than 1 year, so the data of 40 listed commercial banks in China are finally used. This study collects data from the China Stock Market & Accounting Research (CSMAR) Database. R^i is equal to the monthly return of the commercial banks in the PRC and R^s is equal to the monthly return of the financial industry index in the PRC.

4 Systematic Risks and Spillover Effect of Commercial Banks in China

In this paper, the ΔCoVaR value of 40 listed commercial banks in China is measured by the ΔCoVaR model. The ΔCoVaR values of the commercial banks in China are obtained by the weighted average of 40 banks. Figure 1 is a graph of the ΔCoVaR changes of the commercial banks in China from November 2006 to December 2021.

4.1 The Impact of Financial Crisis of 2007–2008 on the Systematic Risk of Commercial Banks in China

According to Fig. 1, the ΔCoVaR index of China's commercial banks dropped significantly in 2008, indicating that China's commercial banks have a large risk spillover to the financial system, which is mainly due to the global financial crisis in 2008 triggered by the US sub-prime crisis. First of all, under the background of global economization

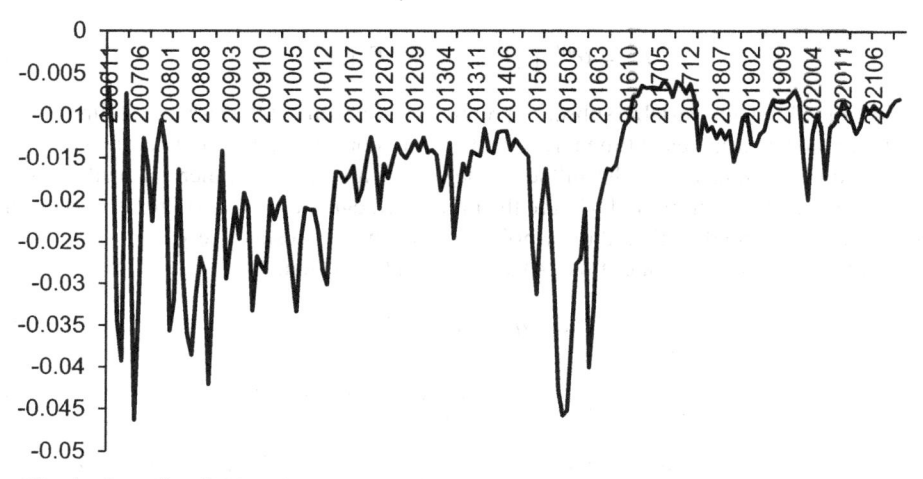

Fig. 1. Overall ΔCoVaR change graph of 2006M11-2021M12 commercial banks in China.

and a clear international division of labor, China's export industry boomed after China's accession to the WTO in 2003. However, during the financial crisis of 2007–2008, the EU and US were China's top two trading partners at that time. Many companies in Europe and the United States went bankrupt one after another and the sharp drop in demand led to China's loss of a vast overseas market. As a result, China's import and export trade suffered setbacks, economic growth slowed down, and the profitability of enterprises declined, which in turn led to the impact on banking operations and systematic risks in the banking system spread to financial markets.

4.2 The Impact of the European Debt Crisis in 2010 on the Systematic Risk of China's Commercial Banks

With the introduction of the 4 trillion stimulus plan, China's economy gradually stabilized and rebounded rapidly. As a result, the ΔCoVaR index of China's commercial banks rebounded, but in 2010, the ΔCoVaR index of China's commercial banks dropped to a certain extent. This is because the European debt crisis has reduced China's commodity exports to Europe. In 2010, China's top trading partner was the EU. Therefore, the European debt crisis caused a great impact on the export of Chinese enterprises to Europe. Enterprises with insufficient profitability and solvency were unable to repay the bank loans, which negatively affected the capital of commercial banks, and further led to an increase in the systematic risk spillover effect of China's commercial banks.

4.3 The Impact of the 2015 Stock Market Crash on the Systematic Risk of Commercial Banks in China

In 2015, the ΔCoVaR index of China's commercial banks dropped again significantly, which is closely related to the stock market crash in 2015. On June 15, 2015, the Shanghai Composite Index suddenly dropped from its high of 5,174.42 points to its closing price of 3,507.19 points on July 8. During the stock market crash from June 15 to August 26, more than 2,500 listed companies in the two cities recorded a daily limit, and most companies recorded a daily limit of more than 7 days. Under such circumstances, the risks in the stock market have risen sharply. At that time, retail investors accounted for the largest share of China's stock market. Unlike rational institutional investors, retail investors often "chase after the rising and kill the falling". Under the herd effect, a large number of companies' stock prices fell or even were suspended, and the financial market collapsed. Banks have a great influence on the real economy and is important in China's financial market. The banking sector accounts for a relatively large proportion of the overall market. When the crisis occurs, the risks in the banking sector will spread to the entire financial market, causing fluctuations in the entire financial market, i.e., the systematic risk spillover effect of China's commercial banks will increase significantly.

4.4 The Impact of China–United States Trade War in 2018 on the Systematic Risk of Commercial Banks in China

In 2018, the ΔCoVaR index of China's commercial banks dropped slightly because China was facing both internal and external pressures. In 2018, under the background of Sino-US trade frictions and China's "de-production, de-inventory, de-leverage" policy, China's stock market faced both internal and external shocks. In 2018, the Shanghai Composite Index fell by 24.59%, the biggest drop since the 2008 financial crisis. China's customs statistics reflected that in 2018, China and the US had a total bilateral trade in goods of 633.52 billion USD, which makes US China's second-largest trading partner and the largest export market. However, with the introduction of the US trade protectionism policy, China–United States trade war started. The US imposed tariffs on goods imported from China and restricted China's investment and merger with the US. As a result, China's export of goods to the United States has been blocked and the real economy has been hit, with the negative impact on high-tech companies being more obvious. These negative impacts have caused a great impact on Chinese enterprises, and thus the banks that provide financial services to enterprises have also suffered a great impact, which in turn has caused fluctuations in bank share prices and shocks in the entire financial sector in China.

4.5 The Impact of COVID-19 Epidemic on Commercial Banks' Systematic Risk in China

In 2020, the COVID-19 epidemic broke out rapidly on a global scale. As a "barometer" of the national economy, China's stock market has been hit and has fallen sharply. The transportation, wholesale and retail, accommodation, catering, tourism, entertainment and other industries have been greatly affected. The banking industry, which supports its financial services, has been hit by the sudden increase in operating pressure, and is under pressure from declining profits, declining asset quality and increasing credit risk. As a result, the ΔCoVaR index of commercial banks dropped. To cope with the pandemic, the central bank has taken a series of measures to rescue the market, such as lowering the money market interest rate, guiding the medium-term borrowing convenience, and lowering the deposit reserve ratio of financial institutions and the interest rate of excess deposit reserve. As a result, the stock market has gradually recovered, the operation of enterprises greatly affected by the epidemic has stabilized, the risk faced by the banking industry has been reduced, and the systematic risk spillover effect of China's commercial banks has weakened.

5 Conclusion

This paper uses the ΔCoVaR model constructed by Adrian and Brunnermeier based on the VaR model to measure the systematic risk and risk spillover effect of listed commercial banks in China [1], and then constructs the ΔCoVaR index of 40 listed commercial banks in China from November 2006 to December 2021. According to the overall ΔCoVaR index of China's commercial banks, this paper finds that the ΔCoVaR index is in good agreement with the actual economic performance of China at different stages. During the 2018 global financial crisis, the 2010 European debt crisis, the 2015 stock market crash, the 2018 China-United States trade war, and the COVID-19 pandemic, the ΔCoVaR index decreased significantly, indicating that the systematic risk spillover effect of China's commercial banks is strong during these periods, which indicates that the ΔCoVaR index better depicts the systematic risk situation of China's commercial banks and has better practical significance.

References

1. Adrian, T., Brunnermeier, M.K.: CoVaR. Am. Econ. Rev. **106**(7), 1705–1741 (2016)
2. Lehar, A.: Measuring systemic risk: A risk management approach. J. Bank. Finan. **29**(10), 2577–2603 (2005)
3. Gray, D.F., Merton, R.C., Bodie, Z.: New framework for measuring and managing macro-financial risk and financial stability. Working Paper No. 09–015, Harvard Business School (2008)
4. Acharya, V.V., Pedersen, L.H., Philippon, T., Richardson, M.: Measuring systemic risk. Rev. Finan. Stud. **30**(1), 2–47 (2017)
5. Girardi, G., Ergün, A.T.: Systemic risk measurement: multivariate GARCH estimation of CoVaR. J. Bank. Finan. **37**(8), 3169–3180 (2013)
6. Reboredo, J.C., Ugolini, A.: Systemic risk in European sovereign debt markets: a CoVaR-copula approach. J. Int. Money Financ. **51**, 214–244 (2015)
7. Sun, X., Liu, C., Wang, J., Li, J.: Assessing the extreme risk spillovers of international commodities on maritime markets: a GARCH-Copula-CoVaR approach. Int. Rev. Financ. Anal. Financ. Anal. **68**, 101453 (2020)

Case Analysis of Kingfisher PLC's Operational Quality Based on the Perspective of Financial Report

Xinyi Song(✉)

Shandong University of Technology, Zibo, Shandong, China
20121491032@stumail.sdut.edu.cn

Abstract. Financial statements are an effective carrier of accounting information, which can reflect the financial status, operating results and cash flow of listed companies in the most authentic and comprehensive way. They have a strong reference value for the internal management of the enterprise and external investors, creditors and other stakeholders. This paper analyzes the industry environment of Kingfisher Plc. Through Porter's five forces model and SWOT analysis model. Then relying on the financial statements, analyze the financial ratio of Kingfisher Plc from four aspects: profitability ratio, liquidity ratio, efficiency ratio, and investment ratio, and compare the ratios with the three-year average of the home improvement industry to evaluate its operating quality. Give investment advice to investors and propose measures for company development. Committed to serving as a reference for companies, stakeholders and potential investors. Through the analysis, this paper believes that Kingfisher's profitability and solvency performance is relatively good, but it has no advantages in operating efficiency, and finally holds an optimistic attitude towards Kingfisher's operating quality.

Keywords: Financial Statements · Operational Quality · Financial Ratio Analysis

1 Introduction

As the business language of economic organizations, financial statements reflect the operating level of the enterprise. The financial situation of a company, the effectiveness of its operations, the management's policies and plans, and insight into its future performance are all covered in great detail in financial statements and the notes that accompany them [1]. Users of financial reports can combine the industry environment of the company, make full use of the information disclosed in the financial report, and dig out the operating quality hidden behind its financial data. This article takes Kingfisher PLC, a listed company in the UK, as an example to analyze its industry background, profitability, asset operation quality, asset liquidity and financial solvency. Comprehensively analyze the operating quality of Kingfisher Plc in the past three years, and predict the company's prospects. Provide reference for companies, stakeholders and potential investors.

2 Literature Review

In recent years, some scholars have used different methods to conduct research on financial statement analysis. For example, in 2019, Petrit Hasanaj and Beke Kuqi adopted qualitative and quantitative analysis methods to analyze the financial statements of "X" company. Deriving financial statement analysis is necessary for businesses to make sound decisions [2]. In 2022, Lan Tianyang used case analysis and Harvard analysis framework research methods to conduct financial analysis on HD shares. The main problems existing in the rubber and plastic products industry and HD shares are analyzed, which can be used as a reference for other enterprises in the industry [3]. In 2022, Wang Ying discussed the application of financial statement analysis in business operations, and explained several commonly used financial statement analysis methods such as ratio analysis, comparative analysis, and trend analysis, but did not conduct a specific analysis [4].

In addition, the author finds that there are few relevant literatures through the search of articles on the value of Kingfisher Plc. In 2020, Silva, Francisco Miguel Duarte da used the absolute valuation method and relative valuation method, conducted equity research on Kingfisher plc through sensitivity analysis and Monte Carlo simulation [5]. Silva made a detailed valuation and forecast of the intrinsic value of the company at the end of 2020, and draw the conclusion that Kingfisher Plc faces medium risk. But Silva's research is highly technical and uses a model architecture that is difficult to understand. When users cannot correctly understand the meaning of each parameter, they will cause some misunderstanding of the results, so the requirements for users are relatively high, which is not suitable for most investors. Therefore, from the perspective of public users, this paper adopts a more simple and understandable way to analyze the management quality of Kingfisher Plc. And is committed to providing reference for users of all parties.

3 Industry Background Analysis

The case company Kingfisher Plc in this article belongs to the home improvement retail industry. This paper uses Porter's five forces model and SWOT analysis to analyze the macro environment of Kingfisher Plc and Kingfisher Plc's own advantages and disadvantages.

3.1 Enterprise Profile

Kingfisher Plc was founded in 1982. Kingfisher Plc is an international home improvement company with over 1,500 stores, supported by a team of 80,000 colleagues. Kingfisher Plc is one of the world's top 500 companies and ranks third in the global home improvement retail industry. They offer home improvement products and services to consumers and trade professionals who shop in their stores and via our e-commerce channels.

3.2 Porter's Five Forces Analysis

Threat of New Entrants. In the home improvement retail industry, although the cost of customer switching is low, it is already a mature market with a high degree of market concentration, making it difficult for new entrants to enter. Network effects play a relatively weak role in the industry and cannot significantly impact the industry. Overall, the threat of new entrants in the home improvement retail industry is low but still exists.

Threat of Substitutes. One of the trickiest problems to solve is the availability of many replacement items, as well as the growing willingness of merchants from different industry to sell the same products at competitive prices.

Bargaining Power of Suppliers. The concentration of suppliers in this industry is low. Several suppliers have identical offers, which limits their negotiating power. Although there is a great demand for raw materials in this industry, many cheap raw material providers worldwide. And the switching costs are relatively low. For these reasons, the paper considers this a low threat.

Bargaining Power of Customers. As a home improvement retail industry, individual consumers are the main customers, and the low concentration of customers reduces the bargaining power of customers. However, at present, the high degree of product homogeneity in the market provides customers with more choices, and the customer switching costs are very low, which enhances the bargaining power of customers. Therefore, the bargaining power of buyers is high in this industry.

Industry Rivalry. The home improvement market is fragmented, highly competitive and has slow industry growth. Kingfishers Plc' competitors are large in scale, have developed economies of scale and often adopt aggressive strategies to acquire market share. For that reason, and considering Kingfisher Plc has a strong presence in several European countries, this paper argues that the rivalry among existing competitors to be a moderate threat to Kingfisher Plc.

3.3 SWOT Analysis

The SWOT analysis of Kingfisher PLC is shown in Table 1.

Table 1. SWOT analysis.

Strengths	Weaknesses
1) In a leading position in the industry 2) Products wide audience, can meet the needs of different customers, have many loyal consumers 3) Cooperate with multiple suppliers to establish a flexible supply chain 4) With the combination of online and offline sales, there are a large number of offline stores and the rapid development of online e-commerce	1) Inventories are high, assets are less liquid and short-term debt service payments are under pressure 2) High dependence on network technology 3) The strategy of reducing the size of physical stores will put a huge pressure on inventory
Opportunities	**Threats**
1) The development of electronic commerce is the general trend. Kingfisher can seize the opportunity to continue to improve in the e-commerce sector 2) As the spread of COVID-19 slows, revenue from offline stores will recover 3) Interest in DIY increased during the Covid-19 pandemic. Kingfisher Plc can continue to make steady progress in this field	1) The status of the economy has a significant impact on the home improvement industry. Due to the present economic crisis, customers downturn, consumers tend to spend less on big-ticket items 2) OEB relies on global supply chains and is highly exposed to geopolitical uncertainties 3) The international market is becoming increasingly competitive, and the competitors are constantly expanding their scale

4 Financial Ratio Analysis

4.1 Profitability Ratio

Profitability refers to the ability of an enterprise to earn profits, that is, to bring about a net inflow of funds. This is an important driving force for the long-term and stable development of enterprises, so the majority of investors attach great importance to profitability. The higher the profitability, the more returns shareholders can get [6].

Since the financial report of 2022/23 has not been disclosed when this paper is written, the financial data of the three years from 2019/2020 to 2021/22 are selected for analysis, and the average value of the home improvement industry in these three years is taken as the benchmark for comparison, as shown in Table 2.

Return on Equity (ROE). From 0.14% to 9.01% and then to 12.44%, it can be seen that the company's return on equity has increased significantly in these three years. It indicates that the profitability of the company has made great progress in recent years, which benefits from the good implementation of Kingfisher strategy. However, this ratio is still low and needs to be further improved.

Return on Asset (ROA). ROA's growth suggests that Kingfisher's prospects are improving. Because it means that there is a potential increase in the profits that the

Table 2. Profitability ratios.

Financial ratios	Jan.31,2022	Jan.31,2021	Jan.31,2020	Industry 3 Year Avg.
ROE (%)	12.44	9.01	0.14	-
ROA (%)	6.82	4.83	0.07	-
ROCE (%)	12.15	10.30	3.54	-
Gross profit margin (%)	37.43	37.05	36.96	34.33
Net Profit margin (%)	6.39	4.80	0.07	8.34
Operating margin (%)	8.68	7.42	2.46	12.01

company makes, which means that he will increase the value of the company. Such positive signals increase investor confidence and make it easier for management to attract capital in the form of shares [7].

Return on Capital Employed (ROCE). ROCE shows how well investors funds are being used to generate profit. The higher the ratio, the better. During the three years from 2019/2020 to 2021/22, ROCE has continued to rise. This is a good sign, which proves that the company's credit rating has improved and it is more likely to be favored by investors.

Gross Profit Margin. It can be seen that the gross profit margin has been improving, and the gross profit margin is higher than the market benchmark (34.33%) in these three years. It shows that the enterprise has good profitability.

Net Profit Margin. The net profit of Kingfisher Plc was far lower than the industry benchmark. But compared with itself, it has shown a good growth momentum in the past three years. The increase was mainly due to the implementation of a compact store strategy, which simplifies physical store operations and helps save management and labor costs.

In conclusion, all ratios listed in this article regarding Kingfisher Plc's profitability have improved over the three years. There are many reasons for this, including employee and equipment innovation, the implementation of the company's OBE strategy. One of the most important factors contributing to the dismal 2020 figures is the global spread of COVID-19. The implementation of some epidemic prevention measures has affected the logistics industry, as well as offline sales, and also caused a certain impact on the development of Kingfisher Plc. Business conditions improved as Kingfisher Plc implemented its response strategy and the spread of COVID-19 slowed. Overall, the company's operating conditions are improving and its profitability is increasing rapidly.

4.2 Liquidity Ratio

The liquidity ratio is a ratio that shows a company's ability to service its short-term debt. It is usually divided into current ratio and quick ratio. The liquidity ratios of Kingfisher plc from 2019/2020 to 2021/2022are shown in Table 3.

Table 3. Liquidity ratio.

Financial ratios	Jan.31,2022	Jan.31,2021	Jan.31,2020	Industry 3 Year Avg.
Current ratio	1.27	1.24	1.12	1.26
Quick assets ratio	0.36	0.46	0.38	0.25

Current Ratio. Kingfisher's current ratio has increased over the past three years. The company's current ratio looks low compared with the usual one of about 2. But with a current ratio of 1.26 against the industry benchmark, the company is in the normal range and showing good growth trends. Generally speaking, the short-term liquidity reserve of enterprises can meet the demand of short-term debt repayment.

Quick Assets Ratio. It has a trend of rising first and then falling. The main reason for the decline in 2022 is an increase in ending inventories, which brings with it a decline in corporate solvency. Too much inventory can tie up money, so the company should probably reduce its inventory. The quick ratio looks low but it is appropriate in the industry.

4.3 Efficiency Ratio

Efficiency ratio reflects the enterprise's operating ability and capital utilization ability. The efficiency ratio analysis is mainly to objectively evaluate the enterprise's operating ability through the turnover rate of relevant indicators, so as to improve the economic efficiency of enterprises and ensure the direction of efficient development [8]. The efficiency ratios of Kingfisher plc from 2019/2020 to 2021/2022are shown in Table 4.

Table 4. Efficiency ratios.

Financial ratios	Jan.31,2022	Jan.31,2021	Jan.31,2020	Industry 3 Year Avg.
Asset turnover ratio	1.07	1.01	1.02	1.75
Inventory turnover ratio	3.00	3.12	2.92	6.79
Receivables turnover ratio	43.94	42.56	39.19	30.81

Asset Turnover Ratio. It can be seen from Table 4 that Kingfisher Plc's asset turnover rate tends to be stable in the three years from 2019/20 to 2021/22, with little fluctuation. The higher the asset turnover rate, the better the utilization efficiency of assets. If the ratio is greater than 1, it proves that the company has a strong sales ability and a relatively high return on asset investment. However, compared with the industry benchmark of 1.75, it shows that Kingfisher Plc still needs to be further improved.

Inventory Turnover Ratio. The inventory turnover rate of Kingfisher has not changed much in the past three years, which is low compared to the industry benchmark. A low inventory turnover rate means that the company's inventory holding period is long, which will result in higher management costs. It also indicates that the inventory turnover speed is slow and there is a high risk of obsolescence. The company was advised to reduce its inventory.

Receivables Turnover Ratio. In the three years from 2019/20 to 2021/22, Kingfisher's accounts receivable turnover rate has shown a slow growth trend. And it has been above the industry benchmark for all three years. A high turnover rate of accounts receivable indicates that the company has a short collection cycle and strong liquidity, which is a good sign.

4.4 Investment Ratio

For investors, they may pay more attention to earnings per share and the debt-to-asset ratio of the company. The EPS ratio describes the state of the company in terms of distributing and generating corporate profits and can have a significant impact on stock prices [9]. The higher a company's EPS, the more profitable it is considered to be. The gearing ratio shows a company's debt load. Moderate debt can enable companies to obtain tax credits to increase corporate value, but excessive debt can lead to financial difficulties and increase the risk of bankruptcy. Simply focusing on the level of gearing ratio may also lead to the abandonment of many investment projects with positive net present value [10]. Therefore, investors should keep their eyes open when examining the gearing ratio. Table 5 shows Kingfisher Plc's earnings per share and debt ratios from 2019/20 to 2021/22.

Table 5. Investment ratio.

Financial ratios	Jan.31,2022	Jan.31,2021	Jan.31,2020
EPS ($)	1.10	0.72	0.01
Gross Gearing ratio (%)	35.29	38.41	56.26

Earnings Per Share (EPS). Kingfisher's earnings per share increased significantly from 2019/20 to 2021/22. This means that the company's asset appreciation ability is enhanced, its profitability is getting better and better, and it has more funds to distribute dividends. A positive sign for investors.

Gross Gearing Ratio. It is generally believed that the optimal gross gearing ratio should be between 25% and 50%. As can be seen from Table 5, Kingfisher's gross gearing ratio in 2020 is relatively high. Combining the previous analysis of various ratios and the background of the 2019/2020 COVID-19 pandemic, it is not difficult to judge that companies are in a downturn in 2019/2020. Later, with the adjustment of the strategy, the company's operations gradually recovered, and the gross gearing ratio reached a relatively moderate state. As far as the current data is concerned, Kingfisher Plc's bankruptcy risk is very low.

5 Conclusion

Judging from the above financial indicators, Kingfisher Plc has developed rapidly in recent years and has a good operating quality. Judging from the results of profitability ratio analysis, Kingfisher Plc's development strategy in recent years has been well implemented, and its profitability has been continuously improved. Combining the characteristics of the industry to look at the liquidity ratio of Kingfisher Plc, it is found that the ratios are appropriate, indicating that the company has a certain short-term solvency. Judging from the results of efficiency ratio analysis, various indicators are relatively stable. However, except for the moderate and fast payment collection, other operating efficiencies do not have obvious advantages in the industry, which will also make it passive in the competition. In terms of investment ratio, both EPS and Gross Gearing ratio performed well. This paper holds a relatively optimistic attitude towards Kingfisher Plc's current operating quality. Investors can combine their own investment needs and comprehensively consider the risk of investment to judge whether to invest.

If Kingfisher Plc wants to ensure its sustainable development, it should conform to the development trend, analyze its own advantages and disadvantages, and formulate and continuously adjust and improve its strategic plan in combination with the development trend of the market economy and the development trend of the group. According to their own financial situation, analyze the financial problems in their own development. Focus on cultivating customer loyalty in the fierce market competition. While strengthening the better experience of offline stores, we will continue to improve the marketing and after-sales service of online products to improve consumer satisfaction. Of course, while innovating and developing, ensure the sustainable development of the consumption ecology and improve the shopping experience of users. Continue to adhere to the strategy of "Source and buy better, reduce costs and same-store inventory", optimize inventory products, and accelerate product sales. Continuously improve its own strength, and eventually become a more powerful Kingfisher Group.

References

1. Fraser, L.M., Ormiston, A., Mukherjee, A.K.: Understanding financial statements, p. 3. Pearson, New York (2016)
2. Hasanaj, P., Kuqi, B.: Analysis of financial statements. Human. Soc. Sci. Res. **2**(2), 17 (2019)
3. Lan, T.: Analysis of HD share financial statements under the Harvard analysis framework. Foreign Econ. Trade **340**(10), 91–93 (2022)
4. Wang, Y.: Application of financial statement analysis in enterprise operations. Qual. Mark. **320**(21), 43–45 (2022)
5. Silva, F.M.D.: Equity research-Kingfisher PLC. Instituto Superior de Economia e Gestão (2020)
6. Zhang, Y.: Financial analysis and performance evaluation of Vanke co., ltd..Natl. Circ. Econ. (08), 117–119 (2021)
7. Dance, M., Imade, S.: Financial ratio analysis in predicting financial conditions distress in Indonesia Stock Exchange. Russ. J. Agric. Soc.-Econ. Sci. **86**(2), 155–165 (2019)
8. Yang, Q., Zhu, J.: Financial analysis of listed companies based on financial statements–taking "Suning Tesco" as an example. Qual. Mark. **317**(18), 25–27 (2022)

9. Bustani, B., Kurniaty, K., Widyanti, R.: The effect of earning per share, price to book value, dividend payout ratio, and net profit margin on the stock price in Indonesia stock exchange. J. Maksipreneur: Manajemen, Koperasi, dan Entrepreneurship **11**(1), 1–18 (2021)
10. Myers, S.C.: Determinants of corporate borrowing. J. Financ. Econ.Financ. Econ. **5**(2), 147–175 (1977)

Comedic Violence Advertisement and Limiting Factors

Yuting Tong(✉)

College of Business and Public Management, Wenzhou-Kean University, Wenzhou 325006, Zhejiang Province, China
`tongyu@kean.edu`

Abstract. In many nations, advertising of violent content was made illegal, although funny advertisements of violent content were widely consumed. The level of acceptance of comedic advertisements featuring violent content could be raised by including funny components in those advertisements. The influence of comic violence advertisement and the useful scope of comedic violence are both investigated in this research using the method of literature review. The investigation is carried out from the viewpoint of latecomers. According to the findings of the paper, humorous violence may be tolerated, but the degree of tolerance varies depending on factors such as gender, age, norm belief, and power distance. This paper can assist readers in gaining a better understanding of the most recent studies in the subject. At the same time, it provides recommendations for businesses who are designing comical violent commercials for various demographics of individuals in order to obtain the best response.

Keywords: Comedic Violence Advertisement · Limiting Factors · Comedic Elements

1 Introduction

Violence is a banned factor in advertisement. Too much violence will lead to disgust in the audience. But comedic violence is on the opposite, violence becomes understandable even welcomed, under the umbrella of comedy.

The studies in this field focus on exploring which impact would influence the popularity of comedic violence advertisements. Researchers used data to find out difference between impacts. This paper focused on conclusion, make a summary of all the factors that may affect the comedic violence advertisement, and provide solutions for different groups for the enterprise's advertisement design.

This paper can help readers get a quicker grasp of current research in the field. At the same time, it gives suggestions when companies design comedic violence advertisements for different groups of people to get best attract. And at the end of the paper, some suggestion would be given to accurate the degree of comedic violence in different situation.

2 Violent Advertisement

"In the last six months of 2006, 916 complaints against violence in commercials were received, referring to 195 ads," according to ASA data. 523 commercials received 1748 complaints between January and October 2007 [1]. Australians worry about violence, sex, sexuality, nudity, and advertising discrimination [2]. David S. and colleagues examined cross-cultural offensiveness of violent advertising [3]. Australian, Canadian, Indian, Kazakhstan, South Korean, and Turkish university students were sampled to support ethical judgment. Analyzed 930 answers. It is not surprising that a convenience sample of students would have a mean age of 21.22 years (96.5% varied from 18 to 25), and that females made up 49.3% of the sample. The high percentages of Muslims (Turkey and Kazakhstan) and Christians (Canada and Australia) in the sample is a direct reflection of those countries' respective populations. 1–5 scales measured all questions. 1 is "strongly disagree" while 5 is "strongly agree". The final interview results are as follows (Table 1).

Table 1. Descriptive Statistics and Variables [3].

Independent variables (continuous) N = 930		Mean (SD)
Age		21.22 (2.87)
Intensity of religious belief		3.00 (1.35)
Political inclination		3.01 (0.86)
Economic inclination		3.37 (0.92)
Individualism		3.73 (0.70)
Offensiveness of advertising promoting social/political groups		3.28 (1.06)
Independent variables (categorical)	Frequency	Valid %
Gender		49.3 female
Religion		
Islam	335	37.02
Christianity	268	29.61
Nonbeliever	130	14.36
Hinduism	88	9.72
Other	43	4.75
Buddhism/Taoism	41	4.53
Country		
Turkey	221	23.76
Kazakhstan	177	19.03
South Korea	151	16.24
Canada	146	15.70
Australia	140	15.05
India	95	10.22
Dependent variables		Mean (SD)
Extent of offensiveness of violent images in advertising		3.54 (1.36)

The initial part of the research consisted of determining the overall circumstances of the people who participated in the study. The political situation is less capitalist (M = 3.01), the religious situation is completely neutral (M = 3.0), and the economic situation is more capitalist (M = 3.37). All of these measures have a value of M = 3. The fact that the dependent variable offensive of violent image is significantly higher than the mean (M = 3.54) indicates that students have a pessimistic outlook on the use of violent imagery in advertising. In addition, the most important reason to avoid violent advertising is that it promotes violent imagery, which is in direct conflict with ethical standards. The audience expressed unease at the sight of those.

3 Comedic Violence Advertisement

Comedic violence, according to Hetherington and Wray [4], is a form of aggressive humor that is always accompanied by the hostile purpose to ridicule, deprecate, or harm. In contrast to more restrained forms of violent advertising, the more extreme the content of such ads get, the more successful they tend to be. Researchers Mark R. Brown and other researchers examined the impact of aggressive behavior on AMI, recall, and transmission rates [5]. We postulate in the first place that "severe consequences will have a more pronounced influence of humorous violence intensity on ad message involvement than moderate ones." This study employed the Coca-Cola brand to conclude a humorous commercial in which two guys fight over a cola and the first man hurts the second man while he works at a typewriter. Most advertising has a similar message; what changes is how the victim responds to being hurt. The high-intensity, high-severity result is that the victim crumples to the ground, hands over his ears as he screams in agony. His reaction to the high-intensity stimulation was to stick his hand to his head and utter "ouch" in an angry tone, but his reaction to the low-intensity stimulus was the same as it was to the first stimulus (he threw his hand over his head and said "ouch"). Finally, a moderately intense ad with middling results. This leads to the following conclusions (Fig. 1).

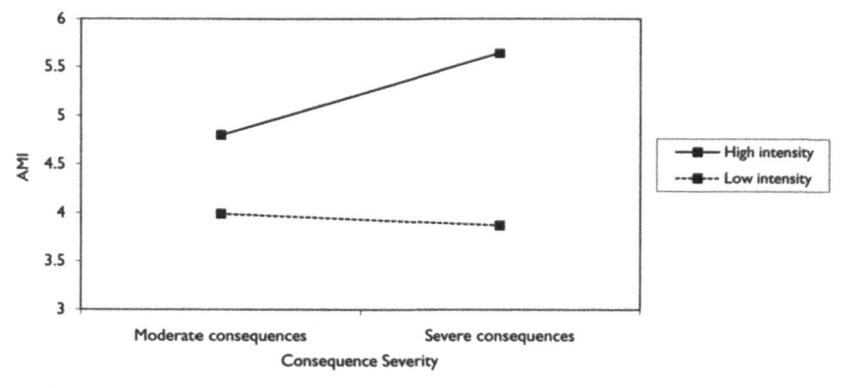

Fig. 1. The relationship between Ad Message Involvement (AMI) and consequence severity [5].

The data shown in the figure indicates that a high intensity (M = 5.21) has a more significant impact on AMI than a low intensity (M = 3.93). Intensity and consequences are found to have a highly significant association (F = 6.25; df = 1, 160; p .05). This relationship can be expressed as intensity consequences. The assumption of high intensity predicts that strong consequences, which have a magnitude of 5.64, will have a higher average damage than mild consequences, which have a magnitude of 4.8. H1 was approved for use. Audiences are becoming more sensitive to advertisements with a high level of intensity. And severe repercussions would generate a greater amount of acute myocardial infarction (AMI) than moderate consequences would against the backdrop of high intensity. And researchers also deal with data about correct recall and recognition for various levels of violence and consequences, in order to address the second hypothesis. This hypothesis states that "comedic violence intensity influences brand remember more when repercussions are severe than moderate (Table 2)."

Table 2. Correct Recall and Correct Recognition of the Advertised Brand for Different Levels of Violence and Consequence Severity [5].

	HiSev	HiMod	LoSev	LoMod	n
Delayed recall					
Incorrect					
n	16	24	28	28	96
%	44.4	70.6	73.7	75.7	
Correct					
n	20	10	10	9	49
%	55.6	29.4	26.3	24.3	
Total					
n	36	34	38	37	145
%	100	100	100	100	
Pearson $\chi^2 = 22.01$, p $< .01$					
Delayed recognition					
Incorrect					
n	9	18	18	21	66
%	25.0	52.9	47.4	56.8	
Correct					
n	27	16	20	16	79
%	75.0	47.1	52.6	43.2	
Total					
n	36	34	38	37	145
%	100	100	100	100	

Note: HiSev = high intensity-severe consequences; HiMod = high intensity-moderate consequence; LoSev = low intensity-severe consequence; LoMod = low intensity-moderate consequence. Pearson $\chi^2 = 15.99$, p $< .05$

From this table, high intensity-serve consequence has high accuracy of recall and recognition than other situations (Recall-HiSev, 55.6%; HiMod, 29.4%; LoSev, 26.3%; LoMod, 24.3%; Recognition-HiSev, 75%; HiMod, 47.1%; LoSev, 52.6%; LoMod, 43.2%). This also prove that the second hypothesis is currect.

This experiment demonstrated how effective humorous depictions of violence can be in advertising. Comedic advertisements for violence take a different approach, reconciling the unpleasant aspects of violent content. And the more graphic and graphically violent an advertisement for humorous violence is, the more popular it is.

4 Limitations in Comedic Violence Advertisement

4.1 The Limitation of Gender on Comedic Violence Advertisement

Comedic violence is not always working, different groups have different reaction about same comedic violence advertisement. Gender, the role of normative beliefs, age, religions, and power distance would influence comedic violence advertisement.

The impact of gender as a moderator on humorous portrayals of violence in advertising has been discussed by Hye Jin Yoon and other researchers [6]. They compare how men and women respond to different levels of humor, ad and brand attitudes, buy and sharing intentions, and other measures of how people identify with a given gender (SI). SI is a crucial metric for gauging the success of an advertisement; one of its questions is "If you saw this advertisement online, how likely are you to recommend it to others? (r = .96)" [6]. Additionally, researchers use a second metric to differentiate between two groups of people. Subjects are not stereotypical males and females but rather men and women who identify as such. T ratio, the difference between masculine and femininity evaluations, was the quantitative approach used [7]. Female subjects with high positive ratings are feminine, whereas male subjects with high negative scores are masculine. Those found to be in the middle range are viewed as possessing qualities of both sexes. Rather than selecting people just based on whether they possessed biologically male or female characteristics, the researchers aimed for subjects who exhibited extremes of both sexisms. They went with a Toyota and a Doritos ad. These ads are amusing and violent as they had predicted, and they may be detected. Perceived levels of comedy and aggression were both above the median value of 4 in the data. The two commercials were generally judged to be equivalent in quality by all participants. In some cases, data may vary between objects. For perceived humor, (Toyota: M masculine = 5.14, SD = 1.98; M feminine = 4.24, SD = 2.43, t (145) = 2.47, p < .05) (Doritos: M masculine = 5.37, SD = 1.78; M feminine = 4.46, SD = 2.40, t (145) = 2.64, p < .01). For SI, the result was like predicted (Toyota: M masculine = 4.53, SD = 2.24; M feminine = 3.27, SD = 2.17, t (150) = 3.45, p < .01) (Doritos: M masculine = 4.83, SD = 2.20; M feminine = 3.94, SD = 2.37, t (150) = 2.37, p < .05). These results also pointed out that masculine audiences could perceive more humor than feminine group, but feminine audiences would not recommend a same advertisement than masculine, maybe feminine could perceived more violence than masculine.

Kunal Swani and other researchers made an experiment discuss the success of an advertisement from the gender perspective [8], draw path form perspective humor to brand attitude. And speculate violations of social norms (VSN) is a possible factor impact the path. The researchers played an advertisement and gave out two questions to test VSN, "I think this commercial is wrong" and "I think this commercial broke societal norms" with five degrees from "strongly disagree" to "strongly agree". As predicted, women thought the high-violence humor advertisement caused more VSN than men (M women = 3.54, M man = 3.02; F = 5.11, [1, 78], p < 0.05) (Fig. 2).

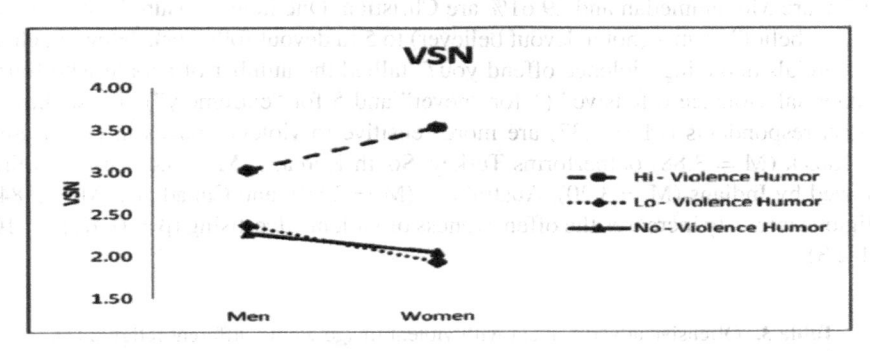

Fig. 2. Violations of Social Norms [8].

High-violence humor would cause more VSN. Meanwhile, women would perspective more VSN than men in Hi-violence Humor. And they draw the path between perspective humor and attitude to brand (Fig. 3).

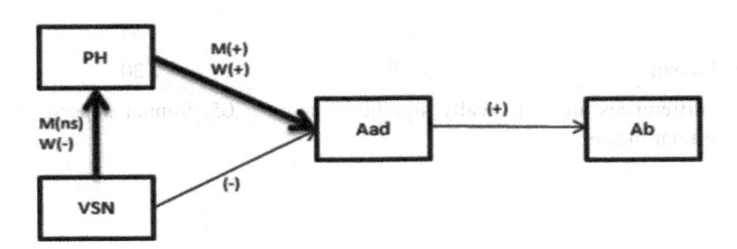

Fig. 3. The path from Perspective Humor to Attitude to Advertisement [8].

They limited VSN's effect on PH and calculated modification index, which was significant (2 (1) = 3.99, p < 0.05; CFI = 0.01), suggesting gender differences in VSN's effect on PH. VSN and PH negatively correlate, according to previous research. This connection was significant for women but not for men ($\beta M = -0.042$, t = 1.16, p > 0.05; $\beta W = -0.149$, t = 3.82, p < 0.01). Gender directly affects VSN and PH, although the road from VSN to PH is free. With RMSEA = 0.064, CFI = 0.99, NFI = 0.98, and $\chi 2(6) = 9.00$, p > 0.05, this model works well.

VSN is one of the reasons for women perspective less humor and more violence than men.

4.2 The Limitation of Religion in Comedic Violence Advertisement

Discussing the effect of religion on comedic violence advertisement. David S. Waller and other researchers had do a cross-cultural study about appeal on offensive advertisement with violent image [3]. Religion is a research subject in this study. Most of 930 respondents were from Turkey, Kazakhstan, Canada and Australia. Among them, 37.02% are Mohammedan and 29.61% are Christian. One item measured "intensity of religious belief" from 1 (not a devout believer) to 5 (a devout follower). "How much do commercials depicting violence offend you?" tallied the number of people who found commercial violence offensive" (1 for "never" and 5 for "extremely"). T-test showed Turkish respondents (M = 4.37) are more sensitive to violent images in provocative ads. Kazak (M = 3.88) outperforms Turkey. South Koreans (M = 3.46) placed third, followed by Indians (M = 3.20), Australians (M = 2.89), and Canadians (M = 2.84). Religious intensity increases the offensiveness of violent advertising ($\beta = 0.07$, $p < .10$) (Table 3).

Table 3. Offensive advertisement with violent image within different religion [3].

Religion	Mean	SD
Islam	4.19^a	1.15
Nonbeliever	3.23^b	1.36
Other religion	3.21^b	1.36
Christianity	3.16^b	1.27
Hinduism	3.14^b	1.54
Buddhism/Taoism	3.13^b	1.30

Note: Mean differences are statistically significant at $p < .05$. Similar superscripts indicate statistically similar means

4.3 The Limitation of Countries in Comedic Violence Advertisement

Comedic violence advertisements have different effects in different countries, and power distance is a standard to distinguish different types of countries. it is said by Kara Chan [9], different countries have different cultural taboo, as China is sensitive about kneel, and German rejected to watch Benetton campaign in advertisement. Even a normal advertisement should consider the region they will be played. Hye Jin Yoona and relevant researchers have done a study test sense of humor on different countries [10]. And they also examined the difference between self and others, with expectation that under different cultural background, individuals would perspective the impact of violent humor on themselves with different results. The subject countries they choose are America, Korea, and Croatia. The comedic violent advertisement they chose is "FedEx or Carrier Pigeon", a real advertisement. ANOVA test show there exist difference about perspective humor among these countries ($F(2, 133) = 4.89$, $p < .01$). American (M = 5.83) thought this aggressive advertisement was funnier than Koreans (M = 4.98) and Croatians (M = 4.92). The difference between Koreans and Croatians was not significant (p > .05). Relationships are indicated by self- and other-perception differences (F (2, 133) = 8.01, p < .01). American self (M self = 5.83) is funnier than others indifferent civilizations (M others = 5.29; F (1, 53) = 7.99, p < .01). Koreans thought others (M others = 5.29) in different cultures were funnier than self (M self = 4.98; F (1, 53) = 7.99, p < 0.01). Croatians found this commercial hilarious to themselves (M self = 4.92) and others (5.01; F (1, 45) = .45, p = n.s.). Americans prefer aggressive humor (Fig. 4).

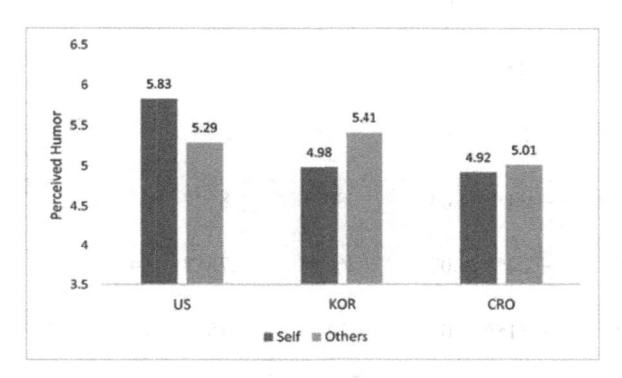

Fig. 4. Perceived Humor in difference countries [3]

This study shows the acceptance level to comedic violent advertisement is different among different types of cultures. And the gap between self and others is different based on culture background. Americans prefer more violent humor than Koreans or Croatians. And this result is also same as past research which was made by Chen et al. [11], people in individualistic cultures are more open to accept comedic violent ad. Than collectivistic cultures.

4.4 The Limitation of Norm Beliefs in Comedic Violence Advertisement

Hye Jin Yoon and Yeuseung Kim made a study about the relation between age, norm beliefs and acceptance level of comedic violent advertisement [12]. As people get older, personality changed. Neuroticism, Extraversion and Openness decreasing, while Agreeableness and Conscientiousness increase [12]. People's attitude towards society become more mature. Younger consumers had a weaker beneficial influence of norm views on perspective humor, according to researchers. With the method of correlation matrix, the result is as this (Table 4).

Table 4. Age, norm beliefs and acceptance level of comedic violent advertisement [12].

	Norm	Age	Norm × Age	Perceived humor	A_{ad}	A_{brand}	PI	SI	Mean (SD)
Norm	1								0.00 (1.60)
Age	−.31**	1							0.00 (17.78)
Norm × Age	.07	−.14**	1						−8.87 (27.40)
Perceived humor	.38**	−.25**	.06	1					4.92 (1.52)
A_{ad}	.37**	−.28**	.07	.91**	1				4.89 (1.53)
A_{brand}	.31**	−.24**	.04	.80**	.86**	1			4.92 (1.37)
PI	.28**	−.22**	.02	.66**	.75**	.84	1		4.52 (1.36)
SI	.32**	−.31**	.00	.71**	.75**	.72**	.71**	1	3.87 (1.83)

The results of the regression analyses are presented below.

Table 5. Regression analyses [12].

	Perceived Humor	A_{ad}	A_{brand}	PI	SI
	β	β	β	β	β
Norm	.29*	.26*	.27*	.28*	.38*
Age	−.18	−.23	−.15	−.11	−.10
Norm x Age	.05	.06	−.01	−.04	−.16
F	26.69***	27.69**	18.18***	15.29***	24.79***
R - squared	.16	.17	.12	.10	.15

Shown in Table 5, norm beliefs had a positive main effect on all outcome variables (β = .29, p < .05; A ad: β = .26, p < .05; A brand: β = .27, p < .05; PI: β = .28, p < .05; SI: β = .38, p < .01). But age and other outcome variables do not have significant relation. Norm belief plays a role as main effect, people thought if it is normal to see violence in advertisement, the acceptance level to comedic violence advertisement would be higher. Age doesn't have significant effect on attitude to violent advertisement, but maybe age have negative effect on norm beliefs. According to the result, it's harder for older people to accept violent advertisement.

5 Discussion

Some studies did not assess subjective factors, such as whether all participants had the same sense of humor. Only having the same sense, the variation in opinion regarding a similar funny violent advertisement makes sense. Almost every trial tests the violent degree of various funny violent advertisements, making the overall research more rigorous. However, one study on discussing gender limitations chose to select an expert to decide the degree of comic violent commercial, then used the results from this people into the next steps. This stage should be improved; the author believes that all data that potentially impact the outcome should come from interviewers. In the gender test, researchers picked feminine or masculine features as the target, rather than regular men and women. Because not every man possesses male characteristics, and not every woman possesses feminine characteristics. And, in the experiment examining the relationship between power distance and acceptability level to comic violence advertisements, perhaps changing the target object would be preferable. The author argues that interviewers from the United States and England are more common.

6 Conclusion

Comedic violent advertising are more popular than violent advertisements. The comic impact would mitigate the negative consequences of the violence. Meanwhile, it is constrained. Different audiences respond differently to comedic violent advertisements. People with feminine characteristics might exaggerate a violent scene in an advertisement. People who hold strong religious convictions are less accepting than others. Liberal countries are more open to comic violent advertising. And consumers' attitudes toward humorous violence advertisements would be influenced by norm belief and transgressions of societal norms. People with strong religious convictions and traditional views are less likely to accept comic violence advertisements. Furthermore, elderly persons always have high norm beliefs. These also provided us some ideas for using comic violence advertisements. When the primary audience is female, comedic violence advertising are not our first choice, and advertisements designed for the elderly should contain fewer violent components. And for young people and guys, it could be a good idea to include some violent components to capture the interest of the audience.

References

1. Practice, A.: What are you looking at? Drawing the line on violence in advertising (2022). https://www.asa.org.uk/resource/Drawing-the-line-on-violence-in-advertising.html. Accessed 12 Oct 2022
2. Complaints about violence in advertising are rising - AdNews (2022). https://www.adnews.com.au/news/complaints-about-violence-in-advertising-are-rising. Accessed 12 Oct 2022
3. Offensiveness of Advertising with Violent Image Appeal: A Cross-Cultural Study (2022). Journal of Promotion Management. https://www.tandfonline.com/doi/full/10.1080/10496491.2013.817220?casa_token=FnUKrUA1XY4AAAAA%3AdBsWtv3N-
4. Gradinaru, C.: Violence dressed in humor: comedic violence in advertising. J. Media Critiques 1(2), 55–73 (2015). https://doi.org/10.17349/jmc115303

5. The Impact of Comedic Violence on Viral Advertising Effectiveness (2022). J. Advertising. https://www.tandfonline.com/doi/abs/10.2753/JOA0091-3367390104?src=recsys
6. The Moderating Role of Gender Identity in Responses to Comedic Violence Advertising (2022). Journal of Advertising. https://www.tandfonline.com/doi/full/10.1080/00913367.2014.880390?casa_token=qKGFiWXRk3IAAAAA%3Auk8K0cMee5OPb6FbuSgd-BpD3AavddP75cdrU4SjiwNWGkd4knHUZ3dlbeVRRdwPmfnTy5VKU1kMjw
7. Lenney, E.: Sex roles: the measurement of masculinity, femininity, and androgyny. Measures Pers. Soc. Psychol. Attitudes, 573–660 (1991). https://doi.org/10.1016/b978-0-12-590241-0.50015-0
8. The Impact of Violent Humor on Advertising Success: A Gender Perspective (2022). Journal of Advertising. https://www.tandfonline.com/doi/full/10.1080/00913367.2013.795121?src=recsys
9. Comedic violence in advertising: cultural third-person effects among U.S., Korean, and Croatian consumers (2022). International Journal of Advertising. https://www.tandfonline.com/doi/full/10.1080/02650487.2020.1827894?src=recsys
10. Chen, G., Martin, R.: A comparison of humor styles, coping humor, and mental health between Chinese and Canadian university students. Hum. Int. J. Hum. Res. **20**(3) (2007). https://doi.org/10.1515/humor.2007.011
11. The effects of norm beliefs and age on responses to comedic violence advertising (2022). Journal of Current Issues & Research in Advertising. https://www.tandfonline.com/doi/full/10.1080/10641734.2016.1171180?casa_token=96fNSAFhUJcAAAAA%3APH1n2XT01VADDXr3YE_k3B8ZrUzCVSljjZ6CvUM0SV19fd9nvgO0Zf_Kzh7wOOV69Jy6upJMIk9GEQ
12. Terracciano, A., McCrae, R.R., Brant, L.J., Costa, P.T., Jr.: Hierarchical linear modeling analyses of the NEO-PI-R scales in the Baltimore longitudinal study of aging. Psychol. Aging **20**(3), 493–506 (2005). https://doi.org/10.1037/0882-7974.20.3.493

The Impacts of Goal Setting on Enterprises from a Corporate Social Responsibility Perspective

Yu Chen(✉)

University of St Andrews, Scotland, UK
yc79@st-andrews.ac.uk

Abstract. With the steady development of the social economy, the responsibility and status of companies in society has gradually increased, thus making the public more interested in goal setting and planning for companies. Moreover, good goal setting also enables employees to understand the organisation's vision and course of action more clearly, thus improving their understanding and effectiveness. This paper will focus on the benefits and drawbacks of goal setting for business, followed by a few case studies to illustrate the impact of the theory on business, with respect to the need for business to meet its goals not only in economic terms, but also in social terms. "Carroll's CSR Pyramid" clearly outlines four types of social responsibility for companies: economic, legal, ethical, and philanthropic. These four areas play a leading role in setting goals for companies. This paper finds out that goal setting has both advantages and disadvantages for companies, and that effective goals can improve performance and employee motivation. Moreover, goals related to social responsibility can also enhance a company's reputation, which can lead to better growth. However, goal setting can also cause companies to lose the trust of their customers by neglecting issues such as ethical aspects while pursuing results. This paper will link the two theories and analyse the social responsibility that companies need to take into account when setting their goals.

Keywords: Goal setting · Corporate social responsibility · Carroll's CSR pyramid

1 Introduction

The twenty-first century world is highly competitive; companies, organisations and individuals are constantly looking for ways to outdo their competitors. Thus, such companies need to consider task performance to identify the best approach. According to Locke and Latham, human behaviour is generally purposeful because it is guided by conscious goals [7]. Goal setting is inherently related to task performance, suggesting that specific and challenging goals with appropriate feedback contribute to higher and better task performance [6]. However, although clear goals do undoubtably help people to be more purposeful in their tasks, certain hazards associated with goals are often overlooked.

Ordóñez et al. identified specific side effects related to goal setting, including a narrow focus on ignoring non-goal areas, distorted appetite for risk, increased unethical behaviour, inhibited learning, corrupted organisational culture, and reduced intrinsic motivation [10].

Carroll's CSR pyramid articulates an intricate relationship between the elements of goal setting, which CSR (Corporate Social Responsibility) is often understood as the policies and practices adopted by managers to ensure that society or stakeholders (rather than owners) are fully considered and protected in their strategies and operations [3]. It includes the four parts of expectations that society has of an organisation at a given point in time, namely economic, legal, ethical, and philanthropic, and a pyramid-shaped graph of CSR that he created can captures the relationship between each part [2]. The establishment of these four responsibilities creates a basis for the objectives of business and describes the framework of corporate responsibility as part of society.

In this era of rapid development, the importance of business is coming to the fore and the public is becoming more concerned about business development. Thus, goal setting has become particularly important. This paper will evaluate the positive and negative impacts of "goal setting theory" on organisations, using Carroll's CSR pyramid to analyse how goal setting influences enterprises through the corporate social responsibility perspective.

2 Literature Review

2.1 Goal Setting

During work and life, planned forms with goals are increasingly being adopted as they are effective in keeping people on a specific track to complete tasks efficiently. The theory of goal setting is based on an important truism: Life is a process of goal-directed action. Originally, goal setting theory was developed by Edwin A. Locke in 1967, emphasising that setting goals affects motivation levels and job performance. This theory suggests that goal setting has a direct impact on performance because goals have a motivational effect: turning human needs into motivation, causing people to act in a defined direction and to adjust and modify their behavioural outcomes in relation to the set goals in order to achieve them [5]. Also, according to Thompson and McEwen, the target positioning of an enterprise is crucial to its survival and development [12]. If an enterprise does not have a rational goal positioning, it will be in a state of blind development and may potentially be replaced by more innovative competitors. Thus, goals play a key role in the development of enterprises, they contribute to performance by influencing the individual's direction of action, level of effort and persistence.

For the employees of organisations, there are two kinds of goals: 1) internal goals, the desire for achievement; and 2) external goals, the results that employees seek, for example, performance levels, sales or promotions. There are three key points in goal-setting theory: goal difficulty, goal clarity, and self-efficacy (and with adjustment variables); they all have the potential to influence employee performance [7]. The difficulty and clarity of the objectives depend on the ability of the staff and the intensity to which each individual is adapted varies. Hence, to achieve expected outcomes, one needs to align the objectives with as many audiences as possible.

However, goal setting is often influenced by a number of factors that can lead to failure to achieve desired goals: 1) Heterogeneous influence: executives and baseline employees have different understandings and perceptions of goals, making it difficult to achieve unity. 2) Short-term orientation: organisations often seem to emphasise the achievement of short-term goals without concerning for long-term ones. Such a perception, if ingrained in the minds of all members of the organisation, is detrimental to the long-term development of the organisation. 3) The one-sidedness of objectives: Organisational objectives may also be set to over-emphasise the economic terms while overlooking the social dimension.

2.2 Corporate Social Responsibility

Corporate social responsibility (CSR) refers to a company's responsibility to consumers, communities, and the environment, in addition to creating profits and assuming legal responsibility for shareholders and employees. Corporate social responsibility requires companies to abandon the traditional concept of profit as the only goal and to emphasise the importance of human values in the production process, as well as the contribution to the environment, consumers, and society [2].

In 1979 Carroll introduced the CSR pyramid, which relates CSR to four different dimensions of the relationship between business and society, namely that "corporate society encompasses the economic, legal, ethical and philanthropic expectations that society has of economic organisations over a given period of time." The following sections will link CSR and goal setting, focusing on the "economic" and "ethical" dimensions of Carroll's CSR pyramid, in an attempt to analyse the positive and negative effects of goal setting on companies from the perspective of long-term goals.

2.3 Inspiration from the Relationship of Goal Setting and CSR

The research of goal setting of Locke and Latham is mainly from a psychological perspective. Indeed, knowing the psychological mechanism of motivation allows managers to set up goals that suit their employees. However, while companies, as investment economies, need to prioritise the maximisation of economic profit, they also have an obligation to take on social responsibility as an important part of society. As a general approach to business development, CSR also needs to be incorporated into the goal setting of individual companies so as to better link business and society.

3 Impacts of "Goal Setting" in Enterprises

3.1 Positive Impacts Through Goal Setting

Cohesiveness and efficiency are important to the company. High or specific goals lead to a higher level of task performance than do easy goals or vague goals, because goals refer to valuable future outcomes, so goal setting is first and foremost a process that generates difference. It implies dissatisfaction with the current status quo and a desire to achieve the goal or outcome [8]. As a business entity, companies need to strive to maximise their profits so that they can be accountable to their shareholders and stakeholders, while leading the social economy forward. As CSR evolves, companies need to consider not only their economic and stakeholder interests, but also their responsibilities to society. Taking CSR into account while setting goals can contribute positively to the reputation of the company.

3.1.1 Case Study of the Babyfood Company

As for organisations, the key moderators of goal setting are feedbacks, through which people can track progress on team tasks under a same goal; achieving commitment to goals is enhanced through self-efficacy and seeing goals as important factors. For example, Italian food company *Babyfood* has reshaped its corporate strategy over three decades by adopting CSR practices and has earned the trust of its stakeholders in food safety and supply chain [4]. Clear goals have not only allowed their shareholders to work more effectively for achieving higher profit, but also made them a flagship for social and environmental responsibility in the food industry over these 30 years.

Babyfood's planning has helped them achieve both economic and ethical components of Carroll's CSR pyramid. The significance of economic responsibility as the foundation of the pyramid, reflecting its importance as a fundamental requirement for business, highlights that the infrastructure of CSR is based on the premise of sound and sustainable economic development [3].

3.1.2 Analysis Through "Economic" and "Ethical" of Carroll's CSR Pyramid

Moreover, society also expects businesses to operate and conduct their affairs in an ethical manner. According to Carroll, one aspect of the ethical expectation is that business conveys a 'spirit' to society, not just the words in law [3]. Another aspect is that business conducts its affairs in a fair and objective manner, even if it does not violate the law, which means that businesses have expectations and obligations to do what is right and fair, in order to minimise harm to all stakeholders. Thus, the case of *Babyfood* shows that goal setting can be very effective for organisations.

However, the process for the organisation to achieve goals is often more complicated than individuals do, as conflicts can occur between members. Simply assigning goals to members of the organisation may not inspire them to take responsibility for them, especially if they are difficult to achieve. One effective way to resolve this is to allow members of the organisation to participate in the goal-setting process, which will help them better understand the goal and hence increase the likelihood of achieving an unanimous commitment to it [9].

In conclusion, goals are related to one's emotions and affects, because they set the main criteria for self-satisfaction [8]. High or hard goals are motivating for organisations because they need members to help them achieving more than just low or easy goals in order to gain satisfaction. When members see that they have abilities to meet the challenges by pursuing and achieving important and meaningful goals, they will likely to develop a sense of success during work.

3.2 Negative Impacts Through Goal Setting

Goal setting in companies has become one of the common ways to improve employee performance and motivation. Managers often believe that challenging goals enhance benefits more than those that are simple and universal, and this has led to the misuse of goal setting. Although many studies have shown that goals have a positive impact on performance, they also have displayed unpredictable negative effects on the organisation. While goals can help focus one's attention and improve cohesion, they may have a detrimental effect on the organisation by blinding managers or members to sacrifice some equally significant factors which may not be closely related, in order to accomplish their goals. A high warp focus can blind employees to issues that seem unrelated to the goal, but are important.

Moreover, while challenging goals can be effective in motivating employees, too many difficulties may in turn tempt them to behave unethically, such as falsifying performance or cheating consumers. This is because specific, difficult goals can create anxiety for members who aspire to pursue them, leading to risk-taking behaviour (such as deception or fraud) that may occur under great pressure. According to Ordóñez and Welsh, this influence appears to be driven by cognitive dissonance caused by unmet expectations [11].

3.2.1 Case Study of the Ford Company

The CEO of Ford Motor Company Lee Iacocca announced an ambitious goal in the 1960s: to produce a new car "under 2,000 pounds and under 2,000 dollars" which should be achieved in 1970 [10]. This tight deadline led the company to sacrifice many opportunities for safety checks. Ford executives, however, remained committed to their goal and did not fix the flawed design, even after being warned of the risks during its design process. While the goal of sales volume and low cost was ultimately achieved, consumer safety and the reputation of the company were compromised. Ordóñez et al. show that while goal setting helps people to be more effective, it is too exclusive [10]. Goals limit attention to one particular area and does not provide a comprehensive overview of one thing, which may lead members to overlook important but unspecific goals. Therefore, members need to re-evaluate the advantages and disadvantages of goal setting in order to reduce risks.

3.2.2 Case Study of Enron

The pursuit of economic and social status goals can exert pressure that might, in turn, drive individuals toward unethical behaviour. The apprehension of failing to meet socially accepted standards could be associated with resorting to criminal activities. Contrary to mere threats, challenges are often conducive to enhanced performance [11]. A notable illustration is the case of Enron's bankruptcy, wherein executives engaged in numerous unethical and illegal actions to fulfil their objectives. This included misrepresenting accounts on the balance sheet, deceiving investors, and pursuing personal gain [13].

Enron's management team deceived investors and inflated the company's share price by creating special purpose entities used to conceal the company's debts and losses. These off-the-books entities were not properly disclosed in Enron's financial statements, providing a misleading picture of the company's financial health. Additionally, Enron employed mark-to-market accounting, a method that allowed the company to immediately estimate the future profits of certain businesses and include them in its current financial statements [1]. This practice further inflated Enron's reported profits, creating an illusion of strong financial performance.

As Enron's stock price soared, executives, including senior officials such as CFO Andrew Fastow, cashed in their stock options and reaped huge personal gains [1]. Meanwhile, uninformed investors, including employees who had invested their retirement savings in Enron stock, suffered devastating losses when the truth about the company's financial problems came to light.

3.3 Analysis Through "Economic" and "Ethical" of Carroll's CSR Pyramid

Enron's anxious for quick results allows it to achieve its goals while laying the foundations for failure. According to Carroll's CSR pyramid, financial responsibility is a fundamental condition for corporate survival and business competition, and the only way to achieve this is through profitability, which provides an incentive and reward for stakeholders or shareholders to continue investing to have sufficient resources to continue operations [10]. Therefore, company executives see demonstrating profitability and return on investment as crucial. Enron's case shows that their executives breech legal and ethical standards in order to achieve economic goals faster, ultimately failing to achieve corporate social responsibility.

Thus, regarding negative side effects of goals, the organisation should carefully shape their target goal, monitoring the process closely and being aware of possible harm [10]. The benefits that performance goals can bring to an organisation are undeniable, so it seems irrational to do away with them. But members (especially managers) need to be vigilant and use such goals properly if they are to realise their value. In order to avoid the negative impact of goal setting on the company, the company should set a system of goals that is suitable for its employees, taking into account the difficulty of the goals, the goal setter and the degree of goal completion. Managers can provide skills training for employees in advance, enabling them to acquire the necessary abilities to achieve the goals and adapt to the goal system. Additionally, allowing more employees to participate in goal setting is beneficial, as people tend to work harder on aspects they are actively involved in.

4 Conclusion

Many research findings and case studies indicate the importance of goals. The example of *Babyfood* shows that clear and challenging goals represent effective and higher quality of work in the view of many companies, leading to higher profits and prestige. However, cases like Ford and Enron illustrate that wrong goals are likely to allow ambitious employees to act unethically and even illegally, which can lead to corruption and bankruptcy. Carroll's CSR pyramid gives companies a representative information of social expectations, anticipating that they can build connections with society in the four areas: economic, legal, ethical, and philanthropic. CSR may help enterprises to have a closer connection with their own customer base and promotes mutual trust, thus achieving a mutually beneficial and better outcome for both companies and society. As an important part of Carroll's CSR Pyramid, the ethical dimension also needs to be taken into account by goal setters. Companies that focus on ethics give their stakeholders a sense of positive corporate culture. In conclusion, goal setting cannot be abolished, but it needs to be used cautiously and wisely in order to achieve the value it deserves.

References

1. Benston, G.J., Hartgraves, A.L.: Enron: what happened and what we can learn from it. J. Account. Public Policy **21**(2), 105–127 (2002). *ScienceDirect*. https://www.sciencedirect.com/science/article/pii/S027842540200042X
2. Carroll, A.B.: Social responsibility: toward the morai management of organizational stakeholders. Bus. Horiz. **34**(4), 39–48 (1991). 1 Diagram, 5 Charts. https://search.ebscohost.com/
3. Carroll, A.B.: Carroll's pyramid of CSR: taking another look. Int. J. Corp. Soc. Responsib. **1**, Article number: 3 (2016). http://jcsr.springeropen.com/articles/10.1186/s40991-016-0004-6
4. Lamberti, L., Lettieri, E.: CSR practices and corporate strategy: evidence from a longitudinal case study. J. Bus. Ethics **87**, 153–168 (2008). https://link.springer.com/content/pdf/10.1007/s10551-008-9876-z.pdf
5. Locke, E.A.: Motivational effects of knowledge of results: knowledge or goal setting? J. Appl. Psychol. **51**(4, Pt.1), 324–329 (1967). https://doi.org/10.1037/h0024771
6. Locke, E.A.: Toward a theory of task motivation and incentives. Organ. Behav. Hum. Perform. **3**(2), 157–189 (1968). https://doi.org/10.1016/0030-5073(68)90004-4
7. Locke, E.A., Latham, G.P.: A theory of goal setting & task performance. Prentice-Hall, Inc (1990)
8. Locke, E.A., Latham, G.P.: New directions in goal-setting theory. Curr. Dir. Psychol. Sci. **15**(5), 265–268 (2006). https://doi.org/10.1111/j.1467-8721.2006.00449.x
9. Lunenburg, F.C.: Goal-setting theory of motivation. Sam Houston State University. Int. J. Manage. Bus. Adm. **15**(1) (2011). https://static1.squarespace.com/static/5b0b8f55365f02045e1ecaa5/t/5b14d215758d46f9851858d1/1528091160453/Lunenburg%2C+Fred+C.+Goal-Setting+Theoryof+Motivation+IJMBA+V15+N1+2011.pdf
10. Ordóñez, L.D., Schweitzer, M.E., Galinsky, A.D., Bazerman, M.H.: Goals gone wild: the systematic side effects of overprescribing goal setting. Acad. Manag. Perspect. **23**(1), 6–16 (2009). http://www.jstor.org/stable/27747490
11. Ordóñez, L.D., Welsh, D.T.: Immoral goals: how goal setting may lead to unethical behavior. Curr. Opin. Psychol. **6**, 93–96 (2015). https://doi.org/10.1016/j.copsyc.2015.06.001
12. Thompson, J.D., McEwen, W.J.: Organizational goals and environment: goal-setting as an interaction process. Am. Sociol. Rev. **23**(1), 23–31 (1958). https://doi.org/10.2307/2088620
13. Thomas, C.W.: The rise and fall of enron. J. Account. **193**(4), 41–48 (2002). https://web.p.ebscohost.com/ehost/pdfviewer/pdfviewer?vid=1&sid=29bdc16b-24a1-42b5-ade5-d1451ee1f11e%40redis- 42b5-ade5-d1451ee1f11e%40redis

Behavioral Economics and Macroeconomics: Relationship Identification by Case of Economy Crisis in 2008

Haocheng Yan(✉)

Ulink College Suzhou Industrial Park, Suzhou, Jiangsu 215000, China
frankdongdy@gmail.com

Abstract. Research in behavioral economics is finding increasing application in the field of microeconomics, which examines how people behave and what they could be thinking while economists do case studies. However, it has been found only rarely that human behavior has a strong relationship with microeconomics, and that is what the purpose of this paper is to investigate using the example of the economic crisis that occurred in 2008. Accordingly, the paper utilized a variety of literature study (desk research) and data base analysis to arrive at the conclusion that behavior economics can be qualitatively applied in macroeconomics; nevertheless, there is a lack of proof in the data base. In addition, as a follow-up on the case from 2008, the paper receives a new formula to identify human behavior in consumption or speculation. This is a new behavior notion that may be used in macroeconomics and in the study of human consumption behavior.

Keywords: Behavior Economics · Government Failure · CDS · New Keynesian Model

1 Introduction

As a result of Richard Thaler's development of the nudge theory in 2017, the influence of behavioral economics surged, attracting more economists to study behavioral economics and expectation. Typically, behavior economics and microeconomics shared a deep interest in individual choice making to prevent market failure and poor decision making. Nevertheless, behavior analysis can also uncover macroeconomic failure, and it is ideally suited for identifying New Keynesian models, which analyze economics from the demand side.

Since the turn of the century, the origins of the 2008 economic crisis have been the subject of never-ending debates, which may be attributed to the theories of Ben Bernanke and Richard Taylor. According to Taylor's theory in 2010, he believed that the financial crisis was the result of a government failure in which they employed a flawed monetary policy between 2006 and 2008 and encouraged a bubble in the real estate market, accompanied by an economic crisis following the collapse of the bubble. Bernanke, on the other hand, believed that an economic crisis would never occur for a single reason, and he argued that policymaking would be delayed until the market was ready [1].

If we reevaluate the concepts of Bernanke and Taylor from the perspective of behavioral economics, we will conclude that both are acceptable, as the behavior of residents in the United States real estate market could have led to a business cycle shock. The goal of this essay is to analyze various consumer, producer, and government actions to determine the causes of the 2008 economic crisis and to introduce a new idea in behavior economics. The essay agrees with Ben Bernanke's view that rationality alone will not cause an economic disaster.

Through qualitative and quantitative research methods, this paper will look into the behavior and decision-making of customers in the real estate market prior to the 2008 financial crisis. This paper will study overconsumption, the New notion of behavior economy, and the New Keynesian AD model, as well as Producers, Wall Street, and policies. In addition to a central bank-based study of government policies, specific reasons for government failure are also given. Moreover, the paper concludes with a DSGE model analysis. The primary purpose of the paper is to establish a connection between behavioral economics and macroeconomics using the 2008 financial crisis as evidence that society can make common errors based on general knowledge and experience.

2 Consumers

This section will discuss the mindset of American customers, including the causes of the economic crisis since 1990. As a result of government and societal directives, comparable consumer behavior on a particular real estate market resulted in market failure, which led to the formation of price bubbles. Some macroeconomic models are consistent with the relationship between utility and consumption that is illustrated by behaviorally influenced social decisions.

Nevertheless, according to a number of studies, utility and expectation of consumers are difficult to collect and calculate, making them unsuitable for macroeconomics models; even the most basic behavioral model includes non-rational sectors to consumers, and detail data cannot be used to calculate the coefficient in any market. According to 2008 lawsuits and real estate market trade data, the government has fostered deceptive overconsumption of homes since 1990. During 20th century, the real estate market was plagued by an unsound trading structure that encouraged a widespread error in judgment. This error transforms the meaning of trade from consumption to speculation.

2.1 Consumption Euler Equation, Utility and Social General Decision

The 2008 economic crisis was primarily caused by the bursting of a price bubble in the United States real estate market, which was linked to the overconsumption of homes before to the catastrophe. According to data from the Federal Housing Finance Agency, the US home price index has been on a decreasing trend since 2006, with the lowest point being in 2008, indicating that the real estate market in 2006 saw a rise in house prices and a decline in housing demand. Prior to 2006, the average price of a new home in the United States indicates an upward trend. Based on this graph, we determined that the distribution of house prices was not normal and that the mean increase of house prices occurred between 2002 and 2005, which we termed the "period of overconsumption."

In reality, the economic crisis was rooted in politics. Bill Clinton issued an executive order in 1995 mandating that Fannie Mae and Freddie (MAC) purchase at least 42% of mortgage bonds from the poor. As a welfare for the poor, the government purchased bonds from MAC and raised money supply (MS) in a certain real estate market, if we interpret the policy from an economic perspective. This expansionary fiscal strategy boosted home purchases and utility satisfaction. On the consumption side (Government policies will be analyzed in Sect. 4 of the government section), housing demand skyrocketed as barriers to purchasing a home decreased, as consumers were able to apply for more credit with fewer requirements, and government supply could lead to a 'zero down payment' trade in which consumers could buy a home with no down payment and mix it with credit. Short-term increases in housing demand were accompanied by skyrocketing house prices and output. In the long run, however, individuals' credit pressure increases as a time bomb due to price change.

From 1995 to 2008, customers committed at least five behavioral errors. If we assume that a poor person with a fixed salary 'y' and he purchased a home following President Clinton in 1995, he was misled by the government into believing that he had limited information about current house prices, that he was eligible for 'zero down payment' with government assistance, and that his salary 'y' was sufficient to pay his credit. The second behavioral error is that he would never fix the interest rate 'r' if he had little information about 'r' or government-secret information regarding inflation expectations 'π^e'. According to research conducted by Calvo Fairy [2], the distinction between the Neoclassical fixed-price model and the New Keynesian aggregate price level function is as follows [2]:

$$\ln P_t = \theta \ln P_t^* + (1-\theta)\ln P_{t-1} \tag{1}$$

'P*' means optimally price level add price price level from last year to get the current year price level. Then if, price level can be comparative, difference of two price level over time can be represent as [2]:

$$\ln P_t - \ln P_{t-1} = \theta(\ln P_t^* - \ln P_{t-1}) \tag{2}$$

As Neoclassical model and New Keynesian model, the function not only can recognize Aggregate Price level over time and expectation, but another result is inflation rate change [2].

$$\pi_t = \theta \pi_t^* \tag{3}$$

Here is differences, 'θ' represents price by firms is fixed in Neoclassic model because several assumptions; thus in the equation, current inflation rate should be equal to the optimal inflation rate (π_t^*). However, in New Keynesian Philips curve, producer price 'θ' would change by labor market which more fit to describe marketing. As a result, consumers' information on the real estate market is obscured by price 'θ' causing them to have erroneous expectations regarding the Aggregate Price level and inflation rate; consequently, government policies on interest rate led by inflation rate would be difficult to discern. This information failure delayed consumers' ability to purchase or sell real estate for a profit, and it also contributed to a market collapse after 2006. (even house price index decreased, several people still purchased houses). Government policies also fail to provide customers with adequate information (specific government site in Sect. 4). According to Hall's theory based on the consumption Euler equation, the link between utility, consumption, and interest rate [3].

$$u' \times C_t = \beta(1 + r_t)u\prime(C_{t+1}) \tag{4}$$

In 2006, the government implemented expansionary policies to boost marketing; as a result, consumption decreased due to diminishing returns (details in government policy Sect. 4); nonetheless, utility is not fixed on the market, resulting in an additional information failure on consumption. According to information cocoons by Cass R. Sunstein (Infotopia), people could only use the information surrounding them to generate expectations [4], hence utility coefficients cannot be determined. Under such conditions, behavior failure has a high probability of leading to market failure.

2.2 Experience Leading Over-Speculation

For the uncertain utility assumption in macroeconomics and the reliance of the main premise of behavioral economics on rational decision-making, experience would be an important concept to discuss in market and individual behavior. The business cycle can be used to determine market logic, such as price change and output gap, for market experience. This is an illogical concept in macroeconomics due to the fact that price change and output gap are never normally distributed as time progresses, but medium time attracts customers to invest or buy. For example, before to 2006, individuals favored the unlimited acquisition of real estate for the pursuit of wealth, disregarding restrictions such as their income and unforeseeable future. According to information cocoon, a psychological concept developed by Sunstein, people have limited exposure to information that conflicts with their preferences. As a result, they can only accumulate a limited quantity of information and experience to make decisions. This is perfectly fit to basic behavior AD model. $a_1 E_t^\wedge y_{t+1}$ mpc $(1 - a_1)y_{t-1}$ mps [5]

$$y_t = a_1 E_t^\wedge y_{t+1} + (1 - a_1)y_{t-1} + a_2(r - E_{\pi+1}^\wedge) + \varepsilon_t \tag{5}$$

According formula, $E^\wedge$ is irrational expectation to do operation on saving, consuming and investing and result is equal to income. Moreover, $a_1 E_t^\wedge y_{t+1}$ is marginal propensity of consume (MPC), and $(1 - a_1)y_{t-1}$ is marginal propensity of saving (MPS). Based on the formula consumption and future expectation are irrational and ε as rational expectation, it is now assumed zero in essay condition (at least in real property market). To properly distribute output, all consumer behavior would be based on income, but customers would not anticipate a future income and price level that favored non-profit distribution. Prior to 2006, in the event of an economic crisis, consumers preferred to invest their money in the purchase of real estate rather than in bank savings. As a less elastic good, consumers expect that the price of housing will continue to rise as a result of a prolonged price increase. Thus, more individuals adopt the behavior of acquiring a home as a means of surviving and earning a living. Such conceptual shifts are referred to as "experience-driven conjecture."

As a Macro Behavioral notion, 'experience leading to over-speculation' must be predicated on the circumstance of consumers pursuing the same objective, such as profit. Overall, the number of consumers should have the ability to influence market price, and their primary objective would be to shift from consumption to speculation. Such a judgment can also be identified by the necessity and liquidity of the product. In the context of the 2008 economic crisis, the law of diminishing returns would lead to a fall in demand and utility with each additional home purchase. However, more people prefer to acquire houses individually, and more than half of U.S. residents had more than two apartments in separate states, indicating that the house has transformed from a necessity into an investment, and that people's purchasing behavior might be described as speculative. In John C. Driscoll and Steinar Holden's work [6], they described various instances in which consumers' behavior changed, such as overreaction to news, incorrect identification of multiple equilibria, and overestimation of bubble asset. It was not difficult to realize that people made decisions based on experience, both market and personal. Behind the housing market, trade times and house prices exhibited a stable rising trend prior to 2006, which misled consumers to speculate on home prices while they rarely considered the causes for the stable market. Moreover, houses as low-liquidity items should be a basic necessity over time, and individuals should never be concerned about housing demand. However, their experience and surrounding knowledge (information cocoon) led them to waste money on housing.

On the basis of income and the New Keynesian AD model, people had less or incorrect expectations of inflation and interest rate changes, and they sometimes disregard income changes in their work. Such entrenched beliefs are bolstered by their experience, which leads individuals to assume they have sufficient authority to accept credits.

3 Producers

This section focuses mostly on the information failures of corporations that led to a price shock and contributed to the economic crisis. The essay's assumption is predicated on the sticky information proposed by N. Gregory Mankiw and Ricardo Reis and their relationship with the New Keynesian AS model and Philips curve [7]. In addition, the overreaction or delayed reaction of a decision maker would be an example of the combination of behavior and macroeconomics.

"Experience contributing to over-speculation" also fits within the Macroeconomics AS part, which the second paragraph will elaborate on. The evidence and case analysis are the 2008 shutdown of Lehman Brothers and the behavior error in the case. The quantitative support is primarily derived from the Lehman Brothers annual report [8], which was an example of excessive speculation on the financial market and market expectation failure. The evidence analyzed only one specific reason for CDO closure and assumed that this was the primary cause. The method for 'Experience-led over-speculation' will guess and explain in Sect. 3.2 which CDOs have the strongest connection to the underlying danger.

3.1 Behavior Mistake by Entrepreneur: Sticky Information Model and Information Delay

According to study conducted by N. Gregory Mankiw and Ricardo Reis on sticky prices and exogenous studies of dynamic models of price adjustment [9], they discovered that the 'New Keynesian Philips curve' is applicable to an economy in which prices are always fluctuating. However, company decision makers may postpone knowledge concerning inflation and other policies, leading to behavioral errors. It depends on currency liquidity and market price change. Thus, the information sticky model was initially dependent on the price sticky model. In part two, Gregory develops a new model from Calvo's model, which has a different curve [9].

$$P_t = \lambda \sum_{j=0}^{\infty} (1-\lambda)^j X_{t-j} \tag{6}$$

The function is more fit to New Keynesian Philips curve because (1-λ) is a percentage of price change. Thus aggregate price can change with individual price change and aggregate adjustment price. Comparatively, inflation π can be renew a new function [9].

$$\pi_t = [\alpha \lambda^2 (1-\lambda)] y^t + E_t \Pi_{t+1} \tag{7}$$

And it can be simplify into original price level change, which $\Pi_t = P_t - P_{t-1}$. The most major reaction to a change in the market is a change in pricing, as inflationary expectations grew increasingly relevant. Infrequently, however, does quantitative research indicate that the probability of a price change is accurate, because, according to Eric Sim's research, output gaps in different countries are unstable and non-normally distributed, meaning that price changes cannot be accurately predicted by mathematics. Moreover, in the majority of cases of market failure, some corporations had a sophisticated structure on price and interest rate reaction, whose economic influence may be effective many months after the decision was implemented, when the market environment had already altered (Case of Lehman Brother is a proof.). After that, Mankiw and Reis formulated the following equation on information stickiness, which is a reluctance of decision makers to commit behavioral errors after receiving knowledge. In addition, they combine three equilibriums into a price-leading equation [9].

$$P_t = \lambda \sum_{j=0}^{\infty} (1-\lambda)^j E_{t-j}(P_t + \alpha y_t) \tag{8}$$

The equation include plan of period ago firms set price and optimal price level in their plan $(E_{t-j}(P_t + \alpha y_t))$. Thus, the prior plan multiplied by the current price change would equal the current price level, and the error would be the difference between the past price change and the present adjustment price change. Thus, not all policies can instantly affect enterprises.

For delayed response, methods of acquiring information are crucial, and individuals must collect current figures, data, and government processes. Jaimovich and Rebelo construct a model that analyzes media and network development to create a more efficient and delay-free information transfer [10], and Bernanke's declaration that a company's simpler structure has a higher efficiency infers that a simple structure can prevent an inner information delay and generate a more efficient information transfer.

3.2 Cases of Economy Crisis in 2008 Caused by Information Delay and 'Experience Leading Over-Speculation'

The failure of Lehman Brothers would be the primary example of an economic crisis in this part. There are various reasons for Lehman brother's demise as a credit firm with insurance survey, but the primary one would be over-leverage rate within the company and death by synthesis CDO, which caused a lack of capital and a domino effect in the insurance market.

According to the book 'Good night & Good Luck' by Li wei [11], the CEO of Lehman Brother announced on 18 March 2008 that the company's net income had declined by 57% and that bond prices had fallen by 20%. On 1 April, they initiated an expansionary policy to avert Bear Streams Cos. Mergers by selling bonds. But after 15 days, Lehman Brother believed that the market had stabilized based on the increase in house prices and the number of people who began to pay their loans. Lehman Brother then began to raise funds and successfully sold 11% of CLO. However, on 4 June, as a result of the increasing number of people who abandoned their homes and stopped paying their loans, Lehman Brother's credit rating dropped by 272 points. For payment of these failed CDS and CDO securities, Lehman Brothers sold their commercial real estate at a loss in the majority of cases, due to the fact that the purchasing period had already been extended, causing the home prices to drop so sharply that nobody wanted to buy them. This is consistent with the information delay indicated in Sect. 2.1, which demonstrates that information had a sticky operation that caused the economic reaction to be delayed and the death of Lehman Brothers.

The error of Lehman brother's April policies ultimately prompted a worse challenge, which was Lehman Brother's CDS skyrocketing to 700 points, which they could not afford by current account, and they ceased operations on 15 April 2008. According to Lehman Brother's (LB) most recent report, in the second quarter of 2008, they had 4.13 billion dollars in Level 3 Assets (another mistake going to analysis) and a total of 2.06 billion in housing credit and pledged assets, but they had to pay over $7.25 billion for pledged assets and broken CDS [13]. Expecting excessive reliance on short-term investment operations in April to lead to market failure in September was logical, as was the occurrence of such a high number of breached CDS, which was yet another behavior error committed by so many businesses.

In 2006, when the home price index peaked and the real estate market was stable, Wall Street firms began to employ leverage to increase their profits. Except for satisfying essential corporate needs, increased competition drove the majority of businesses to engage in CDO and CDS trading. This appears to be a credit insurance in which, if a borrower defaults on a loan, the company must pay for itself as well as an additional sum for the last loaned company, which sum is CDO and is not regulated by the government in terms of price and trade. Under such a solid real estate market, a number of decision-makers opt to gather several CDO cases and sell them at a higher price. The process multiplied the CDO trade risk. In 2006, Morgan Stanley (MS) and Merrill Lynch (MER) had the highest leverage rates at 30% and 27%, respectively, while LB ranked third at 24%. However, there are issues as to why MS and MER had a higher risk of CDS and CDO but survived the economic crisis. According to a survey by the business Markit, over sixty percent of LM's credit portfolio consisted of level 3 assets, which had poor market liquidity and were difficult to sell; this was also the reason why, in 2008, LM had no idea how to sell its assets to survive [14].

According to the case, except for the information-sticky model, LM was insanely focused on profit maximization, to the point where they forgot their own power. This was the general situation in 2008, as over 80% of defunct companies in 2008 had problems with over-credit, as they traded a greater proportion of CDOs than their own assets [15]. Since 2006, businesses have shifted their focus from consumer behavior to speculative behavior, in accordance with the concept of "experience leading to excessive speculation." For instance, the 2006 emergence of synthetic CDOs was premised on a stable market pricing, which misled decision makers into taking additional actions for greater profit. If CDO and CDS rates are a natural rate of investment, we may establish a return on investment and attempt to derive consumption or speculation behavior, as well as the ration or non-ration of policies and the avoidance of over-speculation. If we suppose it is the risk assumed by operation (a coefficient), we can build the following formula:

$$x^e_{t+1} = I_t r_t - I_t \alpha_t \tag{9}$$

According to formula, X can be the real return of CDO (or investment/ consumption) that should fit to go with investment capital and its risk taking. α as a risk taking coefficient, it can be identify by 1. Where $\alpha > 1$. It means more risks taking that result behavior should be speculation; however, $\alpha < 1$ means result behavior would be consumption. Thus, higher risk taking means lower real return, which fit to behavior economics. Moreover, CDO as a less regulation features, r_t here is also various. Furthermore, synthesis CDO can be present by square of X, in which 'j' means times of CDO added into behavior and caused a larger risks. In a neoclassical model, the assumption should be that synthesis CDO must suffer more risks and receive lower rewards.

$$(X^e_{t+1})^j = (I_t r_t - I_t \alpha_t)^j \tag{10}$$

solved

$$(X^e_{t+1})^j = I^j_t (r^j_t - \alpha^j_t) \tag{11}$$

Similar to the business cycle, the addition of additional CDOs results in a new equation in which the expected return X depends more on speculation or consumption. It makes mathematical and economic logic that if it is a consumption approach CDO, the rational decision will have a smaller impact on return expectation, however if it is a speculative approach CDO, a more irrational decision will be made on CDO and the return expectation of X will be lower. Therefore, 'Experience driving over-speculation' is a method for identifying ratio by risk coefficient, and the estimate would be applicable to any investing behavior and its returns.

The rule follows the New Keynesian model's assumption that, on the demand side, interest rates can fluctuate over time and risk has a positive correlation with money input and periods of trade. However, it is still difficult to prove the formula using statistics and different distributions. Connecting real macroeconomics and behavioral economics requires a considerable amount of data base verification, as it is currently merely a qualitative logical finding.

4 Government and Central Bank Behavior Mistake in Case of 2008 Economy Crisis

From 1995 to 2008, this section will discuss government policy and government failure in response to the economic crisis. Government analysis employs the DSGE model to introduce four market shocks and to highlight the relevance of government in influencing consumer and producer behavior. As with other behavior errors, 'experience leading to over-speculation' can be eliminated by government rules, and the government can also rectify various empirical decisions and correct information failure.

To implement contraction or expansion programs, the government must also have access to reliable income data and forecasts of price and inflation change. In 2006, it was incorrect to anticipate a shift in demand, and the government implemented a flawed market operation strategy, which led to an increase in incorrect market behavior. In addition, according to Bernanke's theory, government operations have a lagging effect on the market, as demonstrated by 2008 government contraction policies.

In the United States, house prices are rising at a time when the economy is in a state of crisis because of a discussion about housing costs. Taylor supported the increase in house prices since 2002, while the end of the cyber market led to an economic crisis that was resolved by an increase in demand for real estate and maintained currency liquidity [16]. In 1995, when Ben Bernanke backed a rise in house prices through political means, it made more sense for housing demand to explode. Bill Clinton signed an executive order mandating that MAC purchase at least 42% of mortgage bonds issued by the poor (illustration in Sect. 2), and George W. Bush upped the bond percentage to 55% in 2001. The objective of such programs is to enhance their support for the presidency, but on the economic front, they have increased social welfare for locals [17]. In the near term, work increased the U.S. gross domestic product and people's pleasure. However, the government erroneously predicts future conditions and leads speculation. Therefore, this is a beneficial approach in the short term but not the long term.

Using the DSGE model, the first shock in the market analysis would be the policy shock, which would increase consumption to a higher level. In addition, the government implemented expansionary policies in 2002 to further jolt the market. Thus, in 2002, numerous individuals were aware of a rise in real estate demand and revenue (y). According to 'experience leading over-speculation,' the majority of consumers' house-buying behavior was rational, and such loans were affordable. Nonetheless, in 2006 (Sect. 2), despite a decline in home prices, a number of people nonetheless acquired homes for profit, causing a short-term demand shock. In DGSE model, Π already increased with consumption, furthermore, producer's operation was collect CDO and CDS to trade in second credit market. Thus, actually, consumers' over-consumption actually leaded wrong expectation to credit department and they wrongly expected demand of house and income of people, which both π^e and Y^e were all shock in DGSE model but seldom people found that according to report of MAC (2006), US apartment empty rate start increase, supply already over demand [18].

In government side, the shock would contraction to limit people purchasing house but actually in 2006, government did a expansionary policy again, which shocked an inelastic market. Thus, interest rate setting of government had based on a true Π with a wrong π^e. In addition, government CDS trading was not governed by government regulations, which are never limited by legislation. Thus, the second credit market is actually unprotected and extremely susceptible to over-trading. The final economic crisis occurred in 2008, and the government and central bank had a correct short-term outlook on it. Contractionary policy was initiated, but it was inefficient in that it did not prevent the domino collapse of the second credit market, proving Bernanke's theory that government policy would be delayed in the market thereafter.

5 Conclusion

The paper establishes a connection between behavioral economics and macroeconomics using the 2008 financial crisis as a case study and concludes that behavioral economics may be logically applied to macroeconomics. Because all consumer, producer, and government-encouraged market failures are founded on erroneous conduct, insufficient knowledge, and incorrect expectations. This conforms to the fundamental concept of New Keynesian models, which stands on the side of fluctuating demand to make judgments. However, they do not correspond qualitatively because numerous factors are not distributed or cannot be analyzed statistically. For example, in Sect. 2, the utility of consumers cannot be predicted by the government and producers, and in Sect. 3, the bid price of a good by a corporation is difficult to predict in terms of its rate of change, leading to the conclusion that aggregate prices are difficult to predict.

In addition, the research identifies and explains behavioral errors on different sides in 2008 using macroeconomics results. And we discovered that if the focus of consumers and producers shifted from consumption to speculation, the price of goods and inflation would skyrocket. Such a development can be identified as 'experience leading to over-speculation,' in which people incorrectly evaluate one's ability to invest huge sums of money based on factors such as income, interest rate, and market stability. Prior to the 2008 financial crisis, customers over consumed houses and manufactures over traded CDOs were suitable for rule. Accordingly, return expectation can be expressed as a formula involving interest rate, investment, and risk. If risk can be dispersed and quantified, this can demonstrate that behavioral economics and macroeconomics can be related. The paper can now demonstrate that behavioral economics and macroeconomics can be quantitatively demonstrated but not qualitatively.

References

1. Bernanke, B.S.: Essays on the Great Depression. Lieu de publication inconnu: New Age Publications (Aca) (2007)
2. DSGE New Keynesian Phillips Curve. YouTube (2016). https://www.youtube.com/watch?v=mOZcIYxeQT8. Accessed 15 Nov 15 2022

3. Euler Equation in Economics - Deriving over an Infinite Horizon. YouTube (2020). https://www.youtube.com/watch?v=tx8u1f6VSm0. Accessed 15 Nov 2022
4. Sunstein, C.R.: Infotopia. 2nd edn. Oxford University Press, Incorporated, Oxford
5. Solving a Simple New Keynesian DSGE Model. YouTube (2020). https://www.youtube.com/watch?v=HvJCpHNHqLQ&t=43s. Accessed 15 Nov 2022
6. Driscoll, J.C., Holden, S.: Behavioral Economics and macroeconomic models. SSRN (2014)
7. Mankiw, N.G., Reis, R.: Sticky information versus sticky prices: a proposal to replace the New Keynesian Phillips curve. Quart. J. Econ. **117**, 1295–1328 (2002)
8. United States Securities and Exchange Commission, Lehman Brothers Holdings Inc. 2007. Sec.gov (2007). https://www.sec.gov/Archives/edgar/data/806085/000110465908005476/a08-3530_110k.htm#Item15_ExhibitsFinancialState%E2%80%A6. Accessed 15 Nov 2022
9. Mankiw, N.G., Reis, R.: Sticky information versus sticky prices: a proposal to replace the new Keynesian Phillips curve. Quarterly Journal of Economics -Cambridge Massachusetts-. Massachusetts Institute of Technology Press (1970)
10. Jaimovich, N., Rebelo, S.: Can news about the future drive the business cycle? Am. Econ. Rev. **94**, 1097–1118 (2009)
11. Wei, L. : Bie Le Lei man Xiong Di. Beijing: Zhong xin chu ban she, pp. 326–409 (2009)
12. Taylor, J.B.: Discretion versus policy rules in practice. In: Carnegie-Rochester Conference Series on Public Policy. North-Holland (2002)
13. Driscoll, J.C., Holden, S.: Finance and Economics Discussion Series Divisions of Research & Statistics and Monetary Affairs Federal Reserve Board, Washington, D.C (2014)
14. Dynan, K.E.: Habit formation in consumer preferences: Evidence from panel data. American Economic Review
15. Fuhrer, J.C.: Habit formation in consumption and its implications for monetary-policy models. American Economic Review
16. Grauwe, P.D.: Top-down versus bottom-up macroeconomics, CEPR (2009)
17. Grauwe, P.D.: Booms and busts in economic activity: a behavioral explanation. J. Econ. Behav. Organ. **83**, 484–501 (2012)
18. Taylor, A.M.: The great leveraging, Google Books. Centre for Economic Policy Research

The Impact of Endogenous Sentiment on US Stock Market Trading Volume

Lvqin Huang(✉)

Tianjin University of Finance and Economics, Tianjin, China
Huanglvqin519@163.com

Abstract. Using the popular music of the day to measure people's sentiment, this sentiment is endogenous rather than market sentiment. Through the analysis of endogenous sentiment and the trend of the price and trading volume of the Dow Jones Index, this paper finds that there is a correlation between the endogenous sentiment of the U.S. public and the trading volume of the U.S. stock market, and proposes one path of the influence of endogenous sentiment on stock market activity using VAR models, impulse response analysis models and Granger causality test models, etc. These findings support some theories in behavioral finance.

Keywords: Behavior finance · endogenous sentiment · trading volume

1 Introduction

In a strong efficient market, stock prices change instantaneously when news is given or a change in market information occurs, but this is not the reality; as a form of momentum, the change is slow rather than instantaneous and has a clear curve. Moskowitz, Yao and Lasse Heje [1] find persistence in returns over time horizons of one to twelve months that partially reverses over longer time frames, supporting sentiment theories of initial under-reaction and delayed over-reaction, inconsistently Andrei and Cujean [2] argue that momentum arises primarily because of an increase in the speed of information flow. The faster the flow of information, the more buying and selling operations are performed in response to this information, so the volume of stock trading is an important basis for evaluating the level of stock market activity. In addition, the academic community believes that stock trading volume has a significant impact on stock prices and stock price volatility, so trading volume is an important indicator for studying stock markets. So there are many scholars who are studying the impact of trading volume on the stock market. However, only a relatively small number of articles explore which factors influence trading volume, and most of the articles that examine the factors influencing trading volume start with aspects such as the impact of news and the impact of information dissemination. Although there have also been studies analyzing the relationship between trading volume and under- and over-reaction, which have touched the field of behavioral finance, there is still no direct study of the impact of investors' endogenous interest on trading volume. We therefore aim to close this gap in the literature.

2 Literature Review

Lin [3] Point out that high residual trading volume firms exhibit a stronger drift than low residual trading volume firms. Lee, Charles M. C. and Bhaskaran Swaminathan [4] find that past volume helps to reconcile intermediate-horizon "underreaction" and long-horizon "overreaction" effects. Consistently The opinion in the paper is that investors' endogenous sentiment affects the extent to which investors pay attention to story-related information, which in turn affects the level of stock market trading activity, and that there is also a relationship between sentiment itself and stock market activity and stock price momentum and drift, which is consistent with theories in behavioral finance.

In the field of momentum, a significant number of scholars have studied strategy-related issues from a rational perspective and have not focused primarily on behavioral perspectives, e.g., Chan and Jegadeesh & Lakonishok [5] analyzed the profitability of price momentum strategies based on historical returns, as well as earnings momentum strategies based on standardized unexpected earnings and changes to consensus projections, in particular. Novy-Marx and Robert [6] point out that momentum is not primarily driven by the trend of continued upward or downward stock prices, but by the performance of the firm over the past 7–12 months, both of which are in the rational framework.

Instead of focusing on the effect of news sentiment on the momentum effect and the test of the momentum effect based on historical data, this paper focuses on the change of attention and trading volume of the stock market under the influence of investors' own sentiment. By verifying the effect of investors' endogenous sentiment on trading volume to determine whether endogenous sentiment can be used as a reference for studying momentum strategies, price drift, stock price volatility, etc.

Financial news articles are believed to have impacts on stock price return, Some studies are specific to the content of news articles, for example, Blaufusa, Alexander and Möhlmann [7] point that news about tax evasion has negative anomalous returns, but that news about tax avoidance has no such effects, some scholars use some events to represent people's emotions, such as victory or defeat in sports events, disasters, etc. (Edmans and García [8]; García and Levy [9]), Chen and Li et al. [10] argue that only To take one step further by using the Loughran-McDonald financial mood vocabulary and the Harvard psychological dictionary. The sentiment space is then projected with quantitatively measured textual news stories, and Edmans, Fernandez-Perez, Garel, Indriawan [11] further argue that These events are episodic and discrete, and endogenous emotions are better studied in the area of the relationship between emotions and investment. Although feelings are invisible, they show up in visible acts. However, the great majority of acts that represent people's mood are not covered by datasets, so this paper argues that Edmans' approach is better, they use music to measure people's mood, which has two main advantages, firstly, the data of music charts are continuous, which can help the data analysis more complete, and secondly the mood reflected by music is an endogenous one. In this paper, we want to study whether investors' own good or bad mood affects the momentum effect rather than directly analyzing the optimistic or negative market sentiment, so this method of measuring endogenous sentiment is very suitable. In addition, this measure has been validated to show that music is used to reflect people's moods rather than to influence them, i.e., when people are in a bad mood they use sad music to reflect their sadness rather than cheerful music to cheer them up. On this basis Edmans et al. [11] find that music sentiment is positively correlated with same-week equity market returns and negatively correlated with next-week returns, consistent with sentiment-induced temporary mispricing.

And this paper further finds that this relationship is related to how much investors pay attention to the market, that endogenous sentiment can cause changes in attention, and that increased attention can help increase stock trading volume. These studies help provide behavioral finance dimensions to research related to momentum strategies, stock price drift, under- or over-reaction, stock market liquidity and volatility, among others.

3 Methodology

3.1 Research Data

In order to measure people's endogenous emotions, I contacted Alex Edmans and obtained his permission to use the method of measuring emotions with music that he created in Music sentiment and stock returns around the world [11], Edmans also provided me with the data he had used. Edmans, collect data from Spotify: Daily statistics for the top 200 songs according to total streams (S) were provided by Spotify. Spotify only counts streams when a song is played for at least 30 s; as a result, if a user "passively" listens to a song because it was recommended to them or is in a playlist but skips it right away, it is not included in our data.

Valence(V), a metric offered by Spotify, measures a song's musical optimism. The Echo Nest, a research spin-off from the MIT Media Lab that Spotify eventually purchased in 2014, is the entity responsible for tracking this parameter. The Echo Nest gave a sample of 5,000 songs a positivity score, and then utilized machine learning to develop an algorithm that is then applied to the rest of the world's music. Valence, which goes from 0 to 1, measures the music's optimism rather than the lyrics.

Refer to Admans' method, We construct a stream-weighted average valence (henceforth SWAV) across the top-200 songs for each day d and country i as follows:

$$SWAV_{i.d} = \sum_{j=1}^{200}(S_{j.i.d} \cdot V \div \sum_{j=1}^{j=200} S_{j.i.d})$$

American music-based mood proxy, Sentiment, is given by:

$$\text{Sentiment} = SWAV_t - SWAV_{t-1}$$

where $SWAV_t$ is the stream-weighted average valence for week t. Music Sentiment is thus the total change in the stream-weighted average valence of the top-200 songs American people listen to in week t.

To measure the trading volume (Volume) of the U.S. stock market, this paper obtains daily and weekly frequency data of the U.S. Dow Jones index from 2017.1.1 to 2020.12.31 through the IFind database, which contains the trading volume.

To measure people's attention to stock trading, this paper obtains the search hotness of stock-related terms from Google Trends, which reflects the weekly number of searches for stock-related terms in all fifty U.S. states and Washington, D.C. We use this number of searches(hot) to represent people's attention to stock trading.

3.2 Research Model

First of all, the smoothness test was done for hot, sentiment and volume, and after finding that hot was not smooth, since the VAR model requires the series to be smooth or cointegrated, the Engle-Granger cointegration test was done for hot and other variables, and after confirming the cointegration relationship between the groups of data, the VAR model with lag order of 2 was used to confirm that the best lag order is 1, and then the VAR(1) model was established:

$$\text{sentiment} = \alpha_1 \text{sentiment}(-1) + \beta_1 \text{hot}(-1) + \delta_1 \text{volume}(-1) + \varepsilon_1$$

$$\text{hot} = \alpha_2 \text{sentiment}(-1) + \beta_2 \text{hot}(-1) + \delta_2 \text{volume}(-1) + \varepsilon_2$$

$$\text{volume} = \alpha_3 \text{sentiment}(-1) + \beta_3 \text{hot}(-1) + \delta_3 \text{volume}(-1) + \varepsilon_3$$

Based on the results of the VAR (1) model, after testing the stability of the model, impulse response analysis was conducted to observe the impact of changes in sentiment on attention and trading volume. Finally, the findings obtained from the above analysis were tested using a Granger Causality Test model.

4 Result

4.1 ADF Test

Table 1 and Table 2 show that the time series of sentiment and volume are smooth, but the time series of hot is not smooth, but the first-order difference of each series is smooth, in order to know whether the subsequent VAR model can be built, it is necessary to do further analysis whether there is a cointegration relationship between the series.

Table 1. ADF test results for each series

Variables	t	P	Threshold values		
			1%	5%	10%
sentiment	−16.63	0.000***	−3.462	−2.876	−2.574
hot	−2.455	0.127	−3.462	−2.876	−2.574
volume	−2.978	0.037**	−3.465	−2.877	−2.575

4.2 The Engle-Granger Cointegration Test

Table 3 illustrates that there is a cointegration relationship between hot and volume, and between hot and sentiment, and they are in equilibrium in the long run.

Table 2. ADF test results for the first-order difference of each series

Variables	t	P	Threshold values		
			1%	5%	10%
Sentiment(1)	−7.633	0.000***	−3.462	−2.876	−2.574
Hot(1)	−9.355	0.000***	−3.462	−2.876	−2.574
Volume(1)	−4.521	0.000***	−3.465	−2.877	−2.575

Table 3. Results of covariance test

Variables	Z(t)	P	Threshold values		
			1%	5%	10%
Sentiment and hot	−18.571	0.000***	−3.475	−2.883	−2.573
Volume anf hot	−14.517	0.000***	−3.475	−2.883	−2.573

4.3 Optimal Lag Order

Table 4 shows the table of information criteria obtained from the first VAR model, and according to the principle of choosing information criteria, the lag order is chosen as order 1 from the results of four evaluation indicators: FPE, AIC, SC, and HQ, and the VAR(1) model will be built subsequently.

Table 4. Information Guidelines

Lag order	logL	AIC	SC	HQ	FPE
0	−4630.382	36.038	36.086	36.058	4478761377050001
1	−4350.779	33.639	33.832*	33.717*	406595677310238.4
2	−4319.888	33.631*	33.97	33.768	403417026405532.2*
3	−4296.209	33.693	34.18	33.89	429447359966315.7
4	−4271.234	33.744	34.378	34	451717852388258.6
5	−4244.057	33.773	34.556	34.09	465265396535328.9

4.4 VAR(1)

The VAR (1) model based on the results of the analysis in 4.3:

$$sentiment = -0.213*sentiment(-1) - 0.0*hot(-1) + 0.0*volume(-1) - 0.002$$

$$hot = 71.318*sentiment(-1) + 0.971*hot(-1) - 0.0*volume(-1) + 4.38$$

volume=2346406159.774*sentiment(-1)+7558149.32*hot(-1) + 0.509*volume(-1)+536072767.661

Figure 1 shows that all the eigenroots are within the unit circle, so this VAR model is stable and can continue with the impulse response analysis.

4.5 Impulse Response Analysis

Figure 2 shows the impact of a standard deviation change in sentiment on HOT, that is, the impact of a change in sentiment on the level of attention. It can be found that sentiment has a significant supporting effect on the level of attention, and a rise in sentiment leads to a rise in the level of attention in the short term.

Figure 3 shows the impact of a one standard deviation change in HOT on VOLUME, that is, the impact of a change in the level of attention on trading volume. It can be found that the level of attention has a significant supportive effect on trading volume, and an increase in the level of attention leads to an increase in trading volume, and this effect gradually fades after about a week.

Figure 4 shows the impact of a one standard deviation change in sentiment on volume, that is, the impact of sentiment on trading volume. It can be found that elevated sentiment has a significant supporting effect on trading volume, and elevated sentiment leads to an increase in short-term trading volume. However, at the same time, not all the changes are positive so the results still need further testing.

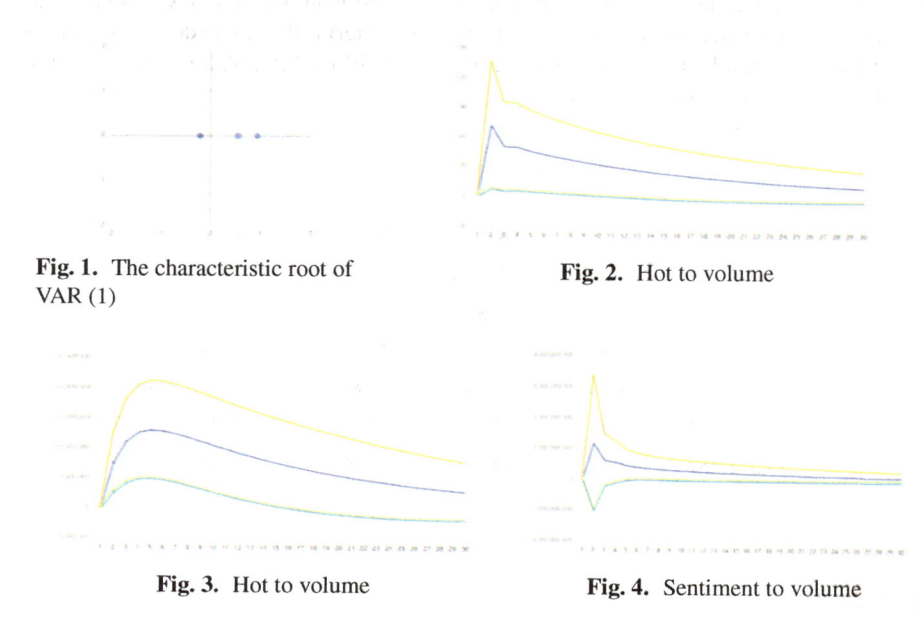

Fig. 1. The characteristic root of VAR (1)

Fig. 2. Hot to volume

Fig. 3. Hot to volume

Fig. 4. Sentiment to volume

4.6 Granger Causality Test

Table 5 shows the results of Granger causality test, based on the variables sentiment and hot, the significance P-value is 0.023**, presenting significance and rejecting the original hypothesis that sentiment can cause changes in hot. Based on the variable hot with volume, the significance P-value is 0.002***, which presents significance and rejects the original hypothesis that hot can cause a change in volume.

Table 5. Result of Granger Causality Test

Paired samples		F	P
hot	sentiment	0.056	0.813
sentiment	hot	5.227	0.023**
volume	sentiment	0.637	0.426
sentiment	volume	1.353	0.246
volume	hot	4.16	0.043**
hot	volume	9.522	0.002***

5 Conclusion

This paper analyzes the effect of investors' endogenous sentiment on stock market activity by building a VAR model, and concludes after verification by Granger causality test that investors' endogenous sentiment can affect investors' attention to the stock market, and the attention to the stock market affects trading volume, i.e. there is an influence path that investors' endogenous sentiment affects trading volume by affecting people's attention to the stock market.

This finding is consistent with the hypothesis of this paper, and is in line with the theories of behavioral finance that sentiment affects information flow and sentiment affects trading, etc. It can provide a reference for the analysis of volume based on trading volume such as the volume/price relationship.

References

1. Moskowitz, T.J., Ooi, Y.H., Pedersen, L.H.: Time series momentum. J. Financ. Econ. **104**(2), 228–250 (2012)
2. Andrei, D., Cujean, J.: Information percolation, momentum and reversal. J. Financ. Econ. **123**(3), 617–645 (2017)
3. Lin, M.-C.: Underreaction, trading volume, and momentum profits in Taiwan stock market. Asia Pac. Manag. Rev. **9**(6), 1115–1142 (2004)
4. Lee, C.M.C., Swaminathan, B: Price momentum and trading volume. J. Finan. **55**(5), 2017–2069 (2000)
5. Chan, L.K.C., Jegadeesh, N., Lakonishok, J.: Momentum strategies. J. Finan. **51**(5), 1681–1713 (1996)
6. Novy-Marx, R.: Is momentum really momentum? J. Finan. Econ. **103**(3), 429–453 (2012)
7. Alexander, B., Möhlmann: The effect of news articles on stock prices. Finan. Res. Lett. **30**, 278–284 (2019)

8. Edmans, A., García, D.: Sports sentiment and stock returns. J. Financ. **62**(4), 1967–1998 (2007)
9. Kaplan, G., Levy, H.: Sentiment and stock prices: the case of aviation disasters. J. Financ. Econ. **95**(2), 174–201 (2010)
10. Li, X., Xie, H., Chen, L., Wang, J., Deng, X.: News impact on stock price return via sentiment analysis. Knowl.-Based Syst. **69**, 14–23 (2014)
11. Edmans, A., Fernandez-Perez, A., Garel, A., Indriawan, I.: Music sentiment and stock returns around the world. J. Financ. Econ. **145**(2), 234–254 (2022)

The Factors Affecting Electric Vehicle Adoption in the United States, 2016–2021

Qing Hou[1](✉), Shuai Zhou[2], and Guangqing Chi[3]

[1] University of Southern California, Los Angeles, CA 90007, USA
Qinghou0520@gmail.com
[2] Department of Agricultural Economics, Sociology, and Education, The Pennsylvania State University, 312 Armsby Building, University Park, PA 16802, USA
[3] Department of Agricultural Economics, Sociology, and Education, Population Research Institute, and Social Science Research Institute, The Pennsylvania State University, University Park, PA 16802, USA

Abstract. Electric vehicles (EVs) provide an innovative solution that may reduce greenhouse gas emissions from transportation and help mitigate environmental problems. While the impacts of technological factors on EV adoption have been analyzed, externalities—such as socioeconomic status, state political alignment, and the number of charging facilities—have not been well studied in the United States. To address this gap in the literature, we employed ordinary least squares models to explore the relationships between external factors and EV adoption using state-level data in the contiguous United States from 2016 through 2021. We found the number of charging stations, level of education, median household income, and percentage of Democrats in state legislatures significantly increased EV market share and that population size significantly decreased state-level EV market share. The number of charging stations had the greatest impact on EV adoption. This study validates the effects of contextual factors on EV adoption, provides insights into facilitating broader EV adoption, and suggests ways of promoting sustainability.

Keywords: Electric Vehicle Adoption · Public Charging Facilities · Political Alignment · Green Transportation

1 Introduction

Increasing global interest in the environment, including air quality, greenhouse gas (GHG) emissions, and the depletion of natural resources, has raised concerns about transportation—one of the largest consumers of petroleum [1, 2]. In response, the electrification of the transportation sector has been proposed as an alternative. In the past decade, the success of hybrid electric vehicles (HEVs) has highlighted the utility of both traditional internal combustion engines and electric motors that use energy stored in batteries [3]. Newer electrified vehicles, such as plug-in hybrid electric vehicles (PHEVs) and battery-operated electric vehicles (BEVs), have an even greater potential to improve fuel efficiency and have been mass produced since 2010 [4]. Compared to PHEVs and HEVs, BEVs are fully electric vehicles with a rechargeable battery serving as the only source of power for the vehicle. Because BEVs are entirely electric and produce no tailpipe emissions, they are also widely considered to be truly electric vehicles (EVs). Since lower CO_2 emissions could be achieved through the wide adoption of EVs (such as BEVs), many governments have employed strategies to enable incremental adoption, thus reducing the discharge of harmful GHGs and dependence on gasoline [5, 6].

A boom in the production of EVs began in 2015, following the sale of one million such vehicles and implementation of various policy incentives [7]. The United States accounted for one-third of global EV, HEV, and PHEV sales before 2011 and has enacted several policies to address market barriers and overcome the initial purchase costs compared to gasoline-equivalent vehicles, but the growth of EV adoption is declining, has fallen short of the initial goals, and has fallen behind the global market [8]. This highlights the urgency with which we must understand how different factors jointly lead to the declining market share of EVs and how to most effectively assess and resolve the barriers consumers face in adopting the use of EVs [9]. Furthermore, it is problematic to do a standard analysis of the energy demand, categorization prices, and accompanying policies for EVs, PHEVs, and HEVs altogether owing to the enormous variations in each of the three categories. Therefore, we concentrate on EV adoption in this study because it has the largest environmental benefits (zero emissions) while also encountering the most obstacles (such as the highest-category pricing and shortest commercial history).

Recent studies have identified intrinsic factors (e.g., vehicle ownership costs, driving range, charging time) that act as impediments to EV adoption, thereby affecting the fluctuation of EV market shares [10]. Moreover, as radical innovations that differ from known products, EVs are associated with greater levels of uncertainty, which drives interactions in ways that differ markedly from the consumer behavior observed in the traditional automobile industry [4]. Thus, the adoption of EVs is more likely to be influenced by external factors, such as increasing oil prices, government financial incentives, or EV-related facilities (i.e., charging stations), than by slow spillover of knowledge or irregular technological progress.

A major challenge that limits research into the relationship between EV adoption and externalities is the lack of isolation regarding the effects of the variables [11]. Absent other factors, such as innovative technologies, the classical pattern of new technology diffusion predicts a gradual increase in the market share of EVs, enabled by both observed and unobserved factors, most of which are correlated with socioeconomic variables. This makes it even more important to isolate the effects of individual variables that have similar effects on EV adoption, which requires longer market histories to regress the effects of predictor variables from time-series data and parametric diffusion curves to establish relevant diffusion models [11]. Most research based on national time-series data lacks long histories, and the observed deviations lead to assumptions that are concerning with respect to future guidance on EV development.

This study hypothesized that several variables, including the number of charging facilities, median income, level of education, population size, and state political alignment, influence EV adoption. We utilized state-level data to isolate and separate those that varied across space but were highly correlated in time, which overcame the inherent limitations of using national time-series data. By analyzing these relationships, we aimed to identify the most critical barriers to EV adoption, provide guidance for governments and EV manufacturers, and contribute to global sustainability.

2 Research Design

2.1 Data

This study analyzed EV adoption in the contiguous United States, including the District of Columbia, from 2016 through 2021, to identify the most critical barriers consumers face in adopting EVs. Table 1 shows the variables and data sources. The data for this study come from four sources. Specifically, we used data from the U.S. Department of Energy to measure state-level EV adoption and charging facilities. The socioeconomic and demographic characteristics, including income, education, and population size, come from the U.S. Census and American Community Survey (ACS). The state political alignments come from the National Conference of State Legislatures. Because of its unicameral legislature and lack of partisan data, we excluded the state of Nebraska from our analyses. The final data consisted of 288 samples from 48 states and the District of Columbia.

2.2 Variables

This paper defines EV adoption as the share of light-duty EVs in the light-duty market. We chose the light-duty vehicle sector over the entire vehicle market for two reasons. First, analyzing the light-duty EV market makes more sense because it has been relatively mature since 2016 and has more samples. Compared to light-duty EVs, medium- and heavy-duty EVs have a shorter market history, this is attributable to the advanced technical requirements to charge heavy-duty batteries [12]. Moreover, according to the Union of Concerned Scientists, medium- and heavy-duty vehicles account for only 10% of U.S. on-road vehicles and 28% of U.S. GHG emissions. Therefore, in this study, we wanted to focus on the adoption of light-duty EVs because they constitute a significant portion of on-road vehicles and are an essential source of GHG emissions [13].

This study used the annual national market share of light-duty EVs in the light-duty market to quantify the dependent variable. The independent variables include state-level charging stations, median annual household income, percentage with a bachelor's degree or higher, population, and the percentage of Democrats in each state's legislature.

2.3 Methods

This study first examined the distribution of the state-level market share of EVs across the contiguous United States. Next, we conducted a correlation analysis of the variables we selected for the analysis. We then fitted OLS models to explore the relationships between EV adoption and state-level contextual characteristics. The formula for our model is as follows:

$$Market\_share = \alpha + \beta_1 Variable1_{it} + \beta_2 Variable2_{it} + \cdots + \beta_n VariableN_{it} + \varepsilon_{it} \quad (1)$$

Table 1. Variables and data sources.

Variables	Description	Source
EV market share (dependent variable)	Annual market share of light-duty EVs in light-duty market	U.S. Department of Energy
Charging facilities	Number of charging stations corrected for population (number of charging stations per 1000 residents)	U.S. Department of Energy
Income	Annual median household income by state (in $1000s)	U.S. Census
Education	Annual educational attainment (percentage of population holding a bachelor's degree or higher, by state)	U.S. Census
Population	ACS five-year estimates for the total population in 1000 units of population (2016–2020) ACS one-year estimates for the total population in 1000 units of population (2021)	U.S. Census
Political parties	Percentage of Democrats in the state legislature	National Conference of State Legislatures

where α is the constant term (the intercept of the regression line), β is the coefficient of the variable, and each subscript indicates the performance of an individual state i at time t, with ε representing error.

2.4 Results

Descriptive Statistics. Figures 1A and 1B show the shares of EVs in the light-duty vehicle market in 2016 and 2021, while Figs. 1C and 1D show the percentage of market share growth from 2016 through 2021 relative to 2016. The results shown in Figs. 1A and 1B reveal that most states have maintained their ranking in EV adoption over the past five years. The overall EV market share has grown more in the west, followed by the east, with markedly lower adoption in the central United States. In the aspect of market share percentage growth shown in Figs. 1C and 1D, the West Coast differs from the rest of the country in that the percentage growth is significantly lower, and a correlation can be observed between the rankings of the states in terms of average growth and total percentage growth. Therefore, it can be seen in Figure that places with higher EV market share have lower growth rates from 2016 through 2021, most notably the U.S. west Coast.

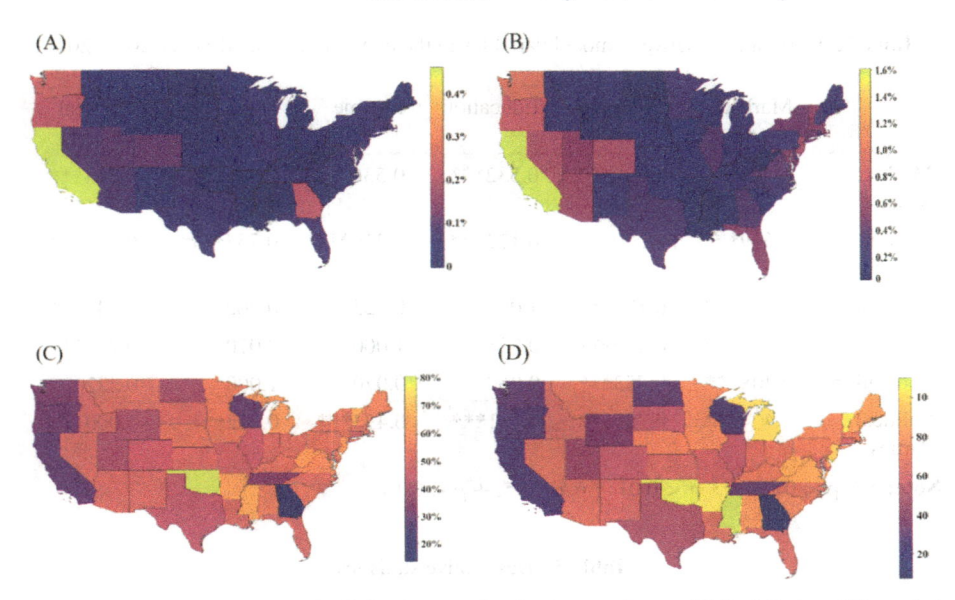

Fig. 1. Annual EV shares of the light-duty market in the contiguous United States. (A) market shares in 2016, (B) market shares in 2021, (C) five-year average annual percentage growth, (D) total growth in market shares. Note: In 2016, no EVs were sold in North Dakota, so the four-year (rather than five-year) average percentage growth for North Dakota was used in Fig. 1C, and the percentage growth for North Dakota from 2017–2021 was used in Fig. 1D (rather than 2016–2021).

We next present the correlation matrix of the variable (Table 2). The interpretation of correlation coefficients depends on the complexity of the tested variable. For easily measured variables, such as socioeconomic status, higher correlations may be expected. In this study, we considered demographic correlations of <.45 to be weak, 0.45–0.75 to be moderate, and > 075 to be strong. The first of two patterns observed was that of moderate to high-moderate correlations between many independent variables. A high correlation (>0.75) was found between two pairs of independent variables—level of education vs. median household income and the number of charging facilities vs. population. The second pattern we observed was that the four independent variables (number of charging facilities, level of education, median household income, and state political alignment) were moderately to high-moderately correlated with the dependent variable (market share of EVs).

Table 3 shows the descriptive statistics. The mean value of the EV market share ranges from 0 to 1.6%, with an average of 0.2%. This suggests that there is still significant potential for EV development. It is also worth noting that the development of charging facilities is significant. The lowest number of charging facilities was in North Dakota in 2016, with only seven charging stations, and the highest number (14,616) was in California in 2021. While the number of charging stations in California is the highest for all six years data were gathered, the number of charging stations in North Dakota were the lowest in the country for the three years data was available.

Table 2. Correlations between model variables in the contiguous United States 2016–2021

	Market Share	Charging Facilities	Education	Income	Population	Political Parties
Market Share	1.000	0.699***	0.532***	0.536***	0.408***	0.464***
Charging Facilities	0.699***	1.000	0.172***	0.219***	0.753***	0.305***
Education	0.532***	0.172***	1.000	0.825***	0.062	0.541***
Income	0.536***	0.219***	0.825***	1.000	0.070	0.473***
Population	0.408***	0.753***	0.062	0.070	1.000	0.222
Political Parties	0.464***	0.305***	0.541***	0.473***	0.222***	1.000

Note: *** $p < 0.001$, ** $p < 0.01$, * $p < 0.05$, + $p < 0.10$

Table 3. Descriptive statistics

	N	Mean	SD	Min	Max
EV Market Share	288	0.002	0.002	0.000	0.016
Charging Facilities	288	0.578	1180.869	0.007	14.616
Education	288	0.327	0.06	0.202	0.636
Income	288	66.992	11294.357	44.100	97.332
Population	288	6.675e+03	7.299e+06	5.788e+02	3.935e+04
Political Parties	288	0.444	0.175	0.114	0.880

Regression Results. Table 4 shows the regression results. We regressed the EV market share on the number of charging stations, level of education, population size, and percentage of Democrats in the state legislature. The adjusted R^2 was 0.685, which indicates that 68.5% of the variation in the EV light-duty market could be explained by the variables in our study. Based on the p-values of each variable, all were statistically significant, and all except for population increased EV adoption. The importance of the variables can be predicted from the standardized and unstandardized β-values (coefficients), where the latter represents the average unit change in the value of EV adoption resulting from a one-unit increase in that variable, with all other variables held constant. In contrast, standardized β-values are often used to rank predictors because they eliminate the units of measurement for both the independent and dependent variables. The results show that charging facility variable has the largest impact on EV adoption, followed by education, suggesting that the two variables are the most important factors affecting state-level EV adoption.

Table 4. OLS regression predicting state-level EV adoption in the contiguous United States 2016–2021

	Coefficients	Standardized Coefficients
Charging Facilities	1.394e−03 (9.690e−08)***	0.755
Education	0.009 (2.020e−05)***	0.272
Income	2.450e−05 (1.150e−08)***	0.127
Population	−6.047e-11 (1.520e−11)**	−0.202
Political Parties	0.001 (0.001)***	0.072
Constant	−0.004 (0.000)	–
Observations	288	
R^2	0.691	
Adjusted R^2	0.685	

Note: *** $p < 0.001$, ** $p < 0.01$, * $p < 0.05$, + $p < 0.10$

3 Conclusion

This study aimed to explore the factors affecting EV adoption and identify measures that may promote the future acceptance of EVs in the United States. To better understand the EV adoption process, we first reviewed the background of EV development and looked at EV adoption in the light-duty vehicle market from 2016 through 2021. From the different visualizations, the EV market share and growth rate showed a spatially correlated pattern. These patterns have remained constant over the years: a high EV market share is found in coastal regions, a high EV market share is associated with low growth percentages and vice versa.

Then this paper applied a regression model to explore variables that are related to EV adoption. Our state-by-state results showed that four variables—the number of charging stations, median household income, level of education, and percentage of Democrats in the state legislature—significantly increased EV adoption, while population size significantly decreased EV adoption. Combined with our descriptive results, we identified the number of charging stations as the most influential factor in EV adoption. The impact of the legislative party on EV market share was also noteworthy. The differences among parties with respect to climate policy have been well-documented [13], and the adoption of EVs is essentially based on social consciousness and a desire to protect the environment.

In EV adoption research, financial incentives are the most popular variable for exploring government influence. However, policies related to EVs go far beyond financial incentives, and the same monetary value obtained by quantifying financial incentives often has different impacts in different regions owing to the socioeconomic environment of the regions. Therefore, it appeared reasonable to use state political alignment to quantify the impact of government power on EV adoption. Our results indicate that a higher percentage of Democrats in the state legislature leads to greater EV adoption. Finally, although party differences are outside the scope of this study, we suggest that both parties increase their support for EVs to better protect the environment.

Acknowledgments. This research was supported in part by the USDA National Institute of Food and Agriculture and Multistate Research Project #PEN04623 (Accession #1013257) and the Eunice Kennedy Shriver National Institute of Child Health and Human Development (Award # P2C HD041025).

References

1. Christensen, C., Salmon, J.: EV adoption influence on air quality and associated infrastructure costs. World Electr. Veh. J. **12**(4), 207 (2021)
2. Tarei, P.K., Chand, P., Gupta, H.: Barriers to the adoption of electric vehicles: evidence from India. J. Cleaner Prod. **291**, 125847 (2021)
3. Adnan, N., Nordin, S.M., Rahman, I.: Adoption of PHEV/EV in Malaysia: a critical review on predicting consumer behaviour. Renew. Sustain. Energ. Rev. **72**, 849–862 (2017)
4. Sierzchula, W., et al.: The influence of financial incentives and other socio-economic factors on electric vehicle adoption. Energ. Policy **68**, 183–194 (2014)
5. Brady, J., O'Mahony, M.: Travel to work in Dublin. The potential impacts of electric vehicles on climate change and urban air quality. Transp. Res. Part D: Transp. Environ. **16**(2), 188–193 (2011)
6. Krause, R.M., et al.: Perception and reality: public knowledge of plug-in electric vehicles in 21 U.S. cities. Energ. Policy **63**, 433–440 (2013)
7. Coffman, M., Bernstein, P., Wee, S.: Electric vehicles revisited: a review of factors that affect adoption. Transp. Rev. **37**(1), 79–93 (2016)
8. Langbroek, J.H.M., Franklin, J.P., Susilo, Y.O.: The effect of policy incentives on electric vehicle adoption. Energy Policy **94**, 94–103 (2016)
9. Carley, S., et al.: Intent to purchase a plug-in electric vehicle: a survey of early impressions in large US cites. Transp. Res. Part D: Transp. Environ. **18**, 39–45 (2013)
10. Onat, N.C., et al.: Exploring the suitability of electric vehicles in the United States. Energy **121**, 631–642 (2017)
11. Diamond, D.: The impact of government incentives for hybrid-electric vehicles: evidence from US states. Energ. Policy **37**(3), 972–983 (2009)
12. Borlaug, B., et al.: Heavy-duty truck electrification and the impacts of depot charging on electricity distribution systems. Nat. Energy **6**(6), 673–682 (2021)
13. Ghandi, A., Paltsev, S.: Global CO_2 impacts of light-duty electric vehicles. Transp. Res. Part D: Transp. Environ. **87**, 102524 (2020)

Assessing Endowment Effect in Different Cooperative Settings

Fengyi Zhang[✉]

Peking University, Beijing 100871, China
zhangfengyi@stu.pku.edu.cn

Abstract. Those who are endowed with certain assets will demand higher compensation to give it up than they would have been willing to pay to obtain it initially. This disequilibrium is known as the endowment effect. Current research on endowment effect mainly focused on influential factors that manipulate the magnitude of endowment effect on individuals, yet this study centered on the occurrence of endowment under group settings, drawing different cooperative status and assessing the existence of the effect. By exploiting a 2-by-2 between-subject design on 51 participants, the experiment verified the endowment effect and discovered that the effect was neutralized under cooperative group settings. Theoretical explanations interpreted the result using the in-group generosity within Asian cultures, yet to which extent the cultural factor had influenced the participants in cooperative group was unknown.

Keywords: Endowment effect · Cooperation · Competition · Collectivism

1 Introduction

The endowment effect is a cognitive bias first described by Richard Thaler in the 1980s. It occurs as individuals ascribe a higher value to an object simply because they own it. This effect has been demonstrated in numerous experiments [1, 2], where participants have been given a good and then asked to trade it for something else. In many cases, the participants were unwilling to trade the item, even when the alternative was objectively more valuable.

The effect is considered to be driven by a combination of loss aversion [3] and status quo bias [4]. Loss aversion refers to people's inclination to prioritize foreseeable losses above potential rewards, while status quo bias emphasizes a propensity of individuals to favor the existing state of events over prospective alternatives. When combined, these biases can lead people to overvalue what they already have, making them reluctant to give it up.

The endowment effect has significant practical implications for economics, as it suggests that people may be less willing to sell the items they own than they would be to buy. This can result in market inefficiencies, as prices may not reflect the true value of goods. The endowment effect elicited inferences for public policy as well, revealing that people may be resistant to manipulations, especially external interferences, in their current situation, even if those changes would be objectively beneficial.

Empirical evidence from previous research had indicated that the endowment effect is a complex phenomenon influenced by a range of factors. For example, the endowment effect has been found to be stronger for goods that are unique or have personal significance to the individual, such as family heirlooms or sentimental objects [5]. Additionally, the social context where the endowment effect occurs can be important as well, since individuals may be more likely to exhibit the endowment effect when they feel a sense of ownership over a good and perceive that others would also value the good. Physical possessions of goods and the strategy of declaring ownerships, though seemed trivial to pricing, imposed significant influence on the endowment effect that could ultimately determine the magnitude of the effect [6].

Cooperation is a fundamental aspect of human social behavior which plays a critical role in a wide range of contexts, including economics. It can be interpreted as a collective action problem, where the interests of the individual and the group are not always aligned. Under certain circumstances, individuals may be enticed by some temptations to favor their own interests over the communal objectives, leading to a suboptimal outcome for everyone involved. Nevertheless, when individuals are willing to cooperate, they can achieve outcomes that are better than what they could achieve on their own.

Noticeably however, few studies had been centered on the interactions between the endowment effect and the status of cooperation, partly because a majority of designs that seek to explore potential interrelations between the endowment effect and other factors had been focusing on individual behaviors. Given previous researcher had verified the existence of endowment effect within both parties of a successful transaction, an explorative research of endowment effect in more generally applicable contexts hence established a possible framework for research on endowment effect.

In short, to verify the existence of endowment effect within the Chinese undergraduates and explore potential interrelations within endowment effect and cooperation status, the experiment exploited a 2-by-2 between-subject design involving ownerships and cooperation status. Based on previous research, the expected outcomes of the experiment are as follows. Firstly, the endowment effect existed among undergraduate participants, as participants of earned ownership was reluctant to spare more money to their counterparts. Secondly, if endowment effect did exist among participants, it would be intensified by the competitive context while mitigated by the cooperative context due to the underlying sense of competition for scarce resource and the influence of collectivism proved to be prominent in Asian cultures. The results had reached these expectations as endowed ownerships decreased participants' willingness to possess properties, and, moreover, cooperative pairs are prone to spare significantly more money to their counterparts. This revealed an initiated endowment effect among participants and an in-group generosity for cooperative pairs.

The following content would elaborate more about the design of the experiment, results from statistical analysis and a brief discussion.

2 Experimental Design

2.1 Design

The experiment exploits a 2-by-2 between-subject design, where Cooperation Status (High/Low) and Ownership (Owned/Not owned) are its independent variables, while the amount of money participant agreed to portion out to its counterpart is the dependent variable. The experiment implements a modified Stroop paradigm [7] in respect of participants' tasks, as two Chinese characters of different size are presented on the screen (For display purposes, the Fig. 1 below was translated to English). Participants are instructed to judge whether the meaning of the larger character cohere with the text color of the smaller one.

In terms of control variables, since the forms and contents of the task feedback may influence participant's achievement goals throughout the experiment (i.e., presenting only correct task results may increase participant's anticipation and confidence, which can further improve their performance), all feedbacks will be presented on screen regardless of the result. Besides, possibilities do exist that social comparisons with high-performing counterparts may impart the participant higher mental stress [8], thus the score of the counterparts is controlled to be lower than the participants (within 3 points). Participants are asked to retain their distance to the screen around 60 cm in order to prevent priming effects. The number of stimuli is evenly distributed among 4 different conditions of position as well as correctness.

To be specific, initially, a pair of participants were designed to enter the experiment simultaneously, both of them had already confirmed that they didn't personally know their counterparts beforehand. The experimenter would first explain the whole procedure of the experiment by clarifying that the experiment was about a task involving reaction time and accuracy, while participants would meet up with each other so as to ensure that both of them were well acknowledged of their counterpart's presence. The pairs in the cooperation group were expected to achieve higher scores as their scores would be summed up as a whole, on the contrary, the pairs in the competition group were asked to achieve higher score individually for their score would be taken into comparison by experimenter afterwards.

Participants were then taken into isolated rooms for further explanation and experiment. For subjects in the owned group, ownership was conveyed by telling them that they already obtained a bonus payment of 15 RMB on account of their odd(even) subject number, which can be redeemed by the end of experiment.

The experiment consisted of 5 test trials and formal experiments. Participants were firstly provided with 5 trials for comprehending the operations within the trials. If participants were not fully familiar with the objectives, another 5 test trials were presented. During the formal experiment, stimulus of different colors and meanings were successively presented, participants were asked to make their judgement and press the designated key on the keyboard in 2000 ms, a feedback showing the correctness of a duration of 1000 ms then followed. 1500 ms after the feedback, the second trial starts. A correct response would be 1 point, given every 20 trials make up a block, the total score for a block would be 20 points, and the experiment have a total number of 3 blocks. Between the blocks, a 30 s rest was provided, at in the meantime, the participant's score in that block would emerge on the screen. Participants were told that their counterparts scored 1–3 points lower than his or her score. A figurative illustration for a single block is shown below (Fig. 1). After the participant completed 3 blocks of trials, another 30 s rest was provided.

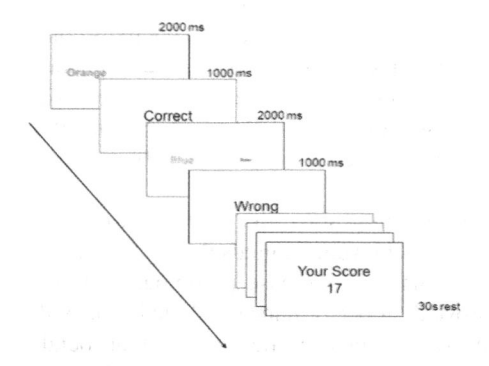

Fig. 1. An illustration for a single block of trails.

For participants with a previous entitlement, the money allocation task was informed by suggesting sparing some money for their counterparts since their subject number didn't meet the criteria. For participants without ownerships, the money allocation task was instructed in a similar manner. Specifically, all individuals were told that their performance had passed the baseline of the task and hence earned themselves (their team) a bonus payment of 15 RMB. And participants are given the right to disperse the money within the pairs. Participants were then given a spreadsheet to fill out the money they are willing to spare.

2.2 Participants

Fifty-two students from the Peking University (statistical descriptions would appear below in Sect. 3.1) participated the experiment for payment or course credit. All participants are recruited online through social medias and gave consent to the treatment of the experiment. The intentional deception of cooperative and competitive environment was clarified immediately by the end of the experiment.

2.3 Materials

The tasks were operated by participants on a desktop computer, which equipped with a 20-in ViewSonic displayer of 1920 × 1080 resolution and refresh rate of 60 Hz. The experiment program was based on PsychoPy-2022.2.4, where a Stroop task and a task of money allocation was presented. The visual stimulus of the experiment consists of eight different colored Chinese characters, as shown in the Fig. 2 and Fig. 3.

Orange **Green**

Fig. 2. An example of stimulus where meaning of larger characters and color of smaller ones are consistent.

Blue **Green**

Fig. 3. An example of stimulus where meaning of larger characters and color of smaller ones are not consistent.

3 Results

3.1 Descriptive Analysis

SPSS 25 was used to process the data, one subject was rejected due to dearth of data, another outlier was rejected as well. The descriptive statistics for the rest of the 50 subjects was shown in the Table 1. The significance level α was set at 0.05.

Table 1. a, b Descriptive statistics for the amount of money subject willing to spare in different treatments.

	Age	Cooperative	Competitive	MD	Observations
Owned	19.847	6.308	5.808	0.499	25
	(1.12)	(2.18)	(2.51)		
Not owned	20.979	6.846	3.000	3.846***	25
	(2.48)	(1.40)	(3.01)		
Total	20.413	6.577	4.404	2.173**	50
	(2.37)	(0.46)	(0.48)		

Note: a. Standard Deviations are listed in corresponding parenthesis.
b. * $p < .05$, ** $p < .01$, *** $p < .001$.

3.2 ANOVA

The experiment exploited a 2(Cooperation status) × 2(Ownership) ANOVA in order to verify the endowment effect and explore possible links between two independent variables. The Levine's test of equal error variances indicates that all data satisfies the null hypothesis of all error variances in distinctive blocks were all equal, hence it may proceed to the ANOVA. The main effect of cooperation status was significant, indicating that the cooperative or competitive experience significantly influenced participant's willingness to spare the money, the main effect of the ownership, though peripherally, was significant. The endowment effect could be, to some extent, verified on the basis of the experiment data and a significance level of 0.10. The interaction between cooperative status and the ownership was significant.

Given the significant interaction effect, a simple main effect analysis adjusted by Bonferroni method was then implemented. The results revealed that, under the competitive conditions, the amount of money spared by different ownerships was significant, as cooperative pairs are prone to spare significantly more money to their counterparts, while no significant difference exist between two ownerships under the cooperative condition. The observed negative mean difference even, in a sense, suggested that the endowment effect might be neutralized by the cooperation status.

Table 2. a. ANOVA result for cooperation status, ownership and their interaction.

	F	Partial η^2	Observations
Cooperation Status	10.901**	0.192	50
Ownership	2.974	0.061	50
Interaction	6.466*	0.123	50

Note: a. *$p < .05$, **$p < .01$, ***$p < 0.001$.

The experimental results indicated that a weak endowment effect existed among the participants, which did not exactly correspond to previous expectations (Table 2). Apart from the apparent scarcity of participants and gender differences [9], the design of the experiment worth taking a closer investigation. Consider the design of establishing a ratio variable as the direct indicator of participants' willingness to pay. It is indeed a more precise measure for evaluating tendencies within the participants, yet effects other than the endowment effect would blend into such tendency, say, participants' attitude toward freeriding or beliefs for social egalitarians [10]. These unobservable factors might equally affect the sensitive indicator, thus more conspicuous influence on verification for Endowment effect compared to a Yes-No judgment. Also, with cooperative and competitive designs combined into the paradigm of endowment effect, several operations that secured the inevitability of the endowment effect was unable to proceed, which would weaken the effect of endowment. For instance, as mentioned, physical possession of the property endowed would be of great significance in initiating the endowment effect. However, the money allocation task was impossible to complete with cash, for a face-to-face allocation might not only bring numerous extra variables into account, but even reverse participants' decisions.

In the meantime, the observed differences between cooperation status were in line with the expectation, suggesting the pairs in the cooperative treatment were likely to spare larger sum of money for their counterparts. Furthermore, the simple main effect test implied a reversed trend, where pairs that eventually earned their bonus ended up distributing the money evenly and resulted in more money spared, occurred within the cooperative group. This phenomenon might be supported, at least partially, by the inclination toward collectivism within the Asian culture. Among numerous consequences proved to be salient in collectivism cultures, a critical one that influenced the outcome of the experiment was that group memberships were assigned and unchangeable, considered as "facts of life" that people had to accommodate; and in-group exchanges were largely founded on notions of equality or even generosity principles [11]. Considering that all participants of the experiment was constraint to Asian, or more specifically, Chinese culture, it could be assumed that the cooperative setting had promptly attributed a group membership to participants, which soon led to the fifty-fifty division of bonus, treating the earned money as a product of collective efforts.

4 Conclusion

In conclusion, the current experiment aimed at verifying endowment effect among Chinese undergraduates and assessing the influence of cooperation setting on endowment effect. By exploiting a 2-by-2 between-subject design where Cooperation Status (High/Low) and Ownership (Owned/Not owned) are its independent variables, this study had successfully carried out an experiment on 51 participants. The results suggested that the relative lower tendency for participants to spare money with endowed ownerships exhibited slight endowment effect, as the design of the experiment left a vent for confounding variables including personal beliefs and preferences to mitigate the endowment effect. While the significant main effect of cooperation status indicated a disposition of participants in cooperative groups to include their counterparts of a same membership, which consequently affected their decisions in the money allocation task. Theoretical explanations interpreted the result using the in-group generosity within Asian cultures, yet to which extent the cultural factor had influenced the participants in cooperative group was unknown.

References

1. Knetsch, J.L., Sinden, J.A.: Willingness to pay and compensation demanded: experimental evidence of an unexpected disparity in measures of value. Q. J. Econ. **99**(3), 507 (1984)
2. Hubbeling, D.: Rationing decisions and the endowment effect. J. R. Soc. Med. **113**(3), 98–100 (2020)
3. Brenner, L., Rottenstreich, Y., Sood, S., Bilgin, B.: On the psychology of loss aversion: possession, valence, and reversals of the endowment effect: table 1. J. Consum. Res. **34**(3), 369–376 (2007)
4. Bruner, J., Calegari, F., Handfield, T.: The evolution of the endowment effect. Evol. Hum. Behav. **41**(1), 87–95 (2020)
5. Gawronski, B., Bodenhausen, G.V., Becker, A.P.: I like it, because I like myself: associative self-anchoring and post-decisional change of implicit evaluations. J. Exp. Soc. Psychol. **43**(2), 221–232 (2007)
6. Knetsch, J.L., Wong, W.-K.: The endowment effect and the reference state: evidence and manipulations. J. Econ. Behav. Organ. **71**(2), 407–413 (2009)
7. Shin, J., Lee, Y., Seo, E.: The effects of feedback on students' achievement goals: interaction between reference of comparison and regulatory focus. Learn. Instr. **49**, 21–31 (2017)
8. Zhou, J., Zhan, Y., Cheng, H., Zhang, G.: Challenge or threat? Exploring the dual effects of temporal social comparison on employee workplace coping behaviors. Curr. Psychol. (2022)
9. Dommer, S.L., Swaminathan, V.: Explaining the endowment effect through ownership: the role of identity, gender, and self-threat. J. Consum. Res. **39**(5), 1034–1050 (2013)
10. Sevdalis, N., Harvey, N., Bell, A.: Affective equilibria in the endowment effect. J. Behav. Financ. **10**(2), 89–100 (2009)
11. Oyserman, D., Coon, H.M., Kemmelmeier, M.: Rethinking individualism and collectivism: evaluation of theoretical assumptions and meta-analyses. Psychol. Bull. **128**(1), 3–72 (2002)

The Primary Performance Trait of Corporations with High Managerial Short-Termism

Yuping Wang(✉)

Adam Smith Business School, University of Glasgow, Glasgow G12 8QQ, UK
2732097w@student.gla.ac.uk

Abstract. The aim of this paper is to investigate and summarize three factors that contribute to short-termism in corporate management: CEO (Chief Executive Officer) equity incentive, takeover threat, and short-term institutional investors. Management short-termism has always been the focus of attention, and this paper also wants to infer the characteristics of management short-termism by analyzing these three factors which have been studied by literatures. First, the analysis of the relationship between CEO equity incentive and management short-termism focuses on demonstrating causality and measuring long-term effects. Second, the analysis of managers' short-sighted behavior prompted by the threat of takeover is conducted primarily through the lens of the impact of takeover protection clauses and managers' willingness to invest in the complexity of investment. Third, the analysis of short-termism promoted by short-term institutional investors focuses on three factors: agency cost between shareholders and creditors, internal control quality, and sensitivity to short-term performance appearances. This paragraph provides a comprehensive overview of the different factors that contribute to managerial short-termism, which is a critical issue faced by organizations in the modern business environment.

Keywords: Managerial Short-Termism · CEO Equity Incentive · Takeover Threat · Transient Institutional Investor

1 Introduction

Managerial short-termism, also known as managerial myopia and defined by several different concepts, has been a concern of both shareholders and researchers in recent years. Short-termism is prevalent in management. Most American CEOs argue that they are willing to forego long-term corporate value in exchange for returns that outperform market expectations [1]. As a result, investigating the primary influencing factors and performance characteristics of managerial short-termism is critical, as it provides a theoretical foundation for other problems caused by managerial short-termism. This paper focuses on three major factors influencing management short-termism: CEO equity incentive, takeover threat, and short-term institutional investors. Each factor is analyzed based on the summary of previous studies, reasoning, and verification through various evidence, and the final result is obtained.

2 Factors Affecting Managerial Short-Termism

2.1 CEO's Equity Incentives

CEOs with higher shareholding in equity incentive portfolios are more inclined to strive to achieve short-term performance targets. Granting stock options that vest over a long period of time means losing the options if the CEO is fired before the interim date, so the long-term vesting horizon encourages the CEO to stay with the company. This is good from an incentive perspective, but at the same time, the pressure on the CEO to assume the forfeiture of options can distort investment decisions for short-term projects. Because boards renew management talent based on short-term results, CEOs reduce their chances of being fired or losing options by seeking ways to improve the board's perception of their abilities. As a result, when a CEO is on the verge of leaving, long-term vesting terms tends to be tied to short-term performance, encouraging short-termism [2]. Many practitioners, scholars, and policymakers have proposed that executive compensation plans are a significant contributor to short-termism. The concern is that short-term pay incentives encourage CEOs to raise stock prices at the expense of the company's long-term value in order to meet short-term objectives. However, proving this theory is difficult. First, the CEO's contract's endogeneity makes proving a causal effect of short-term incentives difficult. Second, measuring the long-term impact of a CEO's specific actions as a result of incentives is difficult [3].

The first challenge was addressed by Edmans, Fang, and Lewellen, who introduced the quantity of shares and options granted in a given quarter as a short-term CEO incentive [4]. They looked into the relationship between actual investment decisions and CEOs' concerns about short-term stock price movements. The study looked at the relationship between vesting equity and CEO investment in long-term R&D and capital growth projects. Analyst forecasts and profit guidance have been revised. The final results show that vesting equity incentivizes CEOs to reduce long-term investments and increase short-term returns. In general, the contracts of CEOs have a causal impact on decision-making. There are three main explanations for the findings. One is that stock price concerns are causing CEOs to sacrifice long-term value and move away from positive net present value investing. The second explanation is that equity grants are an effective deterrent to overinvestment by CEOs. The third reason is that the boards are planning the vesting at a time when investment opportunities are diminishing. It is difficult to separate these assumptions because studies can only observe the amount of investment and not its effectiveness. Edmans, Fang, and Lewellen use indirect tests to evaluate them [4]. It finds no significant changes in the ratios of cost of goods sold to sales, operating expenses to sales, and sales growth rate and concludes that the efficiency hypothesis is unlikely. The results remain robust when the test is run using only data from grants made at least two years ago, which are unlikely to be relevant to current investment opportunities, ruling out the possibility of the third explanation. Eventually, they concluded that the acquisition of equity was strongly associated with reduced investment growth.

The second challenge of measuring the long-term impact of behavior on firms is also addressed. Edmans, Fang, and Huang evaluated the significance of short-term incentives by studying two corporate actions with estimated long-term consequences [3]. The first is a stock repurchase, and the second is corporate mergers and acquisitions. By studying the relationship between vested equity and repurchase and M&A announcements from 2006 to 2015, they found that an increase in vested equity was linked to an increase in the frequency of repurchase and merger and acquisition announcements. This result suggests that impending equity vesting can lead to short-termism behavior by CEOs. In addition, non-observable characteristics may also influence the decision of the company to accelerate option grants and its investment rate. For example, a company with weak corporate governance is more likely to accelerate options to reduce investment, so the causal effect between the two cannot be confirmed. Ladika and Sautner exploit the random variation in compliance dates of FAS123-R to overcome this problem [5]. They discover that accelerated vesting significantly boosts the returns CEOs receive from exercising their options after a short-term increase in stock price. At the same time, it significantly reduced the CEO's overall incentive horizons, leading CEOs to reduce investment. Ultimately, their study confirms a negative relationship between each investment measure and accelerated option increments.

In general, the research on the relationship between equity grants of management ownership and management short-termism has gradually improved and matured. From the gradual breakthrough of the two difficulties of the confirmation of causality and the measurement of long-term influence, many researchers have reached the same conclusion, that is, the equity grant of managers is one of the important factors causing management short-termism.

2.2 Takeover Threat

The increased threat of a takeover will increase pressure on managers to boost profits in the current period and cut their companies' long-term risky investments to fend off takeover attempts. The study of Zhao et al. look at the impact of takeover defense on real earnings management [6]. Defined as a deviation from normal operating practices in order to achieve short-term earnings targets, real earnings management usually overstates short-term reported earnings at the cost of a company's long-term cash flow and is therefore viewed as a form of management myopia. Protection against takeovers is generally seen as a sign of poor corporate governance, which undermines market review of takeovers and exacerbates conflict between shareholders and managers. Real earnings management, on the other hand, is opportunistic behavior that benefits managers while undermining shareholder interests. External governance from the takeover market can reduce opportunistic manipulation, whereas takeover protection strengthens management's real earnings management or managerial myopia. There is also a school of thought that believes real earnings management is a behavior driven by external market pressure, and that acquisition pressure may induce unprotected managers to manipulate activities like reducing long-term investments in pursuit of short-term gains. And takeover protection reduces the takeover threat, managers are then less pressured to improve short-term results. To test these two divergent views, Zhao et al. use the staggered board provision (which makes it difficult for dissidents to acquire and replace existing companies) as the primary proxy for increased takeover protection [6]. The manipulation of the company's actual activity is measured by calculating the company's abnormal cost of production, abnormal discretionary expenditures, and abnormal operational cash flows. They discover that better-protected firms (staggered board firms) engage in less abnormal manipulative activity to achieve short-term gains. They also conducted other tests and found that abnormal real activity is negatively related to future performance when the company does not achieve the target profit, while abnormal real activity is for the company to have better subsequent performance when the company achieves the target profit. Taken together, takeover protection reduces the pressure on fund managers for engaging in authentic earnings management in order to show rising future performance.

In addition, Chatjuthamard et al. summarized two hypotheses about the impact of acquisition risk on corporate complexity from previous literature [7]. The first, the quiet life hypothesis, argues that in an environment without takeover market pressure, fund managers tend to avoid investments of high complexity that require significant management time and effort. More takeover threats induce managers to actively invest in projects with more complex risks. Another hypothesis of managerial myopia holds that the threat of a takeover will reduce the job security of managers and make them focus on the benefits of short-term projects, ignoring more complex long-term investments. Their study demonstrates that vulnerability to acquisitions leads to a reduction in firm complexity, and the evidence thus far does not support the quiet life hypothesis. Their research also suggests that the threat of a takeover exacerbates managerial short-termism, ultimately reducing corporate complexity. According to the findings of Chatjuthamard et al., increased takeover threats significantly reduce asset redeployment [8]. At the same time, their findings are consistent with the management myopia hypothesis. This study also adds to the literature on agency theory by proving how agency problems promote manager myopia in competitive takeover markets. This finding runs counter to the institutional cost mitigation hypothesis, which holds that an active takeover market can reduce institutional conflict and thus limit managerial opportunism. According to research, takeover markets can lead to institutional problems and, as a result, managerial myopia. At the same time, they also take the view that protecting against takeovers has a positive direct effect and a negative dampening effect on innovation, which is particularly evident in small and medium-sized firms and in very competitive industries. Finally, they argue that the effects of the two factors, incentive strategy, and takeover protection, on a firm's innovation are interrelated, and that the impact of incentives on innovation also depends on whether anti-takeover provisions are in place.

In general, there is now a substantial body of literature demonstrating that the threat of a takeover induces managers to prioritize short-term gains over more risky and complex long-term investment projects. Takeover protection would give management more confidence and allow them to invest in more complex, long-term investments that would benefit both the company and its shareholders. Some researchers examined both takeover protection and long-term incentives for management and concluded that in companies with takeover protection clauses, the incentive measures carefully designed by the company for management can play an important role.

2.3 Transient Institutional Investors

A larger proportion of transient institutional investors forces managers to focus more on current profits and thus reduce long-term risky investments. An increase in the ownership of institutional investors tends to reduce the agency conflict between managers and shareholders through incentives and resources to supervise management, thus increasing stock value. However, since institutions within firms are heterogeneous, the characteristics of these investors are different. For example, investment horizons are used to categorize institutions as long-term investments, such as pension funds, whereas mutual funds and hedge funds are short-term investments. Institutions with long-term investment horizons have a tendency to promote corporate long-term value. Furthermore, institutions with short-term investment horizons frequently use their influence on corporate policies and information advantages to achieve short-term trading profits at the expense of the firm's long-term interests. Kim et al. demonstrated that short-term investors will try to change the balance between creditors and shareholders in order to intensify the conflict of interest between them, thereby harming creditors' interests [9]. Moreover, short-term institutional activists will require the company's management to reduce the company's cash storage by selling assets, buying back shares, and increasing dividends, thus weakening the company's solvency and increasing the company's credit risk. Other researchers have discovered that when hedge fund activity is supported by corporate control and financial restructuring, bank loan spreads rise. Kim et al. worked hard in their research to demonstrate the impact of institutional investors' level of investment on debt costs [9]. Long-term investors tend to increase a company's ability to generate cash flow to reduce the cost of debt. While transient institutional investors are more likely to promote short-term management leading to an increase in debt agency fees. They focus on bank lending because banks are more rational and efficient in perceiving increased loan risk when transient institutional investors drive policies that negatively affect the value of debt. The Bank's credit officers will calibrate the terms of the loan using the organization's credit risk information and a risk estimate. Creditors can alleviate conflicts and reduce agency costs between shareholders and creditors by limiting the behavior of managers through the terms of debt agreements. Lenders may control corporate management through supervision and contracts, but agency costs are high, so lenders may need to rely on long-term institutional investors. Short-run institutions, on the other hand, are more likely to induce corporate managers to adopt short-termism strategies in order to increase agency costs between shareholders and lenders. As a result, the study of loan terms can assess the perception of transient institutional investors' debt holders about the potential risk of investing in the company. Kim et al. conclude that banks need more covenants and higher spreads to lend to companies dominated by transient institutional investors because of the higher agency costs between shareholders and creditors of these companies [9]. This study contributes to the understanding of the impact of institutional investors' investment horizons on corporate policies and the cost of capital.

In addition, Chen et al. argue that diversification can incentivize ineffective internal control by managers and that this relationship is affected by the composition of institutional ownership [10]. Transient ownership contributes positively to the relationship between diversification and the weakening of internal control, while dedicated ownership contributes negatively to moderating this relationship. It also demonstrates that committed investors with long-term investment horizons are more likely to monitor corporate behavior and improve corporate internal control quality. The demonstration of this viewpoint also demonstrates that an increase in short-term institutional investors will promote diversification while causing internal control issues, which supports the view that short-term institutional investors promote myopic behavior in management decisions. Moreover, Boo and Kim proposed the hypothesis in the study that myopic marketing management may be due to the presence of powerful institutional investors who are very sensitive to short-term earnings performance in the company [11]. Long-term investors often implement the strategy of buying and holding for a long time, while short-term investors are more inclined to get returns as soon as possible, which is also a source of pressure for fund managers. If a company has a large number of transient institutional investors, shareholders will be highly sensitive to the company's quarterly earnings performance, and fund managers will be under enormous pressure to meet quarterly financial targets, leading to management myopia. Their research also supports the notion that transient institutional investors promote managerial short-termism.

In general, many researchers are interested in the role of institutional investors in corporate governance and have done a lot of empirical research. This paper mainly summarizes three aspects to explain and demonstrate the view that transient institutional investors induce short-termism behavior of managers, from the existence of institutional investors, will increase the agency cost between shareholders and creditors, short-term institutional investors will weaken the quality of corporate internal control, and transient institutional investors will be highly sensitive to the short-term financial performance of the company.

3 Conclusion

In conclusion, this paper summarizes three factors that influence management short-termism: CEO's equity incentive, takeover threat, and transient institutional investors. First, in the analysis of CEO equity incentive, this paper mainly analyzes the breakthrough of two research difficulties, namely, the demonstration of the causal relationship between management equity grants and management short-termism and the measurement of long-term impact. Finally, a large number of literature have contributed evidence and the same conclusion. Second, the analysis of takeover threat mainly concludes that takeover protection will increase managers' sense of security and thus strengthen the company's long-term investment, while a takeover threat will force managers to pay attention to short-term interests and give up a long-term investment with greater risk and complexity. Moreover, studies have proved that the long-term incentive of management is more effective under the takeover protection clause. Third, the impact of short-term institutional investors on management is examined primarily through the agency costs of shareholders and creditors, the quality of the company's internal control, and the sensitivity of short-term financial performance. According to the study, the rise in short-term institutional investors is positively correlated with the three aforementioned factors, leading to managers' short-termism. This paper primarily summarizes three factors influencing management myopia, and these three aspects can also be viewed as performance characteristics of the company with management myopia.

References

1. Marinovic, I., Varas, F.: CEO horizon, optimal pay duration, and the escalation of short-termism. J. Financ. **74**(4), 2011–2053 (2019)

2. Laux, V.: Stock option vesting conditions, CEO turnover, and myopic investment. J. Financ. Econ. **106**(3), 513–526 (2012)
3. Edmans, A., Fang, V.W., Huang, A.H.: The long-term consequences of short-term incentives. J. Account. Res. **60**(3), 1007–1046 (2022)
4. Edmans, A., Fang, V.W., Lewellen, K.A.: Equity vesting and investment. Rev. Financ. Stud. **30**, 2229–2271 (2017)
5. Ladika, T., Sautner, Z.: Managerial short-termism and investment: evidence from accelerated option vesting. Rev. Financ. **24**(2), 305–344 (2020)
6. Zhao, Y., Chen, K.H., Zhang, Y., Davis, M.: Takeover protection and managerial myopia: evidence from real earnings management. J. Account. Public Policy **31**(1), 109–135 (2012)
7. Chatjuthamard, P., Boonlert-U-Thai, K., Jiraporn, P., Uyar, A., Kilic, M.: Hostile takeover threats, managerial myopia and asset redeployability. Corporate Governance: The International Journal of Business in Society (ahead-of-print) (2022)
8. Chatjuthamard, P., Ongsakul, V., Jiraporn, P.: Corporate complexity, managerial myopia, and hostile takeover exposure: evidence from textual analysis. J. Behav. Exp. Financ. **33**, 100601 (2022)
9. Kim, H.D., Kim, Y., Mantecon, T.: Short-term institutional investors and agency costs of debt. J. Bus. Res. **95**, 195–210 (2019)
10. Chen, G.Z., Keung, E.C.: Corporate diversification, institutional investors and internal control quality. Account. Financ. **58**(3), 751–786 (2018)
11. Boo, C., Kim, C.: Institutional ownership and marketing myopic management. Appl. Econ. Lett. **28**(2), 148–152 (2021)

Research on the Factors Affecting Inequality – Evidence from China

Gengqiang Xiao[✉]

University of Liverpool, Liverpool L7 7JB, UK
Xiao15181675275@outlook.com

Abstract. Income inequality in China is a prominent issue, especially in the regional area. Infrastructure development has been used as an important tool to boost regional economic development and reduce the income inequality problem. The aim of this paper is to examine whether the level of infrastructure development has an impact on regional income inequality in China, using inter-provincial data from China from 2008, 2013 and 2018. Three variables, namely road network density, railway density and postal road density were selected for statistical analysis in this paper. Considering the influence of the time dimension, the article uses the panel data method as the analysis method to analyze the factors of income inequality. The results show that infrastructure development is significant in reducing regional income inequality.

Keywords: Income Inequality · China · Infrastructure

1 Introduction

The Gini index (coefficient) is a commonly used indicator of income disparity among residents and reflects the extent of regional income inequality of a country or a region. Income inequality in China, one of the fastest-growing economies in the world, is also expanding rapidly [1, 2]. China's Gini index has risen apace over the past decades, expanding rapidly from 32.2 in 1990 to 43 in 2008, and has only begun to decline year on year since 2008 [3–5]. Income inequality within China is concentrated in regional inequalities, such as urban-rural and provincial differences [1]. In terms of geographical differences, China's eastern coastal provinces are growing very fast, while some western provinces are doing it much more slowly [1]. This issue is also found in urban and rural areas at the same time, Liu, Liu and Zhou pointed out that rural poverty in China has developed a clustering character in its spatial distribution [6]. They also suggest that inequalities between regions can be reduced by implementing specific regional development strategies [6]. Implementing specific regional development strategies, e.g., public services such as investment in building a new transport network. In addition to this, the transport network may also affect the participation of the region in globalisation and have an impact on inequalities between regions [7].

In the area of infrastructure, Zhou, Hu and Lin use the construction of a highway network in the Yangtze River Delta region of China as an example to show that the construction of a road network can improve transport efficiency and increase regional advantages, thus effectively boosting the regional economy [8]. In addition, the construction of railway networks can also help to improve regional economies by stimulating manufacturing and increasing transport, as illustrated by Wang and Wu with the construction of the Qinghai-Tibet Railway program [9].

In terms of the urban-rural wealth gap, China's precise poverty alleviation policy has effectively reduced poverty rates in both rural and urban areas [4]. One of the most effective ways of doing this is through industrial poverty alleviation, which increases the income of residents and raises employment rates and regional economic levels by developing industries with local characteristics [6]. As most industries in poor villages are concentrated in agricultural products and tourism, i.e., the main products are sold through e-commerce platforms, the construction of roads and postal routes can greatly help industrial development and reduce the poverty rate [6].

The main task of this paper is to examine the impact of the level of infrastructure on income inequality income inequality. This paper selects road density, railway density and postal line density as explanatory variables to find the effect and impact of the level of infrastructure on reducing the level of income inequality between regions. This paper finds that infrastructure development has an impact on income inequality between regions in China.

2 Methodology

2.1 Model and Method

The purpose of this paper is to examine the causal relationship between road density, rail density and postal line density and variations in income inequality. Data relating to each of the thirteen provinces or administrative divisions of the same level were selected and a panel data set was created [10]. Regression analyses were carried out using panel methods.

We conducted individual effects tests and random effects tests and concluded that both were significant. We then conducted a heteroskedasticity test and concluded that there was a between-group heteroskedasticity. We then performed a Hausman test using robust standard deviations and decided to use a fixed effects model.

Based on the basic fixed-effects model, we introduced the Gini index, which is the Gini coefficient multiplied by 100, as the dependent variable. We also introduce road density, rail density and postal line density as the independent variables x_{1t}, x_{2t} and x_{3t} respectively (Table 1). a_i is the amount of influence that is constant over time and u_{it} is the amount of influence that varies over time. The fixed-effects model is as follows:

$$lnY_{it} = \beta_0 + \beta_1 lnx_{1t} + \beta_2 lnx_{2t} + \beta_3 lnx_{3t} + a_i + u_{it}$$

For all independent variables, we used the total length of the route divided by the land area of the whole province, hence the unit is kilometers per square kilometer. Given the differences in province size, we use density rather than total length to ensure that the figures are comparable. Also, we take logarithms to measure their elasticities.

For the dependent variables, because GINI index cannot be less than zero, we take the logarithm to make sure that the distribution of error term is close to normality.

Table 1. Variable definition.

Variable Definition	
Y	GINI INDEX
x1	Road density
x2	Rail density
x3	Postal network density

2.2 Data

In this paper, thirteen provinces were selected from the east, west, south, north and central parts of China for three years of data. The provinces selected here include Beijing, Tianjin, Shanxi, Liaoning, Shanghai, Jiangsu, Zhejiang, Fujian, Hubei, Guangxi, Hainan and Yunnan. The years are 2008, 2013 and 2018. As infrastructure construction, is often a long-term project, that takes several years to complete, especially in China, so there is no option here for consecutive years.

At the same time, decisions within provinces regarding the construction of road, rail and postal networks may be influenced by several indicators, such as the number of prefecture-level cities, the number of natural villages and the number of important transport hubs. After taking this part of the variables into control as far as possible, we can roughly assume that the sample can be considered as randomly assigned. The above data are obtained from the World Bank, the National Bureau of Statistics of China and the Sixth China Land Survey. The following are descriptive statistics for each variable in the data table (Table 2).

Table 2. Descriptive statistics for variables [5, 10].

Variable	N	Mean	p50	SD
GINIINDEX	36	42.95	41.66	4.748
Roaddensity	36	1.025	0.964	0.380
Raildensity	36	0.726	0.775	0.343
Postalnetw~y	36	0.916	0.559	0.902

3 Results and Analysis

3.1 Result

Individual effects, random effects and Hausman tests were all significant (Table 3) (Table 4). As this paper use a fixed-effects model, it focuses on columns (2) and (3) (Table 5). In the previous section, we found that this panel dataset has between-group heteroskedasticity, so we use robust standard deviations instead of general standard deviations in the second column for the fixed effects model.

Table 3. Individual effects, random effects and hausman tests results.

	FE	RE
lnx1	−0.319*	−0.0820
	(−2.44)	(−1.42)
lnx2	−0.095**	−0.122***
	(−2.85)	(−4.95)
lnx3	−0.0400	−0.046*
	(−1.73)	(−2.20)
cons	3.677***	3.673***
	(334.28)	(160.35)
N	36	36
Ftest	0	
xttest0		0.0012
Hausman Test		0.0095

t statistics in parentheses.
*p < 0.05, **p < 0.01, ***p < 0.001.

Table 4. The results of our respective regressions.

	(1)	(2)	(3)	(4)
	OLS	fe robust	fe	re
lnx1	−0.0614	−0.319*	−0.319**	−0.0823
	(0.0428)	(0.159)	(0.131)	(0.0580)
lnx2	−0.0624**	−0.0948**	−0.0948***	−0.122***
	(0.0293)	(0.0326)	(0.0332)	(0.0247)
lnx3	−0.0410**	−0.0399*	−0.0399*	−0.0465**
	(0.0198)	(0.0184)	(0.0231)	(0.0211)
cons	3.703***	3.677***	3.677***	3.673***
	(0.0191)	(0.00827)	(0.0110)	(0.0229)
N	36	36	36	36

Standard errors in parentheses.
*p < 0.1, **p < 0.05, ***p < 0.01.

In column (2) (Table 4), it can be seen that the estimated coefficients for all three variables show negative values, indicating that road density, rail density and postal network density have a contributory effect in reducing the Gini index. This is in line with the effect suggested by previous literature above.

Because of the small sample size, this paper chose the significant level of the coefficients of each variable at 10%. And all coefficients are found to be significant at the 10% level in both the robust standard deviation and the general standard deviation fixed-effects

Table 5. Regression results robust FE test.

lnY	Coef	St.Err	t-value	p-value	[95% Conf	Interval]	Sig
lnx1	−.319	.159	−2.01	.069	−.669	.03	*
lnx2	−.095	.033	−2.91	.014	−.166	−.023	**
lnx3	−.04	.018	−2.17	.053	−.08	.001	*
Constant	3.677	.008	444.68	0	3.659	3.695	***
Mean dependent var		3.754		SD dependent var		0.110	
R-squared		0.906		Number of obs		36	
F-test		91.346		Prob > F		0.000	
Akaike crit. (AIC)		−151.313		Bayesian crit. (BIC)		−146.563	

*** $p < .01$, ** $p < .05$, * $p < .1$.

models. This suggests that all three variables are effective in explaining the variation in the Gini index. Note that the author have used the log-log form of the equation, so the coefficients are all interpreted as elasticities.

3.2 Analysis

The coefficient for road density is −0.319, which means that every 1% increase in road density reduces the Gini index by 31.9%. The coefficient for rail density is −0.0948, meaning that a 1% increase in rail density reduces the Gini index by 9.48%. The coefficient for postal line density is −0.0399, meaning that a 1% increase in postal line density reduces the Gini index by 3.99%.

The results of the test illustrate that an increase in road density, railway density and postal line density can effectively reduce the Gini index, with the construction of a road network being highly effective, probably due to the flexibility of the road network and the financial agglomeration effect it brings. Extensive road construction links developed and less developed regions well, making the financial spillover effect from central cities more pronounced.

In addition to this, the road network can link various infrastructure facilities, such as motorways that can connect railway stations and airports, making the infrastructure transport network more efficient. In addition, the development of logistics networks is greatly dependent on the road network. Finally, the construction of roads itself generates many jobs and funds, which can greatly contribute to the level of internal circulation.

4 Limitations

There are some limitations to this paper. Firstly, infrastructure development encompasses many aspects, including a range of basic public construction, such as airline construction and bridge construction, in addition to the three factors mentioned in this paper. The three variables in this paper do not represent the level of infrastructure construction very completely. Moreover, there is a difference in the level of road and rail construction. For example, there may be a difference in the impact of effects brought about by highways versus secondary roads. Furthermore, there may be macro policy influences on the infrastructure planning of the provinces, such as the central government's Western Development Plan, which focuses on raising the level of infrastructure in the western provinces. These limitations will hopefully be addressed in further research in the future.

5 Conclusions

This paper uses the level of infrastructure in selected Chinese provinces as a factor to examine its impact on regional income inequality. In addition, the Gini index was chosen as a measure of income inequality and uses road density, railway density and postal line density as indicators of infrastructure levels. This paper uses a panel data approach with data from thirteen provinces in China for 2008, 2013 and 2018, while trying to control for some of the determinants to reduce selection bias. To address the issue of heteroskedasticity, the author chose to use robust standard deviations instead of general standard deviations.

The results show that an increase in the level of infrastructure significantly reduces the Gini index and reduces regional income inequality. The expansion of infrastructure networks reduces transport costs and increases transport efficiency, which in turn increases market potential. The development of local economies also increases incomes and reduces inequality. The most effective way of doing this is through the construction of road networks. The road network is more flexible and can effectively cover less developed rural areas, thus helping to develop special industries, increase employment and reduce poverty rates. Because of the agglomeration effect of China's current poor areas, connecting them to the national transport network can enhance the mobility of people, capital and technology, effectively activating local economic activities.

Acknowledgement. Thank you to all the teachers who have guided me, and the HTT band.

Firstly, I would like to show my deepest gratitude to my teachers and professors in my university, who have provided me with valuable guidance in every stage of the writing of this thesis. Further, I would like to thank all my friends and parents for their encouragement and support. Without all their enlightening instruction and impressive kindness, I could not have completed my thesis.

References

1. Zhang, X., Hu, Y., Lin, Y.: The influence of highway on local economy: evidence from China's Yangtze River Delta region. J. Transp. Geogr. **82**, 102600 (2020). https://doi.org/10.1016/j.jtrangeo.2019.102600
2. Knight, J.: Inequality in China: an overview. World Bank Res. Observer **29**(1), 1–19 (2014). https://doi.org/10.1093/wbro/lkt006
3. Sutherland, D., Yao, S.: Income inequality in China over 30 years of reforms. Camb. J. Reg. Econ. Soc. **4**(1), 91–105 (2011). https://doi.org/10.1093/cjres/rsq036

4. Tian, W.: Measurement of the Gini coefficient of provincial income and analysis of its trend. Econ. Math. **02**, 48–59 (2012). https://doi.org/10.19523/j.jjkx.2012.02.004
5. Gini index - China | Data. https://data.worldbank.org/indicator/SI.POV.GINI?locations=CN. Accessed 28 July 2022
6. Liu, Y., Liu, J., Zhou, Y.: Spatio-temporal patterns of rural poverty in China and targeted poverty alleviation strategies. J. Rural. Stud. **52**, 66–75 (2017). https://doi.org/10.1016/j.jrurstud.2017.04.002
7. Wan, G., Lu, M., Chen, Z.: Globalization and regional income inequality: empirical evidence from within China. Rev. Income Wealth **53**(1), 35–59 (2007). https://doi.org/10.1111/j.1475-4991.2007.00217.x
8. Zhou, Y., Song, L.: Income inequality in China: causes and policy responses. China Econ. J. **9**(2), 186–208 (2016). https://doi.org/10.1080/17538963.2016.1168203
9. Wang, Y., Wu, B.: Railways and the local economy: evidence from Qingzang railway. Econ. Dev. Cult. Change **63**(3), 551–588 (2015). https://doi.org/10.1086/680091
10. National Data. https://data.stats.gov.cn/english/easyquery.htm?cn=E0103. Accessed 28 July 2022

Accounting Measurement and Recognition of Digital Cryptocurrencies: Challenges, Practices, and Recommendations

Jiajun Ma(✉)

Department of Accounting, The London School of Economics and Political Science,
London WC2A 2AE, UK
631401040211@mails.cqjtu.edu.cn

Abstract. The emergence of digital cryptocurrencies has disrupted traditional financial systems and challenged existing methods of measuring and recognising financial transactions. This paper aims to explore the different methods and reasons for the accounting measurement and recognition of digital cryptocurrencies worldwide, summarise the findings, and provide recommendations for the accounting treatment of digital cryptocurrencies. Through a review of recent literature on accounting for digital cryptocurrencies and reference to the decisions made by various organisations and governments worldwide, this paper discusses the challenges posed by volatile prices, complex valuation methods, and the lack of uniform accounting standards. Additionally, the paper highlights the potential for fraud and accounting confusion created by cryptocurrencies, using real-world examples. The paper concludes that recognising digital cryptocurrencies as intangible assets and measuring them at fair value is the most appropriate accounting treatment, with proper disclosures to address the inherent risks. This paper provides valuable insights for academics, practitioners, and regulators in understanding the accounting treatment of digital cryptocurrencies.

Keywords: Digital Cryptocurrencies · Accounting Standards · Worldwide · Recommendations

1 Introduction

Digital cryptocurrencies have become a global phenomenon that has transformed the way we view and use money. Cryptocurrencies are defined as digital or virtual tokens that use cryptography for security and operate independently of central banks [1]. These currencies have disrupted traditional financial systems, presenting an alternative to decentralised fiat currency that operates on a peer-to-peer network. Cryptocurrencies utilise blockchain technology, a distributed ledger that records transactions securely and transparently. This technology provides an unparalleled level of security and anonymity, making it an attractive option for individuals seeking a high level of privacy in their financial transactions. Bitcoin, the first and most well-known cryptocurrency, was created in 2009 and has since paved the way for a multitude of other cryptocurrencies to emerge. Ethereum, Litecoin, and Ripple are just a few examples of the many cryptocurrencies that have gained significant traction in recent years [2]. These currencies offer unique features and benefits that have attracted a wide range of users, from tech enthusiasts to investors.

Cryptocurrencies have disrupted traditional financial systems, challenging the existing methods of measuring and recognising financial transactions. Cryptocurrencies' decentralised nature and lack of regulation have raised concerns over their use in illegal activities and the potential for fraud. Additionally, cryptocurrencies' accounting measurement and recognition pose significant challenges due to their volatile prices, complex valuation methods, and lack of uniform accounting standards. For example, in 2019, the US Securities and Exchange Commission (SEC) charged a cryptocurrency startup with defrauding investors out of over $25 million by making false statements about its product and exaggerating its profitability [3]. Another example of the potential accounting confusion created by cryptocurrencies is the issue of forks, which occur when a blockchain splits into two separate chains, resulting in the creation of a new cryptocurrency. The accounting treatment of forks can be complex, and the lack of clear guidance has led to inconsistencies in accounting practices across organisations. For instance, when Bitcoin underwent a hard fork in 2017, resulting in the creation of Bitcoin Cash, some organisations treated the new cryptocurrency as a dividend, while others recorded it as a separate asset [4].

This paper will examine the various methods and reasons for the accounting measurement and recognition of digital cryptocurrencies across different jurisdictions worldwide. It will explore the challenges posed by the volatile nature and lack of standardisation across markets and provide insights into the different accounting treatments for cryptocurrencies. Additionally, this paper will review the recent literature on accounting for digital currencies, including academic research, industry publications, and regulatory guidance.

To achieve this objective, this paper will reference the decisions made by various organisations and governments worldwide regarding the accounting treatment of cryptocurrencies. These include the International Accounting Standards Board (IASB), the US Financial Accounting Standards Board (FASB), International Financial Reporting Standards (IFRS), the Australian Accounting Standards Board (AASB), and others. This paper will also provide recommendations for the accounting treatment of digital cryptocurrencies based on a critical analysis of the current accounting practices and potential issues.

In summary, this paper aims to provide a comprehensive overview of the accounting measurement and recognition of digital cryptocurrencies worldwide. By examining the current accounting practices and providing recommendations, this paper will contribute to developing a standardised and transparent accounting framework for cryptocurrencies, ensuring accurate financial reporting and preventing potential fraud.

2 Literature Review

2.1 Accounting Recognition

There is still no consensus among countries and organisations on classifying cryptocurrencies. However, most accounting groups believe cryptocurrencies should be recognised as assets. It is also recognised as a liability in rare cases. According to a study by Hsu et al. [5], digital cryptocurrencies should be recognised as assets as they meet the definition of an asset under the International Financial Reporting Standards (IFRS). The study argues that digital cryptocurrencies possess monetary value, are controlled by the holder and can generate future economic benefits.

However, accounting groups have differing views on whether cryptocurrencies should be classified as intangible assets, financial instruments, inventories, or cash and cash equivalents.

2.2 Intangible Asset

According to Zinatullina et al. [6], the AASB has recognised digital cryptocurrencies as intangible assets. The AASB issued an interpretation in 2019 that clarified the accounting treatment of digital cryptocurrencies under Australian accounting standards. The interpretation states that digital cryptocurrencies meet the definition of an intangible asset and should be measured at fair value.

Pettersson et al. [7] found that the Swedish Financial Supervisory Authority (SFSA) issued guidelines in 2020 to treat digital cryptocurrencies as intangible assets and value them at fair value. Additionally, the European Securities and Markets Authority (ESMA) issued similar guidelines in 2019 for the treatment of digital cryptocurrencies as intangible assets.

In the United States, the FASB has not issued specific guidance on the accounting treatment of digital cryptocurrencies. However, Brink et al. [8] found that many companies in the United States have recognised digital cryptocurrencies as intangible assets. The study analysed the financial statements of 80 companies holding digital cryptocurrencies and found that 68 recognised digital cryptocurrencies as intangible assets.

Finally, a study by Ng et al. [9] found that the Singaporean government has recognised digital cryptocurrencies as intangible assets for tax purposes. This approach allows businesses and individuals to deduct expenses related to digital cryptocurrencies, such as mining and trading fees.

Overall, these articles suggest that various organisations, companies, and governments worldwide have recognised digital cryptocurrencies as intangible assets. The reasons for this recognition vary but often relate to the lack of physical form and the volatile nature of digital cryptocurrencies. Recognising digital cryptocurrencies as intangible assets allows businesses and investors to account for them more accurately and transparently.

2.3 Financial Instruments

Several studies have examined the recognition and measurement of digital currencies in various countries. Fanning and Gao [10] conducted a study on the accounting treatment of cryptocurrencies in Australia and found that they are recognised as investment instruments and valued based on fair value measurement. Biasioli and Malafronte [11] investigated the accounting treatment of Bitcoin by Italian companies and found that most companies recognise it as an investment instrument. Benkherouf [12] provided an overview of cryptocurrencies' accounting and financial reporting worldwide and found that most countries recognise digital currencies as investment instruments. Niranjan and Naik [13] compared the accounting standards for digital currencies in the United States, Europe, and Asia and found that most countries recognise them as investment instruments. Alkhazraji and Islam [14] examined the accounting treatment of digital currencies in the United Arab Emirates and found that they are considered investment instruments.

In summary, these studies highlight that digital currencies are recognised as investment instruments in accounting by various organisations, companies, and governments worldwide. There are three main reasons. Firstly, digital cryptocurrencies have been shown to possess monetary value, an essential characteristic of investment instruments. Secondly, digital cryptocurrencies are controlled by the holder, meaning that they can be bought and sold in the same way as traditional investment instruments. Finally, digital cryptocurrencies are capable of generating future economic benefits, as they can be used to purchase goods and services or exchanged for traditional currencies. These factors contribute to the recognition of digital cryptocurrencies as investment instruments for accounting purposes.

2.4 Inventory

A study by Iqbal et al. [15] investigated the accounting treatment of cryptocurrencies by the Malaysian government. They found that the Malaysian government recognises digital cryptocurrencies as inventory, which is consistent with their definition of tradable assets. The study also concluded that the Malaysian government measures cryptocurrencies at a lower cost and net realisable value.

Another study conducted by Oh and Kim [16] explored Korean companies' accounting treatment of cryptocurrencies. They found that Korean companies also recognise digital cryptocurrencies as inventory and measure them using the historical cost method.

Also, Adams and Booth [17] found that US firms recognise digital cryptocurrencies as inventory, reflecting their status as tradeable assets. They measure cryptocurrencies at market value.

Choi et al. [18] conducted a study on Japanese companies' accounting treatment of cryptocurrencies. They found that Japanese companies recognise digital cryptocurrencies as inventory and measure them using the FIFO (first in, first out) method. The study concluded that this method provides a reliable measure of the value of cryptocurrencies, especially during periods of high volatility.

Finally, a study by Hu et al. [19] investigated the accounting treatment of cryptocurrencies by the Chinese government. The study found that the Chinese government recognises digital cryptocurrencies as inventory and measures them using the weighted average method. The study suggests that this method is used because it provides a more stable measure of the value of cryptocurrencies.

In summary, the reviewed literature suggests that various organisations, companies, and governments worldwide recognise digital cryptocurrencies as inventory, which is consistent with their status as tradeable assets. Furthermore, the accounting measurement of cryptocurrencies is determined by the organisation, company or government and may vary according to different methods such as historical cost, market value, FIFO, and weighted average.

2.5 Cash and Cash Equivalents

Studies by Leoni and Santandrea [20], Kourtidis and Kakavas [21], Viljoen and Smith [22], Bhatia and Garg [23], and Oyeyiola and Adebisi [24] have explored the classification of cryptocurrencies as cash or cash equivalents. Their findings suggest that the classification of digital currencies depends on their specific characteristics, liquidity, and intended use. Factors such as the ability to convert quickly into cash and use it as a means of payment are also taken into consideration. The literature suggests that digital currencies can be classified as cash and cash equivalents, but the specific accounting treatment may vary depending on the jurisdiction and accounting standards used.

This analysis highlights that the acceptance of digital currencies as cash and cash equivalents for accounting purposes is being acknowledged by various organisations, businesses, and governments globally. It is manifest that the categorisation of digital currencies as cash and cash equivalents is contingent upon their liquidity and purpose.

2.6 Liability

Digital currencies are considered liabilities due to their nature as debt. The FASB defines a liability as an obligation for an entity to transfer assets or provide services to other entities in the future which arises from past transactions or events and is likely to result in a sacrifice of economic benefits. Therefore, digital currencies are classified as liabilities because they represent an obligation for the issuer to transfer assets or provide services to the holder in the future in exchange for the value received at the time of issuance [25]. Digital currencies can be considered a liability because they represent a promise by the issuer to deliver a certain amount of cryptocurrency in the future in exchange for something of value (e.g. fiat currency or goods and services).

For example, the IFRS Foundation asserts that digital currencies should be categorised as financial liabilities if they satisfy the criteria for a financial liability, which is an agreement that requires an entity to transfer cash or some other financial asset to another entity or to exchange financial assets or liabilities with another entity under terms that may be disadvantageous. In other words, if a digital currency involves a contractual obligation to deliver cash or another financial asset, or to exchange financial assets or liabilities, and the terms of the contract have the potential to put the issuer at a disadvantage, it meets the definition of a financial liability and should be recognised as such [26]. The United States Securities and Exchange Commission (SEC) has also recognised digital currencies as liabilities under certain circumstances, such as when they are offered in Initial Coin Offerings (ICOs) and represent a future obligation to deliver a certain amount of cryptocurrency to investors [27].

One example of digital cryptocurrencies being recognised as liabilities can be found in Facebook, Inc.'s accounting policies. In its 2021 annual report, Facebook states that it recognises its Libra digital currency as a liability, with the obligation to redeem the currency for its underlying assets. The accounting treatment aligns with Financial Accounting Standards Board (FASB) Accounting Standards Codification (ASC) Topic 480, which defines liabilities as obligations arising from past transactions or events and require settlement by providing goods, services, or other assets [28].

In summary, recognising digital currencies as liabilities in accounting practices is based on their nature as a form of indebtedness. Moreover, fair value measurement is commonly used to measure their value. As the use of digital currencies continues to grow, accounting standards need to keep pace with these developments and provide clear guidance on their accounting treatment.

3 Accounting Measurements

There are various reasons why the accounting measurement of digital cryptocurrencies differs from traditional financial assets. One primary reason is the decentralised nature of cryptocurrencies, which allows users to transact directly with each other without the need for intermediaries such as banks. This characteristic makes it difficult to trace and track transactions, leading to concerns over the accuracy and completeness of financial reporting. Additionally, the lack of regulation and standardisation in the cryptocurrency market makes it challenging to establish uniform accounting principles.

Another reason is the volatile and speculative nature of cryptocurrencies. The market value of digital currencies can fluctuate rapidly, resulting in significant gains or losses in a short period. This volatility presents challenges for accounting measurement, as the fair value of digital cryptocurrencies can be challenging to determine due to the lack of liquidity and transparency in the market.

Furthermore, the unique features of digital cryptocurrencies, such as the use of blockchain technology, add complexity to accounting measurement. The decentralised and distributed nature of blockchain technology makes it challenging to track and verify transactions, leading to difficulties in measuring and recognising digital currencies' value.

Overall, the reasons for the differing accounting measurement of digital cryptocurrencies are multifaceted, including decentralisation, lack of regulation, market volatility, and complex technological features.

3.1 Initial Measurement

According to the IFRS, digital cryptocurrencies should be initially measured at their fair value, which is defined as the amount for which an asset could be exchanged between knowledgeable and willing parties in an arm's length transaction [29]. However, the fair value of cryptocurrencies can be difficult to determine due to their volatile nature and lack of standardisation across markets.

Some organisations have taken alternative approaches to the initial measurement of digital cryptocurrencies. For example, the FASB in the United States has stated that digital cryptocurrencies should be initially measured at their cost, which is the amount paid to acquire the asset [30]. This approach is similar to the cost method used for inventory accounting, and it may be easier to implement than fair value accounting.

3.2 Subsequent Measurement

Subsequent measurement of digital cryptocurrencies can also be challenging due to their volatility. To address this, various organisations have developed different approaches. For example, the IASB proposed in 2019 to require the reclassification of digital currencies as inventory, with the subsequent measurement at lower cost and net realisable value [31]. In contrast, the FASB proposed to classify digital currencies as intangible assets, with the subsequent measurement at cost or fair value, whichever is more relevant [32].

3.3 Reasons Behind the Methods

The choice of the accounting treatment for digital cryptocurrencies is influenced by factors such as the purpose of holding the asset, the entity's business model, and the regulatory environment. Some organisations may prefer the fair value method for initial measurement because it reflects the asset's true market value, while others may prefer the cost method because it is easier to implement. Similarly, some organisations may prefer the fair value method for subsequent measurement because it provides a more accurate reflection of the asset's value at each reporting date, while others may prefer the intangible asset method because it reduces the need for frequent adjustments to the value of the asset.

4 Discussion

This paper has reviewed the existing literature on the accounting measurement and recognition of digital cryptocurrencies. The review indicates that there is an ongoing debate on how to classify and measure digital currencies in accounting records. Despite the widespread acceptance of digital currencies as assets, there is still a lack of consensus on whether they should be treated as cash and cash equivalents, inventory, financial instruments, or intangible assets. In addition, there are differing views on how to measure digital currencies, particularly with regard to initial and subsequent measurement.

Based on the literature review, this paper argues that the accounting recognition and measurement of digital currencies should not be rigidly defined. Rather, it should take into account the intent of the company holding the digital currencies. This means that companies should be flexible in classifying and measuring digital currencies based on their specific circumstances.

4.1 Cash and Cash Equivalents

Digital currencies can be used as a medium of exchange and are often held as a store of value. In some instances, they may be readily convertible into cash, making them functionally equivalent to cash or cash equivalents. For example, a company may hold Bitcoin as a means of payment to suppliers or to make investments. In such instances, digital currencies can be recognised as cash and cash equivalents.

4.2 Inventory

Digital currencies can also be held as inventory. In some cases, companies may mine digital currencies or acquire them for resale purposes. In such instances, they can be classified as inventory and measured at cost or net realisable value.

4.3 Financial Instruments

Digital currencies can also be classified as financial instruments. If a company holds digital currencies with the intent of trading, they should be recognised as financial assets or financial liabilities, depending on the nature of the transaction. Measurement of financial instruments will depend on the classification and fair value measurement principles.

4.4 Intangible Assets

Finally, digital currencies can also be recognised as intangible assets. In cases where digital currencies are held as long-term investments, they can be classified as intangible assets and measured at fair value.

5 Conclusion

In the face of the accounting dilemma of digital cryptocurrency, this paper puts forward the following suggestions for policies:

1. Companies should be allowed to classify and measure digital currencies based on their intent to hold them.
2. Companies should disclose the classification and measurement basis used for digital currencies in their financial statements.
3. Standard-setters should provide guidance on classifying and measuring digital currencies based on the company's intent and circumstances.
4. Regulators should continue to monitor the development of digital currencies and guide their accounting recognition and measurement as needed.
5. In conclusion, the accounting recognition and measurement of digital currencies are complex issues that require careful consideration. This paper suggests that there is a lack of consensus on how to classify and measure digital currencies. This paper argues that companies should be allowed to classify and measure digital currencies based on their specific intent and circumstances. Policymakers should provide guidance and monitor the development of digital currencies to ensure that accounting standards remain relevant and informative.

References

1. Nakamoto, S.: Bitcoin: A Peer-to-Peer Electronic Cash System (2008). Bitcoin.org. https://bitcoin.org/bitcoin.pdf
2. Chiu, J., Koeppl, T.: The economics of cryptocurrencies-bitcoin and beyond. Bank Canada Rev. **2018**(4), 52–60 (2018)
3. Securities and Exchange Commission.: SEC Charges Issuer With Conducting $25 Million Ponzi Scheme (2019). https://www.sec.gov/news/press-release/2019-189
4. BDO USA, LLP.: Accounting for Cryptocurrency: How to Apply Existing GAAP to Today's Transactions (2018). https://www.bdo.com/insights/assurance/accounting-for-cryptocurrency-how-to-apply-existin
5. Hsu, J., Li, Y., Yang, T.: Should digital currencies be recognised as assets? Evidence from the International Financial Reporting Standards. J. Int. Financ. Manag. Acc. **30**(2), 92–114 (2019)
6. Zinatullina, A., Voronova, L., Krivchenko, E.: Recognition of digital assets in accounting practices of Australia. J. Account. Manag. **11**(2), 47–57 (2021)
7. Pettersson, J., Olofsson, T., Hultén, P.: Accounting treatment of cryptocurrencies: evidence from Sweden. J. Appl. Acc. Res. **22**(4), 630–651 (2021)
8. Brink, M., Barlow, R., Malafronte, I.: Digital assets in financial statements: an analysis of reporting practices among US public companies. J. Inf. Syst. **34**(1), 23–39 (2020)
9. Ng, J.H., Tan, W.K., Wong, P.: Singapore's approach to digital currencies: income tax implications. J. Int. Tax. **31**(2), 29–39 (2020)
10. Fanning, J., Gao, B.: The accounting treatment of cryptocurrencies - an Australian perspective. Aust. Account. Rev. **29**(3), 390–401 (2019)
11. Biasioli, F., Malafronte, E.: Cryptocurrencies in the financial statements: an empirical study on the accounting treatment and disclosure of Bitcoin. J. Appl. Acc. Res. **21**(5), 749–764 (2020)
12. Benkherouf, A.: The accounting and financial reporting of cryptocurrencies: an analytical study. J. Bus. Res. **134**, 397–407 (2021)
13. Niranjan, A., Naik, N.: Cryptocurrency accounting: a comparative analysis of the accounting standards in the United States, Europe, and Asia. Int. J. Financ. Econ. **27**(1), 47–65 (2022)
14. Alkhazraji, S., Islam, M.: The accounting treatment of digital currencies in the United Arab Emirates. Int. J. Account. Audit. Perform. Eval. **19**(1), 1–16 (2023)
15. Iqbal, M., Ali, S., Hasan, M.: Accounting treatment of cryptocurrencies by the Malaysian government. J. Financ. Reporting Account. **17**(2), 244–257 (2019)
16. Oh, W.Y., Kim, H.: Accounting treatment of cryptocurrencies by Korean companies. J. Asian Financ. Econ. Bus. **7**(10), 181–188 (2020)
17. Adams, S.J., Booth, P.: Accounting treatment of cryptocurrencies by US firms. Int. J. Account. Inf. Manag. **29**(1), 48–63 (2021)
18. Choi, H.J., Kim, J.Y., Park, Y.H.: Accounting treatment of cryptocurrencies by Japanese companies. J. Account. Public Policy **41**(4), 106994 (2022)
19. Hu, Y., Chen, C., Wang, Y.: Accounting treatment of cryptocurrencies by the Chinese government. China Financ. Rev. Int. **13**(1), 92–107 (2023)
20. Leoni, F., Santandrea, G.: Are cryptocurrencies a new type of cash? J. Money Laundering Control **22**(4), 476–484 (2019)
21. Kourtidis, C.D., Kakavas, E.P.: The accounting treatment of cryptocurrencies as cash and cash equivalents: a review of the current literature. Int. J. Econ. Account. **11**(3), 210–231 (2020)
22. Viljoen, E., Smith, A.: Digital currencies: a review of the accounting treatment and disclosure requirements in South Africa. J. Econ. Financ. Sci. **14**(1), 1–15 (2021)

23. Bhatia, T., Garg, R.: Accounting treatment of cryptocurrencies: a comparative study of IFRS and US GAAP. J. Appl. Acc. Res. **23**(1), 135–151 (2022)
24. Oyeyiola, S.S.,Adebisi, O.M.: The accounting treatment of cryptocurrencies in Nigeria: a review of the current practice. Int. J. Account. Auditing Perform. Eval. (2023)
25. Financial Accounting Standards Board (FASB). Accounting Standards Update 2019-02—Entertainment—Films—Other Assets—Film Costs (Subtopic 926-20) and Entertainment—Broadcasters—Intangibles—Goodwill and Other (Subtopic 920-350) (2019). Improvements to Accounting for Costs of Films and License Agreements for Program Materials. https://www.fasb.org/jsp/FASB/Document_C/DocumentPage?cid=1176169778466&acceptedDisclaimer=true
26. International Financial Reporting Standards (IFRS) Foundation (2021). IFRS 9 Financial Instruments. https://www.ifrs.org/issued-standards/list-of-standards/ifrs-9-financial-instruments/
27. SEC. Framework for 'Investment Contract' Analysis of Digital Assets. US Securities and Exchange Commission (2019). https://www.sec.gov/files/digital-asset-framework.pdf
28. Facebook, Inc. Form 10-K Annual Report for the Fiscal Year Ended December 31, 2020. Securities and Exchange Commission (2021). https://www.sec.gov/ix?doc=/Archives/edgar/data/1326801/000132680122000012/fb-20211231.htm
29. International Accounting Standards Board (IASB). IFRS 13 Fair Value Measurement (2018). https://www.ifrs.org/issued-standards/list-of-standards/ifrs-13-fair-value-measurement/
30. Financial Accounting Standards Board. Accounting for digital assets. FASB Staff Q&A (2020). https://www.fasb.org/cs/ContentServer?c=FASBContent_C&cid=1176169376261&d=&pagename=FASB%2FFASBContent_C%2FGeneralContentDisplay
31. Dixon, R.: IASB proposes clarifications to IFRS 9, IFRS 7 and IFRS 16. J. Account. **228**(4), 14 (2019)
32. Peng, K.: FASB proposes accounting guidance for digital assets. CPA J. **90**(8), 18 (2020)

Study on the Spillover Effect of Shanghai Crude Oil Futures Price Fluctuations on New Energy Stock Prices

Zhang Xinyu(✉)

Hunan Normal University, Changsha 410000, Hunan, China
sylvia1011zhang@qq.com

Abstract. The impact of crude oil price fluctuations on the economic operation and development of a region is concretely reflected in macroeconomic indicators such as real GDP and its growth, inflation level, unemployment rate, and exchange rate. This paper focuses on the spillover effect of crude oil futures price fluctuations on new energy stock prices, and mainly selects Shanghai crude oil futures and China new energy stock index as the research objects. The former is selected from the daily closing price of Shanghai Crude Oil Futures and the latter is selected from the CSINE Index. The data sample period is from January 4, 2022 to June 30, 2022, and 117 sets of data are obtained. In addition, this paper mainly uses VAR model and GARCH-BEKK model to analyze the volatility spillover effect of Shanghai crude oil futures and China new energy stocks from the variance and covariance of the two markets. The research results show that the volatility of Shanghai crude oil futures price has a positive impact on the volatility of China's new energy industry stock price in the short term, and the contribution of Shanghai crude oil futures price to the new energy industry stock price is increasing and the degree of mutual influence is gradually increasing.

Keywords: Shanghai Crude Oil Futures Prices · New Energy Stock Prices · Spillover Effects · VAR Model · GARCH-BEKK Model

1 Introduction

In 1981, New energy sources were defined at the United Nations Conference on New and Renewable Sources of Energy as: the modern development and utilization of traditional renewable energy sources based on new technologies and materials, replacing fossil energy sources with inexhaustible and recurring renewable energy sources that have limited resources and are polluting to the environment. New energy is also known as energy other than conventional energy. For decades, crude oil, the representative of traditional energy, has continued to develop as a pillar industry of the national economy. However, recent years, people's awareness of environmental protection is gradually rising, and the government has introduced many favorable policies regarding new energy sources, which has led to a constant influx of various creative new energy vehicles into the Chinese market. Especially in the first half of 2022, as oil prices continue to rise in the Chinese market, more and more people are choosing new energy sources. These show that people's choice of new energy sources is influenced by traditional energy sources.

In previous studies on the impact of oil price fluctuations on new energy prices, scholars have mostly focused on the causal relationship and spillover effects between the two. However, considering the time-varying nature, the relationship between old and new energy sources is also in flux, which is why opposite findings are obtained at different times. Therefore, this report focuses on the relationship between old and new energy in the first half of 2022. And most of the existing related studies take international crude oil futures and new energy stock prices around the world as the research objects, while China's Shanghai crude oil futures market only started to be officially listed for trading in 2018, and there are few articles directly studying domestic crude oil futures and new energy stock prices, considering that the prices of domestic crude oil futures are somewhat different from those of international crude oil futures, this paper hereby studies the relationship between Shanghai crude oil futures market and China The relationship between the Shanghai crude oil futures market and the Chinese new energy market is studied in this paper. The specific method is chosen to combine the time-varying nature mentioned earlier, and a VAR model is first established in the study of the spillover relationship between the two, and then a GARCH-BEKK model is established in combination with volatility.

The old and new energy sources are alternative to each other, and the change in the pattern of the two reflects the change in the global economic development mindset today, which is to reduce carbon emissions and pursue long-term development. In China, the development of the new energy sector cannot be separated from the background of the huge increase in demand for crude oil. This study will help policy makers to provide incentives for the development of new energy, and provide reference for investors in their investment strategies, and provide suggestions for new energy listed companies to avoid crude oil market risks and better raise capital in the future.

2 Literature Review

Research on the relationship between crude oil prices and new energy share prices was first conducted abroad by Henriques and Sadorsky [1], who found that crude oil prices are the Granger cause of share prices of alternative energy companies [1]. Subsequently, Tang and Tang [5] conducted a cointegration test on oil prices and new energy consumption and found that new energy consumption increases with crude oil prices [5]. Both studies point to a relationship between the price of crude oil and the price of new energy stocks. So, in 2012, Kumar [2] explored the interaction between crude oil prices and new energy stock prices based on a VAR model and concluded that there is a positive relationship between the two [2]. However, subsequent domestic studies gave less similar results. Qin [6] studied the impact of traditional energy prices on the share prices of new energy companies based on VAR model and CAPM-GARCH model and found that the impact of oil prices on the share prices of new energy companies was limited and it was mainly influenced by coal prices [6]. Soon after this, domestic research results of significant relationship between the two were given, Hu and Ding [7] used VAR-Asymmetric-BEKK model to compare the volatility spillover effect between international crude oil prices and new energy stock prices under the condition of considering China's stock market quotes and without stock market quotes, and the results showed that when the factor of stock market quotes was excluded, the volatility spillover effect of international crude oil prices on new energy stock prices in China was significant [7]. And in Dutta [3, 4], the analysis shows that the crude oil volatility index has a significant impact on U.S. clean energy stock returns and is a better predictor of clean energy stock price volatility [3]. Meanwhile Reboredo et al. [4] developed a wavelet analysis model to study the relationship between oil prices and clean energy company stock prices and reconfirmed that: crude oil prices are the Granger cause of clean energy company stock prices [4]. Subsequently, in China, Wang et al. [8, 11] conducted a study on the spillover effect of oil price on the share price of new energy in China. The findings show that there is a unidirectional spillover of oil prices on stock prices of the new energy industry in China. In this paper, we directly study the spillover effect between old and new energy sources in China based on this and choose VAR-GARCH-BEKK model to conduct the related study [11].

3 Spillover Effect

Spillover effects are widely distributed in the fields of environmental development, knowledge technology, economic production, and finance. In the financial field, they mostly refer to the situation in which the price of a product caused by a price change in other related markets is influenced by time, information transmission, and other signals, resulting in price fluctuations in other markets as well, i.e., the price of a product is not only related to its own factors, but also influenced by the prices of related product markets. Therefore, each crude oil futures market is influenced by information such as supply and demand within the market and between neighboring markets, national policies, and market movements [13]. The transmission of information spillover in the Shanghai crude oil futures market may include the price impact of the domestic crude oil futures market with the domestic new energy stock market. For the capture of this spillover, this study analyzes it through the mean spillover effect resulting from the change in the mean market price and the volatility spillover effect due to the change in market price volatility.

4 Data Selection and Processing

CSI New Energy Index (CSINE) data from CSI (https://www.ine.cn/) and Shanghai Crude Oil Futures daily closing price data from Sina Finance (https://finance.sina.com.cn/). The sample of Shanghai crude oil futures data covers the period from January 4, 2022 to June 30, 2022, with 117 sets of data. CSI New Energy Index is selected based on the date and number of the Shanghai crude oil futures data sample, and both are selected from the daily closing prices. In the empirical process, to reduce the serial correlation of the time series data for better data analysis, the logarithm of each starting data is taken from [8]. Subsequently, the daily closing price of Shanghai crude oil futures in SHYY and the stock price of new energy industry in ZZXN will be used in this paper.

Figure 1 shows the series trend of China's new energy stock price and the daily closing price of Shanghai crude oil futures before logarithmization. Shanghai crude oil

[Figure showing two line series: Shanghai Crude Oil Futures Closing Price and CSI New Energy Index Closing Price, with data points labeled. Crude oil futures values shown: 444.74, 529.5, 565.2, 627.1, 650.5, 629.7, 636, 700.2, 734.9, 691.5. New Energy Index values: 4133.47, 3789.37, 4249.41, 4020.16, 3660.35, 2889.49, 3377.74, 3698.65, 4293.4. Dates from 20220104 to 20220620.]

Fig. 1. China's new energy stock price and Shanghai crude oil futures daily closing price series chart.

futures prices are less volatile overall, compared to new energy stock prices which are a bit more volatile.

The descriptive statistics in Table 1 show that the ZZXN series is right-skewed with a cusp distribution and a small probability of outliers in the current data. The SHYY series is right-skewed with a flat broad-peaked distribution and a small probability of outliers in the current data.

Table 1. Descriptive statistics results.

Variable Name	Sample size	Maximum value	Minimum value	Average value	Standard deviation	Median	Variance	Kurtosis	Skewness	Coefficient of variation (CV)
ZZXN	117	8.428	7.947	8.256	0.102	8.288	0.01	0.132	−0.825	0.012
SHYY	117	6.653	6.181	6.456	0.13	6.491	0.017	−0.865	−0.572	0.020

5 Methods

5.1 VAR Model

Smoothness test. To avoid the phenomenon of "pseudo-regression", the ADF unit root test is used in this paper. The following regression equations are available.

$$y_t = \partial + \emptyset_1 y_{t-1} + \emptyset_2 y_{t-2} + \ldots + \emptyset_p y_{t-p} + u_t \tag{1}$$

Extended definitions can be checked at:

$$\begin{cases} H_0: \mu = 0 \\ H_1: \mu < 0 \end{cases} \tag{2}$$

In (3) and (4), y_t is the column vector of endogenous variables, which represents the closing price of Shanghai crude oil futures or CSI New Energy Index at time t, respectively; p represents the previous p periods; ∂ is the intercept vector; $\emptyset_p$ and H are the coefficient matrices to be estimated; u_t is the error term with zero mean and constant variance distribution, independent of the other vectors; H represents the conditional covariance matrix.

VAR Model. Expression (3) with VAR(p)

$$y_t = \emptyset_1 y_{t-1} + \ldots + \emptyset_p y_{t-p} + H x_t + \varepsilon_t, t = 1, 2, \cdots, T \tag{3}$$

In (3), y_t, x_t, ε_t are column vectors and $\emptyset_p$ and H are coefficient matrices to be estimated. Generally speaking, each variable has smoothness is a prerequisite for building VAR, and if the variables are not smooth, they need to be differenced to obtain smoothness or there is a cointegration relationship between the variables to build VAR model.

Impulse Response Function. As an Example, Take the Binary VAR.

$$\begin{cases} x_t = a_1 x_{t-1} + a_2 x_{t-2} + b_1 z_{t-1} + b_2 z_{t-2} + \varepsilon_{1t}, \\ z_t = c_1 x_{t-1} + c_2 x_{t-2} + d_1 z_{t-1} + d_2 z_{t-2} + \varepsilon_{2t} \end{cases} t = 1, 2, \cdots, T \tag{4}$$

(4) where a_i, b_i, c_i, d_i is a parameter, x_t and z_t denote the closing prices of Shanghai crude oil futures and CSI New Energy Index at time t, and the perturbation term $\varepsilon_t = (\varepsilon_{1t}, \varepsilon_{2t})'$, set the following white noise vector.

$$\begin{aligned} & E(\varepsilon_{it}) = 0, & \forall ti = 1, 2 \\ & \text{var}(\varepsilon_t) = E(\varepsilon_t \varepsilon_t') = \{\sigma_{ij}\}, & \forall t \\ & E(\varepsilon_{it} \varepsilon_{is}) = 0, & \forall t \neq s i = 1, 2 \end{aligned} \tag{5}$$

5.2 GARCH-BEKK Model

GARCH(p, q) The mathematical expression of

$$y_t = x_t' \gamma + \mu_t, \mu_t \sim N\left(0, \sigma_t^2\right) \tag{6}$$

$$\sigma_t^2 = \varepsilon_0 + \sum_{i=1}^{p} \alpha_i \mu_{t-1}^2 + \sum_{j=1}^{p} \beta_j \mu_{t-1}^2 \tag{7}$$

where (6) is the mean equation, (7) is the variance equation, y_t and x_t denote the closing price of Shanghai crude oil futures and the closing price of CSI New Energy Index at time t, and p and q are the orders of the GARCH and ARCH terms, respectively. The equation of BEKK is as follows.

$$\begin{aligned} h_{11,t} &= c_{11}^2 + a_{11}^2 \varepsilon_{1,t-1}^2 + 2a_{11}a_{21}\varepsilon_{1,t-1}\varepsilon_{2,t-1} + a_{21}^2 \varepsilon_{2,t-1}^2 + b_{11}^2 h_{11,t-1} + 2b_{11}b_{21}h_{21,t-1} + b_{21}^2 h_{22,t-1} \\ h_{21,t} &= c_{11}c_{21} + a_{11}a_{21}\varepsilon_{1,t-1}^2 + (a_{21}a_{12} + a_{11}a_{22})\varepsilon_{1,t-1}\varepsilon_{2,t-1} + a_{21}a_{22}\varepsilon_{2,t-1}^2 + b_{11}b_{21}h_{11,t-1} \\ & + (b_{11}b_{22} + b_{21}b_{12})h_{21,t-1} + b_{21}b_{22}h_{22,t-1} \\ h_{22,t} &= c_{21}^2 + c_{22}^2 + a_{12}^2 \varepsilon_{1,t-1}^2 + 2a_{12}a_{22}\varepsilon_{1,t-1}\varepsilon_{2,t-1} + a_{22}^2 \varepsilon_{2,t-1}^2 + b_{12}^2 h_{11,t-1} + 2b_{12}b_{22}h_{21,t-1} \\ & + b_{22}^2 h_{22,t-1} \end{aligned} \tag{8}$$

where $h_{11,t}$ and $h_{22,t}$ denote the conditional variance of Shanghai crude oil futures and CSI New Energy at time t, respectively, and $h_{21,t}$ denotes the conditional covariance between the two markets at time t. In the structural equation of the conditional variance of Shanghai crude oil futures, the coefficients a_{11} and b_{11} are the ARCH and GARCH effects of the closing price of Shanghai crude oil futures, respectively, while a_{21} and b_{21} are the respective effects of the stochastic disturbance and conditional variance from CSI New Energy Index on the ARCH and GARCH effects of Shanghai crude oil futures. Similarly, a_{22} and b_{22} are the ARCH effect and GARCH effect of the closing price of CSI New Energy Index, respectively, while a_{12} and b_{12} are the ARCH effect and GARCH effect of CSI New Energy from the random disturbance and conditional variance of Shanghai Crude Oil Futures, respectively. Therefore, the volatility spillover effect between Shanghai crude oil futures price and CSI New Energy Index price can be determined by whether the corresponding coefficients are significantly zero.

6 Empirical Study and Analysis

6.1 VAR Model

Table 2. CSI new energy index data ADF test.

ADF Inspection Form							
Variables	Difference order	t	p	AIC	Threshold value		
					1%	5%	10%
ZZXN	0	−1.26	0.647	−464.268	−3.488	−2.887	−2.58
	1	−9.904	0.000***	−459.976	−3.489	−2.887	−2.58
	2	−6.465	0.000***	−436.034	−3.493	−2.889	−2.581

Note: ***, **, * represent 1%, 5%, 10% significance levels, respectively

Table 3. ADF test for Shanghai crude oil futures data.

ADF Inspection Form							
Variables	Difference order	t	p	AIC	Threshold value		
					1%	5%	10%
SHYY	0	−2.027	0.275	−417.167	−3.491	−2.888	−2.581
	1	−6.382	0.000***	−409.769	−3.491	−2.888	−2.581
	2	−7.485	0.000***	−386.592	−3.493	−2.889	−2.581

Note: ***, **, * represent 1%, 5%, 10% significance levels, respectively

Table 4. Comparison of different lag orders.

Lagging order	logL	AIC	SC	HQ	FPE
0	182.033	−8.753	−8.706	−8.734	0
1	508.29	−14.336*	−14.193*	−14.278*	0.0*
2	505.817	−14.299	−14.06	−14.202	0
3	501.233	−14.224	−13.888	−14.087	0
4	499.409	−14.196	−13.762	−14.02	0
5	495.99	−14.14	−13.606	−13.923	0
6	493.343	−14.096	−13.462	−13.839	0
7	496.86	−14.164	−13.428	−13.865	0
8	493.306	−14.103	−13.264	−13.763	0
9	490.169	−14.049	−13.106	−13.667	0
10	485.762	−13.97	−12.921	−13.545	0
11	484.012	−13.94	−12.784	−13.472	0

Table 5. Model parameter estimation table.

Parameters	Estimated volume	ZZXN	SHYY
ZZXN(-1)	Coefficient	0.979	−0.007
	Standard deviation	0.024	0.03
	t-statistic	40.327	−0.228
SHYY(-1)	Coefficient	0.015	0.954
	Standard deviation	0.019	0.023
	t-statistic	0.819	40.668
Constants	Coefficient	0.075	0.355
	Standard deviation	0.27	0.335
	t-statistic	0.279	1.061

From Table 2 and Table 3, it can be seen that the significance P-value of both ZZXN series and SHYY series is 0.000*** at the level of significance at the difference of order 1, and the original hypothesis is rejected, and both ZZXN series and SHYY series can be considered as being smooth time series (Tables 4 and 5).

The stability test results of the VAR (1) model of SHYY and ZZXN are shown in Fig. 2 below: all the points are located within the unit circle, from which it can be judged that the VAR system is stable, and the model can further do impulse response analysis and variance decomposition (Figs. 3 and 4).

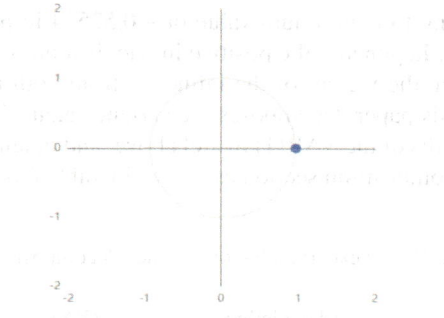

Fig. 2. Unit circle test results of VAR model.

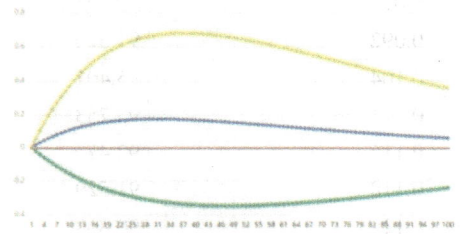

Fig. 3. SHYY (yellow) impacting ZZXN (green).

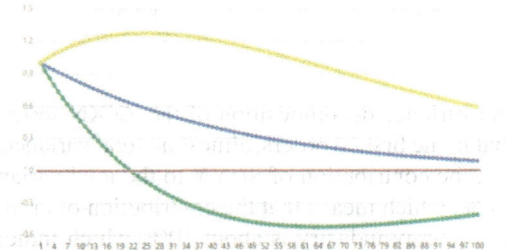

Fig. 4. ZZXN (yellow) impacting ZZXN (green).

According to the results of the above graph, it can be seen that the response of ZZXN to the shock from SHYY starts to fall rapidly to a negative value in the first period and drops to a minimum value of -0.34755 in period 48, after which it enters a slow rising phase, and according to the trend it can be inferred that it tends to 0 after a longer period of time, and the adjustment of ZZXN to the shock from SHYY ends, which indicates that the movement of crude oil futures price brings a negative impact on the new This indicates that the movement of crude oil futures price brings reverse shock to the stock price of new energy industry, and the futures price has a negative effect on the stock price movement in the initial stage, and this negative effect lasts for a long time. The response of ZZXN to its own shock, on the other hand, reaches a maximum in the first period, and then enters a long-term downward channel, dropping to a negative value in period 22 and falling to a minimum value of −0.52514 in period 65, after which it slowly converges to 0. In general, the positive impact is more significant.

In order to analyze the weight of the influence from both itself and SHYY in the variation of ZZXN, this paper decomposes the variance analysis of the ZZXN forecast error based on the results of the VAR(1) model above, and obtains some results selected from the variance decomposition section as shown in Table 6 below.

Table 6. Partial excerpt table of variance decomposition results.

Number of steps	Standard deviation	ZZXN%	SHYY%
1	0.025	100	0
10	0.071	99.163	0.837
20	0.092	97.326	2.674
30	0.104	95.401	4.599
40	0.111	93.753	6.247
50	0.116	92.47	7.53
60	0.118	91.529	8.471
70	0.12	90.867	9.133
80	0.121	90.415	9.585
90	0.122	90.114	9.886
100	0.122	89.918	10.082

Table 6 shows the variance decomposition of the ZZXN series within the order of 100. It can be seen that in the first 10 orders, almost no total variance comes from SHYY. as the order increases, the contribution of SHYY to the total variance increases slowly and finally stays at 10%, which means that the contribution of crude oil futures price to the stock price of new energy industry is about 10%, which indicates that SHYY has some influence on ZZXN but not much i.e. the price transmission shock is not obvious and the trend expectation of ZZXN has a great influence on own market has a great impact.

6.2 Estimation Results of the GARCH-BEKK Model

Many literatures proved that the GARCH(1,1) model has a better fit, so a GARCH(1,1)-BEKK model was established to study the volatility spillover relationship between Shanghai crude oil futures prices and China's new energy stock prices, and the empirical results were realized through WinRATS, as shown in Table 7 below.

Table 7. GARCH-BEKK estimation results.

Variable	Coeff	Std Error	T-Stat	Signif
Mean(1)	6.520668	0.010969	594.47978	0.00000000
Mean(2)	8.294104	0.005919	1401.29799	0.00000000
C(1,1)	−0.023213	0.005470	−4.24382	0.00002197
C(2,1)	0.004614	0.006162	0.74880	0.45398054
C(2,2)	0.016623	0.002793	5.95265	0.00000000
A(1,1)	0.988715	0.089392	11.06043	0.00000000
A(1,2)	0.025062	0.023959	1.04606	0.29553483
A(2,1)	−0.009904	0.030760	−0.32197	0.74747558
A(2,2)	1.020570	0.082679	12.34371	0.00000000
B(1,1)	−0.242329	0.201039	−1.20539	0.22805406
B(1,2)	0.072744	0.028570	2.54619	0.01089070
B(2,1)	0.059278	0.039268	1.50956	0.13115665
B(2,2)	0.093270	0.178004	0.52398	0.60029543
Shape	635295.469917	1129554.628550	0.56243	0.57382305

Note: Convergence in 93 Iterations.
Final criterion was $0.0000000 \leq 0.0000100$.
Usable Observations 117.
Log Likelihood 336.93765280.

A, B, C, and D in the first column of Table 7 are matrix elements, where C(i, j) represents the elements of the constant term matrix C, A(i, j) is the element of the measurement ARCH effect matrix A, and B(i, j) is the element of the measurement GARCH effect matrix B. i, j = 1, 2, where 1 is the closing price of Shanghai crude oil futures and 2 is the closing price of CSI Xinjiang Energy Index. The following results and analysis can be obtained from Table 7.

(1) Firstly, the elements A(1,1), A(2,2) on the diagonal of matrix A and B(1,1), B(2,2) on the diagonal of matrix B are significant at the same level and the coefficients are not zero, indicating that the Shanghai crude oil futures market as well as China's new energy stock market have ARCH effects as well as GARCH effects on their own historical fluctuations. In terms of coefficients, the absolute value of the coefficient of matrix A is larger than the absolute value of the coefficient of matrix B, indicating that the spillover effect of shocks in the two markets is significantly stronger than the variance spillover effect of the two markets themselves. In terms of risk accumulation, the diagonal elements are all significant, indicating a stronger risk accumulation effect in the two markets, but it is known above through the VAR(1) model: price transmission shocks in the two markets in the price transmission relationship are not significant. This indicates that the stronger risk accumulation in both markets is not expressed through price transmission.

(2) A(1,2) and A(2,1) and B(1,2) and B(2,1) are compared numerically under T-stat, and we can find that Shanghai crude oil futures price volatility has a greater effect on CSI New Energy Index price volatility in the short term. Meanwhile, we can find that the price fluctuation of Shanghai crude oil futures has a positive effect on the price fluctuation of CSI New Energy Index regardless of the long term or short term, while the price fluctuation of CSI New Energy Index has a negative effect on the price fluctuation of Shanghai crude oil futures in the short term and a positive effect in the long term based on the positive and negative nature of the data.

7 Conclusions and Recommendations

In this paper, VAR and GARCH-BEKK models are used to analyze the spillover effect of Shanghai crude oil futures price volatility on new energy stock prices. Both models suggest that Shanghai crude oil futures price volatility has an impact on new energy stock price volatility. However, the empirical results in this paper are not quite the same as those shown in previous related studies, probably because the specific indices and sample intervals selected by different studies are different. As time changes, the world is also changing all the time: new policies, changes in market demand, etc., which closely affect the spillover effect between Shanghai crude oil futures price fluctuations and new energy stock prices. The GARCH-BEKK model also demonstrates the different performance of the relationship in the long and short term. The reason for the positive results is perhaps because the new energy is more negatively affected by the epidemic, while the crude oil futures have some policy control, and only finally in the VAR (1) model, it is presented that the impact of crude oil futures is not very large.

Based on the above analysis, the following recommendations are made: from the government's perspective, promote the construction of China's energy futures price system represented by Shanghai crude oil futures, the price guidance and discovery function of futures can also promote the improvement of China's energy market; at the same time, also strengthen the support for the new energy industry, provide preferential policies to investors in the new energy industry to encourage investment. From the company's experience perspective, it is necessary to continuously pay attention to domestic and international energy price changes, conduct professional planning as well as risk management, while strengthening internal management, making prudent investment decisions, and taking advantage of national policies as well as its own advantages to plan future development. From the investor's point of view, it is important to have a sensitive insight and pay attention to the situation in time, so that you can take the initiative to understand some factors that can easily affect crude oil futures and new energy stock prices, flexibly match the assets in your hands, and hedge the stock market through crude oil futures to effectively hedge the risks.

Although this paper studies the spillover effect of Shanghai crude oil futures price volatility on new energy stock prices, the choice of model and data selection are different from other studies, resulting in different research results. And although this paper has studied that price transmission has a certain role, it is not the main factor of risk accumulation between old and new energy, and these shortcomings still need to be solved by subsequent related studies.

References

1. Henriques, I., Sadorsky, P.: Oil prices and the stock prices of alternative energy companies. Energy Economics **30**(3), 998–1010 (2008)
2. Kumar, S., Managi, S., Matsuda, A.: A stock prices of clean energy firms, oil and carbon markets: a vector autoregressive analysis. Energy Econ. **34**(1), 215–226 (2012)
3. Dutta, A.: Oil price uncertainty and clean energy stock returns: new evidence from crude oil volatility index. J. Cleaner Prod. 1157–1166 (2017)
4. Reboredo, J.C., et al.: Wavelet-based test of co-movement and causality between oil and renewable energy stock prices. Energy Econ. 241–252 (2017)
5. Tang, J.C., Tang, Y.J.: An empirical analysis of the impact of oil price fluctuations on new energy development and utilization. Price Monthly **4**, 11–14 (2010)
6. Qin, T.C.: Traditional energy and carbon trading prices and new energy stock prices: an analysis based on VAR and CAPM-GARCH models. Technol. Econ. Manag. Res. **12**, 120–124 (2014)
7. Hu, Q.L., Ding, M.Y.: Study on the volatility spillover effect of international crude oil prices on stock prices in China's new energy industry. Financ. Financ. **3**, 78–84 (2016)
8. Shen, J., Yang, Z.W., Qiao, J.L.: Forecasting analysis of forestry output value based on seasonal time series model. J. Nanjing Forestry Univ. (Nat. Sci. Ed.) **42**(5), 185–190 (2018)
9. Bi, Y.M.: Study on the Risk Spillover Effect of China's Crude Oil Futures Price and Energy Stock Index in the Context of Epidemic. Chongqing University of Technology and Industry, Chongqing (2021)
10. Si, X.L., Yang, A.J.: Study on the correlation between Shanghai crude oil futures prices and China's new energy stock prices. China Forestry Econ. **2**, 103–106 (2021)
11. Wang, C.Y., Chen, Y.F., Jin, X.: Study on the transmission effect of international oil prices on China's new energy market. Quant. Econ. Technol. Econ. Res. **4**, 131–146 (2018)
12. Zang, X.J.: Analysis of the Correlation Between Domestic and International Energy Prices and China's New Energy Stock Prices Based on Multivariate VAR-GARCH-BEKK. Sichuan University, Sichuan (2021)
13. Yang, S.X.: Study on the Linkage Between Shanghai Crude Oil Futures Prices and International Crude Oil Futures Prices. Guizhou University of Finance and Economics, Guizhou (2020)

Exploring the Impact of Social Economic Status on Migrant Workers' Sense of Social Equity from the Economic Sociology Perspective

Hu Xinrui(✉)

China University of Labor Relations, No.45, Zeng Guang Road, Hai Dian District, Beijing 100089, People's Republic of China
h854931965@163.com

Abstract. Society is greatly influenced by whether social members perceive social resources as being distributed in a reasonable manner. This is known as the level of social equity. Here, starting from the perspective of economic sociology, socioeconomic status is decomposed into subjective socioeconomic status and objective socioeconomic status, and community integration is decomposed into three dimensions: community identity, community interaction, and community participation. The method of multiple regression is used to analyze socioeconomic status. The study found that both subjective and objective socioeconomic status had an impact on migrant workers' sense of social equity, and the three dimensions of community integration had statistical significance for migrant workers' sense of fairness. The more frequent the interaction, the more frequently the community organization is provided with comments or suggestions, and the greater the sense of fairness. Finally, based on the research conclusions, some countermeasures and suggestions are put forward to enhance the sense of social equity for migrant workers.

Keywords: Socioeconomic Status · Community Integration · The Sense of Social Equity

1 Introduction

Since the mid-1990s, tens of millions of migrant workers have come to cities to do business and work every year. Although the vast majority of them have not yet obtained official status compared to urban residents, they have gained a certain amount of economic income [1]. But due to the restrictions of the household registration system and human capital, migrant workers cannot achieve free movement in the labor market and enjoy the same social services that urban residents have, especially in the next generation's education, and this policy causes many social problems. Among them, the most important is migrant workers' social integration. There are two types of groups of migrant workers, one is traditional migrant workers, and the other is the new generation. Compared to the traditional population, the new generation of migrant workers has different motivations and lifestyles, and a different degree of willingness to integrate into the city [2]. Thus, the problem is becoming more complex.

From the perspective of economic sociology, this paper intends to analyze the impact of socioeconomic status and urban community integration on migrant workers' sense of social equity.

A sense of social equity is an important goal pursued by individuals. Socialism with Chinese characteristics has entered a new era, and people's needs for a better life are becoming more and more extensive. Understanding migrant workers' sense of social equity will help governments know the limitations of current work and understand how to improve in the next stage to build a more harmonious society.

2 Literature Review

2.1 Social Justice of Migrant Workers

The theoretical explanation of fairness can be examined from a variety of perspectives, including the economy, management, society, and psychology. Among them, Adams Du's comparative theory is the main representative, and social equity is perceived through social comparison. In addition, the structure-determination theory states that equity is perceived through position Y in the social structure. Finally, the theory of life experience analyzes equity from the perspective of daily life practice, which helps special groups such as migrant workers to sense the equity of electricity. The social equity that affects migrant workers mainly comes from the experience of fairness in life practice. It is a subjective concept that is difficult to define absolutely but can be obtained through relative comparison.

This will be the research content of this paper. One of the purposes of social security is to maintain fairness. The goal of establishing a social insurance system is to promote social equity; migrant workers are socially marginalized groups, and their sense of social equity is important. In this paper, the dependent variable is the sense of social justice of migrant workers, mainly to study the impact of social security.

2.2 Research Gap

Social equity is an important goal of human society. People's need for a better life is becoming more extensive. It not only puts forward higher requirements for material and cultural life but also has increasing requirements in democracy, rule of law, fairness, justice, security, and the environment. People's demands for fairness and justice are related to the sound development of society. With the change of migrant workers into the city and their occupation and status since the reform and opening up, the income level of migrant workers has improved, and the social communication objects and communication methods have also changed accordingly [3]. Urban communities have become an important field for migrant workers' lives. This paper intends to analyze the impact of socioeconomic status and urban community integration on the sense of social equity of migrant workers from the perspective of economic sociology. Political philosopher Rawls believes that justice is the primary value of the social system and that, including opportunities, income, wealth, and self-esteem, all social values should be equally distributed. Fairness and justice are distinct but related concepts. Although justice also contains the meaning of fairness, with more value orientation, focusing on the basic values of society is justified. Although the focus on fairness and justice is different, both have the meaning of fairness, justice, and equality.

On the influencing factors of social equity, there are three main ways to explain the current academic circles: one is the social comparison theory, according to which people's sense of social equity comes from social comparison, which includes comparison with others and comparison with their own past. That is, compared with others or their own past situation, the higher the evaluation of their social and economic status, the higher the sense of social equity. The second is attribution theory. This view holds that the sense of social equity depends on the attribution of social inequality. Different attributions have an important impact on people's fair judgement and subsequent emotions and behaviors. These factors include personal ability, education level, family background, wealth gap, unfair treatment, organizational factors, and so on. In the attribution of social inequality, the relationship factor is very important. The more social inequality is attributed to the relationship factor, the more society is considered unfair.

The previous works of literature focused on the unique perspective of social psychology to study the subjective aspects of social equity issues. Feeling and judging a sense of equity is a subjective experience and an internal process, and the standard of a sense of equity is a socially constructed, shared psychological reality that is maintained and constructed through different levels of individuals, groups, or organizations, and society. On the one hand, social institutions or social norms can prompt people to form a sense of equity or inequity; on the other hand, equity or inequity experiences can prompt people to form important social attitudes and bring about corresponding behavioral consequences. Migrant workers are a special group produced in the process of contemporary China's modernization [4], and they have an important impact on China's social and economic development. With the rapid development of China's economy [5], generations of migrant workers have flocked to the cities, and their problems in urban life, urban adaptation, and urban integration have been paid more and more attention by all parties. Among them, the issue of equity is the most basic and important issue. From the subjective feelings of migrant workers about the sense of social equity, discussing the individual reasons and deep-seated social reasons that affect their sense of equity, as well as the relationship between their sense of equity and their behavioral tendencies, will help people analyze the historical and dynamic issues. From the standpoint of grasping migrant workers' sense of equity, combine their individual psychology with their social background, and combine their psychology and behavior to more accurately understand migrant workers' real situation [6].

Among them, socioeconomic status refers to the position of an individual or group in society, which is generally measured in two ways: one is through objective indicator measurement, that is, based on income, education level, and occupation; the other is through objective mixed indicator measurement, which includes both objective and subjective indicators such as self-assessment of socioeconomic status, income perception compared with others, or one's own past. Many disciplines are focusing on the concept of social equity. There are related studies in economics, psychology, management, and sociology. Different disciplines have different research priorities and research methods. Economics focuses on the study of social equity from the perspective of distribution;

psychology focuses on the psychological level, such as the impact of individuals' views of equity on social equity; and management mainly focuses on inequality in organizations, such as the values of employees and the relationship between employees. How trust level and corporate performance affect employees' sense of equity, etc. Sociology studies the sense of social equity from a macro perspective, including social class, the household registration system, social interaction, and social integration, and this paper will choose the subjective indicators.

3 Theoretical Foundation

The theoretical basis of this paper is mainly researched and analyzed from the following three aspects; the specific contents are as follows:

3.1 The Sense of Social Equity and Its Influencing Factors

The political philosopher Rawls believes that justice is the primary value of social institutions and that all social values, including opportunity, income, wealth, and self-esteem, should be distributed equally. Equity and justice are both distinct and related. Fairness emphasizes the "same scale" of measurement standards, which is used to prevent double standards in social treatment; although justice also includes the meaning of fairness, it has more value orientations, focusing on whether the basic values of society are legitimate. Although fairness and justice have different emphases, both have the meanings of fairness, justice, and equality. The fairness discussed in this paper mainly refers to a subjective judgement of social members on whether the distribution of social resources is reasonable. The concept of fairness includes both value orientation and evaluation criteria.

The sense of social equity is an essential aspect of human emotional development, a basic attitude and moral value judgement of human beings, and a subjective feeling for the whole society. The sense of social equity is a hot spot of concern in many disciplines. There are related studies in economics, psychology, management, and sociology. Different disciplines have different research priorities and research methods. Economics focuses on the study of social equity from the perspective of distribution; psychology focuses on the psychological level, such as the impact of an individual's view of justice on social fairness; and management mainly focuses on inequality in organizations etc. Sociology mostly studies the sense of social equity from a macro perspective, with more representative perspectives including social class, the household registration system, social interaction, and social integration [7].

Regarding the factors affecting the sense of social equity, there are three main ways to explain the current academic circles: one is social comparison theory, that is, people's sense of social equity comes from social comparison, which includes comparison with others and comparison with their own past. That is, compared with others or their own past situation, the higher the evaluation of one's own socioeconomic status, the higher the sense of social equity. The second is the attribution theory, which holds that the sense of social equity depends on the attribution of social inequality. Different attributions have an important impact on people's fair judgement and subsequent emotions and behaviors.

These factors include personal ability, education level, family background, wealth gap, unfair treatment, organizational factors, etc. In the attribution of social inequality, relational factors are crucial. The more social inequality is attributed to relational factors, the more unfair society is considered. The third is structural determinism, that is, people's sense of sense of social equity depends on their social status. The higher the social status, the more social resources they have, and the higher the sense of social equity. At the same time, some scholars' research on the new generation of migrant workers found that people with a relatively high position in the social structure have a lower sense of social equity.

Regarding migrant workers' sense of social equity, studies have found that factors such as their socioeconomic status, personal income, and social interactions may all have an impact on the group's sense of social equity.

3.2 Research on Socioeconomic Status

Socioeconomic status refers to the position of an individual or group in society and is generally measured in two ways: one is through objective indicator measurement, that is, based on income, education level, and occupation; the other is through a mixture of subjective and objective The indicator measurement method includes both objective indicators and subjective indicators such as self-assessment of socioeconomic status and income perception compared with others or oneself in the past. Socioeconomic status not only measures an individual's social mobility but also influences the attitudes and daily behaviors of members of society. Existing studies on the urbanization of migrant workers have found that the socioeconomic status of migrant workers will affect the support of their children and the elderly, which in turn affects the mobility of individual migrant workers and their families; migrant workers found in their interactions with urban residents that their own income, treatment, and many other aspects are at a disadvantage, which in turn creates a sense of relative deprivation and social injustice.

3.3 Research on Community Integration

Community integration is an extension of social integration. Early social integration focused on the nature of integration, emphasizing that integration has the cohesive characteristics of individuals and groups. Research in recent years has emphasized that social integration is a process. Through mutual influence, mutual integration, and emotional exchange between different subjects, different subjects are finally integrated into a common culture. Domestic research on integration issues mainly focuses on the social integration of migrant workers. The social integration of migrant workers generally refers to the urban integration of migrant workers, which mainly includes the aspects of economy, culture, identity, social participation, and social interaction. Specifically, it refers to non-discrimination in employment, no difference in housing, and social interaction. Non-territoriality, equivalence in social security, etc.

Although "integration" and "integration" have similar connotations, the two concepts can reflect differences in research perspectives. The term "integration" is more commonly used in foreign studies on immigration, focusing on the social integration of immigrant labor, including physical, social, and psychological integration, which is often linked to the rights of immigrants and emphasizes that immigrants should be treated equally in terms of rights. Domestic scholar Yang Juhua has made a systematic analysis of "integration" and "integration" [8]. She believes that "fusion" has been systematically analyzed. She believes that "integration" is two-way, referring to the fusion of the two cultures of the inflow and the outflow, mutual influence and mutual penetration, no distinction between primary and secondary, reflecting the equal relationship between the two cultures; "integration" is a one-way process. Rather, it is a two-stage process in which the floating population actively adapts to the culture of the flowing place. In her opinion, the current direction of China's floating population is from the countryside to the city, and the disadvantaged culture flows into the mainstream culture. Therefore, the use of the word "integration" can better reflect the real situation of migrant workers. However, at present, the demographic composition of migrant workers has undergone great changes, and the identities of migrant workers in different age groups are also different. The old generation of farmers has a preference for the identity of "farmer," while the new generation of farmers has a preference for the identity of urban "community members." Staying in cities in the future will be the choice of most of the new generation of migrant workers. In view of the changing times and the dominant position of the new generation of migrant workers in the composition of the entire migrant worker group, this paper uses the concept of "integration," which emphasizes the two-way interaction process between migrant workers and urban residents in the integration of urban communities. See the two as having an equal relationship. There are two main research paths on the community integration of migrant workers: one is to regard community integration as the condensation of social integration; the other is to discuss community integration from the perspectives of humanistic spirit, value recognition, and interpersonal interaction. This study belongs to the former, which regards community integration as a condensation of social integration [9].

4 Method

The research assumptions and relevant empirical measurement variable analysis methods are employed in this case. The specific details are as follows:

4.1 Research Hypothesis

Socioeconomic Status and Sense of Social Equity. There have been some studies on the relationship between socioeconomic status and a sense of social equity, but the conclusions of the studies are quite different. Regarding education, some studies have shown that education has a positive impact on the sense of social equity, i.e., the higher the education level, the stronger the sense of social equity. Regarding income and occupation, some studies show that high-income earners have a higher sense of social equity than low-income earners, and some studies show that income and occupational status have no significant impact on sense of social equity. Regarding subjective socioeconomic status, existing studies have found that social comparison is the main source of a sense of social equity. Compared with others or with oneself in the past, the higher the evaluation of one's own socioeconomic status, the stronger the sense of social equity. Given that socioeconomic status has an impact on the perception of fairness, we propose the following assumptions:

Hypothesis 1: The higher the education level of migrant workers, the greater the sense of social equity.

Hypothesis 2: Compared with ordinary households living in cities, the higher the household income of migrant workers, the higher their sense of social equity.

Hypothesis 3: Compared with ordinary families in their hometowns in rural areas, the higher the family income of migrant workers, the higher their sense of social equity.

Community Integration and Migrant Workers' Sense of Social Equity. Existing studies have shown that the degree of urban integration of migrant workers is related to their perception of fairness, and the migrant unions with a higher degree of integration believe that society is more fair. From the perspective of economic sociology, an individual's economic life and social life will affect and restrict each other. The individual's "economic man" attribute will make him pay attention to his own interests and changes in his social and economic status; the individual's "social man" attribute will make them pay attention to their own well-being in society and community life. Therefore, the individual's life experience in the community and the change in the individual's socioeconomic status compared with others have become the main factors affecting the individual's sense of social equity. Therefore, we make the following guess:

Hypothesis 4: The higher the degree of community integration of migrant workers, the higher their sense of social equity.

4.2 Analysis of Relevant Empirical Measurement Variables

Data Sources and Sample Composition. The data for this study are mainly from the questionnaire survey data of the National Social Science Fund Project "Urbanization of Migrant Workers from the Perspective of Social Quality." From January to March 2016, the research group conducted a large-scale interview-style questionnaire survey with migrant workers in Xiamen, Suzhou, Dongguan, Shenzhen, and other places. Quota sampling was conducted according to age, gender, and occupation, and a total of 1,370 questionnaires were distributed; 1356 questionnaires were recovered, and 1291 valid questionnaires were obtained. The basic composition of the samples is shown in Table 1.

Variable Measurement. This study starts from the perspective of economic sociology and explores migrant workers' sense of social equity from the perspective of socioeconomic status and urban community integration. Therefore, the independent variables of this study are socioeconomic status and community integration, and the dependent variable is sense of social equity. Each variable is measured as follows:

This study employs both subjective and objective measures of socioeconomic status in order to measure socioeconomic status. Considering that most of the occupational categories of migrant workers are manual labor and the level of their occupations is not very different, in terms of objective indicators, occupational indicators are not used and only education is used. The degree and income are used as measurement indicators, and income includes "personal wage income, total household income, and income from rural areas"; the subjective measurement indicators use "comparison with ordinary households in the city" and "economic income compared with ordinary households in the rural hometown". Status, the answers include five levels of "very low," "lower," "average," "higher," and "much higher," with 1 to 5 points assigned, respectively.

It is important to note that urban communities are mainly the primary places where urban residents live. The essence of community integration is psychological identification and behavioral interaction. Therefore, this study adopts the measurement method of Lu Zirong and Xu Jinyan and measures migrant workers along three dimensions: community identification, community interaction, and community participation. The degree of community integration and the specific indicators are as follows:

Community identity refers to residents' preference, trust, and sense of belonging to community space, interpersonal, cultural, and management models due to life interaction within a certain geographical scope, which reflects community members' recognition of the community and the trust among community members. This research operationalizes it as "Do the following conditions apply to your community: you are proud to be a resident of your community; community residents trust each other; community neighbors often help each other; the community accepts people from different backgrounds; and migrant workers can participate in community affairs?" The answers are divided into five levels of "do not understand," "very inconsistent," "somewhat inconsistent," "somewhat consistent," and "very consistent," and assign 1 to 5 points, respectively. The Cronbach's alpha reliability coefficient for the five items was 0.908. The factor analysis was carried out according to the principal component analysis method, and the maximum variance method was used for rotation. A total of one factor was extracted, and the explained variance was 73.3%.

Community communication mainly refers to the communication between migrant workers and local residents in their daily lives, which is specifically operationalized as "the frequency of contacting local residents in the following places: residential quarters, vegetable markets, shopping malls, restaurants, etc., and public places such as squares and parks." The answer includes four levels of "very little," "few," "more," and "very much," and assigns 1 to 4 points, respectively. The Cronbach's alpha reliability coefficient of these three items was 0.776. In order to simplify the project, the factor analysis method was used, and the maximum variance method was used to rotate. A total of one factor was extracted, and the explained variance was 69.5%.

Community participation refers to the participation of community residents in various public activities organized by the community. This study operationalized the community participation of migrant workers as: "frequency of providing opinions or suggestions to community organizations" and "whether to participate in community residents' joint proposals." The former measures the individual community participation of migrant workers, which is quantified as " There are three levels of "never participation," "occasional participation," and "frequent participation," which are assigned 1 to 3 points respectively; the latter measure is the collective community participation of migrant workers and urban residents under the joint cooperation, which is quantified as "never thought about," "never participate," "may participate," and "have participated," assigning 1 to 4 points respectively.

Socioeconomic status not only measures an individual's social mobility, but also influences the attitudes and daily behaviors of members of society. Community integration mainly focuses on the nature of integration, emphasizing that integration has

Table 1. Basic information of sample composition.

categorical variable		Number of samples	Percentage (%)	continuous variable	mean	standard deviation
gender	male	618	48.6	age	42.3	140
	female	653	51.4			
political status	party member	55	4.7	personal monthly income	3574	3538
	non-party member	1122	95.3			
Account type	rural	1215	96.4	monthly household income	6923	6812
	City	46	3.6			
education level	Elementary school and below	121	9.5	monthly consumption expenditure	3044	2379
	junior high school	520	40.9			
	High School/Transit	464	36.5			
	college	133	10.5			
	Undergraduate and above	33	2.6			

the cohesive characteristics of individuals and groups. As the gap in socioeconomic status becomes more obvious, the corresponding community integration process will be slower. There is a certain degree of discrimination in socioeconomic status in some aspects, but community integration makes up for this discrimination. Community integration is non-discriminatory and non-differentiated in some aspects, and the community is the basic unit of society. To build a harmonious social state, it is necessary to reduce the sense of difference in socioeconomic status and enhance community integration. Therefore, socioeconomic status and community integration have a mutually reinforcing relationship.

Migrant workers' sense of social equity is the dependent variable of this study. Regarding the measurement of migrant workers' sense of social equity, we measure it by constructing an index system. This article uses the subjective measurement method to concretely operationalize migrant workers' sense of social equity as an indicator of "do you think today's society is fair?" The answers include "very unfavorable." fair, relatively unfair, average, fairly fair, and very fair. Through frequency analysis, it can be seen that the sense of social equity among migrant workers is shown in Table 2 below.

From the data in Table 2, nearly 40% of migrant workers believe that their sense of social equity is average, and the proportion of people who feel unfair is 37.7%, far

Table 2. Status Quo of Migrant Workers' Sense of social equity.

degree	Frequency	effective percentage
very unfair	147	11.7
more unfair	326	26.0
generally	501	39.9
fairer	250	19.9
very fair	31	2.50
total	1255	100

exceeding the proportion of people who feel fair (22.4%). It can be seen that, in general, migrant workers do not have a high sense of social equity.

This study employs a multiple linear regression model to examine the main factors influencing the sense of social equity of the new and old generations of migrant workers, with socioeconomic status and community integration as independent variables. The main reason for selecting these two factors is that socioeconomic status receives more emphasis from the material economy and personal income angles. Another independent variable focuses on the individual's subjective feelings. They are two different perspectives on how to measure migrant workers' sense of social equity. Then we chose migrant workers' sense of social equity as dependent variables; gender, age, and living conditions were included in the model as control variables.

5 Results

On the influence of control variables. In the three models in Table 3, neither gender nor age have statistical significance on migrant workers' sense of social equity. In Models 1 and 2, living conditions are statistically significant; that is, the better the living conditions, the greater the sense of social equity among migrant workers. However, the statistical significance disappears after adding the independent variable of community integration, indicating that community integration has a greater impact on migrant workers' sense of social equity. The data for this study are mainly from the questionnaire survey data of the National Social Science Fund Project "Urbanization of Migrant Workers from the Perspective of Social Quality."

This paper focuses on the effects of independent variables. First, let's look at the impact of socioeconomic status on migrant workers' sense of fairness. From models 2 and 3, it can be found that the three indicators of family income, income compared with ordinary urban households, and education level have statistical significance on migrant workers' sense of social equity. The higher the family income, the stronger the sense of social equity; the higher the evaluation of one's own income compared with the average urban family, the stronger the sense of social equity; compared with the primary school and below, the college degree and above have a higher sense of social equity. a sense of fairness, thereby verifying hypotheses 1 and 2. Among these three indicators, family income has a relatively greater impact on migrant workers' sense

Table 3. Multiple regression analysis (standard regression coefficient).

predictor variable	model one	model two	model three
gender	0.016(0.008)	0.035(0.018)	0.022(0.011)
age	−0.005(−0.005)	−0.005(−0.001)	−0.005(−0.008)
living conditions	0.100(0.087)***	0.072(0.062) **	0.036(0.031)
personal city income		0.006(0.008)	0.016(0.024)
Average monthly household income		0.126(0.113)***	0.056(0.099)***
household rural income		0.045(0.057)*	0.046(0.054)*
Income compared to the average urban household		0.078(0.062)*	0.068(0.055)*
Income compared to the average rural household		0.000(0.021)	0.000(0.016)
education level:			
junior high school	0.079(0.039)	0.079(0.039)	0.079(0.039)
high school or secondary school	0.108(0.053)	0.150(0.073)	0.150(0.073)
college	0.279(0.086)**	0.321(0.099)**	0.321(0.099)**
Undergraduate and above	0.536(0.086)**	0.481(0.071)**	0.481(0.071)**
community identity			0.187(0.182) ****
community engagement			0.090(0.088) ***
Community Involvement:			
individual participation			0.150(0.120) ***
group participation			−0.094(−0.071) *
constant	3.506****	3.619****	3.313****
N	1255	1255	1255
Adjusted R square	0.005	0.025	0.081
F	2.622**	3.227****	6.633****

Note: * $P < 0.1$, ** $P < 0.05$, *** $P < 0.01$, *** *$P < 0.001$

of social equity. Compared with ordinary rural households, income is not statistically significant for social equity, and Hypothesis 3 has not been tested. And it can be seen that the survival status data in the predictor variables is basically consistent with the existing research conclusions and that there is not much difference.

Secondly, looking at the impact of community integration on migrant workers' sense of fairness. In Model 2, the three dimensions of community identification, community interaction, and community participation have statistical significance on migrant workers' sense of fairness, and Hypothesis 4 is verified. Judging from the standard regression coefficient, the standard regression coefficient of the community identity dimension reaches 0.182, which has the greatest impact on migrant workers' sense of social equity.

The stronger migrant workers' community identity, the more frequent their interactions with local residents, and the greater their sense of social fairness. From the perspective of community participation, the higher the frequency of providing opinions or suggestions to community organizations, the higher the sense of social fairness, but the indicator of "joint proposals" presents a negative impact, that is, the frequency of participating in community residents' joint proposals. The higher the value, the lower the sense of social equity, indicating that individual community participation helps migrant workers to improve their sense of social equity, while group community participation is the opposite. Community residents provide opinions or suggestions to their community organizations, which is an act of actively participating in community public affairs and expressing community civil rights. Participation in such activities can enhance participants' sense of political efficacy and thus improve migrant workers' sense of social equity. Group participation will reduce migrant workers' sense of social fairness. It may be because the event, which was jointly proposed with community residents, is tricky. For example, the joint proposed event involves a larger scope and involves more interest groups, and community members are generally passive. Status, even if the community residents are all organized, it cannot be reasonably resolved, thus creating a sense of unfairness. The purpose of migrant workers participating in joint proposals is generally to protect their own interests. However, due to the lack of sound laws and regulations on the protection of labor rights and interests in my country, the interests of migrant workers are often suppressed, and a good result cannot be obtained. Therefore, the greater the participation in the joint proposal, the stronger the sense of unfairness.

6 Discussion

According to the research analysis of this paper, the following discussions can be made on this topic from the following three aspects:

6.1 Migrant Workers Generally Have a Low Sense of Social Equity

Due to the existence of the household registration system, migrant workers cannot obtain urban household registration and can only exist as others in the city. The system hinders the integration of migrant workers and urban residents. However, some scholars believe that even if migrant workers obtain urban hukou, it cannot guarantee a good integration between migrant workers and urban residents, and the hukou system is only one aspect. To enhance the sense of social equity of migrant workers, we must start from the perspective of combining the macrosystem and community governance, promote the community integration of migrant workers and urban residents, and enhance the dominant position of migrant workers in urban communities. The macrosystem design includes education, fair distribution of medical resources, and increased housing subsidies. From the perspective of community governance, it is necessary to enhance community capabilities by improving community service levels, innovating community management, and promoting the participation of migrant workers in their communities.

6.2 Socioeconomic Status Affects Migrant Workers' Sense of Social Equity

The sense of social equity of migrant workers is affected by subjective and objective socioeconomic status. Family income and education level are important factors that affect the sense of fairness. Meanwhile, social comparison also affects migrant workers' sense of social fairness. Since the reform and opening up, people's income levels have been continuously improved, and educational opportunities have also increased compared with the previous generation. At the same time, the gap between urban and rural areas has continued to widen. When migrant workers arrive in the city, their welfare reference group shifts from rural to urban ordinary families. When compared to ordinary urban families, it is easy to feel unfair. The research of Li Lulu et al. shows that in today's social transformation, people's mentality towards wealth distribution has changed to "worrying about inequity and even more injustice." So, while migrant workers' incomes should keep going up, the gap between the rich and the poor should get smaller, and there should be a more even distribution of income. These things are very important for giving migrant workers a better sense of social fairness.

6.3 Community Integration is an Important Factor Affecting Migrant Workers' Sense of Social Equity

This study found that community integration is an important factor affecting migrant workers' sense of social equity. The higher the degree of community integration, the stronger the migrant workers' sense of social equity. A higher degree of community integration can reduce the cost of community governance, adjust the interests and conflicts of various groups in the community, and maintain the harmony and stability of the community. It is an important measure to maintain community harmony and stability and promote community governance by enhancing the sense of belonging of migrant workers in the community, increasing the opportunities for migrant workers to participate in the community, and creating conditions for social interaction between migrant workers and local residents. Therefore, it is necessary to give full play to the roles of all parties through a comprehensive approach to jointly promote the community integration of migrant workers.

First, from the point of view of community identity, it is important to make sure that migrant workers and urban residents have the same rights at the level of system design and share the main role in community governance and community building. This can not only lower the cost of community governance, but it can also help migrant workers feel more like they belong in the community.

Secondly, from the perspective of community communication, it is necessary to build a community-based social network. For migrant workers in cities, due to social mobility, their old social networks dominated by rural communities have been broken, and new social networks dominated by urban communities cannot be quickly established. The situation will inevitably hinder the process of urbanizing migrant workers. Therefore, the community neighborhood committee must play the role of an advocate and facilitator in promoting the social interaction of the community residents.

Finally, from the perspective of community participation, conditions must be created so that migrant workers have more opportunities to participate in community development and community construction. What can really reflect substantive community participation is participation in community public welfare affairs. Creating conditions for migrant workers to participate in community public welfare affairs is an important measure to promote the integration of migrant workers in the community. Urban communities established from top to bottom under the will of the state must go through bottom-up governance. Therefore, community organizations such as community neighborhood committees organize collective activities to mobilize all community residents, including migrant workers, to participate in collective activities and community public affairs, which can not only enhance the daily communication between migrant workers and urban residents but also promote the transformation of urban communities into autonomous organizations.

7 Conclusion

The data analysis in this study shows that the accumulative number of migrant workers who feel that their sense of social equity is "average" or "unfair" is at a very high rate, indicating that migrant workers generally have a low sense of social equity. Social equity is an important condition for the benign operation and coordinated development of society. Improving the sense of social equity of migrant workers is of great significance not only to individual migrant workers, but also to the smooth operation of the entire society. Whether social members feel reasonable about the distribution of social resources, that is, the level of social fairness, is of great significance to the smooth operation of society. Here, starting from the perspective of economic sociology, socioeconomic status is decomposed into subjective socioeconomic status and objective socioeconomic status, and community integration is decomposed into three dimensions: community identity, community interaction, and community participation. Multiple regression methods are used to analyze socioeconomic status. The impact of community integration on migrant workers' sense of social equity. The study found that both subjective and objective socioeconomic status had an impact on migrant workers' sense of social equity, and the three dimensions of community integration had statistical significance for migrant workers' sense of fairness. The more frequent the interaction, the more frequently the community organization is provided with comments or suggestions, and the greater the sense of fairness. And the sense of social equity of migrant workers is affected by subjective and objective socioeconomic status. Family income and education level are important factors that affect the sense of fairness. Participation in such activities can enhance participants' sense of political efficacy and thus improve migrant workers' sense of social equity.

References

1. Mingzhong, L., Ziyu, L.: Internet use, class identity and happiness of rural residents. China Rural Economy, **2022**(08), 114–131 (2022). http://kns.cnki.net/kcms/detail/11.1262.f.20220902.1250.014.html
2. Jian, L., Tangbiao, X.: How does the sense of sense of social equity affect political participation?—Analysis based on CSS2019 national sample survey data. J. Cent. China Normal Univ. (Humanit. Soc. Sci. Ed.) **60**(06), 10–20 (2021)
3. Jinhua, L.: How does public service supply affect residents' life satisfaction?—analysis of moderating effect of social fairness. J. Sichuan Admin. Inst. **05**, 62–76 (2021)

4. Yunliang, Z., Jiankun, L.: Internet use, sense of social equity and doctors' trust: an empirical analysis based on CSS2013 data. News Univ. **08**, 18–34+117–118 (2021)
5. Yue, X.: Sense of social fairness, redistribution preference and welfare attitude: an empirical analysis based on CGSS2015 data. J. Dalian Univ. Technol. (Soc. Sci. Ed.) **42**(03), 101–109 (2021). https://doi.org/10.19525/j.issn1008-407x.2021.03.012
6. Feng, G., Bofeng, L., Xin, L.: Does university enrollment increase the sense of social equity? A breakpoint regression analysis based on subjective sense of fairness. Finan. Trade Econ. **42**(03), 111–127 (2021). https://doi.org/10.19795/j.cnki.cn11-1166/f.20210308.001
7. Yuanqi, Y.: Socioeconomic status and sense of social fairness: political participation under subjective perception—an empirical analysis based on CGSS2015. Secretary **06**, 37–47 (2020)
8. Yanfang, Z., Can, L., Zhenhua, H., Xian, J.: Analysis of influencing factors of civil society's sense of fairness under the new normal—based on CGSS2015 China comprehensive social survey data. Econ. Res. Guid. **17**, 178–184 (2020)
9. Zhengwu, M., Yudong, S., Wenzhang, L.: The level of equalization of public services and the sense of fairness in the civil society: an analysis based on CGSS 2013. Finan. Trade Res. **31**(04), 63–74 (2020). https://doi.org/10.19337/j.cnki.34-1093/f.2020.04.005

Microeconomic Study of the Digital Economy's Importance on Manufacturers' Management

Yuyan Wang(✉)

Beijing University of Technology, Beijing 100124, BJ, China
yuyan.wang@ucdconnect.ie

Abstract. With the advent of the area of the digital economy, digital factors provide new impetus for the production and investment of manufacturers. This article aims to explain the theories of firms using digital factors to earn profits through microeconomic theory and empirical data. It analyzes the character of the data as an emerging production factor and demonstrates theoretical and empirical research on scale economies. After analyzing the fixed cost effect of the supply-side and the network effect of the demand-side, the characteristics of increasing returns to scale of digital factors are obtained through the mathematical proof under Bertrand equilibrium. With the empirical evidence in the field of artificial intelligence and the data of Ali's e-commerce, this article confirmed the role of investment in the scale of statistics in the short run and long run. In addition, in order to cope with the implementation of manufacturers under a realistic business background, this article explains the application of price discrimination based on the binary selection model. Finally, from the perspective of the existing development problems in China, some prospects are put forward.

Keywords: Digital Economy · Returns to Scale · Price Discrimination

1 Introduction

Originating from network intelligence, the digital economy is a kind of new economy with information technology as its core and modern network as its carrier. It comes from a series of economic activities aimed at effectively applying communication technology and improving the economic structure [1]. With the rapid development of the new generation of information and intelligence technologies, the types, scale, and applications of data in human society are expanding at an unprecedented speed. Digital factors have been transformed from mere carriers of information into valuable resources and assets. Global economic governance is entering a new era through digital transformation. The resulting business model innovations have fundamentally changed consumer expectations and behavior, putting pressure on traditional firms and disrupting numerous markets [2]. As a pioneering branch of the economy, the digital economy requires a scientific knowledge base, which can exactly represent the transformation of global economic growth mode and the important impact of digital technology on the upgrading of industrial structure.

The fourth Plenary Session of the 19th CPC Central Committee highly affirmed the role of digital factors as a production factor that has the same importance as land, labor, technology, and capital. Through the analysis and arrangement of many theoretical proofs and empirical literature around the world, this article analyzes the characteristics of digital factors, proves the nature of increasing economies of scale, analyzes the theory of price discrimination, and provides some suggestions for future development.

According to the characteristics, the digital factors are non-competitive and the marginal cost of data tends to be zero. Digital factors can be easily replicated and disseminated at a low cost. There is no congestion caused by an additional person using it. In the long term, the exclusivity of the data may not be guaranteed. Business warfare happens unless it is hushed up. Under this perspective, digital factors even have the character of a public good. Additionally, the cost of data transmission and replication could be negligible. With the continuous selection of hardware and software generation, chip computing and storage capacity will enhance continuously, and the cost of data creation is falling. As a result, the cost of secondary authoring of raw data will fall, and the marginal cost of digital factors will be increasingly lower [3].

2 Scale Economy Theory Analysis

In microeconomics, traditional factors of production like capital and labor, are included in the Cobb-Douglas production function to describe the characteristics of constant return to scale or diminishing marginal return. However, digital factors are different from traditional factors of production. For manufacturers using data elements, economies of scale refer to the total profit of manufacturers increasing with the enlargement of scale. This section will use microeconomic theories to verify why the return to scale of digital factors shows an increasing trend.

2.1 The Supply and Demand Theory

From the fixed cost effect on the supply side, the replication and transmission cost of the data is almost negligible, and the variable cost of the manufacturer is low. However, the realization of data analysis and processing needs to invest enormous capital in preparing technological equipment and software. Therefore, fixed cost accounts for a relatively high proportion of the total cost of digital factors input. The larger input can share a higher proportion of fixed costs, which could reduce the average cost and bring increasing returns on the scale of data elements [4].

In terms of the demand-side network effects, digital production factors reveal strong network effects. For the direct network effect, consumers naturally choose products that already have more users. For the indirect network effect, systems with more users and content tend to attract more users. The existence of direct and indirect network effects enables vendors with larger data volumes to collect more potential data by attracting more users, which could provide more profits for the firms.

2.2 Expansion of Returns to Scale Theory

Hagiu and Wright assume that two firms compete in the background of the Bertrand Model [5]. Different from the Cournot model and the Stackelberg model, this model takes the price factors of production as a means of competition.

Assuming that the products of enterprises A and B are completely substitutable, consumers will always choose the products of the enterprise with lower prices if the prices are different. Therefore, the two enterprises will cut their prices to get more customers. Only when the price falls to $P_A = P_B = MC$ (the price equals its marginal cost) can a firm achieve the Bertrand equilibrium.

Definite γ as the correlation coefficient of economies of scale and make $\alpha(\gamma) \in (0, 1)$ as a market share function that is positively correlated with economies of scale. From the perspective of the post-pricing enterprise, by simplifying the formula of the Bertrand model, the price was defined as the following formula:

$$P_B = \frac{f_B(min\{Y_B - \overline{Y_B}\})}{1 - \alpha(\gamma)} \tag{1}$$

where $f_B(min\{Y_B - \overline{Y_B}\})$ is a digital factor learning function, Y_B represents the output and sales volume of digital factors, $\overline{Y_B}$ is the optimal learning effect level of production and sales.

The manufacturer's profit (π) is explored as follow:

$$\begin{aligned}\pi &= P_B \cdot Y_B - f_B(min\{Y_B - \overline{Y_B}\})Y_B \\ &= \frac{f_B(min\{Y_B - \overline{Y_B}\})}{1 - \alpha(\gamma)} \cdot Y_B - f_B(min\{Y_B - \overline{Y_B}\})Y_B \\ &= \frac{f_B(min\{Y_B - \overline{Y_B}\}) \cdot \alpha(\gamma)}{1 - \alpha(\gamma)} \cdot Y_B\end{aligned} \tag{2}$$

On the condition that other factors remain unchanged and are all positive constants, the derivative of manufacturer's profit can be shown as:

$$\frac{\partial \pi}{\partial \alpha(\gamma)} = f_B(min\{Y_B - \overline{Y_B}\}) \cdot Y_B \cdot \frac{1}{(1 - \alpha(\gamma))^2} \tag{3}$$

Since $\alpha(\gamma) \in (0, 1)$ π and $\alpha(\gamma)$ are positively correlated, which demonstrates that the profit of the manufacturer increases with the expansion of scale. It should be noted that this methodology is different from our previous testify (of using the Cobb-Douglas function) to prove the scale effect of traditional factors of production: suppose $q = f(K, L)$ is the production function, where K is the capital input of factors of production and L is the labor input of factors of production. When the capital and labor inputs are increased to λ times (λ is a constant) in the same proportion, the new output is $q' = f(\lambda K, \lambda L)$. If $q' = f(\lambda K, \lambda L) > \lambda q = \lambda f(K, L)$ exists, then the production function has the characteristic of increasing returns to scale.

However, in the hypothesis of Hagiu and Wright (2020), the Bertrand model is not a production pricing model, starting from the price elements. In other words, due to the different nature of digital factors and traditional factors of production, we cannot prove the effect of scale from the yield side. Meanwhile, the hypothetical $\alpha(\gamma)$ is a direct function related to the economies of scale. Therefore, the positive relation between π and $\alpha(\gamma)$ can prove the characteristic of increasing returns to scale.

2.3 Empirical Study on Economies of Scale

By conducting an empirical study on the marginal returns of data elements in the artificial intelligence industry, Posner and Weyl clarified that complex analysis functions only could be realized through large-scale data input. The input of digital production factors presents a periodical and wavy form of "increasing marginal return - decreasing marginal return", as Fig. 1 shown [6].

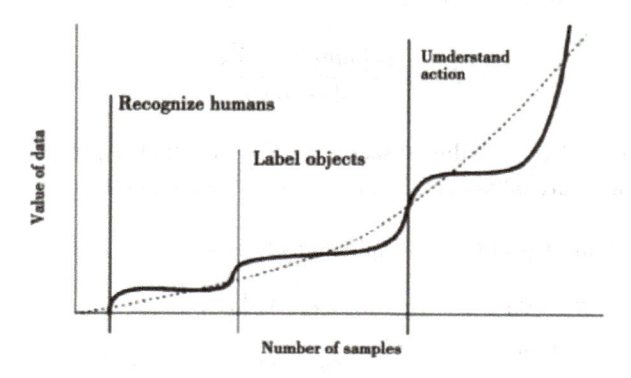

Fig. 1. Sample scale and data value in the artificial intelligence field [6].

Taking Ali's e-commerce platform as the research object, this section analyzes the scale economy level and turnover from 2003 to 2013 (see Fig. 2). The correlation between the digital economy and the firm's investment in the scale of the economy can be analyzed from the short term and long term [7].

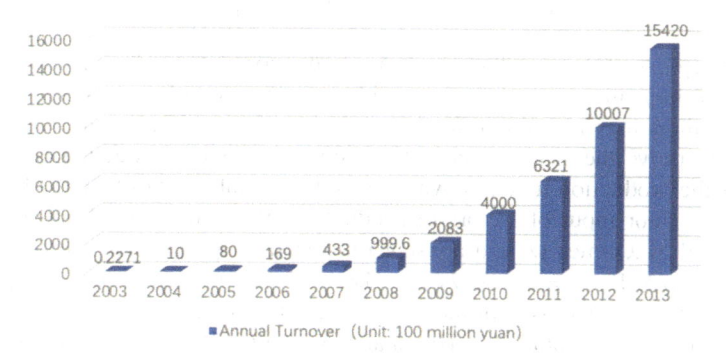

Fig. 2. Annual turnover of Ali's e-commerce.

Gross margin reflects the proportion between operating cost and operating revenue. The larger the sales gross margin is, the smaller the proportion of operating cost in net operating revenue is, and the stronger the enterprise's ability to obtain profits through sales is. As can be seen from Table 1, Ali's e-commerce presents an increasing trend in gross profit.

Table 1. Profitability ratios of Ali's e-commerce.

	2006	2007	2008	2009	2010
Profit margin	79.69%	79.80%	79.64%	79.40%	79.95%
The net profit margin on sales	42.54%	41.92%	41.43%	41.82%	42.17%
Return on equity (ROE)	22.26%	28.11%	43.69%	57.72%	67.12%
Return on total assets (ROA)	5.94%	6.58%	11.25%	15.32%	17.75%

Asset-liability ratio, debt service ratio, and interest service multiple reflect the company's long-term debt service ability, while liquidity ratio reflects the company's short-term debt service ability. From Table 2, Ali's e-commerce asset-liability ratio is decreasing year by year, reducing to 0.03 in the fifth year, and the company is in good financial condition. Interest coverage multiple is used to measure the ability to pay interest on loans, and it is an indicator to measure the ability of enterprises to pay interest on debts. From the above tablet, the company's interest guarantees multiple increases year by year in the next five years, with strong financial strength.

Table 2. Solvency ratios of Ali's e-commerce.

Long-term solvency ratios					
	2006	2007	2008	2009	2010
Asset-liability ratio	9.05%	7.96%	5.90%	4.21%	3.07%
Debt Service Coverage Ratios	0.35	0.19	0.09	0.05	0.03
Interest coverage ratio	227.13	331.61	705.25	1306.93	2049.87
Short-term solvency ratios					
	2006	2007	2008	2009	2010
Current ratio	58.11	63.24	80.89	106.37	134.95

In the short term, taking the stage of 2003 to 2005 as an example, users reached ten thousand levels for the first time and the profit capability is low. Artificial intelligence used by small manufacturers in the initial stage is established, but manufacturers cannot make a huge leap in the technical level of applied data elements in a short period. The investment and operation of manufacturers in the short term are weakly correlated with the digital economy model, which implies that the digital economy model will not be affected by manufacturers' application of big data and artificial intelligence technology in the short term.

However, in the long run, the digital economy is strongly related to the investment and management of manufacturers. The reason is that vendors will continue to upgrade their technology levels using big data and blockchain. For example, from 2005 to 2009, the number of Ali's users reached 100,000, which realized a small order of magnitude growth with an increasing economy of scale. From 2009 to 2013, driven by the scale economy of digital factors, the business users have spread by millions, and the profit showed a large order of magnitude growth. On the other hand, the competition inherent in the operation of the digital economy will drive manufacturers to develop new technologies to improve the technological hierarchy. Therefore, it can be concluded that the digital economy will react to the long-term investment management of the manufacturers [8].

Through the above theoretical and empirical analysis, we can know that the digital production factors have economies of scale in the long run. When the information density of data elements of an enterprise is small, it can play a smaller role. Only large-scale data elements can play a comprehensive role. Meanwhile, with the expansion of data elements, people can mine more value from data, and the profit for manufacturers will also show an increasing trend. Therefore, for companies that use data as an important factor of production, scaling up data and improving analytical capabilities can make a big difference in the long run.

3 Price Discrimination Theory

In the real business background, increasingly more manufacturers classify customers and discriminate them by using the information brought by digital factors. The essence of the operating mechanism of algorithmic price discrimination is the binary selection model [9].

Since the purpose of price discrimination is to determine whether consumer i is willing to pay a given price t_i for a given product (or service), the vendors can modify the price between consumers or groups of consumers [10]. The discrete choice model (DCM) is used for specific analysis, in which the consumer's response y_i is "1" or "0", respectively indicating whether they are willing to pay a given price t_i. . Assumes that consumers' willingness to pay (WTP_i) can be expressed as linear model, expression is:

$$WTP_i(z_i, u_i) = z_i\beta + u_i \qquad (4)$$

where z_i represents the vector of independent explanatory variables, the importance of each variable is contained in the coefficient β, and u_i is the error term used to describe the interfering factors in the measurement. If $WTP_i > t_i$, that is, consumer WTP is higher than the given price t_i, then consumer I will agree to pay the given price t_i. The corresponding probability can be expressed as:

$$P(y_i = 1|z_i) = P(WTP_i > t_i) = P(z_i\beta + u_i > t_i) = P(u_i > t_i z_i\beta) \qquad (5)$$

When consumers are divided into different groups, sellers can calculate the probability that each group will buy a product at a given price. Since each cluster is made up of consumers with similar attributes (independent variables), their probability of buying at a given price will be very similar or vary within a small range. On the contrary, the probability of a consumer buying will be different in different clusters. Hence, enterprises can charge different fees to different consumer groups by forming group pricing. Table 3 is a summary of the price discrimination which has already existed in the realistic market.

Table 3. Types of discrimination.

	Manner of execution	Suitable products
First-degree price discrimination	1. Big data analysis of consumption tendency and demand (to achieve "personalized customization") 2. Online bidding auction	Products can be customized products and services such as computers, digital products, etc
Second-degree price discrimination	1. Price varies according to quantity 2. Pricing varies according to the discount rate 3. Establish a membership system 4. Bundling sale	Almost all of the commodities can be implemented second-degree price discrimination, such as all kinds of physical goods and network derivatives
Third-degree price discrimination	1. Implementation based on the demand elasticity 2. Implement according to the time effect 3. Implement differentiated services	The same price is charged to different consumers within each group, but the price varies from group to group. Common examples: airline tickets and cinema ticket pricing online

4 Conclusion

With the continuous development of the digital economy, big data, blockchain, artificial intelligence are continuing to accumulate the application of digital factors in manufacturers' production. However, anti-monopoly acts on the internet platform have become increasingly popular among the policies since 2020. Many documents point out that the increasing returns to scale is the domain reason which leads to the differentiation of the firms and the monopoly of the internet platforms. Therefore, when designing the anti-monopoly rules, the policy makers should take the anti-competition effect into consideration. In addition, Chinese internet consumers have little awareness of protecting their privacy. Hence the digital marketization trade like "privacy swap service" springs up. Concerned both benefits and reputation, manufacturers should attach more importance to the laws and ensure the safety of consumers' privacy. In conclusion, although the digital economy is not mature and perfect, the whole tendency is still thriving and the manufacturers should make use of advanced digital technology to make more profit for society.

References

1. Pan, W., Xie, T., Wang, Z., Ma, L.: Digital economy: an innovation driver for total factor productivity. J. Bus. Res. **139**, 303–311 (2022)
2. Verhoef, C., Broekhuizen, T., Bart, Y., et al.: Digital transformation: a multidisciplinary reflection and research agenda. J. Bus. Res. **122**, 889–901 (2021)
3. Feng, K.: Economic analysis of data production factorization in the era of digital economy. J. Beijing Technol. Bus. Univ. (Soc. Sci.) **37**(1), 1–12 (2022)
4. Carter, D.: Urban regeneration, digital development strategies and the knowledge economy: Manchester case study. J. Knowl. Econ. **4**(2), 169–189 (2013)
5. Hagiu, A., Wright, J.: Platforms and the exploration of new products. Manage. Sci. **66**(4), 1527–1543 (2020)
6. Posner E., Weyl E.: Radical Markets, Princeton University Press, New York (2018)
7. Jallouli, R., Zaïane, O.R., Bach Tobji, M.A., Srarfi Tabbane, R., Nijholt, A. (eds.): ICDEc 2017. LNBIP, vol. 290. Springer, Cham (2017). https://doi.org/10.1007/978-3-319-62737-3
8. Xiao, H.: Analysis on the stage profit model of alibaba group. Eastern Enterp. Culture **3**, 193 (2015)
9. Bar-Gill, O.: Algorithmic price discrimination when demand is a function of both preferences and (Mis)perceptions. Univ. Chicago Law Rev. **86**(2), 12 (2019)
10. Ezrachi, A., Stucke, E.: Virtual Competition: The Promise and Perils of the Algorithm-Driven Economy. Harvard University Press, Cambridge (2016)

Fintech Development and Corporate Innovation

Chen Huan[✉]

Software Engineering Institute of Guangzhou, Guangzhou 510980, China
chh@mail.seig.edu.cn

Abstract. Companies generally face difficulties in raising capital. The emergence of Fintech brings new opportunities to the reform of the financial system. It remains to be seen whether Fintech promotes corporate innovation performance. To explore this question, this paper uses data of A-share listed enterprises in Shanghai and Shenzhen markets in China from 2011–2017, and a prefecture cities level Fintech development index constructed on the data retrieved from The Peking University Digital Financial Inclusion of China (PKU-DFIIC), to examines the impact of Fintech on innovation performance. The result shows that Fintech development significantly improve corporate innovation performances through alleviating corporate financing constraints. The enriching literature on the determinants of the corporate innovation and the consequences of the Fintech was contributed by the current research. Meanwhile, this study also provides practical implications for policy makers and for investors to reduce financial barriers for listing of promising enterprises, so as to improve their independent innovation capacity.

Keywords: Fintech Development · Innovation Performance · Financial Constraints

1 Introduction

Innovation effects an all-round improvement of enterprises. By reinforcing the foundational role of enterprises, all essentials to innovation could be allocated to enterprises, so as to embrace better development in economy. Digital transformation is the process of utilizing emerging information communication technologies (ICTs), such as big data and artificial intelligence (AI), to reform the way of production and operation [1], which poses challenges in all industries and business sectors. The development of digital transformation has also contributed to the emergence of Financial technology (Fintech) initiatives. Fintech is produced by the organic fusion of information technology and finance, some of the most important innovations which greatly affect financial institutions, markets and service supplies. On the strength of Fintech development, enterprises are able to integrate information, strengthen communication and improve innovation performance. Meanwhile, Fintech development helps further reduce barriers, enhance efficiency, alleviate information asymmetry as well as ease financial constrains for enterprises, a result of which, providing financial supports for enterprises possessing innovative potentials and talents. Due to its powerful financing capacity and comprehensive service capability,

Fintech can effectively match up enterprises demands for long- and short-term capital in the course of innovation, which creates a sound financial ecology for corporate innovation. In the context of the popularity of 5G network, emerging information technologies, such as Blockchain, Artificial Intelligence, Internet of Things, has gradually penetrated into segments in finance, which would have a much more greater role to play in corporate innovation. However, research in the filed of Fintech remains in its infancy. Scarce studies have conducted research to further clarify the correlation between Fintech and corporate innovation performance. This provides opportunities to more closely examine Fintech development research challenges and trends. Based on that, this paper is aiming to look deeper into how Fintech development affect corporate innovation, which provides significant theoretical and practical implications. Firstly, this paper enriches the literature on determining factors of corporate innovation and consequences generated from Fintech development. There has been research regarding the impact of macro-policies on corporate performance on innovation, and how Fintech development affects information constraints on corporate funding. But, scare research exists on the influences of Fintech development on corporate innovation performance. The research gap is narrowed by identifying the impact of Fintech development on corporate innovation in the context of Chinese market. Secondly, this paper also provides practical implications for policy makers as well as corporate managers on promoting the integration of financial technology and enterprises, and help firms to improve their independent innovation capacity by reducing the barriers and provide financial support.

Organized as followed, Sect. 2 of this paper is the literature review and hypotheses, while Sect. 3 elaborates details of research design, and presents data and the definition of variables. The fourth section is the verification of constructed model and the results analysis. The last section is a conclusion of this paper.

2 Literature Review and Hypothesis Development

These days digital transformation has attracted increasing attention from academic circle, all industries and governments. Due to its complex nature, there has been no consensus on the definition of digital transformation. Nambisan et al. suggests that digital transformation is a process when enterprises employ ICTs to generate innovate product, process or business models [2]. Drawn on Diffusion of innovations theory, Boland et al. defines digital transformation as the process that enterprises employ new digital channel, tool and related method to improve corporate operations and efficiency [3]. Digital transformation drives the emergence of Fintech. According to Navaretti et al., Fintech refers to a novel processes and products provided by financial institutions, e.g. banks, owing to digital technological advancement [4]. Specifically, the term is coined by Financial Stability Board as "technological enabled financial innovation that could result in new business models, applications, processes or products with an associated material effect on financial markets and institutions and the provision of financial services". The development of emerging ICTs, such as Artificial intelligence, Blockchain and Big data, gradually integrate with financial industrial, which become financial product innovation, help improve financial efficiency and lower financial transaction costs [5].

Traditional financial institutions have long been blamed for less efficiently providing services, or not providing at all, which has created barriers to transformation and upgrading of economic structure. However, this also provides an opportunity for the integration of financial and technology. On the one hand, the advancement and application of Fintech offers more financial products and services in a different and unbundled way, which help greatly lower services and operation costs. On the other hand, by reducing information asymmetry, it also offers more financing channels and methods for enterprises which may suffer from difficulties in financing and hence hinder their innovative activities.

There are many factors that may hinder corporate innovation. One of the most important question lies in whether enterprises have enough spending on research and development to keep up with growing demand. Filled with uncertainties, corporate innovation is usually a long-term process that requires a huge amount of money for the continuous research. Some of that money will be spent on self-developed research while the other will go towards gaining innovative resources either from mergers and acquisitions, or purchase for patents [6]. However, internal capital is not always sufficient to meed the demand of long-term investment for corporate innovation. For this reason, enterprises are trying to find external financing to invest into research and innovation. Generally speaking, enterprises get loans from banks and financial institutions, or issue shares and bonds as their main external financial channels. Abundant existing research evidences indicate that financing constraints is the most critical barriers to corporate technology innovation [7].

Promoted by the occurrence of Fintech, financing constraints shall be reduced from corporate innovation. Firstly, Fintech development alleviates information asymmetry between the investment side and the financing side. The existence of information asymmetry has attributed to incomplete, distorted and misdescribed information received by the two sides during the transaction. Precisely, it is not uncommon that enterprises tend to be cagey about details of their innovative activities because of the increasingly competitive business. A lack of sufficient information can result in investors' misjudgment in the value of enterprises' innovative activities. Hence, information asymmetry is seen as the major obstacle that generate financing constraints between the two sides, because it can easily lead to 'reverse selection' or trigger 'moral hazard'. Furthermore, a high number of small firms have greater difficulties in financing mainly because their finances is not so transparent that may lead to higher cost in supervision for banks and other financial institutions. By employing ICTs like Big data and artificial intelligence, the depth and the scope of financial services offered by banks and financial institutions become more obvious than ever, which helps alleviate information asymmetry between traditional financial institutions and enterprises. Secondly, Fintech development provides more channels for corporate financing. Thanks to the low cost and high efficient of ICTs, banks and other financial institutions can build up new businesses, attract higher numbers of small investors that are not spread evenly across financial market, as a result of which, help compensate for the shortage of traditional financial services while expanding the scope of services. In this way, Fintech development helps enrich the supply of funds in financial markets and broaden financial channels for corporate innovation.

Fintech development widens the scope of financing, alleviates financing constraints for enterprises by reducing information asymmetry arise among banks, enterprises and other financial institutions, a result of which, promotes corporate innovation. Based on the discussion above, following hypothesis is proposed:

Hypothesis 1. Fintech development has a positive effect on corporate innovation.

3 Research Design

3.1 Sample and Data

Adapting an index provided by a research team from the Institute of Digital Finance at Peking University and Ant Financial Services Group, Fintech development is measured in this paper. This index includes provincial level, prefecture city level and county level data from 2011–2017. Prefecture city-level data is included for more observations in this research. The data indicating firm-level variables, including enterprise financial data and the patent data, is obtained from the China Stock Market& Accounting Research (CSMAR) database. The sample period of A-share listed firms covers from 2011 to 2017.

The sample data are processed as follow to be more representative: (i) data from financial industry is excluded; (ii) data from ST firms is deleted. Afterwards, 13438 observation samples were obtained and every continuous variable is winsorzied at the 1% and 99% levels to mitigate the effects of outliers. Summary statistics of the variables used in the model is demonstrated in Table 1.

3.2 Selection of Variables

(1) **Dependent Variable.** Corporate innovation performance: Innovation input and output are mainly used in previous research to measure the level of corporate innovation performance. R&D input is used as a significant indicator of corporate innovation input, while the number of patents applied and the number of newly-developed products are used as corporate innovation output to measure enterprise innovation performance. Drawing on the study of Dosi et al. [8], Hall & Harhoff [9], Tong et al. [10], corporate innovation performance in this paper is measured by the total of patents applied and granted, which better reflects the results of R&D investment and the transformation efficiency of corporate innovation performance. In this paper, the total of patent applied and granted (*Patent*) is comprised of two categories: patent for invention (*Patenti*) and patent for utility and design (*Patentud*).

(2) **Core Explanatory Variable.** Fintech development: As previous research suggest, this paper applies the prefecture-level cities China Digital Financial Inclusion Index complied by the Digital Finance Research Center of Peking University as a proxy variable for Fintech development. A general picture describing the level of digital financial development is illustrated by this index with three comprising dimensions: breath of digital financial coverage, depth of digital financial usage, the degree of digitization, and other sub-index, including payment, insurance, credit, investment and monetary fund. Used as a proxy variable, the total Digital Inclusive Finance Index demonstrates Fintech development in this paper.The breath of digital inclusive finance coverage and the depth of usage are also used for measuring.

(3) **Control variables.** Several control variables are included in this study for the regression model, so as to avoid the influences of other non-core variables as much as possible. These include firm size (*Size*), the proportion of independent directors (*Indep*), the scale of director board (*Board*), *HHI*, Duality (*Dual*), and other financial indicators: cash flow operating (*Cfo*), and Leverage ratio (*lev*). Table 1 summarizes definitions of major variables selected.

Table 1. Variable Definitions.

Variable	Definition
Patent	The total of patent applied and granted (including patent for invention, utility and design) annually
Patenti	The total of invention patent applied and granted annually
Patentud	The total of utility and design patent applied and granted annually
Size	Logged value of total assets
Cfo	Logged value o net cash flow generated from operational activities
Lev	Ratio of long-term debt plus debt in current liabilities to total assets
Indep	The proportion of independent directors
Board	The number of shareholders
HHI	Herfindahl-Hirschman Index
Dual	Duality of CEO and chairman

3.3 Modal Setting

To investigate the association between the Fintech development and innovation performance, we employ the following model:

$$Patent = \alpha 0 + \alpha 1 Digital + \alpha 2 Controls + YearFixedEffect + IndustryFixedEffect + e \quad (1)$$

4 Research Result

4.1 Descriptive Statistics

In our research, a total of 13438 samples is observed. Table 2 shows the distribution of amount of samples during the sample period from 2011 to 2017. It is indicated that the proportion of samples almost evenly distribute in the sample period, with 11.13% in 2011, 12.06% in 2012, 12.58% in 2013, 13.41% in 2014. The amount of samples from 2015 to 2017 is 14.91%, 16.62% and 19.25%, respectively.

Table 2. Sample distribution.

Year	N	Percentage
2011	1,495	11.13
2012	1,621	12.06
2013	1,691	12.58
2014	1,802	13.41
2015	2,009	14.95
2016	2,233	16.62
2017	2,587	19.25
Total	13,438	100

Table 3 describes the statistics of the key dependent and independent variables in the model. It is indicated that the mean value of Total Digital Inclusive Finance index is 180.973, while the mean of Digital inclusive finance coverage index and the Digital inclusive finance usage depth index are 181.479 and 178.78, respectively. With respect to the total of patent applied and granted, the mean value is 61.334 and the standard deviation of patent is 147.877, indicating a variation in patent. The mean values are patenti and patentud are 23.050 and 37.458, respectively. In terms of controlled variables, the mean value of Size is 22.123 and the standard deviation of Size is 1.378, suggesting the variation in total asset of firms. The mean value of the PPE is 0.213. The mean values of Cash flow and Leverage are 0.412, where as those of proportion of independent directors and shareholders are 0.384 and 2.296, respectively. The mean value of HHI is 0.313 and that of Duality of CEO and chairman is 0.28.

4.2 Main Results

Table 4 presents the regression result of Fintech on corporate innovation performance. Columns (1) and (2) use the number of patents as the dependent variable. Aiming to control the number of patent applied and granted at the firm level with disturbing factors, this study controlled for Size, PPE, Cfo, Leverage, Indep, Board, HHI and Duality effects. As given in column (1) of Table 4, the regression coefficient estimates of Total Digital Inclusive Finance Index is positive and significant at the 1% level (coefficient = 0.539 with t = 7.96), indicating that a significant positive effect on corporate innovation performance has been generated by Fintech performance. In column (2), the coefficient estimates of Total Digital Inclusive Finance Index remains positive and significant at the 1% level (coefficient = 0.410 with t = 6.60). With respect to controlled variable, the coefficient estimates of Size, Cfo, Indep, HHI and Dual are positive and significantly at the 1% level (Coefficient = 61.273 with t = 27.58; Coefficient = 76.263 with t = 4.56; Coefficient = 66.525 with t = 3.81; Coefficient = 109.433 with t = 5.23; Coefficient = 8.056 with t = 3.38). The coefficient estimates of PPE, Leverage, Board are negative and significant at the 1% level (coefficient = −58.177 with t = −6.28; coefficient = −38.360 with t = −6.09; coefficient = −20.060 with t = −3.75). The results for the control

Table 3. Descriptive statistics.

Variable	N	Mean	S.D.	25th	Median	75th
Total Digital Inclusive Finance Index	13438	180.973	59.859	137.830	189.260	227.898
Digital inclusive finance coverage index	13438	181.479	57.316	144.880	189.090	229.014
Digital inclusive finance usage depth index	13438	178.780	65.746	130.750	175.830	226.055
Payment	13438	194.494	81.549	124.850	199.240	266.980
Insurance	13438	325.955	137.591	255.130	348.110	427.685
Credit	13431	131.131	40.555	98.160	124.050	171.174
Digitization level	13438	183.764	74.747	146.660	215.941	247.580
Patent	13438	61.334	147.877	7.000	18.500	49.000
Patenti	13438	23.050	59.207	2.000	5.000	17.000
Patentud	13438	37.458	92.117	3.000	11.000	30.000
Size	13438	22.123	1.378	21.143	21.879	22.812
PPE	13438	0.213	0.152	0.097	0.183	0.299
Cfo	13438	0.041	0.067	0.003	0.039	0.081
Lev	13438	0.412	0.213	0.238	0.396	0.570
Indep	13438	0.384	0.073	0.333	0.364	0.429
Board	13438	2.296	0.251	2.197	2.303	2.485
HHI	13424	0.313	0.135	0.233	0.291	0.319
Dual	13438	0.280	0.449	0.000	0.000	1.000

variables are largely consistent with previous literature. As evidenced by Hypothesis 1, it can be concluded that Fintech development indeed brings a significant driving effect on corporate innovation performance.

Table 4. Regression results.

Variable	(1)	(2)
	Patent	Patent
Total Digital Inclusive Finance Index	0.539***	0.410***
	(7.96)	(6.60)
Size		61.273***
		(27.58)
PPE		−58.177***
		(−6.28)
Cfo		76.263***
		(4.56)
Lev		−38.360***
		(−6.09)
Indep		66.525***
		(3.81)
Board		−20.060***
		(−3.75)
HHI		109.433***
		(5.23)
Dual		8.056***
		(3.38)
Industry	YES	YES
Year	YES	YES
N	13438	13424
R2	0.065	0.287

5 Conclusion

In the era when digital economy is rapidly developing, it is indispensable to explore the impact of financial environment on corporate innovation. This paper empirically examines the association between Fintech development and corporate innovation performance adopting data from A-share listed enterprises in Shanghai and Shenzhen markets in China between 2011 and 2017. Impact of Fintech development on corporate innovation performance is confirmed by the findings, while empirical results indicating such an effect is indeed positive and significant. Fintech development contributes to corporate innovation development mainly through alleviating corporate financing by reducing information asymmetry among banks, enterprises, and other financial institutions.

Based on the analysis above, following implications for policy makers and investors are proposed: Firstly, active policy support should be put into effect to facilitate Fintech development. Emerging ICTs such as artificial intelligence and big data play an active role in promoting digital transformation of the financial industry and deepening the reform of the financial system. Secondly, the all-round integration between financial technologies and enterprises should be promoted. The introduction of emerging financial technologies encourages the cost reduction of financing for enterprises and improve their profitability, a result of which, lay a solid foundation for corporate innovation. Thirdly, Fintech should increase its efforts to encourage financial institutions to reduce the barriers and support the research and development of enterprises financially, increasing their chances to seize the opportunities brought by technological advancement and improve their capacity of innovating independently.

The limitations of this paper lies in two aspects. Firstly, the Peking University Digital Inclusive Finance Index compiled by transaction data of individual users from Ant Financial Services Group, as a proxy variable for Fintech, may result in a representativeness bias in that this index could not comprehensively measure the regional Fintech development level to a certain extent. Secondly, this paper provides empirical evidence of the impact of Fintech development on corporate innovation performance, however, there is still limited research in this field and future study is needed of the possible impact mechanism of it.

References

1. Ilvonen, I., Thalmann, S., Manhart, M.: Reconciling digital transformation and knowledge protection: a research agenda. Knowl. Manag. Res. Pract. 16(2) (2018)
2. Nambisan, S., Lyytinen, K., Majchrzak, A., Song, M.: Digital innovation management. MIS Q. **41**(1), 223–238 (2017)
3. Boland, R.J., Lyytinen, K., Yoo, Y.: Wakes of innovation in project networks: the case of digital 3-D representations in architecture, engineering, and construction. Organ. Sci. **18**(4), 631–647 (2007)
4. Navaretti, G.B., Calzolari, G., Mansilla-Fernandez, J.M., Pozzolo, A.F.: Fintech and banking. Friends or foes? Friends or Foes (2018)
5. Liu, Y., Peng, J., Yu, Z.: Big data platform architecture under the background of financial technology: In The Insurance Industry As An Example. In Proceedings of the 2018 International Conference on Big Data Engineering and Technology (BDET 2018), pp. 31–35. Association for Computing Machinery, New York, NY (2018).https://doi.org/10.1145/3297730.3297743
6. Atanassov, J.: Do hostile takeovers stifle innovation? Evidence from antitakeover legislation and corporate patenting. J. Finan. **68**(3), 1097–1131 (2013)
7. Brown, J.R., Fazzari, S.M., Petersen, B.C.: Financing innovation and growth: cash flow, external equity, and the 1990s R&D boom. J. Finan. **64**(1), 151–185 (2009)
8. Dosi, G., Marengo, L., Pasquali, C.: How much should society fuel the greed of innovators?: on the relations between appropriability, opportunities and rates of innovation. Res. Policy **35**(8), 1110–1121 (2006)
9. Hall, B.H., Harhoff, D.: Recent research on the economics of patents. Ann. Rev. Econ. **4**(1), 541–565 (2012)
10. Tong, T.W., He, W., He, Z.L., Lu, J.: Patent regime shift and firm innovation: Evidence from the second amendment to China's patent law. In Academy of management proceedings (Vol. 2014, No. 1, p. 14174). Briarcliff Manor, NY 10510: Academy of Management (2014)

Analysts' Characteristics and Forecast ability–An Empirical Study from China's A-Share Market

Mengyan Lei[✉]

Beijing Quantex Technology Co., Ltd, Beijing 100044, China
lmy.beckham@hotmail.com

Abstract. Using a sample earnings forecast from China's A-Share Market over the 5 years from 2016 to 2020, This article finds that analysts' characteristics are related to their forecast ability. Specifically, analysts' gender conditional on educational background and experience significantly affects their forecast ability. This paper also investigates the relationship between analysts' effort, attention, and forecast ability and finds effort has a positive relationship with accuracy and relative accuracy but is negatively associated with optimism. Attention also has positively related to accuracy and optimism.

Keywords: Analyst characteristics · Forecast ability · Accuracy Optimism

1 Introduction

Financial analysts are an integral and intermediate part of the modern financial market and they usually provide information interpretation and information discovery in the capital market [1, 2]. Thus, their earnings forecasts influence the investors' decisions and alleviate the information asymmetry of the financial market, and further, improve the allocation efficiency of resources. However, whether their predictions are valuable and accurate has not reached a consensus [3].

A key aspect of previous research concerning forecast accuracy is analysts' traits or characteristics. Existing literature usually focuses on analysts' gender, educational background, firm-specific, and general experience, and identifies the relationship between these factors and their forecasting accuracy. However, few of the prior studies examine the interactive effect between gender and educational background and experience. Besides, analysts' efforts and attention are often treated as the control variables.

Using a sample of earnings forecasts from China's A-share market over 5 years from 2016 to 2020, this paper seeks to illuminate the effect of analysts' traits and subjective characteristics on analysts' forecast ability. Following the classical previous studies, this research measures the forecast ability as three: forecast accuracy, relative forecast accuracy, and forecast optimism [4, 5]. It also inspects the interactive effect of analysts' traits, such as gender, educational background, and relevant working experience on analysts' forecast ability by regression analysis. Besides, I also use the number of forecasts that analysts issued as the proxy variable of analysts' effort and the number of firms that analysts followed as the proxy variable of their attention to explore their effect on forecast ability, which indicates this research takes the subjective characteristics into account as well. The result shows males and females perform differently in their forecast accuracy, but for relative accuracy and optimism, results vary on their experience and educational background. In addition, forecast ability is also affected by analysts' hard-working and attention. More effort implies better forecast results, however, more followed listed companies, less forecast accuracy, and less optimism.

This study contributes to the analysts' performance literature by providing new insights into the interactive effect of their characteristics on forecast performance and highlights analysts' subjective traits like effort and attention also affect the result of analysts' predictions.

2 Literature Review and Hypotheses Development

The previous research on factors that affect the accuracy of the securities analysts' earnings forecasts could be divided into three different dimensions. Analysts' decisions to initiate coverage may be associated with analyst, brokerage, and firm characteristics [6].

The first one is based on the analysts' characteristics. Generally, Analysts' characteristics can affect their forecast accuracy [7]. Behavior finance study shows there is a difference between females and males in solving problems, risk preference, and cognitive style, thus gender influences the relationship between the analysts' accuracy and experience [8]. Male analysts with firm-specific experience and female analysts with general experience perform differently in forecast accuracy [9]. The gender of analysts also plays a role in their followed firms' social well-being activity [10]. Because there is gender discrimination in the analyst labor market, only females with superior forecasting abilities can enter this profession. Besides, female analysts make bolder and more accurate forecasts [10]. Recommendations made by female analysts produce similar abnormal returns but with lower idiosyncratic risks [11].

Experience and educational background is also regarded as factors that affect the forecast accuracy of securities in the prior literature. Security analysts do improve their forecasting ability through their experience and there is no performance difference between honored analysts and non-honored ones [3]. Analysts with more firm-specific and general experience and more accurate forecasts experience, tend to revise forecasts later in the quarter, this also happens to analysts employed by larger brokerage firms. These analysts' characteristics are negatively related to relative forecast errors [12]. Some existing literature combines gender and educational background to explore these personal characteristics and the forecasting results. The proportion with prestigious universities degree in female analysts sample is higher than male counterparts, and female analysts make more effort in their earning forecasting work. Besides, both the overseas background and the effort of female analysts have a negative relationship with stock return synchronicity [13]. Thus, based on the above previous foundation, this proposes our first hypothesis.

H1. The difference in forecast ability between male and female analysts is conditional on experience and their educational background.

The effort is also regarded as an indicator of personal traits in analyst work and if analysts put more energy into the firms that they followed, the number of the listed companies that are followed decreases accordingly [14]. Female analysts put more effort than their counterparts into work [13]. The number of analysts following is positively correlated with the accuracy of the forecast [15]. It is more difficult to follow a larger set of firms and industries which renders analysts to devote less attention to each firm [4].

H2. Analysts' effort is positively related to forecasting accuracy and relative accuracy but negatively associated with optimism

H3. Analysts' attention is negatively correlated with forecast accuracy and relative accuracy but positively related to optimism

Financial indicators, such as firm size, change in stock price, the standard deviation of earnings, and leverage also affect the analyst forecast performance [16]. Meanwhile, analysts are keen on research firms that have stable earnings, better operating abilities, and leverage levels, historic volatility is also correlated with the accuracy of earnings forecasts [17]. For firm-specific variables, the firm market value of equity at month-end before the revision and book-to-market ratio as of month-end before the revision is redeemed as control variables [18]. Recommendation changes are more likely to be influential if they are from leaders, stars, or previously influential analysts [19].

Based on the above, the size of the listed enterprises, liquidity of brokerage firms, and forecast Horizon may also affect their forecast ability. Therefore, I include these factors as control variables.

3 Methodology

3.1 Sample and Data

The sample used to examine the impact of analysts' characteristics and followed firms on analyst forecast ability includes 51,230 observations on all Chinese A-share firms listed on the Shanghai and Shenzhen stock exchanges from 2016 to 2020.

I collect forecast data and financial indicators of followed firms from the CSMAR database and limit the firms to non-financial stock and non-special treated ones. All the data is analyzed by Python.

3.2 Variable Definitions and Model Specification

Analysts' Forecast Ability. Following previous literature, this paper uses three measures for forecast ability:(1)$Ferri_{jtk}$, forecast accuracy [20], more accurate, the smaller value $Ferri_{jtk}$; ; (2) Considering analysts' forecasts may be influenced by other analysts or the mood of the whole stock market, I also use relative forecast accuracy $RFerri_{jtk}$ [4] as a measurement of analysts' forecast compared with other analysts; (3) $Foptimi_{jtk}$ forecast optimism [5].

Analysts' Characteristics. Based on the existing literature, this research includes analysts' gender, experience, educational background, analysts' effort, and attention in our model and measures variables as the following:

Variable Definitions. The following Table 1 defines all variables.

Table 1. Variable definitions.

Variable Definitions	
Dependable Variables	
$Ferr_{ijtk}$	$Ferrijt = |FEPSijtk - EPSjt|/|EPSjt|$, $FEPSijtk$ is the earnings forecast k analyst i issues for firm j at fiscal year t. $EPSjt$ is the annual earnings announced by firm j at fiscal year t
$RFerr_{ijtk}$	$RFerrijtk = (AFEijtk - \overline{AFEijtk})/\overline{AFEijtk}$, $AFEijtk = |FEPSijtk - EPSjt|$ is the absolute forecast error for analyst i's forecast k of firm j at year t. $\overline{AFEijtk} = \frac{1}{N}\sum_N AFEjtk$ is the mean absolute error of all forecasts that are issued by other analysts for firm j. It measures the forecast accuracy of analyst i compared with other analysts that followed firm j
$Foptim_{ijtk}$	$Foptimijtk = \frac{FEPSijtk - EPSjt}{EPSjt}$ $FEPSijtk$ is the earnings forecast k analyst i issues for firm j at time t, $EPSjt$ is the annual earnings announced by firm j at fiscal year t
Independent Variables	
Male	Dummy variable, equal to one if male analysts, zero otherwise
$Exper_{it}$	The number of quarters between the date analyst i issued the first forecast and the end date of the fiscal year t
Mst_{it}	Dummy variable, the final degree of analyst i at fiscal year t, equal to one if the final degree is post-graduate, zero otherwise
$Fnum_{it}$	The Proxy variable of effort. The number of forecast reports between the date analyst i issued the first forecast and the end date of the fiscal year t. A Higher value indicates more effort
$FlCNum_{it}$	The Proxy variable of attention. The number of firms that analyst i followed between the date analyst i issued the first forecast and the date of the fiscal year t. A higher value indicates less attention
Control Variables	
$FHorizon_{ijkt}$	The number of days between the date forecast k made by analyst i and the date of the official fiscal report released by firm j
$Flanalysts_{jt}$	The number of analysts that followed firm j at the end of fiscal year t
$Firmsize_{jt}$	Natural log of total assets of firm j at the start date of fiscal year t
$Netcapital_{it}$	Natural log of net capital of brokerage firm that analyst i employing at the date of brokerage official report at fiscal year t

3.3 Testing Methodologies and Empirical Results

Descriptive Statistics. Table 2 presents the overall variables' descriptive statistics. It reports the number of the sample is 51,230 and the average gender is 0.84, this indicates that 84% of the analysts in our sample are male and the average working experience of earning forecast of analysts is 17.84 quarters. For educational background, the mean

Table 2. Descriptive statistics.

	Mean	SD	Minimum	Maximum
Male	0.839	0.367	0.000	1.000
Exper$_{it}$	17.838	11.752	0.770	67.120
Mst	0.955	0.207	0.000	1.000
FNum$_{it}$	74.004	48.943	1.000	213.000
FlCNum$_{it}$	23.362	11.633	1.000	85.000
FHorizon$_{ijkt}$	284.313	95.089	81.000	479.000
Flanalysts$_{jt}$	25.716	13.788	2.000	49.000
Netcapital$_{it}$	24.348	0.667	18.878	25.186

value of the variable degree is 0.96, which implies that 96 % of analysts have a master's or above degree. The mean value of analysts' forecast number is 74 and the maximum forecast number for an analyst is 213 during the 5 years.

Testing Methodologies. To test Hypotheses 1 and 2 and 3, Eqs. (1) to (3) are computed using ordinary least squares (OLS) estimators.

$$Ferr_{ijt} = \alpha_0 + \alpha_1 Male + \alpha_2 Exper + \alpha_3 Mst_{it} + \alpha_4 Male * Exper_{it} + \alpha_5 Male * Mst_{it} + \alpha_6 FNum_{it} + \alpha_7 FlCNum_{it} + \alpha_8 Cont_{ijkt} + \varepsilon_t \tag{1}$$

$$RFerr_{ijt} = \alpha_0 + \alpha_1 Male + \alpha_2 Exper + \alpha_3 Mst_{it} + \alpha_4 Male * Exper_{it} + \alpha_5 Male * Mst_{it} + \alpha_6 FNum_{it} + \alpha_7 FlCNum_{it} + \alpha_8 Cont_{ijkt} + \varepsilon_t \tag{2}$$

$$Optim_{ijt} = \alpha_0 + \alpha_1 Male + \alpha_2 Exper + \alpha_3 Mst_{it} + \alpha_4 Male * Exper_{it} + \alpha_5 Male * Mst_{it} + \alpha_6 FNum_{it} + \alpha_7 FlCNum_{it} + \alpha_8 Cont_{ijkt} + \varepsilon_t \tag{3}$$

Regression Results. Table3 shows the main results of the impact of factors on analysts' forecast ability, year fixed effect and industry fixed effect are included in all specifications.

The results of the regression model show there is a gap in forecast accuracy between male and female analysts at 1% significance level. But for relative accuracy, column (2) reports the result is also conditional on experience (*Experit*) and educational background (*Mstit*). With more working experience, less incremental accuracy of male analysts than their counterparts, suggesting that working experience could narrow the relative accuracy gap between male and female analysts, and for analysts with post-graduate degrees, this effect could be magnified. Column (3) demonstrates optimism is conditional on experience and educational background. Specifically, male analysts are more optimistic than female ones but with more experience and higher educational background, this discrepancy in optimism tends to be closer. This result is consistent with H1, but not with previous literature concerning gender in forecast accuracy in the U.S. stock market. However, in China's A-share market, male analysts usually have social skills in connecting with the management of the firms that they followed due to the social-cultural atmosphere. Thus, they could get more undisclosed information than their counterparts [9], and 'the observed performance improvement attributes to the close association between security companies and the listed firms rather than other enhancement of ability to predict' [3].

Table 3. Regression results.

Variables	Column (1) Forecast Accuracy	Column (2) Relative Forecast Accuracy	Column (3) Forecast Optimism
Male	0.000*** (0.135)	0.001*** (1.3544)	0.000*** (0.002)
Mst_{it}	0.653 (0.088)	0.019** (0.258)	0.056* (0.001)
$Exper_{it}$	0.000*** (0.002)	0.036** (0.007)	0.000*** (3.45e−05)
$Male*Mst_{it}$	0.673 (0.121)	0.003*** (0.354)	0.000*** (0.002)
$Male*Exper_{it}$	0.499 (0.003)	0.000*** (0.007)	0.004*** (3.92e-05)
$FNum_{it}$	0.000*** (0.000)	0.000*** (0.001)	0.000*** (5.56e-06)
$FlCNum_{it}$	0.000*** (0.001)	0.141 (0.004)	0.000*** (2.25e-05)
$Firmsize_{jt}$	0.000*** (0.012)	0.255 (0.036)	0.000*** (0.000)
$Netcapial_{it}$	0.000*** (0.018)	0.000*** (0.054)	0.139 (0.000)
$FHorizon_{ijkt}$	0.000** (0.000)	0.000*** (−0.0062)	0.002*** (1.93e-06)
$Flanalysts_{jt}$	0.000*** (0.001)	0.000*** (-0.000)	0.000*** (1.75e-05)
Industry FE	Y	Y	Y
Year FE	Y	Y	Y

Note: Robust standard errors, clustered at the industry level, are reported in parentheses. *, **, and *** denote significance at the 10%, 5% and 1% level, respectively

The forecast number ($FNumit$) is measured as analysts' effort. The positive coefficient (0.002 and 0.006, respectively) demonstrates more reports that analysts issued, more accuracy, and relative forecast accuracy as well. Thus, from this perspective, hardworking rewards. Besides, optimism is negatively related to forecasting number, suggesting that with more effort, analysts issue forecast report more cautiously. This finding is consistent with the expectation of H2.

Since different listed firms have different operating strategies, and in some cases, may belong to different industries. Thus, the number of listed firms ($FlCNumit$) measured analysts' attention. Regression reports the number of listed firms that analysts followed is a negative association with forecast accuracy (t = −0.018) at 1% significance level. More followed companies, less forecast accuracy. However, there is no significant association with relative forecast accuracy. It implies working in different firms does not empower the ability to stand out from other analysts. Column (3) indicates there is a negative relationship between optimism (t = −0.0002) and the number of followed firms, suggesting that following more companies cause analysts more cautious in making forecasts. This finding is consistent with H3, except for relative accuracy.

For control variables, forecast horizon (*FHorizonikt*) is positively related to accuracy but negatively associated with relative accuracy and optimism indicating that compared with other analysts, longer horizons alleviate herd effect and lead to better performance compared with other analysts. However, it also implies longer horizon does not make more accurate forecast result compared with their results. The number of analysts that follow (*Flanalystsjt*) the same firms, which represents the listed firms' attractiveness, shows a negative relationship with forecast ability (forecast accuracy, relative accuracy, and optimism). This result is consistent with previous literature [5]. *Firmsizejt* shows there is a negative relationship between the size of listed firms and forecast accuracy but a positive association with relative accuracy and optimism, which reflects the bigger size of firms doesn't make analysts perform better compared with themselves but are more accurate than their counterparts and more cautious in making predictions. *Netcapitalit* is 1% positive with forecast accuracy but negative with relative accuracy implying analysts employed by stronger and better liquidity brokerage perform better.

Robust Test. In the robust test part, this research limits our sample period to 2018–2020, which includes a systematic stock market crash in 2018 and an outbreak, post of covid-19 from 2019 to the end of 2020. I find the results of the main explanatory variables still stand, except for the difference between males and females in accuracy. In the robust test, due to potential financial risk during this special time - period, the disparity of accuracy between males and females is also narrowed by final degree and experience.

4 Conclusion

Using a comprehensive sample of analysts' forecasts, this research investigates differences in male and female analysts' forecast ability conditional on educational background and experience plus analysts' effort, and attention to the forecast performance over 5 years.

Compared with male and female analysts' earning forecasts, this paper finds there is a performance gap between male and female analysts' forecast accuracy and this result is probably due to the social-cultural atmosphere in China--male analysts could get more undisclosed information than their counterparts since they have an advantage in social connection with the management of followed firms.

In addition, our empirical results further indicate that the difference between male and female analysts' relative forecast accuracy is conditional on their experience and educational background and our empirical results further imply that male analysts are more optimistic than female analysts, though this result is also relative to their experience and educational background. This finding is consistent with the previous literature that female analysts are more cautious compared with their counterparts [13].

Analysts' effort and attention also influence forecast ability. With more hard-working on predictions, analysts tend to perform better in their forecasts. More following listed firms indicates a distraction of analysts' attention, and lead to a negative relationship with forecast accuracy and optimism.

Unlike research that solely focuses on analysts' objective characteristics, this paper adds to the literature on the interactive effect of analysts' objective traits that may influence their prediction performance. In addition, this study also explores the effect of subjective characteristics like analysts' effort and attention on forecast ability. The results further provide insights for investors who could benefit from understanding the relation between analysts' characteristics and their prediction ability.

References

1. Ramnath, S., Rock, S., Shane, P.: Financial analyst forecasting literature: a taxonomy with trends and suggestions for further research. Int. J. Forecast. **24**(1), 34–75 (2008)
2. Chen, X., Cheng, Q., Lo, K.: On the relationship between analyst reports and corporate disclosures: exploring the roles of information discovery and interpretation. J. Account. Econ. **49**(3), 206–226 (2010)
3. Zhang, Z.X., Yao, P.Y.: Gifted, skilled, or associated. Econ. Theory Bus. Manage. **7**, 64–76 (2017)
4. Clement, M.B.: Analyst forecast accuracy: do ability, resources, and portfolio complexity matter? J. Account. Econ. **27**, 285–303 (1999)
5. Tan, S.T., Cui, X.Y.: Can investigation and research on listed firms improve the accuracy of analysts' forecasts? J. World Econ. **4**, 126–145 (2015)
6. Ertimur, Y., Muslu, V., Zhang, F.: Why are recommendations optimistic? Evidence from analysts' coverage initiations. Rev. Account. Stud. **16**, 679–718 (2011)
7. García-Meca, E., Sánchez-Ballesta, J.P.: The influence of the board on firm performance: an empirical vision in the Spanish capital market. Corp. Ownership Control **3**(3), 199–204 (2006)
8. Hardies, K., Breesch, D., Branson, J.: Are female auditors still women? Analyzing the sex differences affecting audit quality. Working paper (2010). available at SSRN: http://ssrn.com/abstract=1409964
9. Shi, X.W., Li, Z.G., Liu, Z.: The difference of analysts' characteristics and forecast accuracy. Friends Accou. **8**, 53–58 (2015)
10. Wang, Y.: Emerging markets review (2022).https://doi.org/10.1016/j.ememar.2022.100941
11. Kumar, A.: Self-selection and the forecasting abilities of female equity analysts. J. Account. Res. **48**(2), 393–435 (2010)
12. Li, X., Sullivan, R.N.: Sell-side analysts and gender: a comparison of performance, behavior, and career outcomes. Finan. Anal. J. **69**(2), 83–94 (2013)
13. Kim, Y., Lobo, G.J., Song, M.: Analyst characteristics, timing of forecast revisions, and analyst forecasting ability. J. Bank. Finan. **35**(2011), 2158–2168 (2011)
14. Yi, Z.H., Li, Y., Jiang, X.Y.: Female analysts' coverage and stock return synchronicity. J. Finan. Res. **425**, 175–189 (2015)
15. Barth, M.E., Kasznik, R., McNichols, M.F.: Analyst coverage and intangible assets. J. Account. Res. **39**(1), 1–34 (2001)

16. Yue, H., Lin, X.C.: Financial analyst vs. statistical model: the relative accuracy of analyst forecasts and its determinants. Account. Res. **8**, 40–95 (2008)
17. Matolcsyz, Z., Wyatta, A.: Capitalized intangibles and financial analysts. Account. Finan. **46**, 457–479 (2006)
18. Wang, H.F., Li, C.C.: An empirical study on the accuracy of securities analysts' earnings forecast in China. J. Nanjing Audit Univ. **6**, 51–59 (2016)
19. Livnat, J., Zhang, Y.: Information interpretation or information discovery: which role of analysts do investors value more? Rev. Account. Stud. **17**, 612–641 (2012)
20. Loh, R.K., Stulz, R.M.: When are analyst recommendation changes influential? The Review of Financial Studies. **24**(2), 593–627 (2011)
21. Crichfield, T., Dyckman, T., Lakonishok, J.: An evaluation of security analysts' forecasts. Account. Rev. **53**(3), 651–668 (1978)

Is There Salary Discrimination by Race and Nationality in the NBA? A New Approach

JiaYou Liang[✉], ShuaiJie Zhao, and HaoYuan Zhu

Beijing Normal University - Hong Kong Baptist University United International College, Zhu Hai, China
q030018038@mail.uic.edu.cn

Abstract. This study seeks to investigate the existence of salary discrimination in the National Basketball Association (NBA). According to Gary Becker's theory of discrimination in labor economics, this study focuses on employer discrimination. While previous research has examined discrimination based on race and nationality separately, this paper combines them to analyze the issue comprehensively. Specifically, the study focuses on whether salary discrimination occurs among American-white, American-nonwhite, other country-white, and other country-nonwhite individuals. Therefore, based on the data collected from Basketball Reference for the 2021–2022 season, a Mincer equation has been constructed to predict the effect of experience, races, nationality, and players' performance on earnings. The OLS regression result provides the evidence that there was no such race or nationality discriminations in NBA.

Keywords: NBA · Salary Discrimination · Mincer Equation · OLS

1 Introduction

As one of the most popular sports in the world, the National Basketball Association (NBA) has been plagued by discrimination, particularly in terms of salaries. Previous research has looked at the differences between white and black players. According to Kahn and Sherer [1], customer discrimination led to a racial gap in salaries for black players in the 1980s, with some teams making discriminatory salary offers because fans preferred white athletes. In the 1990s, Matthew [2] found that the NBA had become a racially equal labor market, and there was no longer a difference between white and black fans. Similarly, when Hisahiro and Yu [3] revisited the issue of a racial gap in the NBA, they found that the racial salary gap had disappeared in the 1990s and 2000s, but another racial gap began to emerge in the 2000s and reached about 20% in the 2010s. They suggested that this emergence may have been caused by the globalization of teams, the introduction of luxury taxes, and minor leagues.

After the 2000s, more and more international players entered the NBA, leading to a new salary discrimination between American and international players. During the 2000s

---

Liang, J., Zhao, S., Zhu, H—These authors contributed equally.

© The Author(s), under exclusive license to Springer Nature Singapore Pte Ltd. 2024
X. Li et al. (Eds.): ICEMGD 2023, AEPS, pp. 391–399, 2024.
https://doi.org/10.1007/978-981-97-0523-8_38

and 2010s, international players received lower salaries than their U.S.-born counterparts [4]. However, the tide has quickly turned, with Hoffer and Freidel [5] finding that not only have wages for foreign players caught up to those of their American counterparts, but foreign-born players have actually received higher average wages.

We believe that previous research on salary discrimination has not adequately addressed the issue in today's context. Most studies have analyzed discrimination separately based on nationality and race, but our idea is to combine them in order to get a more comprehensive understanding of the issue. Specially, our work focuses on examining whether salary discrimination occurs among American-white, American-nonwhite, other country-white, and other country-nonwhite individuals.

2 Conceptual Framework

Discrimination is a longstanding and significant topic in economics and society. In The Economics of Discrimination [6], Gary Becker discusses discrimination from an economic perspective. The author identifies three main types of discrimination in the labor market: employer discrimination, employee discrimination, and consumer discrimination. Becker's theory suggests that discrimination occurs when employers or workers have a preference for or against a certain group of people, leading to unequal treatment in the labor market. Discrimination can arise from various factors, including prejudice, stereotypes, and beliefs about the abilities and characteristics of different groups. Becker also notes that discrimination can be rational or irrational, and can occur in both competitive and non-competitive labor markets.

Our research focuses on employer discrimination, specifically whether there is a salary discrimination in the sports league. The Mincer equation is a well-known economic model that describes the relationship between an individual's earnings and their education and experience. The equation was developed by economist Jacob Mincer in the 1970s [7] and is widely used in labor economics to predict the effect of education and experience on earnings [8]. To investigate this issue, we use the Mincer equation to build a model and perform OLS regression. Our data comes from the 2021–2022 season and includes player productivity statistics as well as individual characteristics such as height, weight, race, and nationality. We create four new dummy variables by combining race and nationality to further analyze the data: American-white, American-nonwhite, other country-white, and other country-nonwhite. By using the Mincer equation and regression analysis, it is easily for us analyses to determine whether employer discrimination exists in the NBA. Our research is significant because it sheds light on the issue of employer discrimination and provides evidence of its existence or lack thereof in a specific context. By understanding the factors that contribute to discrimination in the labor market, we can better address and combat it.

3 Data

The data for this research project was collected from Basketball Reference, a website that maintains comprehensive statistics on NBA players. In order to obtain information on players' race, we used a combination of methods, including looking at photos, examining players' family backgrounds, and visiting their individual pages on Basketball Reference. The data pertains to the 2022–2023 season and the dependent variable in the analysis is player salary, which was converted to the natural log in order to avoid issues with heteroscedasticity due to the high range of values.

To control for potential factors that might influence player salary, we included a number of variables in the analysis. These include player age, age squared, team, position, height, weight, games started, and minutes played. We also created several dummy variables to identify whether a player is white, American, or from another country. These dummy variables were used to create three interaction terms: American nonwhite, other country white, and other country nonwhite. The reference category for these interaction terms is American white.

Initially, we calculated the mean salary for white and non-white players in order to assess whether there was any preliminary evidence of discrimination. We found a $400,000 difference in mean salary between the two groups. However, when we examined the average player stats for the two groups, we found that black athletes had higher scores in most categories, with the exception of total rebounds. Given that black athletes tend to have better performance statistics overall, it is not surprising that they would be paid more. Therefore, we cannot definitively conclude that there is discrimination in the NBA based on these findings alone, and further regression analysis is needed.

Table 1. Independent variable value list.

Variables	Count	Mean	Std	Min	Max
GS	408	31.669	30.672	0	154
PER	408	10.091	6.0785	0	36.094
GDPpop	408	599.96	196.84	3.1029	934.329
AW	396	0.1085	0.3115	0	1
AN	396	0.6439	0.4794	0	1
OW	396	0.1111	0.3146	0	1
ON	396	0.1363	0.3436	0	1
Gift	405	0.0958	0.0688	0.003	0.29241
Age	408	25.713	4.3005	19	41
Age2	408	679.62	233.27	361	1281

In total, after we drop the nan value in dataset our regression included 392 observations, which are summarized in the Table 1 "Independent variable value Lists" and described in detail in Table 2 "Data Description."

4 Econometric Models and Testing

4.1 Econometric Models

To study whether there is discrimination against race and country in NBA salary, we introduced three dummy variables in the regression model. We used the interaction term to represent athletes of different races and countries. Considering that the dependent variable is salary, we use the Mincer earnings function as the basic model and further optimize the NBA salary problem on its model. The following are the equations used in the regression model [9]:

$$lnsalary = \beta_0 + \beta_1 GS + \beta_2 PER + \beta_3 GDP_{pop} + \beta_4 AN + \beta_5 OW + \beta_6 ON + \beta_7 Gift + beta_8 Age + \beta_9 Age^2 u \quad (1)$$

The dependent variable is lnsalary, which is the natural log of the players' 2022–2023 salaries. Calculation by natural logarithm, which can reduce the range of salary and make it closer to normal distribution.

The first independent variable GS is the number of starts for the player in the 2021–2022 season. Usually, we think that a player's appearance in the starting lineup reflects their stronger ability and better skills. We generally think that starting players will have higher wages, which can also be understood as a proxy variable of the star effect.

The second independent variable is PER, which is the player's efficiency rating in the 2021–2022 season. Calculated as follows:

$$PER = \frac{(PTS + TRB + AST + STL + BLK) - (2PA + 3PA - 2P - 3P) - (FTA - FT) - TOV - PF}{G} \quad (2)$$

For the PER which is a factor developed by ESPN's John Hollinger to measure a player's per-minute production in the NBA. PER includes all good performances and bad performances of players in the game, which are summed and averaged for each game. We believe that PER is the embodiment of a player's overall strength.

The third variable is GDP Pop, interpreted as the GDP per capita of the athlete's home country. Calculated as follows:

$$GDP_{pop} = \frac{GDP}{Population} \quad (3)$$

It is generally believed that countries with higher per capita GDP tend to have more resources and wealth, which can translate into higher salaries for athletes, including basketball players. This is because these countries may have more disposable income and a greater willingness to spend money on sports, including supporting their national teams and investing in the development of athletic talent. Additionally, higher per capita GDP may also be indicative of a larger market for basketball and other sports, which can lead to higher revenue streams for teams and leagues and ultimately result in higher salaries for players. However, it is worth noting that there are many other factors that can influence an athlete's salary, such as the individual's skill level, popularity, and negotiating power.

Table 2. Data description.

Data name	Description	Unit
Pos	The position of the player on the field	non
Age	Player's age on Feb 1st of the season	years
G	Games	times
GS	Games Started	times
MP	Minutes Played	minutes
FG	Filed Goals	points
FGA	Filed Goal Attempts	times
3P	3-pointed filed goal	points
3PA	3-Pointed Field goal Attempts	times
2P	2-Pointed Field goal	points
2PA	2-Pointed Field goal Attempts	times
FT	Free Throw	times
FTA	Free Throw Attempts	times
ORB	Offensive Rebounds	times
DRB	Defensive Rebounds	times
TRB	Total Rebounds	times
AST	Assists	times
STL	Steals	times
BLK	Blocks	times
TOV	Turnovers	times
PF	Personal Fouls	times
PTS	Points	points
white	= 1, if the player is white	non
country	= 1, if the player is American	non
Salary	Salary of player in 2021–2022	dollars
lnsalary	= ln(Salary)	non
Position	the position that the players were selected	number
Height	the height of player	cm
weight	the weight of player	kg
Age2	square of Age	non
AW	American white	non
AN	American nonwhite	non

(*continued*)

Table 2. (*continued*)

Data name	Description	Unit
OW	Other country white	non
ON	Other country nonwhite	non
Gift	position/(height + weight)	number
GDP	The GDP of one country in 2021	$1 billion
Population	The population of one country in 2021	10 million
GDP Pop	GDP/Population	$10
PER	[(PTS + TRB + AST + STL + BLK)-2PA + 3PA-2P-3P-(FTA-FT)-TOV-PF]/G	points

The fourth to sixth independent variables are dummy variables. AN represents non-white Americans, OW represents non-white Americans, and ON represents non-white non-Americans, so the base of the model is black Americans. We use these three variables to divide the athletes in the NBA into four categories. If a certain category is met, the variable value is 1, and the other dummy variable values are 0.

The seventh independent variable is Gift, which is used to represent the player's physical talent. The lower the Gift value, the better the physical talent we think. The calculation formula is as follows:

$$Gift = \frac{Position}{Height + Weight} \quad (4)$$

The eighth independent variable and the ninth independent variable are age and the square of age respectively. According to the thinking of the Mincer earnings function, we believe that wages will show a trend of rising first and then falling with age. The same is true in terms of subjective understanding. Athletes will reach a peak period as they grow older, and their performance will decline with age, and their salary will also decline.

To summarize, our research aims to investigate whether there is salary discrimination in the NBA based on race and nationality. We use the Mincer equation as a foundation and incorporate various independent variables that we believe may impact salaries. Our results will provide insight into the prevalence of discrimination in the NBA and may help to inform policies and practices to address such discrimination in the future.

4.2 Testing

We conducted several statistical tests to assess the validity and reliability of our multiple linear regression (MLR) model. First, we checked for collinearity among the independent variables by performing a correlation test. The results which are shown in the following Table 3.

Next, we conducted a RESET test to check for misspecification in the model. The RESET test compares the fit of a full model, which includes all the independent variables,

Table 3. Correlation.

Variables	lnsalary	GS	GDPpop	PER	AW	AN	OW	ON	Gift	Age	Age ^2
lnsalary	1	0.61	0.08	0.74	0.07	0.08	0.01	0.06	0.43	0.31	0.29
GS	0.61	1	0.09	0.07	0.11	0.11	0.01	0.03	0.27	0.15	0.13
GDPpop	0.08	0.09	1	0.03	0.17	0.64	0.53	0.56	0.04	0.02	0.02
PER	0.74	0.7	0.03	1	0.11	0.08	0.02	0.03	0.42	0.17	0.16
AW	0.07	0.11	0.17	0.11	1	0.47	0.12	0.14	0.07	0.03	0.01
AN	0.08	0.11	0.64	0.08	0.47	1	0.48	0.53	0.01	0.02	0.01
OW	0.01	0.01	0.53	0.02	0.12	0.48	1	0.14	0.02	0.06	0.06
ON	0.06	0.03	0.56	0.03	0.14	0.53	0.14	1	0.03	0.05	0.05
Gift	0.43	0.27	0.04	0.42	0.07	0.01	0.02	0.03	1	0.03	0.02
Age	0.31	0.15	0.02	0.17	0.03	0.02	0.06	0.05	0.03	1	1
Age2	0.29	0.13	0.02	0.16	0.01	0.01	0.06	0.05	0.02	1	1

with a reduced model that omits certain non-significant variables. The p-value of the RESET test was 0.0664, which passed the test at a confidence level of 0.05. This suggests that the model is reasonable and does not suffer from misspecification.

Finally, we performed the White test and the BP test to check for heteroscedasticity in the model. Heteroscedasticity occurs when the variance of the error term is not constant across the range of the independent variables and can lead to biased and inconsistent estimates of the regression coefficients. The p-values of both the White test $= 0.1951$ and the BP test $= 0.3588$ were above the 0.05 confidence level, indicating that there is no heteroscedasticity in the model.

Overall, the results of these tests suggest that the MLR model is valid and reliable for making predictions or inferences about the relationship between the independent variables and the dependent variable.

5 Result

Table 4 shows the OLS model estimates for the 2021–2022 NBA season. As can be seen from Table 4, the model is significant, with a F-statistic of 77.24. And the model with basic variable AW equation is:

$$lnsalary = 9.4929 + 0.0070GS + 0.0004GDP_{pop} + 0.0001AN + 0.06980OW + 0.0286ON - 3.1944Gift + 0.3326Age - 0.0052Age2 \quad (5)$$

The coefficient for games started (GS) was positive and statistically significant, indicating that players with a higher value in this variable may receive higher salaries. This could be due to the"star" effect, where the starting lineup of each team is perceived as having a stable level of productivity and receives a lot of attention from the public. As a result, teams may be willing to spend more to retain these players in order to improve their chances of winning and attract more fans. Player efficiency rating (PER)

Table 4. Regression results.

Factors	OLS(AW)	OLS(AN)	OLS(OW)	OLS(ON)
GS	0.007(0.002)	0.007(0.002)	0.007(0.002)	0.007(0.002)
PER	0.0886(0.008)	0.0886(0.008)	0.0886(0.008)	0.0886(0.008)
GDPpop	0.0004(0.0003)	0.0004(0.0003)	0.0004(0.0003)	0.0004(0.0003)
AW	-	−0.0001(0.114)	−0.0698(0.193)	−0.0286(0.182)
AN	0.0001(0.114)	-	−0.0697(0.167)	−0.0285(0.155)
OW	0.0698(0.193)	0.0697(0.167)	-	0.0412(0.139)
ON	0.0286(0.182)	0.0285(0.155)	−0.0412(0.139)	-
Gift	−3.194(0.569)	−3.194(0.569)	−3.194(0.569)	−3.194(0.569)
Age	0.3326(0.091)	0.3326(0.091)	0.3326(0.091)	0.3326(0.091)
Age2	−0.0052(0.002)	−0.0052(0.002)	−0.0052(0.002)	−0.0052(0.002)
constant	9.4929(1.225)	9.4931(1.203)	9.5627(1.203)	9.5216(1.198)
n	392	392	392	392
R2	0.645	0.645	0.645	0.645
Adj. R2	0.637	0.645	0.645	0.645
F-statistic	77.24	77.24	77.24	77.24

were statistically significant and related to player performance which imply that that one player can receive a larger wage from his great performance.

However, the result of GDP Pop coefficient differs from the conclusion of Yang & Lin. We found that the GDP Pop has a positive impact on salary but it's not statistically significant. We also included a factor called "Gift" to measure player talent, including draft pick, height, and weight, with a lower Gift indicating greater talent. The coefficient for Gift was negative and statistically significant, which aligns with the definition of the variable. Based on the Mincer equation, we also included Age and Age2 in the model, both of which were statistically significant and had reasonable signs. The Age factors suggest that a player's salary may increase as they get older, but may decrease after reaching their peak physical fitness. It is worth noting that the OLS model only takes into account the variables included in the analysis and may not capture all factors that influence a player's salary. Further research could explore other variables that may affect salary in the NBA.

Moreover, the results of the OLS model estimate for the 2021–2022 NBA season suggest that there is no salary discrimination in the league. This conclusion is based on the coefficients for each dummy variable, which were all statistically insignificant. This finding differs from previous research, which may be due to the "winner's curse" disappearing in recent years. It is possible that teams have gained more experience in evaluating the talent of players, including international talent, and as a result, discrimination has decreased [10]. Additionally, society has become more focused on promoting ethnic equality, and managers may be more aware of the consequences of discrimination. The banishment of Donald Sterling from the NBA serves as an example of the league's commitment to addressing discrimination and promoting inclusivity. Overall, it is important to continue efforts to eliminate discrimination and promote fairness in the NBA and other sports leagues.

6 Conclusion

Salaries discrimination in the National Basketball Association (NBA) has been a long-standing issue. In order to better understand the problem of salary discrimination in the NBA, we conducted research using data from the 2021–2022 season and the Mincer equation to build a model and perform OLS regression analysis. Our data include player productivity statistics as well as individual characteristics such as race and nationality. The result shows that there was no salary discrimination caused by race and nationality in the NBA based on the coefficients for the dummy variables in our OLS model, which were all statistically insignificant. While our research provides evidence that salary discrimination does not currently exist in the NBA, it is important to continue monitoring this issue and addressing any potential instances of discrimination that may arise.

References

1. Kahn, L.M., Sherer, P.D.: Racial differences in professional basketball players' compensation. J. Labor Econ. **6**(1), 40–61 (1988)
2. Dey, M.S.: Racial differences in national basketball association players' salaries: a new look. Am. Economist, **41**(2), 84–90 (1997)
3. Naito, H., Takagi, Y.: Is racial salary discrimination disappearing in the NBA? Evidence from data during 1985–2015. Int. Rev. Appl. Econ. **31**(5), 651–669 (2017)
4. Yang, C.H., Lin, H.Y.: Is there salary discrimination by nationality in the NBA? Foreign talent or foreign market. J. Sports Econ. **13**(1), 53–75 (2012)
5. Hoffer, A.J., Freidel, R.: Does salary discrimination persist for foreign athletes in the NBA?. Appl. Econ. Lett. **21**(1), 1–5 (2014)
6. Becker, G.S.: The Economics of Discrimination. University of Chicago Press, Chicago (1971)
7. Chiswick, B.R.: Jacob mincer, experience and the distribution of earnings. Rev. Econ. Household **1**, 343–361 (2003)
8. Heckman, J.J., Lochner, L.J., Todd, P.E.: Earnings functions, rates of return and treatment effects: The Mincer equation and beyond. In: Hanushek, E., Welch, F. (eds.) Handbook of the Economics of Education, vol. 1, pp. 307–458. Elsevier, Amsterdam (2006)
9. Chiswick, B.R., Mincer, J.: Experience and the Distribution of Earnings. Springer, New York (2006)
10. Eschker, E., Perez, S.J., Siegler, M.V.: The NBA and the influx of international basketball players. Appl. Econ. **36**(10), 1009–1020 (2004)

Choice Overload Paradox in Online Shopping Environment

Jiaxin Wang[1(✉)], Fang Han[2], Manting Ding[3], and Jia Zhang[4]

[1] Department of Economics, Xi'an Jiaotong-Liverpool University, Suzhou 215123, China
Jiaxin.WANG20@student.xjtlu.edu.cn
[2] Chengdu Shude High School Foreign Language Campus, Chengdu 610066, China
[3] Department of International Economics and Trade, Beijing Foreign Studies University, Beijing 100089, China
[4] Department of Economic Management, Northeast Agricultural University, Harbin 150006, China

Abstract. Choice overload appears to be the norm in the age of big data. The trend in consumer spending has been from offline to online over time. When given both extensive and limited options, Iyengar and Lepper performed a field experiment on jam purchases. Limited choice typically increases the urge to purchase, whereas extensive choice initially draws customers but does not encourage subsequent purchases. Has the proliferation of online shopping models that offer more options than traditional offline shopping models been hampered by choice overload? A simple mathematical model and a field experiment were used to demonstrate this paradox. A combination of quantitative and qualitative approaches was used in the experiment and data analysis. It was discovered that merchants might maximise consumer utility while still achieving their own goals of profit maximisation by interfering with consumer choices.

Keywords: Choice overload · Online · Paradox · Merchants · Utility

1 Introduction

Global retail e-commerce sales were estimated at 5.2 trillion dollars in 2021. By 2026, this amount is expected to have increased by 56%, totalling roughly 8.1 trillion dollars (see Fig. 1). The rapid development of e-commerce has also gradually allowed online shopping to replace traditional offline shopping methods [1, 2]. Khan and Sharmin found that people chose to shop online during Covid-19 Pandemic mainly because of the lack of transport or to avoid crowds [3]. Consumers are more concerned with the variety of products and the global nature of the online shopping model. Consumers are faced with more choices than offline shopping, they do not need to spend much time in the

---

J. wang and F. Han—These authors contributed equally to this work and should be considered co-first authors.
M. Ding and J. Zhang—These authors contributed equally to this work and should be considered co-second authors.

© The Author(s), under exclusive license to Springer Nature Singapore Pte Ltd. 2024
X. Li et al. (Eds.): ICEMGD 2023, AEPS, pp. 400–413, 2024.
https://doi.org/10.1007/978-981-97-0523-8_39

supermarket to select the products they are happy with, and they do not need to worry about the opening hours. The convenience of online shopping allows consumers to shop without leaving home. However, the choice overload theory proposed by behavioural economics needs to offer a reasonable explanation for this phenomenon. The choice overload theory is a paradox in an online shopping model with a more significant number of choices and a more comprehensive range of options. Under the assumption of choice overload, consumers would not make subsequent purchases with such a large number of choices, and the growth of e-commerce would therefore be curtailed. However, the reality is the opposite, and e-commerce has continued to grow in the last decade. The purpose of this paper is, therefore, to examine whether choice overload has a positive or negative impact on the two main shopping methods, offline and online, as well as to analyse the internal factors that influence it - the clarity of consumer preferences - and the external factors - some of the measures taken by merchants to promote consumer shopping. It is crucial to discover, analyse and understand this phenomenon's theoretical underpinnings and practical implications for two main reasons: on the one hand, it is vital to examine whether the choice overload theory is outdated or has its limitations and to study the factors that influence it to combine theory and reality in the analysis. On the other hand, consumer preferences are subject to external intervention by businesses.

Understanding how businesses can maximise their profitability by maximising consumer utility is also essential. Iyengar and Lepper conducted a field experiment on jam purchasing and found the negative impact of choice overload on subsequent purchases. Although extensive research has been carried out on choice overload, studies have yet to be conducted that especially explain the reasons for the real paradox caused by choice overload. A combination of quantitative and qualitative approaches was used in the experiment and data analysis. The present research explores, for the first time, the analysis of the factors influencing choice overload only in terms of consumer preference and merchant intervention. However, due to practical constraints, this paper cannot provide a more comprehensive analysis of consumer preferences but only a theoretical analysis from a simple mathematical model and a field experiment.

2 Literature Review

In the age of the information explosion, people's choice of online and offline shopping is expanding, and consumers' decision-making power and purchasing power are constantly influenced by intrinsic (subjective) and extrinsic (objective) factors when faced with a plethora of choices. According to Fig. 2, choice set complexity and decision task difficulty are the main extrinsic factors, and preference uncertainty and decision goal are the main intrinsic factors. Iyengar and Lepper conducted a field experiment in an upscale grocery store. It offers a limited (6) or an extensive (24) selection of different jam flavours. This experiment included several methods of controlling variables, including choice of location and jam brand, removal of the effect of the jam flavour itself, etc. By observing the initial attractiveness of the two displayed products to customers (how many consumers passing by were willing to try the jam) and the subsequent purchasing behaviour (how many consumers passing by were ready to buy the jam), it was concluded that extensive choices have the characteristic of being more attractive to customers; this

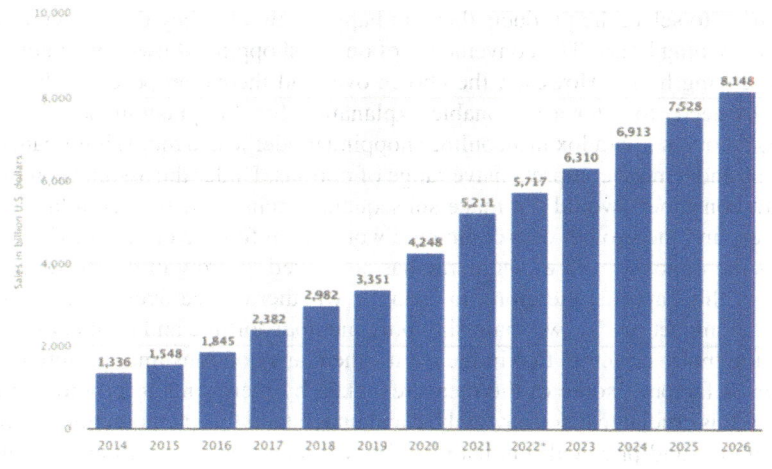

Fig. 1. Retail e-commerce sales worldwide from 2014 to 2026 (in billion U.S. dollars) [2].

is because a more comprehensive variety can occupy more of the customer's attention, and multiple options can settle more of the user's field of vision and the user's mind than a smaller arrangement of products, making them want to try and learn more; at the same time, limited choices make it easier for the user to make a purchase decision and the difference in the user's purchase decision is greater than the difference in attractiveness. However, is there only a negative impact of too many choices? The choice overload hypothesis states that increasing options will hurt choice motivation and the final decision [4, 5]. Contrary to popular belief, selecting from a large assortment might result in weaker preferences. Nagar found that the rapid growth of the Internet has allowed consumers to move from offline retail shops to a broader choice and range of online shopping platforms [6]. While Aparicio and Prelec found that online shopping platforms have contributed to the rapid development of the Internet economy [7]. A paradox has arisen: the negative impact of too much choice, as revealed by choice overload, is why the growth of online shopping platforms with more options has not stagnated; on the contrary, the online shopping approach has become the primary way of choice for consumers today. It is crucial to verify the positive and negative effects of choice overload and the factors influencing it considering this paradox.

3 Research Design and Methods

Iyengar and Lepper confirmed the existence of the demotivating effect of too many choices using three experiments. They also analysed the cause of this phenomenon—choosers in extensive-choice contexts feel more responsible for their choices, resulting in more significant frustration and dissatisfaction. However, they did not explain the question quantitatively. Prior literature did build numerical models to account for choice overload. The complexity of them prevents further discussion in this work. So, it is significant to build a mathematical model explaining choice overload that is simpler and easier to understand. A mathematical model has the merit of being objective, so to

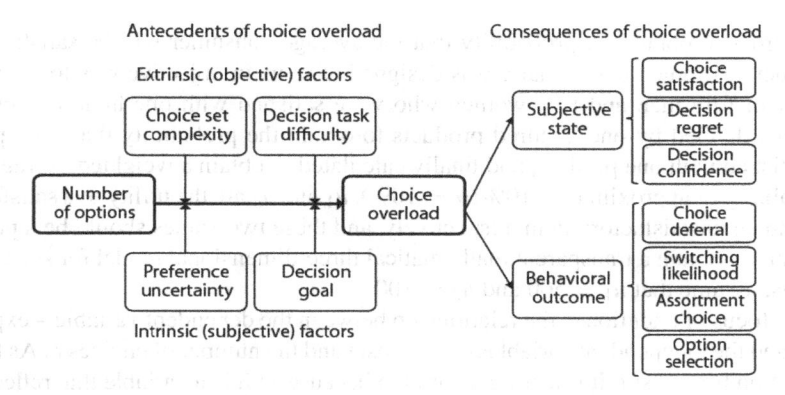

Fig. 2. Conceptual model of the impact of assortment size on choice overload [4].

preserve this objectivity, customer's utility is measured in "time" instead of "reported satisfaction", which can be subjective. As prior studies confirm choice overload, an inverted-U relation can be assumed between the number of choices and expected utility. Such a relation usually results from two opposed mediating processes, both monotonic. Based on this claim, a model was built synthesising a large assortment's positive and negative effects.

In this model, the selecting scenario is as follows: A customer comes to buy an item either offline or online, following three steps. 1) Before purchase, he will verify every item to see whether it is satisfactory, and this verification process costs time. 2) After verifying all the items, if there exists any satisfactory item, he will buy one; if no item is satisfactory, he will buy an unsatisfactory item. 3) After the purchase, he consumes the item and gets a specific utility. Satisfactory items will render him significantly higher utility than defective items do. How to connect utility with time can be understood as: after consuming an item, whether satisfactory or not, the customer's utility will rise, and therefore some amount of time can be saved.

Note that there are two critical premises in this hypothesis used to simplify the model:

1. The customer will check every item before purchase. He still needs to continue verification after finding a satisfactory item.
2. The customer will only choose one item. Also, time is assumed to be well-spent on hovering and hesitating.

Then is to set the parameter:

1. Considering one customer, the probability of each item being satisfactory to him is α.
2. The number of items is n.
3. The verification time cost to see whether an item is satisfactory is t.
4. The utility of a satisfactory item is u_1. The utility of an unsatisfactory item is u_2.

Therefore, the expected utility is:

$$u_1\left[1 - (1 - \alpha)^n\right] + u_2(1 - \alpha)^n - tn \tag{1}$$

In order to obtain the probability that the average consumer will be satisfied with a product, a simple questionnaire was designed. The main objective was to obtain the number of fifty men and fifty women who were satisfied with one hundred common products, divided by one hundred products to obtain the probability that each person was satisfied with one product, and finally calculated to obtain a weighted average with a probability of approximately 10% ($\alpha = 10\%$). u_1 and u_2 are the utility of a satisfactory item and an unsatisfactory item, respectively, and these two values should be a positive constant. To obtain a transparent mathematical three-dimensional model for subsequent analysis, assume that $u_1 = 500$ and $u_2 = 100$.

The focus of attention is the relationship between the dependent variable – expected utility and the independent variables – time cost t and the number of choices n. As for the verification time cost t, it is a critical variable because 1) It is a variable that reflects the intensity of preference. The clearer a customer's preference is, the less time he will need to verify each item. If the customer has a clear preference, then t is close to 0; therefore, the expected utility increases with n. 2) It also reflects the influence of online shopping. Due to the time-saving convenience and rating system of online shopping, verification time cost t will be significantly reduced.

The new expected utility function is:

$$500(1 - 0.9^n) + 100 * 0.9^n - tn \qquad (2)$$

And it is shown in Fig. 3:

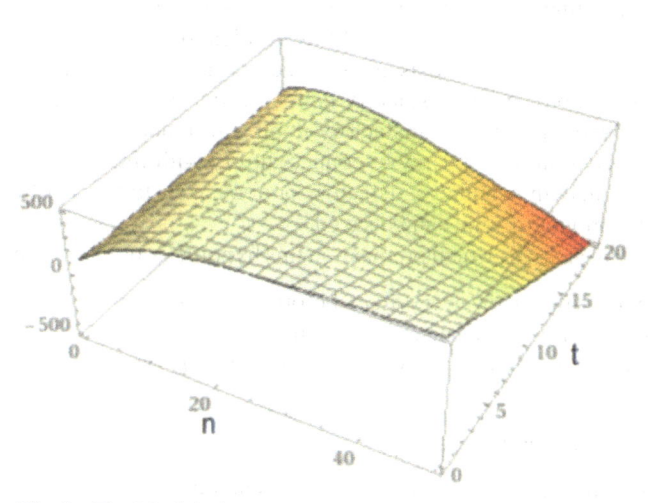

Fig. 3. The Model of Expected Utility Function [Owner-draw].

Three notable features can be seen from the graph that the function has:

1. For any same n, the function value decreases as t increases.
2. For any $t > 0$, the function value first increases and then decreases as n increases, suggesting the existence of choice overload, a maximum expected utility and an optimal number of choices.

3. The lower t is, the larger the optimal n is, suggesting that if verification time cost can be somehow reduced, the demotivating effect of too many choices will be significantly reduced.

Although customers will not do the detailed calculation in the offline scenario, they still need to learn by intuition and experience choice overload. Their expected utility will not permanently rise as the number of choices rises. Hence, they will likely be discouraged from buying by too many choices. However, in the online scenario, the fact that customers do not need to spend time going to physical stores and the rating system combine to reduce significantly verification time costs. Consequently, the expected utility increases and the arrival of the inflexion point is delayed. Also, the online shopping filter helps restrict the number of choices. All these functions unique to online shopping combine to alleviate the effect of choice overload that is almost unavoidable offline.

4 Methodology

So far, this paper has focused on verifying the effect of choice overload based on a numerical model designed on the grounds of an assumed shopping scenario from an offline-conducted jam experiment. When many options exceed inflexion, customers would be discouraged from consuming the goods as the increase in variable indicating the number of goods (n) on items "$(1 - \alpha)^n$" and "$t * n$" would always numerically lead to a fall in expected utility. Once the tendency of being affected by choice overload cannot be avoided despite scenario differences, online businesses may take marketing means from another potentially new dimension---helping to clarify customers' preferences. Given that the two variables "$t * n$" jointly affect the expected utility, it is likely that as verification time reduces, the impact of choice overload on the overall expected utility will diminish. This is because a shorter verification time (t) may offset the impact of a more significant number of choices (n). It is necessary to experimentally verify the hypothesis deduced from numerical analysis in a reproduced-reality online scenario.

4.1 Preliminary Analysis and Assumption

In this study, the centre of interest is finding how preferences could be clarified online. This would then cause a fall in verification time and, therefore, hypothetically correlates with reduction-being-controlled expected utility. As verification time may numerically reflect the degree to which customers are clear about their preferences, online shopping platforms indirectly take measures to help the customers cut down the time it takes to make choices by intervening in consumers' preferences. This carefully designed presentation may refer to a choice architecture. Previous studies mainly defined choice architecture as a specific environment that affects choice-making. However, Thaler pointed out that choice architecture often works in the shopping scenario when nudges are designed accordingly [8]. Nudge is a term that defines any aspect of choice architecture that predictably alters behaviour without forbidding options or significantly changing economic incentives. Some nudges could be realised in online shopping by offering complex choices or setting a filter system.

The increase in complexity of choices may refer to, for instance, the addition to the credit of online shop owners which provides a reference for how honestly the shop owners may have behaved on the online shopping platform. Adding more complex information may positively impact clarifying customers' preferences and thereby lead to reduced time for verification (t), since they are free to choose products based on specific reference standards. Another form of nudge is a filter system set. A filter system refers to a navigation system carried out by official online shopping companies and applied to a specific platform, which breaks down long lists of products into manageable results. Assuming that, with results being affected by filter systems, the reduction of expected utility could be retarded with limited choices (n). The initial round of selection performed by the filter system has also decreased the verification time simultaneously. In this study, how the two nudges based on choice architecture affect expected utility will be respectively researched.

4.2 Participants and Experimental Site

The study involves two field experiments that research whether/how changes in choice architecture may help to neutralise the effect of choice overload on expected utility in online shopping scenarios. The main experimental sites are an offline convenience store and an online platform. Considering the companies' user profiles, publicity and unique features, the experimental platform is Jindong. For the user profile of Jindong, most users are young grown-ups between 18–45, which takes up 87%. According to the report provided by China Chain-Store & Franchise Association (CCFA) in 2022, the user group could be representative despite platform differences since the user base is extensive and accords with the constitution of buyers in offline scenarios whose leading group are people aged between 21–49(92%) [9]. Besides, according to a data report released by Alibaba in 2021, there were 0.53 billion active users annually buying goods on Jindong in 2021 [10]. This indicates the relatively constant reputation it is likely to enjoy among citizens and the high publicity it possibly holds now and soon, which could, thus, to some extent, ensure the long-term ecological validity of the study and results.

One unique feature of Jindong is that the company runs offline convenience stores around China. It does sound to set the experimental site both in online and offline scenarios; by setting the context in the convenience stores run by Jindong company itself, the conditions, prices, brands of products, and the service mechanism applied could be, to a great extent the same as on the Jindong online platform. Also, as the offline context is labelled as Jindong, the brand trust, which would easily be affected by brand familiarity, that participants hold towards two scenarios could be controlled to a certain level. In other words, with offline and online scenarios set in Jindong, the influence of factors such as management and brand trust could be minimised. At the same time, the variables to be studied could still be adjusted to be different. The participants selected with opportunity sampling are 50 students attending the same university, 25 men and 25 women. A specific feature about the participants is that they seldom or never had online shopping but tend to have offline shopping more frequently. The age interval of participants is set based on considerations about the user profile of Jindong, where university students aged between 18–25 make up 40%. The purpose of choosing participants who are lovers of offline shopping is to minimise their familiarity with the online shopping mechanism. In this way, once exposed to online shopping, the effect of nudges is more significant.

4.3 Product Selection - Initial Selection

The product is instant noodles. Considering minimising the effect of prices and brands, using instant noodles as the products for participants, the differences between price and brands, which are usually the main features for consumers to choose goods, could be relatively small. There are two benefits. On the one hand, prices and brands are not the main features to be studied when it comes to identifying differences between offline and online scenarios since they would always have primary effects regardless of context. Since people may directly use simplifying heuristics and are more likely to be influenced by present bias, such as choosing the significantly cheapest option or the option with the most prominent brand, the difference between prices and brands should be minimal when determining the impact of choice overload. On the other hand, since no clear preferences participants would have towards instant noodles, the effect of nudges may be more clearly shown.

4.4 Product Preference Survey and Specific Selection

An instant noodles preference survey would be conducted before the primary procedure to ensure participants could accept all the brands and categories of chosen instant noodles. It is significant to survey individual preferences with thirty brands and thirty flavours. In the first round of the survey, participants would be asked to choose their favourite and least favourite flavours. The favourite and least favourite options would then be excluded. This survey ensures no clear preferences would have influenced the primary procedure as the ones towards which participants show relatively strong love or hate are presented outside the primary buying process. The price of instant noodles is around 5–6 RMB. The price difference is relatively small, but participants could still have some trade-offs between price and other noodles features. There would be a limited-choice group of a total of 6 choices, among which every two products are of one particular brand and one specific flavour that participants feel neutral. As for prices, three of the six would be 5 RMB while another three would be 6 RMB. In other words, participants would face a selection between six products from 3 similar brands, three commonly accepted flavours and two similar price levels. There would be another extensive-choice group of 24 choices, among which every four products are of one particular brand and one specific flavour that participants feel neutral. As for prices, 12 of the 24 would be 5 RMB, while another 12 would be 6 RMB. In other words, there would be a selection between 24 products of six similar brands, six commonly accepted flavours and two similar price levels.

4.5 Designed Procedures

Procedure 1. Procedure 1 is set to be a non-participant and structured observation. It aims to discover whether the change in the complexity of choices might reduce the effect of choice overload on expected utility with decreasing verification time by clarifying preferences. Procedure 1 may last for about two months. During the two months, there would be six days for the experiment. However, an interval of at least seven days between each experiment day would be set. If the experiments were conducted less frequently, participants might be fed up with buying instant noodles. This is also to prevent participants from realising the study's aim and thus grow demand characteristics, which would hurt the selection process. The first and second groups of experiments would determine whether a fall in expected utility suggests a longer verification time (t) taken.

Experiment 1. The first two experiments conducted in an offline convenience store involved two control-treatment groups for verifying the hypothesis that the increase in the verification time (t) caused by the increased provision of choices could lead to a fall in expected utility, which indicates choice demotivating. The experiment time would be set at 5 pm, one hour before the typical dinner time. On Day 1, the participants were successively told to have a 20% discount if they entered the offline Jindong convenience store to choose one instant noodle to buy while provided with a limited-choice group (6). Participants may buy one noodle or give up this chance to buy instant noodles at a discount. After one participant leaves the convenience store, the vacant left would be filled before the next participant enters. Each participant would not be aware of others' choices. An inconspicuous observer would act as a shopper on the nearby shelf, recording the time for participants to make the final decision. Time recording would start from the instant the participants are standing in front of the shelf where the instant noodles are set, and end as the customer moves their eyes off and start to leave with/without any chosen noodles. On Day 2, all procedures would be the same as on Day 1 except for the treatment added. The limited-choice group (6) would replace the extensive-choice group (24).

Experiment 2. The second two control-treatment groups would be conducted online for the same research purpose as in the offline scenario. However, it is for verifying the hypothesis that the increase in verification time caused by the increased provision of choices correlate with a fall in expected utility in a specific online scenario. The experiment time would be set at about 3 pm, and the participants would be informed to have the chosen product delivered in three hours. This time interval is designed to simulate in-city delivery service in online shopping. Moreover, participants would be aware that they are also ordering their dinner. Participants would gather in one classroom in the university. On Day 3, all participants were again told successively to order instant noodles with a 20% discount. However, the ordering process is through searching for instant noodles on the Jindong application on a new phone. In this scenario, participants would search within Jindong online shop, where the limited-choice group (6) would be presented. Observers would run the new online shop. Another observer acts as another student participant would start time recording from the instant the participant has the search result to the instant the participant has paid for the chosen noodles or has decided to give up. This time, the only information provided would be the pictures and information about the ingredients and manufacturers of the products. This minimises the difference in features between the goods in online and offline scenarios since the information provision differs from the study's centre in experiment 2. The only variable in this scenario is the number of choices provided. There would be 50 new accounts registered in advance.

Every individual participant would search with a new account logged in. This is to avoid the memory of user preferences. On Day 4, all procedures would follow that of Day 3. However, the choice group provided would be the extensive-choice group (24).

Experiment 3. Experiment 3 involves a change in the complexity of choices. The control group would be the experiment on Day 4, where participants were required to have a choice among an extensive-choice group. The treatment condition would be a change in the complexity of choices which may be presented as an addition to information. The change in the complexity of choices would be the addition to the shop owner's choices (saying the shop owner recommends the good) and the comments left by former buyers. This group of experiments would be conducted in the same scenario as the second group. After the second group of experiments, qualitative data will be collected. The participants who had bought instant noodles would be required to leave comments on the online platform. The comments could be "good" or "bad" optional feedback or descriptions of their feelings for the product.

On Day 5, all participants were again told successively to order instant noodles with a 30% discount in another online shop run by observers. This time, the online shop would be set to be different. The brands and flavours would be changed to others still from the choice pool of instant noodles that participants all feel neutral about (the number of noodles of each flavour and brand would remain the same). This prevents participants from being affected by the previous shopping experience and may have a present bias about certain online shops or products. The choice group presented this time would be an extensive-choice group (24).

With the feedback collected from the last group of experiments, observers leave reviews under some products with their own Jindong accounts (reviews would exactly be repeated from participants). However, the proportion of "good" or "bad" reviews would vary. After that, some products with relatively not that great ratings by buyers would be labelled as "shop owner's choice", which suggests this is the product the shop owner recommends the customers buy. In contrast, the products with a relatively good reputation among former buyers (with a large proportion of "good" reviews) would not be labelled as "shop owner's choice". Again another observer acts as another student participant would start time recording from the instant the participant has the search result to the instant the participant has paid for the chosen noodles or has decided to give up.

Procedure 2. Procedure 2 is set to be a non-participant and structured observation. It verifies the effect of the filter system on the expected utility. The filter system may be assumed to reduce the verification time (t) and the number of choices (n) simultaneously. Nevertheless, this time, the participants may be required to search for instant noodles on a search engine, and the conditions of instant noodles cannot be controlled. It is assumed to last for one month. Furthermore, there would be two days for the experiment.

Experiment 4. On Day 1, all participants were again told successively to order instant noodles with a 20% discount through the Jindong application. In this scenario, participants would not make the selection in a private online shop but directly through a search engine. The Jindong filter system, which might assist users in finding items via categories like "price level from highest to lowest", "the best sold", "the best rated", or "imported or domestic", would be set to "blocked" in this method. This time, the phone screen for the experiment would be monitored through a remote recorder. The action of the participants on the phone would be recorded. Moreover, the time interval between the instant participants having the search result and the instant participants having paid or given up making choices would also be recorded. On Day 2, all procedures follow that of Day 1. However, this time participants would be informed about the filter system and be allowed the freedom to conduct it if necessary since all participants are the nearly green hand of online shopping. It is assumed that participants would choose to use the filter system for the selection or at least have some tries. The action of the participants on the phone would be recorded. Moreover, the time interval between the instant participants having the search result and the instant participants having paid or given up making choices would also be recorded.

Operationalization. To make the dependent variable accurately quantified, the expected utility would be measured by the giving up rate in one experiment (the rate of participants choosing to give up buying noodles).

4.6 Dependent Measures and Predicted Results

Two measures would be taken for assessment in the three experiments in procedure 1. In Experiments 1 and 2, the time it takes for participants to have the final decision (t) and the rate of giving up buying noodles would be recorded and then calculated. The result is predicted that with more choices provided, the verification time (t) for participants to make choices may be longer. Moreover, as the verification time (t) increased, the giving-up rate was also likely to increase, showing a fall in the expected utility. In Experiment 3, the decision-making time and the giving-up rate would also be recorded and calculated. The increased complexity is predicted to occur with a quicker decision made. Furthermore, the giving up rate would also fall in line with the fall in verification time. Two measures would be used for assessment in the one experiment in procedure 2. In Experiment 4, through the recorded action of participants on the phone, the number of products browsed by participants before making final decisions (n) and the time it takes for participants to make choices (t) would be calculated, which are the two items that would affect the expected utility. It is predicted that the number of products being browsed, and the amount of time needed to make decisions would decrease with a filter system. This is a simultaneous decrease in the verification time (t) and the number of options (n) in correlation with the fall in expected utility being controlled.

4.7 Limitations

Ecological Validity: The experiment might not be a full-field experiment since informed consent is ensured to a large extent. Though the environmental settings "the convenience store" and "the classroom" are natural, the participants' behaviours may not reflect that of real life for some extraneous variables in specific experimental situations.

Experimental Design: Repeated measure is conducted. Participants may have greater exposure to demand characteristics since they go through all levels of independent variables. Besides, participants may grow tired of eating instant noodles during the procedures. Some alternate participants should be available.

Dependent Measures & Data: It should be argued whether the giving up rate could be used as a measure for the expected utility since it only reflects the overall expected utility and individual expected utility is not studied.

5 Conclusion

The experimental results show that when people face the situation of choice overload, their purchasing power will increase because of the help of sellers. Sellers will use some measures to make consumers choose the products they are more satisfied with. In most cases, the seller's help is some joint activities businesses make to consumers. The positive reciprocity enables consumers to respond positively; that is, they are more likely to buy goods from sellers. The assortment's feature complementarity is significant because it affects customers' preferences and evaluations of the choices they ultimately select [11]. When an assortment's features are complimentary as opposed to non-complementary, consumers benefit more from it. For more enormous assortments, choice overload may result from the increased trade-offs and challenging decision-making caused by complementing characteristics in the choices in the assortment. Through the creation of choice environments, choice architecture interventions seek to encourage individuals to engage in personally and socially beneficial conduct [12]. Sellers take some measures to help consumers make choices better, faster and easier by changing their choices without changing the option pool. Expert opinion guide consumers to make choices more efficiently by giving opinions on specific options [13]. "Expert" may be any trusted person, organisation or business. A filter may be a simple and effective tool for the overly complex option pool. Information filtering systems are created for unstructured or semi-structured data, and the basis for filtering is descriptions of individual or group information preferences [14]. To prevent customers from making poor judgements due to the complexity of choosing, let them remove the most superfluous possibilities by giving them limited options. In order to improve the experience for both customers with and without preferences, the filter also performs the task of dividing the selection pool of those with clear and ambiguous preferences. When there are many parameters to be compared in the selection, adding a comparison panel can help consumers better understand the differences and commonalities of various products to make better choices. Vivid choice allows customers to comprehend numerous possibilities naturally and assists them in making better decisions. Adding images, assessment movies, and user feedback are covered in this section. Some firms attempt to give a "try before you buy" service by providing clients with various samples from which to choose.

The relationship between decision utility and experienced utility of recreational nature visits is assessed by the travel cost (TCM) and subjective well-being (SWB) [15]. A similar measurement can be applied to consumer preferences. The abstract concept of preference is translated into a tangible cost of time to measure the maximum utility of the experience for the consumer. If customers' experienced utility and objective happiness rise, the likelihood of subsequent purchases will increase dramatically. Enterprise exists only to increase profits. Welsch and Ferreira found that if customers are satisfied throughout the consumption process, there will be a greater likelihood of repurchasing, which will boost the operational profit of businesses [16]. As previously said, businesses may take various steps to boost client satisfaction in the online buying environment. As a means of enhancing the offline shopping experience, several shopping malls provide shoppers with snacks and modest presents or conduct lottery activities at the final checkout.

A person's happiness over a given period is equal to the total of their momentary utilities during that time or the temporal integral of momentary utilities. According to the peak-end rule, people tend to focus more on the final (end) episode and the episode with the highest intensity when reflecting on an event than they do on other episodes. In retrospective evaluations, the length of painful or uncomfortable episodes was disregarded entirely, and many emphases were placed on the experience's conclusion and its peak or trough. Doi and Yamaoka explored the use of the peak-end rule in assessing the product user experience in the context of overall satisfaction with smartphone applications, a chronological evaluation of previously special episodes with the usage of applications, and the level of satisfaction of each episode [17]. The Peak-End Rule means that our memory of a thing is limited to the peak and the trough, but the event process has little influence on the memory. It is mainly divided into two parts: the peak part and the trough part. An examination of the variables' correlations showed that the end and the peaks were related to overall satisfaction. A person's overall experience of an event depends on the peak moment (especially good or bad) in the whole event process and the end feeling. That is to say, in the process of shopping, when consumers enter the mall at the beginning, it is "peak", and when they check out at the end, it is "trough". Most people feel happy when they purchase something and a little down when they see a massive payment at the cash register. Certain shopping malls will take some proactive actions after customers have finished shopping to boost their sense of consumption happiness and, as a result, the businesses' revenues. This is done to lessen the depressed mood of customers in the malls.

As mentioned before, future conduct is formed by memory. As a result, how people recall a particular experience may be just as significant as the experience itself. The peak-End rule contends that the peak and emotional valence after an experience in the present is the best predictor of recalled memories. People's memories will eventually lose track of the laborious process of things. Consumers may have less than favourable or uninteresting experiences while shopping at the mall, Such as spending much time in line to make a purchase. When they finish shopping, many might need to pay attention to this tedious process. Merchants, therefore, need to carefully evaluate every aspect of the shopping experience and design a peak and end value to help consumers choose their preferences among a large number of options, shorten the time spent choosing and reduce time costs, thereby maximising consumer utility and happiness, and ultimately maximising their profits.

Acknowledgment. Jiaxin Wang and Fang Han contributed equally to this work and should be considered co-first authors, Manting Ding and Jia Zhang contributed equally to this work and should be considered co-second authors.

References

1. Iyengar, S.S., Lepper, M.R.: When the choice is demotivating: can one desire too much of a good thing? Constr. Preference 300–322 (2006). https://doi.org/10.1017/cbo9780511618031.017
2. Stephanie Chevalier. Retail e-commerce sales worldwide from 2014 to 2026 (in billion U.S. dollars) [Graph]. In Statista (2022). https://www-statista-com.heyworld.top/statistics/379046/worldwide-retail-e-commerce. Accessed 25 Feb 2023
3. Khan, M.M., Shams-E-Mofiz, M., Sharmin, Z.A.: Development of E-commerce-based online web application for COVID-19 pandemic. iBusiness **12**, 113–126 (2020)
4. Chernev, A., Böckenholt, U., Goodman, J.K.: Choice overload: a conceptual review and meta-analysis. J. Consum. Psychol. **25**, 333–358 (2015)
5. Scheibehenne, B., Greifeneder, R., Todd, P.M.: Can there ever be too many options? A meta-analytic review of choice overload. J. Consum. Res. **37**, 409–425 (2010)
6. Nagar, K.: Drivers of E-store patronage intentions: choice overload, internet shopping anxiety, and Impulse Purchase Tendency. J. Internet Commer. **15**(2), 97–124 (2016). https://doi.org/10.1080/15332861.2016.1148971
7. Aparicio, D., Prelec, D.: Choice overload in online platforms. SSRN Electron. J. (2017). https://doi.org/10.2139/ssrn.3044096
8. Thaler, R.H., Sunstein, C.R.: Nudge: Improving Decisions about Health, Wealth, and Happiness. Yale University Press (2008)
9. CCFA. China Shopping Mall Consumer Insight Report 2020–2021 (2022)
10. Alibaba Group. Filing of Annual Report on Form 20-F for Fiscal Year 2021 (2021)
11. Zhu, Q., Sarkis, J., Geng, Y., Fujita, T., Hashimoto, S.: Feature complementarity and large assortments: role of feature complementarity in developing product assortment (2018)
12. Mertens, S., Herberz, M., Hahnel, U.J., Brosch, T.: The effectiveness of nudging: a meta-analysis of choice architecture interventions across behavioral domains. In: Proceedings of the National Academy of Sciences of the United States of America, vol. 119 (2021)
13. Ribeiro, T.P., Corsi, A., Lockshin, L., Louviere, J.J., Loose, S.M.: Analysis of consumer preferences for information and expert opinion using a discrete choice experiment. Port. Econ. J. **19**, 67–80 (2019)
14. Belkin, N.J., Croft, W.B.: Information filtering and information retrieval: two sides of the same coin? Commun. ACM **35**, 29–38 (1992)
15. Börger, T., Maccagnan, A., White, M.P., Elliott, L.R., Taylor, T.: Was the trip worth it? Consistency between decision and experienced utility assessments of recreational nature visits (2022)
16. Welsch, H., Ferreira, S.: 1 environment, well-being, and experienced preference (2014)
17. Doi, T., Doi, S., Yamaoka, T.: The peak–end rule in evaluating product user experience: the chronological evaluation of past impressive episodes on overall satisfaction. Hum. Factors Ergon. Manuf. Serv. Ind. **32**, 256–267 (2022)

The Influence of Endowment Effect on the Investment Decisions in Hybrid Funds

Huiqi Zhang[✉]

Southwest Jiaotong University, Chengdu 611756, Sichuan, China
2020117101@my.swjtu.edu.cn

Abstract. Fund purchasing has become a hot field and topic in the financial industry in recent years. Investors realize the preservation and appreciation of assets by trading fund shares. As an important member of fund products, hybrid fund has been favored by many investors by virtue of its strong liquidity. However, current studies rarely involve the result that investors' decisions are affected by endowment effect when facing large varieties funds. Therefore, this paper starts from the considerations of investors when purchasing hybrid funds taking into account the influence of endowment effect on purchase conditions and fund performance as independent variables. Due to the endowment effect, the influence of investors' decision to buy mixed funds is studied. This paper bases on the data obtained from previous studies and combined with theoretical analysis then come to a conclusion. Due to the endowment effect, investors are more inclined to buy star funds and retain funds with good performance, even if their status quo is not in an excellent situation. This paper studies the irrational decisions investors make when buying funds, and the impact of these decisions on investment behavior. At the same time, this paper also explains the causes of "irrational" decisions, so that investors can properly use analytical thinking to adjust and avoid irrational decisions in the future investment, so as to obtain higher investment returns and fund returns.

Keywords: Endowment Effect · Hybrid Funds · Investment Decision · Irrational Decision

1 Introduction

With the vigorous development of local economy, fund purchase has become a hot field and topic in the financial industry in recent years. Investors realize asset preservation and appreciation by trading fund shares. While institutional investors make profits by constantly adjusting their portfolios, so the fund industry plays a vital role in promoting the rapid development of the capital market, maintaining the stability of the financial market and reducing systemic risks [1]. As an important member of the fund products, hybrid fund has gained a lot due to its advantages of being able to buy and redeem at any time and strong liquidity Investors like it.

Through the study and summary of previous research results, the author finds that most of the papers are discussing whether this type of fund is worth buying based on the fund itself, or evaluating fund performance based on data analysis, or how to buy funds. However, current studies rarely involve the result that investors' decisions are affected by endowment effect when they are faced with many types of funds. Therefore, this paper will start from the factors that investors consider when making purchase decisions.

In the previous studies, Data Envelopment Analysis (DEA) model is used to analyze the efficiency value, technical progress efficiency, pure technical efficiency and scale efficiency of partial stock hybrid fund, partial debt hybrid fund and balanced hybrid fund from static and dynamic aspects, taking the influence of endowment effect on purchase conditions and fund performance as independent variables. The previous data will be used in this paper to analysis the influence of endowment effect on consumption decision making. The influence of investors' decision to invest in mixed funds is studied. The research results show that, due to the existence of endowment effect, investors will be affected by peer pressure, star effect and other factors before buying to enhance their purchase intention, while in the case of purchased funds, they will make "irrational" judgments on the original funds due to the influence of endowment effect. In general, the author finds that due to the effect of endowment effect, investors are more inclined to buy star funds and keep the funds with good performance, even if their current situation is not excellent.

This paper analyzes and summarizes the influence of endowment effect on the public's decision to buy mixed funds by taking the influence of pre-purchase conditions on purchase intention, the influence of fund performance on purchase decision and the role of endowment effect in these two influences as research points.

2 Analysis on Investment Decisions in Hybrid Funds

2.1 Conceptual Framework

Below, in Fig. 1, there presents a conceptual framework of investment decision-making in hybrid funds. In accordance with this logical framework, this paper will discuss the factors that affect investors' decisions. The main part of this paper will make an analysis of the fund purchase decision according to this logical framework. Firstly, the influences of pre-purchase conditions and fund performance on investors' investment decisions and the influencing process will be obtained based on previous research and analysis. At the same time, this paper will demonstrate the role and effect of endowment effect on how pre-purchase conditions and fund performance affect investors' decisions.

2.2 The Influence of Pre-purchase Conditions on Purchase Decision

This section summarizes the reasons why people have the impulse to buy, and the correlation between these reasons and the decision of fund purchase in the fund market by reviewing the literature.

It is clear that consumers are often not rational when making decisions. In many cases, some external factors will cause them to consumption impulse. According to previous studies, analytical thinking is negatively correlated with purchase intention. When people's analytical thinking is awakened, their consumption impulse will decrease significantly [2]. It is expected that the reason of purchase intention and purchase antecedents will affect the invest decision.

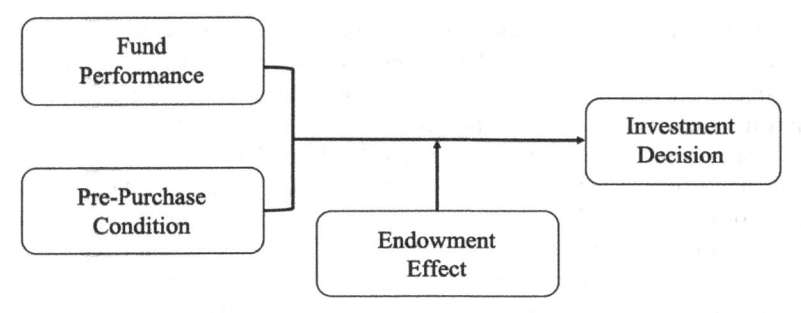

Fig. 1. Conceptual Framework of Investment Decisions in Hybrid Funds.

Pre-purchase Conditions. As mentioned above, the influence of pre-purchase conditions on consumers' decision-making is mainly through influencing consumers' analytical thinking. In terms of the selection of influencing factors, this paper will make a choice by judging the influence of such factors on rational analytical thinking. A preliminary judgment can be made by referring to the previous literature. Therefore, this paper will comprehensively discuss the influence of pre-purchase conditions on investors' purchase decisions from the perspectives of the star effect of funds, the influence of "boredom" on consumption impulse and the influence of pre-purchase ritual behavior on consumption.

Boredom on Impulse Spending. According to the previous studies, from the perspective of cognition, when consumers make purchase decisions, factors such as maintaining mood and repairing emotions will exert cognitive load, thus resulting in ego loss [3]. Fund as a kind of non-physical products, investors before buying the lack of stimulation of boredom and excessive analysis of the product will make consumption decisions tend to be "irrational". The boredom caused by insufficient stimulation will make consumers obtain instant gratification through impulse consumption. At this time, consumers focus on negative emotions, but not fully mobilize their analytical thinking, and ignore the problem of thinking about the purchase itself. However, if there is too much product analysis before purchase, especially when purchasing financial products, consumers tend to collect more information before making decisions. This will cause, in the final decision, they tend to consume too much energy in the early stage to produce cognitive load, which leads to impulsive consumption.

Star Effect. In the investigation of funds, individual investors tend to be "irrational" due to their limited attention and ability to acquire information cost in decision-making, so the "star funds" are more favored by investors in the decision-making of fund selection. In particular, star funds with excellent historical performance will be favored by investors. However, the fund's income will be affected by the market, if the market is good, the fund often can have a stable performance. However, these potential earnings due to market factors should not be ignored, so blindly choose star funds and have a higher performance expectation is irrational.

According to previous studies, the anticipated emotions before purchase will promote the generation of psychological ownership and the generation of guilt about the anticipated non-purchase [4]. Therefore, when investors analyze the historical performance of star funds, if the market is in a good period, consumers will feel guilty about not being able to purchase enough. If in the general market period, investors will produce high psychological expectations of the star fund and produce the purchase intention. In a word, investors under the star effect are more likely to reduce the consumption impulse caused by the endowment effect.

2.3 The Influence of Fund Performance on Purchase Decision

In order to reduce evaluation costs, investors of open-end funds would preferentially choose funds with good performance. At the end of the 20th century, some scholars have shown that performance is positively correlated with net fund inflow [5]. When making decisions, investors have obvious "loss aversion", which means, investors are more sensitive to losses than profits, which makes investors make "irrational" choices when making decisions.

In this section, the influence of fund performance on investors' decision-making is obtained by comparing the numerical changes of fund performance obtained by DEA model analysis during the investigation period and the amplitude of fund profit and loss.

It is expected that, in the purchase decision of hybrid funds, investors tend to prefer more stable partial debt funds than partial stock funds with large ups and downs.

Evaluation on Fund Performance. Among the evaluation methods of fund performance, the traditional evaluation methods based on Mean value--Variance (MV) theory and Capital Asset Pricing Mode (CAPM) theory model usually only apply to those funds with positive excess returns. However, in the current fund market, it is impossible for a fund or portfolio to have only positive excess returns. When facing funds with negative returns, traditional evaluation methods are not suitable [6]. At the same time, in the evaluation of fund performance, the traditional method has the defect of not taking into account multiple factors due to the relatively simple evaluation index. However, if researcher use the DEA model, these problems can be solved. Because DEA model can carry out weighted processing of indicators, so that the results are more objective. On this account, this paper chooses to use the DEA model which can analyze fund performance from multiple input and output indicators to evaluate and judge the performance of hybrid fund.

According to the performance of 172 hybrid funds selected from the Choice financial terminal from the beginning of 2019 to the end of 2019, the DEA model is used to analyze the conclusion that under the significance level of 5%, the smaller the risk fluctuation of fund assets, the easier the fund performance is to improve, that is, investors are more inclined to choose this kind of fund [6].

Market Fluctuations. Based on previous studies,60 open-ended stock funds of four different styles established over eight years are selected as sample funds to study their performance from 2014 to 2018. The research shows that the overall fund performance is better than that in the stable market period, and market fluctuations not only affect the overall fund performance and return. Moreover, the input-output efficiency gap among funds will be increased, among which, input-output efficiency of inefficient funds is most affected by market period [7]. Thus, during periods of market volatility, investors tend to choose funds with a low probability of loss.

Starting from the direction of market volatility, it is found that the overall performance of the fund market is better in the stable period. From the perspective of fund performance itself, funds with more stable fluctuations of income and loss can attract more investors. It is not difficult to find that mixed funds with good performance and stable volatility are more favored by investors.

2.4 The Role of Endowment Effect

The endowment effect is the idea that once an individual owns something, he values it much more than he did before. This leads to another concept that plays an important role in investment decisions called loss aversion. As people tend to increase their evaluation of the value of their existing goods, when facing risks, the pain caused by the loss of the existing goods will be greater than the happiness generated by the acquisition of the same value goods, thus resulting in the loss aversion mentality.

The Choice of Fund Holders. As mentioned above, since investors prefer to stay in the status quo, and the amount of information they can process over a period of time is limited, they are more likely to stay in the funds they hold, even if they are currently not doing well, than to change their investment decisions in response to changes in the market and fund performance. The reason behind this kind of investor psychology is the effect of endowment. When the investor holds a certain fund, they will increase the value of the fund psychologically, so that they are not willing to give up the fund when the fund performance is poor, and try to reason for this decision. For example, the fund performance is poor because of market fluctuations, or they think that the fund performance can be improved in the future. The seemingly "safe" choice of staying put is actually an irrational one, because qualified investors will react significantly to the alpha of a fund, not based on past experience. Therefore, in essence, the deviation of fund holders' decisions is often caused not by the fund itself, but by the constraints faced by investors [8]. As a result, investors who pay more attention to safety prefer low-risk assets, while investors who seek high returns prefer high-yield assets, but still follow the investment criterion of "safety first" [9].

The Choice of Non-holders. For investors who do not hold funds, they will have endowment effect on their assets, which leads to their loss aversion of loss and risk. As the previous study shows, investors exhibit the endowment effect for non-instrumental information, and so value information more, simply by virtue of "owning" it [10]. In the classic experiment of loss aversion, investors are more likely to choose a portfolio with less risk when faced with different probabilities of gains and losses, even if the mathematical expectations are the same. As the phenomenon mentioned in Sect. 2.3 above, this results in generally better fund performance in stable market periods, and funds with small risk fluctuations are often favored by investors.

In the selection of funds, investors often need to invest a lot of time and energy in the market, policy, fund and other aspects of research. However, people's learning ability is limited, which leads to that if they do not do enough analysis and investigation in the early stage, they will often miss the better options due to careless thinking when making decisions. However, if a investor do too much preparatory work in the early stage, when it comes time to make a decision, even if there is no choice that meets the expectation, he will force to make a decision because of loss aversion and sunk costs, or because he do not have enough energy to make a reasonable choice because of too much investment in the early stage. In both cases, the decision will be guided by a pre-existing mindset, namely, loss aversion. This kind of decision will inevitably lead to people ignoring some objective factors, such as market influence and star effect. While avoiding risk, investors ignore the impact of other factors on fund performance, resulting in the above-mentioned phenomenon that funds with stable returns are more popular.

3 Discussion

The star effect and peer pressure appearing in the pre-purchase will alleviate the endowment effect by improving the investor psychology of ownership and guilt of not buying enough expected, thus generating consumption impulse. For investors who already hold funds, the decision of whether to continue to hold the original fund is not entirely based on fund performance. Affected by the endowment effect, investors will be more optimistic about the original fund and are more willing to maintain the investment status quo to some extent.

This study analyzes the "irrationality" of investors' decisions under the influence of endowment effect. Different from the assumption that "human beings are rational" in traditional economics, this paper studies the decision-making behavior under the influence of investor psychology. The disadvantage is that the number of independent variables is still not enough, and the direction of thinking is not perfect, does not take into account the conversion cost when changing investment decision, and the difference of people's decision on fund investment when the principal is different.

4 Conclusion

This paper selects hybrid fund as the research object, starts with pre-purchase condition and fund performance, firstly demonstrates the influence of the previous two on fund investment decision, and then analyzes the crucial role of endowment effect in the process of influence. This paper explores the causes and processes of "irrational" decision making in the process of investment and its impact on the final decision. Through research and analysis, the author draws the conclusion that under the endowment effect, people are affected by fund performance, fund star effect, loss aversion and other psychological factors, so as to make irrational investment decisions. According to the conclusion of this study, investors can avoid "irrational" decisions with rational thinking in time, so as to make a more reasonable judgment. However, this paper has not taken into account the conversion cost generated when the decision is changed in the investment process, as well as the influence of investors' income level and social status on the investment decision. It is hoped that there will be further research on this subject from the perspective of psychology in the future.

References

1. Qiang, G.: How to do well the education and investment company of fund investors. China Credit Card (01), 72–76. (2021)
2. Zeng, T., Ma, W., Sun, M., Mo, L.: The influence of analytic thinking on impulse buying intention. Stud. Psychol. Behav. (04), 536–541 (2022)
3. Yan, S.: The effect of boredom on impulsive buying: evidence from eye movement. Ludong University (2022)
4. Cai, P.: Research on the influence of consumers' pre-purchase ritual behavior on endowment effect (2021)
5. Lan, Z.: Fund performance and investor behavior: whether there is redemption vision and star effect in Chinese open-end equity funds (2020)
6. Li, Y.: Performance evaluation and driving factors analysis of hybrid funds: based on DEA-Tobit model. Sci. Technol. Ind. (08), 8–13 (2021)
7. Hu, D.: Research on performance evaluation of open-end stock funds in china based on DEA method (2020)
8. Liu, Y.: A study of the behaviors of the Chinese mutual fund investors: from the perspectives of investors' limited attention and endowment constraints (2022)
9. Zhan, Z., Wu, Z.: Mental accounting, loss aversion and behavioral asset allocation empirical study. Oper. Res. Manage. Sci. (08), 177–184 (2022)
10. Litovsky, Y., Loewenstein, G., Horn, S., Olivola, C.Y.: Loss aversion, the endowment effect, and gain-loss framing shape preferences for noninstrumental information. Proc. Natl. Acad. Sci. U.S.A. **119**(34), e2202700119 (2022)

Research on Empowering Huawei's Financial Transformation by Financial Shared Service Center

Yiru Su(✉)

School of Accountancy, Zhongnan University of Economics and Law, Wuhan 430073, China
`suyr@stu.zuel.edu.cn`

Abstract. With the innovation of science and technology and the development of the economy, the financial management mode of enterprises has gradually been changing. In the context of the economic downturn and the high pressure of market competition, in order to achieve cost reduction, efficiency increase of financial operation, and improve the operating conditions, some multinational group companies had begun to set up Financial Shared Service Centers with the help of the rapidly developing Internet technology to empower the financial transformation of enterprises. Taking Huawei as an example, by sorting out the construction process of Huawei's Financial Shared Service Center and analyzing its overall financial situation, this paper introduces how the Financial Shared Service Center can help Huawei achieve successful financial transformation and create economic benefits. At the same time, the author analyzes the possible problems in the development of the Financial Shared Service Center and puts forward some relevant suggestions.

Keywords: Huawei · Financial Shared Service Center · Financial Transformation

1 Introduction

With the development of the economy and the change in science and technology, the financial situation of enterprises is becoming more and more complex. The traditional financial management mode and accounting method have no longer adapted to the era trend of the rapid development of information and digitalization. The requirements for financial personnel have also increased. In order to achieve the financial accounting of process standardization with high efficiency, low cost, and concentration, create greater economic benefits, carry out more effective management of the financial affairs of enterprises, and assist in financial decision-making, the Financial Shared Service Center came into being to help many large enterprises gradually realize financial transformation.

At present, many achievements have emerged in the research field of the Financial Shared Service Center. The concept of financial shared service originated in the United States in the 1980s, but different people put forward different views on its specific definition. As early as 1993, Robert W. Gunn of Gunn Partners and others proposed that the essence of financial shared service is a change in the organizational structure of enterprises. In 1998, Barbara Quinn proposed that shared service is a business operation. In 2003, Bryan Bergeron believed that shared service is a semi-self-service management business unit. Domestic scholars later contacted the concept of financial shared service but still summarized some views. In 2004, Hanjin Liu proposed that it is a semi-market-oriented internal organization. In 2009, Hu Chen and Hao Dong proposed that the shared service center is an innovative and customer-oriented management model. Based on the definition, scholars at home and abroad have also put forward some views on the mode and operation of the Financial Shared Service Center. In 1998, Barbara Quinn proposed that financial shared service can be divided into the basic mode, market mode, advanced market mode, and independent operation mode from primary to advance. Denburgh further explained these four modes in 2001 and pointed out their characteristics. In 2009, Hu Chen, Ruijun Zhang, and Yongji Zhang proposed three stages of building a Financial Shared Service Center based on their practice in ZTE and discussed the relevant design concepts. In general, foreign scholars' research is mainly based on theoretical deduction. In contrast, Chinese scholars' research on Financial Shared Service Centers is mainly based on practical applications and more in combination with China's national conditions [1].

This paper mentions the background and development of the Financial Shared Service Center. It takes Huawei as an example to introduce the general situation of Huawei's establishment of the Financial Shared Service Center. It also discusses the functions of the Financial Shared Service Center, explains how it helps Huawei achieve financial transformation, analyzes the problems that may arise during its operation, and puts forward development suggestions.

2 Overview of Financial Shared Service Center

2.1 Background

The Financial Shared Service Center (FSSC) is a financial management model based on the ERP system, traced back to the early 1980s. At this time, developed countries had just passed the economic crisis of the 1970s. Although the stagflation problem had been solved, the economy had not improved significantly. The growth rate was slow and unstable. Multinational group companies were facing huge economic market competition pressure. In order to seek new development, some transnational group companies gradually expanded their business to emerging economies and realized the transfer of investment markets. With the increasing number of companies following this path, emerging economies gradually become saturated, and transnational group companies are again facing the situation of increasing competitive pressure. At this time, some leaders of transnational group companies were keenly aware of the root cause of the problem. The transfer of the market can only temporarily relieve the pressure but cannot really improve economic efficiency [2]. Instead, it needed to carry out internal strategic reform, starting from reducing the operating costs, to make the company rejuvenate. At that time, it was also at the juncture of the rapid development of Internet technology. Ford Company had seized the opportunity under serious losses and large personnel changes. Expecting to integrate and plan internal resources, the reform direction was to realize the collaborative sharing of information and resources of all departments and business units and reduce the cost of human resources, thus, the Financial Shared Service Center was born [2].

2.2 Development Situation

In the early 1980s, Ford Company of the United States turned its losses into profits using the Financial Shared Service Center. In the early 1990s, Europe began to use the Financial Shared Service Center. Some large international groups, such as General Electric and DuPont, basically achieved success here. By the late 1990s, IBM, HP and other Fortune 500 enterprises had widely applied financial shared services in financial management [3]. In 1999, the location of Motorola's "Asian Settlement Center" in Tianjin marked the official landing of the Financial Shared Service Center in China. Some large domestic companies, such as ZTE, Haier, and Huawei, have also started the construction of the first batch of local Financial Shared Service Centers since 2005. According to the research results from Everest Group in 2011, more than 70% of the top 500 companies adopted the shared service mode to carry out accounting work, and more than 50% of European multinational enterprises have set up shared service centers. Financial Shared Service Centers have rapidly expanded globally and are favored by many large companies [3]. Today, more than 90% of the world's top 500 enterprises have built financial sharing centers.

2.3 Technology Application

Today, the Financial Shared Service Center is still developing due to technological innovation. And it gradually integrates with various digital technologies. RPA is widely used in Financial Shared Service Centers. RPA financial robot is widely used in reconciliation, document review, archiving and other aspects, mainly because it automates and standardizes these processes, significantly improves efficiency, and reduces error rate [4]. It can also operate around the clock and free the financial staff from repetitive and simple work. In addition, RPA is "non-intrusive". In other words, RPA can be designed independently. When it is connected to the original system, it will not change the structure of the original information system, which reduces the coordination cost of linking RPA into the existing system [4]. In addition to RPA, there are also image intelligence recognition technology that can be used to scan and identify invoices, cloud computing technology that can be used to declare taxes automatically, and so on.

3 Research Method

In the writing process, this article mainly adopts the literature research method and case analysis method.

3.1 Literature Research Method

The literature research method refers to the method of collecting, identifying, and sorting out the literature, studying the literature, and finally forming a scientific understanding of the relevant research fields. Before writing, the author first looked up a large amount of data about the Financial Shared Service Center, understood its background, development process, and related technology applications, and sorted them out. After determining to take Huawei as an example for research, the author also looked up many Huawei's own information and the data of Huawei's construction of the Financial Shared Service Center, combined with the author's own understanding, analyzed it, and finally reached a conclusion.

3.2 Case Analysis Method

The case analysis method uses a specific relevant case as the object of analysis in the selected research field to summarize the results of individual research with broad applicability. In this article, the theme of the author's research is how the Financial Shared Service Center empowers the financial transformation of enterprises. On the one hand, Huawei, as a well-known enterprise that built the Financial Shared Service Center earlier in China, its relevant information is relatively easy to obtain. On the other hand, the role of the Financial Shared Service Center in Huawei's financial transformation is of certain representative significance. Therefore, the author chooses to research by exploring the process and achievements of Huawei's construction of the Financial Shared Service Center.

4 FSSC and Huawei's Financial Transformation

4.1 Huawei's Financial Shared Service Center Construction

Before Huawei built the Financial Shared Service Center, its traditional financial model was no longer suitable for the development of the company. There were many drawbacks, such as complex and repetitive processes, blocked information transmission paths, and disjointed financial services, which made the management and operation inefficient [5]. Huawei urgently needed to find solutions to the problems [5].

Huawei has been building its Financial Shared Service Center since 2005 and is one of the first enterprises to build a Financial Shared Service Center in China. Although the Financial Shared Service Center can also be used as an external service, in Huawei, it mainly responds to the internal management needs. Since 2006, Huawei has gradually established seven regional Financial Shared Service Centers in the world, distributed in Chengdu, Shenzhen, Malaysia, Brazil, and other places. Figure 1 is the basic structure of Huawei's Financial Shared Service Center. Its seven regions are roughly divided into global and regional regions [6]. As shown in Fig. 1.

The Global Financial Shared Service Center mainly deals with businesses with standardized processes and accurate data such as accounts receivable and fixed assets. In contrast, the Regional Financial Shared Service Center mainly deals with businesses with non-standard processes, such as accounts payable and inventory costs or businesses involving tax [6].

Although many resources have been invested in the construction of the Financial Shared Service Center in the early stage and accompanied by a series of changes in the

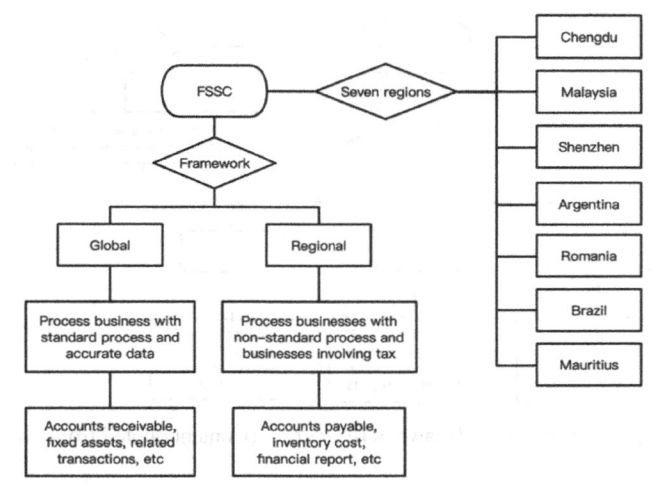

Fig. 1. Basic structure of Huawei FSSC (Some contents are quoted from [6]).

internal organizational structure of the enterprise, the results have not been achieved in the early stage [7]. But statistics show that after the formal and stable operation of Huawei's FSSC, the processing cost of a single invoice has decreased by 75%, while the audit adjustment rate is only 0.01% [7]. Since implementing internal control over financial statements in 2013, a total of US $7.8 billion has been monitored for various types of front-end non-compliance data, avoiding a capital loss of $945 million. Currently, relying on FSSC, Huawei has achieved a global 7×24-h cycle checkout mechanism. And more than 170 systems are seamlessly connected. It only takes one hour to process 40 million lines of data, greatly improving the efficiency of financial management [8].

4.2 Huawei's IFS Reform

Huawei began to cooperate with IBM in 2007 to implement an eight-year IFS reform, also called integrated financial reform. The reform project is expected to deal with the uncertainty of the results with the certainty of rules. It covers all major financial fields of Huawei in the world, which can strengthen Huawei's management and operation capabilities, promote future business development and help Huawei establish a more thorough and in-depth partnership with top operators. As shown in Fig. 2, the IFS reform can be divided into three stages, IDS1, IDS2 and IDS3. IDS is an integrated service. From the transaction level to the project management, and then to the responsibility center, it gradually promotes the integration of business and finance at all levels of the enterprise. The IFS reform has opened Huawei's refined management, laying a solid foundation for its steady development [9].

4.3 Functions of FSSC in Huawei's Financial Transformation

First, improve accounting efficiency and reduce labor costs. The FSSC makes simple financial accounting, tabulation, and other work automated and streamlined according to

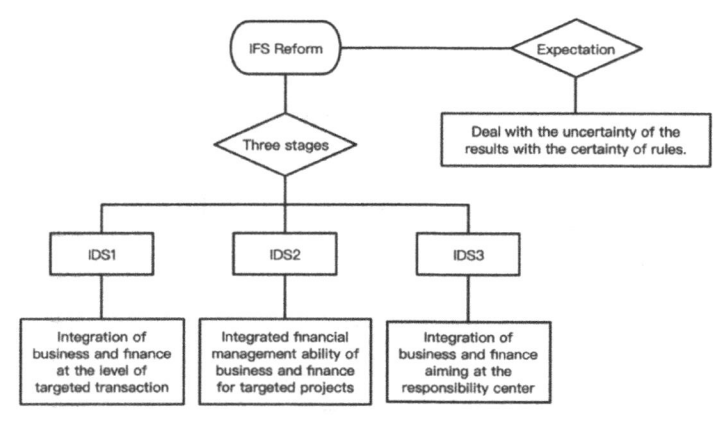

Fig. 2. Overview of Huawei's IFS reform (Content quoted from [9]).

the set standards. And it operates 24 h. Compared with the traditional manual accounting mode of Huawei, this greatly improves the efficiency and ensures the standardization of data and lower error rate. The consequent reduction of labor costs can be reflected in two aspects. On the one hand, which is the most intuitive, in basic financial work, the FSSC is far more efficient than the manual work. So many traditional financial personnel will be replaced, and the labor costs will be reduced. On the other hand, the FSSC has a lower error rate than manual work, which reduces the hidden costs of the enterprise in error detection and correction.

Second, promote the transformation of financial personnel. The FSSC basically solves the accounting problems of enterprises and is more efficient and accurate than manual work. Financial personnel who can only do traditional accounting work lose their living space under the pressure of the FSSC. Therefore, financial personnel first transform to financial management and prediction in their functions and assist the management in making more effective and rapid decisions. Second, financial personnel cannot only understand finance but should also understand the specific business and actively communicate with the business department, reflecting the difference between human and digital platforms in flexibility. Finally, in order to coordinate with the construction of the FSSC and better use various data and technologies, financial personnel should have a basic understanding and application ability of Python, SQL, and so on. Only financial personnel who meet the above three points can have a place in a large enterprise like Huawei. Therefore, the FSSC has promoted the transformation of financial personnel.

Third, integration of business and finance, information sharing, integration of resources, and effective allocation of resources. The FSSC connects finance and business and reduces the loss of economic benefits brought by the information transmission time. The FSSC utilizes the scale effect to integrate financial resources. After completing the filing and publishing process, it prepares financial accounting reports. It uploads them to the system, so that Huawei can grasp the enterprise's overall operation in a timelier manner [10]. Huawei's internal financial department once revealed that "every day in advance of the report, it is worth one billion yuan". The FSSC brings the benefits of financial management and decision-making to Huawei's self-evident.

4.4 Huawei Financial Profile Analysis

The financial indicators in Fig. 3 can directly reflect Huawei's overall financial situation, reflecting its good profitability and capital liquidity. The improvement in 2007 and the steady development since then reflect Huawei's asset management capability enhancement. From this time point of view, this is not unrelated to Huawei's FSSC.

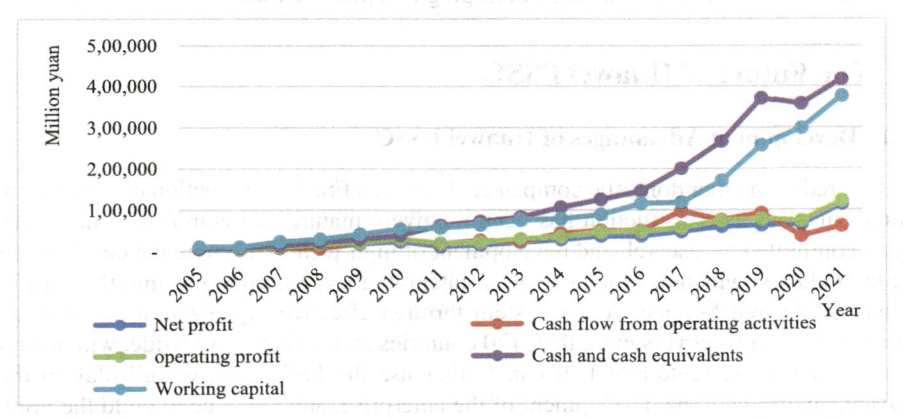

Fig. 3. Huawei's main financial indicators from 2005 to 2021 (Data from Huawei's annual report).

The FSSC has improved the financial management efficiency and financial work efficiency of the enterprise through the refined management of creditor's rights and debts so that the funds can be used more reasonably and the settlement process can be effectively shortened, which has a positive impact on the financial performance of the enterprise. As can be seen from Fig. 4, the turnover days of accounts receivable and accounts payable have generally declined, reflecting the enhancement of Huawei's operational capacity [7].

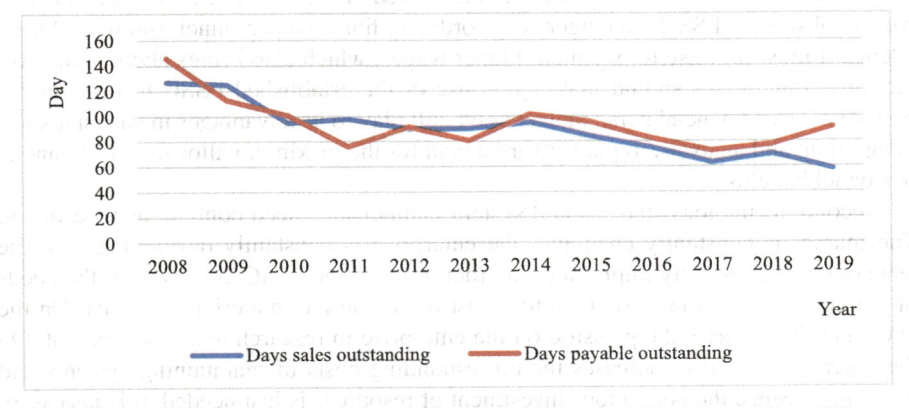

Fig. 4. Some financial indicators of Huawei in 2008–2019 (Data quoted from [7])

Since the construction of the FSSC in 2005, although the initial construction cost had increased and was not mature enough, there have been no obvious economic benefits. But with the continuous improvement and the further implementation of the IFS reform in 2007, the effect of the FSSC has been demonstrated, improving Huawei's economic benefits significantly. In addition to the impact of exchange losses in 2011, the impact of increased pressure on the chip supply chain, and the impact of the epidemic in 2020, these main financial indicators are developing in a positive trend as a whole [7].

5 The Future of Huawei FSSC

5.1 Development Advantages of Huawei FSSC

Compared with other domestic companies, Huawei's FSSC construction has been at the forefront. And its construction has been relatively mature and complete. Huawei has been committed to research and development of high-tech to promote the development of the industry, which also helps Huawei integrate these technologies into the existing Financial Shared Service Center system through effective organization and linkage. Huawei's business covers more than 170 countries and regions worldwide, with a large volume and good scale effect. It can further use the FSSC to give full play to this advantage, promote the development of the enterprise, and continue to build the FSSC that is more suitable for the needs of enterprise management in the process. The two complement each other.

5.2 Problems and Development Suggestions

Although the FSSC has effectively promoted Huawei's financial transformation and integration of business and finance, it has successfully translated into practical economic benefits. But it has also brought some new problems. Next, the author will briefly describe these problems and propose corresponding development suggestions.

First, the ability of financial personnel is required to be improved, and compensation and benefits need to be rebalanced. As mentioned earlier, Huawei, an enterprise that has established an FSSC, no longer needs ordinary financial personnel. But when hiring talents, it must promise to pay them higher wages, which also brings about some cost recovery. Enterprises should make good use of the established FSSC to monitor the performance of financial personnel and give full play to its advantages in data statistics, integration, and analysis, to put forward a plan for the maximum allocation of financial personnel benefits.

Second, technology updates and system maintenance need continuous investment. The market is constantly changing, the enterprise is constantly developing, and the technology is constantly improving. In order to make the FSSC always meet the needs of the enterprise, it must continue to invest in human and material resources. On the one hand, it increases the pressure on the enterprise in research and development. On the other hand, it also increases the corresponding costs of maintaining systems and equipment. Since the continuous investment of resources is just needed, it is necessary to consider how to exchange the minimum investment for the maximum return. This requires enterprises to clarify the development direction and coordinate the synchronous development of the FSSC and the organizational structure, to reduce the loss caused by the friction between the two.

Third, the FSSC has the risk of developing into saturation by mistake. The author believes there is a misunderstanding in the development of the FSSC. That is, the FSSC may reach saturation. This saturation does not mean it can no longer progress, but that when people face too detailed data and reports, it may be difficult to make effective decisions, and much information is redundant. The FSSC is not only the centralized management of financial information. If this happens, its serviceability cannot be reflected. Of course, the author pointed out that there might be such risks as a reminder.

6 Conclusion

The Financial Shared Service Center has been widely recognized and applied worldwide. Its integration with digital technology has greatly affected the financial management mode of Huawei and other enterprises, promoted the financial transformation of enterprises, increased efficiency, and reduced costs. The refined management mode it brings can bring huge economic benefits to enterprises and help them develop steadily. Suppose we adhere to continuous innovation and seek progress in a stable manner, by making full use of human's subjective initiative. In that case, we can adapt to the changing world and develop well with the help of the FSSC.

This paper introduces the background, development, and technology of the FSSC. It mainly takes Huawei as an example to sort out its construction. Through the analysis of Huawei's financial situation, it summarizes its functions in the enterprise's financial transformation. At the same time, it puts forward some general problems and suggestions according to Huawei's situation. The case selected in this paper is Huawei, one of China's earliest enterprises to establish a Financial Shared Service Center. Although it is representative, the content discussed in this paper is still limited due to the different circumstances of each enterprise, and Huawei's FSSC is mainly for the internal service of the enterprise. Therefore, this paper has some deficiencies in reflecting the external service of the FSSC. Later research can focus on this aspect.

References

1. Zeng, Z.Z., Liu, X.Y.: Financial sharing literature review. Natl. Circ. Econ. (32), 140–141 (2018)
2. Yan, J.H.: Analysis on the construction and operation of the financial shared service center of the group company. Shandong University (2018)
3. Li, M.: Research on the construction of international financial sharing service center. Chin. Foreign Entrep. (01), 18–19 (2018)
4. Zhang, J.: Research on the application of RPA robot in the financial shared service center of central enterprises. China Chief Account. (10), 88–90 (2022)
5. Fu, B.W.: Application and thinking of financial shared service center in multinational corporations – taking Huawei as an example. Mod. Mark. (Bus. Edn.) (08), 221–222 (2019)

6. Zong, W.J., Wang, B.L.: Research on the enterprise financial sharing model based on the integration of business and finance – taking huawei as an example. Financ. Account. Commun. (12), 173–176 (2020)
7. Hu, A.P., Zhang, C.Y., Zhou, S.: Research on the impact of financial sharing on corporate financial performance – taking Huawei as an example. Friends Account. (19), 14–19 (2021)
8. An, N.: Research on the application of financial sharing in financial management of private enterprises, Contemp. Account. (20), 58–60 (2021)
9. Zhu, T.Q.: Huawei's practice of business-finance integration. China Manage. Account. (03), 20–33 (2022)
10. Deng, Y.: Application of financial robot RPA in financial shared service center. China Agric. Account. (05), 86–87 (2022)

A Study on the Relevance of Corporate Solvency – A Case Study of Procter & Gamble

Huangzhiyi Zhang[✉]

Department of Management, Shenyang Urban Construction University, Shenyang 110000, Liaoning, China
631402090103@mails.cqjtu.edu.cn

Abstract. In recent years, Chinese daily necessities companies have faced fierce market competition alongside rapid and steady growth. In order to strengthen their competitiveness and advantage in the market, the companies are constantly developing new products, expanding into new markets, and increasing their capital requirements. As debt ratios increase, the company's financial risk increases, and it falls into more significant financial distress. By analyzing the solvency of the daily goods companies, it is possible to determine the current repayment capacity of the daily goods companies and to estimate whether they can repay their loans and interest. This paper is based on Procter & Gamble's (P&G)'s financial data from 2017 to 2021, and short-term solvency and long-term solvency are selected for the analysis of P&G's solvency. The short-term solvency analysis includes the current ratio, realization of inventory and receivables, and cash flow ratio. In contrast, the long-term solvency analysis includes gearing ratio, equity ratio, and interest coverage multiple to analyze the current problems of P&G's solvency. The paper found that P&G has problems, such as a lack of financing channels and an unreasonable debt structure. Furthermore, it finally proposed corresponding improvement methods and measures for P&G. For example, P&G can exploit bank loans to adjust the corporate financing structure, improving the enterprise's profitability. Moreover, optimize the overall debt structure to increase the efficiency of capital flow to enable P&G to develop in a long-term and healthy manner.

Keywords: Procter & Gamble · Short-Term Solvency · Long-Term Solvency

1 Introduction

1.1 Research Background

Since China's reform and opening up, the household goods industry has grown faster than other domestic industries and become a significant economic driver. However, China's household goods manufacturing industry is at the end of the global industrial chain and is labor-intensive. Raw materials and labor are a big part of the cost of a finished product because they have low added value, require manual labor, and use a lot of raw materials and energy. The rising costs of raw materials and labor, as well as the rising value of the RMB, are quickly driving up the prices of finished goods and making them much less competitive. This has caused a crisis and problems for Chinese companies that make household goods that have never been seen before. Many small and medium-sized businesses are right on the edge of going out of business [1, 2].

Strategically changed enterprises are significant in the daily chemical industry. With the consent of the Yunnan Provincial People's Government, eight businesses established Procter & Gamble (P&G), a market leader in the household chemical sector. Its production and operation report released at the end of 2021 showed that its annual revenue had reached approximately 109 billion yuan, an increase of 11.2% over the previous year [3]. Before this, several scholars conducted studies on P&G [3]. In order to investigate the financial problems of P&G, a study of the company's financial performance was conducted based on an in-depth understanding of the company's operating conditions. The entropy method was used to determine the weights of the selected indicators objectively, calculate the scores of each financial capability and governance capability of the company in each year, and arrive at a total evaluation value of financial performance [4].

Several researchers have looked at how Chinese consumers see P&G's "localization" marketing strategy and how often they buy P&G products. By ranking the factors. They determine whether P&G's marketing localization strategy in China is successful in the eyes of consumers, which ones have been implemented most effectively, and which ones still need improvement [5]. In recent years, P&G has combined the problems of poor business conditions and declining profits with the exploitation of debt. This approach is not just a borrowed one but a way to maximize the company's profits. Such a situation does not make the company's financial situation any worse.

On the contrary, it is also suitable for the company [6]. Hence, a company's future growth depends on its solvency, which requires adequate liquid assets to satisfy its short- and long-term responsibilities. P&G's solvency fluctuates with business conditions. Therefore, P&G's long-term success depends on investigating its solvency.

1.2 Research Gap

In economic globalization and integration, the credit economy is gradually gaining ground. Solvency analysis has an important place in the financial indicators of modern enterprises and is an essential guarantee for the smooth growth of their economic efficiency. The solvency of an enterprise can be strengthened by improving its asset structure, strengthening the liquidity of liquid assets, and raising awareness of timely debt repayment [7]. Debt-servicing capability is related to the survival and development of an enterprise and is of great significance to the enterprise itself and all stakeholders. By comparing the evaluation indicators with industry averages and assigning different weighting factors to each indicator, solvency can be improved by optimizing the structure of long- and short-term liabilities, planning capital requirements in the long term, and improving the operating capacity of assets [8]. How can P&G effectively reduce its risks in financial management and make the company's development more qualitative and efficient? This paper will explore and analyze the solvency of P&G, identify the risk factors affecting its development, and provide references to solve the problem according to the actual situation.

1.3 Structure of This Paper

By looking at P&G's financial data from 2017 to 2021 and analyzing the daily goods company's solvency, it is possible to figure out the daily goods company's current repayment capacity and whether or not it will be able to pay back the loan and interest. Through comparative and ratio analysis, this paper gives a full analysis and evaluation of P&G's financial health. It starts with long-term and short-term solvency, identifying the shortcomings of P&G's debt repayment and proposing corresponding countermeasures to ensure the long-term and healthy development of P&G's enterprise.

2 Case Description

2.1 Company Profile

Founded in 1837, P&G is one of the world's largest consumer goods companies, with annual sales of US$51.4 billion in fiscal 2003–2004 [3]. It is ranked 86th in Fortune magazine's latest list of the world 500 largest industrial and service companies. Employing nearly 100,000 people worldwide, P&G has factories and subsidiaries in more than 80 countries and operates more than 300 brands of products sold in more than 160 countries and regions, including fabric and home care, hair and beauty, baby and home care, health care, food, and beverages. During 2017–2021, P&G's solvency was unstable and frequently faced weakened or insufficient solvency. When P&G's solvency is weakened, it also means fewer convertible funds, and P&G often has a backlog of inventory when the pressure to service debt is more significant.

2.2 The Issues of P&G's Short-Term Solvency

Current Ratio: From the company's point of view, the current assets are twice as much as the current liabilities, and the current ratio is more than 2. As shown in Table 1 and Fig. 1, P&G's current ratio is generally low and unstable from 2017 to 2021. From 2019 to the middle of 2020, the change in P&G's current ratio becomes important. This indicates that the company has not paid off its short-term liabilities during these three years and needs more debt servicing capacity. According to statistics, the company's current ratio was 1.23 in 2018 and 1.13 in 2019. In just one year, the company's current ratio has decreased by 0.1, which indicates that the company's short-term debt servicing capacity has weakened. This also means the company will have even fewer convertible funds in 2019.

Realizability of Inventories and Accounts Receivable: Table 2 shows that P&G's inventory and accounts receivable turnover are trending downward from 2017–2021. This indicates that the company's liquidity turnover of inventory and accounts receivable has continued to decline. According to the statistics, the current ratio is also statistically higher in 2021, only 0.01 less than in 2020. However, inventory and accounts receivable have the highest turnover times, at 50 and 127 days, respectively. This indicates a backlog in P&G's inventory during the year, with fast-moving assets dominated by accounts receivable. The liquidity of accounts receivable is even worse than in 2020, putting more pressure on P&G's short-term debt this year.

Table 1. P&G current ratio calculations [3].

Item (RMB million)	2017	2018	2019	2020	2021
Total current assets	1298746	1328984	1415795	1382838	1542596
Total current liabilities	1096467	1080927	1253047	1031374	1166645
Current ratio	1.18	1.23	1.13	1.34	1.32

Data source: Based on P&G's annual financial statements

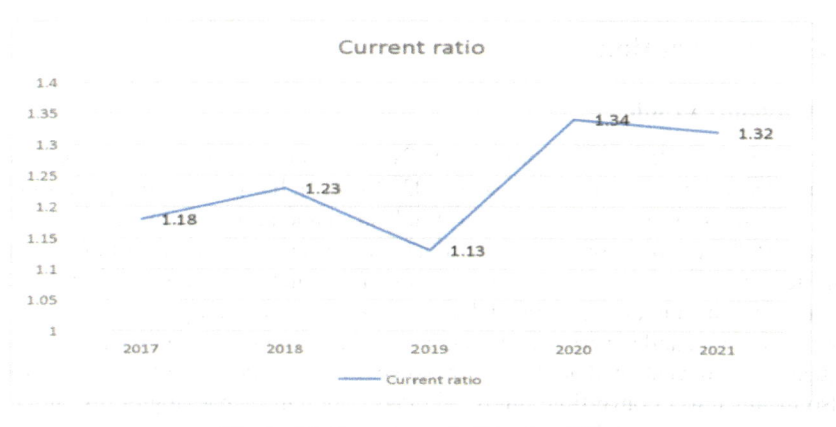

Fig. 1. P&G current ratio line chart [3].

Table 2. Inventory and accounts receivable turnover at P&G [3].

Item	2017	2018	2019	2020	2021
Inventory turnover ratio (times)	8.652	8.894	8.365	9.471	7.348
Inventory turnover days (days)	42	41	44	39	50
Accounts receivable turnover (times)	22.08	10.73	6.43	5.61	2.87
Turnover days of accounts receivable (days)	17	34	57	65	127

Data source: Based on P&G's annual financial statements

Cash Flow Ratio: For P&G to meet its investment and debt service needs, its operating income needs to go up. The data in Table 3 shows that the company has a negative cash flow ratio for three out of the five years from 2017 to 2021. It is −2.99% in 2017, −4.87 in 2020, and −5.42% in 2021. During these three years, P&G's operating income could not offset its current liabilities. As can be seen from the data in the table, P&G makes minimal profits from its operations, and the company lacks sufficient financial support of its own. As a result, due to the company's deteriorating financial position, its operating activities do not generate enough cash to cover its short-term liabilities, which has a significant negative impact on the company's production and operations and some impact on short-term capital.

Table 3. P&G cash flow statement [3].

Item	2017	2018	2019	2020	2021
Net cash flow from operating activities (RMB million)	−32835	36823	74278	−50256	−63222
Current liabilities at the end of the period (RMB million)	1096467	1080927	1253047	1031374	1166645
Cash flow ratio	−2.99%	3.41%	5.93%	−4.87%	−5.42%

Data source: Based on P&G's annual financial statements

2.3 The Issues of P&G's Long-Term Solvency

Gearing Ratio: P&G is at risk of having a high gearing ratio, which could lead to it not having solvency guarantees. From the relevant data and information shown in Fig. 2, it can be seen that Procter & Gamble's companies operate with a high debt ratio of 59.30% in 2017 and 59.68% in 2018. By 2019, it was 65.46%. In 2020, P&G had a total debt of 60.51%. This shows that from 2017 to 2021, P&G has a high debt ratio with a large percentage of total debt to total assets. In 2019, the operating debt ratio increased significantly, which means that the company cannot generate more revenue through financing while the debt ratio is high. If more than profits are required, the risk of debt is high.

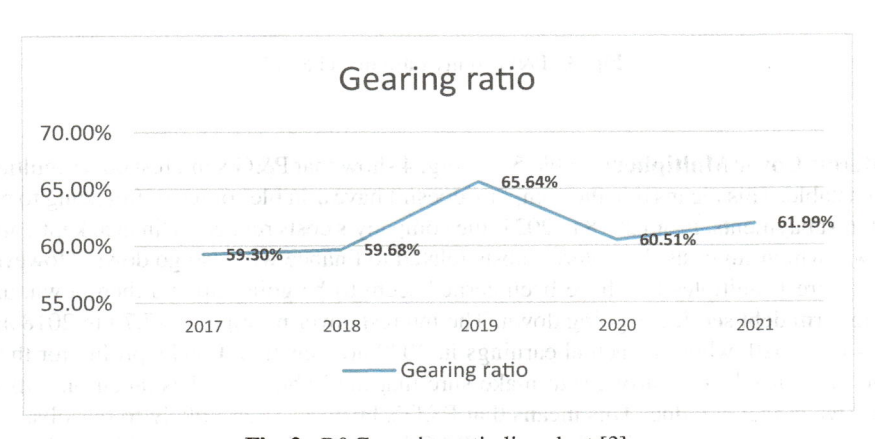

Fig. 2. P&G gearing ratio line chart [3].

Equity Ratio: As seen from the data in Table 4 and Fig. 3, the equity ratio of P&G changes relatively significantly from 2018 to 2020, reaching a peak in 2019. A higher equity ratio indicates the company has less capital and cannot service its long-term debt. The company wasn't strong enough to handle market shocks from the outside, which led to a lot of interest in debt and financial risk.

Table 4. P&G equity ratio [3].

Item	2017	2018	2019	2020	2021
Total liabilities (RMB million)	1152678	1206637	1409498	1076374	1216851
Total owners' equity (RMB million)	791249	815159	740958	702419	746122
Equity ratio	145.68%	148.02%	190.23%	153.24%	163.09%

Data source: Based on P&G's annual financial statements

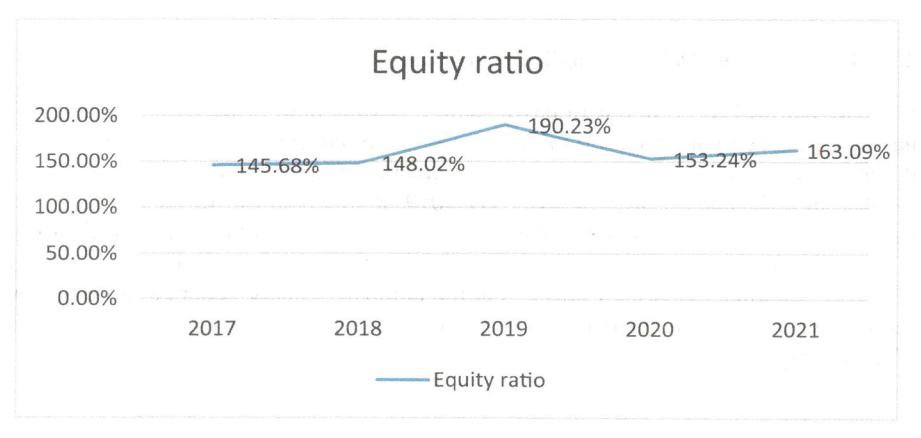

Fig. 3. P&G equity ratio line chart [3].

Interest Cover Multiplier: Table 5 and Fig. 4 show that P&G's interest cover multiple is unstable. This means that the company doesn't have a stable source of financing to pay interest payments. From 2018 to 2021, the company's costs related to finance kept going down, which suggests that interest costs related to finance will also go down. However, the interest multiples that have been earned seem to be going up and then down, and long-term debt service is going down. The interest cover multiple is 17.79 in 2018 and 11.41 in 2020, while the actual earnings in 2020 are negative. P&G's profits for these two years need to be stronger to make sure that the liabilities it has taken on will be paid when they are due. This means that P&G's business is less likely to be solvent in the long run than it was in other years. P&G had an exciting cover multiple of −3.06 in 2017 and −15.94 in 2021. During this period, the company has earned a negative interest multiplier. Interest expense is harmful because many companies make steady profits through bank deposits and investing in bonds, yielding enough interest income to exceed interest expense. The interest multiples already earned are harmful because they are much more profitable than the company's profits from bank loans, bonds, and other financing methods, so they do not represent poor repayment [9].

Table 5. P&G interest cover multiples [3].

Item	2017	2018	2019	2020	2021
Total profit (RMB million)	19634	27602	10415	−11889	49196
Finance costs (RMB million)	−4841	1645	116	−1143	−2905
Interest cover multiplier	−3.06	17.79	91.56	11.41	−15.94

Data source: Based on P&G's annual financial statements

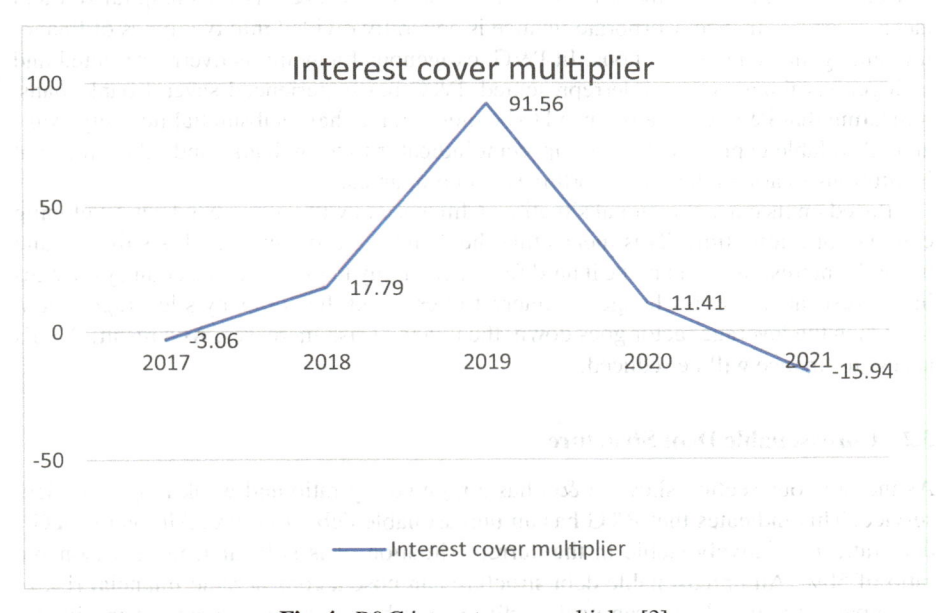

Fig. 4. P&G interest cover multiples [3].

3 Analysis on Problems

P&G's current problems are mainly in solvency, focusing on financial issues and deficiencies in how liabilities are repaid. The literature shows that solvency is closely related to a company's access to finance and debt structure. The way a company is financed will directly determine the final financing structure of the company, with different financing structures indicating different financing methods and, thus, the final capital structure of the company [10]. Banks grant loans in favor of companies that can afford to pay the interest rate on their loans, so the amount of capital a company has directly determines its ability to pay the interest rate on its loans [11]. P&G is a daily goods company utilized for personal care and household cleaning. The recent increase in the variety of such daily products has hit its sales industry hard, resulting in a significant drop in gross profit [12]. The debt structure has a non-negligible influence on a company's business operations. P&G itself has to be aware of the risk to earnings due to prolonged and short-term debt risk when adjusting its debt structure, and sound risk management in this area is crucial to the company's liquidity [13].

3.1 Lack of Access to Finance

The description of P&G's short-term solvency in this paper shows that P&G has a low current ratio, a decline in the realization of deposits and accounts receivable, and a low cash flow ratio. All these phenomena indicate that P&G is undercapitalized and lacks access to finance. Corporate finance is generally divided into two types of financing: endogenous and exogenous. In P&G, exogenous financing is overrepresented and endogenous financing is underrepresented. P&G has experienced several bank loans, indicating that P&G companies need to be more vital to have substantial liquidity available. Available capital is also an important indicator used by banks and other financial institutions to assess the creditworthiness of companies.

Based on its current national situation, China is and will continue to be a developing country for a long time. This means that the country's economic level is still low, and unstable interest rates can make it hard for the economy to grow. So, the country changes its interest rate system. Changes in interest rates affect the company's leverage factor, and when the leverage factor goes down, the financial risk increases. As a result, P&G's access to finance will be reduced.

3.2 Unreasonable Debt Structure

As the previous section shows, P&G has a high equity ratio and weak long-term debt service. This indicates that P&G has an unreasonable debt structure. Although P&G's debt ratio is relatively stable in the current situation, it is still far from a reasonable ratio of 50%. An unreasonable debt structure can pose a considerable financial risk to a company. Financial risk can profoundly impact business projects and even directly determine a company's long-term business and profitability.

The Yunnan State-owned Assets Supervision and Administration Commission owns and controls P&G. P&G's growth has boosted the local economy, created many jobs, helped the government solve the social employment problem, and paid many taxes. Based on this, the company has won the full support of society and the government. At present, faced with the development of the daily necessity industry, P&G needs to meet the challenges of the new situation through industrial upgrading. The local district government has repeatedly allocated $998 million to help P&G upgrade technology, boost productivity, and develop projects for the circular economy. In addition, the government will play a series of indirect roles to guide P&G in properly allocating and exploiting funds, thus promoting the healthy and sustainable development of P&G's enterprises. Through a series of operations with the help of the government, the debt structure of

P&G enterprises has changed significantly, and its non-current liabilities have been significantly reduced. A series of government policy interventions can profoundly impact the changes in the capital structure of listed companies. However, an unbalanced capital structure can lead to a company's financial collapse.

4 Suggestions

At this point, it is clear how important the ability of solvency is for a business. Maintaining the stability of a company's repayment capacity requires optimizing its capital structure. Optimizing the capital structure requires balancing the company's financial leverage, stabilizing the cost of capital, managing financial risks, and maximizing the company's value. In addition, it is also necessary to constantly improve the solution to optimize corporate capital in a changing economic environment to better respond to unexpected challenges. This paper indicates some suggestions for optimization based on the analysis and discussion of P&G's corporate capital structure.

4.1 Restructuring Corporate Finance to Improve Profitability

Using Bank Loans: In addition to the money the company has saved, it can apply the financial markets to get money from outside the country. Company funding usually comes from bank loans. P&G companies must use lower bank lending rates to optimize their capital structure and reduce their debt to ensure liquidity. If it needs loans, P&G should monitor bank interest rates [14]. Project financing must account for the time it takes to raise funds for fast-growing companies. Equity financing is slow, and capital eligibility is limited. P&G chose debt financing because it is fast, but the capital structure needed to meet expectations. P&G may issue convertible bonds to optimize its capital structure. Only internal conditions allow this. Convertible bonds convert into shares of the bond issuer at a lower coupon rate. P&G must exploit government and bank financing, develop long-term debt markets, change or update its long-term borrowing facilities, and adjust its capital structure to meet unique needs in the new economic environment.

Improving the Profitability of the Company: A company's profitability is an important indicator of its financing, and it can be financed in various ways, including equity, debt, internal, and other financing modes. Chinese listed companies prefer equity financing, but their profitability could be higher. Policy restrictions make equity financing unavailable, so debt financing is often chosen. If P&G chooses to increase debt, it will increase the company's risk and cost, ultimately negatively impacting its value. However, P&G could increase profits by reducing costs, which would require the designation of better marketing policies to increase P&G's profitability. By doing so, the company can improve its capital structure to the greatest extent possible, thus achieving its long-term and stable growth goals and creating more excellent value for society.

4.2 Optimizing the Overall Structure of Liabilities and Increasing the Efficiency of Capital Flows

The current ratio is the ratio of current assets to current liabilities. Generally speaking, the higher the current ratio, the stronger the company's short-term solvency and the more secure its debts are. Current liabilities are the debt facilities on which listed companies in China rely. A company's solvency is influenced by its capital liquidity, which affects the credit valuation of creditors and, therefore, its overall financing decisions. Therefore, P&G can realize inventory and increase capital liquidity through various channels, such as technological innovation and the development of new products.

Current assets minus inventories minus current liabilities is the quick ratio. A higher ratio means a company has fewer current liabilities and can service its debt better. If P&G can show it is generating more cash flow from operations, its credit rating will improve, and more debt will be guaranteed for the duration of this contract. P&G's credit rating will improve as it shows its ability to repay its debts. Rate flow gives companies more financing options and helps them adapt to change [15]. P&G's ability to service its debts in other business projects may be affected if it yields in large quantities, which increases stock and non-liquid costs. Thus, first, yield moderately. To reduce waste and improve debt servicing, P&G should improve accounts receivable management.

The quick ratio is between current assets, inventories, and liabilities. A higher ratio indicates that a company has fewer current liabilities and a more vital ability to service its debt. If P&G can demonstrate that it is generating more cash flow from operations, the higher the credit rating the business will receive and the more debt will be guaranteed for this contract. The greater P&G's ability to repay its debts, the better the credit rating the creditor firm will have, and the more it can demonstrate its ability to repay its debts. Therefore, focusing on rate flow is something that companies must do in their economic activities because it will give them more options for financing their business and not always be reactive to change [15]. If P&G yields in large quantities, P&G will increase the accumulation of goods in stock and the accumulation of non-liquid costs, which will reduce realization and even affect the company's ability to service its debts in other business projects. Therefore, care must be taken to yield in moderation first. P&G should also strengthen accounts receivable management to avoid unnecessary business and enhance debt servicing capacity.

The only way for a company to avoid financial risks is for it to use balance sheet control. So, the debt structure becomes another area that companies need to pay attention to, especially the mix of current and non-current liabilities and the possibility of restructuring to increase debt and avoid short-term payment risks in the most cost-effective way.

5 Conclusion

Solvency is an important part of a company's ability to stay in business in a competitive market. The finance department must also manage the operating earnings of a company. Suppose a company needs to have adequate financial capital management capabilities and levels. In that case, it will significantly negatively impact the development of the company's debt capacity in the future. Because in today's society, a company's solvency is essential, directly impacting its development and progress. As a result, the analysis of a company's financial position and solvency is important and merits careful consideration by significant companies.

This paper selects the solvency of P&G as a case study. It conducts a systematic study of the financial problems of P&G and the deficiencies of its debt repayment methods in light of the relevant theories of solvency. The conclusions are as follows: P&G's problems in terms of solvency are mainly due to the poor quality of its assets, its weak profitability, and its single source of financing. It recommends that P&G establish a system to manage cash flow, improve profitability through innovative business practices, and establish a well-managed financing system.

In terms of short-term solvency, P&G's short-term solvency is high. The enterprise has a solid ability to repay short-term debts compared to leading enterprises in the same industry. P&G should strengthen and exploit current assets, improve asset utilization efficiency, and maximize corporate profits. In terms of long-term solvency, P&G's is relatively strong. However, compared with short-term solvency, the enterprise's ability to repay In terms of long-term solvency, P&G's is relatively strong. However, the company's ability to repay long-term debt needs to be more vital than its short-term solvency. Thus, it can compensate for the lack of long-term solvency by using idle current assets to repay long-term debt. Overall, P&G's debt servicing capacity over the past five years has been in the upper-middle range of its industry. Although there is no apparent financial risk for the time being, the debt structure is relatively unreasonable. Thus, the company needs to optimize the overall structure of its liabilities and increase the efficiency of its capital flow to actively improve its debt servicing capacity and profitability. The company needs to optimize its liabilities' overall structure and increase the efficiency of its capital flows to actively improve its solvency and earnings.

References

1. Zhai, W.Z.: Analysis of the solvency of enterprise X from the perspective of sustainable development. Mark. World (2021)
2. Nora, D.M.S., Alberto, B.O.: The financial impact of the implementation of Solvency II on the Mexican insurance sector. Geneva Pap. Risk Insur.-Issues Pract. (2021)
3. Procter & Gamble Company. Procter & Gamble Company Financial Statements (2021). https://www.pg.com.cn
4. Pang, B.: Research on the financial performance of Procter & Gamble based on the entropy value method. Tianjin Univ. Financ. Econ. (2019)
5. Xu, P.U.: Research on P&G's marketing localization strategy in China. Nanjing Agric. Univ. (2020)
6. Liu, Z.H., Yu, S.J.: The impact of capital structure on corporate solvency: the case of listed commercial properties in China. China Bus. J. (2021)
7. Suo, W.J.: An empirical analysis of the solvency of listed enterprises–Qingdao Haier enterprises as an example. Mod. Enter. (2021)
8. Zhang, Y.Y.: Analysis of real estate enterprises' solvency and sales growth capacity. China Mark. (2021)
9. Wang, M., Fan, H., Chen, L.T.: Analysis of the solvency of small and medium-sized enterprises based on sustainable development perspective. J. Sci. Technol. Econ. (2021)
10. Li, X.L.: Research on solvency analysis and coping strategies of Tibetan Yiming medicine. Rural Econ. Technol. (2021)
11. Liu, X., Guo, S.Q.: On the impact of corporate solvency on enterprises' sustainable operation and development: the example of enterprises A and B in the iron and steel industry. J. Econ. Res. (2021)

12. Zhou, C.B., Li, Y., Yang, X.F.: The impact of debt servicing ability on the financial leasing decisions of listed enterprises in China: an empirical study of 2089 listed enterprises from the Shenzhen stock exchange. Financ. Financ. (2021)
13. Liu, L.: Analysis of corporate solvency based on strategic management perspective–Sichuan Changhong as an example. J. Tianjin Bus. Vocat. Coll. (2020)
14. Zhang, X.H.: Balancing solvency in the rapid expansion of enterprises–analysis and reflection on the default of Guoyu Logistics bonds. Chin. Foreign Entrep. (2020)
15. Che, G., Gu, F.R.: Analysis of solvency and profitability of Procter & Gamble. Guangxi Qual. Supervision Herald (2020)

ESG Performance Under Economic Policy Uncertainty: An Empirical Study of Chinese Corporations

Song Qiuge(✉)

University of Putra Malaysia, Jalan Universiti 1, 43400 Serdang, Selangor, Malaysia
`song.lindy@student.upm.edu.my`

Abstract. ESG is an investing philosophy including enterprise environment, society, and governance, and it is crucial for determining whether publicly traded corporations take appropriate social responsibility. Using annual data from 2011 to 2020 from 5,271 companies, this study examines the impact of economic policy uncertainty (EPU) on Chinese companies' environmental, social, and governance (ESG) practices. Our results show that companies tend to be more conservative in their overall ESG performance, environmental performance, and corporate governance in times of high uncertainty. A robust check has been done to verify the results. This study contributes to the existing knowledge of the effects of economic policy uncertainty and the ESG drivers. This report also gives implications for assisting the government in enhancing the ESG performance of businesses.

Keywords: ESG Performance · Economic Policy Uncertainty · China Market

1 Introduction

According to officials, China's newly issued advice for business disclosure criteria on environmental, social, and governance (ESG) activities intends to develop a framework that is more favourable to analysing risk and performance indicators for domestic investors. One of the three main pillars of sustainable development in ESG practice has attracted significant attention in Chinese academic circles over the past decade. Most academics are interested in the relationship between ESG policy and trade policy. At the same time, the vast majority of research focuses on the relationship between the environment and corporate social responsibility (firm value, performance, risk, cost of financing, and equity). Nevertheless, there needs to be more research on corporate ESG engagement and its implications for business needs. Even while much research has proven the correlation between firms and social responsibility and the relationship between firms and social responsibility, it has yet to be confirmed that the EPU directly influences ESG in the Chinese market. This study aims to fill the gap between ESG involvement in China and economic instability [1, 2]. After several robustness checks, the study's results held up, including alternate assessments of crucial factors. This paper's significant contributions are as follows: (1) This research adds to the literature on the consequences of economic policy uncertainty; (2) this study adds to the literature on the drivers of ESG; and (3) this study has implications for supporting the government in improving enterprises' ESG performance.

2 Literature Review and Hypothesis Development

2.1 EPU and Corporation Financial Performance in China

Economic policy uncertainty (EPU) is the risk that government policies and regulatory frameworks will be unclear for the foreseeable future [3]. By tracking the occurrence of keywords in newspaper articles published in the United States beginning in 1985, Baker's team created the first index of economic policy uncertainty [4]. According to new research, shocks that interact with poor policy design, political turmoil in the aftermath of financial mismanagement, tax reforms aimed at promoting economic development, natural disasters that raise questions about how policymakers will respond, and state-specific exposures to significant national effects and policy actions, all cause the EPU index to rise sharply [5]. Economic growth will decelerate due to the EPU, reducing the economy's balance sheet and business profits. Guo et al. discovered that EPU reduces business investment and profitability by investigating panel vector autoregression models (PVAR) [6]. Furthermore, business behavior and policies tend to be risk-averse in uncertain conditions. This propensity is based on top management's risk aversion and correlates positively with the level of uncertainty. EPU can drastically diminish Chinese enterprises' risk appetite, particularly those with little financial resources. This is because these companies become more risk-averse when confronted with EPU shocks. It may also force companies to postpone or even cancel part of their initiatives [7]. During periods of high uncertainty, corporate mergers and acquisitions are also severely impacted, with two significant shifts emerging: the quantity of such deals decreases, while the time needed to complete these procedures increases. Borthwick et al. examined a sample of Chinese enterprises from 2003 to 2017 and discovered that the chance of future year mergers and acquisitions activities (M&As) decreases with policy uncertainty among Chinese firms. Results confirm that irrespective of institutional variations. Political uncertainty harms subsequent mergers and acquisitions [8]. Worse, the EPU's harmful impact extends beyond corporate policy to business innovation. Cui et al. found strong evidence for a significant negative association between EPU and green business innovation in a sample of Chinese A-share listed companies from 2005 to 2019. According to their mitigation impact analysis, financial limitations magnify the negative effects of EPUs on green innovation, but government environmental subsidies considerably alleviate the negative effects of EPUs [9]. The COVID-19 epidemic has boosted economic policy uncertainty to 2.7 times its pre-COVID-19 level [5]. Even in the slow recovery stage from the epidemic, the high EPU index is not the only new challenge facing enterprises today.

2.2 ESG and Corporation Financial Performance in China

ESG performance refers to environmental, social, and corporate governance performance in business choices. The United Nations Environment Program Finance Initiative (UNEP

FI) has worked to incorporate environmental, social, and governance (ESG) considerations into financial institutions' decision-making processes since 1992. Since then, ESG has steadily evolved into one of the three most important criteria the global community uses to assess economic organizations' ability to achieve sustainable development [10]. However, previous research on the advantages of ESG investment has yet to reach an agreement. Notably, China is a typical developing nation where ESG operations by corporations are in their infant stages, and there are fewer solid institutional or regulatory mechanisms in place. Hence, theory and practice must soon offer more exact answers to this issue search.

On the one hand, some scholars suggested that ESG investing will be beneficial. According to Bai et al., the good ESG performance of non-state-owned listed Chinese enterprises in the secondary and tertiary sectors encourages institutional investors to expand their holdings, giving good signals to the market and supporting businesses in decreasing financing limitations [11]. Moreover, ESG performance increases the quantity and quality of company innovation by decreasing budget limits and agency costs [12, 13]. Furthermore, environmental, social, and corporate governance performance might contribute to the expansion of small businesses. [14] Zhang et al. Before 2016, ESG was not a priority in the investment process, but it has been increasingly crucial for boosting portfolio performance since then. Equities with firm ESG profiles yield much greater abnormal returns [15].

Other experts believe that ESG investments would harm a company's financial success. From 2015 to 2019, Ruan and Liu examined samples of ESG rating data from China's Shanghai and Shenzhen A-share listed enterprises and discovered that corporate ESG activities significantly negatively impacted company performance. Moreover, they observed that non-state-owned and non-environmentally sensitive enterprises give more evidence to support the initial findings than state-owned and environmentally sensitive firms. [16]. Additionally, Liu et al. used the panel regression analysis method to investigate a sample of 191 listed enterprises in China's Yangtze River Delta region from 2015 to 2020. They found that environmental performance has an enormously detrimental impact on a corporation's financial success, whereas government performance has a considerable positive impact, and social performance has less impact [17]. S. Zhang et al. studied the impact of ESG performance on the financialization of China's non-financial listed enterprises since 2011. They observed that short-term financial arbitrage is the driving force behind this phenomenon. Long-term return greater than sensible savings or financial arbitrage until 2020. Furthermore, a study of internal and external factors influencing the relationship between ESG performance and firm financialization discovered that corporate ownership and marketing harmed this linkage [18].

2.3 Relationship Between EPU and ESG Performance of Chinese Firms

Uncertainty over the direction of macroeconomic policy has grown in light of recent macroeconomic swings in China. Economic, social, and environmental policy is also a crucial challenge in China today. Meanwhile, academics have studied the connection between monetary policy uncertainty or ESG practice with China's financial market performance. Nonetheless, additional study on the influence of economic policy uncertainty on Chinese enterprises' ESG performance is required. While corporations in rich European nations enhance their ESG policies in times of uncertainty to limit their pursuit of corporate risk-taking and value-added activities [19], the situation in undeveloped countries may differ. Hence, this study will investigate the Chinese firm's ESG performance under the direct and indirect effects of EPU.

In an era of unpredictable economic policies, worsening external funding conditions have exposed Chinese businesses to more significant risks and increased financing costs. As investors consider the ESG performance and index as an indicator of firms' future success and risk mitigation [20], Chinese enterprises may decide to improve their ESG practices and ESG index in order to lessen the negative impact of EPU on corporate finance and improve their stock market performance [21]. Regardless, given that ESG performance may enhance financial flexibility greatly, that would be one of the solutions [22]. In addition, most Chinese enterprises now recognize the strategic importance of digital transformation [23]. Statistics suggest that EPU substantially influences a company's digital transformation in this digital era [24], whereas digital finance can improve ESG performance by removing corporate financial constraints [25]. The following economic policy uncertainty and ESG research hypothesis are generated from the initial theoretical analysis:

Hypothesis H1a: Economic policy uncertainty increases corporate ESG performance.

Considering the conservative character of Chinese culture, Ahsan et al. propose an approach in that Chinese businesses adopt a defensive or analytic business strategy to offset the negative impact of policy-related uncertainty on Corporates' sustainable growth [26]. Specific defensive strategies, however, may have a detrimental influence on a firm's ESG performance. For instance, in response to growing EPU, industrial enterprises prefer to employ cheap and polluting fossil fuels, which increase carbon emissions [27]. Moreover, according to the real options theory, in the presence of adjustment costs during firms' ESG practices, the enterprise investment implies the execution of a call option. In contrast, the investment cost reflects the option's execution price. As a result, corporations may prefer short-term investment above the right to wait for better future investment opportunities if this right is valuable to them [28]. Nevertheless, in the near run, ESG fulfillment has a detrimental impact on firm performance, particularly for small and medium-sized businesses [29]. Besides, Feng et al. discovered that policy-related economic uncertainty negatively impacts Chinese company investment, employment, and revenue [30]. Hence, high economic policy uncertainty will also cut off the capital used for firm ESG activities. Therefore, the subsequent study hypothesis on "economic policy uncertainty and business ESG performance" is developed from the initial theoretical analysis.

Hypothesis 1b: Economic policy uncertainty decreases corporate ESG performance.

3 Research Design

3.1 Sample and Data (Period Country Data Source)

The sample, launched in 2011, covered all Chinese businesses registered on the A-share market between 2011 and 2020. However, the variables utilized in this investigation need more data. Therefore, the Bloomberg ESG rating database, which contains 1062 listed businesses and 6720 firm-years, is utilized to acquire ESG data, while the China Stock Market and Accounting Research (CSMAR) database is used to gather financial and corporate governance information.

3.2 Dependent Variable

Bloomberg ESG Ratings are a proxy for a company's environmental, social, and governance performance. Bloomberg ESG Ratings are based on the accuracy of the information given. The score examines how corporations disclose their ESG operations across three dimensions, including environmental, social, and governance of public information, using 21 indicators and 122 sub-indicators. The greater the ESG rating, the better the total score.

3.3 Independent Variable

The EPU index of China used in this study is taken from Baker et al. [5]. Both national and international reports incorporate a monthly calculation of an unknown short-term delivery amount. Following that, each month, the same number of articles on the same report will be published in the same EPU report, and the series will be standardized until 2011. Ultimately, as of 2011, the average score of other national periodicals was modified to 100. Figure 1 shows the China EPU Index 2021–2020.

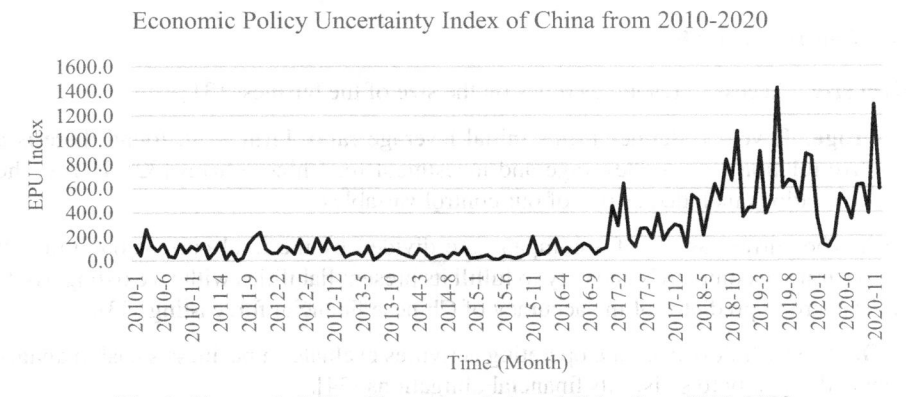

Fig. 1. Economic Policy Uncertainty Index of China from 2010–2020.

Table 1. Variable Definitions.

Variable	Definition and measurement
Panel A: Dependent variables	
Overall ESG performance	Score for overall ESG performance
Environmental performance	The score of a company's resource utilisation and environmental impact
Social performance	The score of a company interaction with consumers, workers, and communities
Governance performance	The average of management, shareholders, and CSR strategy scores
Panel B: Independent variable	
EPU	The weighted average of last three months' EPU index values' natural logarithm
Panel C: Control variables	
Firm size	Natural logarithm of total assets
Leverage	Total debt/total asset
PPE	A firm's total current assets are divided by its total current liabilities
CFO	The amount of money a company brings in from its ongoing, regular business activities
Independent director ratio	Outside director of a total number of directors
Board size	Total number of board members
Industry	Industrial fixed effect
Year	Year fixed effect

3.4 Control Variables

Firm size. Access to resources relies on the size of the business [31].

Leverage. Leverage defines firm's initial leverage ratio. Firth et al. found there is a negative relation between leverage and investment for Chinese firms [32]. Hence, the leverage ratio is included as one of our control variables.

PPE. The current assets of a company are divided by the total current liabilities. It demonstrates a company's capacity to fulfill its present liabilities with its existing assets and is a strong predictor of the accuracy of Chinese financial forecasting [33].

CFO. The cash flow from the operating activities evaluates a business's cash management and capacity to satisfy its financial obligations [34].

Independent Director Ratio. A director with independence may provide clarity, perspective, and the capacity to conduct impartial board debates. In China, the fraction of independent directors is adversely correlated with the chance of financial hardship [35].

Board Size. According to Huang and Wang, board size has a detrimental effect on the risk-taking of Chinese firms [36].

Year-Fixed Effects. The year-fixed effects are involved in accounting for macroeconomic changes.

Industry-Fixed Effects. The industry-fixed effects of accounting for unobservable industry-invariance aspects on prediction accuracy and bias across analysts.

3.5 Model Specification

This research measures the influence of economic policy uncertainty on the ESG performance of Chinese enterprises from 2011 to 2020. The natural choices impact channel is initially used to assess the transmission path of economic policy uncertainty (EPU) on environmental, social, and governance (ESG). The introductory panel model is then created as follows:

$$ESG = \alpha_0 + \beta_1 EPU_t + \sum Control_i + IndustryFE + YearFE + \varepsilon_i \qquad (1)$$

Equation (1) represents i-industry ESG performance in t-year, and EPU t represents China's economic policy uncertainty index in t-year. The yearly EPU index is calculated by taking the geometric mean of the China EPU index. Control for other variables impacting ESG, such as firm size, Leverage (Lev), a firm's total current assets is divided by its total current liabilities (PPE), the amount of money a company brings in from its ongoing (CFO), independent director ratio and board size. What is more, year-fixed and industry-fixed impacts of accounting for unobservable industry-invariance components on prediction accuracy and bias among analysts are considered. Table 2 shows descriptive statistics for all variables. The ESG performance of A-share listed companies in China from 2011 to 2020 was between 1.000 and 9.000, with an average of 6.053.

4 Empirical Results and Discussion

4.1 Effect of EPU on ESG

A panel regression model was used to experimentally estimate the influence of economic policy uncertainty on the Chinese corporate ESG performance. According to the study, the regression model's standard errors are considered the robust standard errors of clustering for companies. In addition, the fixed effect model was chosen for investigation using the Hausmann test.

In addition, a robustness test is also done in this study. According to related research [37], the arithmetic means of the Chinese monthly EPU indices and the weighted mean of the monthly EPU indices are employed for regression estimation instead of the geometric mean. The primary empirical simulation is shown in Table 3.

According to Table 3, the EPU diminishes overall ESG performance. All coefficients are statistically significant and positive at the 1% level. Regarding economic effect, each standard deviation increase in the EPU leads to a loss of 4.17 units in total ESG

Table 2. Descriptive Statistics.

Variable	N	Mean	SD	Min	p25	p50	p75	Max
ESG	25888	6.503	1.154	1.000	6.000	6.000	7.000	9.000
EPU	25888	381.485	239.988	113.897	170.636	363.874	460.470	791.874
Size	25888	22.254	1.446	19.569	21.241	22.039	23.017	27.273
PPE	25888	0.208	0.165	0.001	0.079	0.173	0.301	0.703
Cfo	25888	0.042	0.072	−0.197	0.005	0.042	0.084	0.242
Lev	25888	0.438	0.219	0.050	0.262	0.428	0.599	0.944
Indep	25888	0.381	0.072	0.250	0.333	0.364	0.429	0.600
Board	25888	2.296	0.259	1.609	2.197	2.303	2.485	2.944
HHI	25885	0.288	0.120	0.202	0.213	0.258	0.298	0.829
Dual	25888	0.260	0.439	0.000	0.000	0.000	1.000	1.000

performance. Based on these facts, we cannot reject Hypothesis 2 for overall ESG, environmental performance, and governance performance.

This demonstrates that the Chinese firm's ESG performance is consistent with the real option theory. When economic policy uncertainty increases, businesses hesitate to take on greater ESG responsibilities. Furthermore, the research findings revealed that the regression coefficients of business size, cash flow from operations, and independent director ratio on ESG are 0.367, 0.828, and 0.035, respectively, indicating a strong beneficial influence. That is, the scope of the enterprise's operations, R&D spending, and strategy-making abilities all significantly influence ESG practice. One probable explanation is that the larger a firm is, the more money it spends on ESG to attract additional investment. As a result, more finances would be available to practice ESG, improving ESG performance.

On the contrary, at the 1% significance level, leverage has a statistically significant negative impact on the total ESG score. In addition, the data reveal a negative link between firm ESG policies and the EPU, indicating that managers prefer to make conservative decisions during periods of high uncertainty. The ESG performance and PPE under high economic policy uncertainty show a negative correlation. When environmental uncertainty is high, the investment risk of investors, creditors, and other stakeholders increases, risk-averse investors' investment readiness decreases, and risk-inclined investors' investment decisions become more cautious, reducing the availability of company financing.

4.2 Robustness Test

The following measurement approach was utilized to replace the key variables and was substituted into Eq. (1) for the regression analysis to ensure the study's robustness. Table 3 displays the results of the robustness test. The impact coefficients of EPU on ESG performance were -0.000 and -0.001, respectively, according to the robustness test

Table 3. Baseline Results and Robustness Tests.

Baseline Results			Robustness tests		
	(1)	(2)		(1)	(2)
	ESG	ESG		ESG	ESG
EPU	−0.000***	−0.001***	EPU	0	−0.000***
	(−4.17)	(−13.90)		(−1.45)	(−6.69)
Size		0.367***	Size		0.233***
		−32.32			−11.48
PPE		−0.123	PPE		0.021
		(−1.29)			−0.2
Cfo		0.828***	Cfo		0.088
		−6.07			−0.88
Lev		−0.847***	Lev		−0.684***
		(−11.82)			(−8.89)
Indep		0.035	Indep		0.129
		−0.28			−1.4
Board		−0.06	Board		−0.193***
		(−1.40)			(−6.23)
HHI		0.543***	HHI		0.695***
		−3.17			−3.7
Dual		−0.109***	Dual		−0.007
		(−4.30)			(−0.28)
Constant	6.137***	−1.281***	Constant	6.471***	1.952***
	−38.05	(−4.49)		−278.16	−4.48
Industry	YES	YES	Firm	YES	YES
Year	YES	YES	Year	YES	YES
N	25888	25885	N	25888	25885
Adj R^2	0.088	0.232	Adj R^2	0.015	0.039

Note: The findings of staggered DID regressions evaluating the effects of ESG ratings on analysts' forecast inaccuracy and optimism bias are presented in this table. Standard errors at the firm level are denoted by parenthesis. *, **, and *** denote significance at the 10%, 5%, and 1% (two-tailed) levels, respectively. Table 1 contains the variable definition and measurement

results. This result matches the underlying estimates, showing that the core regression findings are consistent and reliable.

4.3 Herfindahl–Hirschman Index Test

The Herfindahl-Hirschman index is commonly used to measure industry concentration (HHI). It is computed as a percentage of a firm's market share in an industry [38]. Considering the acquired empirical data, the industry concentration favorably improves Chinese firm's ESG performance.

4.4 Discussion

According to the findings of this study, a rise in macroeconomic uncertainty would lead to a reduction in Chinese firms' ESG performance. This demonstrates that while increasing ESG performance can lower equity costs and enable firms to achieve long-term excess returns, investing in ESG performance is not a reasonable option for Chinese companies with high EPU. This, however, contrasts with the findings published by Vural-Yavaş. At times of significant uncertainty, companies in industrialized European countries use ESG practices to reduce risk, akin to insurance [19]. Moreover, Ilyas et al. discovered that American firms would opt to raise their ESG investment in response to high EPU as part of the firm's competitive strategy [39]. Several variables contribute to the disparities in decisions made by Chinese corporations and those in developed nations such as Europe and the United States under high EPU. To begin, the development of ESG in China saw several economic policy upheavals immediately after it began. As previously stated, ESG has a short-term negative impact on business performance, particularly for small and medium-sized firms, which have greater trouble financing under high EPU. Second, the complicated structure of Chinese enterprises impedes improving ESG performance in the face of high EPU. Big Chinese corporations frequently have vast and complicated shareholders. As a result, corporate management tends to minimize risks and make more cautious decisions, especially amid heightened economic policy uncertainty. Finally, it is influenced by cultural context. According to the model results, with high EPU, Chinese firms' investment decisions are more compatible with the Real options theory. In contrast, European and American nations' decisions are more consistent with the stakeholder theory.

5 Conclusion

From 2011 to 2020, data on Chinese A-share businesses was used in the study. This study studies strategic ESG decision-making in economic policy uncertainty and discovers correlations between macroeconomic policy uncertainty and Chinese company ESG performance. According to research, economic policy uncertainty might harm a company's ESG performance. Basic research indicates that businesses take a wait-and-see attitude to socially responsible investing in times of high economic uncertainty. The following policy implications are provided based on the preceding study.

The government levels. To begin, the government must develop more detailed and standardized environmental rules based on the peculiarities of China's economic complexity to enhance the ESG performance of various types of firms. For example, different taxation degrees are implemented based on firms' carbon emissions and environmental pollution; incentives for high-quality green invention patents and enterprises are encouraged to increase employee job satisfaction. Second, the government should preserve economic and environmental policy stability and consistency. On the one hand, the government should decrease the negative impact of EPU through policy stability. At the same time, on the other, it also should consider the implementation of environmental rules to avoid slack oversight. Third, the government must rigorously punish some corporations that have profited from "green-washing" practices.

The firm levels. Enterprises should not mindlessly fulfill their ESG performance. Following macroeconomic policy, management should establish acceptable ESG strategies. ESG should complement core business expansion and long-term stability maintenance, especially when EPU grows. Fulfilling the ESG needs of diverse stakeholders is always vital for firms trying to accomplish their long-term financial goals.

The society levels. The notion of ESG has to be extensively publicized and educated. As ESG becomes the mainstream value choice, a positive cycle might emerge.

6 Limitations and Future Research Suggestions

6.1 Limitations

In considering the results mentioned above, it is crucial to recognize the limits of this study. It is conceivable that our EPU measurements need to be revised due to limited data. A news-based approach estimates EPU using keyword searches by Baker et al., which has limitations due to the possibility of unreported issues or confusing phrases [19]. In addition, this study is relatively broad and does not focus on specific geographical distribution features of Chinese enterprises or particular industries. Therefore, at this time, the results of this study apply solely to the influence of EPU on the overall ESG performance of Chinese businesses.

6.2 Future Research Suggestions

Future studies can assist local governments in creating support and supervisory policies by refining the association between the ESG performance of Chinese enterprises in various locations and the EPU. In addition, future studies emphasize public education and corporate human resource management of ESG in China to address this research vacuum.

References

1. Zhao, T., et al.: Economic policy uncertainty and corporate social responsibility performance: evidence from China. Sustain. Account. Manage. Policy J. **12**(5), 1003–1026 (2021). https://doi.org/10.1108/sampj-05-2020-0158
2. Su, F., et al.: The impact of economic policy uncertainty on corporate social responsibility: a new evidence from food industry in China. PLOS One **17**(6), e0269165 (2022). https://doi.org/10.1371/journal.pone.0269165
3. Al-Thaqeb, S.A., Algharabali, B.G.: Economic policy uncertainty: a literature review. J. Econ. Asymmetries **20**, e00133 (2019). https://doi.org/10.1016/j.jeca.2019.e00133

4. Baker, S.R., et al.: Measuring economic policy uncertainty*. Q. J. Econ. **131**(4), 1593–1636 (2016). https://doi.org/10.1093/qje/qjw024
5. Baker, A.C., et al.: How much should we trust staggered difference-in-differences estimates? J. Financ. Econ. **144**(2), 370–395 (2022). https://doi.org/10.1016/j.jfineco.2022.01.004
6. Guo, A., et al.: Enterprise sustainability: economic policy uncertainty, enterprise investment, and profitability. Sustainability. **12**(9), 3735 (2020). https://doi.org/10.3390/su12093735
7. Wen, F., et al.: How does economic policy uncertainty affect corporate risk-taking? Evidence from China. Financ. Res. Lett. **41**, 101840 (2021). https://doi.org/10.1016/j.frl.2020.101840
8. Borthwick, J., et al.: Does policy uncertainty influence mergers and acquisitions activities in China? A replication studies. Pac.-Basin Financ. J. **62**, 101381 (2020). https://doi.org/10.1016/j.pacfin.2020.101381
9. Cui, X., et al.: Economic policy uncertainty and green innovation: evidence from China. Econ. Model. **118**, 106104 (2023). https://doi.org/10.1016/j.econmod.2022.106104
10. Zhao, C., et al.: ESG and Corporate financial performance: empirical evidence from China's listed power generation companies. Sustainability **10**(8), 2607 (2018). https://doi.org/10.3390/su10082607
11. Bai, X., et al.: ESG performance, institutional investors' preference and financing constraints: empirical evidence from China. Borsa Istanbul Rev. **22**, S157–S168 (2022). https://doi.org/10.1016/j.bir.2022.11.013
12. Tang, H.: The Effect of ESG performance on corporate innovation in china: the mediating role of financial constraints and agency cost. Sustainability. **14**(7), 3769 (2022). https://doi.org/10.3390/su14073769
13. Wang, F., Sun, Z.: Does the environmental regulation intensity and ESG performance have a substitution effect on the impact of enterprise green innovation: evidence from China. Int. J. Environ. Res. Public Health **19**(14), 8558 (2022). https://doi.org/10.3390/ijerph19148558
14. Ge, G., et al.: Does ESG performance promote high-quality development of enterprises in China? The mediating role of innovation input. Sustainability **14**(7), 3843 (2022). https://doi.org/10.3390/su14073843
15. Zhang, X., et al.: Do green policies catalyze green investment? Evidence from ESG investing developments in China. Econ. Lett. **207**, 110028 (2021). https://doi.org/10.1016/j.econlet.2021.110028
16. Ruan, L., Liu, H.: Environmental, social, governance activities and firm performance: evidence from China. Sustainability. **13**(2), 767 (2021). https://doi.org/10.3390/su13020767
17. Liu, H., et al.: Whether and how ESG impacts on corporate financial performance in the yangtze river delta of China. Sustainability **14**(24), 16584 (2022). https://doi.org/10.3390/su142416584
18. Zhang, S., et al.: Effect of environmental, social, and governance performance on corporate financialization: evidence from China. Sustainability **14**(17), 10712 (2022). https://doi.org/10.3390/su141710712
19. Vural-Yavaş, Ç.: Economic policy uncertainty, stakeholder engagement, and environmental, social, and governance practices: the moderating effect of competition. Corp. Soc. Responsib. Environ. Manag. **28**(1), 82–102 (2020). https://doi.org/10.1002/csr.2034
20. Broadstock, D.C., et al.: The role of ESG performance during times of financial crisis: Evidence from COVID-19 in China. Financ. Res. Lett. **38**, 101716 (2021). https://doi.org/10.1016/j.frl.2020.101716
21. Deng, X., Cheng, X.: Can ESG indices improve the enterprises' stock market performance?—an empirical study from China. Sustainability **11**(17), 4765 (2019). https://doi.org/10.3390/su11174765
22. Zhang, D., Liu, L.: Does ESG performance enhance financial flexibility? Evidence from China. Sustainability **14**(18), 11324 (2022). https://doi.org/10.3390/su141811324

23. Yan, M., et al.: The status quo of digital transformation in China: a pilot study. Hum. Syst. Manag. **40**(2), 169–183 (2021). https://doi.org/10.3233/hsm-200917
24. Cheng, Z., Masron, T.A.: Economic policy uncertainty and corporate digital transformation: evidence from China. Appl. Econ. 1–17 (2022). https://doi.org/10.1080/00036846.2022.2130148
25. Mu, W., et al.: Digital finance and corporate ESG. Financ. Res. Lett. **51**, 103426 (2023). https://doi.org/10.1016/j.frl.2022.103426
26. Ahsan, T., et al.: Economic policy uncertainty and sustainable financial growth: does business strategy matter? Financ. Res. Lett. **46**, 102381 (2022). https://doi.org/10.1016/j.frl.2021.102381
27. Yu, J., et al.: Economic policy uncertainty (EPU) and firm carbon emissions: Evidence using a China provincial EPU index. Energy Econ. **94**, 105071 (2021). https://doi.org/10.1016/j.eneco.2020.105071
28. Arasteh, A.: Considering the investment decisions with real options games approach. Renew. Sustain. Energy Rev. **72**, 1282–1294 (2017). https://doi.org/10.1016/j.rser.2016.10.043
29. Chen, L., et al.: Fulfillment of ESG responsibilities and firm performance: a zero-sum game or mutually beneficial. Sustainability **13**(19), 10954 (2021). https://doi.org/10.3390/su131910954
30. Feng, X. et al.: Economic policy uncertainty and firm performance: evidence from China. J. Asia Pac. Econ. 1–18 (2021). https://doi.org/10.1080/13547860.2021.1962643
31. Brammer, S., Millington, A.: Firm size, organizational visibility and corporate philanthropy: an empirical analysis. Bus. Ethics: Eur. Rev. **15**(1), 6–18 (2006). https://doi.org/10.1111/j.1467-8608.2006.00424.x
32. Firth, M., et al.: Leverage and investment under a state-owned bank lending environment: evidence from China. J. Corp. Finan. **14**(5), 642–653 (2008). https://doi.org/10.1016/j.jcorpfin.2008.08.002
33. Chen, J., et al.: Financial distress prediction in China. Rev. Pac. Basin Financ. Mark. Policies **09**(02), 317–336 (2006). https://doi.org/10.1142/s0219091506000744
34. What Are Some Examples of Cash Flow From Operating Activities?. https://www.investopedia.com/ask/answers/032615/what-are-some-examples-cash-flow-operating-activities.asp
35. Li, H., et al.: Ownership, independent directors, agency costs and financial distress: evidence from Chinese listed companies. Corp. Govern.: Int. J. Bus. Soc. **8**(5), 622–636 (2008). https://doi.org/10.1108/14720700810913287
36. Huang, Y.S., Wang, C.-J.: Corporate governance and risk-taking of Chinese firms: the role of board size. Int. Rev. Econ. Financ. **37**, 96–113 (2015). https://doi.org/10.1016/j.iref.2014.11.016
37. Guan, J., et al.: Economic policy uncertainty and corporate innovation: evidence from China. Pac. Basin Financ. J. **67**, 101542 (2021). https://doi.org/10.1016/j.pacfin.2021.101542
38. Modi, S.B., Mishra, S.: What drives financial performance-resource efficiency or resource slack? J. Oper. Manag. **29**(3), 254–273 (2011). https://doi.org/10.1016/j.jom.2011.01.002
39. Ilyas, M., et al.: Economic policy uncertainty and firm propensity to invest in corporate social responsibility. Manag. Decis. **60**(12), 3232–3254 (2022). https://doi.org/10.1108/md-06-2021-0746

Relationship Between Macroeconomy and Stock Market in the United States

Lixiang Zheng(✉)

College of Arts and Sciences, Boston University, Boston, MA 02215, USA
lixiangzheng0619@gmail.com

Abstract. This paper aims to find out the relationship between the stock market and the macroeconomy. This paper finds that the GDP growth rate, M2 growth rate, and 10-year treasury bond yield growth rate are all the Granger causes of the S&P 500 index growth rate. In addition, for one unit increase in GDP_gr, M2_gr, the first lag usually leads to a significant increase in the current SP_gr, and the earlier lags lead to a significant decrease in the current SP_gr. For an increase in the yield_gr, the second and third lags all lead to a significant increase in the S&P 500 index growth rate. In this paper, we present findings to provide investors with a guide to forecast stock market fluctuations and to provide the government with guidelines for making fiscal and monetary policy decisions to enhance and stabilize the economy in the long run.

Keywords: VAR · GDP · M2 · S&P 500 Index · 10-Year Treasury Bond Yield

1 Introduction

There is no doubt that a relationship exists between the stock market and the macroeconomy. However, there has yet to be a consensus on the exact relationship, and examining the exact relationship is very important. On the one hand, investors investing in the stock market rely on macroeconomic variables such as the consumer price index and interest rate to help them forecast the stock price and make rational decisions. On the other hand, stock market investments comprise a large proportion of investment in the Gross Domestic Product (GDP). Therefore, understanding the relationship between the stock market and macroeconomy helps the government make fiscal and monetary policies to boost the economy. This is especially important given the current downturn in the global economy.

This paper aims to examine the relationship between the stock market and the macroeconomy. By using 10-year data, it finds out which exact period of macroeconomic variables has influenced the current stock price. In addition, the Granger test is performed to examine the order of causality. The last part of this paper focuses on developing a vector autoregressive (VAR) system for forecasting future stock prices and testing its reliability.

The rest of the paper is structured as follows: Sect. 2 reviews the relevant literature. Section 3 discusses the data selection and the model used in the paper. Section 4 presents the empirical results. Finally, Sect. 5 summarizes the paper.

2 Literature Review

The relationship between the macroeconomy and the stock market has always been a popular topic among economists, and there are tons of research about it. It is said that the stock market is a barometer for the macroeconomy and can forecast the macroeconomy to some extent (Li, 2020). According to Ruixi (2020), macroeconomic variables and stock prices in China exhibit a stable intrinsic relationship.

There is a relationship between GDP and the stock market, but the relationship is different in different countries. For China, Suying (2010) concludes that macroeconomic change, partly reflected by the GDP growth rate, has an uncertain influence on Chinese stock market fluctuation. When the macroeconomy is strong, income increases, which incentivizes more investors to go into the market, leading to high fluctuations in the stock market.

On the contrary, when the macroeconomy is down, investors have low expectations of the stock market, which leads to a low transaction amount in the stock market. Since most investors in China are individual investors who do not have enough professional knowledge to help them make rational decisions, they cannot fully take advantage of the information reflected in the macroeconomy when investing in the stock market. As a result, the influence of the macroeconomy on the stock market is uncertain in China. However, for a more mature stock market like that in the United States, a clear positive relationship between GDP and the stock market, reflected by Don & Jones Index, has been detected (Jareño & Negrut, 2015).

Furthermore, the change in interest rates also influences the stock market. The interest rate negatively impacts the stock market in China (Chen et al., 2010) and the United States (Humpe & Macmillan, 2009; Bhargava, 2014). The logic behind this is intuitive. When the interest rate increases, investors invest through low-risk investments such as depositing money in the bank, so they have less money or are less enthusiastic about investing in the stock market, which decreases the stock price. In addition, the interest rate also influences the discount rate, which affects the present value of future cash flows and influences stock prices.

Finally, money supply plays a key role in the stock market. Chen et al. (2010) conclude that the money supply influences the stock market positively in China. When the money supply increases, investors have an increasing amount of money on hand, prompting them to invest, including in the stock market. As a result, stock prices fluctuate. However, the situation is different in the United States, where the money supply does not have an important influence on the stock market (Humpe & Macmillan, 2009).

This paper contributes to the existing literature in three ways. First, it takes the approach of taking the growth rate of each variable instead of differencing like many other pieces of literature to make the non-stationary time series stationary. Using the growth rate has a better economic interpretation. In particular, the stock price growth rate is the stock return. Second, the VAR system built in this paper passes many tests, such as the autocorrelation test, the Eigenvalue stable test, and the Wald test. Therefore, this system is valid for further interpreting the ontologized impulse response function. Lastly, this paper divides the sample into training and testing groups to test the VAR's ability to predict the future.

3 Methodology and Data

3.1 Methodology

In order to investigate the relationship between the stock market and macroeconomic variables (VAR), this paper implements the vector autoregression model (Suying, 2011), which is expressed as:

$$Y_t = c + \Pi_1 Y_{t-1} + \Pi_2 Y_{t-2} + \cdots + \Pi_p Y_{t-p} + \varepsilon_t, \ t = 1, \ldots, T$$

where Y_t represents the column matrix of the dependent variable. Π_1, Π_2, and Π_p are the coefficient matrix for each lag order of the variables, Y_{t-p} represents the column matrix for the p lags of the explanatory variable, ε_t and is the vector white noise process. Y is the column matric for intercept. In particular, the Y_t and the Y_{t-p} in this paper are the column matrix for SP_gr (growth S&P 500 index), GDP_gr (growth rate of GDP), M2_gr (growth rate of M2), and yield_gr (growth rate of 10-year treasury bond yield).

One prerequisite of VAR is that the data must be stationary since non-stationary data might give us a spurious correlation. To find out whether the original time series is stationary, this paper performs the unit root test by completing the Dickey-fuller test. If the dataset is non- stationary and we still want to perform regression analysis, we can make it stationary by computing the difference or growth rate. This paper uses the growth rate method, which has a better economic interpretation.

In addition, this paper performs the Granger test to examine the order of causality. After testing the reliability of the VAR system, this paper produces Ontologized Impulse Response Function (OIRF) to analyze the effect of one standard deviation of a positive impulse to one variable on other variables. Lastly, the forecasting and testing of the VAR model are performed.

3.2 Data Selection

Standard and Poor's 500 (S&P 500) is comprehensive since it tracks the performance of 500 companies in the United States, so this paper selects S&P 500 as the variable to reflect stock market fluctuation.

This paper selects GDP, M2, and the US 10-year treasury bond yield for the macroeconomic variables. GDP is the monetary value of all final goods and services produced and sold in a country, thus reflecting the big picture of how a country performs. M2 is used as an indicator of the money supply and the target of monetary policy in the United States, which includes cash, checking deposits, and near-money. The U.S. 10-year treasury yield is the interest rate that the government will pay investors if they buy the bond today. It typically reflects the borrowing rate, such as the mortgage rate, which is why investors pay so much attention to monitoring it.

All the data are from the Federal Reserve Economic Data. Considering the availability of datasets, the data selected for this paper span from 2013 Q1 through 2022 Q3.

4 Empirical Results

4.1 Stationary Test

According to the DF tests, test statistics for all the variables are larger than the 5% DF critical value. Therefore, we reject the null hypothesis and conclude that all the original data are not stationary (Table 1).

Table 1. Unit root test.

Variable	Test Statistics	Dickey-Fuller Critical Value 5%	Machinnon Approximate p-value	Conclusion
S&P 500	−0.386	−2.964	0.9124	Non-stationary
GDP	0.853	−2.964	0.9924	Non-stationary
M2	1.720	−2.964	0.9982	Non-stationary
10-year treasury bond yield	−1.303	−2.964	0.6279	Non-stationary

To make these variables stationary, this paper calculates the growth rate for each variable. The DF tests after the transformation indicate that the growth rate for each variable is stationary (Table 2). Thus, they are ready to be used to build a VAR model.

Table 2. Unit root test after transformation.

Variable	Test Statistics	Dickey-Fuller Critical Value 5%	Machinnon Approximate p-value	Conclusion
SP_gr	−4.508	−2.964	0.0002	Stationary
GDP_gr	−7.455	−2.964	0.0000	Stationary
M2_gr	−4.144	−2.964	0.0008	Stationary
yield_gr	−3.894	−2.964	0.0021	Stationary

4.2 Building Var Model

Before building the VAR model, we need to select the appropriate lag order according to the lag selection criteria. More specifically, this paper focuses on the Akaike information criteria (AIC). The lag order that minimizes AIC is the appropriate order we should choose. According to the results (Table 3), four lags give the smallest AIC, meaning we should choose four lags.

Table 4 shows the result of the VAR model. As shown in the table, there are 17 variables for each equation, and 23 of all estimated coefficients are significant, at least at

Table 3. Lag-order selection criteria.

lag	LL	LR	df	P	FPE	AIC	HQIC	SBIC
0	243.499				8.9e−12	−14.0882	−14.0269	−13.9086
1	282.146	77.296	16	0.000	2.4e−12	−15.4204	−15.1142	−14.5225*
2	298.901	33.509	16	0.000	2.4e−12	−15.4648	−14.9136	−13.8486
3	326.697	55.593	16	0.000	1.3e−12	−16.1587	−15.3626	−13.8242
4	348.708	44.022*	16	0.000	1.2e−12*	−16.5122*	−15.4712*	−13.4595

the 10% significant level. According to the coefficients, one unit increase in the L2.SP_gr and the L4.SP_gr leads to 0.246 and −0.539 changes in the current SP_gr, respectively. This means that an increase in the second lag of SP_gr and the fourth lag of SP_gr leads to a significant increase and decrease in SP_gr, respectively. One unit increase in the L1.GDP_gr, L3.GDP_gr, and L4.GDP_gr leads to 1.984, −1.464, and −1.141 changes in the current SP_gr, respectively. This means that an increase in the first lag of GDP_gr leads to a significant increase in the current period of SP_gr, but an increase in the third and fourth lag of GDP_gr leads to a significant decrease in the current period of SP_gr. Past lags of the M2_gr also affect the current SP_gr. One unit increase in the L1.M2_gr and L2.M2_gr leads to 2.976 and -1.231 changes in the current SP_gr. This means that an increase in the first lag of M2_gr leads to a significant increase in the current SP_gr, but an increase in the second lag of M2_gr leads to a significant decrease in the current SP_gr. As a result of the influence of the past lags of yied_gr, an increase in the second and third lag will also result in a significant increase in the current period of SP_gr. Since all the variables are in growth rate, an increase or decrease in the growth rate means an increase or decrease in the level of those variables.

4.3 Testing VAR

The autocorrelation test shows that there is no autocorrelation in the VAR model. In addition, the VAR stable test shows that all eigenvalues lie in the unit circle, so the model is stable. The Wald test shows that for the SP_gr equation, we can safely reject the null hypothesis that all four endogenous variables are zero at all four lags. Although we cannot reject null hypotheses for other individual equations at all lags, we can strongly reject the hypothesis that all endogenous variables are zero in all four equations jointly at the 1% significance level.

4.4 Orthogonalized Impulse Response Analysis

Considering the large number of variables in the VAR model, it is somewhat difficult to interpret all of the coefficients in all of the equations. Therefore, it is reasonable to interpret based on the Orthogonalized Impulse Response Function (OIRF) to see the effect of one positive standard deviation of shock on one variable on other variables in the VAR model.

Table 4. Vector Autoregression.

variables	(1) SP_gr	(2) GDP_gr	(3) M2_gr	(4) Yield_gr
L.SP_gr	−0.045	−0.001	0.024	−0.077
	(−0.29)	(−0.01)	(0.25)	(−0.08)
L2.SP_gr	0.246*	−0.112	0.143	0.251
	(1.79)	(−1.34)	(1.62)	(0.31)
L3.SP_gr	0.053	−0.165	0.141	−1.297
	(0.32)	(−1.63)	(1.33)	(−1.31)
L4.SP_gr	−0.539***	−0.133	0.090	−0.958
	(−3.41)	(−1.38)	(0.88)	(−1.02)
L.GDP_gr	1.894**	0.577	−0.946*	−1.684
	(2.43)	(1.21)	(−1.89)	(−0.36)
L2.GDP_gr	−0.872	0.419	−0.428	3.326
	(−1.42)	(1.12)	(−1.09)	(0.91)
L3.GDP_gr	−1.464**	−0.481	0.528	−2.032
	(−2.49)	(−1.34)	(1.40)	(−0.58)
L4.GDP_gr	−1.141***	−0.523**	0.401	−1.208
	(−2.60)	(−1.96)	(1.43)	(−0.46)
L.M2_gr	2.967***	1.690***	−1.184**	1.972
	(4.10)	(3.83)	(−2.55)	(0.46)
L2.M2_gr	−1.231**	−0.157	0.514	5.840*
	(−2.25)	(−0.47)	(1.47)	(1.79)
L3.M2_gr	−0.342	−0.649*	0.926**	−2.631
	(−0.53)	(−1.67)	(2.26)	(−0.69)
L4.M2_gr	−0.672	−0.173	0.385	2.619
	(−1.02)	(−0.43)	(0.91)	(0.67)
L.yield_gr	−0.011	0.069***	−0.090***	0.637***
	(−0.29)	(3.15)	(−3.89)	(2.97)
L2.yield_gr	0.174***	0.037	−0.021	−0.065
	(4.39)	(1.52)	(−0.85)	(−0.28)
L3.yield_gr	0.065**	0.064***	−0.052***	−0.006
	(2.20)	(3.55)	(−2.73)	(−0.03)

(*continued*)

Table 4. (*continued*)

variables	(1) SP_gr	(2) GDP_gr	(3) M2_gr	(4) Yield_gr
L4.yield_gr	0.041	0.052**	−0.038*	0.623***
	(1.21)	(2.54)	(−1.78)	(3.11)
Constant	0.034***	0.008	0.002	−0.071
	(2.84)	(1.04)	(0.29)	(−0.98)
Observations	34	34	34	34

z-statistics in parentheses
*** p < 0.01, ** p < 0.05, * p < 0.1

According to the OIRF (Fig. 1), if we give one standard deviation positive shock to GDP_gr, the SP_gr will decrease in the next period. If we give one standard deviation positive shock to the M2_gr, the SP_gr will increase in the next period and decrease in the future second period. We will see a decrease in the SP_gr in the future sixth period if we provide a standard deviation positive shock to the yield_gr.

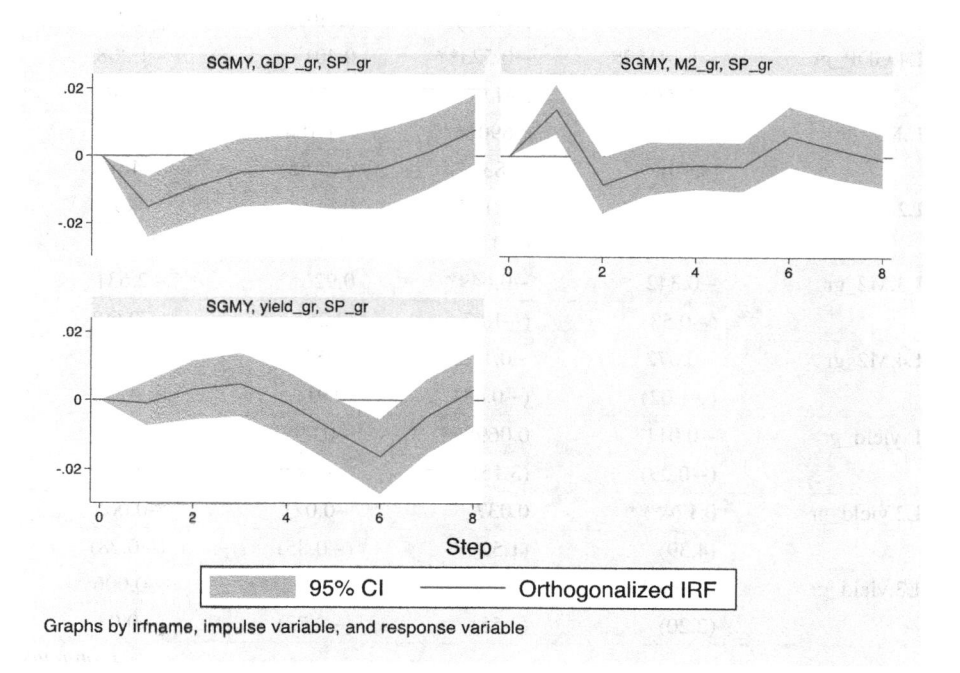

Fig. 1. Orthogonalized impulse response function.

4.5 Forecasting

To forecast and test the forecast result, this paper splits the dataset into a training group and a testing group. The training group, ranging from 2013 Q1 to 2021 Q4, is for building the VAR model for forecasting, and the testing group, ranging from 2022 Q1 to 2022 Q3, is for testing the forecast by comparing the predicted with the actual.

The results (Fig. 2) show that the 95% confidence interval of the estimated SP_gr covers the actual SP_gr; thus, the forecasting is reliable. However, others are not so reliable, as even the 95% confidence intervals do not cover the actual data.

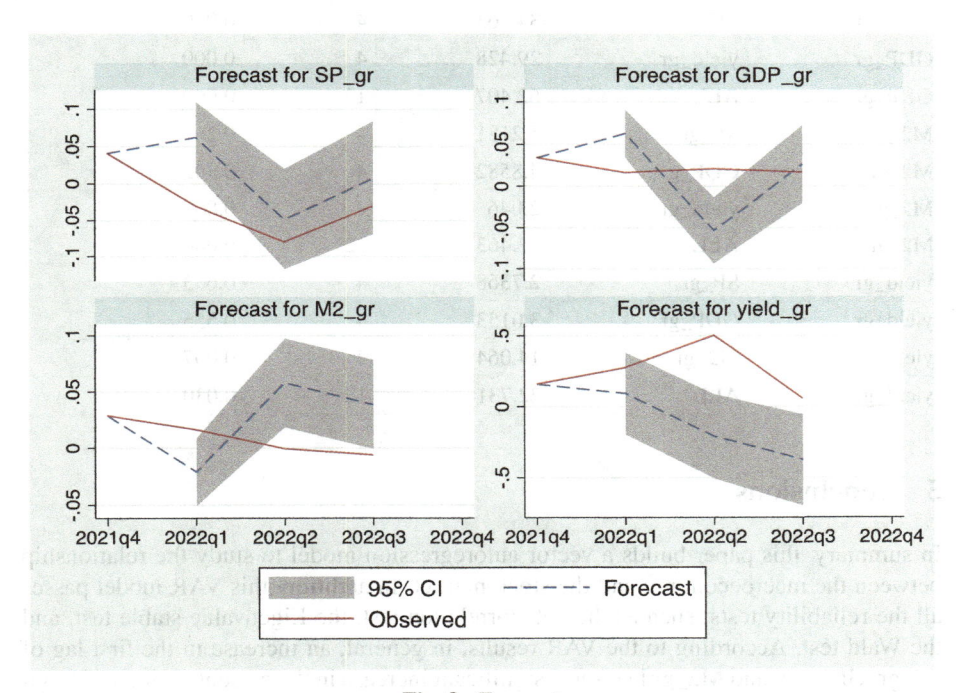

Fig. 2. Forecast.

4.6 Granger Test

The Granger test (Table 6) shows that when excluding GDP_gr, M2_gr, or yield_gr individually from the SP_gr equation, the p-value is smaller than 0.01. In addition, when excluding SP_gr in all other three equations, the p-values are all larger than 0.1. Therefore, we can conclude that the GDP_gr, M2_gr, and yield_gr are all Granger causes of the S&P 500 index growth rate (Table 5).

Table 5. Granger test.

Equation	Excluded	chi2	df	Prob > chi2
SP_gr	GDP_gr	20.354	4	0.000
SP_gr	M2_gr	33.258	4	0.000
SP_gr	yield_gr	32.705	4	0.000
SP_gr	ALL	80.988	12	0.000
GDP_gr	SP_gr	5.9266	4	0.205
GDP_gr	M2_gr	34.763	4	0.000
GDP_gr	yield_gr	29.428	4	0.000
GDP_gr	ALL	62.407	12	0.000
M2_gr	SP_gr	5.2181	4	0.266
M2_gr	GDP_gr	4.8582	4	0.302
M2_gr	yield_gr	23.46	4	0.000
M2_gr	ALL	37.463	12	0.000
yield_gr	SP_gr	2.7368	4	0.603
yield_gr	GDP_gr	3.0153	4	0.555
yield_gr	M2_gr	14.064	4	0.007
yield_gr	ALL	22.731	12	0.030

5 Conclusions

In summary, this paper builds a vector autoregression model to study the relationship between the macroeconomy and the stock market. In addition, this VAR model passes all the reliability tests, such as the autocorrelation test, the Eigenvalue stable test, and the Wald test. According to the VAR results, in general, an increase in the first lag of SP_gr, GDP_gr, and M2_gr leads to a significant increase in the current period of SP_gr. However, an increase in the earlier lags of these variables usually leads to a significant decrease in the current period of SP_gr. For yield_gr, an increase in the second and the third all lead to a significant increase in the current SP_gr. In addition, the VAR model built in this paper provides a good forecast for the SP_gr in the future.

When looking at the Orthogonalized Impulse Response Function, a positive shock on GDP_gr and M2_gr leads to a significant decrease and increase in the next period of SP_gr, respectively. In addition, an increase in the yield_gr, which can be considered a long-term interest rate, leads to a decrease in the future sixth period of the SP_gr.

Given the current downturn of the global economy, the results of this paper provide a framework for investors to forecast stock market fluctuations based on macroeconomic variables and make rational decisions when investing. Moreover, understanding the relationship between the macroeconomy and the stock market also helps the government make fiscal and monetary policies to boost the economy.

References

Bhargava, A.: Firms' fundamentals, macroeconomic variables, and quarterly stock prices in the US. J. Econom. **183**(2), 241–250 (2014). https://doi.org/10.1016/j.jeconom.2014.05.014

Chen, Q., Zhang, Y., Liu, X.: Macro economic environment, government regulation policy and stock market fluctuation—empirical evidence from Chinese stock market. ECONOMIST (02), 90–98 (2010). https://doi.org/10.16158/j.cnki.51-1312/f.2010.02.015

Humpe, A., Macmillan, P.: Can macroeconomic variables explain long-term stock market movements? A comparison of the US and Japan. Appl. Financ. Econ. **19**(2), 111–119 (2009). https://doi.org/10.1080/09603100701748956

Jareño, F., Negrut, L.: US stock market and macroeconomic factors. J. Appl. Bus. Res. **32**(1), 325 (2015). https://doi.org/10.19030/jabr.v32i1.9541

Liu, R.: The co-integration relationship between macroeconomic variables and stock price index. Zhongguo Shuiyun (Second Half Month) (08), 22–23+37 (2020). (In Chinese)

Li, Z.: Chinese stock market and macroeconomic analysis. China J. Commer. (13), 178–180 (2016). (In Chinese)

Yang, S.: Study of relationship between stock market and macroeconomic variables (2011). https://kns.cnki.net/KCMS/detail/detail.aspx?dbname=CMFD2012&filename=1012301397.nh

Research on the Activated Utilization and Digital Innovation Development of Cultural Heritage Under the Concept of Sustainable Development

Yuting Yu(✉)

University College London, Gower St, London WC1E 6BT, UK
yuting.yu@outlook.com

Abstract. This paper aims to uphold the premise of the concept of sustainable development and explore the new direction of the digital development of cultural heritage. The involvement of digital technology not only stimulates dynamic inheritance power but also brings a variety of benefits. This paper elaborates on the time machine project and the digital protection of the capital of Zheng and Han states, further excavates the new mode of digital management and inheritance of contemporary cultural heritage, and looks forward to the innovative development of cultural heritage in the future against the background of the metaverse era.

Keywords: The Idea of Sustainable Development · Cultural Heritage · Digital Innovation · Metaverse

1 Introduction

In the present era, cultural heritage still has certain limitations in terms of protection and inheritance, which are embodied in the increasingly serious homogenization trend and the gradual increase of communication barriers. Therefore, we should uphold the concept of sustainable development for the follow-up protection and development of cultural heritage. At the same time, digital technology is rapidly popularizing and being integrated into many fields. Digital innovation also brings new opportunities for the development of cultural heritage. In addition, the innovative development and living inheritance of data intelligence under the concept of sustainability not only provide a new method for the protection of cultural heritage but also bring the audience a new interactive experience and immersive visiting mode. In this paper, starting from the concept of sustainable development, the author expounds on the importance of sustainable cultural heritage. Secondly, this paper analyzes the status quo of digital development and the advantages brought by digital technology intervention. Thirdly, this paper presents two new forms of digital management and inheritance through practical case analysis. In the end, this paper puts forward the prospect of future cultural heritage innovation and development from the concept of the metauniverse.

2 Sustainable Development of Cultural Heritage

2.1 The Idea of Sustainable Development

The idea of sustainability originated in ecology. In 1731, Hans Carl von Carlowitz first used the term "sustainability" in German forestry circles to emphasize the importance of environmental carrying capacity [1]. Since then, the concept of sustainability has been given a higher priority in cognition and practice. Sustainability in the four directions of environment, economy, society, and culture has adopted as the four pillars to promote innovation and reduce risks by maintaining the dynamic balance between these four fields so as to meet the development needs of the contemporary population to the greatest extent possible without wasting future natural capital. At the same time, the sustainable development strategy has been gradually established and improved in different social forms. The United Nations has also set clear Sustainable Development Goals (SDGs) [2]. Based on the concept of sustainable development, this paper studies some cultural heritage with environmental management problems and development risks, which are embodied in the activation, utilization, and digital innovative development of heritage with the help of various digital tools or platforms.

2.2 The Importance of Sustainable Development of Cultural Heritage

To some extent, the sustainable development of cultural heritage promotes the active reuse of cultural heritage, which is mainly reflected in three aspects. To begin with, it promotes the inheritance of excellent spiritual and cultural connotations as well as the guarantee of authenticity in the protection and inheritance of intangible cultural heritage of traditional skills, thereby resolving the contradiction between alienation of heritage and authenticity. Secondly, in the aspect of material cultural heritage, the objective subject is protected in a more comprehensive way by means of the theory of cultural positive circulation and the construction of an activation path [3]. Finally, sustainable development also promotes the transformation and upgrading of the local industrial structure, transforming it from a traditional labor-intensive industry to a "tourism plus technology" cultural industry chain, alleviating the conflict between tradition and modernity, and providing a new digital transformation path for the long-term development of cultural heritage. In short, in the view of all-round social development, a broad consensus has been reached on the importance of the sustainable development of cultural heritage, which not only includes the inheritance of contemporary and future excellent intrinsic cultural values but also makes a significant contribution to social innovation, economic progress, environmental protection, and other aspects.

3 The Intervention of Digital Technology: A New Direction of Activation Inheritance

3.1 Current Situation of Digital Development of Cultural Heritage

At present, with the increasing proportion of commercial development, serious homogenization and the loss of some minority intangible cultural heritage appear to be part of the process of development. The innovation and upgrading of digital technology have brought new vitality to its development, which is mainly reflected in the expansion of the communication mode, the expansion of the expression form of the unknown field, and the enrichment of the development system. Furthermore, digitalization opens up new avenues for the preservation and transmission of cultural heritage, such as visual analysis of user behavior, human-machine emotional interaction expression, and so on. This not only strengthens the intellectual support of digital protection for cultural heritage but also broadens the breadth and depth of consumption around cultural heritage. The popularity of digital media and big data satisfies the trend of personalized consumption in cultural tourism. At the same time, it also makes use of the characteristics of fast information transmission in the era of "we media" to strengthen viewers' loyalty, improve user experience to the greatest extent possible [4], and radiate core users. Therefore, the digital culture industry centered on heritage will continue to iterate and upgrade.

3.2 The Advantages of Digital Technology Intervention

Immersion and Interactivity: Strengthening the Characteristic Image of Cultural Heritage. This refers to the immersive atmosphere created by the secondary developers of cultural heritage using digital technology and the enhancement of the immersive experience of viewers. The specific manifestation is to develop high-value and high-quality consumption forms such as personalized experiences with the help of artificial intelligence and other digital equipment and scientific and technological design tools, so as to strengthen the image characteristics of cultural heritage among individuals and groups. At the same time, digital technology emphasizes interactivity and integrates interactive tools into a specific cultural environment. Cultural heritage experts, guided by tourist experience, explore appropriate human-computer interaction technologies to enhance interactive tools so as to deepen tourists' understanding of heritage elements and satisfy their curiosity and desire for knowledge [5]. For example, in the case of Piet Mondrian's painting (Fig. 1), the cultural heritage agency uses the work itself and the environment in which the artist worked and lived as entry points to create a story composed of ten virtual scenes. With the help of interactive tools, users are guided into this space to interact with the painting, gain an in-depth understanding of the fine structure of the original painting, and experience the whole process of painting from conception to creation [6].

Unbounded: Breaking the Bonds of Time and Space. The intervention of digital technology breaks the "fourth wall" between the cultural heritage itself and the viewer in the traditional sense. The use of emerging virtual reality technologies such as VR, AR, and blockchain has increased the scope of cultural transmission, broken the limitations of the traditional static presentation of regional restrictions and cultural restoration difficulties, and promoted the cultural heritage from local cognition to wide dissemination so as to obtain efficient protection and inheritance. In terms of time, it further extends the intrinsic cultural value of the heritage, making it an "eternal art." In terms of space, the new digital technology provides more potential customers with in-depth understanding and remote experience opportunities, greatly shortening the space and time distances and even realizing "zero distance".

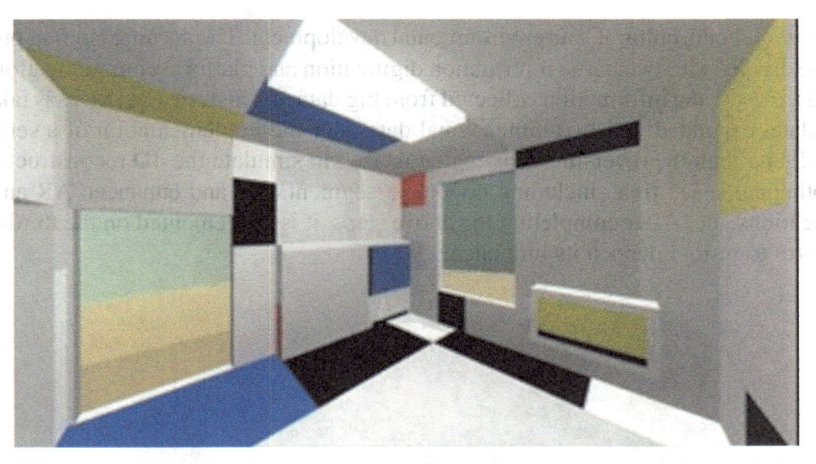

Fig. 1. 3D painting interior space perspective. (Picture Source: https://monvr.psychologyresearch.co.uk/index.php/virtual-space/)

Sustainability: The Inheritance and Protection of Cultural Heritage. Digitization preserves the strong inheritance value contained in cultural heritage itself, which is conducive to the sustainable development of heritage. Through the collection of scattered pieces of information, visual modeling is used to carry out three-dimensional reconstruction and cultural representation so as to promote the inheritance of cultural heritage. At the same time, the establishment of a cultural gene information base also makes the protection of cultural heritage more systematic and protects the characteristic cultural heritage resource system to a certain extent. Information and communication technologies (ICTs) for visitors, for example, and highly configurable and user-friendly applications have become key tools for achieving sustainable development at world heritage destinations [7]. Such tools can be used to collect and disseminate historical and cultural resources, which indirectly promotes the green development of cultural heritage.

4 The Manifestation of Digital Management and Inheritance

4.1 European Time Machine Data Intelligent Innovation Protection and Development

"Time Machine" refers to the re-use of past heritage resource data to revitalize the history of Europe, which belongs to the digital humanities project of urban time and space retrospection. Europeana and Time Machine are working together to design and implement advanced new digitalization and artificial intelligence technologies to further explore the intrinsic value of Europe's vast cultural heritage system, provide fair and free access to information, and provide more possibilities and multi-dimensional display platforms for the sustainable development of cultural heritage.

The European Time Machine project aims to combine Europe's rich human and historical resources with emerging digital technologies to build an integrated digital management and inheritance system, depicting the intergenerational evolution of Europe's economic, social, cultural, and environmental development. The specific landing process can be divided into two parts: information digitization and platform communication (see Fig. 2). Firstly, the information collected from big data and historical archives is taken as metadata, expanded into two-dimensional data after the implementation of a semantic model, and then the diversification engine is used to simulate the 4D reconstruction of hypothetical space-time, including document segmentation and enhanced AR and VR applications, etc. After completing the above steps, it is implemented on the third-party platform to further deepen its influence.

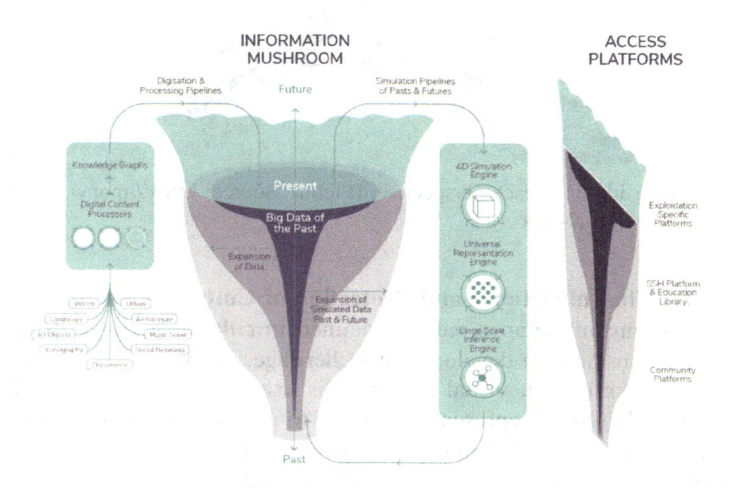

Fig. 2. Time machine digital content processing model. (Picture Source: https://www.timemachine.eu/)

In addition, the basic digital architecture of the historical and cultural heritage of this project is implemented into several local time machine branch projects or urban heritage protection projects according to local conditions through the framework of the European Time Machine and through cooperation with one or more stakeholders to develop strategic plans so as to achieve the sustainability of the time machine project and the economic independence of the TMO institutional management framework. Its representative local time machine projects include the 4D reconstruction of historic cities, the visualization of heritage wisdom data, and the construction of digital platforms and tools.

One of TMO's sub-projects is a collaboration with EURECA on the enrichment of urban archives and collections in the European region. Its main goal is to closely link LBS (location-based services) and personalized development trends, to find traces and origins that shape the urban heritage of contemporary Europe, and to activate and explore with digital tools. In addition, the spatio-temporal metadata automatically generated by this innovative tool can be used to conduct new research while establishing a broader mass base, thus attracting new personalized cultural heritage consumers.

LBS run by the EURECA project offer visitors the chance to explore the history of a specific city. Visitors can combine natural language processing (NLP), semantic intelligence technology, and mobile devices as mediators to link a city's cultural heritage to its cultural origin area, known as RoO [8]. In Ghent, for example, visitors can explore traces of the city's original Austrian heritage. At the same time, the RoO heat map of cultural heritage points of interest (POI) generated by the project (see Fig. 3) can be used to compare and achieve mutual achievements in relation to different time and spatial locations in the current era through GIS, remote intelligent computing, and other technologies, so that more people can trace back to the source of culture, realize cultural exchanges between cities, and indirectly promote the innovative development of cultural heritage.

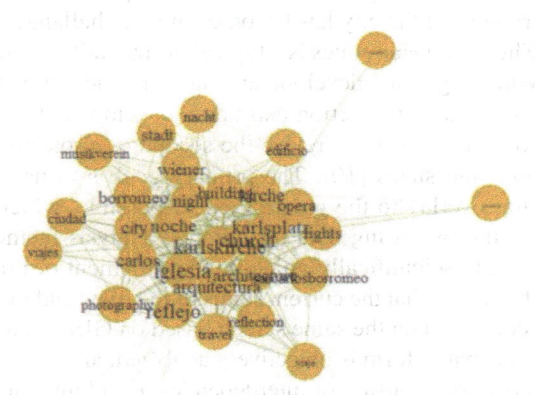

Fig. 3. Word graph for RoA of points of interest. (Picture Source: European Time Machine EURECA project)

In addition, this project also uses the network kernel density estimation method (NKDE) to analyze the cultural heritage travel preferences and footprint distribution of different sources of tourists in a specific city so as to enrich the virtual collections and digital heritage resource reserves of the local city [9]. Figure 4 shows the footprint distribution of NKDE in Vienna for three groups, including all users and RoO in Belgium and Spain.

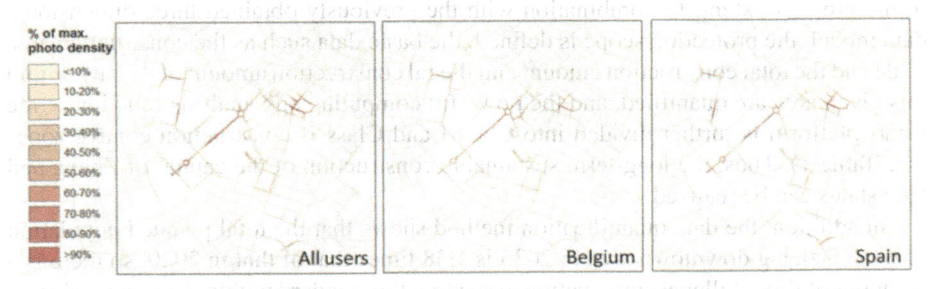

Fig. 4. NKDE Footprints for Vienna. (Picture Source: Delso, J., Martin, B., Ortega, E., & Van De Weghe, N. 2019)

4.2 Data Quantification and Intelligent Analysis Protection Strategies for the Capital of Zheng and Han States

Nowadays, there are some difficulties in the protection of large urban overlay sites. The main reason is the general contradiction between urban modernization and rapid economic development. Some local urban planning and coordination departments believe that large-scale urban sites squeeze and occupy limited urban development space, thus hindering the process of urbanization. However, the protection of traditional sites is mainly from the perspective of cultural connotation and inheritance, so there is a certain conflict between the two. Finding a reasonable balance point to realize the sustainable development of heritage and the city has become a major challenge.

The capital of Zheng and Han states is a typical horizontally scattered superimposed site (see Fig. 5). With the gradual development and construction of Xinzheng City, the relationship between heritage protection and urban development is becoming increasingly rigid. Therefore, it is urgent to revise the secondary protection planning for the capital of Zheng and Han states [10]. The primary goal is to use digital technology to protect the cultural overlay to the greatest extent possible, which entails analyzing the conflict between the two using data quantitative analysis methods and an intelligent analysis platform to scientifically guide the development of protection strategies. Specifically, it can be shown that the current status of the ruins and the planning scope of Xinzheng City are compared on the same screen based on GIS and historical maps, and the evolution of urban spatial form is objectively analyzed, and it is concluded that they belong to the dialectical relationship of interdependence and mutual restriction [11].

The innovative quantitative research on data from Zheng and Han states capital is primarily reflected in three aspects. The first is the innovation of digital technology, including the use of airborne laser remote sensing mapping to obtain accurate geographic information, the collection of sites and new towns within the overlaying range of image data and surface information, and then the construction of three-dimensional models; Simultaneously, an information resource database is being built to analyze the status quo of Zheng and Han states' rich historical and cultural heritage resources above and below ground, as well as data from various urban business types. The second is a quantitative analysis of the relationship between cities and ancient cities. On the premise of ensuring the steady development of the city, the authenticity of cultural sites should be preserved to the greatest extent. In combination with the previously obtained three-dimensional data model, the protection scope is defined, the basic data such as the construction area scale and the total construction amount and illegal construction amount of the city within this given area are quantified, and the powerful computing and analysis function of the smart platform is further divided into Class I and Class II construction control zones (see Table 1). Thus, the long-term sustainable construction of the capital of Zheng and Han states can be realized.

In addition, the data quantification method shows that the total planned population of the Xinzheng downtown area in 2035 is 1.38 times that of that in 2020, so there is a great possibility of illegal construction exceeding the standard within the protected area. This has affected the scientific protection of the original cultural heritage. Based on the analysis of the above data, the following conclusions can be drawn about the overall protection planning of the capital of Zheng and Han states: The established regional

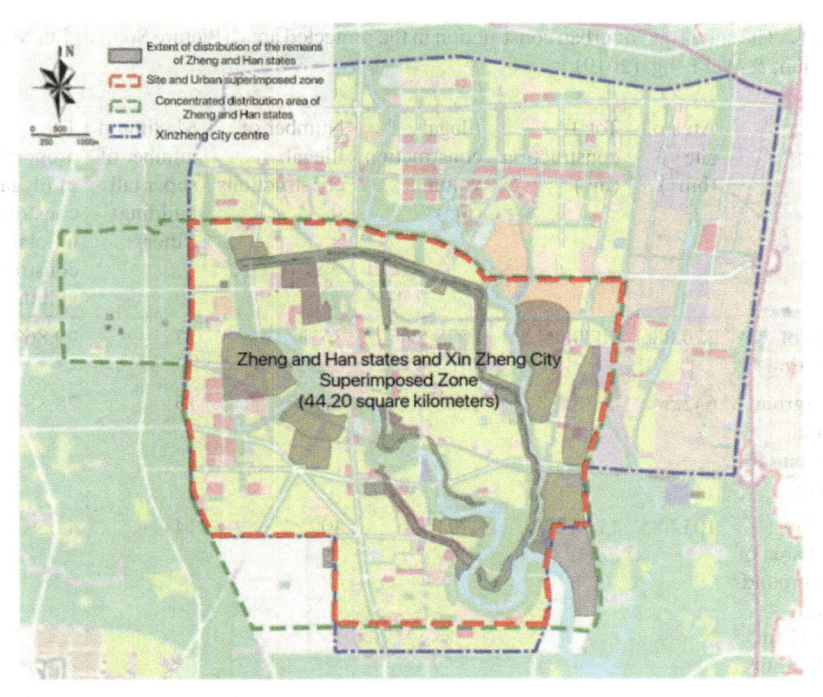

Fig. 5. The location relationship between Xinzheng City and the capital of Zheng and Han states. (Picture Source: Wang Qinglan & An Lei. (2022). Conservation Planning Methods for Urban Superimposed Large Sites: A Case Study of the Capital of Zheng and Han States. Urban Studies. (07), 117–127+2+37).

scope of the capital of Zheng and Han states cannot meet the development demands of Xinzheng City. Therefore, it has become an inevitable and necessary trend to shift the development direction of some new cities away from cultural sites and gradually outward [12]. In a word, the capital of Zheng and Han states has developed a new planning scheme guided by the results of digital quantitative analysis that retains the characteristics of the original heritage buildings to a great extent and meets the needs of new urban development on this basis. It reconciles the contradiction between old and new cities in the process of modernization and proves that digitalization is the inevitable trend toward sustainable development of cultural heritage.

5 Prospects for Future Innovation and Development

5.1 The Cultural Products of the Metaverse

In recent years, the concept of "metaverse" (Neal Stephenson, 1992) has gradually come into people's view. It is essentially a multiple, superimposed world of physical and virtual digital synergistic interaction [13]. The popularity of metaverse cultural products is also rising, among which the NFT (non-fungible token) digital collection is the most typical.

Table 1. The status quo of urban construction in the protected area. (Picture Source: Cui Minmin, Xie Lijun, & Wei Feng. (2019).)

District Names	Area of site (hm^2)	Total construction (m^2)	Illegal construction volume (m^2)	Number of illegal constructions	Maximum number of super tall buildings (floor)	The proportion of illegal construction in total construction volume
Scope of protection	370.88	1079864	1078364	3633	27	99.86%
Underground cultural relics burial reserve	642.5	4328498	1250151	1961	15	28.88%
Possible burial area of underground cultural relics (24m height limit area)	1032.85	11774376	477167	409	14	4.05%
Class I construction control zone	183.78	414230	314866	831	17	76.03%
Class II construction control zone	373.2	2313411	841604	1010	26	36.38%
grand total	2603.21	19910379	3962152	7844	27	19.90%

It represents the digital assets of physical objects such as artwork and collectibles. The main form of expression is to truncate the data node of a cultural product as a selling point [14]. Compared with traditional digital products, users have the sole "property right" and strong liquidity. For cultural heritage, the emergence of NFT products in this field not only broadens the possibility of artistic creation but also has great advantages in the protection of heritage-related intellectual property rights. In addition, due to the recent impact of the epidemic, some cultural heritage organizations find it difficult to maintain the original funding chain, which hinders the sustainable development of cultural heritage to a certain extent. Some museums and cultural attractions have been forced by the severe economic situation to suspend the original heritage development and protection plans, so there are problems such as the withdrawal of museums and the breakdown of the funding chain for cultural heritage restoration plans. "NFT plus traditional culture IP" changes this situation. It proves that digital innovation and development provide new ideas for cultural survival, open up a new path for cultural transmission, and realize the transformation from traditional coordinates to the emerging NFT dimension [15].

In addition, the Artificial Human Project within the Metaverse Ecosystem is also progressing. If it is combined with the development of cultural heritage, such virtual characters can accurately capture the characteristic culture of the heritage site, including the minority's intangible cultural heritage, and can quickly respond to the dialogue and make real expressions like real people. Users can comprehensively deepen their understanding of cultural heritage through this kind of immersive experience, thus promoting the sustainable development of cultural heritage.

5.2 The Creation of Exclusive Digital Identity

The creation of exclusive digital identities for individual cultural heritage has also become a new avenue for future growth. Based on different types of cultural structures, the blockchain digital identity of cultural heritage can be created in a targeted way, and the information security of a single cultural heritage can be protected through practical application [16], so as to effectively avoid the trend of homogenization, which is conducive to long-term protection and management. At the same time, it can also build a multiverse ecological system and use big data to analyze its correlation to build a visual chart, so that each independent identity module can correspond with the network relationship one by one and realize the coordinated development of cultural heritage. In addition, the modal digital identity mechanism will also cover the multi-modal characteristic information of the identified object as far as possible, so as to promote the essential transformation of the memory resources of an object from plane to three-dimensional [17], making the social image of cultural heritage more rounded, and realizing the transformation from "identity" to "cultural identity" in a real sense. For example, traditional villages have rich historical and cultural heritage, and there is overall consistency and local differences among ancient village groups. With the progress of the times, some minority cultural heritage resources are on the verge of disappearing. Therefore, it has become a necessary trend to establish a safe and effective digital identity authentication mechanism for ancient villages to protect and inherit traditional culture. The first is to collect digital information from multiple sources; the second is to use blockchain technology to integrate resources, establish a digital information sharing platform, and apply the concept of sustainable development to achieve a high degree of information interoperability.

5.3 The Building of Characteristic Smart City

With the emergence of emerging technologies such as artificial intelligence, metaverse has redefined the concept of the original smart city: it is not only limited to changing the existing urban lifestyle and basic functions through digital means but also includes the effective use of intelligent vision [18], GIS modeling, ARM cloud technology, and other means to seamlessly integrate the virtual city and the real city. As a result, the realization of digital sustainable development of cultural heritage can also build a distinctive smart city around the diverse heritage, i.e. the formation of digital cultural communities. In this way, the scene-oriented construction of the meta-universe based on cultural heritage can be realized, and an interactive system of virtual interaction and virtual symbiosis can be created, thus comprehensively upgrading the viewer experience. At the same time, it can also break the fourth wall between cultural heritage and viewers due to time, space, and other factors and realize the digital development of heritage on the basis of preserving the original urban construction to the maximum extent.

6 Conclusion

In a word, based on the concept of sustainable development, this paper summarizes the mainstream development trend by analyzing the current situation of digital inheritance and the protection of cultural heritage. Then the paper discusses the new form of digital management through the study of two practical cases. Finally, the paper puts forward several possibilities for the future innovation and development of digital cultural heritage against the backdrop of the meta-universe sweeping the world. As a result, the spiritual connotation and existence value of cultural heritage should be explored to the greatest extent possible in order to capitalize on the opportunity to achieve leapfrogging development.

References

1. Du Pisani, J.A.: Sustainable development: historical roots of the concept. Environ. Sci. **3**(2), 83–96 (2006)
2. Cordova, M.F., Celone, A.: SDGs and Innovation in the business context literature review. Sustainability **11**(24), 7043 (2019)
3. Wang, F., Huang, Y., Wu, B.: Study on the model construction of tourism activation path of traditional art cultural heritage. Tour. Tribune/Lvyou Xuekan **36**(2) (2010)
4. Chen, Z., Ma, J.: From interpretation to deduction: a study on the experience design method of digitized communication of cultural heritage. In: Kurosu, M. (ed.) HCI 2018. LNCS, vol. 10902, pp. 281–289. Springer, Cham (2018). https://doi.org/10.1007/978-3-319-91244-8_23
5. Maye, L.A., Bouchard, D., Avram, G., Ciolfi, L. Supporting cultural heritage professionals adopting and shaping interactive technologies in museums. In: Proceedings of the 2017 Conference on Designing Interactive Systems, pp. 221–232 (2017)
6. Toscano, J.J.R., Fondón, I., Sarmiento, A.: The Experience "mondrian from inside". A immersive and interactive virtual reality experience in art. In: De Paolis, L.T., Arpaia, P., Bourdot, P. (eds.) AVR 2021. LNCS, vol. 12980, pp. 275–289. Springer, Cham (2021). https://doi.org/10.1007/978-3-030-87595-4_20
7. Ramos-Soler, I., Martínez-Sala, A.M., Campillo-Alhama, C.: ICT and the sustainability of world heritage sites. Analysis of senior citizens' use of tourism apps. Sustainability **11**(11), 3203 (2019)
8. Verstockt, S., Milleville, K., Ali, D., Porras-Bernandez, F., Gartner, G., Van de Weghe, N.: EURECA: EUropean region enrichment in city archives and collections. In: 14th ICA conference: Digital Approaches to Cartographic Heritage, pp. 161–169. Aristoteleio Panepistimio Thessalonikis (APTh) (2019)
9. Delso, J., Martin, B., Ortega, E., Van De Weghe, N.: Integrating pedestrian-habitat models and network kernel density estimations to measure street pedestrian suitability. Sustain. Cities Soc. **51**, 101736 (2019)

10. Xue, M.: Spatialization of time: a comparison of Xi'an horizontally scattered sites and roman vertically superimposed sites on the shape of urban style. Archit. J. **96**, 51–70 (2016)
11. Cui, M., Xie, L., Wei, F.: A study on the evolution of urban spatial form based on GIS and historical maps: a case study on the relationship between the capital of Zheng and Han states and the urban development of Xinzheng. Chin. Overseas Archit. **4** (2019)
12. Wang, Q., An, L.: Conservation Planning methods for urban superimposed large sites: a case study of the capital of Zheng and Han states. Urban Stud. (07), 117–127+2+37 (2022)
13. Mystakidis, S.: Metaverse. Encyclopedia **2**(1), 486–497 (2022)
14. Nadini, M., Alessandretti, L., Di Giacinto, F., Martino, M., Aiello, L.M., Baronchelli, A.: Mapping the NFT revolution: market trends, trade networks, and visual features. Sci. Rep. **11**(1), 1–11 (2021)
15. Valeonti, F., Bikakis, A., Terras, M., Speed, C., Hudson-Smith, A., Chalkias, K.: Crypto collectibles, museum funding and OpenGLAM: challenges, opportunities and the potential of non-fungible tokens (NFTs). Appl. Sci. **11**(21), 9931 (2021)
16. Tan, J., Lu, X.: Research on the design of blockchain digital identity establishment and management system of material cultural heritage. Decoration (6), 104–106 (2018)
17. Wang, X., Zheng, X., Wang, Y.: Digital memory: a new form of library social memory. Libr. Res. Work (12), 30–37 (2022)
18. Allam, Z., Sharifi, A., Bibri, S.E., Jones, D.S., Krogstie, J.: The metaverse as a virtual form of smart cities: opportunities and challenges for environmental, economic, and social sustainability in urban futures. Smart Cities **5**(3), 771–801 (2022)

Analysis of the Reasons for the Development of the New Energy Vehicle Industry and Prospects —Taking BYD as an Example

Boyu Liu[✉]

Beijing Normal University & Hong Kong Baptist University United International College, Zhuhai 519000, GuangDong, China

boyuliu222220@gmail.com

Abstract. Recently, the new energy vehicle industry has been a popular field. Many nations are trying to catch this tendency. The paper uses references and observation as measures to research. Then, the paper analyzes green development and energy resources safety. The broadening of new energy vehicles is helpful for reducing the emission of carbon dioxide and decreasing oil imports. What are the positive conditions encouraging the development of the new energy vehicle industry? There are two potential aspects which are policy support and the maturation of related industry chains. By operating a series of supporting policies like financial subsidies, the Chinese government encourages the development of the new energy vehicle industry. Moreover, the maturation of related industries like new energy vehicle batteries and telematics systems also motivates the improvement of the new energy vehicle industry. To prove the supposes above, take BYD as an example. As the biggest new energy vehicle producer in China, BYD has a mature industry chain like Fin dreams factories. For the financial data in recent years, BYD has brilliant performance, its income and market sustained an increase from 2017 to 2022. Moreover, its other financial index also keeps a great performance like PB and ROE. It can represent that the new energy vehicle industry has a development in recent years. Finally, there are still many existing problems about new energy vehicles like charging time. In the future, the new energy vehicle would be broadened and automatic driving would be a new tendency.

Keywords: New Energy Vehicle · New Energy Industry Supply Chain · New Energy Policy · Cars · BYD

1 Introduction

Nowadays, the new energy vehicles are able to quantitative production and achieve market orientation. A series of related new energy industry chain also mature than before. For example, the new energy vehicle battery has achieved a long duration. However, technologies like automatic driving have not been applied. The new energy vehicle appeared many years ago but was not paid attention to. What are the reasons that the new energy vehicle companies are developing so fast in recent years? Based on different references, the paper concluded some potential reasons in different aspects and support some relative data as evidence. Firstly, dividing the paper into three parts, external reasons, industry reasons, and company analysis (BYD as an example). For external reasons, supporting two possible reasons: green development and reducing the dependence on oil imports. Then, collecting some policies about a new energy to research their effect on the development of the new energy vehicle industry. In addition, supporting that the evolution of the new energy industry chain contributes to the development of the new energy vehicle industry. Then, taking BYD as an example, analyzing the major businesses of BYD and its past financial paper to prove the development of the new energy vehicle industry, through its company strategy to discover the relationship between the development of BYD and the elements above. Finally, based on the research above, concluding some existing problems and giving out prospects for the new energy vehicle industry. By the paper, it is able to discover what are the motivations for the new energy vehicle industry and the potential prospect of the industry. Additionally, it could also give some inspiration about what may be the crucial elements for the development of an emerging industry.

2 Macro Conditions

2.1 Green Development

In 2018, the State Council released the Three-Year Action Plan to Win the Blue-Sky Defense War, which requires provinces, municipalities, and autonomous regions to adjust their energy structures and promote the scope of application of new energy vehicles and other clean energy vehicles [1].

The other important goals of green development are carbon peaking and carbon neutral. At the seventy-fifth session of the United Nations General Assembly in 2020, the Chinese government proposed that China strive to achieve carbon peaking by 2030 and carbon neutrality by 2060. Carbon peaking means that China would achieve a peak in carbon dioxide emissions, and carbon neutral represents the emission of carbon dioxide would be balanced by the production of oxygen.

Thus, to achieve the goals above, the Chinese government requires to guide the consumption behavior of citizens. The Green consumption pattern refers to the public's green consumption behavior at the micro level, which is mainly manifested in the public's initiative to choose green products and services, consciously reduce the consumption of energy and resources in the process of consumption, and minimize the pollution to the environment [2]. Encouraging the consumption of the new energy vehicle is one of the methods done by the Chinese government.

2.2 Reduce the Dependence on Energy Resources

As we all know, oil is a kind of crucial energy resource and an unrenewable resource. Once the energy resources like oil imports suffer from interruption, it would cause serious economic and social unstable. And, only a little part of nations like Brazil can be energy resource independent. General Secretary Xi Jinping emphasized in the sixth meeting of the Central Leading Group of Finance and Economics in 2014 that energy security is a global and strategic issue involving the national economy and social development, which is significant to national prosperity and development, improving people's lives, and long-term social stability, and put forward the "four revolutions and one the new energy security strategy of "four revolutions and one cooperation" was proposed [3]. Meanwhile, according to <the bp World Energy Statistics Yearbook (2021)>, the status of China's energy resource endowment is "rich in coal, poor in oil and less in gas". The proven oil reserves in China account for only 1.5% of the total worldwide, the reserves-to-production ratio is 18.2 years which is lower than the world average of 53.5 years. Proven natural gas reserves in China account for 4.5% of the global total, the ratio of reserves to production is 43.3 years, which is lower than the world average of 48.8 years [4]. Meanwhile, with the Outbreak of the Russia-Ukraine War, energy safety has become more serious since Russia is one of the major Natural Gas Exporters.

Based on the paper of Xinquan Li, developing new energy and focusing on clean, low-carbon, energy-efficient, intelligent, and comprehensive energy security are two means of increasing energy safety [3]. One of the major applications of oil is in transportation. By developing the new energy vehicle and reducing the dependence on oil, it could reduce the relationship between the economy and oil, motivating oil back to the common goods.

3 Supporting Conditions

3.1 Policies

Policy encouragement is an important requirement for industry development, especially in China. Based on the paper of Jingcheng Zhang [5], divided the development of the new energy vehicle industry into four periods from 1991–2021 which are Technology exploration, demonstration, and promotion, rapid development, and quality development. In different periods of development, the Chinese government adopted different policy supports for the new energy vehicle companies. In the research of Haojun Wu, he classified the policies into three kinds, which are the Promotional effect of financial subsidies; the complementary effect of transportation preferences; and the accelerating effect of promotion areas. According to some researchers' reports by Haojun Wu, financial subsidies have a positive relationship with the sales of new energy vehicles [1]. However, financial subsidies for the new energy vehicles have weakened since 2016 because the motivative elements have transformed from policy orientation to market orientation. The complementary effect of transportation represents there are fewer restrictions on the new energy vehicles, and the user cost of the new energy vehicles is relatively lower compared to the traditional fuel vehicles. Accelerating the effect of promotion areas means that the government acts as a role model by purchasing new energy vehicles (Table 1).

3.2 The New Energy Vehicle Industry Chain

The new energy vehicle industry is based on the new energy industry. Thus, some breakthroughs happening in the new energy industry are significant for the new energy vehicle industry. Moreover, with the advancement of the 5G technique and the intelligent network, the new energy vehicle should be redefined (Fig. 1).

Table 1. The new energy vehicle policies.

Summary of important policies related to the promotion of NEV in China

Time	Policy	Issuing Agency
2009.01.23	Notice of the Pilot Project of Demonstration and Promotion of Energy-saving and New Energy Vehicles	Financial Ministry, Science and Technological Ministry
2014.07.14	Guiding Opinions on Accelerating the Promotion and Application of New Energy Vehicles	Office of the State Council
2016.02.17	Notice of Guidance on Promoting Green Consumption	National Development and Reform Commission, Ministry of Propaganda, Science and Technological Ministry, etc
2018.02.12	About adjusting and improving the financial subsidy policy for the promotion and application of new energy vehicles Notice on Adjusting and Improving the Financial Subsidy Policy for the Promotion and Application of New Energy Vehicles Notice on Adjusting and Improving the Financial Subsidy Policy for the Promotion and Application of New Energy Vehicles	Financial Ministry, Industry and Information Technological Ministry of, Ministry of Science and Technology, Ministry of Development and Reform Commission
2020.06.15	Average Fuel Consumption of Passenger Vehicle Enterprises and New Energy Vehicle Credits Parallel Management Measures" (2020)	Ministry of Industry and Information Technology, Ministry of Finance, Ministry of Commerce
2020.10.20	Notice on the Issuance of the Development Plan for the New Energy Vehicle Industry (2021–2035) (2021–2035) Notice	Office of the State Council
2021.01.01	About improving the financial subsidies for the promotion and application of new energy vehicles Notice of the Policy	Financial Ministry, Industry and Information Technological Ministry, Science and Technological Ministry, Development and Reform Commission

Battery. The new energy vehicle battery is the most important upper industry part of the new energy vehicle industry. The cost of the battery takes up nearly 1/3 of the new energy vehicle. Undoubtedly, the advance in the new energy vehicle battery pushes the development of new energy vehicles. Three major batteries are used in the new energy vehicle: the Trithium battery, LiFePO$_4$ battery, NiMH battery, and the Trithium battery are used broadly.

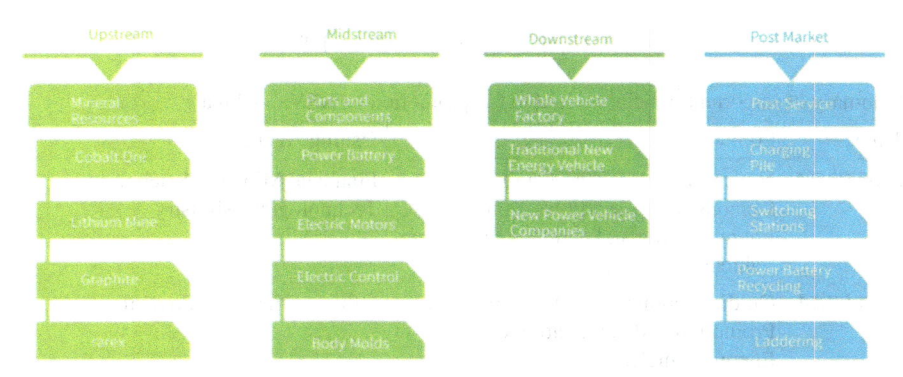

Fig. 1. The new energy vehicle industry supply chain.

The battery's installed capacity is a crucial standard of battery storage capacity. According to the industry paper, it is estimated that in 2022 the global power battery installed capacity is about 436 GWh (+47%), and China's power battery installed capacity is about 237 GWh (+53%) [6]. The industry growth rate is fast. It is expected that in the next three years the global/China power battery installed capacity will also maintain more than 20% compound annual growth, almost equivalent to three years and then doubled, in 2025 the global power battery installed capacity is close to 1000 GWh, meet the "TWh era". The Chinese new energy battery industry has a Possession advantage compared to other nations.

Additionally, Chinese battery companies also take up an important role worldwide, and it also motivates the development of new energy vehicle companies in China. Taking Ningde times as the representation of the new energy battery company, the biggest new battery company in China. Through Table 2, Ningde times is also the biggest new energy vehicle battery producer in the world, which could support a solid upstream industry chain for the new energy vehicle companies.

Recently, Ningde Technology established a new battery product called Kirin Battery, which adapts the CTP (Cell To Pack) technique. The Kirin Battery's principle is that, through structural innovation, the water-cooled plate is integrated from a horizontal single-sided working condition to a vertical structure so that the water-cooled plate is installed and the volume of the water-cooled plate is greatly increased.

The Intellectualization. Intellectualization belongs to the lower supply chain of the new energy vehicle industry which is also a crucial part of the new energy vehicles. There is a word, the new vehicle should be redefined as the third space for people. Especially, because of the development of the 5G technology and cloud storage technology, telematics systems of the new energy vehicle can be performed safer and work faster.

According to Wang's research, people prefer to use in-vehicle smart network systems to achieve human-machine interaction, with the voice assistant being one example [7]. In the research, nearly 73% of interviewees prefer to use the voice assistant to control the car. Many software companies support the software for the telematics system such as Baidu and Patio, and the companies like Gaode map or Baidu map support navigation services for the telematics system.

Table 2. Top 10 ranking of global power battery installed capacity (GMV) in 2021.

Ranking	Company Name	2021 Installed capacity	2020 Installed volume	2021/2020 Year on Year	2021 Market share	2020 Market share
1	Ningde Times	96.7	36.2	167.50%	32.60%	24.60%
2	LG New Energy	60.2	34.3	75.50%	20.30%	23.40%
3	Matsushita	36.1	27	33.50%	12.20%	18.40%
4	BYD	26.3	9.8	167.70%	8.80%	6.70%
5	SK on	16.7	8.1	107.50%	5.60%	5.50%
6	Samsung SDI	13.2	8.5	56.00%	4.50%	5.80%
7	China Inniovation Aviation	7.9	3.4	130.50%	2.70%	2.30%
8	Guoxuan High-Tech	6.4	2.4	161.30%	2.10%	1.70%
9	Vision Power	4.2	3.9	7.80%	1.40%	2.70%
10	Hive Energy	3.1	0.6	430.80%	1.00%	0.40%
Total of TOP10		270.8	–	–	91.20%	–
All companies		296.8	146.8	102.30%	100%	100%

The other popular topic about the telematics systems of the new energy vehicle is automatic driving. According to the paper of Wang, the automatic parking function is welcome by the customers [7]. Furthermore, even though the TJA Traffic Congestion Assist is still not being used broadly enough, people have used it and tend to use it frequently. There are five levels used to classify automatic driving, L1 is the lowest level and L5 is the highest level which means the telematics system can finish driving tasks by itself. Most of the new energy vehicle companies are trying to achieve automatic driving at levels higher than L2. The AI chip companies like ShangTang can help the new energy vehicle companies to apply AI technology to telematics systems.

However, since the safety and law problems, automatic driving still not be used broadly.

4 BYD Company

4.1 The Introduction of BYD (The Major Business)

BYD was established in 1995 by Chuanfu Wang, and its major business is battery production in the early stage. In 2003, BYD became the second biggest battery supplier in the world and purchased the QinChuan car to enter the vehicle industry. Nowadays, BYD has become the second biggest new energy vehicle battery supplier in China.

Through Fig. 2, there are three major businesses of BYD nowadays, they are vehicle production, the second charge battery, and cell phone parts production and assembly. We can see that the vehicle production business takes up the biggest shares, then is cell phone parts production and assembly, and the last one is the second charge battery.

According to the paper by Wang, from 2015 to 2020, BYD's company income increased from 80 billion to 156.6 billion, and its income increased by more than 20% per year after the IPO [8]. BYD's gross margin benefit rate of vehicle production is 22% higher than other new energy vehicle companies, which is 15%.

Then, BYD did much hard work on arranging the industry chain. Fin dreams System Factory is a typical example, which are Affiliated Company of BYD. Through the Fin dreams system factory, BYD could expand its External cooperation on core components with big vehicle production companies like TOYOTA. The Fin dreams system factories master a series of Segmented Technologies respectively. By doing so, BYD deeps in the industry supply chain and have a chance to develop other potential businesses.

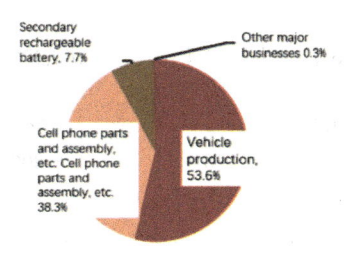

Fig. 2. Share of businesses.

4.2 The Financial Report of BYD

Through the financial data from the stock trade company platform East Information Co Ltd, we can see the financial data of BYD in the first half year 2022 [9].

Through the Fig. 3, 4 and 5 below, we can find that the total operating revenue of BYD has increased from 105.91 billion to 216.14 billion from 2017 to 2021, which has increased by more than 105.7%. The first half year's total operating revenue has increased 65.7% compared to the last year. Moreover, the net profit attributable to and the net profit after deduction to the non-mother company also have an increase. It means BYD's revenue and income have kept a continued raise.

In Fig. 6, we can see that the major income comes from vehicle production and related businesses, which contribute more than 70% of income. In addition, in Fig. 7, vehicle production and related businesses also have the highest main gross profit and gross profit margin rate, which is higher than other businesses in a big degree. It means the new energy vehicle production and related business are potential businesses, which can help the company to profit. On the other side, it presents that the new vehicle business has transformed into market-orientation leading.

In Fig. 8 financial ratio, compared to the mid-year report data in 2021, the financial indexes of BYD in the 2022 mid-year report are better in five dimensions which are

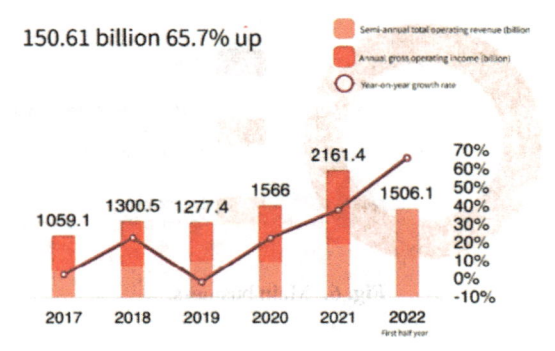

Fig. 3. Total operating Revenue.

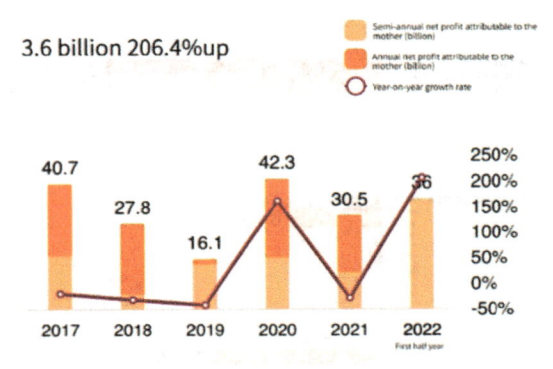

Fig. 4. Net profit attributable to.

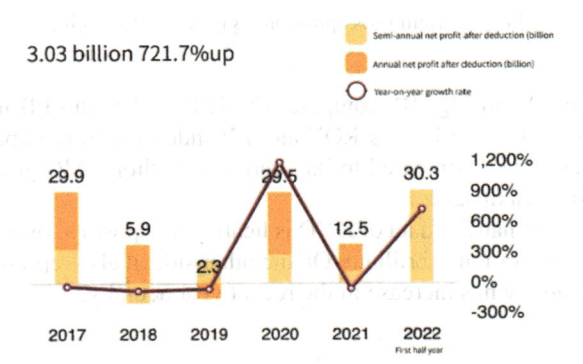

Fig. 5. Net profit after deduction of non-mother.

profitability and weighted return on net assess, solvency and gearing ratio, cash acquisition ability, and sales cash ratio, operating capacity and total asset turnover ratio, growth capacity and year over year growth rate of income contribute to the mother company.

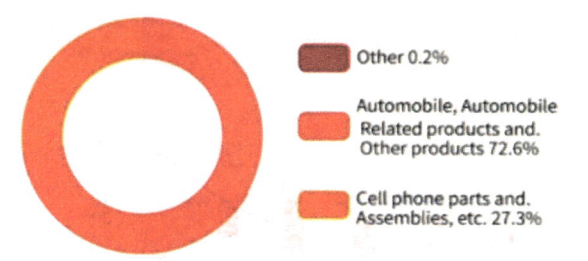

Fig. 6. Main business.

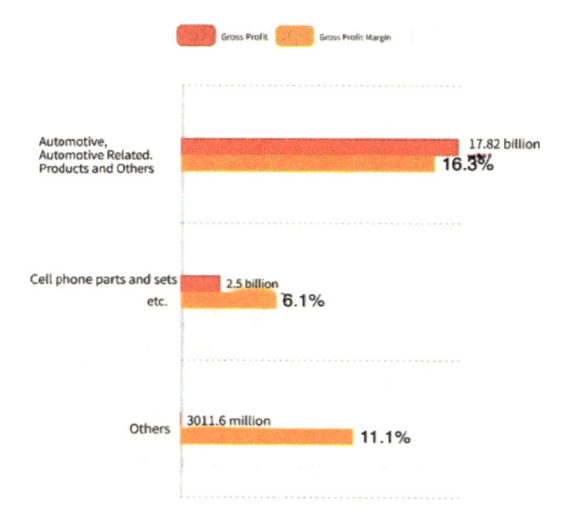

Fig. 7. Main gross profit and gross profit margin.

Finally, in Fig. 9 and Fig. 10, compares the ROE index and PB index in the new energy vehicle industry, the BYD's ROE and PB index are in the upper middle level in the industry. However, compared to its major competitor SAIC group and WeiChai power, BYD still has a distance.

To conclude, the financial data of BYD is healthy and positive over years. One side, is because BYD's operation is brilliant. On the other side, it also represents that the new energy vehicle industry has increase in the recent year actually.

5 Prospects

There are still many problems with the new energy vehicles, which are major concentrated in the continuity of new energy vehicles and charging. In the low-temperature condition, the battery's continuity would be declined seriously. Charging is also a significant problem. On the one side, charging piles are not popular enough in some remote places which would reduce customers' purchasing intention. Moreover, charging time

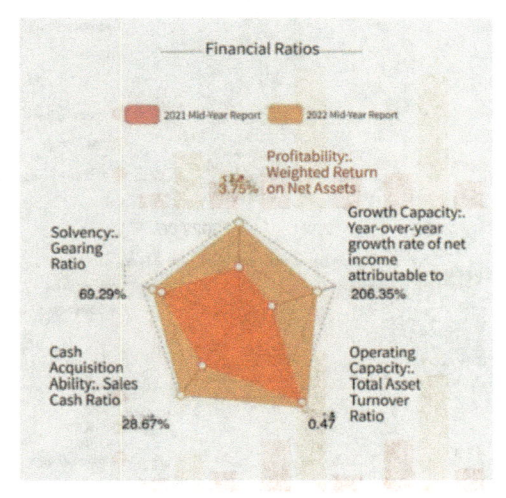

Fig. 8. Financial ratios.

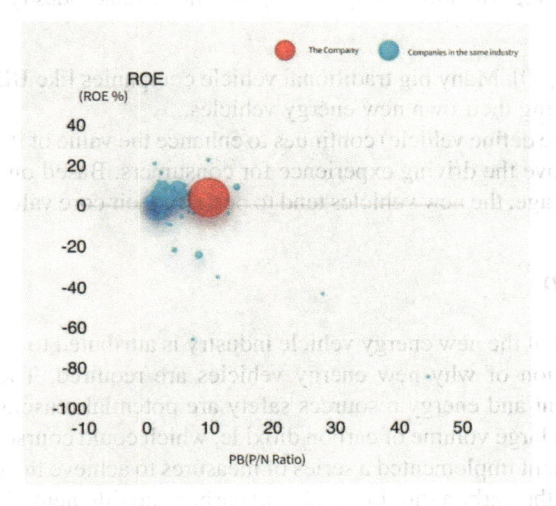

Fig. 9. Industry earnings and valuation comparison.

is the other problem, many people complain they have to wait near the car when the car is charging.

For automatic driving, because of technology and legal issues, is still not applied in telematic systems broadly. There is no doubt that automatic driving must be popular in the future. The companies like TESLA are trying to achieve L5. Similarly, the Chinese government is also trying to establish regulations for automatic driving.

With the promotion of new energy vehicles, the production of traditional fuel vehicles would suffer a decline in the future. According to the report of IRESEARCH, it is expected that by 2035, the automotive industry may largely achieve the transformation

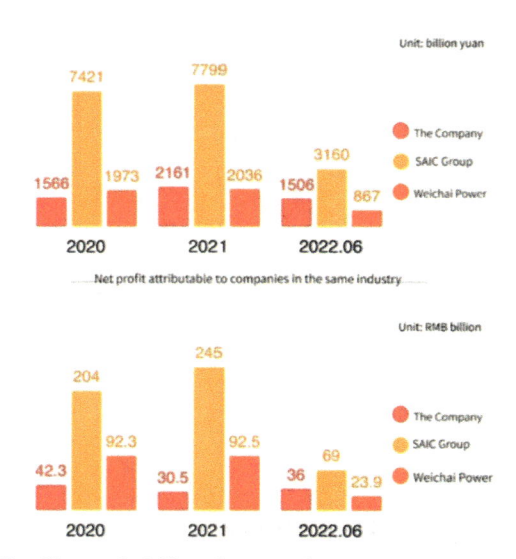

Fig. 10. Profitability of companies in the same industry.

of electrification [10]. Many big traditional vehicle companies like BBA and Mercedes-Benz are developing their own new energy vehicles.

SDV (software define vehicle) continues to enhance the value of its software and will continue to improve the driving experience for consumers. Based on the technology of 5G and cloud storage, the new vehicles tend to perform their core values by the software.

6 Conclusion

The development of the new energy vehicle industry is attributed to several dimensions. Firstly, the question of why new energy vehicles are required. The requirements of green development and energy resources safety are potential reasons. Traditional fuel cars would emit a large volume of carbon dioxide, which could course air pollution. The Chinese government implemented a series of measures to achieve the goal, starting with the giving out of the carbon dioxide peak and carbon dioxide neutral. Encouraging the use of new energy vehicles could reduce carbon dioxide emissions and motivate green development. Moreover, oil as an unrenewable energy resource takes up a significant strategic role, once the irruption of oil import happens, it would threaten social stability and economic safety. Encouraging the development of the new energy vehicle industry helps to reduce the dependence on the energy resources like oil and motivates oil back to the common-goods characteristic.

This paper takes BYD as the representation of new energy vehicle companies to prove the development of the new energy vehicle industry. As the biggest new energy vehicle producer, vehicle production and secondary charging are its major businesses. In recent years, BYD established Fin dreams system companies to expand its businesses, every Fin dream companies are able to produce a kind of core parts for new energy vehicles. BYD also has a personal battery called blade battery. Then, BYD's financial data sustained a healthy situation overall. The revenue and income sustain an increase from 2017 to 2022. The vehicle production business attributes the largest part of its income and has a great gross profit margin rate. Compared to the other companies in the new energy vehicle industry, the PB and ROE of BYD also be in the upper middle level. It can be proved that BYD has a stable increase in those years.

Firstly, the research method is too simple and lacks variety, the conclusion is major comes from references and observation results. Then, the research target is too less which only focuses on BYD. There are many other new energy vehicle companies like TESLA or XiaoPeng. For the different companies, the research results would be different. Moreover, with the mutualization of the industry, some potential conditions may be changed and it is possible that there are other more effective elements existing that we have not found.

As the biggest new energy vehicle company, the success of BYD can be used to prove the development of the new energy vehicle industry in a certain degree.

However, there are several problems of new energy vehicles required to solve like battery charging time. These problems are being tried to be solved. In the future, new energy vehicles would be more intelligent like automatic driving, and being used more broadly.

References

1. Haojun Wu, W.C.: Policy Support, Environmental Pressure, and New Energy Vehicle Promotion - A Panel of 31 Provinces and Cities Based on Spatial Durbin Model. Transportation energy saving and environmental protection (2022)
2. Xue, H.: Research on the driving mechanism and policy of public green consumption pattern–take new energy vehicles as an example. J. Univ. Sci. Technol. Beijing 325–334 (2022)
3. Xinquan, L., Yang, X.: Challenges of China's energy security strategy and international experience. Globalization 107–136 (2022)
4. World Energy Statistics Yearbookbp 2021. (July 8, 2021). bp World Energy Statistics Yearbook. Search Source: bp China Website
5. Jing, C., Zhang, F.W.: Research on the evolution of innovation ecosystem from the perspective of policy change –taking the new energy vehicle industry as an example. Sci. Technol. Manag. Res. 173–182 (2022)
6. Zhengping, W.: New energy vehicle industry chain boom is high, power battery is the core track–new energy vehicle industry chain research report series. Xiangcai Secur. 1–34 (2022)
7. Wang, B.: Smart Car Market Research 2022. IDG, pp. 1–22 (2022)
8. Wang, J.: Start from the "core" and move towards the "new" BYD In-depth Report. Zheshang Secur. 1–66 (2021)
9. Eastmoney. (2022). Eastmony. Search Source: Eastmoney website. https://emweb.eastmoney.com/PC_HSF10/NewFinanceAnalysis/Index?type=web&code=sz002594
10. IRESEARCH. (2020). China New Energy Vehicle Industry White Paper 2020. I RESEARCH, 1-57

Challenges of Stock Prediction Based on LSTM Neural Network

Rufeng Chen(✉)

University of California, San Diego 92122, USA
ruc003@ucsd.edu

Abstract. For a long time, many scholars and researchers have tried stock forecasting. Stock forecasting has always been the most concerned and challenged in time series forecasting. People have different opinions on whether the stock market can be accurately predicted. Some scholars believe that stocks cannot be predicted, while others believe that using LSTM for stock prediction has high accuracy. In this work, the author experimented with whether LSTM could accurately predict stocks and found hysteresis in the prediction results. The author believes that although the prediction error of LSTM is small, it cannot provide support for actual transactions due to the hysteresis. In the last part of this paper, the author provides possible solutions to solve the hysteresis problem. These results explain how to improve the usability of stock market predictions and put forward suggestions and directions for future development.

Keywords: Long and Short-term Memory Network (LSTM) · Stock Prediction · Hysteresis · Time Series Analysis

1 Introduction

Investigations in stocks is one of the most complex business activities. The military, political, and corporate decisions can affect the stock market and other factors to produce anomalies. Building an accurate model of the stock market is very difficult. Investors and stock analysts often trade stocks through personal experience and decision-making, which is more likely to lead to erroneous analysis and economic losses due to personal limitations. A stable and accurate forecasting method has always been the most desired by stock market participants. Long short-term memory neural network (LSTM) is favoured by investors due to its high adaptability to time series data. Many authors apply LSTM to financial market forecasting. Some authors have proved that LSTM is more accurate than traditional algorithms [1]. Other authors compared the performance of different types of LSTMs for stock market forecasting [2, 3]. This paper aims to analyze the accuracy of predicting stock prices using LSTM and propose possible solutions to the problems that arise. Many studies have proved the excellent performance of LSTM in stock market forecasting. This paper focuses on the following questions: Is LSTM accurate for stock market predictions? Are LSTM's predictions helpful for actual transactions? After discovering the hysteresis of LSTM predictions, the author proposes possible solutions on how to solve the hysteresis problem. The results of this paper demonstrate the inability of using LSTMs to be practically helpful for stock market forecasting, and make suggestions for improving the practicality of forecasting in the future.

2 Long-Short Term Memory Neural Network

2.1 The Structure of LSTM

LSTM is a type of Recurrent Neural Network (RNN). RNN is one of the most suitable forms of neural networks for stock forecasting [4]. The most significant feature of LSTM is that it can solve long-term dependencies. For RNN, the farther the information is from the current node, the more difficult it is for RNN to obtain. However, specially designed LSTMs allow information from the past to be passed on to the present. The structures can be compared in the following two figures (Figs. 1 and 2):

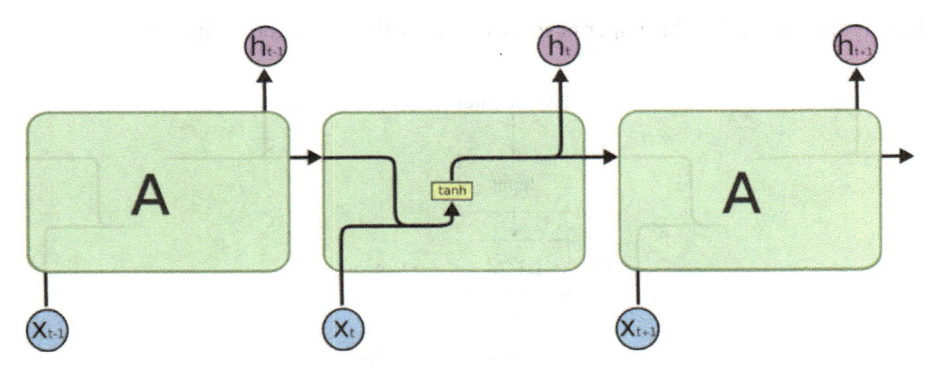

Fig. 1. RNN internal structure [5].

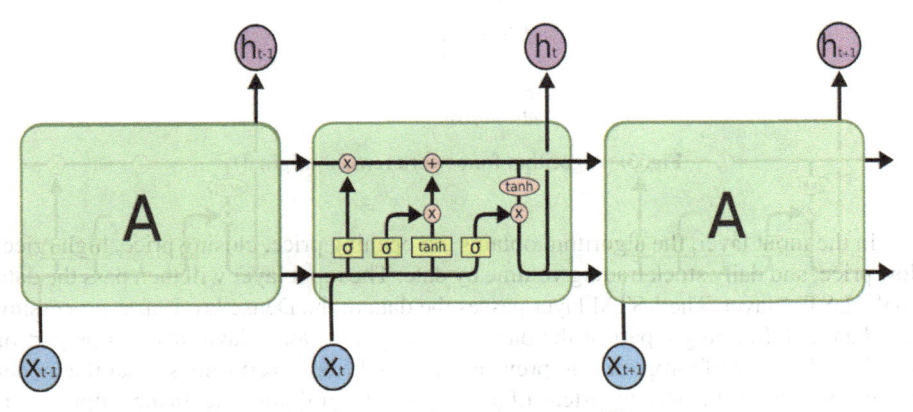

Fig. 2. LSTM internal structure [5].

Different from RNN, the more complex structure of LSTM allows it to choose to forget or store the information of previous nodes.

2.2 Related Work

Siami-Namini and Tavakoli et al. compared the performance of ARIMA and LSTM in predicting time series, and pointed out that LSTM has a lower error rate [1]. Sunny and Maswood et al. used LSTM and bidirectional LSTM for stock market prediction [3]. They believe that the better performance of bidirectional LSTMs can help companies or individuals make market predictions. Dwivedi and Attry et al. used S-Arima, CNN and LSTM for stock market forecasting [10]. They concluded that deep learning based models outperformed machine learning in time series prediction.

The author examines the performance of the LSTM model in stock market forecasting and points out that the accuracy of the model is high, but the lag of forecasting makes the forecasting results unhelpful.

3 Algorithm

The algorithm used in this paper is shown in the following figure (Fig. 3):

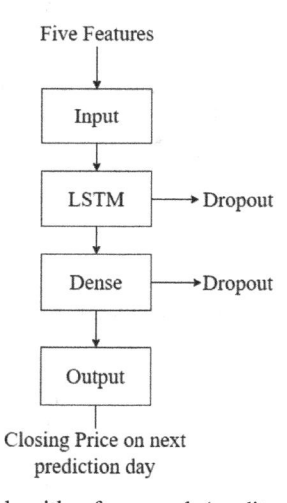

Fig. 3. Algorithm framework (credit: original).

In the input layer, the algorithm obtains the opening price, closing price, high price, low price, and daily stock trading volume by date. The input layer will then pass the data to the LSTM layer. The LSTM layer passes the data to the Dense layer after processing the data and dropping a part of the data. Similarly, the Dense layer also drops part of the data. The role of Dropout is to prevent the model from overfitting so that the model learns the patterns in the data instead of memorizing the training data. In the output layer, the algorithm outputs the closing price of the forecast day (Fig. 4).

During training, the author used different short-term memory intervals to expect the best short-term memory interval length for each model. Again, the author set different prediction days. The different prediction days prevent the forecast days from being too

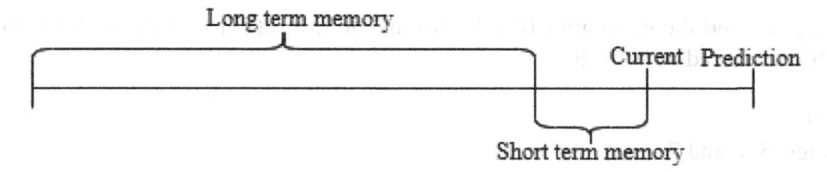

Fig. 4. Time diagram (credit: original).

close to the current time to observe possible problems. Extending forecast days can magnify possible problems. To facilitate understanding, a simple example is presented: if the current date is August 1, 2022, Short term memory is 5, and Prediction Day is 5, then the short-term memory interval of LSTM will be set to five days, and the output of the algorithm will be 2022 The closing price on August 6.

To judge how well the model performs, the author used mean absolute percentage error (MAPE) as the metrics and mean squared error (MSE) as the loss function. MAPE is defined as:

$$MAPE = \frac{100\%}{n} \sum_{t=1}^{n} \left| \frac{A_t - F_t}{A_t} \right| \qquad (1)$$

MSE is defined as:

$$MSE = \frac{1}{n} \sum_{i=1}^{n} \left(Y_i - \widehat{Y_i} \right)^2 \qquad (2)$$

The reason for choosing MAPE is that it is easy to interpret and understand the magnitude of the error. Percentage error can avoid the misjudgment factor caused by too high or too low the stock price.

4 Methodology

Data: the data include Google and Apple stock data provided by stooq. Google data covers the period from August 19, 2004, to August 8, 2022. Apple data is from January 3, 2000, to August 1, 2022. Stock information includes the date, opening price, closing price, high price, low price, and daily trading volume.

Data normalization: Since the order of magnitude of the daily transaction volume is different from that of other data, the data needs to be normalized. The normalization of the data can guarantee the weight and influence of all eigenvalues. Normalization formula:

$$X_{\text{scaled}} = \frac{X - \text{mean}}{\text{sd}} \qquad (3)$$

Training: This paper sets three PredictionDays, which are [1, 5, 10]. At the same time, three different short-term memory intervals are also set: [5, 10, 15]. For each PredictionDay of each stock, try to train for 50 epochs for each short-term memory interval, and then select the one with the best effect. 90% of the data is used as the training set, and the remaining 10% is used as the test set. The model with the lowest MAPE is selected as a result.

Result

See Figs. 5, 6 and 7.

Table 1. Training result (credit: original).

Company	PredictionDays	MemoryDays	Metrics (%)
Google	1	5	2.916
	5	5	3.890
	10	15	4.276
Apple	1	10	3.128
	5	5	4.450
	10	5	4.865

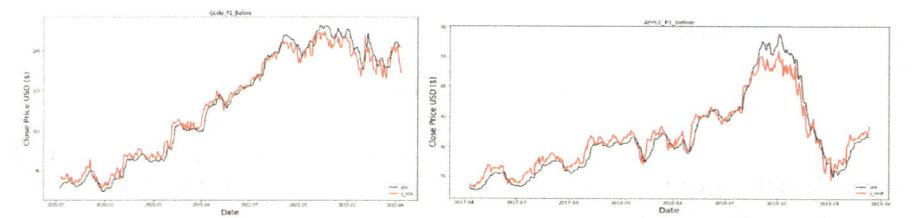

Fig. 5. Curve comparison when PredictionDays = 1(Left: Google; Right: Apple) (credit: original).

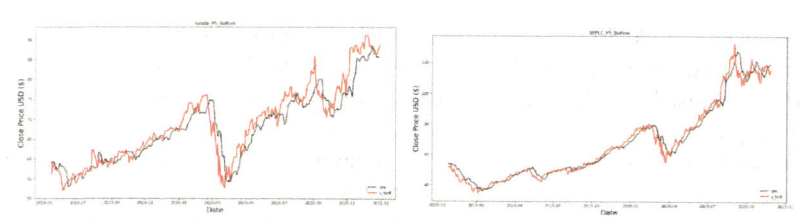

Fig. 6. Curve comparison when PredictionDays = 5(Left: Google; Right: Apple) (credit: original).

It can be seen from Table 1 that the MAPE of all models is lower than 5%, that is, the average accuracy of all models has reached more than 95%. In the following table, it is easy to observe that the shapes of the Prediction Lines and the test lines are very similar. However, as PredictionDays increases, so does the hysteresis of Prediction Lines. This hysteresis behavior makes the LSTM produce results that are more like shifting the test

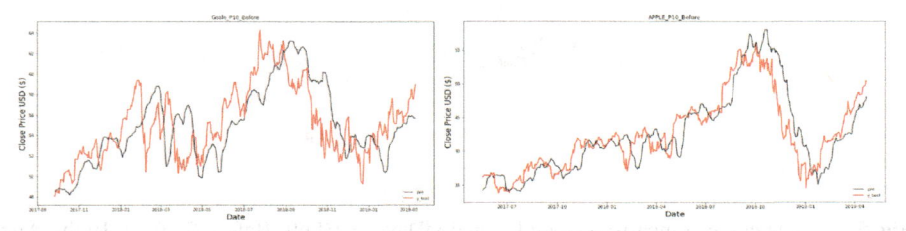

Fig. 7. Curve comparison when PredictionDays = 10(Left: Google; Right: Apple) (credit: original).

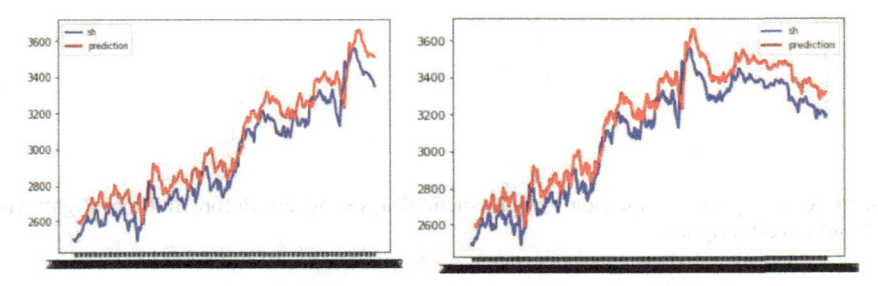

Fig. 8. Shanghai stock index prediction by Wei D [6].

data to the right than actually making predictions. The following is the data with similar performance in the paper by Wei D [6] (Fig. 8).

To verify the hysteresis generation, the author shifted the actual test line to the right and recalculated the MAPE between the predicted line and the test line after the shift. The author chose the number of days to shift as (Figs. 9, 10, 11, 12, 13 and 14 and Table 2).

Table 2. Moving result (credit: original).

Company	PredictionDays	MemoryDays	Metrics(%)	MoveDays	MAPE_After
Google	1	5	2.916	3	1.902
	5	5	3.890	7	1.489
	10	15	4.276	17	2.026
Apple	1	10	3.128	3	2.441
	5	5	4.450	7	1.839
	10	5	4.865	12	1.550

It can be observed that after moving the test line to the right, the MAPE between the two lines drops significantly, that is, the average error between the two lines is more minor. Compared with the images before and after the translation, the prediction and test lines are more coincident after the translation. The above results show that the LSTM's

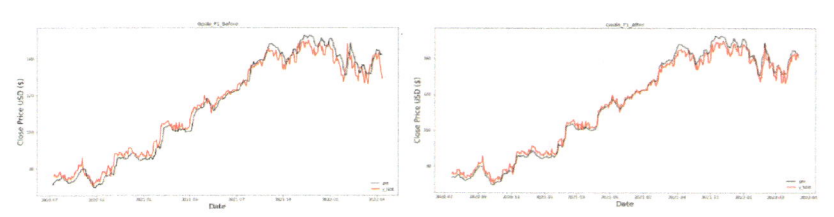

Fig. 9. Google curve comparison when PredictionDays = 1(Left: Before Shifting; Right: After Shifting) (credit: original).

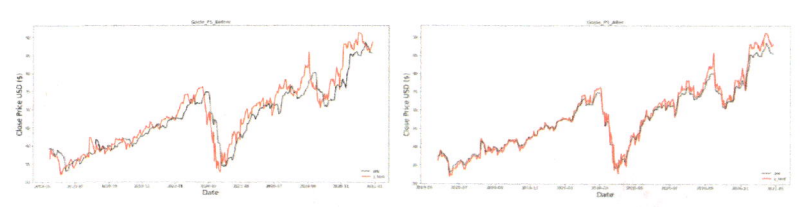

Fig. 10. Google curve comparison when PredictionDays = 5(Left: Before Shifting; Right: After Shifting) (credit: original).

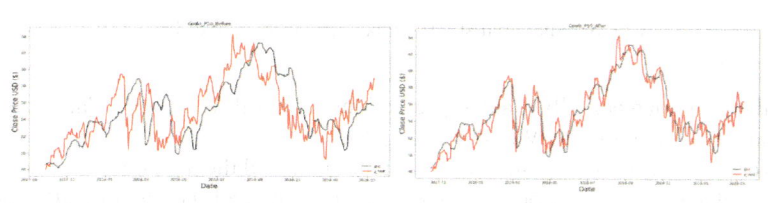

Fig. 11. Google curve comparison when PredictionDays = 10(Left: Before Shifting; Right: After Shifting) (credit: original).

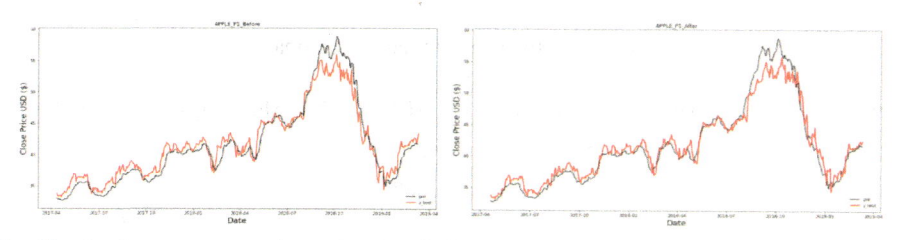

Fig. 12. Apple curve comparison when PredictionDays = 1(Left: Before Shifting; Right: After Shifting) (credit: original).

prediction of stock prices is actually a translation of historical data. LSTM analyzes the data in the short-term memory interval and combines the changes of historical data to give a number similar to the data in the short-term memory interval to reduce MAPE. Such behavior and results are not helpful for stock market analysis.

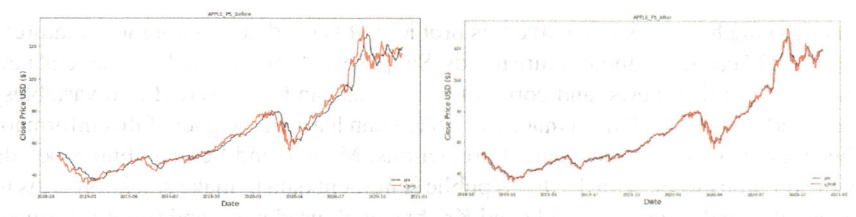

Fig. 13. Apple curve comparison when PredictionDays = 5(Left: Before Shifting; Right: After Shifting) (credit: original).

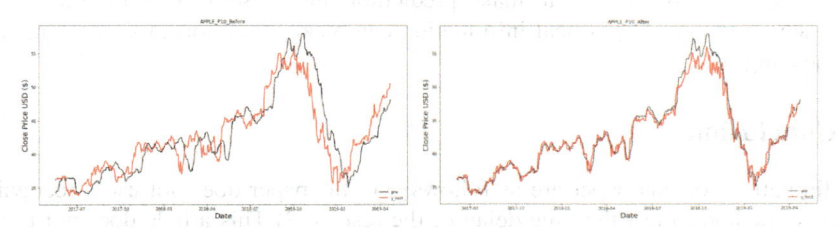

Fig. 14. Apple curve comparison when PredictionDays = 10(Left: Before Shifting; Right: After Shifting) (credit: original).

5 Possible Solutions

To address the hysteresis problem, the author proposes possible solutions for reducing the hysteresis and making actual predictions.

5.1 Reducing Hysteresis

Stock data is a non-stationary time series. The price of a stock is affected by many factors, including time and trends. Modeling non-stationary data is less effective than stationary data. This is one of the reasons for hysteresis. Authors such as Lina Li pointed out that accurate prediction of non-stationary time series is still difficult to solve [7]. To reduce the hysteresis, it is needed to difference the data, thereby removing the non-stationarity of the data. Differencing removes horizontal variation in a time series and reduces the trend of the data by calculating the difference between consecutive observations. In Lina Li's paper, the data is first differentiated, and then the training results are better [7]. The Augmented Dickey-Fuller test (ADF test) can be used to test the stationarity of the time series before and after differencing.

5.2 Making Real Predictions

At present, people using machine learning methods to predict the stock market usually rely on the historical data of the stock. However, stock investors and analysts tend to weigh more on factors such as recent financial news and company decisions. The correlation between future data and historical data of stocks is not enough for LSTM to learn the prediction rules. This is also the fundamental problem of LSTM prediction results showing hysteresis. To solve this problem, it is needed to input more features so that the LSTM can learn about future trends. Suppose information such as financial news, military and political news, and corporate decisions can be converted into variables as features and input to LSTM. In that case, LSTM can learn the impact of this information on the stock market and make actual predictions. Mehtab and Sen combine stock data from the previous week with Twitter's public sentiment data to make stock forecasts that are a valuable endeavor [8]. Hegde and Krishna et al. used news and tweet information combined with historical data to make predictions, and the results had extremely high accuracy and low hysteresis [9]. These studies provide neural networks with information different from historical data to make predictions more useful. It is foreseeable that more news and current political information can make stock forecasts more accurate and meaningful.

6 Conclusion

The limitations of this paper are as follows: 1) This paper does not use a recognized effective method to test the time delay of the results. 2) This article does not use the forecast results to simulate stock trading to prove the low practicability of the forecast results.

Unlike other time series, stock market trends are less dependent on historical data than financial, political, and other news. LSTMs that rely on historical stock data produce results with hysteresis. Stationarity of the data may reduce hysteresis but does not solve the underlying problem. Feeding relevant news as features into an LSTM may yield actual predictions. When the model can accept news information, the next stage is to predict the psychology of other investors. Market trading relies not only on historical data and news information, but it is also essential to predict the psychology of other participants in playing the game. After more and more AIs that can accurately predict the market appear, AI has to learn to play games with other AIs. Although there is still a long way to go, it can be predicted that the future stock market will be a game between AIs.

References

1. Siami-Namini, S., Namin, A.S.: Forecasting economics and financial time series: arima vs. LSTM (2018). arXiv preprint arXiv:1803.06386
2. Joshi, A., Deshmukh, P.K., Lohokare, J.: Comparative analysis of Vanilla LSTM and Peephole LSTM for stock market price prediction. In: 2022 International Conference on Computing, Communication, Security and Intelligent Systems (IC3SIS), pp. 1–6 (2022). https://doi.org/10.1109/IC3SIS54991.2022.9885528
3. Istiake Sunny, M.A., Maswood, M.M.S., Alharbi, A.G.: Deep learning-based stock price prediction using LSTM and Bi-directional LSTM model. In: 2020 2nd Novel Intelligent and Leading Emerging Sciences Conference (NILES), pp. 87–92 (2020). https://doi.org/10.1109/NILES50944.2020.9257950
4. Vasudevan, J.P.N.B.: Effective implementation of neural network model with tune parameter for stock market predictions. In: 2021 2nd International Conference on Smart Electronics and Communication (ICOSEC), pp. 1038–1042 (2021). https://doi.org/10.1109/ICOSEC51865.2021.9591781

5. Olah, C.: Understanding LSTM networks–Colah's blog. Colah (2015). github. Io
6. Wei, D.: Prediction of stock price based on LSTM neural network. In: International Conference on Artificial Intelligence and Advanced Manufacturing (AIAM), 16–18 October 2019
7. Li, L., Huang, S., Ouyang, Z., Li, N.: A deep learning framework for non-stationary time series prediction. In: 2022 3rd International Conference on Computer Vision, Image and Deep Learning & International Conference on Computer Engineering and Applications (CVIDL & ICCEA), pp. 339–342 (2022). https://doi.org/10.1109/CVIDLICCEA56201.2022.9824863
8. Mehtab, S., Sen, J.: A robust predictive model for stock price prediction using deep learning and natural language processing. Econom. Model. Cap. Mark. Forecast. eJ. (2019). n. pag
9. Hegde, M.S., Krishna, G., Srinath, R.: An ensemble stock predictor and recommender system. In: 2018 International Conference on Advances in Computing, Communications and Informatics (ICACCI), pp. 1981–1985 (2018). https://doi.org/10.1109/ICACCI.2018.8554424
10. Dwivedi, S.A., Attry, A., Parekh, D., Singla, K.: Analysis and forecasting of Time-Series data using S-ARIMA, CNN and LSTM. In: 2021 International Conference on Computing, Communication, and Intelligent Systems (ICCCIS), pp. 131–136 (2021). https://doi.org/10.1109/ICCCIS51004.2021.9397134

Explore the Impact of Natural Factors on the Use of Shared Bicycles

Liu Jiamei(✉)

Central South University of Forestry and Technology, Changsha, China
Cristinazoo@163.com

Abstract. In the last several years, the "bike sharing" model has rapidly become popular in major cities around the world, but with the gradual ebb of capital, bike sharing enterprises need to seek new profit models, and the primary task is to figure out the factors affecting the use of shared bicycles. In order to explore the degree of influence of various factors related to the use of shared bicycles in Seoul, and better optimize the amount of shared bicycles, the article takes the use of shared bicycles in Seoul as an example, selects temperature, humidity, wind speed and visibility as independent variables, and constructs corresponding linear regression models with the help of STATA software, so as to explore the specific degree of influence of various factors on the use of shared bicycles in Seoul. The results show that air temperature, humidity, wind speed and visibility have a certain degree of influence on the use of shared bicycles, and among the four factors, air temperature is the most influential one.

Keywords: Sharing Bicycles · STATA · Linear Regression Model · Relative Importance Analysis

1 Introduction

In order to solve the problem of "the last mile", shared bicycles came into being. Because of its convenient connection with the bus and subway, bike sharing has gradually become an indispensable means of travel in the daily life of residents. Unlike online car hailing, the rental of shared bicycles is greatly affected by weather conditions, user needs and other factors. Based on the mining and analysis of big data, this paper selects the use data of shared bicycles in Seoul, temperature, humidity, wind speed and visibility as key variables, builds multiple linear regression models with the help of STATA software, and uses standard coefficient method and R^2 method to study the relative importance, so as to study the impact of natural factors on the use of shared bicycles.

2 A Review of Domestic and International Research

Gebhark [1] found that low temperature, rain and high humidity will reduce people's willingness to use shared bicycles and travel time to some extent. The study presented by the author analyzed the influence of weather factors on the use of shared bicycles in Washington, D.C. The researcher uses the data set of all journeys in the system, a statistical model of the number of connected users and the duration of use was estimated, and the results showed that low temperature, rain and high humidity will reduce people's willingness to use shared bicycles and travel time to some extent. Kim [2] introduced the temperature and humidity index (THI), also known as the discomfort index, which is a composite indicator that combines air temperature and air humidity for estimating the degree of heat, and the heat wave indicator variable is also introduced to represent the interaction between temperature and humidity, and to measure the impact of high temperatures. From the research results, we can know that the impact of high temperature and non-working days on the demand for shared bicycle usage changes over time. Ashqar [3] creatively proposed a method to quantify the impact of weather conditions on the predicted number of bicycle stations in the San Francisco Bay Area bike-share system, using Poisson regression models (PRM) and negative binomial regression models (NBRM) to predict the number of bicycles in the network. Results of this research showed that time of day, temperature and humidity levels were important predictors of counts. Campbell [4] et al. used a predictive preference survey and multi-metric analysis to analyze the factors influencing the choice to shift from existing transportation modes to bike-share and bike-share in Beijing, and the study found that the impact of cycling distance, heat and air quality on bike-sharing usage is small, and precipitation is a higher negative factor for bike-sharing usage.

Xie [5] et al. used backward selection method to input independent variables to establish a multiple linear regression model and obtained the regression equation. The study shows that as the temperature rises in mid-August, the demand for bike-sharing trips decreases. However, because the author only selected the bike-sharing usage data for August in Shanghai, the overall temperature in August is high, so the results may differ significantly from this paper. Li Peng [6] constructed a BP neural network-based prediction model of weather factors on bike-sharing ridership, combining user tidal riding patterns and geospatial interest point data under relatively stable conditions, and trained a "day-by-day" and "hour-by-hour" model of bike-sharing ridership and weather data in a region of Chengdu. "The experimental results show that the ridership is influenced by temperature and rainfall at different times. In order to find out the factors affecting the short-time demand of bicycle sharing and make a descriptive statistical analysis, Zhang Manlin [7] selected weather conditions such as high temperature and cold, rain and snow, as well as related psychological factors and bicycle sharing condition variables in an empirical study. Wang [8] selected key influencing factors such as air temperature and air quality were studied in detail by selection factor analysis, grey correlation degree and multiple linear regression analysis, and found that variables such as temperature and heavy rain were the main factors affecting travel. Wei [9] et al. established an ordered logit model through statistical analysis of SP survey data of bike-sharing riders under adverse weather conditions to analyze the effects of gender, age, rainfall, and temperature on the selection behavior of bike-sharing distance willingness, and the results showed that both rainfall and temperature had significant effects on bike-sharing distance willingness. Using factor analysis, Zhu Yan [10] obtained five influencing factors of cycling awareness and weather, road conditions, traffic conditions, travel cost and travel comfort, and the results of the study showed that weather was the primary factor influencing whether travelers chose bicycle for short-distance travel.

At present, most researches on shared bicycles are aimed at forecasting the demand for shared bicycles, and there are few designs to explore the extent to which natural factors affect the use of shared bicycles. By using big data to explore the impact of natural factors on the travel demand of shared bicycles, it not only helps to find out the impact of natural factors on residents' socio-economic activities, but also provides support for more accurate research on the impact mechanism of urban users' use of shared bicycles.

3 Data Source and Preprocessing

In order to ensure the quantity of data and the accuracy of data sources, I selected the number of public bicycles rented per hour in the bicycle sharing system in Seoul, as well as the corresponding weather data and holiday information. The original data contains 14 attributes, totaling 8760 pieces of data.

According to the research content, the dependent variable of this paper is defined as the amount of shared single car rental. The natural factors involved in this paper include temperature, humidity, wind speed and visibility. Since these factors are numerical variables, they are defined as follows (Table 1):

Table 1. Definition and coding of numerical variables.

Code	Variable	Unit
Y_i	Rented Bicycle Count	Vehicles
G_{i1}	Temperature	°C
G_{i2}	Humidity	%
G_{i3}	Windspeed	m/s
G_{i4}	Visibility	km

4 Basic Statistical Analysis

4.1 Temperature Distribution of Shared Bicycle Usage

See Fig. 1.

It can be seen from the above histogram that, on the whole, the usage of shared bicycles increases first and then decreases with the increase of temperature. Taking [20, 25] as the dividing point, the use of shared bicycles before this temperature range shows a positive correlation with the temperature, and the change speed is fast first and then slow; the use of shared bicycles after this temperature range shows a negative correlation with the temperature.

This may be because when the ambient temperature is between 18 °C and 25 °C, it is the most comfortable temperature for the human body, and everyone is willing to use the shared bike at the most comfortable temperature.

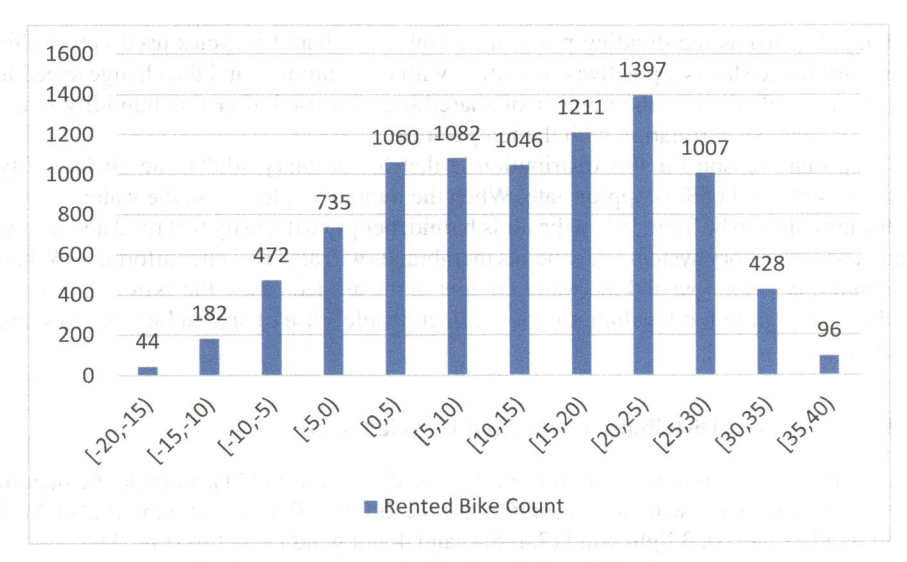

Fig. 1. Temperature distribution of shared bicycle usage.

4.2 Humidity Distribution of Shared Bicycle Usage

See Fig. 2.

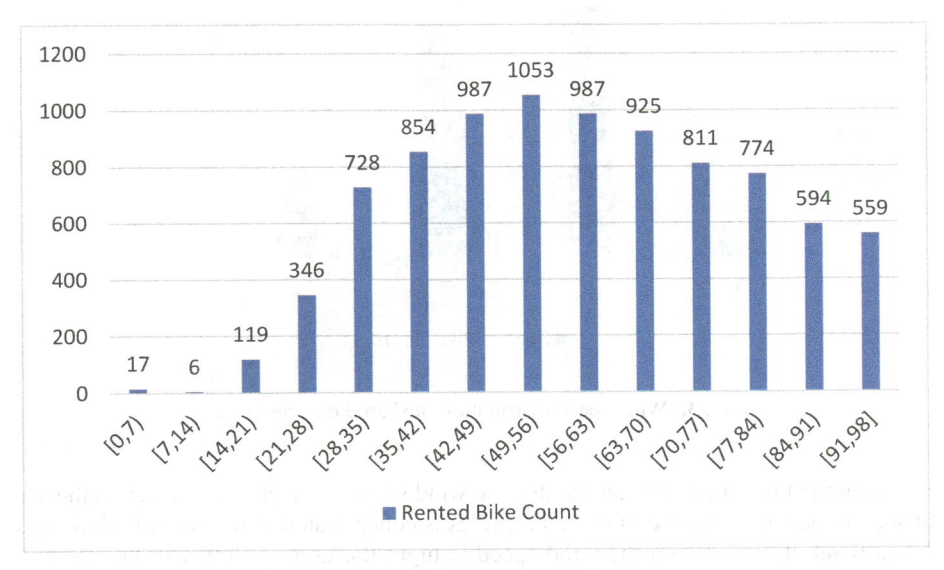

Fig. 2. Humidity distribution of shared bicycle usage.

It can be seen from the above histogram that, in general, the use of shared bicycles also shows a trend of first increasing and then decreasing with the increase of humidity.

Taking [49, 56) as the dividing point, the number of shared bicycles used before this humidity range shows a positive correlation with the humidity, and the change speed is fast first and then slow; the number of shared bicycles used after this humidity range shows a negative correlation with the temperature.

The main reason for this distribution is that for ordinary adults, the air humidity between 45% and 65% is appropriate. When the humidity is too high, the water content in the air will also be high. When the air is humid, people will easily feel tired and heavy, and their respiratory system and mucous membranes will also feel uncomfortable; When the humidity is too low and the water content in the air decreases, the skin will be easy to dry. Too high or too low humidity will affect people's use of shared bicycles to some extent.

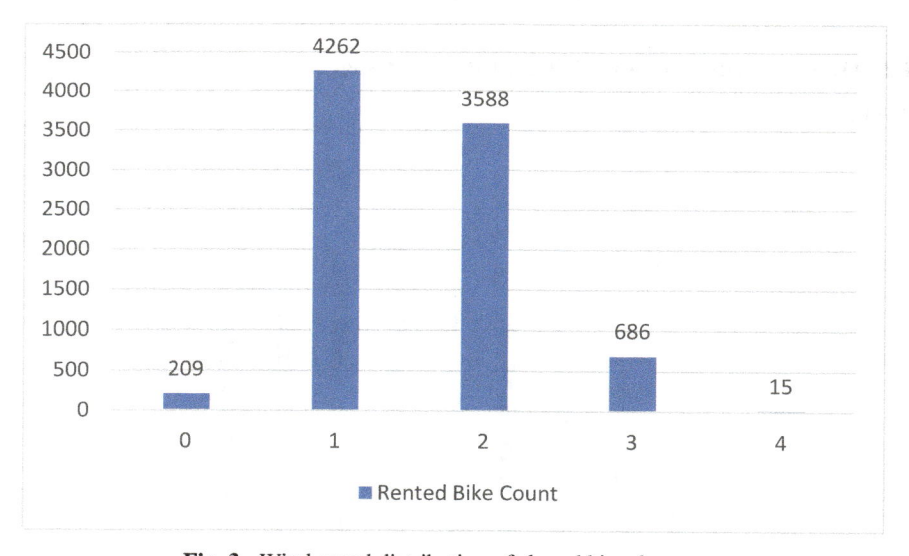

4.3 Wind Speed Distribution of Shared Bicycle Usage

According to the reference table for wind grade classification [11], I divide the data in the database into five wind levels (unit: m/s): 0 calm (0.0–0.2), 1 soft wind (0.3–1.5), 2 light wind (1.6–3.3), 3 light wind (3.4–5.4) and 4 and wind (5.5–7.9) (Fig. 3).

Fig. 3. Wind speed distribution of shared bicycle usage.

From the histogram, we can see that the wind speed has a greater impact on the use of shared bicycles. The use of shared bicycles is concentrated in the case of wind class 1 and wind class 2. When the wind speed is high, the user's safety will be affected, and when the wind is calm, the user's experience will be affected. Therefore, the use of shared bicycles will be concentrated in the windy but low wind speed.

4.4 Visibility Distribution of Shared Bicycle Usage

General visibility is divided according to the following criteria: 1. Visibility 20–30 km: excellent visibility, clear vision; 2. Visibility 15–25 km: good visibility and clear vision; 3. Visibility 10–20 km: average visibility; 4. Visibility 5–15 km: poor visibility and unclear vision; 5. Visibility 1–10 km: light fog, poor visibility and unclear vision; 6. Visibility 0.3–1 km: heavy fog, poor visibility; 7. Visibility less than 0.3 km: heavy fog, poor visibility; 8. Visibility less than 0.1 km: dense fog, poor visibility; 9. Visibility less than 100 m is usually considered as zero.

I have divided the visibility in the database into five intervals, corresponding to: 1. The visibility is less than 0.3 km, and the visibility is extremely poor; 2. The visibility is 0.3–1 km, which is very poor; 3. The visibility is 1–10 km and poor; 4. The visibility is 10–20 km, with average visibility; 5. The visibility is 15–25 km and good (Fig. 4).

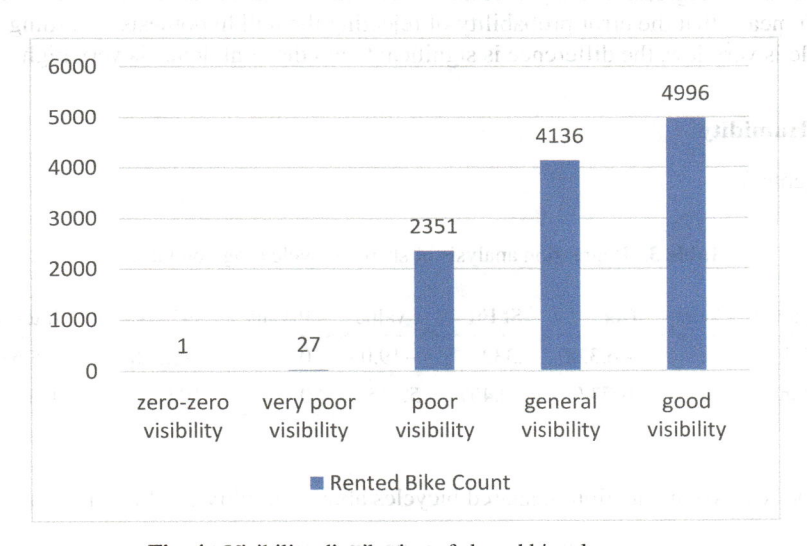

Fig. 4. Visibility distribution of shared bicycle usage.

From the above figure, we can also see that visibility has a great impact on the amount of shared bicycle rentals. When the visibility is less than 0.3 km, the use of shared bicycles can be approximately regarded as zero. In this case, no one chooses to use shared bicycles. When the visibility is 10–25 km, the number of bike sharing rentals is huge. The number of bike sharing rentals is positively correlated with visibility. The higher the visibility, the more bike sharing rentals. The higher the visibility, the better the vision when using the shared bike, and the more the usage will be.

5 Regression Analysis

5.1 Temperature

See Table 2.

Table 2. Regression analysis of shared bicycle usage on temperature.

Rented Bike Count	Coef	St Err	t-value	P-value	[95% Conf	Interval]
Temperature	29.081	.486	59.82	0	28.128	30.034
Constant	329.953	8.541	38.63	0	313.21	346.695

The regression equation of shared bicycles about temperature can be written as

$$Rented\ Bike\ Count = 329.953 + 29.081 \bullet Temperature \quad (1)$$

The above regression analysis results show that the statistical value of P is $0 < 0.01$, which means that the error probability of rejecting the null hypothesis according to the sample is very low, the difference is significant, and the confidence is very high.

5.2 Humidity

See Table 3.

Table 3. Regression analysis of shared bicycle usage on humidity.

Rented Bike Count	Coef	St Err	t-value	P-value	[95% Conf	Interval]
Humidity	−6.328	.332	−19.08	0	−6.978	−5.678
Constant	1073.07	20.457	52.45	0	1032.969	1113.172

The regression equation of shared bicycles about humidity can be written as

$$Rented\ Bike\ Count = 1073.07 - 6.328 \bullet Humidity \quad (2)$$

The above regression analysis results show that the statistical value of P is $0 < 0.01$, which means that the error probability of rejecting the null hypothesis according to the sample is very low, the difference is significant, and the confidence is very high.

5.3 Wind Speed

See Table 4.

The regression equation of shared bicycles about Windspeed can be written as

$$Rented\ Bike\ Count = 574.581 - 75.378 \bullet Windpeed \quad (3)$$

The above regression analysis results show that the statistical value of P is $0 < 0.01$, which means that the error probability of rejecting the null hypothesis according to the sample is very low, the difference is significant, and the confidence is very high.

Table 4. Regression analysis of shared bicycle usage on windspeed.

Rented Bike Count	Coef	St Err	t-value	P-value	[95% Conf	Interval]
Windspeed	75.378	6.602	11.42	0	62.437	88.319
Constant	574.581	13.284	43.25	0	548.541	600.622

Table 5. Regression analysis of shared bicycle usage on visibility.

Rented Bike Count	Coef	St Err	t-value	P-value	[95% Conf	Interval]
Windspeed	.211	.011	19.03	0	.19	.233
Constant	400.997	17.324	23.15	0	367.038	434.955

5.4 Visibility

See Table 5.

The regression equation of shared bicycles about visibility can be written as

$$Rented\ Bike\ Count = 400.997 - 0.211 \bullet Visibility \quad (4)$$

The above regression analysis results show that the statistical value of P is $0 < 0.01$, which means that the error probability of rejecting the null hypothesis according to the sample is very low, the difference is significant, and the confidence is very high.

5.5 Multiple Regression Analysis of Four Factors

See Table 6.

Table 6. Multiple regression analysis of four factors.

Rented Bike Count	Coef	St Err	t-value	P-value	[95% Conf	Interval]
Temperature	31.356	.467	67.18	0	30.441	32.271
Humidity	−8.22	.341	−24.13	0	−8.888	−7.552
Windspeed	30.939	5.58	5.54	0	20.001	41.877
Visibility	.031	.011	2.91	.004	.01	.053
Constant	680.78	34.033	20.00	0	614.068	747.492

From the above series of regression equations, we can draw a conclusion that temperature, humidity, wind speed and visibility all affect the use of shared bicycles to some extent. Among the four factors, temperature, wind speed and visibility are positively correlated with the use of shared bicycles from an overall perspective, while humidity is negatively correlated from an overall perspective.

6 Relative Importance Analysis

At present, there are two main methods to study this problem: standardized coefficient method and R^2 method. I first use the R^2 method to analyze the degree of impact.

A very important issue in empirical economics is to explore the specific contribution of different explanatory variables to the explained variables. For example, in the paper by Ye Dezhu [12] and others, the three authors tried to figure out which cultural factors have greater impact on happiness. The more common method in the literature is stepwise regression, that is, gradually introduce explanatory variables into the regression and significance test. However, in the stepwise regression method, the order in which explanatory variables are introduced is very subjective. The significance test does not always rank different explanatory variables according to their importance. Based on this, Isarelli [13] proposed the method of importance analysis on the basis of previous studies, mainly based on Fields [15] and Shorrocks [15]. This approach aims to determine the magnitude of the effect of the different explanatory variables in the linear regression on the coefficient of determination R^2, that is, it aims to find out which of the individual explanatory variables is the most important. In fact, the magnitude of the effect on the coefficient of determination R^2 also reflects the contribution of the different explanatory variables to the variance of the explained variable.

From the regression data mentioned above, the results show that temperature, humidity, windspeed and visibility are significantly related to the explained variable at the level of 1%. After this result is obtained, the relative importance analysis is carried out, and the results are as follows (Table 7):

Table 7. Dominance analysis.

Rented Bike Count	Dominance Stat.	Standardized Dominance. Stat.	Ranking
Windspeed	0.3075	0.8166	1
Humidity	0.0411	0.1092	2
Windspeed	0.0083	0.0220	4
Visibility	0.0196	0.0522	3

In this linear regression, the relative importance of each variable is ranked as: Temperature > Humidity > Visibility > Windspeed. In other words, temperature is the most important factor among the factors affecting shared bicycles, followed by humidity, visibility and wind speed.

Then the standard coefficient method is used for analysis, and the results are as follows (Table 8):

From the standard coefficient method, we can get the relative importance order of each variable: Temperature > Humidity > Windspeed > Visibility. In other words, temperature is always the most important factor among the factors affecting shared bicycles, followed by humidity.

Table 8. Standardized coefficient method.

Rented Bike Count	Coefficient	Std. Err.	t	P > |t|	Beta
Windspeed	31.35598	.4667188	67.18	0.000	.5806872
Humidity	−8.220033	.3406584	−24.13	0.000	−.2595044
Windspeed	30.93927	5.579933	5.54	0.000	.0497093
Visibility	.0314025	.0107743	2.91	0.004	.0296158
_cons	680.7797	34.03263	20.00	0.000	

7 Conclusion

From the above analysis results, we can draw a conclusion:

1. Temperature, humidity, wind speed and visibility have a certain impact on the use of shared bicycles;
2. Temperature, wind speed and visibility are all positively correlated with the use of shared bicycles from an overall perspective, while humidity is negatively correlated with the use of shared bicycles from an overall perspective;
3. Among the four factors, temperature is the most influential one.

The reason for the above phenomenon may be that the temperature gives everyone the most intuitive feeling, and the change of temperature is easy to bring changes in other factors, such as: the temperature drops below the dew point to generate fog, such as advection fog and radiation fog; The change of surface temperature makes the air on the surface expand and cool, and this air flow generates wind; The higher the temperature, the more water vapor, so the relative degree of humidity will be lower. On the contrary, the lower the temperature is, the higher the relative degree of humidity will be. According to the results of this paper, bike sharing suppliers should put the temperature first when placing bikes. When the temperature is too high or too low, they should not place too many bikes. When the temperature is 18 °C–25 °C, they can put more bikes.

As this study only collects data from Seoul, if we can obtain data on the use of shared bicycles in other cities at the same time, we can better explain the impact of various factors on the use of shared bicycles after large-scale data processing. In addition, when using the standardized coefficient method and R2 method respectively to test the importance, it is found that the impact of wind speed and visibility is different, and further relevant research and analysis can be conducted from this aspect.

References

1. Gebhart, K., Noland, R.B.: The impact of weather conditions on bikeshare trips in Washington, DC. Transportation **41**, 1205–1225 (2014)
2. Kim, K.: Investigation on the effects of weather and calendar events on bike-sharing according to the trip patterns of bike rentals of stations. J. Transp. Geogr. **66**, 309–320 (2018)
3. Ashqar, H.I., et al.: Modeling bike counts in a bike-sharing system considering the effect of weather conditions. ArXiv abs/2006.07563 (2019). n. pag

4. Campbell, A.A., et al.: Factors influencing the choice of shared bicycles and shared electric bikes in Beijing. Transp. Res. Part C-Emerg. Technol. **67**, 399–414 (2016)
5. Xie, G., Qian, L., Tang, W.: Research on the relationship between the weather and the demand for shared bicycle travel in cities. Logist. Sci.-Tech. **45**(04), 84–90 (2022)
6. Yan, P.-Y., Zhang, H., Wang, X., Li, P., Liu, Y.-X., Yang, D.: Predicting the riding volume of shared bikes based on weather factors. J. UESTC (Soc. Sci. Edit.) **23**(06), 1–9 (2021)
7. Zhang, M.: Analysis of factors affecting short term demand for shared bicycles. China J. Commer. (05), 103–104+155 (2020)
8. Wang, Y.: The Influence of Weather Factors on Travel Characteristics of Urban Shared Bike. Beijing Jiaotong University (2019)
9. Wei, Z., Zhou, H., Chen, G., Jia, Z.: The influence of bad weather on the desire of shared bicycle riding distance. Eng. Constr. **32**(05), 645–647+672 (2018)
10. Zhun, Y., Gan, H.: Research on decision-making willingness of short distance bicycle travel mode. Logist. Sci.-Tech. **44**(01), 94–97 (2021)
11. Nie, R.: Reference table of wind power classification. Meteorol. Hydrol. Oceanograp. Instrum. (01), 67 (2007)
12. Ye, D., Ng, Y.K., Lian, Y.: Culture and happiness. Soc. Indic. Res. **123**(2), 519–547 (2015)
13. Israeli, O.: A shapley-based decomposition of the R-square of a linear regression. J. Econ. Inequal. **5**(2), 199–212 (2007)
14. Fields, G.S.: Accounting for income inequality and its change: a new method, with application to the distribution of earnings in the United States. In: Worker Well-Being and Public Policy, pp. 1–38. Emerald Group Publishing Limited (2003)
15. Shorrocks, A.F.: Decomposition Procedures for Distributional Analysis: A Unified Framework Based on the Shapley Value (mimeo). University of Essex (1999)

Economic Dynamics Analysis of Higher Education Development

Tian Mo[✉]

Faculty of Social Sciences, University of Sheffield, Sheffield S10 2TN, UK
3100400050@caa.edu.cn

Abstract. Nowadays, with the national education double reduction policy and the epidemic in China, higher education is currently showing signs of better health and green financing. This research aimed to investigate the factors that can influence higher education. For the research, data from 31 provinces in China between 2019 and 2021 were studied using a quantitative analytical method, and a linear regression equation was developed. Higher education development was found to be unaffected by economic indicators such as the Gross Domestic Product (GDP) and the high school system; however, it was significantly and positively affected by tertiary industry workforces and the number of college faculty, and significantly and negatively affected by fiscal finance expenditure. It was implied that there was a connection between the development of the higher education system and economic growth, the centralization between the national government and local provinces, and the correlation between different departments. This highlighted the significance of higher education and assisted more families and students in meeting their educational goals during the epidemic.

Keywords: Higher Education · Quantitative Analysis · Budget Expenditure per Student · Employment in Tertiary Industry

1 Introduction

1.1 Research Background

From 2019 through an epidemic period in China, the higher education industry needs to face a series of social restrictions and psychological pressure problems. In 2021, the national government has issued a "double reduction" policy, which means effectively reducing the burden of students' off-campus training and heavy homework in the education stage. The implementation of this educational policy has effectively helped alleviate the pressure on families in the stage of the closure during epidemic time. Education plays a fundamental, leading, and sustainable role in building a socialist, harmonious society, which is a bridge for human resources to spread knowledge and culture. Provincial education bureaus have introduced programs such as "cloud teaching" and "autonomous learning" to ensure a normal high education. The promotion of the "double reduction" policy has shown children a good state and trend, which suggests several positive outcomes including better health, a green economy, and the importance of education.

Some literature reviews indicated that the development of higher education is mainly due to the needs of economic improvement, especially the needs of the development of the knowledge economy for training high-quality talents. Some people also state that higher education is the result of enrollment demand and has practical significance [1]. In China, local governments are competing not only for economic development indicators such as GDP but also for other social development indicators such as enrollment rate [2]. From the perspective of institutional science, there is no close relationship between the development of higher education and the economic system but only a loose coupling [3]. Although the above explanations are reasonable, the analysis objects are all on the expansion of higher education, while in my paper, the analysis content and period are different in terms of specific behaviors.

1.2 Research Gap

Previous literature is unclear as to whether, during an economic downturn and implementation of the government's double reduction policy, the economic impact affects the expansion of higher education and what factors exactly determine the growth and development of higher education even through the recession. Therefore, to make up for the exploration gap in this area, this paper will further clarify and explore "what factors can affect higher education".

At the stage around COVID-19 pandemics, the task of higher education development and reform is concerning, such as in terms of popularization and GDP, government fiscal financial support investment, the scale of education universities, and the employment rate of tertiary industry. This has highlighted the importance of high education and helped more children and families raise their educational expectations during economic downturns.

1.3 Structure of This Paper

To construct higher education, this paper will use rational and realistic analysis to investigate the important factors in the process of higher educational development. This paper applies the national economy as the theoretical basis to study what factors determine the growth of higher education and to collect secondary data in a quantitative way and analyze it in the form of linear regression equation. This study focuses on statistical analysis and modeling to detect whether the development of positive and negative correlation factors before and during the epidemic has a significant impact on higher education development.

2 Literature Review

2.1 Definition and Development

The theoretical paradigms of higher education development, of which the human capital model and signaling model are the most famous, are respectively explained from the perspective of rational choice and institutional theory. The Human Capital Model was formalized by Nobel laureate Gary Becker and economist Adam Smith, who describe the main principle of human capital, the ways that it is different from physical capital, and the influence of these differences on education markets [4]. The investment model of human capital reveals the decision to get a higher education in terms of a discounted cash flow of costs (government fiscal financial investment support or private) as well as benefits. This basic model provides for the development of the national economy by requiring talents with specific knowledge and skills to study, thus promoting the expansion of the scale and improvement of the quality of higher education. An alternative to human capital is the signaling model, which provides a major challenge to the opinion that educational development generates productive skills or human capital. Michael Spence found the classic exposition of the signaling model, which regards asymmetric information factors as impacting incentives to improve in higher education [5]. According to the signaling institutional theory, the expanding scale of higher education is independent of the direct role of the economic system to a certain extent [6]. As a result, the improvement of higher education in some countries or regions is out of line with the actual needs of the local economy. Some developing countries even call it "Over education". While higher education can serve a private investment function in both signaling models and human capital, the social returns are more likely to be different from those of models, with significant implications for policy design [6].

2.2 Important Results

Meyer in 1977 clarifies that the expansion of higher education can be defined from the following three dimensions: first, the increase in the number of students in higher education [7]. Second, the establishment of higher education as a social center [7]. Third, the growth of practical knowledge generated by higher education [7]. In the 20th century, the scale of higher education and its students has significantly developed. In 1950, about 110 countries had the academic system of universities; in 1995, the number of countries with universities increased to 170 [8]. In 1900, less than 1% of the world's population received higher education; in 2000, the ratio increased to 20% [8].

Schofer and Meyer in 2005 analyzed the scale of development of higher education in different countries in the 20th century from a global perspective [9]. They found that since 1960, the scale of higher education in the world has shown an accelerated trend of development [9]. School knowledge and school education are considered necessary and appropriate qualifications to play various social roles. If a country's organizational form meets the characteristics of "world society" (high level of popularization of secondary education, high level of economic development, and low degree of government control over the education system), it will tend to expand its higher education model [9].

Drori and Moon found that the number of students in different disciplines of higher In 2006, education in different countries had increased in all disciplines through the analysis of statistical data collected by UNESCO from 1965 to 1995. This shows that while the scale of higher education has expanded, its internal structure has also changed significantly [10]. With the formation of a new world culture related to the development of higher education, everyone is regarded as suitable for higher education, and "education for all" has become a common phrase of international institutions such as UNESCO [10]. Similarly, under the boost of institutional mechanisms, employers tend to hire people who have received higher education. Thus, the role of the education diploma increases, leading to the emergence of diploma inflation [11].

2.3 Summary

According to the above literature review, the idea of formal rationality is applied with reference to foreign literature and theoretical explorations and then extended to China's higher education system. The basic idea of this study is that in addition to the needs of national economic development, the employment rate of the tertiary industry, and the number of secondary education graduates, government financial support and the number of full-time teachers in colleges and universities are also important factors affecting the expansion of the scale of higher education.

3 Method

3.1 Research Design

This paper exploits a quantitative analytical approach to collect relevant secondary data and make a linear regression equation for the analysis object. The analysis object is at a high educational level. To explore what factors affect the degree of higher education, this paper will search for data on economic and educational aspects of the year range 2019–2021. In addition, based on the factors assumed to affect it, the data of the relevant 31 provinces (municipalities) in China, which suggests the regional situation of higher education development during the pandemic, also needs to be searched and investigated. The reason for choosing quantitative analysis is that the results of the collection and analysis of data on higher education and the national economy are often reliable and effective, which can establish the causal relationship between issues and data.

3.2 Data Collection

The way of data collection is mainly from the national website. From the website of the National Bureau of Statistics website, the number of college enrollment, GDP, population, full-time teachers, employment in the tertiary industry revealing the most likely employment destination of college graduates in 31 various provinces and municipalities from period year 2019 to 2021 were collected [12]. In addition, the number of senior high school graduates was collected from the Statistical Yearbook of China's Education, from the Finance Department of the Ministry of Education web-site [13]. This paper will obtain the education funds in the average student budget of universities in the same period.

3.3 Data Analysis

The data obtained from multiple time series selected from 31 provinces belongs to panel data, which calculates the model measurement by using the software STATA. When verifying the investigation assumptions,

$$HEE = a0 + a1 * GDP_{it} + a2 * EXP_{it} + a3 * TEC_{it} + a4 * GRA_{it}$$

$$+ a5 * WOR_{it} + TIME_i + WHERE_T + E_{it}$$

In the above model, t indicates the year, with the varied range of year 2019–2021, and i indicates the province, with a varied range of 1–31.

HEE: College and university enrollment
GDP: GDP per capita
EXP: Budget expenditure per student
TEC: Number of full-time teachers
GRA: Number of high school graduates
WOR: Employment in tertiary industry
TIME: Time disturbance factors respectively
WHERE: regional areas disturbance factors respectively
E: Other influencing factors not considered

4 Results

4.1 Descriptive Statistics

To determine how the economy impacts higher education, the data's maximum, minimum, median, mean value, standard deviation, and sample size were analyzed. According to Table 1, the descriptive statistical properties of the data are within a suitable range, allowing correlation analysis to be conducted.

Table 1. Results of descriptive statistics.

	N	MEAN	SD	MIN	MEDIAN	MAX
HEE	93	12.3369	0.9593	9.2663	12.5421	13.6718
GDP	93	11.1215	0.3823	10.4041	11.0304	12.1226
EXP	93	16.1051	0.6615	14.5209	16.2050	17.5485
TEC	93	10.8306	0.9261	7.8671	11.0580	12.1564
GRA	93	6.7811	0.8289	4.3940	6.9126	8.2306
WOR	93	12.1384	0.8855	9.8605	12.3332	13.4837

4.2 Correlation Analysis

Next, through correlation analysis in Table 2, It can be found that the degree of correlation between various factors of education and economics. The correlation test for each variable is performed by using software STATA for Pearson coefficient test and Spearman coefficient test. The results are shown in the Table 2, where the numbers reveal the results of Pearson test and * reveal the results of the Spearman test.

Applying Table 2's correlation analysis, it can be determined that there is a degree of association between various education and economic parameters. STATA is used to conduct both the Pearson coefficient test and the Spearman coefficient test. Each correlation test is performed on each variable separately. The results are presented in Table 2, where the numbers represent the Pearson test results and the asterisks represent the Spearman test results.

When the absolute value of the correlation coefficient between variables is larger than 0.75, the Pearson test indicates that the degree of correlation between variables is greater. When the absolute value of the correlation coefficient falls between 0.5 and 0.75, it implies that the variables are highly connected. When the absolute value of the correlation coefficient between variables falls between 0.25 and 0.5, it implies minimal correlation. When the absolute value of the correlation coefficient between two variables is less than 0.25, the variables are either uncorrelated or loosely associated.

The following findings can be seen in Table 2: First, the number of full-time teachers and high school graduates has a substantial effect on the fluctuations in enrolment in higher education. Higher education expenditures and employment in the tertiary industry have undergone minor changes. In conclusion, the GDP has no appreciable effect on the expansion of higher education.

Table 2. Results of correlation analysis between data.

	HEE	GDP	EXP	TEC	GRA	WOR
HEE	1.0000	0.1826^{*}	0.8554^{***}	0.8721^{***}	0.9201^{***}	0.9336^{***}
GDP	0.1490	1.0000	0.3754^{***}	0.4397^{***}	0.3826^{***}	−0.0151
EXP	0.8790^{***}	0.3491^{***}	1.0000	0.8623^{***}	0.9418^{***}	0.8264^{***}
TEC	0.9443^{***}	0.3548^{***}	0.8849^{***}	1.0000	0.8855^{***}	0.7203^{***}
GRA	0.9529^{***}	0.3099^{***}	0.9567^{***}	0.9329^{***}	1.0000	0.8456^{***}
WOR	0.9060^{***}	−0.1658	0.8119^{***}	0.7702^{***}	0.8539^{***}	1.0000

Note: The results of Spearman test, through two-tailed test *, **, *** respectively reveals significantly at the level of 10%, 5%, 1%

4.3 Regression Analysis and Hypothesis Test

Considering China's epidemic situation, detailed regression analysis and hypothesis testing were conducted for the years 2019, 2020, and 2021, when the economic impact was severe.

According to the regression results in 2019 in Table 3, GDP will have a positive impact on HEE, although this impact will be minor; specifically, if everything else remains constant, HEE will grow by 0.0384% for every 1% increase in GDP. EXP has a negative impact on HEE, and this impact is significant at the 1% level. Specifically, if all else remains constant, HEE will decrease by 0.3738% for every 1% rise in EXP. TEC has a positive impact on HEE, and this impact is significant at the 1% level. Assuming everything else remains constant, HEE will increase by 0.7293% for every 1% increase in TEC. GRA has a beneficial effect on HEE, however it is insignificant. With all other circumstances held constant, for every 1% increase in GRA, HEE increases by 0.15 percent. WOR has a positive impact on HEE, and this impact is considerable at the 1% level. With all other circumstances held constant, a 1% rise in WOR results in a 0.4349% increase in HEE.

According to the regression results in 2020, GDP will have a positive impact on HEE, although this impact will be minor; specifically, if everything else remains constant, HEE will grow by 0.1178% for every 1% increase in GDP. EXP has a negative impact on HEE, and this impact is significant at a 10% level; specifically, for every 1% rise in EXP, HEE will decrease by 0.2700%. TEC has a positive impact on HEE, and this impact is substantial at the 1% level; specifically, with all other variables held constant, HEE increases by 0.7015% for every 1% increase in TEC. GRA has a positive impact on HEE, but this impact is not significant. With all other circumstances held constant, a 1% rise in GRA results in a 0.1427% increase in HEE. WOR has a favorable effect on HEE, and this effect is significant at the 1% level. With all other circumstances held constant, a 1% rise in WOR results in a 0.4626% increase in HEE.

According to the regression results in 2021 in Table 3, GDP will have a positive impact on HEE, and this impact will be significant at the 10% level. If everything else remains constant, HEE will rise by 0.2523% for every 1% growth in GDP. EXP has a negative impact on HEE, which is considerable at the 1% level. If everything else remains constant, HEE will decrease by 0.3885% with every 1% rise in EXP. TEC has a favorable effect on HEE, and this effect is evident at the 1% level. If everything else remains constant, HEE will grow by 0.681% for every 1% increase in TEC. GRA has a positive impact on HEE, but this impact is minor. With all other circumstances held constant, each 1% rise in GRA increases HEE by 0.0587%. WOR has a positive impact on HEE, and this impact is considerable at the 1% level. With all other circumstances held constant, a 1% rise in WOR results in a 0.6787% increase in HEE.

The following outcomes can be seen in Table 3: Secondly, in 2019, 2020, and 2021, WOR and TEC always have a positive impact on HEE, and this impact is considerable at the 1% level; nevertheless, EXP always has a significant negative impact on HEE. GDP and GRA have a favorable impact, although they are not statistically significant. Second, while looking at each year, the most particular factor is TEC, which has the greatest favorable impact for each subsequent year. Thirdly, GDP and EXP have shifted in the last three years. GDP is positive at the 10% level in 2021, although it was not significant in 2020 or 2019. EXP is the only negative impact that is considerable at 10% in 2020, and at other times at 1%.

Table 3. Results of Regression.

	2019	2020	2021
	HEE	HEE	HEE
GDP	0.0384	0.1178	0.2523*
t-value	(0.36)	(0.77)	(1.80)
EXP	−0.3738***	−0.2700*	−0.3885***
t-value	(−3.39)	(−1.96)	(−2.79)
TEC	0.7293***	0.7015***	0.6801***
t-value	(9.12)	(7.55)	(7.08)
GRA	0.2015	0.1427	0.0587
t-value	(1.39)	(0.71)	(0.27)
WOR	0.4349***	0.4626***	0.6787***
t-value	(5.45)	(3.91)	(6.09)
E	3.4434*	1.2793	−0.3597
t-value	(2.03)	(0.52)	(−0.14)
N	31	31	31
R^2	0.990	0.987	0.987
adj. R^2	0.988	0.984	0.984
F	494.6690	374.6006	366.2237

5 Discussion

First, the results of the analysis indicate that the number of full-time teachers and employment in the tertiary sector have a significant favorable impact on changes in higher education enrollment. Each province has accounted for the quantity of full-time teachers and employees when formulating a plan to increase university and college enrollment. Second, the effect of budgetary education expenditures on the number of admissions to higher education is notably negative, showing that education expenditures in some provinces have declined rather than increased with the expansion of the higher education enrollment scale. The actual effect is a drop in education funding because the increase in education funding within the budget is slower than the increase in high school enrolment. Third, the GDP and the number of high school graduates have a somewhat beneficial effect on the expansion of higher education. Ignoring the effects of inflation, the GDP is significantly positive at 10% in 2021.

For the study of factors affecting higher education, various analytic approaches can be used to examine various logical behaviors, such as the relationship between the changing higher education system and the economy, the relationship between the central government and local provinces, and the relationship between different government departments. Considering the relationship between the changing higher education system and the economic system, factors such as GDP, population, and the national economy may compel economically developed provinces to open the higher education supply market to economically underdeveloped provinces and invest enrollment quotas in other provinces. Second, considering the relationship between the government and local provinces in terms of the extension of higher education on a wide scale, provincial governments are responsible for regional higher education development. Focusing on the growth of high-level higher education, the central government is responsible for macro regulation and direct management of numerous directly associated high schools, central universities, and national full-time instructors with good educational conditions and high standards. Thirdly, considering the relationship between different government departments, the majority of expenditures for higher education come from the finance department; therefore, the higher education expenditures provided by the local finance department should have as much of a miraculous effect as possible in solving the problem of local higher education enrollment opportunities. Per-student career financing at colleges and universities is smaller than per-student costs. Hence, the greater the scope of higher education, the greater the financial strain it places on universities and colleges. Scale growth is not a primary driver of development.

6 Conclusion

This research investigates the level of higher education in the context of the epidemic and the government's double reduction program. It investigates how factors like as economic development, high school education, the number of university faculty, and financial investment affect higher education. By confirming and restructuring earlier perspectives on higher education and the national economy, higher education and global society, the higher education system, and human capital, this paper arrives at the conclusion that all theories are essentially the same as this paper. The measuring approach examines the numerous elements influencing higher education, descriptive statistics for a reasonable range, the Pearson coefficient test and Spearman coefficient test for each variable, and extensive regression analysis and hypothesis testing. During the epidemic period of 2019–2021, employment in the tertiary industry and the number of full-time teachers usually have a substantial positive impact on higher education expansion; nevertheless, budget expenditure per student always has a major negative impact on higher education. GDP per capita and the number of high school graduates have a positive but not statistically significant impact on higher education development.

This research adds to the government's and local higher education systems' understanding of the severe economic impact of the epidemic period, as well as the relative importance of GDP and financial education funds on higher education during tough times. It also provides government decision-makers with a complete examination of the scale and dynamics of higher education from a variety of perspectives, including the economy, politics, fairness, and quality. Because the data were only collected during the pandemic era, the paper has a limited sample size. Further data may be gathered in the future to compensate for the accuracy of this paper.

References

1. Li, Y.: Research on Educational Investment Decision, pp. 119–127. Peking University Press, Peking (1992)
2. Zhang, J.: The Political Economy of China's Growth, pp. 1–9. People's Publishing House, New Delhi (2008)
3. Fusarelli, L.D.: Tightly coupled policy in loosely coupled system. J. Educ. Adm. 561–575 (2022)
4. Checchi, D.: The Economics of Education: Human Capital, Family Background, and Inequality, pp. 1–35. Cambridge University Press, Cambridge (2006)
5. Spence, M.: Job market signaling. Q. J. Econ. 355–356 (2012)
6. Lovenheim, M.: Economics of Education, pp. 42–44. Worth Publishers, New York (2018)
7. Meyer, J.: The effects of education as an institution. Am. J. Sociol. 55–77 (1977)
8. Hesser, W.: The Dual System of Higher Education in Countries, pp. 157–185. ResearchGate Publication, Charlottesville (2019)
9. Schofer, E., Meyer, J.: The World-Wide Expansion of Higher Education, p. 3. Stanford publications, Redwood (2012)
10. Drori, G., Moon, H.: The Changing nature of tertiary education: cross-national trends in disciplinary enrollment, pp.157–185 (2006)
11. Preckler, M.: Education for all 2015: achievements and challenges. J. Supranatl. Polic. Educ. 328–330 (2015)
12. National Bureau of Statistics of China Homepage. http://www.stats.gov.cn/tjsj/ndsj/. Accessed 13 Mar 2023
13. National education statistics. Ministry of National Education of China Homepage. http://www.moe.gov.cn. Accessed 13 Mar 2023

The Impact of Fintech on Enterprise Innovation: Take Companies that Issue Fintech Concept Stocks as an Example

Yuyao Sun(✉)

Tianjin University of Finance and Economics, Tianjin, China
sunyuyao2002@stu.tjufe.edu.cn

Abstract. This study reviewed 151 Chinese enterprises that issued fintech concept stocks, and selected fintech-related company data from 2017 to 2021 as a sample. The study used crawler software to crawl relevant data and keyword word frequency from the company's annual reports, use the CSMAR database and WIND database, and use econometrics software STATA for analysis. Through the enterprise R&D input and output, the enterprise innovation level is reflected. The method of establishing multiple linear regression formula, is used to reveal the current fintech development to help the innovation of Chinese enterprises. The fintech development level has more obvious effect on investment of enterprise innovation. After replacement of the explanatory variables, fintech affects the innovation output by indirectly influencing inputs. Through concept stock research, we found that fintech can help transform the fictitious economy into the real economy. Specifically improves the real economy through influence. Meanwhile, the profitability, debt, total assets and age also have different effects to the enterprise innovation.

Keywords: Fintech · Enterprise Innovation · Concept Stock

1 Introduction

Fintech originated from the synthesis of finance and technology. Defined by Bettinger, fintech is related to modern management science and is a new field born out of computer technology. With the help of professional experience in the banking industry, it is an important channel for the development of new finance [1]. Which is ultimately an iterative product of the combination of technological innovation and the financial industry.

With the intention of adapt to the incessant changing environment, Enterprises must have the ability to continuous update their own technology. As the core of "dynamic capabilities theory", innovation is the crucial to maintain a competitive advantage in any enterprise's growth. Some scholars have suggested that, today's entrepreneurs are triggering a wave of innovation with their technology and creativity. This heralds a fintech revolution [2]. Carney was proposed that Fintech will lead to a huge innovation from consumers to small and medium-sized businesses, to banking services, even to the entire financial system.

With emerging technologies as back-end support, digital HP finance, digital assets and currencies, artificial intelligence (AI), big data, blockchain, 5G technology and cloud computing, have become an important part of the financial technology system. They have played a significant role in the emergence of emerging financial institutions and services, and there are also emerging front-end financial products and models [3]. The digital financial system has hundreds of millions of people every year, and the ability of fintech to improve the world economy development has become an indisputable fact.

Individual investors are the leading force in China's stock market, most of them do not have a sound professional knowledge system, because of access to information channels, analysis of information ability and own capital restrictions are in a disadvantageous position, vulnerable to relevant rumors and themes in the market, always to pursue stocks related to hot events and policies in the market [4].

These market rumors, defined as "noisy information" [5], are the culprits behind most irrational investment practices. Irrational trading behavior based on the influence of "noise" is widespread in the Chinese stock market. When the market proposes a concept, a small number of concept stocks will become the target of most investors in the market, triggering a series of hype. For example, fintech concept stocks.

As a new generation of intelligent technology in the financial field, Fintech is changing the traditional financial format, it also has a significant impact on the real economy [6].

Fintech can help transform the fictitious economy into the real economy by influencing the real economy. The stock market essentially has the characteristics of a fictitious economy. As a hot word in recent years, fintech concept stocks issued by listed companies, have undoubtedly become the target of most investors. The trend of the A-share market can affect the future company development obviously, and most companies' business relies on fintech. Which help the real economy ability through the fictitious economy. The enterprises growth trend has a vital way to measure, that is, the investment and results of enterprise innovation.

As a classic topic that has been talked about, innovation is the main method of creating new productivity and production tools, and it is also an important driver of human progress.

For enterprises, digital innovation is not an illusory and distant technology. It can fundamentally solve the complex structural problems of some new products and services. In this way, new methods of value creation have been born, and improve the labor appropriation pathways [7]. As previous studies show, the digital revolution can better assist the innovation and development of enterprises, and strengthen the impact of fintech on enterprise innovation in multiple dimensions.

This research will focus on the balance sheet and income statement annual reports of 151 A-share listed companies which have issued fintech concept stocks. As well as the annual K-line data of the stock market, and make three main contributions: First, from the angle of concept stocks, this paper studies the enterprises that issue "fintech" concept stocks. Second, this paper crawls the annual report of the enterprises with the word frequency of "fintech", uses patent applications quantity and R&D investment as the indicators to measure innovation of the enterprise and studies the influence of the fintech development to the innovation of enterprises. Third, this paper also crawls the data in the company's balance sheet, income statement and annual K-line., which will study the fintech effect on enterprise innovation from multiple variable perspectives.

2 Theoretical Analysis and Research Hypotheses

Through the revolution and iteration of artificial intelligence (AI), blockchain, cloud computing, big data and digital application, fintech can analyze and predict enterprise information more accurately. Reduce various risks of enterprise development intelligently. With these technologies, listed companies will no longer be silos. Increased information transparency will also help the market increase trust in enterprises. Therefore, the enterprise annual report has numerous disclosures of fintech and related words. These can further show the enterprise development degree of fintech, and provide reference data for studying the fintech development to enterprises.

In this study, the degree of enterprise innovation is taken as the core research variable. The R&D spending and the patents application quantity are mainly used as indicators to measure the enterprise development.

Corporate R&D and innovation are risky, there are risks in decision-making, and most of them remain confidential. Once a company has a major financial problem, the first thing to do is to reduce the risky decisions. However, fintech has become a new trend technology to the economy development. The attention of enterprises to fintech can reduce the risk considerations, it can also reflect the enterprises' understanding of innovation output. Based on these existing theoretical analyses, following hypothesis is being proposing:

Hypothesis 1: With other control variables constant, fintech can help companies innovate.

Not only that, the issuance of stock information by enterprises also effects the enterprises development trend. Before buying a stock, investors usually calculate the liquidity, market capitalization, and closing price of the stock in different periods, to measure the purchase value of the business. This also determines the degree to which relevant industries are valued by the market.

As a concept stock, "fintech" is the biggest signboard of this type. Studying the relevant indices of the stock market, that can reflect the level of society trust in the hot word "fintech" accurately. This affects the enterprise investments in their own "fintech" development, which also creates a better environment for the enterprise fintech growth. Based on these existing theoretical analyses, following hypothesis is being proposing:

Hypothesis 2: With other control variables unchanged, fintech development can enhance the liquidity and value of fintech concept stocks issued by enterprises, and can further influence the innovation level of enterprises.

3 Research Design

3.1 Sample Selection and Data Source

The final sample selected in this study, which is 151 fintech concept-related companies among China's A-share enterprises, from 2017 to 2021. By inquire many enterprise websites. The company-level data such as R&D expenditure in the annual reports is crawled through web crawler technology, patent data comes from SOOPAT, fintech-related word frequency statistics come from CSMAR database, and stock market-level data comes from WIND database.

3.2 Core Variable Definition

Innovation Outputs. The R&D spending can measures the input of enterprise innovation, which displayed in the income statement from the annual report of the enterprises. At the same time, the patent application quantity is used to measure the annual innovation results [8]. In the empirical analysis, this study treats the natural logarithm of the invention patent application quantity held by the company plus 1.

The Fintech Development Level. The study quotes the frequency of fintech-related technologies' sub-indicators in the enterprise reports. Take this frequency data as an indicator to help measuring the impact of fintech on enterprises level [9]. Such as artificial intelligence (AI), blockchain, cloud computing, big data, digital technology application, coming from the "Digital Economy Data" of the CSMAR database. In the empirical analysis, use the sum of the frequencies related to the fintech in the same year, added by 1 to take the logarithmic treatment.

3.3 Controls Variable Selection

In order to make the regression model more accurate, this article adds corresponding control variables to the model, the specific meaning is report in Table 1 [6]:

Table 1. Introductions to the meaning of variables.

Variable type	Variable name	Variable abbreviation	Variable description
The variable being explained	R&D expenses	RD	Annual R&D expenses in the income statement of listed companies, unit: million
	Patent Applications	Patent	To measure the enterprise innovation result and development level, the natural logarithm of the invention patent applications quantity held by the company plus 1

(continued)

Table 1. (*continued*)

Variable type	Variable name	Variable abbreviation	Variable description
Explanatory variables	The level of financial technology development	FinTech	Artificial intelligence (AI), blockchain, cloud computing, big data, digital technology application in the data. Use the sum of the frequencies related to the fintech in the same year, added by 1 to take the logarithmic treatment
Control variables	Turnover Rate	TR	Measure the liquidity of fintech concept stocks
	Annual closing price	ACP	The year-end closing price of the stock
	Return on equity	ROE	Measure profitability
	Operating cash ratio	OCR	To measure the quality of earnings, operating cash ratio = net operating cash flow/gross operating income
	Corporate debt ratio	Debt	Gearing ratio
	Enterprise age	Age	The period of operation of the company from the date of registration to 2021
	Enterprise size	Size	Total assets of the enterprise, unit: billion

3.4 Metrology Model Setting

Using the assumptions of the analysis described above, this article constructs the following benchmark regression model:

$$Patent i, y(RDi, y) = \alpha_0 + \alpha_0 FinTech_{i,y} + CONTROLs + \varepsilon \quad (1)$$

In model (1), the subscript i indicates the listed company, and y represents the year; CONTROLS represent the control variables in the model. Enterprise research expenditure (RD) and innovation output patent applications (Patent) are used as explanatory variables, and the core explanatory variables of Eq. (1) are the estimated coefficients of fintech development level (FinTech).

To further investigate the relationship between the explanatory and the explainable variables, the model is built again:

$$Patent_{i,y} = \beta_0 + \beta_0 RD_{i,y} + CONTROL_s + \varepsilon_0 \quad (2)$$

In model (2), the subscript i indicates the listed company, and y represents the year; CONTROLS represent the control variables in the model. Innovation output patent applications (Patent) are used as explanatory variables, and the core explanatory variables of Eq. (2) is the patent applications.

3.5 Descriptive Statistics

Table 2 report the descriptive statistics of the variables. The average R&D spending is 163.5 million and the average total assets is 20.82 billion. It shows that, R&D expenses accounts for 0.7853% of the total assets. Compared with before, enterprises attach much more importance to R&D and innovation.

Table 2. Descriptive statistics.

VARIABLES	(1)	(2)	(3)	(4)	(5)
	N	mean	Sd	min	max
RD	600	163.5	163.5	0	2,139
Patent	600	0.705	0.705	0	2.796
FinTech	600	1.553	1.553	0	2.736
ROE	600	−0.00669	−0.00669	−2.750	0.488
OCR	600	0.0945	0.0945	−4.321	7.232
Debt	600	0.421	0.421	0.0360	0.967
Age	600	19.66	19.66	8	37
Size	600	20.82	20.82	0.171	1,870
ACP	600	14.78	14.78	1.070	225
TR	600	688.2	688.2	2.388	3,987

4 Inspection Results and Analysis

4.1 Correlation Analysis

In this study, without considering the causal connection between variables, the correlation between variables will be studied through correlation analysis. R&D spending and the patent application quantity will be the main correlation study as the explanatory variables.

As shown in Table 3, if the explanatory variable is the R&D expenditure, the estimation coefficient of the patent is significantly positive at the 1% level. It shows that, the annual patent application status of enterprises can affect the enterprise scientific innovation to a certain extent, and then increase R&D investment. Meanwhile, if the core explanatory variable is the fintech development level, its estimation coefficient is also significantly positive at the level of 1%. This proves that the enterprise fintech development can indeed help enterprises attach importance to scientific research and development technology.

When the patent applications were used as the explanatory variable, the estimated coefficient of the level of fintech development (FINTECH) was significantly positive at the level of 5%. Obviously, the fintech development can help enterprises to innovate output.

Return on equity (ROE), is a commonly used stock selection indicator for "stock god - Buffett". Value investors often use a company's ability to maintain a high ROE over a long period of time, as a criterion for selecting stocks [10].

As an important indicator reflecting the profitability of enterprises, it can reflect the enterprise development level to a certain extent. As shown in the Table 3, both R&D spending and patent application quantity were used as explanatory variables, and the estimated coefficients for ROE were significantly positive at the 1% level. Therefore, the profitability of a firm can also assist the enterprises with the innovation input and output.

The enterprise debt ratio (Debt), is the ratio of all liabilities of to all fund sources, reflecting the ability of an enterprise to repay debts. In Table 3, the estimated coefficient of the enterprise debt ratio is significantly negative at the 1% level, using the number of patent application quantity as the explanatory variable. It shows that the lower the debt ratio get, the more innovation output the enterprise has. When the company's long-term capital is stable and independent, it can promote the stable output of innovative products.

Company age (Age). If the explanatory variable is the R&D spending, the estimated coefficient for company age was significantly positive at the 10% level. Using the patent applications as the explanatory variable, the estimated coefficient of age is significantly negative at the level of 1%. It illuminates that, the longer the company operates, the more senior management attaches importance to scientific research and innovation. However, based on the life cycle theory of enterprises, at different stages, the R&D capabilities and experience of enterprises will change, which directly affects the innovation efficiency of enterprises. So, the innovation intensity varies with the age of companies. "There is the problem of path dependence due to organizational memory, and the decline of cooperative innovation efficiency due to organizational rigidity." Moreover, it is not strong in adaptability to the rapidly changing external environment, and the enterprise innovation performance will be shocked because of the "short board" effect of the scientific research stage [11]. Therefore, the age of the enterprise has a counter-effect on the amount of innovation output.

Company size (Size). If the explanatory variable is the R&D expenditure, the estimated coefficient for size is significantly positive at the 1% level. If the explanatory variable is the patent applications, the estimated coefficient for company size is significantly negative at the 10% level. The larger the company, the more investment in scientific research will increase. But scale also has the problem of organizational rigidity, and there will be an inverse impact result to the oversized companies on the innovation output efficiency.

Annual closing price (ACP), if the explanatory variables are the R&D expenditure and patent applications, the estimated coefficients are significantly positive at the levels of 1% and 5%. Turnover Rate (TR), if the explanatory variable is the R&D expenditure, the estimated coefficient is significantly negative at the 5% level. When the patent applications are used as the explanatory variable, the estimated coefficient is significantly positive at the 5% level. It shows that the liquidity of concept stocks positively affects the innovation output, but will reduce the innovation investment. Because the annual closing price can reflect the enterprise development, it has a positive effect on both output and input.

Table 3. Correlation analysis results.

	RD	Patent	FinTech	ROE	OCR	Debt	Age
RD	1						
Patent	0.277***	1					
FinTech	0.164***	0.081**	1				
ROE	0.173***	0.175***	0.0140	1			
OCR	0.0360	−0.0180	−0.0180	0.103**	1		
Debt	0.0300	−0.257***	−0.152***	−0.310***	−0.0370	1	
Age	0.074*	−0.129***	−0.0510	−0.070*	0.0120	0.282***	1
Size	0.255***	−0.068*	−0.091**	0.0600	0.00900	0.171***	0.240***
ACP	0.298***	0.082**	0.116***	0.260***	0.115***	−0.159***	−0.139***
TR	−0.096**	0.085**	0.151***	−0.00600	0.070*	−0.192***	−0.163***
	Size	ACP	TR				
Size	1						
ACP	0.0480	1					
TR	−0.096**	0.146***	1				

(*** $p < 0.01$, ** $p < 0.05$, * $p < 0.1$).

4.2 Benchmark Regression

The estimation consequences of the benchmark regression model established in this study, are shown in Table 4. It examines the fintech development level influence on innovation. Columns (1) to (6), they reflect the fintech development level consequences to the enterprise innovation input and output. Control variables were gradually added from the stock level and the company level, to control the different variables impact.

The regression consequences in column (1) of Table 4 present that, the estimated coefficient of fintech development (FINTECH) is significantly positive at the level of 1%, with R&D expenditure as the explanatory variable, and no deliberate control for other variables. Columns (2) and (3) show that the estimated coefficient for the fintech development level (FINTECH) has been significantly positive as the control variables increased. Therefore, we conclude that, enterprise fintech development can promote attention to the scientific innovation, and then increase R&D.

The regression consequences in columns (4) to (6) show that, without controlling other influencing factors. Using patent applications as an explanatory variable, the estimated coefficient of fintech development (FINTECH) is significantly positive at the level of 5%. However, after controlling for the influencing factors at the stock and firm levels, the enterprise fintech development (FINTECH) has not significantly promoted the total innovation output.

Therefore, it can be speculated that, the fintech development level plays an important part in improving the innovation growth of enterprises. But mainly from the incentive impact on enterprise R&D spending.

Table 4. Benchmark regression results (1).

VARIABLES	(1)	(2)	(3)	(4)	(5)	(6)
	RD	RD	RD	Patent	Patent	Patent
FinTech	58.796***	54.982***	64.987***	0.097**	0.043	0.046
	(5.48)	(5.05)	(6.42)	(2.35)	(1.05)	(1.11)
ACP		3.458***	3.081***		0.001	0.000
		(3.36)	(3.13)		(0.87)	(0.29)
TR		−0.067***	−0.050***		0.000	0.000
		(−4.31)	(−3.51)		(0.70)	(0.82)
Debt			67.303		−0.873***	−0.690***
			(1.63)		(−6.65)	(−4.67)
Age			1.617			−0.007
			(1.27)			(−1.42)
Size			0.381***			−0.000*
			(5.58)			(−1.66)
ROE			91.234***			0.324***
			(3.13)			(3.98)
OCR			2.877			−0.068
			(0.17)			(−1.27)
Constant	72.165***	72.812***	−16.041	0.554***	0.959***	1.044***
	(4.14)	(3.55)	(−0.39)	(7.98)	(9.22)	(7.82)
Observations	600	600	600	600	600	600
R-squared	0.027	0.132	0.202	0.007	0.070	0.085
F test		9.92e-09	0	0.0189	1.04e-10	0
r2_a		0.127	0.191	0.00487	0.0636	0.0722
F		13.83	13.45	5.543	13.72	16.60

(Robust t-statistics in parentheses *** $p < 0.01$, ** $p < 0.05$, * $p < 0.1$).

Relied on the less significant influence of the fintech development level on patent applications. We reset the multiple linear regression formula. We reset the variables to take the patent application volume as the explanatory variable and the R&D expenditure as the core explanatory variable to obtain Table 5.

Table 5 convey that, the estimated coefficient for R&D expenditure is significantly positive at the 1% level. It shows that, fintech indirectly affects the total enterprise innovation output, by impacting the enterprise R&D investments.

Table 5. Benchmark regression results (2).

VARIABLES	(1) Patent	(2) Patent
RD	0.001***(6.27)	0.001***(6.88)
CONTROL	No	Yes
Constant	0.554***(15.78)	1.023***(8.15)
Observations	600	600
R-squared	0.077	0.174
F test		0
r2_a		0.163
F		17.97

(Robust t-statistics in parentheses *** $p < 0.01$, ** $p < 0.05$, * $p < 0.1$).

4.3 Robustness Test

Exclude Companies that Have Never Applied for a Patent. Table 6 changes the patent applications to exclude companies with zero patent applications from the sample [12]. A new variable was generated: "patent0". It better reflects the influence of the investment in the enterprise's innovative business on output. Table 6 illuminate that the estimated coefficient of R&D spending is positive at a significant level of 1%. It means fintech has a positive influence in the innovation results, indirectly.

Table 6. Robustness test Patent' RD.

VARIABLES	(1)Patent0	(2)Patent0
RD	0.001***(5.20)	0.001***(5.81)
CONTROL	1.090***	1.207***
Constant	No	Yes
	(31.69)	(9.64)
Observations	384	346
R-squared	0.063	0.132
F test		5.75e-10
r2_a		0.116
F		9.800

(Robust t-statistics in parentheses *** $p < 0.01$, ** $p < 0.05$, * $p < 0.1$).

Adding a New Variable (RD/Sales), the Proportion of R&D Spending to Total Expenditure of Enterprises. Introduce a new variable, the ratio of R&D spending to total operating expenditure. On the basis of the foregoing, the fintech development level is taken as the core explanatory variables, as shown in Table 7.

Table 7 tests robustness by replacing the explanatory variables. The new variables can better reflect the importance that enterprises attach to innovative research and development. It confirms that innovation investment is indeed affected by fintech development, which is positive and favourable.

Table 7. Robustness test: RD/Sales fintech.

VARIABLES	(1)	(2)	(3)
	RD/Sales	RD/Sales	RD/Sales
FinTech	0.036***(6.67)	0.024***(5.00)	0.017***(3.85)
ACP		0.003***(5.01)	0.002***(4.81)
TR		0.000**(2.53)	0.000(0.82)
Debt			−0.178***(-8.79)
Age			−0.000(-0.30)
Size			−0.000(-1.46)
ROE			−0.026(-1.56)
OCR			0.008(0.91)
Constant	0.028***(3.53)	−0.004(-0.41)	0.095***(5.11)
Observations	599	599	599
R-squared	0.047	0.306	0.421
F test		0	0
r2_a		0.302	0.413
F		30.17	32.97

(Robust t-statistics in parentheses *** $p < 0.01$, ** $p < 0.05$, * $p < 0.1$).

And then, use the patent applications as the variable being explained. A new benchmark regression model is established, using the new variable as the core explanatory variable. Shown in Table 8.

Table 8 takes the new variable as the core explanatory variable and the patent applications as the explanatory variable. It discusses how fintech positively impacts the innovation output of firms through indirect impact.

Table 8. Robustness test: Patent RD/Sales.

VARIABLES	(1)Patent	(2)Patent
RD_	1.416***(3.88)	0.839*(1.91)
CONTROL	0.588***	1.005***
Constant	No	Yes
	(14.97)	(7.42)
Observations	599	599
R-squared	0.038	0.090
F test		0
r2_a		0.0780
F		16.03

(Robust t-statistics in parentheses *** $p < 0.01$, ** $p < 0.05$, * $p < 0.1$).

5 Conclusion

Fintech benefits from the rapid development of emerging technologies, is a new generation of intelligent technology in the financial field. While helping the real economy, it will help improve the traditional financial industry system by enhance risk management and reduce information collection costs. This research focuses on the fintech development importance. Through the input and output of enterprise R&D, reflected the enterprise innovation degree.

This paper is relied on a sample of enterprises that have issued fintech concept stocks from 2017 to 2021. Using web crawler technology, CSMAR database and WIND database. Study the mechanisms by which enterprise innovation is affected and how fintech works on these mechanisms. The fintech development level impact to the enterprise innovation is positive, specially to the enterprise innovation investment (R&D). After replacing the explanatory variables, it was found that, fintech affects the innovation output of enterprises by indirectly influencing inputs. After the robustness test, the above conclusion still holds.

The longer the company operates, the more senior management attaches importance to scientific innovation, but most of them are not well adapted to the rapidly changing external environment. Internal organizational rigidity arises, affecting the overall performance of enterprise innovation. Therefore, it is believed that, the age of the enterprise has a reverse effect on innovation.

As stocks that develop on their concepts, concept stocks can accurately reflect the social impact of a "concept". Further research finds that, the liquidity of fintech concept stock is affected by the fintech development, which will also promote enterprise innovation effectively. And for the future enterprise growth, we need to build a fit environment so as to further improve the world economy development.

References

1. Bettinger, A.: FINTECH: a series of 40 time shared models used at manufacturers hanover trust company. Interfaces (4), 62–63 (1972)
2. Carney, M.: The promise of FinTech-something new under the sun?. Speech Given by Governor of the Bank of England, Deutsche Bundesbank G20 Conference on "Digitising Finance, Financial Inclusion and Financial Literacy", Wiesbaden, 25 January (2017)
3. Xue, Y., Hu, J.: Fintech promotes high-quality economic development: theoretical logic, practical basis and path choices. Reform **313**(03), 53–62 (2020)
4. Brad, M., Barber, T.O.: Trading is hazardous to your wealth: the common stock investment performance of individual investors. J. Financ. **55**(2), 773–806 (2000)
5. Zhang, Y., Zhao, Y., Gao, Y., Xiong, X.: Has the launch of concept stocks improved the pricing efficiency of the Chinese stock market? – Take COVID-19 concept stocks as an example. Syst. Eng. 1–18 (2023)
6. Liu, Y., Hua, G.: Can fintech boost corporate innovation? Empirical evidence from listed companies in strategic emerging industries. Jiangsu Soc. Sci. **325**(06), 149–158 (2022)
7. Nambisan, S., Lyytinen, K., Majchrzak, A., Song, M.: Digital innovation management: reinventing innovation management research in a digital world. MIS Q. **41**(1), 223–238 (2017)
8. Li, W., Zheng, M.: Is it substantive innovation or strategic innovation? – Impact of macroeconomic policies on micro-enterprises' innovation. Econ. Res. J. **4** (2016)
9. Wu, C., Zhang, F.: Digital M&A, digital transformation and enterprise innovation. Mod. Financ. Econ. J. Tianjin Univ. Financ. Econ. (03), 21–38 (2023)
10. Xinyi, Z., et al.: Are dividends all for rewarding investors? Evidence from payouts induced by return on equity targets. Account. Res. **406**(08), 107–123 (2021)
11. Xiufeng, Z., Chen Guanghua, H., Beibei, Y.G.: The analysis of the impact of life cycle of enterprise on the performance of industry-university-research institute collaborative innovation. Forum Sci. Technol. China **230**(06), 44–48 (2015)
12. Chun-tao, L., Xu-wen, Y., Min, S., Wei, Y.: Fintech and corporate innovation –evidence from Chinese NEEQ-listed companies. China Ind. Econ. **382**(01), 81–98 (2020)

Resilience Assessment of the South-to-North Water Diversion Central Route Project by Using Urban Futures Method

Qiaozhi Zhang[✉]

School of Architecture and Urban Planning, Beijing University of Technology, Beijing 100124, China
zhangqiaozhi69@gmail.com

Abstract. The South-to-North Water Diversion Project is a significant initiative of China to address water scarcity. Due to the long-term drought and water shortage in the northern region, the economic and social development in the Huang-Huai-Hai region has been limited. The South-to-North Water Diversion Project has laid the foundation for sustainable development. In this study, the Urban Futures Method was used to analyze the performance of the five necessary conditions for the South-to-North Water Diversion Central Route Project under four future social scenarios constructed by the Global Scenario Group, in order to evaluate the project's resilience in the future. The results showed that the scheme had excellent resilience in the "policy reform" scenario, performed well in the "New Sustainability Paradigm" scenario, and had poor resilience in the "Market Forces" and "Fortress World" scenarios. Government-led construction is more suitable for this project, but market-based resource allocation can be improved in the future. In terms of maintenance, two aspects should be involved: resisting social conflicts and preventing river pollution. In addition, the government and relevant departments need to constantly improve and innovate, adapt to the technological development under the new sustainable concept, and timely enhance the sustainability and resilience of the South-to-North Water Diversion Central Route Project.

Keywords: The Urban Futures Method · South-to-North Water Diversion Project · Sustainability Solution · Resilience Assessment

1 Introduction

The "South-to-North Water Diversion Project", which has been divided into three routes, is a substantial and strategic endeavor in China. Located in the upper and middle sections of the Han River, the starting point of the central route project is the Danjiangkou Reservoir. This route is responsible for delivering water to Henan, Hebei, Tianjin, and Beijing [1]. Although China's total water resources rank sixth in the world, the distribution is uneven, and the southern regions are prone to floods while the northern regions suffer from drought. Especially in Beijing, the per capita water resources are only about 150 cubic meters, far below the minimum water shortage limit of 1,000 cubic meters per capita [2].

There is a growing of focus on making our cities more sustainable. However, a short-term focus on implementing solutions instead of considering their long-term performance under changing conditions is hindering our ability to fully reap the benefits of sustainability initiatives. If the expected benefits cannot be ensured during their expected life cycle, it will not only worsen urban problems but also cause huge waste of social resources [3]. The South-to-North Water Diversion project is currently only being implemented, but it cannot guarantee and predict whether the plan can be operated normally in the long term. Urban future scenarios are always changing, if the loopholes in the plan can be predicted in different future scenarios, preventive measures can be taken in advance to reduce economic and urban losses [4]. This research will combine the Urban Futures Method with the project's reality and incorporate four potential future scenarios provided by GSG (Global Scenario Group), indicators will be predicted to explore the loopholes of the South-to-North Water Diversion Central Route Project under future scenarios to improve the sustainability of the plan.

2 Literature Review

2.1 The Global Scenario

Since the end of the twentieth century, global society has been facing a series of serious challenges, including climate change, resource depletion, social inequality, international tension, trade conflicts, and the failure of global governance systems. These problems are interrelated and have far-reaching impacts on global social and economic development. In order to better analyze global issues and trends and provide references for future sustainable development planning, the GSG systematically summarizes and explores global trends from social, economic, and environmental perspectives. In addition, this organization tracks and studies new factors and issues related to the development patterns of different countries and regions. Based on these, GSG has built six possible future scenario simulations, including "Market Forces", "Policy Reform", "Breakdown", "Fortress World", "Eco-Communalism", and "New Sustainability Paradigm" [5]. These scenario simulations comprehensively reflect the diversified choices and different outcomes of global development and provide important ideas and references for achieving global sustainable development.

2.2 The Global Scenario in UFM (Urban Future Method)

The simulations conducted by GSG have analyzed key factors such as human values and needs, knowledge and understanding, power structures, and culture. It is expected that such factors will have varied impacts on population, economy, technology, and governance [6]. GSG's work combines detailed data sets with rich scenario narratives, providing a solid methodological framework for considering fundamental changes in global development [7]. Based on GSG research, Electris and others have provided the latest data for four GSG scenarios, namely the New Sustainability Paradigm, Policy Reform, Market Forces, and Fortress World [8]. These scenarios have subsequently been used as references for future scenarios in "The Urban Futures Method".

New Sustainability Paradigm. Through the adoption of an "one planet living" ethos, a common goal to promote sustainable living and improve quality of life can be established. This principle encourages changes to urban industrial civilization through new socioeconomic arrangements. While local perspectives are valued, a global perspective is also acknowledged. Consequently, new values, development models, and active participation from civil society have facilitated the emergence of a more equitable and sustainable future.

Policy Reform. Effective policy reform for poverty reduction and environmental sustainability necessitates the implementation of comprehensive and coordinated government action. Such action must counteract the prevailing trends toward increasing inequities. However, the values of consumerism and individualism, which continue to persist, often create tensions with policies that prioritize sustainability.

Market Forces. Market forces are dependent on the self-correcting mechanisms of competitive markets. Demographic, economic, environmental, and technological trends are currently unfolding in expected ways. The development of the world is primarily driven by competitive, open, and integrated markets. Social and environmental concerns are considered secondary to market-driven progress.

Fortress World. In the face of resource scarcity and social breakdown, powerful individuals, groups, and organizations may adopt an authoritarian response by forming alliances to protect their own interests. The defense of resources is of paramount importance to the privileged, wealthy elite who inhabit fortresses, while the impoverished majority exists outside of these protected enclaves. Existing policies and regulations may exist, but their enforcement may be limited. Armed forces may act to impose order, protect the environment, and prevent societal collapse.

3 Methodology

3.1 The Urban Future Method

The Urban Futures Method can be used throughout the entire lifecycle of urban development and reconstruction projects to evaluate the resilience of sustainable solutions that are being implemented—from pre-feasibility to design and construction, and then to use, maintenance, and updates. It is worth noting that UFM (Urban Futures Method) focuses on the process—it is about expanding the scope of future risks. The effectiveness of the results depends on posing the correct questions. The Urban Futures Method does not have the ability to directly assess the current benefits of sustainable solutions, nor does it address the obstacles to implementing solutions today [3] (Fig. 1).

3.2 STEEP Analysis

STEEP analysis is a method to estimate the necessary conditions in future scenarios based on the social, technical, economic, environmental, and political factors. Thinking through these aspects may help in identifying a broad and comprehensive set of necessary conditions. Implementing this analysis in a group or workshop setting that includes different professions may lead to a more robust list of conditions.

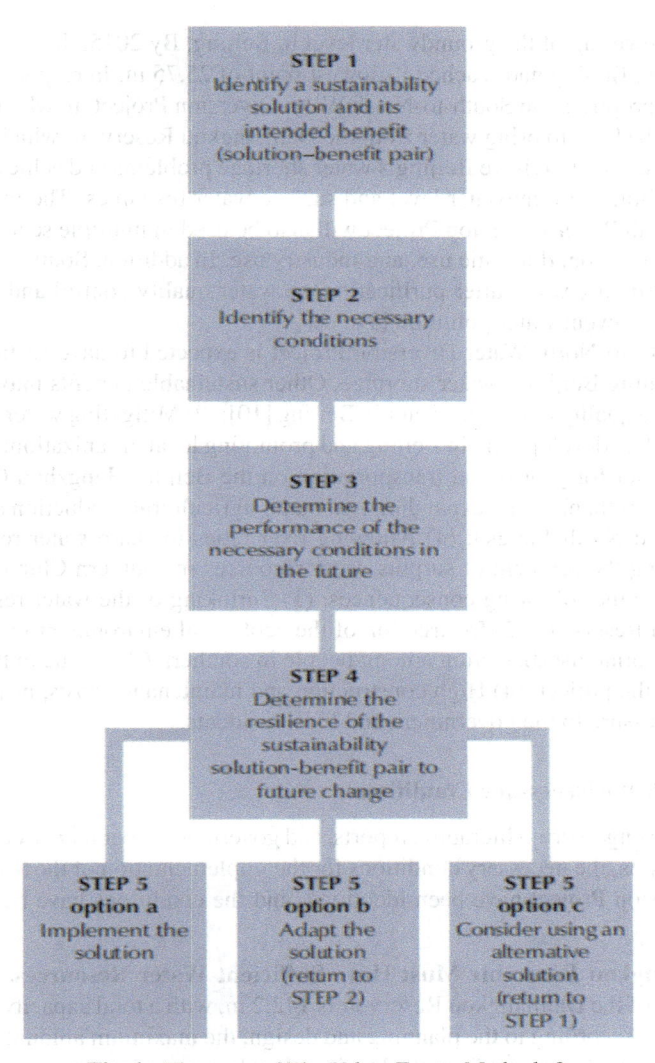

Fig. 1. The steps of The Urban Future Methods 3.

4 The Urban Future Method

4.1 Identify a Sustainability Solution and Its Intended Benefit

The surface runoff in Beijing is insufficient to meet the increasing demand for urban water use. At the same time, due to pollution problems caused by rapid urban development in the early stages, surface water in Beijing had serious water pollution problems. Therefore, Beijing started large-scale groundwater extraction since the 1970s. By 2000, groundwater supply accounted for 67% of Beijing's total water supply, while surface water only accounted for 33%. However, over-exploitation of groundwater has led to continuous lowering of the groundwater level in Beijing. By 2015, the average groundwater depth in Beijing had reached its lowest point of 25.75 m. In response, the central government proposed the South-to-North Water Diversion Project, in which an artificial canal would be built to bring water from the Danjiangkou Reservoir, which is 1,080 km away from Beijing, to relieve Beijing's water shortage problems and achieve the goal of restoring Beijing's groundwater level and surface water resources. The water from the South-to-North Water Diversion Project will also be used in multiple sectors, including agriculture irrigation, domestic use, and industry use. In addition, South water will also be used as drinking water after purification, so water quality control and maintenance are crucial to prevent water pollution [9].

The South-to-North Water Diversion Project is expected to have sustainable benefits in alleviating Beijing's water shortage. Other sustainable benefits may include: (1) Improving the quality of potable water in Beijing [10]; (2) Mitigating water scarcity constraints on urban development in Beijing and promoting local urbanization; (3) Ensuring consistent water for year-round transportation on the Beijing-Hangzhou Grand Canal, as well as strengthening and expanding two major agricultural production areas in West Shandong and North Jiangsu; (4) Allowing river cities to share water resources; and (5) Alleviating the problem of surplus water resources in southern China. However, it may also have the following consequences: (1) Shrinking of the water resource in the Danjiangkou Reservoir; (2) Destruction of the ecological environment in Danjiangkou [11]; (3) Potential dissatisfaction among people in southern China due to the long-term operation of the project; (4) High construction and maintenance costs, bringing certain economic pressure to the government and local residents.

4.2 Identify the Necessary Conditions

After reading engineering literature, reports, and government documents, combined with STEEP analysis, the necessary conditions for the implementation of the South-to-North Water Diversion Project have been identified, and the conditions have been explained below.

The Danjiangkou Reservoir Must Have Sufficient Water Resources. The normal storage level of the Danjiangkou Reservoir is 142.2 m, with a total capacity of 25 billion cubic meters. According to the planning and design, the maximum amount of water that can be diverted to the project from the Danjiangkou Reservoir is no more than 30% of its total capacity [12], which is 750 million cubic meters. During the 10-year period from 2011 to 2020, the average storage capacity of the Danjiangkou Reservoir was 1.3 billion cubic meters, so it has a certain buffer and utilization space for water supply.

Beijing's Water Resource Demand Must Be Greater than Its Local Supply. This is the core reason for the implementation of the South-to-North Water Diversion Project. Over the past decade, Beijing has faced a water shortage where the annual average water supply has been less than 2.1 billion cubic meters, while the demand has been as high as 3.6 billion cubic meters. This has resulted in an annual water resource deficit of 1.5 billion cubic meters [13].

Continuous Maintenance and Protection of the River Channel. The South-to-North Water Diversion Project is approximately 1,080 km long, and some of the water diverted to Beijing will be used for drinking water, so it is important to protect the water channel from becoming polluted during transportation. In addition, basic maintenance of the river channel, including cleaning, water quality monitoring, fault diagnosis, etc., is also necessary.

The Project Must Be Economically Feasible. Ensuring the necessary funding for the start-up and operation of the South-to-North Water Diversion Project is a necessary condition. In this regard, it is necessary to consider the government's financial expenditure.

The Project Must Be Accepted by Society. The social acceptability of the project is directly affected by the balance of interests between residents in the water source and receiving areas, increasing the satisfaction of residents in the water source area with the South-to-North Water Diversion Project, which will help to elevate the social acceptability of the project.

4.3 Determine the Performance of the Necessary Conditions in the Future

The performance of the five necessary conditions under four different scenarios in the future has been listed in Table 1.

4.4 Resilience of the Sustainability Solution to Future Change

The performance under each scenario will be summarized and the resilience of the middle Route of the South-to-North Water Diversion Project will be comprehensively evaluated under this scenario.

Overall Evaluation of the New Sustainable Paradigm. In the NSP scenario, the necessary conditions of the middle route of the South-to-North Water Diversion project perform well. Increased social attention to the themes of sustainable development and environmental protection has helped to restore and increase the Danjiangkou reservoir's water reserves. Residents and the government are also paying more attention to water conservation and environmental protection, thus reducing the demand for water in Beijing. However, as Beijing's water shortage is too large to achieve self-sufficiency in the short term, the impact on the program will not be significant. On the economic side, although the construction investment of the project is difficult to solve under the NSP scenario, one can predict the sustainable benefits after construction, and under this driving force, new forms of financing may be born. In terms of social recognition, people attach great importance to the sustainable management of resources, so they have high expectations for the optimization of resource allocation, which also makes the project gain a high degree of social acceptance.

Overall Evaluation of the Policy Reform. In the PR scenario, the necessary conditions of the middle route of the South-to-North Water Diversion project perform excellently. The government has introduced various measures to limit the excessive use of water resources and control environmental protection. This will help ease the pressure on Beijing's water supply, but the government will still guarantee everyone a minimum amount

Table 1. Performance of Necessary Conditions under Four Scenarios in the Future [3]

South-to-North Water Diversion Project - Alleviating Beijing's Water Shortage				
Necessary conditions	New Sustainability Paradigm	Policy Reform	Market Forces	Fortress World
The Danjiangkou Reservoir must have sufficient water resources	The importance of water conservation and environmental protection is on the rise. Along with ecological restoration around its vicinity, can increase its water storage capacity.	The government will implement measures to limit water usage and protect the environment while ensuring citizens minimum water requirements are met. This could result in insignificant changes to the water storage capacity.	The water storage capacity of the Danjiangkou Reservoir may continue to decrease due to the growth of market demand.	The government will prioritize local water resource management and construction to benefit the riches, and the poor may not benefit, resulting in decreased water demand in the region.
Beijing's water resource demand must be greater than its local supply.	Sustainable water consumption behaviors have become more prevalent. The adoption of high-efficiency water-saving technologies has significantly reduced the demand for water resources. Therefore, the water resource shortage problem in Beijing has been alleviated.	By implementing various measures to restrict over-extraction of water resources and controlling environmental protection, and the adoption of water-saving technologies among residents, the supply pressure on Beijing's water resources will be alleviated to some extent.	The rapid economic development and population growth in Beijing have increased the city's demand for water resources. The demand from high water-consuming groups leading to continued high demand for water resources.	There is high demand for water within the fortress, while water demand outside the fortress is relatively low, which only basically the domestic water. This results in an overall decrease in the water demand level.
Continuous maintenance and protection of the river channel.	The society attaches great importance to sustainable development and adopts sustainable ways of river maintenance to improve the overall environment of river channels and reduce the impact of human activities on river channels through ecological restoration and river regulation.	The government will adopt really strong policies and regulations, strengthen the supervision of enterprises and environmental protection agencies through a deterrent punishment mechanism, and maintain the waterways of the project.	Water usage and sewage discharge are increasing in all regions, while air pollution is also worsening, resulting in further deterioration of water quality in rivers. The government may under pressures from enterprises, making it difficult to maintain the river system.	Efforts will be intensified to invest in and manage the protection and management of river systems, with a focus on establishing effective long-term mechanisms and systems. The military will be enlisted to help safeguard the environment and water quality, prevent illegal acts of vandalism.
Project must be economically viable.	Though the project can provide longer-term and stable profits for future production and development, it places a significant economic burden on enterprises and the government in the construction term.	Considering the significance and long-term nature of the project, the fiscal expenditure will be tilted towards the project. The financial burden will be borne by government finance and state enterprises, and new tax policies may be introduced simultaneously.	Due to the large investment, long cycle, low predictability and rapid changes in market demand, it is difficult to carry out the financing and construction of the project.	The investment in construction and maintenance of the project is facing greater pressure. Additional security investment will be unique to the Fortress World, and the allocation of funds and resources will need to be rediscussed to keep operating costs affordable.
Project must be acceptable to the community.	A highly acceptable solution, as people prioritize sustainable resource management, and optimal resource allocation is desirable nationwide.	The acceptability is variable. Since the program itself is proposed by the government and serves the overall interests of the country, the government will cooperate with a series of official publicity and education to make it widely accepted by the public.	The acceptability of water receiving area is high, while it is uncertain in water source area. The allocation of resources will be more precise under the guidance of the market, and regions will pay more attention to the local interests.	The rich are concerned about the economic benefits and returns brought by the project, while the poor are more concerned about the water supply brought by the project. However, the poor will dispute the proportion of water allocated.

key:
- 🟥 condition highly unlikely to continue in the future
- 🟩 condition highly likely to continue in the future
- 🟧 condition is at risk in the future

of water, so the amount of water in the Danjiang River is likely to remain unchanged. At the same time, the awareness of civil social responsibility will be strengthened to promote the implementation of the policies. The economic feasibility of the construction of the project needs to be considered more carefully, so as not to create huge financial pressure on the government and enterprises. Socially, the project proposed by the government will be accepted by the public through official propaganda and education.

Overall Evaluation of the Market Force. In the MF scenario, the necessary conditions of the middle route of the South-to-North Water Diversion project are very poor. Each region pays more attention to its own economic growth, and is more inclined to use market price to control the problem of uneven distribution of the water resources, rather than the overall optimization of resource distribution. Therefore, different regions' recognition of the plan will be significantly differentiated. The water-receiving areas are willing to accept the supplement of resources, while the water-source areas may question the plan. They believe that the allocation of resources will be more accurate under the market, and faster and more convenient water resource utilization can bring more economic growth than the policy-led remote allocation. The Danjiangkou reservoir's water reserves are likely to decrease as market demand increases, water consumption and sewage emissions increase in various regions, and air pollution will worsen, leading to a decline in river quality.

Overall Evaluation of the Fortress World. In the FW scenario, the necessary conditions of the middle route of the South-to-North Water Diversion project are moderate. Due to the concentration of technology and industry in the fort, the water demand inside the fort is high, while the water outside the fort is mostly minimal domestic water, which may reduce the overall water demand. At the same time, the government will strengthen the protection of the river and adopt military protection to prevent criminals from stealing water resources or damaging the water quality of the river. Therefore, under the polarized social environment, the maintenance input of the middle route of the project is facing greater economic pressure, and it is necessary to rediscuss the allocation of funds and resources to ensure that the operating cost is controlled within the affordable range.

Overall Evaluation of the Four Scenarios. Under PR and NSP scenarios, the middle route of the South-to-North Water Diversion Project performs relatively well, but under MF and FW scenarios, it does not perform well. The main reason is that the government pays too much attention to economic benefits and cost control while ignoring market demand and social environment and other factors when formulating and implementing programs. The project is an extremely large and complex project. If it cannot operate well in the market environment and promote economic development, its role in solving the contradiction between the supply and demand of water resources may be affected. This requires governments to pay more attention to social and market factors in project formulation and implementation to ensure the feasibility and durability of projects.

5 Conclusion

In general, the middle route of the South-to-North Water Diversion project has strong toughness. However, the future scenario is a mixed one that may require appropriate improvement programmes to meet economic and sustainability challenges. Through this analysis, it can be seen that the economic feasibility is the most prone to loopholes in the project. With high investment, long cycle and low predictability, the project is more suitable for government-led construction. But when the scale of the project is too large, the government's adoption of appropriate marketization can also make the project more sustainable and efficient. When the future favors PR scenarios, new taxes and new management positions will be created to achieve a more accurate allocation of resources. When the society tends to FW, the maintenance of the river will require additional security investment; when the society tends to MF, attention should be paid to protecting the river from pollution in time. Although the project has sustainable benefits, it is not a new sustainable project and its competitiveness will be reduced, while the scheme constructed under the new urban concept will be more advantageous. Although the water resources of Beijing under the NSP scenario cannot be fully met in the short term, the project is still competitive, but in the future, the government needs to continuously update and enhance this project, making it adaptable to new sustainable technologies and theories, so as to ensure the sustainability and toughness of the South-North Water Diversion project.

There are also some limitations in this paper. This study used a qualitative method to describe the necessary conditions for the implementation of the middle route of South-to-North Water Diversion project, but there was no quantitative analysis of these conditions. Future researchers may consider using quantitative models to further study how these necessary conditions behave in future scenarios. The models and data based on this study are not the latest. The world scenario model data have not been updated since 2012. These models and data may no longer be accurate and need to be updated in real time. In addition, although The Urban Future Method can be applied to the sustainability program research of various countries in the world, its scenario simulation is based on the data prediction of the UK. Therefore, when studying sustainability programs in other countries, it is necessary to combine local indicator data to build a more realistic future scenario simulation. The conclusions of this study need to be further verified and improved in order to better guide the implementation and sustainable development of the middle route of the South-to-North Water Diversion project.

References

1. Feng, Y., Ling, L.: Water quality assessment of the Li Canal using a functional fuzzy synthetic evaluation model. Environm. Sci. Proc. Impa. (2014)
2. Ministry of Water Resources, People's Republic of China. Why Implement the South-to-North Water Transfer Project. China Water Conservation and Hydroelectric Power Press (2010)
3. Lombardi, D.R., Leach, J.M., Rogers, C.D.F., The Urban Futures Team: Designing Resilient Cities: A Guide to Good Practice (2012)
4. Boyko, C.T., Gaterell, M.R., Barber, A.R.G., et al.: Bench marking sustainability in cities: the role of indicators and future scenarios. Global Environmental Change **22**(1), 245–254 (2012). https://doi.org/10.1016/jgloenvcha.2011.10.004

5. Raskind, P., et al.: Great Transition: The Promise and Lure of the Times Ahead. Stockholm Environment Institute (2002)
6. Raskin, P., Banuri, T., Gallopin, G., et al.: Great Transition: The Promise and Lure of the Times Ahead, Polestar Series Report no.10. Stockholm Environmental Institute, Boston (2002)
7. Hunt, D., Lombardi, D.R., Atkinson, S., et al.: Scenario archetypes: converging rather than diverging themes. In: Proceedings of the 1st World Sustain. Forum, Sciforum Electronic Conferences Series, 1–30 November (2011)
8. Electris, C., Raskin, P., Rosen, R., Stultz, J.: The Century Ahead: Four Global Scenarios. Technical Documentation. Tellus Institute (2009)
9. Management Regulations on Water Supply and Use of the South-to-North Water Diversion Project, Order of the State Council No.647 (2014)
10. Xu, H., Zhao, L., Sun, H., et al.: Water Quality Analysis of the Beijing Section of the South-to-North Water Diversion Middle Route Project. Chinese Academy of Environmental Sciences 2017 Annual Conference (2017)
11. Li, W., Lu, J., Wang, M.: The Impact of the South-to-North Water Diversion Project on the Ecological Environment in Danjiangkou. Ju She (2018)
12. Ge, J., Li, X., He, T.: Study on the Long and Short-term Forecasting Model of the Water Quantity Process of Danjiangkou Hydrological Station. China Water Resources (2014)
13. Zhang, Z., Zhang, Y., Zhao, W.: Study on the Limitations and Compensation Mechanism of Beijing Water Resources Bureau. Journal of Tongji University (Natural Science Edition) (2017)

Research on Factors Influencing the Rewarding Behavior of Virtual Anchors' Fans

Xinran Zhao(✉)

School of Material Science and Technology, Jilin University, Changchun 130022, People's Republic of China
zhaoxr1620@jlu.edu.cn

Abstract. In recent years, virtual anchors have emerged as a new trend on video websites, and their fan-rewarding consumption power has exceeded expectations. This paper aims to summarize academic research on virtual anchors and their fan communities, live streaming rewards, and fan consumption behavior characteristics. It summarizes the factors influencing the fan rewarding behavior of virtual anchors from each participant of the live broadcast process, such as live content, platforms, anchors, and fans, on the basis of an overview of the characteristics of fan consumption behavior and the specific forms of fan rewarding in the live broadcast of virtual anchors. This study fills a gap in this cross-sectional field and reveals that the surge of virtual live-streaming reward is largely attributed to the interaction between the platform, anchors, live content, and fans. The findings have significant implications for the healthy development of the industry, the formulation of future profit strategies for live-streaming platforms, and the enhancement of fans' understanding of reward mechanisms.

Keywords: Virtual Anchors · Live Rewarding · Fan Consumption Behavior

1 Introduction

Since the boom of live streaming in 2016, the industry has seen a significant rise in popularity, presenting both opportunities and challenges. While live streaming has contributed to social and economic development, we cannot ignore its potential for setting poor examples for viewers and even violating consumer rights. The importance of rewards in the live streaming economy underscores the need to examine their effects on industry development and regulation. Furthermore, virtual anchors have emerged as a popular trend on video websites, with fan-rewarding consumption levels on the rise. Therefore, this paper aims to summarize the factors influencing virtual anchor fan rewards, including live content, platforms, anchors, and fans, on the basis of summarizing the characteristics of fan consumption behavior.

A virtual anchor is an anchor who uses an avatar to initiate casting and live streaming on video sites. The main construction process involves capturing and processing the movements and voices of a Nakanojin (translated from the Japanese term for an actor inside a doll costume) in a performance through software to form an image with a complete, independent personality. It can be observed that virtual anchors, as an emerging type of anchor, retain the personality of real anchors but are given the appearance of virtual images, resulting in a compound effect [1]. Virtual anchors are characterized by aerial settings, 2-D images, and background imagination, and their live broadcasts are characterized by interaction, imagination, immersion, emotion, and creativity [2].

Rewarding, i.e., payment for virtual gifts in live broadcast, is the primary source of income for anchors and live broadcast platforms. The 2019 anchor career report shows that 79.4% of users will pay for gifts to anchors in live streams every month, with 28.4% of users spending more than $500 per month. Rewarding is a unique consumption behavior that emerged in the context of live streaming.

The term "fans" can be defined broadly or narrowly, but all types of fans share common characteristics such as financial, time, and emotional investments, as well as a personalized sense of meaning based on their object of affection [3]. In a broad sense, fans refer to supporters of a specific object or person, while in a narrower sense, they refer to individuals who show extreme enthusiasm and display unconventional behavior [4]. This paper focuses on fans in the broad sense, particularly those who support virtual anchors within their live broadcasts.

In the literature review section, this paper compares the research on virtual anchors and their fan groups, live-streaming rewarding, and the characteristics of fan consumption behavior, along with a summary of the specific forms of fan rewarding in virtual anchors' live-streaming. Furthermore, we conduct an analysis of the factors that may influence the rewarding behavior of virtual anchors' fans from four aspects: content, platforms, anchors, and fans. In the concluding section, practical suggestions are put forward to improve the tendency of fans to reward, along with speculations on the future research directions in the relevant academic field.

2 Literature Review

2.1 Virtual Anchors and Their Fans Group

When exploring how virtual idols, as data collections, carry fans' emotions and thus build consumption values, Lu, Xinlei, and Yu, Wen found that fans' deep emotions are actually just laid down by the fact that their idols are anthropomorphic but also at an appropriate distance from real humans. This distance allows fans to freely project their emotions and lets the virtual anchors surpass the boundaries of symbolism that real idols can reach [5].

Song, Chen-Ting, and Qiu, Sang-Kyu argue that in online social interaction, people often feel overwhelmed by the intersection of space due to the high overlap of acquaintance communities online and offline [2]. In contrast, the stranger community mode of interaction in the virtual anchor's live broadcast provides a natural seclusion for the audience, while at the same time presenting the audience's common interests and accepting the projection of their ideal selves through the virtual anchor's presence and symbolic persona.

From the development of virtual idols, it's easy to deduce that people's emotions are gradually changing from being passively stimulated from the objective world and projected to the outside to being actively stimulated from the subjective world and reflected to the inside, which can be summarized as "emotional realism": the formation of an imaginary intimate relationship between the subject and the object is not because the object is real, but because the emotions are real. Rather than describe it as a kind of escape and indulgence, it is a search for a way to transcend the shackles of real-virtual dualism [6].

2.2 Live Rewarding

Reward is a special form of consumption in the context of the rise of live streaming and a kind of recognition by the audience for the performance of the anchor. The anchors show talents and specialties, share knowledge and experience, and satisfy the spiritual needs of the audiences in the live broadcast room, so the latter voluntarily pay for them. The increase in the length of entertainment companionship has been confirmed to facilitate this process [7]. Meng Lu, Liu Fengjun, Duan Shen, and Zhao Yijun derived the main seven factors of information sources influencing rewarding as interactivity, entertainment, attractiveness, skill, usefulness, trustworthiness, and professionalism through quantitative analysis of Python crawler pop-ups [8].

Fans generally do not seek returns but try to get the attention of the anchor through rewarding, which is also an efficient way to show off and seek recognition for their status, thus gaining psychological satisfaction [9]. Hu et al. found that interactions between the two parties in the live room, such as the anchor reading out the ID of the rewarders and expressing gratitude to satisfy their demand to seek status, increased the audiences' willingness to reward more [10]. Gros et al. found that for internet rewarding behavior, socialization factors are more important than entertainment factors, while the former mainly include identity proofing, social comparison, and social identity [11].

In the special online social scene of live streaming, a mimetic social relationship (quasi-social interaction) may be formed between the anchor and the audience, which refers to a special subjective relationship formed between the media user and the media figure. It has been found that although the media persona only performs to the audience indiscriminately, the audience has a personalized, one-way virtual emotional projection towards them that is rooted in their internal imagination [12].

Due to similar interests and driven by social behaviors such as rewarding, communities of interest are easily formed among audiences in live broadcast rooms. Studies have shown that after forming a sense of community belonging, users develop the will to maintain and coalesce the community, i.e., to contribute to it. For example, Shu-Yun et al. found that users' sense of community within a group-buying website in Taiwan, China, helped promote consumption behaviors [13].

In exploring the intensity of live-streaming reward, Liao Li, Wang Xincheng, Wang Zhengbit, and Zhang Jinyan found that the reward of head rewarders would enhance the willingness and the reward intensity of other rewarders, which shows the existence of the herd effect [7]. The herd effect refers to a group of people interacting with similar thoughts or behaviors [14]. This also confirms the rationality of Article 12 of the Measures for the Administration of Online Performance Brokers (Draft for Public Comments): online performance institutions shall not induce users to consume through false consumption or initiative reward.

Through the observation of the virtual anchor live broadcast room, this paper believes that the specific forms of fan-rewarding among them are mainly: (1) The super chat (SC for short), that is, paying to post a separate highlighted, longer-staying, pop-up, eye-catching message. Usually the anchor will read out the account ID and give thanks after the reward. (2) Specifying anchor behavior: For virtual anchors, this is generally a request for the anchor to perform a specific scenario or change the display settings of the avatar (the avatar of virtual anchor Shoto wearing cat ears). (3) Virtual gifts: These are often "physical" items with animated effects that can be chosen from a wide selection in a live room. (In anchor Shoto's studio, gifts from fans are "smashed" into the anchor's avatar, creating a special comedic effect.)

3 Fan Consumption Behavior Characteristics

Academics believe that consumption is a means for fans to construct meaning in their lives actively and creatively. Fans are thus regarded as a typical representative of consumerist culture [4]. According to a summary of relevant studies already conducted in this field by Kang-Hwa Lee, the main characteristics of fans' consumption behavior are as follows [15]:

3.1 Avid Consumption

Introduced by Holbrook, it refers to the consumption behavior of fans who are internally obsessed with their favorite objects and externally show compulsive and addictive behavior [16]. This uniqueness allows fans to distinguish themselves from ordinary consumers and build their own identities. The purpose of this consumption is not external functionality, but consumption itself. Smith, Fisher, and Cole argued that fans' frenzied performances provide a strong support point for the construction of their personal value system and that sharing this lifestyle also allows fans to develop self-and group-identities [17]. Thorne and Bruner pointed out that other characteristics of avid consumption in terms of specific behaviors include: (a) Intrinsic addiction: Fans invest time, energy, and resources to gain emotional satisfaction. (b) Extrinsic obsession: Fans express their fondness through actions, such as actively speaking out in the community and purchasing related paid products and services. (c) Possessiveness: Fans show their fan status by possessing objects related to their favorite objects, and the number of such objects is used as a measure of the seniority of fans. (d) Attribution and identity seeking: Fans want emotional support and a sense of belonging from peers with similar interests [18].

3.2 "Religious" Enthusiasm

According to Pimentel and Reynolds, specific religious enthusiasm behaviors include: (a) Buying, collecting, and displaying: Fans will buy to collect and display the peripheral products of their favorite objects; the products that are harder to get due to limited time and other reasons often make fans show extraordinary motivation to occupy. When they receive the products, fans will display them carefully, just like believers display the statues of their gods. (b) Sacrifice and sharing: Fans will sacrifice other commitments in order to participate in the activities of the community they belong to and look forward to sharing with other members in an enthusiastic and unreserved way during that assembly. (c) Ritualistic expression: Fans of the same community often have specific dress codes, code words, and periods of revelry. These ritualistic elements allow fans to communicate and share their loyalty with each other when celebrating these exclusive holidays. (d) Creative devotion: Fans will actively conduct creative promotion on the basis of events to attract other fans to join and seek the chance to expand the size and influence of their community. This type of emotion-led consumption may deify the fan's object of worship, thus further stimulating fans to escalate their enthusiasm and devotion [19].

3.3 Rational Addiction

A quantitative analysis of American baseball fans shows that, from an economic perspective, according to rational addiction theory, fans' consumption behavior is habitual, relatively stable, and predictable addictive consumption behavior [20]. It is worth noting that this kind of rational addiction consumption by fans is characterized by the anti-generic law of "increasing marginal". Based on the perspective of avid consumers, this is due to the fact that for fans, consumption is an end in itself and can provide emotional satisfaction. Therefore, the marginal utility, i.e., the pleasure of consumption, also increases gradually with the accumulation of consumption behaviors, which leads to the fans' drug-addicted attitude toward consumption.

3.4 Differences and Relations

Avid consumption and religious enthusiasm are very similar in their behavioral manifestations, but the former focuses on distinguishing fans from other consumers in terms of both their external consumption behavior and internal nature, while the latter focuses on portraying fans' religious behavior and psychology. Rational addiction, on the other hand, explains the connection between fans' intrinsic emotions and their external consumption behaviors. Such characteristics of fan consumption behavior arise from fans' strong emotional attachment to their favorite objects and the resulting need to construct self and group identity; in turn, such characteristic consumption behavior provides emotional satisfaction and deepens fans' emotional attachment.

3.5 Summary of Review

The current academic research focuses on analyzing how virtual anchors evoke fans' emotional recognition, exploring the influencing factors of live-streaming fan rewards, and summarizing the characteristics of fans' consumption behaviors from a communication perspective, respectively. Therefore, to address the research gap in the intersection of factors influencing virtual anchor fans' rewarding behavior, this paper explores the influence of four parties: communication content, platform, communicator (anchor), and audience (fans) on virtual anchor fan rewarding behavior, focusing on the influence generated by anchor and fans, each and the connection between them. This is based on the paper's view that the interplay of the key elements of anchors, fans, and fans' rewarding behavior is crucial in the live rewarding process, and they form a network that intersects with each other. This can, to a certain extent, explain the causes of the high popularity of virtual anchor live streaming in recent years.

4 Factors Influencing Virtual Anchor Fans' Reward

Based on the consideration and selection of relevant elements involved in the process of transmitting information through the medium of live streaming, this paper will analyze the factors that may influence the rewarding behavior of fans from four aspects: communication content, platform, anchor, and fans, respectively.

4.1 Content

The characteristics of communication content can be roughly classified into seven points: interactivity, entertainment, attractiveness, skill, usefulness, credibility, and professionalism within the live broadcast, and the relative tendency of communication content among these main content factors may influence fans' rewarding behavior. According to academic empirical analysis, the influence of these seven features on rewarding behavior is ranked as interactive > entertainment, attractive > skillfulness, usefulness > trustworthiness, and professionalism.

The finding that credibility and professionalism do not significantly influence rewarding behavior is contrary to previous research on traditional media, which tends to suggest that credibility and professionalism can play a key role in influencing individual consumption decisions. The reasons for this are speculated as follows: Rewarding is very different from traditional consumption, i.e., consumers do not need to consider the quality of the product and the risk of consumption, so the results of the studies on the influential factors will be different. In addition, the sample live broadcast rooms selected for the study are those of Feng Timo (Douyu: Music and Face), Zhang Daxian (Hu Ya: Games), Sichuan Cola (Racer: Entertainment), and a small pudding OvO (Dragon Ball: Star Show). It can be seen that the types of rooms selected are popular and entertaining, so their live content may be homogeneous and bias the results of pop-up collection. However, this paper concludes that the results of this study still have good applicability to the same type of live broadcast rooms, which include the rooms of most virtual anchors.

Given that the tone of virtual anchors' live broadcasts is generally popular and entertaining, this finding is still of great reference value in studies about virtual anchors. This also reveals that when their teams consider ways to enhance fans' rewarding willingness from the perspective of content, planning live content with interactive, entertaining, and attractive factors will be useful suggestions, which are more likely to positively influence fans' rewarding or provide a sense of worthiness for fans who have already rewarded, building a virtuous cycle of output and income.

4.2 Platform

The factors that may positively influence fans' rewarding behavior in the aspect of platform are as follows: rewards within the platform can be redeemed for sweepstakes participation or other "benefits", which enhances rewarders' sense of gain and willingness to reward; free virtual resources for rewarding can be obtained by signing in or watching for a certain number of minutes within the platform [21], which promotes both the extension of fans' online time and the cultivation of fans' consumption habits; the low starting amount of rewarding set by the platform lowers the threshold of rewarding consumption; and a harmonious atmosphere, a concise interface, and convenient operation of platforms enhance the overall user experience. The active integration of different platforms and synchronization through the same anchor account are conducive to the joint development of the number and stickiness of fans, consolidating their emotional dependence on the anchor and arousing their rewarding willingness at the same time. The platform sets up special effects and viewing seats ("virtual ride" and "guest seat") for fans with high consumption, and when such fans enter the live room, this "special status" symbol is displayed to the whole audience, precisely satisfying their psychological demand to flaunt; fans will trigger animation effects when they reward, which can change the atmosphere of the live broadcast room and even further drive other fans to reward [22].

In addition, there are some negative factors that need to be added: there may be some "hidden operations" in the live broadcast platform; that is, the rewarding is not from the real fans, but from the internal staff of the anchors' team or the platform and other interested parties, to take advantage of the herd effect in the way of rewarding to attract more traffic for the anchor and more fans to pay. This behavior is contrary to Article 12 of the "Management Measures for Network Performance Brokers (Draft for Public Comments)", which states that "network performance brokers shall not induce users to consume by false consumption or initiative reward, etc.". It is likely that the fans' enthusiasm for rewarding will be diminished, and this can even make them resent the particular platform or live broadcast room [21].

4.3 Virtual Anchor

The behaviors and characteristics of virtual anchors can more significantly influence the trends and rhythms of their fans' rewards, and have certain particularities relative to real anchors. This paper summarizes the relevant factors in this regard.

During the live broadcast, the virtual anchor will provide an immersive companionship experience for the fans, which will lead them to form an emotional dependency. Inside and outside the live broadcast room, the virtual anchor will establish an intimate pseudo-social relationship with the fans, which is in stark contrast to the cold and distant interpersonal relationship that the fans may face at any time in reality. Ultimately, the virtual anchors create an exclusive utopia for their fans, making the anchors themselves occupy an irreplaceable position in the spiritual world of the fans, and it is logical that fans will top up their rewards for this. It is worth noting, however, that real anchors can also do this to promote fan rewards.

Virtual anchors always pay attention to the pre-determined idealized persona with meaningful symbols and thus lead their fans to form a sense of identity with them at the value system level. Compared with real anchors, virtual anchors are the ultimate expression of "symbolization". As the purest carrier of fans' idealized self-projection and the ideal object of value system identification, the virtual anchors cannot be successfully transcended by the real anchors in this aspect due to the latter's inherent attributes. This reflects the unique influence of virtual anchors on the spiritual world and the rewarding behavior of their fans.

Virtual anchors will engage in additional interactions with their fans (usually through the medium of language) to maintain emotional ties and provide good rewarding experience. For example, virtual anchor Shoto often "thanks SC" by reading out the ID of the "super chat" payer to show his appreciation, which satisfies the fans' consumption psychology of pursuing status and helps to increase their willingness to reward again.

4.4 Fan

Based on the observation of the virtual anchors' live broadcast booths, this paper initially divides the influence of fans on rewarding into two aspects, as summarized below: fans (individuals themselves and between different individuals); and between fans and virtual anchors.

Fans Themselves and Among Fans. Fans need rewards as an effective means of establishing their self-identities and proving their identities as fans. The act of rewarding is an important capital for social differentiation in Bourdieu's sense as a "differentiating symbol" of consumption, which allows fans to effectively show their own special characteristics and those of the group they belong to, as Baudrillard suggests, in line with people's search for the meaning of consumption in consumer society [5].

Rewarding helps fans gain special interaction with the anchor, which becomes a social currency, a bargaining chip, in comparison, and a symbol of seniority and status within the community of fans centered on the virtual anchor. At the same time, fans create a group identity within this community of interest, which creates a need for fans to consolidate this identity and sense of belonging through rewards.

According to the herd effect, fan rewarding will cause other fans to follow and compare themselves, thus arousing other fans' willingness to reward and may even induce them to reward heavily on impulse [23].

Between Fans and Virtual Anchors. From the fans' perspective, rewarding is an important mode of interaction with virtual anchors. Through the immersive companionship of the anchor, fans become attached to this intimate mimetic social relationship; they identify with the anchor at the level of their value systems and project their ideal selves onto the anchor through the symbolic stacking and persona maintenance of the latter. Corresponding to the anchor's emotion-guiding behavior, fans develop multi-dimensional emotional connections with him or her and then hope to build further connections through rewarding.

Fans take the initiative to "pay tuition" in order to express their inner sense of responsibility to the anchor: to compensate the anchor's labor, as a payment for what they have gained from it or just in return for the anchor's satisfaction; to support the anchor's development, hoping to make their own contribution to the virtual anchor's popularity and recognition in the form of rewarding, which reflects a sense of self-driven responsibility [21].

When the fans' expectations for the live broadcast and the anchor's persona are not adequately addressed and satisfied by the operator, the reward becomes an effective bargaining chip to play a game against the manipulative power behind the anchor. It can be seen that this is the result of some fans forming a clear and rational understanding of the social identities of the virtual anchors and themselves, reflecting a progressive desire for self-empowerment and breaking the old power structure between idols and fans [5].

As virtual idols are still on the rise, questions about their value from non-fans can still persecute fans. For example, some music arrangers use virtual idols as impersonal instruments from the sound bank, which, it is worth considering, was instead the original intention of the development team. To fans, this certainly represents a questioning of the rationality for the existence of virtual idols and the entire subcultural community they form. At this point, consumption centered on virtual idols, such as rewarding, becomes an effective and practical means for fans to prove the value of their idols and themselves.

4.5 Summary

In terms of the psychological mechanism of fan rewarding behavior, the psychological influence of virtual anchors and fan groups on fan rewarding behavior is more emotional, such as emotional dependence, ideal self-projection, status-seeking and showing-off psychology, self-identification, group identification, and the herding effect. However, there are also rational psychological reasons that ultimately contribute to the fans' rewarding behavior, mainly compensation for efforts, contributions for their idols' public recognition, a means to play against the capital manipulation power behind the anchors, etc. This paper speculates that the factors influencing the rewarding behaviors in the live broadcast booths of the virtual anchors are different from those in the booths of the real anchors as follows: due to the special influence of the highly symbolic virtual idols themselves, these emotional connections do not work only in the live broadcast booths as they do for the real anchors, but more outside the booths, within the subcultural communities of interest centered on the virtual idols, and within the ideology of the fans themselves, which may be even more profound than that in the booths of the real anchors.

5 Conclusion and Discussion

This paper summarizes the factors influencing the rewarding behavior of virtual anchor fans from each participating party of live broadcast, which, to a certain extent, reveals that the rise of virtual live broadcast rewarding is the result of the interactive influence of content, platform, anchor, and fans; this paper plays a role in the further healthy development of the industry, the future profit strategy formulation of live broadcast platform, the clarification of the rewarding influence mechanism, and the formation of behavioral consciousness in fans.

Based on the findings, this paper suggests that the following recommendations will possibly help virtual anchors increase their fans' propensity to reward and optimize their reward experience: 1. The anchor outputs high-quality content and emphasizes the need for entertainment, interactivity, and attraction within it. 2. The anchor carefully sets up and maintains a persona to deepen the emotional connection with fans. 3. The platform establishes and maintains a high-quality community of interest, advocates friendly communication, and consolidates the group identity within it. 4. The platform builds a good usage environment and provides a high-quality rewarding experience; it resists false rewards and cultivates users' trust.

At a time when live rewarding, especially virtual live streaming, is on the rise, the existing research findings are still not enough to support its steady and rapid development, and the gaps in the guiding theory still need to be further filled by scholars. As we can see, some virtual idol-related communities or video comment sections are still generally exhibiting controversy and bewilderment, which requires scholars to further explore the psychological mechanisms of fans, guide the public to form healthy perceptions, and lead fans to find a stable home for their emotions across the virtual and real worlds. At the same time, the frequent occurrence of huge blind bounty in recent years, which often further induces violations of the law, also requires scholars to discuss in depth the extreme psychology of the rewarding payers and correctly help the public establish a good perception of moderate bounty.

References

1. Chen, Y.B., Song, Y.S.: The dual role of real and virtual--the evolution, problems and prospects of virtual anchors. Youth Journalist (08), 95–97 (2022)
2. Song, C.-T., Qiu, S.-K.: Digital-real interaction and cyber-clusters: identity construction in live virtual image. New Horizons (06), 54–61 (2022)
3. Jindra, M.: Star Trek fandom as a religious phenomenon. Sociol. Relig. **55**(1), 27–51 (1994)
4. Liu, W., Wang, X.X.: An Exploration of the Frontiers of Research on Fans' Consumption Behavior, Community Culture and Psychological Characteristics as Extraordinary Consumers. Foreign Economics and Management (07), 41–48+65 (2011)
5. Lu, X.L., Yu, W.: A study on the consumption culture of virtual idol fan groups--taking virtual singer Luo Tianyi as an example. Contemporary Communication (06), 75–78+112 (2020)
6. Xue, J.: I love therefore I am: virtual idols and emotional realism. Literary Theory and Criticism **06**, 115–126 (2022)
7. Liao, L., Wang, X.C., Wang, Z.B., Zhang, J.Y.: An empirical study of factors influencing Netflix live streaming rewarding income. Financial Research **08**, 138–151 (2021)
8. Meng, L., Liu, F.J., Duan, S.H., Zhao, Y.J.: The impact of live webcast on audience's willingness to consume virtual gifts from the perspective of information source characteristics. Manage. Rev. **05**, 319–330 (2021)
9. Perretti, F., Negro, G.: Filling empty seats: how status and organizational hierarchies affect exploration versus exploitation in team design. Acad. Manag. J. **49**(4), 759–777 (2006)
10. Hu, M., Zhang, M., Wang, Y.: Why do audiences choose to keep watching on live video streaming platforms? an explanation of dual identification framework. Comput. Hum. Behav. **75**(10), 594–660 (2017)
11. Gros, D., Wanner, B., Hackenholt, A., et al.: World of Streaming. Motivation and Gratification on Twitch. In: International Conference on Social Computing and Social Media. Springer, Cham (2017)
12. Horton, D., Richard Wohl, R.: Mass communication and para-social interaction: observations on intimacy at a distance. Psychiatry **19**(3), 215–229 (1956)
13. Cheng, S.-Y., et al.: Predicting intention to purchase on group buying website in Taiwan: virtual community, critical mass, and risk. Online Information Review **36**(5), 698–712 (2012)

14. Shiller, R.J.: Conversation, Information, and Herd Behavior. Am. Econ. Rev. **85**(2), 181–185 (1995)
15. Lee, K.-H.: Fan consumption and the construction of fan economy. Henan Social Science (07), 72–78 (2016)
16. Holbrook, M.B.: An audiovisual inventory of some fanatic consumer behavior: the 25-cent Tour of a Jazz Collector's Home. In: Wallendorf, M., Anderson, P. (eds.) Advances in Consumer Research. Association for Consumer Research, Provo, UT (7), 144–149 (1986)
17. Smith, S., Fisher, D., Cole, S.J.: The lived meanings of fanaticism: understanding the complex role of label sand categories in defining the self in consumer culture. Consum. Mark. Cult. **10**(2), 77–94 (2007)
18. Thorne, S., Bruner, G.C.: An exploratory investigation of the characteristics of consumer fanaticism. Qualitative Market Research **9**(1), 51–72 (2006)
19. Pimentel, R.W., Reynolds, K.E.: A model for consumer devotion: Affective commitment with proactive sustaining behaviors. Acad. Mark. Sci. Rev. **5**, 1–45 (2004)
20. Lee, Y.H., Smith, T.G.: Why are americans addicted to baseball: an empirical analysis of fandom in korea and the United States. Contemp. Econ. Policy **26**(1), 32–48 (2008)
21. Gao, H., Yan, X.: Factors influencing users' rewarding behavior in online game live streaming. Journalism and Communication Review (06), 108–124 (2022)
22. Yu, T.: Theatre performance and emotional involvement: a study on the phenomenon of online live gift rewarding--an analysis based on more than 30 typical cases. China Youth Studies **288**(02), 92–99 (2020)
23. Zhu, Z., Yang, Z., Dai, Y.: Understanding the Gift-Sending Interaction on Live-Streaming Video Websites. International Conference on Social Computing and Social Media. Springer, Cham (2017)

Analyzing the Reasons of BYD's Low-Profit Margin Through Financial Data

Tianqi Ma(✉)

School of Business, Zhuhai College, Jilin University, Zhuhai 519000, Guangdong, China
sara1220@stu.zcst.edu.cn

Abstract. In recent years, the new energy vehicle industry has developed rapidly. This article took Build Your Dreams (BYD), the leading company of new energy vehicles in China, as the investigation object to explore the reasons for its low profit margin while its sales volume and sales volume are far ahead in the industry. Based on the relevant financial data of the past three years, this paper analyzes the reasons for BYD's low profit margin. It turned out that the issues were mainly due to the high operating costs, the large proportion of R&D expenses, and the high proportion of government subsidies to operating profits. The research further gave reasonable suggestions for optimizing profit margins for these three aspects. Firstly, to reduce costs by reducing raw material costs, operating costs, and various expenses. Secondly, to continuously develop new patented technologies to improve the company's competitiveness in the industry, improve product quality, and increase sales to increase operating income. Thirdly, to make full use of government subsidies and reduce dependence on them to improve the company's profit margin. Through the discussion of BYD's low profit margin, this paper hoped to play a certain practical guiding role for BYD in optimizing the profit margin and promoting the development of the enterprise.

Keywords: Profit Margin · BYD · Operating Costs · Government Subsidies

1 Introduction

1.1 Research Background

With the proposal and gradual advancement of carbon peaking and carbon neutrality, addressing climate change and developing a green economy have become a broad global consensus. Therefore, the new energy automobile industry is a hot industry that has flourished in China and even around the world in recent years. As a leader in the new-energy automobile industry, BYD Co., Ltd. is also developing vigorously in line with market trends. In today's energy crisis, with rising oil prices and increasingly prominent environmental pollution, automobile manufacturers in various countries regard the development of energy-saving and environmentally friendly new energy vehicles as a major strategic measure to improve industrial competitiveness. In the field of new energy vehicles, Tesla, founded in 2003 in Silicon Valley, USA, as a luxury electric vehicle manufacturer, led the development of the world electric vehicle industry, and Tesla still occupies an important position in the field of trams. European countries that have always attached great importance to environmental protection are also vigorously developing pure electric vehicles, and Germany's BMW also launched its first pure electric vehicle in 2013; Japan's Leaf as a result. One of the pure electric vehicle manufacturers, its sales volume is second only to Tesla. However, at the same time, the penetration rate of the new energy automotive industry has reached 30%, and this industry track is very crowded, with opportunities and challenges.

As can be seen from Fig. 1, BYD sold 1.86 million new energy vehicles in 2022, 500,000 more than second-place Tesla, becoming the world's "sales champion" of new energy vehicles [1]. According to BYD's 2022 financial report, BYD's daily revenue and net profit continued to rise, increasing revenue and profit. Behind the seemingly green light, BYD's gross profit margin growth rate is very slow, and the net profit margin is not even 4% [2]. Compared with Tesla, whose operating income is almost the same as BYD's, his gross profit margin is as high as 25.6% and his net profit margin is 15.45%, which is about four times that of BYD [3]. Secondly, 97% of BYD's sales of 1.86 million vehicles in 2022 will come from the Chinese market [3]. The problem of "low gross profit" and market limitations has limited BYD's development. BYD still has a long way to go to truly become a global giant of new energy vehicles.

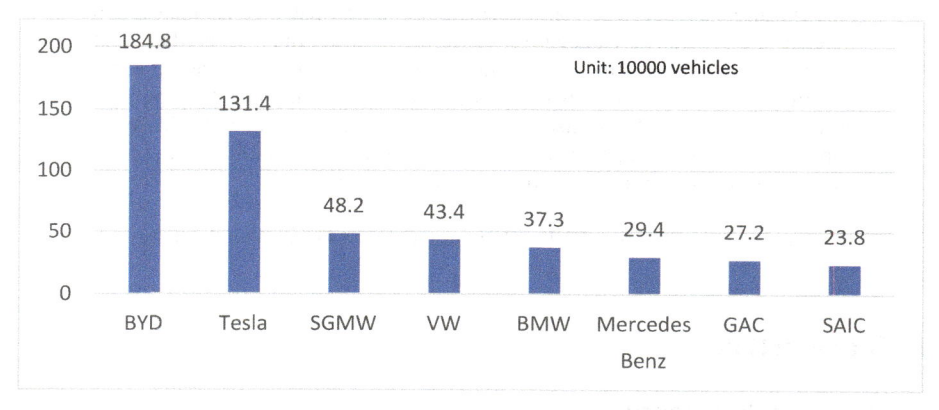

Fig. 1. 2022 Global sales of new energy vehicles [1].

Journal articles have looked at the financial risks and business strategies of BYD companies, and many have done financial analyses of the company. Zhong used BYD as his object of analysis. He chose financial data from 2017 to 2021 and looked at the company's financial status and methods for evaluating risk [4]. Dong looked at the financial risk of BYD's cash flow using three dimensions and five cash flow indicators [5]. Lian introduced EVA economic added value based on the financial index evaluation method and deeply analyzed BYD's financial performance from multiple angles [6].

1.2 Research Gap

BYD's gross profit margin has always been very low, and in recent years, when sales volume and operating income are far ahead, what is the reason why the profit margin is still very low? Although there are many investigations on BYD's corporate financial data, including analysis of the reasons for the low gross profit margin, the latest investigation on BYD's profit margin is also stuck in 2021, the financial data analysis in 2022 is in a blank state, the comprehensive financial analysis for the three years from 2020 to 2022 is also in a blank state, and there is no clear journal paper to analyze the company's operating ability in these three years. The investigation question could be set up as: "What is the reason for BYD's low gross profit margin in the case of considerable sales volume and operating income? The questions studied in this paper are intended to provide a reference for the analysis of BYD's low gross profit margin, in the hopes that enterprises can realize long-term stable development and provide reference significance for the profit analysis of enterprises in the new energy automobile industry.

1.3 Structure of This Paper

To solve the problems and fill the investigation gap in BYD, this paper takes BYD, the "leader" of the new energy automobile industry, as the investigation object and calculates the public financial data such as the balance sheet and cash flow statement of BYD Co., Ltd. From 2020 to 2022. Analyze the reasons behind BYD's low profit margin and give optimization suggestions according to the reasons, hoping that BYD can develop in the long term and overcome the hinderance of a low profit margin.

2 Case Description

BYD Co., Ltd. (Fig. 2) was established on February 10, 1995, and is headquartered in Shenzhen, Guangdong Province, China. BYD's full English name is "Build Your Dreams" It was listed on the main board of Hong Kong on July 31, 2002, and on the Shenzhen Stock Exchange in 2011. In 2003, it became the world's second-largest manufacturer of rechargeable batteries, and in the same year, BYD Auto was established. The company's overall business spans five major industries: electronics, new energy, rail transit, semiconductors, and automobiles. BYD announced in March 2022 that it would officially discontinue the production of fuel vehicles, and the delivery volume has reached record highs. BYD has now formed a complete model matrix in the fields of plug-in hybrids and pure electric vehicles. Such a matrix has promoted the acceleration of BYD's globalization process, and passenger cars have successively entered Norway, Australia, Thailand, and other countries in 2022.

BYD's total operating revenue in the third quarter of 2022 reached RMB 267.7 billion (Table 1), a year-on-year increase of 84.37%, and its net profit was RMB9.311 billion, a year-on-year increase of 281.13% [7]. The total operating income is an amount that has not been reached in previous years. BYD's share of China's new energy vehicle market has further increased, with BYD's auto sales reaching 1 868543 units in 2022, a year-on-year increase of 137.3% [8]. In 2022, a total of 55916 units were exported [8].

Fig. 2. Brand of BYD [picture source: www.logonews.cn].

The company's annual operating income exceeded RMB 420 billion, and the net profit attributable to shareholders of listed companies was RMB 16 billion ~ 17 billion yuan, a year-on-year increase of 425.42% ~ 458.26% [9]. Secondly, the cash flow in a single quarter reached 19.933 billion, which is unprecedented in BYD's history [7]. BYD has increased its revenue and profits, and its sales volume ranks first in the world In recent years. However, the reasons for BYD's low gross profit margin still need to be explored.

Table 1. Some financial indicators from September 2020 to September 2022.

¥ in hundred million	2022/9/30	2022/3/31	2021/12/31	2021/9/30	2021/3/31	2020/12/31	2020/9/30
Total operating income	2677	668.3	2161	1452	409.9	1566	1050
Net profit attributable	93.11	8.084	30.45	24.43	2.374	42.34	34.14
Gross Margin (%)	15.89	12.4	13.02	12.97	12.59	19.38	20.75
Net Profit Margin (%)	3.73	1.36	1.84	2.27	1.25	3.84	4.67
Net cash flow from operating activities	910.4	119.3	654.7	318.7	1.419	453.9	286.6

3 Analysis on the Problems

3.1 The Issues of High Operating Costs

High operating costs are the primary reason for BYD's low gross profit margin. In the economic calculation, the formulate of gross margin could be written as follows:

$$Gross\ margin = (selling\ price - cost)/selling\ price. \qquad (1)$$

Figure 3 shows that during the first three quarters of 2020–2022, BYD's operating costs were too high if operating income didn't change and operating costs went up from one year to the next. This caused operating profit and gross margin to go down. According to the data in Fig. 3, operating costs increased by 12.67%, 51%, and 78%, respectively, from 2019 to 2022, with an average annual increase of about 30%. Among them, it is worth noting that between 2020 and 2021, operating income increased by 27.6% compared to the previous period, but because operating costs increased by 51% compared to the previous period, the profit growth ratio directly decreased to -50%. As a company with a market capitalization of hundreds of billions of dollars, such performance makes investors and the market unsatisfied. The issue of operating costs has been mentioned in many of BYD's papers on financial data analysis. Jiang once pointed out in a published paper that BYD introduced strategic cost management to the gross profit margin [10].

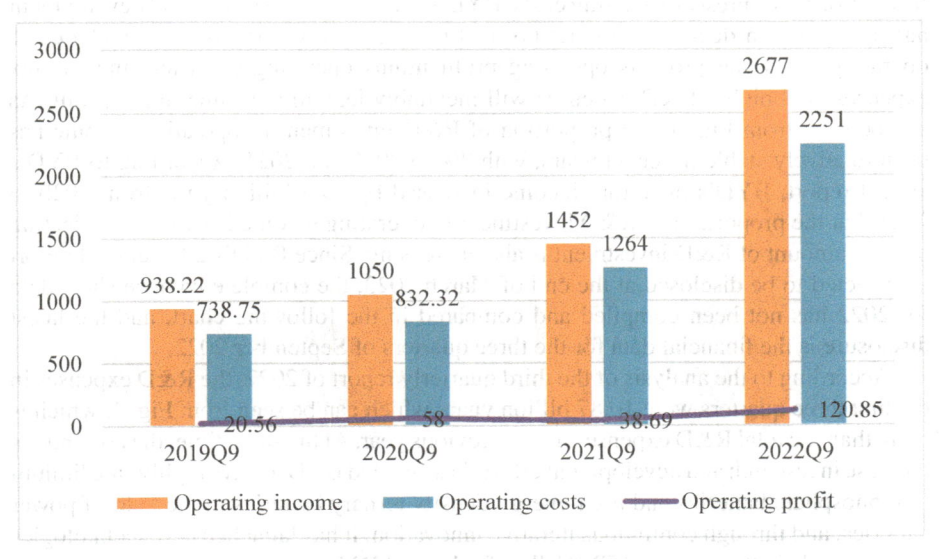

Fig. 3. 2020-2022Q3 operating profit analysis [10].

From the industry background analysis, the price of upstream raw materials has skyrocketed. Raw materials belong to production costs, and changes in raw material prices are directly proportional to production costs and sales prices. Since 2021, the price of raw materials for power batteries has maintained an upward trend. The core component of new energy vehicles is the power battery, which accounts for the majority of the cost of new energy vehicles, and the raw material lithium carbonate is the main component of the battery. Before the price increase, the price of lithium carbonate was still 50,000 yuan a ton, but after several years, it is now 500,000 yuan a ton. To this end, BYD's financial report also explained that the main raw materials required for the company's products include steel, plastic, and other metal raw materials, such as lithium and cobalt, and the fluctuation of their prices directly affects the production cost of the main business. At the same time, BYD is also actively looking for solutions and continues to acquire new mines in the international market. It is worth mentioning that after two years of a crazy rise, the price of lithium carbonate finally ushered in a round of rapid decline. Since December 2022, lithium salt prices have loosened significantly. On January 9, 2023, the price of battery-grade lithium carbonate fell below the 500,000 yuan per ton mark, and the price of lithium carbonate was still falling in February. Data show that the price of battery-grade lithium carbonate fell by 2,000 yuan per ton on February 13, 2023, with an average price of 453,000 yuan per ton. The fall in raw material prices in the new year is good news for the entire new energy battery industry, and whether it can break the curse of "working for upstream raw materials" depends on the operating results of all battery industries, including BYD, in 2023.

3.2 The Issues of High R&D Costs

In addition to the pressure of rising costs, BYD's investment in research and development has also led to a decline in its net profit. Enterprise R&D expenses are included in operating costs, net profit is operating profit minus operating costs and income tax expenses, and higher R&D expenses will inevitably lead to a decline in net profit. As can be seen from Fig. 4, the proportion of R&D investment to operating income has been relatively stable in recent years, with 7% in 2020 and 2021. According to BYD's annual report, BYD's operating income increased by 59.5 billion yuan from 2020 to 2021, but the proportion of R&D investment in operating income is still 7%, indicating that the amount of R&D investment is also increasing. Since BYD's 2022 annual report is expected to be disclosed at the end of March 2023, the complete balance sheet data for 2022 has not been compiled and compared in the following chart, and the latest disclosure is the financial data for the three quarters of September 2022.

According to the analysis of the third quarterly report of 2022, the R&D expenses in the first three quarters were 10.87 billion yuan, which can be seen from Fig. 4, which is more than the total R&D expenses in any previous year. At the same time, the continuous increase in research and development efforts has enabled BYD to have highly safe lithium iron phosphate batteries and high-energy-density ternary batteries in the field of power batteries, and through continuous iterative innovation, it has launched core technologies such as blade batteries and CTB (Cell to Body) and DM-i.

3.3 The Issues of Government Subsidies Account for a Large Proportion

Profit margins have also gone down because of the large amount of government aid. Based on an analysis of how businesses work from the inside, the new energy automobile

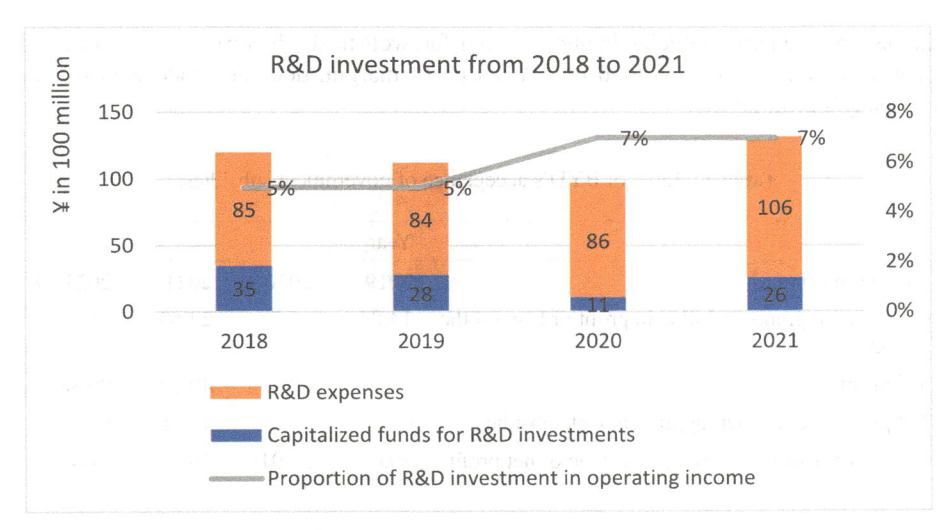

Fig. 4. R&D investment from 2018 to 2021 [10].

industry, especially industries that are strongly supported by the government and are good for the environment, will get a lot of help from the government in the daily research and development process. This will include tax refunds, special industry support funds, and other large subsidies. Through the interpretation of BYD's annual, semi-annual, and quarterly reports, it can be seen that a large amount of BYD's sales revenue comes from state subsidies, and BYD, as a high-tech enterprise, also enjoys the preferential tax policy of "income tax reduction of 15%". As seen from Table 2, after 2019, the government subsidies received by BYD will continue to increase. Still, because the 2022 annual report has not yet been disclosed, only government subsidies for the first three quarters of 2022 can be seen.

As can be seen from Table 2, the percentage of government subsidies in net profit is declining, indicating that enterprises are becoming less and less dependent on government subsidies and their profit margins are becoming more and more optimistic. The percentage of government subsidies in net profit decreased from 70.07% to 27.91% and rose to 56.32% between 2019 and 2021. The reason for the sharp increase in 2021 may be due to the steady annual increase in government subsidies, and in 2021, due to the repeated impact of the epidemic in China, the net profit declined, resulting in an abnormal increase in the percentage of government subsidies in net profit. In 2022, the percentage of government subsidies to net profit in the first three quarters is very small, and the last quarter's financial statements have not yet been published, but the last quarter of government subsidies has no great impact on the overall government subsidies in 2022.

In addition, according to China's national policies, taking into account the development plan of the new energy vehicle industry, market sales trends, and the smooth transition of enterprises, the 2022 new energy vehicle purchase subsidy policy will be terminated on December 31, 2022, after which the licensed cars will no longer be subsidized. Subsequently, the number of new energy vehicle purchases will decline significantly, which may indicate that this "dividend" accompanying the development of

China's new energy vehicles is about to bid farewell to the historical stage. The end of government subsidies, based on BYD's profit margin, does not bode well for the company's profitability.

Table 2. Table of BYD's acceptance of government subsidies.

	Year			
¥ in 100 million	2019	2020	2021	2022Q9
Government grants included in profit or loss for the period	14.84	16.78	22.63	11.4
Net profit	21.18	60.13	40.18	99.88
Net profit after deducting government subsidies	6.34	43.35	17.55	88.48
Government subsidies as a percentage of net profit	70.07%	27.91%	56.32%	11.41%

4 Suggestions

4.1 The Issues of Reduce Costs and Increase Performance

For the problem of high cost, BYD should alleviate the pressure generated by the high price of upstream raw materials through the two aspects of cost reduction and efficiency increase.

Boosting efficiency should come first, followed by improving sales and productivity. BYD, a frontrunner in the new energy automobile industry, overcame a complex and severe external environment to accomplish strong year-over-year growth in new energy vehicle sales, win the world's first new energy vehicle sales, and promote a significant improvement in profitability that can effectively alleviate the cost pressure generated by the rise in upstream raw material prices. Consistently weak demand in the consumer electronics sector led to low-capacity utilization in the mobile phone components and assembly businesses, putting downward pressure on profitability. However, the business segment benefited from an increase in the share of key customers based in overseas markets and, through the optimization of its structure, was able to realize long-term stable and healthy growth.

Second, reduce costs and reduce them through various channels. First of all, continuing to mine the international market, 80% of China's battery raw materials rely on imports, and affected by many uncontrollable factors, import prices are rising. In addition, through technology iteration to reduce the cost of lithium batteries, which account for 40% of the cost of the whole vehicle, and improve energy density, thereby reducing the number of lithium batteries for the purpose of reducing the cost of raw materials, BYD's blade battery has been completed. In terms of technological research and development breakthroughs, BYD has performed well, and there is still room for continuous progress. Hao has also proposed targeted solutions to the problems of high externally related costs, which have reference significance for effectively dealing with BYD's strategic cost management problems [11].

4.2 The Issues of Innovate Technology and Improve Competitiveness

As for R&D expenses, there is no way to decrease R&D costs, and the only method for increasing profit margins is to raise net income. Given that it's generally accepted that automakers should spend vast sums on research and development, BYD, which is a technology-based company, has become the world's most competitive new energy manufacturer with its technology.

Falling behind in terms of technology will make a car company's car manufacturing level quickly lag, and it is difficult to create electric vehicles with reliable quality and strong technology. BYD's current leadership is inseparable from investment in research and development. Wang et al. also conclude that, as the main body of innovation, the core driving force of enterprises is technological innovation, and R&D expenditure is indispensable [12]. For BYD, R&D expenses are expected to reach an unprecedented 16 billion yuan in 2023. Behind BYD's rapidly growing R&D expenses is the whole system at work. Compared with other competitors, BYD's research and development expenses are not much. R&D investment expense will include R&D expenditure in the current income statement, that is, as a costly expense and a one-time inclusion in the current expense, which has a very good benefit in that reducing the current profit can reduce the payment of corporate income tax. Companies with strong profitability like to spend their R&D investments. From the perspective of the proportion of capitalization and expense of BYD's R&D expenses, BYD's R&D investment is real.

In conclusion, it can't cut back on spending on research and development because it needs technology to live. Businesses need to cut expenses to make sure they get as many operating results as possible. This way, they can invest in technological innovation and competitiveness to increase sales and operating income, which increases the value of the business and lets it keep growing.

4.3 The Issues of Make Full Use of Government Subsidies

For government subsidies, reducing dependence on subsidies is key. With the maturity of the new energy industry market, government subsidies will become less and less, which also puts a test on BYD. In the past, BYD's technology research and development invested a lot of research and development expenses, which can be offset over time with government subsidies, but government subsidies cannot essentially improve BYD's growth ability. Too many government subsidies will make enterprises dependent on subsidies, affecting the speed and ability of enterprises to develop. Wang also has the same view in the paper; she asserts that improving the efficiency of government subsidy utilization, strengthening the synergy effect of government subsidy, and reducing the dependence on government subsidy can improve BYD's profitability and development [13].

Therefore, BYD should establish a special R&D fund, reduce dependence on government subsidies, retain talent, and have sufficient R&D funds. These are good goals for enterprises. Concurrently, BYD also needs to make the most of the government-provided subsidies by adhering to strict standards of quality, technology, and regulations, as well as by understanding how the money moves and making full use of every dollar. The need to repay increases when annual cuts are made to government subsidies, and businesses can also seek capital through stock placement, spin-offs, and listing. Duan introduced the implementation of government subsidies, tax incentives, and government procurement preferential policies for BYD, a representative enterprise of the new energy vehicle industry, and compared the impact of different government support policies on BYD's innovation performance, including the effect and impact mechanism [14].

5 Conclusion

With the idea of carbon neutrality and carbon peaking and its slow but steady progress, more and more businesses have joined the new energy industry. This article conducts exploration in the context of the vigorous development of the new energy automobile industry, takes BYD, a leading enterprise in the field of new energy, as the investigation object, analyzes the public financial data such as BYD's balance sheet and cash flow statement, and explores the reasons for BYD's low profit margin under the rapid growth of sales and revenue in recent years. Analyzing BYD's operating costs, R&D investment, and government subsidies, this paper puts forward relevant suggestions for optimizing BYD's profit margin.

To some extent, this article fills the gap in BYD's latest financial data analysis between 2020 and 2022, and the questions studied in this article are intended to provide a reference for analyzing the reasons behind BYD's low profit margin. It is hoped that enterprises can realize long-term stable development, and it is also hoped that this investigation can provide reference significance for the profit analysis of enterprises in the new energy automobile industry.

This article has certain limitations in analyzing data because BYD's complete 2022 annual report has not yet been disclosed, resulting in a lack of completeness in year-to-year data comparison. Because the data was obtained mainly from the Internet, news sources, and corporate annual reports, etc., the information obtained may be incomplete and inaccurate, which may affect the pertinence and effectiveness of recommendations. Therefore, in future investigations, it will be more convincing to compare and analyze the data for the whole year and screen for more accurate data. Secondly, at the limited investigation level, there is a certain subjectivity in the selection of relevant financial indicators, and some other financial indicators and analysis methods may be ignored, which has a certain degree of impact on the evaluation results. Therefore, in the next investigation, combine the industry background and the characteristics of the enterprise in a more scientific way to select indicators and fully consider the impact of various aspects on the profit margin of the enterprise and explore it.

References

1. Automobile vertical and horizontal: Global new energy vehicle sales ranking in 2022. http://news.sohu.com. Last accessed: 16 March 2023
2. BYD Co., Ltd. Semiannual report for 2022. http://www.szse.cn/. Last accessed: 17 March 2023
3. Expound finance and economics: The decline continues, and 130 billion yuan evaporated in January. Is BYD's "big move" useful? https://m.thepaper.cn/. Last accessed: 05 March 2023

4. Zhong, S.H.: Investigation on BYD's corporate financial risk evaluation based on improved power coefficient method. Jiangxi University of Finance and Economics (2022)
5. Dong, L.L.: Investigation on BYD's financial risk analysis and control based on cash flow. Yunnan Normal University (2022)
6. Lian, J.X.: Investigation on BYD's Financial Performance under the Background of Diversified Management. Yunnan Normal University (2022)
7. Qianzhanyan: https://stock.qianzhan.com/. Last accessed: 05 March 2023
8. Securities Times: BYD's net profit last year exceeded 16 billion, an increase of more than four times. https://baijiahao.baidu.com. Last accessed: 03 March 2023
9. 21st Century Economic Reporter. "Sales Champion" BYD achieved results in 2022: revenue exceeded 420 billion, and net profit increased fourfold year-on-year. https://new.qq.com/rain/. Last accessed: 17 March 2023
10. Jiang, H.Y.: BYD Strategic Cost Management Investigation. Kunming University of Science and Technology (2022)
11. Hao, T.Y.: Investigation on Strategic Cost Management of BYD New Energy Vehicles. Hebei Enterprise **396**(07), 59–61 (2022)
12. Wang, C.Y., Jin, J.L., Zhang, J.C.: Analysis of the influencing factors of BYD's R&D investment based on VAR model. National Circulation Economy **2311**(07), 90–93 (2022)
13. Wang, Q.Y.: Investigation on the profitability of BYD based on the perspective of government subsidies. Liaoning University of Engineering and Technology (2021)
14. Duan, W.J.: Investigation on the influence mechanism of government support on enterprise innovation performance. Inner Mongolia University (2022)

Analysis and Forecast of USD/EUR Exchange Rate Based on ARIMA and GARCH Models

Jiatong Li[1], Jiawen Yin[2], and Rui Zhang[3(✉)]

[1] Department of Economy, Simon Fraser University, Vancouver V6B 5K3, Canada
[2] Department of Business, Hubei University, Wuhan 430062, Hubei, China
[3] Department of Economics, University of Washington, Seattle 98105, USA
`rzhang32@uw.edu`

Abstract. This article examines the use of ARIMA and GARCH models to predict and analyze the fluctuations in the USD/EUR exchange rate over the next 53 weeks, based on historical data from 2013 to 2023. The study concludes that the ARIMA model is not well-suited for forecasting exchange rate fluctuations and that the GARCH (1,1) model is a good fit for analyzing volatility in finance. This research provides valuable information for investors and multinational corporations involved in international trade and finance, and can help mitigate the risks associated with financial decision-making. However, this study has limitations, including the use of data from a limited period and the failure to consider external factors that may affect exchange rate movements. This article suggests that future research could focus on integrating more recent data and exploring the use of more variable models to predict exchange rates. Overall, this study aims to serve as a reference for financial investment risk decision-making.

Keywords: USD/EUR Exchange Rate · Forecast · ARIMA · GARCH

1 Introduction

1.1 Research Background and Motivation

Exchange rates are important economic indicators that reflect the relative strength of currencies and their corresponding economic conditions. The USD/EUR exchange rate is one of the most important determinants of the global economy. The U.S. dollar is the most widely used currency in the world for international transactions, and the euro is the second most popular. The exchange rate between these two currencies not only affects the economies of the United States and Europe but also the economies of many other countries that trade with these two regions. Forecasting exchange rates are difficult because the underlying economic factors and their interactions are complex. However, accurate forecasts of exchange rates can have important implications for international trade, investment, and monetary policy. This article used two popular time series models,

---

J. Li, J. Yin and R. Zhang—These authors contributed equally.

© The Author(s), under exclusive license to Springer Nature Singapore Pte Ltd. 2024
X. Li et al. (Eds.): ICEMGD 2023, AEPS, pp. 566–575, 2024.
https://doi.org/10.1007/978-981-97-0523-8_54

Autoregressive Integrated Moving Average (ARIMA) and (Generalized Autoregressive Conditional Heteroscedasticity) GARCH, to analyze and forecast the USD/EUR exchange rate. ARIMA models are extensively used in forecasting and time series analysis, especially for stationary data. ARIMA models capture linear relationships between the past and current or future values of a time series. On the other hand, the GARCH model is well suited for forecasting volatility and modelling, an important aspect of exchange rate fluctuations.

The study first uses historical data from January 2013 to January 2023 to provide a comprehensive analysis of the USD/EUR exchange rate. This article then applies ARIMA and GARCH models to forecast exchange rates for the next 53 weeks based on this 10-year exchange rate data. The main purpose of this article is to provide reliable and accurate USD/EUR exchange rate forecasts to help businesses, investors, and policymakers make informed decisions.

1.2 Literature Review

For decades, economists, researchers, and financial practitioners have been interested in currency exchange rate forecasts. Many scholars have also conducted a lot of research to develop and improve forecasting models, determine the factors that affect exchange rate movements, and evaluate their accuracy [1–4]. One of the earliest and most influential models for forecasting exchange rates is the random walk model, which assumes that the current exchange rate plus a random error term equals the future exchange rate. However, the poor prediction results make the random walk model questionable, the biggest problem is in the long-term prediction. In recent years, time series models such as ARIMA and GARCH have gained popularity in exchange rate forecasting due to their good predictive capabilities. A study by Sarno and Taylor compared the performance of several models, including ARIMA and GARCH, in predicting the dollar/euro exchange rate. They found that the combination of ARIMA and GARCH models outperformed the other models in terms of predictive accuracy [5]. Another study by Narayan applying various time series models to forecast the USD/EUR exchange rate also found that a GARCH model with a skewed t-distribution produced the best forecasting results [6]. They also found that incorporating macroeconomic variables such as interest rates and inflation improved forecast accuracy. Recently, machine learning algorithms such as Artificial Neural Networks (ANN) and Support Vector Regression (SVR) have also been applied in the direction of exchange rate forecasting. A study by Sermpinis and Laws compared the performance of various machine learning algorithms with traditional time series models in forecasting the exchange rate of USD/EUR [7]. They found that the ARIMA showed the result of exponential smoothing, and the best results were produced by a mixed model. In addition to time series models and machine learning algorithms, several studies have explored the application of basic analysis and market sentiment in exchange rate forecasting. A study by Heiden and Klein used a mixed model that combined the sentiment index with a GARCH model to predict the USD/EUR exchange rate and found that the sentiment index significantly improved the prediction accuracy [8]. Overall, numerous kinds of literature show that, in terms of exchange rate forecasting, no fixed model or method can always be superior to other models or methods. Many external factors affect exchange rate movements, such as the choice of model as well as macroeconomic variables and market sentiment. These uncertainties affect specific exchange rates and forecast horizons. By utilizing ARIMA and GARCH models, this study seeks to forecast the USD/EUR exchange rate and assess the fluctuations of the USD against the euro solely based on past exchange rate information for the upcoming 53 weeks [9].

2 ARIMA Materials and Model

2.1 Data

As shown in Fig. 1, a time series plot of the exchange rate of USD/EUR from January 2013 to January 2023, there is no unusual observation, and a downward trend can be witnessed. Also, this fluctuation time series is obviously non-stationary.

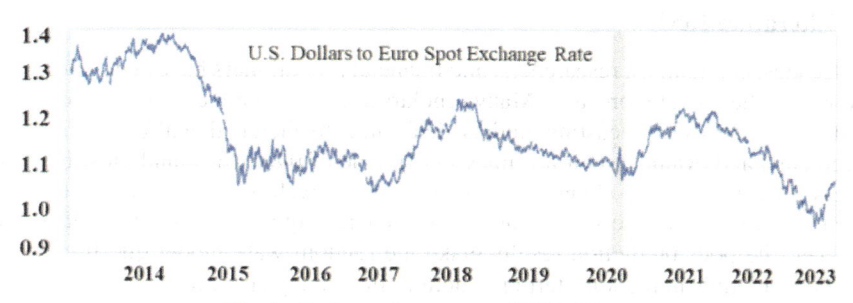

Fig. 1. Daily exchange rate of USD/EUR.

2.2 ARIMA(p,d,q)

The autoregressive integrated moving average model, commonly referred to as ARIMA model, is a very commonly used and popular statistical model for time series data to analyze and forecast patterns in data that change over time. The ARIMA model is a combination of the Autoregressive (AR) model, Moving Average (MA) model and Integration (I) model.

The Autoregressive (AR) component:

$$yt = c + \varphi 1yt - 1 + \varphi 2yt - 2 + \cdots + \varphi pyt - p + \varepsilon t \tag{1}$$

where εt is white noise. The Autoregressive component can be described as a multiple regression that utilizes lagged values of yt as predictors in a time series model.

The Moving Average (MA) component:

$$yt = c + \varepsilon t + \theta 1\varepsilon t - 1 + \theta 2\varepsilon t - 2 + \cdots + \theta q\varepsilon t - q \tag{2}$$

where εt is white noise. The Moving Average component is a multiple regression with past errors, rather than past values of the dependent variable as predictors.

Table 1. Notion of each character.

AR	p	Order of the autoregressive part
I	d	Degree of first differencing involved
MA	q	Order of the moving average part

Integration (I) component: This component models the difference between the current observation and the previous observation to achieve stationarity. To construct a fitted ARIMA model, every parameter of the model should be set carefully. Table 1 presents the meaning of each parameter in ARIMA (p,d,q) model.

The selection of values of p and q is determined by Autocorrelation (ACF) and Partial Autocorrelation (PACF). The selection of differencing parameters in an ARIMA model is typically determined through a combination of visual inspection of the data and the utilization of statistical tests such as the augmented Dickey-Fuller (ADF) test.

2.3 Selection of ARIMA Model Parameters

By using R, these parameters can be determined by auto.arima(). The auto.arima function choses p, d, q by selecting the model with the smallest AICc. The results are show in Table 2.

Table 2. ARIMA(2,0,1) [52] with the smallest AIC.

	AR(1)	AR(1)	MA(1)	
Coefficients	(0.4883)	0.0176	0.7206	
s.e	0.1346	0.0621	0.1267	
Sigma^2	Log likelihood	AIC	AICc	BIC
7.408e -05	1736.28	(3464.56)	(3464.48)	(3447.54)

The metrics used to evaluate the accuracy of a model include the mean percentage error (MPE) and mean absolute percentage error (MAPE). From Table 3, MPE is 97.356, and MAPE is 138.19. The values of MPE and MAPE obtained for the model were found to be very large. Based on the analysis, it turns out that the ARIMA model is not a suitable fit for the data. This implies that the ARIMA model is inadequate in capturing the inherent patterns and trends within the data. For these reasons, an alternative model should be considered for better accuracy and efficiency. The GARCH model will be introduced in the following paper.

Table 3. Results of auto.arima function.

	ME	RMSE	MAE	MPE	MAPE	MASE	ACF1
Training set	(0.0004)	0.0086	0.0067	97.356	138.19	0.6934	(0.0010)

3 GARCH Materials and Methods

3.1 GARCH(P,q)

The GARCH model has two main points. One aspect of the GARCH model is that the random errors are not independent and lack serial correlation [9]. The other aspect of the GARCH model is that the dependence between the random errors can be described by a simple quadratic function of its lagged variation [10].

GARCH model, as a modern model of financial event series, is predicated on the principle of volatility aggregation, which suggests that current volatility is influenced by past volatility. This leads to the concept of conditional variance, where variance is considered in the context of past information. In GARCH(p,q) models, p is the parameter representing the squared residuals while the parameter q refers to the volatility at the time point. Among the different GARCH models, the GARCH (1,1) is the most popular due to its simplicity. To analyze the volatility of the USD/EUR exchange rate, a GARCH (1,1) model will be employed.

3.2 Data

As the GARCH model is utilized in this paper to fit the volatility of the USD/EUR exchange rate. The variable chosen in this paper is the USD/EUR exchange rate, which has been analyzed in the previous part to know that the time series has a large volatility in the index during the sample period (2013.1–2023.1), it is a non-stationary series and GARCH models the volatility, therefore, this paper treats the USD/EUR exchange rate series as follows:

$$RC_t = ln(R_t) - ln(R_{t-1}) \qquad (3)$$

where RC_t is the weekly rate of change of the USD/EUR exchange rate in period t, R_t is the USD/EUR exchange rate in period t, and R_{t-1} is the USD/EUR exchange rate in period t−1.

The following empirical results are output by R studio application.

3.3 Empirical Analysis Process and Results

Foundational Statistical Characteristics. In Table 4 about RC_t, respectively, the minimum and maximum values are −0.0380 and 0.0278, the mean value is −0.0004, which means that there is an overall negative trend. The standard deviation of is 0.0089, which indicates that it is small and relatively stable.

Table 4. Statistical characteristics of RC_t.

Descriptions	Results
Minimum	−0.0380337
Maximum	0.0278041
Mean	−0.0004099
Median	−0.0006133
Std. Dev.	0.008863004

Standard Normal Test. In Table 5, the P-values of the Asymptotic one-sample kolmogorov-smirnov Test and jarque-bera Test below the critical value of 0.05, which points to the that the distribution of the time series is significantly different from the standard normal distribution.

Table 5. The results obtained from the K-S and Jarque Bera Test in R studio.

K-S Test		Jarque Bera Test	
P-value	< 2.2e-16	P-value	1.293e-06

Unit Root Test. Table 6 shows that the results of the ADF test show that the P-value is lower than 0.05, which indicates that the time series is stationary. This can also be seen in Fig. 2.

Table 6. The ADF test of RC_t.

ADF Test		
data: RC_t		
DF = −6.2915	Time Lag = 8	P-value = 0.01
Warning: P-value within the printed P-value		
Alternative hypothesis: stationary		

ARCH Effect Test. From Table 7, ARCH LM-test P-value within 0.05 significance level, therefore, the void hypothesis is disproved, i.e., there is an ARCH effect in the RC_t series.

Results. From Table 8, it can obtain the variance model of GARCH (1,1):

$$\sigma_t^2 = 0.1058 u_{t-1}^2 + 0.8663 \sigma_{t-1}^2 \tag{4}$$

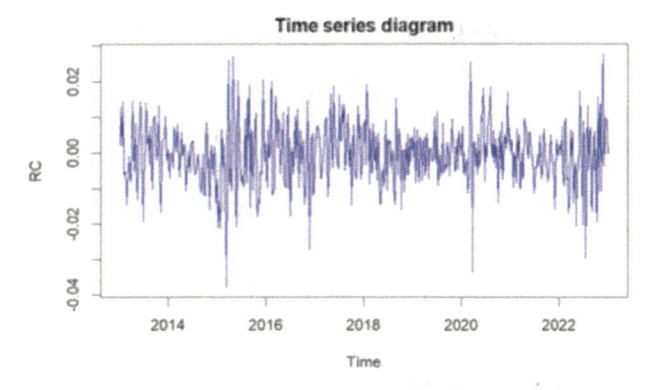

Fig. 2. Time series of RC_t.

Table 7. ARCH LM-Test.

ARCH LM-Test		
data: RC_t		
Null hypothesis: no ARCH effects		
Chi-squared = 46.304	DF = 12	P-value = 6.149e-06

where u_{t-1} is the residual term with lag 1, σ_t is variance in period t, σ_{t-1} is variance in period t−1.

Table 8. Coefficients results of GARCH(1,1).

	Prediction	Std. Error	T-value	Pr(>|t|)
a0	2.529e-06	1.409e-06	1.795	0.0727
a1	1.058e-01	2.491e-02	4.248	2.15e-05 ***
b1	8.663e-01	3.627e-02	23.884	< 2e-16 ***

Note: *** represent the significance level of 1%.

There's a notion of sort of persistence in volatility. As a1 scales between 0 and 1, the closer a1 is to 1 the more persistent the volatility is. And the fact that a1 equals to 0.1058 means that the volatility is more sensitive to short-term moving average contributions. The b1 equals to 0.8663 which shows that today's volatility is greatly affected by the sort of change in volatility from the last day rather than by the volatility.

The GARCH(1,1) model fits well, there are three reasons can be concluded from the result in Table 9. Firstly, the fitted parameters a1, b1 are significant. Secondly, the residuals of the model are not serially correlated. Thirdly, the residual series obeyed a normal distribution.

Table 9. Coefficients results of GARCH (1,1).

Jarque Bera Test		
data: Residuals		
X-squared = 3.2422	DF = 2	P-value = 0.1977
Box-Ljung Test		
data: Residual Sum of Squares		
$X^2 = 0.1613$	DF = 1	P-value = 0.688

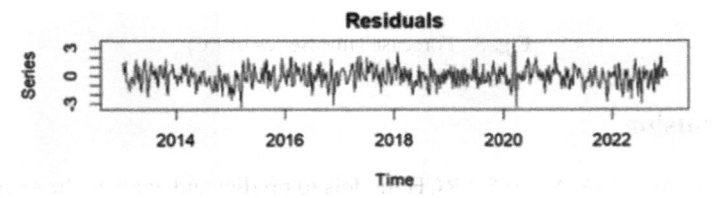

Fig. 3. Time Series of residuals.

From Fig. 3 and Fig. 4, there is no obvious trend in the residual plot, the residuals fluctuate more randomly, and the auto-correlation plot converges quickly, which indicates that the GARCH(1,1) model works well.

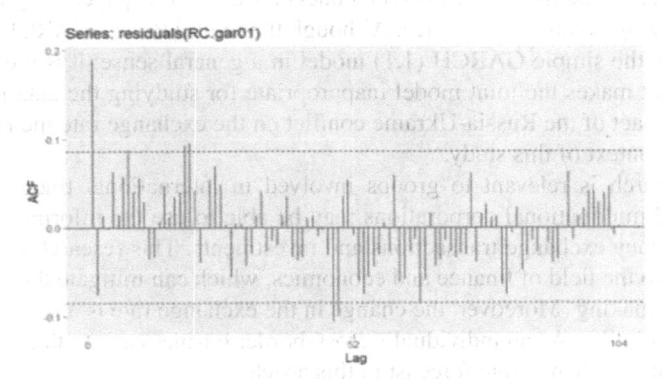

Fig. 4. ACF of residuals.

Forecasting of GARCH (1,1). As shown from Fig. 5, the forecasts of exchange rate volatility in the next year generally have similar characteristics of continuous fluctuations as the historical exchange rate volatility. The different color areas correspond to different confidence intervals, and the size of the confidence interval corresponds to the size of the area in the Fig. 5.

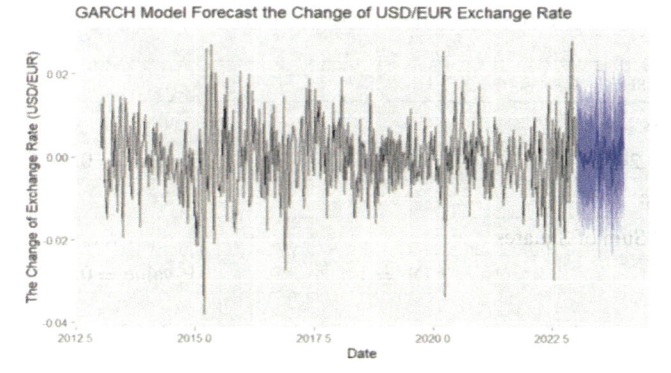

Fig. 5. Forecast Time Series of RC_t.

4 Conclusion

This article uses ARIMA and GARCH models to predict and analyze the exchange rate changes of USD/EUR in the next 53 weeks based on historical data from 2013 to 2023. Although the ARIMA model is widely used in many fields to forecast future values, identify trends, and detect seasonality in the data, it can be concluded that the ARIMA model is not well fitted for forecasting exchange rate fluctuations of USD/EUR. The high values of MPE and MAPE indicate that the model's forecasts deviate significantly from the actual values, indicating poor performance. The GARCH model fits the data well in this paper, and the GARCH (1,1) model chosen for this paper is a good model to use for analyzing volatility in finance. Although the joint ARIMA-GARCH model may fit better than the simple GARCH (1,1) model in a general sense, it is the presence of this factor that makes the joint model inappropriate for studying the data in this paper due to the impact of the Russia-Ukraine conflict on the exchange rate mentioned in the background context of this study.

This research is relevant to groups involved in international trade and finance. Investors and multinational corporations may be able to use the information provided here for currency exchange transactions and investments. This research makes a small contribution to the field of finance and economics, which can mitigate the risk of financial decision-making. Moreover, the change in the exchange rate is also closely related to people's daily life. As an individual's cross-border business asset allocation, you can also refer to the exchange rate forecast in this article.

However, this study has many limitations. First of all, the data used in this article is limited to the period from January 2013 to January 2023, and the data of only ten years may not fully reflect the overall market conditions. In addition, the study's forecasting model is only based on exchange rate data and does not consider other factors that may affect exchange rate movements. External factors such as wars, inflation, interest rate changes, global epidemics, and policy adjustments may affect currency exchange rate changes. Future research in this area could focus on integrating more recent data and exploring the use of more variable models to predict exchange rates. Overall, this article aims to provide valuable insights and references for the exchange rate of the US dollar to the euro, hoping to become a reference tool in financial investment risk decision-making.

References

1. Jonathan, F.P.: Exchange rate forecasting with advanced machine learning methods. J. Risk Financial Manag. **15**, 2 (2022)
2. Florian, M.: Analyst forecasts and currency markets. SSRN Electronic Journal (2020)
3. Alfred, H.W., Richard, A.H.: Volatility smile and one-month foreign currency volatility forecasts, Inc. Jrl Fut Mark. **37**, 3 (2016)
4. Piotr, L.: Low and high prices can improve covariance forecasts: the evidence based on currency rates. J. Forecast. **37**, 6 (2018)
5. Sarno, L., Taylor, M., Frankel, J.: Currency unions, pegged exchange rates and target zone models. In: the Economics of Exchange Rates 170–201 (2003)
6. Narayan, P.K.: Estimating exchange rate responsiveness to shocks. Review of Financial Economics **17**, 4 (2008)
7. Sermpinis, G., Laws, J., Karathanasopoulos, A., Dunis, C.L.: Forecasting and trading the EUR/USD exchange rate with gene expression and psi sigma neural networks. Expert Syst. Appl. **39**, 10 (2012)
8. Heiden, S., Klein, C., Zwergel, B.: Beyond fundamentals: Investor sentiment and exchange rate forecasting. Eur. Financ. Manag. **19**, 3 (2013)
9. Dhinakaran, K., Divya, J., Indhumathi, C., Asha, R.: Cryptocurrency exchange rate prediction using ARIMA Model on Real Time Data. IEEE 914–917 (2022)
10. Bollerslev, T.: Generalized autoregressive conditional heteroscedasticity. Journal of Econometrics **31**(3), 307–327 (1986)

Forecasts on Euro-to-USD Exchange Rate Based on the ARIMA Model

Qiaoyu Xie(✉)

IBSS, Xi'an Jiaotong-Liverpool University (XJTLU), Suzhou 215028, China
`Qiaoyu.XIE20@student.xjtlu.edu.cn`

Abstract. In the past few years, the Euro-to-USD exchange rate fluctuated significantly. Especially during periods of the Russia-Ukraine conflict and the European energy crisis. Since 2021, a clear downward trend in the USD/EUR exchange rate has been witnessed. This rate reached a historically low of 0.9616 on September 27, 2022. In 2023, the rate bounced back slightly to around $1.07 for the moment. The Euro-to-USD exchange rate forecast is conducted in this paper. Data from the Federal Reserve was applied as the training data. ARIMA models were constructed in R to do the predictions with examinations. Both the seasonal ARIMA model and the non-seasonal ARIMA model provided similar results. The Euro-to-USD exchange rate was predicted to maintain at 1.06 for the next eight weeks. The fluctuations of the predicted time series were within 0.01. Exchange rates are critical in the economy worldwide as International trade, investment activity, fiscal and monetary policy are all closely related to exchange rates. This research paper aims at providing forecasting results for both investors and policy-makers. Ideally, they can be inspired to adjust their strategies and contribute to a better economic environment.

Keywords: Forecast · Euro-to-USD Exchange Rate · ARIMA

1 Introduction

The Euro and the USD have inched closer to parity in recent years. The Euro-to-USD exchange rate fell below parity in September, 2022 for the first time in two decades before slowly recovering. The Euro fell below one to the dollar shortly after its creation in 1999, but as its international usage grew rapidly, it rose above the dollar since 2002.

In terms of foreign trade, the relative increase in the purchasing power of US dollar can promote the export of European goods and improve the international balance of payments of EU countries. Furthermore, it is relatively cheaper for Americans to travel and study in Europe, which is conducive to promoting the development of European service industries such as tourism and education. For US, the cost of importing most industrial raw materials from Europe will decrease. The enhanced ability of American people to invest abroad will help the United States to buy high-quality assets in Europe, such as finance and real estate investment, or taking advantage of the purchasing power of the dollar to invest in some advanced manufacturing and service industries in Europe.

There are two arguments that might explain this phenomenon. Firstly, the dollar has strengthened on risk aversion as investors have turned to traditional safe assets, concerning the conflict in Ukraine, supply chain obstacles, rocketing inflation, sluggish economic growth, and tighter monetary policy in Euro zones. Secondly, the narrowing of the gap between the two currencies is also due to differences in monetary policy among central banks. The Fed has been raising rates for the past year. In stark contrast to the US Federal Reserve, the European Central Bank has been slow to raise interest rates despite record inflation in the Eurozone.

The deteriorating terms of trade in the Eurozone, a slowing global economy, and increased turbulence ahead have made the Euro more vulnerable to fiscal tightening by the fragility of peripheral bond markets, further fuelling the argument for a weaker Euro. Excessive Euro weakness threatens price stability in the Euro area, increases the cost of dollar-denominated imports and commodities, and further exacerbates already high price pressures in the Euro area. A break below parity signals an imminent recession in the Eurozone and a more negative impact on trade from the energy crisis. In addition, a weaker Euro could make assets such as equities less attractive. At the margin, this will make Europe less attractive. A sharp fall in currencies, a proxy for confidence in a country, is a warning sign for foreign investors. The motivation for this paper is to examine the future trend of the Euro-to-USD exchange rate and provide some potential suggestions based on the forecasting model applied.

There has been abundant research on Euro-to-USD exchange forecasting. In previous practice, structural exchange rate models performed badly. As technology developed, positive short-term forecasting results by innovative estimation frames, panel forecasting, better out-of-sample test statistics and models with new structures were reported. The predictor, sample period, forecast horizon, model, and forecast evaluation method were all factors to judge the predictability of the model [1, 2]. The exchange rate was rendered to be stochastic, and technical analysis and time series procedures became key roles in exchange rate forecasting. In one research, economic theory was introduced through a chaotic model. Generally, minuscule evidence of chaotic dynamics in economic time series was found [3]. In another research, the FAVAR framework was applied. It improved forecasting accuracy through the expanded information set of the VAR models, which were widely applied before. A flexible model was constructed so that money demand instability and structural breaks in the data were adjusted. For all forecasting horizons, other structural models and the Random Walk were outperformed by the specified models [4].

A hybrid model using a neural network was developed to make volatility forecasting of better accuracy. To improve the results, the GARCH model with calibrations is used [5]. In a comparative research, Recurrent Neural Network (RNN) of the Elman type, Autoregressive Integrated Moving Average (ARIMA), and Long Short-Term Memory (LSTM) models were constructed to predict the Euro-to-USD exchange rate with several forecasting periods. It was found that in the short forecasting period, LSTM was the best forecast model; while Elman fitted the long term forecast best [6]. A linear econometric error correction model (ECM) model was also constructed with the goal of describing the dynamics of the euro-to-dollar exchange rate and offering accurate forecasts. It was based on estimates for GDP growth, short interest rates, and inflation differentials. It was found that for fitting in-sample and out-of-sample, the non-linear model performed better than its linear version [7].

For this paper, the method to construct the model is introduced at first. Then ARIMA models are constructed in R with examinations and comparisons. After passing serval tests, forecast on the Euro-to-USD exchange rate by these models are conducted with interpretations. Discussions on these results and advice are provided. Finally, a conclusion is made to reemphasize this paper's main ideas.

2 Method

Firstly, the data was collected from the FDR website (https://fred.stlouisfed.org/) as a reliable source of information [8]. On this website, the time period and frequency of the Euro-to-USD exchange rate series can be freely adjusted. The Euro-to-USD exchange rate on a weekly basis for ten years from January, 2013 to January, 2023 was selected as training data in this article. These choices of time range and frequency are common in exchange rate research.

A downward trend of the Euro-to-USD exchange rate can be witnessed in Fig. 1. Moreover, there appeared to be a seasonal pattern. Initially, the rate was at a high of over 1.3 in January, 2013. Then it decreased with some fluctuations in the next decade. It was noticeable that the rate dropped below 1 and then bounced back in the last quarter of 2022. On September 27, 2022, a trough of 0.96 was witnessed. Moving into 2023, the exchange rate increased slightly to around 1.07 currently, which is still regarded as a relatively low value in Euro-to-USD exchange rate history.

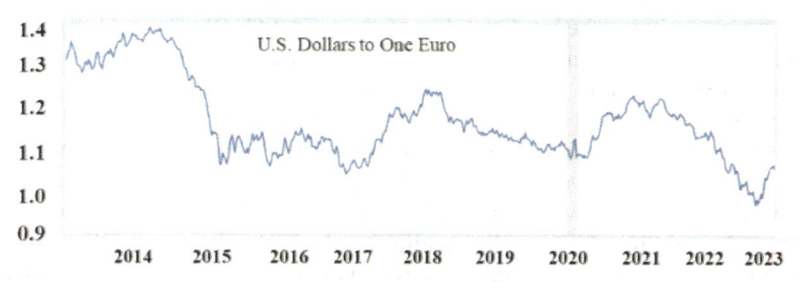

Fig. 1. Euro-to-USD exchange rate Source: Board of Governors of the Federal Reserve System (https://fred.stlouisfed.org/)

To implement a forecast on the Euro-to-USD exchange rate, an ARIMA model is applied in this paper. Autoregressive integrated moving average, or ARIMA, combines autoregression, differencing, and a moving average model. The same stationarity and invertibility are required by ARIMA models as autoregressive and moving average models [9]. Its mathematical formula is expressed as Eq. (1). The interpretation of the reference in the formula is shown in Table 1.

$$y'_t = c + \phi_1 y'_{t-1} + \cdots + \phi_p y'_{t-p} + \theta_1 \varepsilon_{t-1} + \cdots + \theta_q \varepsilon_{t-q} + \varepsilon_t \tag{1}$$

Table 1. Parameters of the ARIMA mathematical formula

Parameter	Interpretation
y'_t	value at time t
c	constant
p	order of the autoregressive part
d	degree of first differencing involved
q	order of the moving average part
ε	disturbance of the series
ϕ, θ	parameters for the model

With backshift notation b, ARIMA is in the form of:

$$(1 - \phi_1 b - \cdots - \phi_p b^p)(1-b)^d y_t = c + (1 + \theta_1 b + \cdots + \theta_q b^q)\varepsilon_t \qquad (2)$$

In real practice, the R process ARIMA model as:

$$(1 - \phi_1 b - \cdots - \phi_p b^p)(y'_t - \mu) = (1 + \theta_1 b + \cdots + \theta_q b^q)\varepsilon_t \qquad (3)$$

$$y'_t = (1-b)dy_t \qquad (4)$$

and μ is the mean of y'_t, set

$$c = \mu(1 - \phi_1 - \cdots - \phi_p) \qquad (5)$$

In real practice, several steps above are complemented in R to acquire the final ARIMA model. The following content will strictly conform the standard procedures through the assistance of R [9].

3 Result

Figure 2 depicts several abrupt shifts, especially the significant decline from 2014 to 2015. The changes in the European economic climate are mostly to blame for these shifts. Other than that, the time plot contains no outliers. This time series is obviously not stationary because it continuously moves up and down.

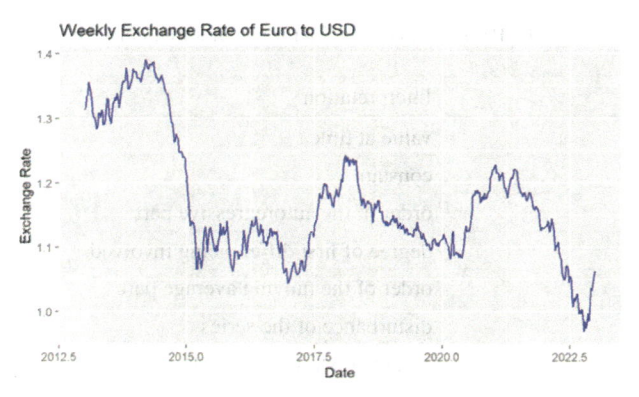

Fig. 2. Weekly exchange rate of euro to USD

Consequently, a series with first order differentiation is used as Fig. 3.

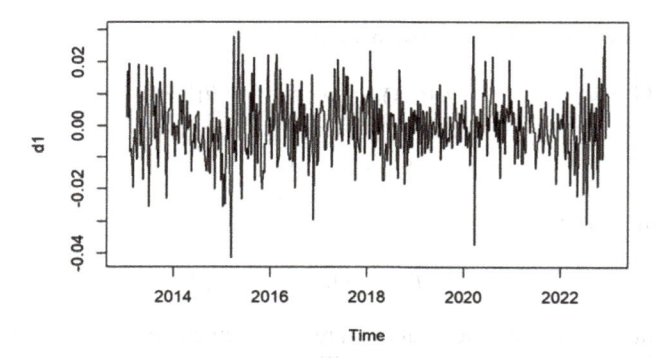

Fig. 3. First differenced time series

After taking the first difference, the time series is concluded to be stationary through Augmented Dickey-Fuller Test. From Table 2, the P-value of this test is 0.01, proving it is statistically significant to accept the alternative hypothesis that the series is stationary instead of the null hypothesis (Table 2).

Table 2. ADF test

Augmented Dickey-Fuller Test		
Lag order = 8	Dickey-Fuller value = −6.2482	p-value = 0.01
Null hypothesis: nonstationary Alternative hypothesis: stationary		

In the standard model selection frame, the next step is done by R through the auto-ARIMA function. This function uses the Hyndman-Khandakar algorithm with a variation. It mixes minimisation of the AICc, unit root tests and MLE to obtain a best-fitted ARIMA model [10].

Table 3. Seasonal ARIMA model

ARIMA (1,1,1) (1,0,0) [52]				
Coefficients	AR (1)	MA (1)	SAR (1)	
	(0.4318)	0.6640	0.0046	
Standard error	0.1320	0.1107	0.0480	
Sigma squared	Log likelihood	AIC	AICc	BIC
9.644e−05	1667.72	(3327.4)	(3327.3)	(3310.4)

The best ARIMA model is generated as Table 3. It is suggested that p, d and q are all 1. Moreover, a seasonal pattern is uncovered with P equals 1, D and Q both equal 0. Fifty-two describes the frequency of the seasonal part.

Table 4. Ljung-Box test

Ljung-Box test		
Data: Residuals from ARIMA(1,1,1)(1,0,0) [52]		
Q* = 88.901	df = 101	p-value = 0.799
Model df: 3		Total lags used: 104

Table 4 shows the residuals have no remaining autocorrelations. From Fig. 4, the ACF plot of the residuals from the ARIMA (1,1,1) (1,0,0) with weekly frequency model depicts that all autocorrelation values are smaller than threshold limits. Thus, the residuals are concluded to be white noise. The last graph in Fig. 4 depicts the randomness of the residuals since they fit the normal distribution well. In summary, the ARIMA model passes tests successfully and there is no systematic bias within the model.

The math expression of this ARIMA model is formula (6), the results of point forecast and confidence intervals from the seasonal ARIMA model are show in Fig. 5 and Table 5.

$$(1 - \phi_1 B)(1 - \Phi_1 B_{52})(1 - B)yt = (1 + \theta_1 B)\varepsilon t \qquad (6)$$

In alignment with previous observations of the Euro-to-USD exchange rate plot, seasonality is discovered by the Hyndman-Khandakar algorithm from R in selecting the best fitting model.

This seasonal part illustrates that the regression against itself is at the first order. Basically, it figures out the connection between the Euro-to-USD exchange rate of one

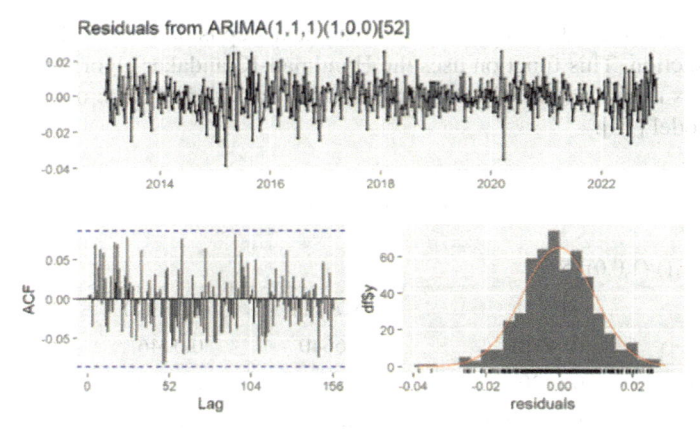

Fig. 4. Residual plots

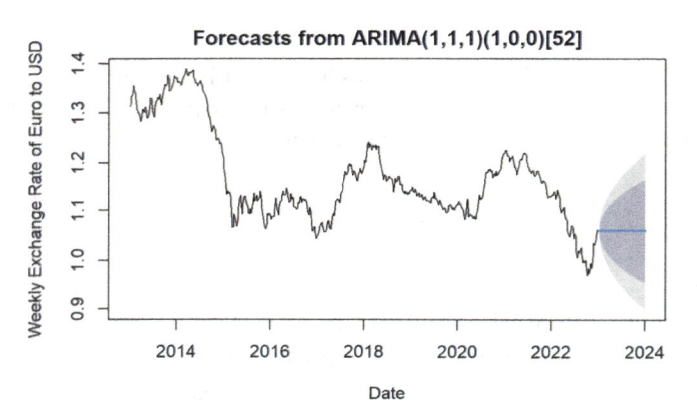

Fig. 5. Forecasts from the seasonal ARIMA model

week and the next year's counterpart (P = 1). This seasonal ARIMA model might be controversial under further analysis, which will be discussed later. D and Q are zero in the seasonal part of the model.

The normal part of the ARIMA model suggests that to keep the time series stationary, first-order differencing is necessary (d = 1). In addition, in the auto-regression part, the next week's value is calculated through a linear combination of the past week's exchange rate and some constant (p = 1). The moving average part uses a one-period past error to forecast the future values (q = 1).

The forecast from the ARIMA model indicates that the Euro-to-USD exchange rate is approximately 1.06 USD to 1 Euro for the next year starting from January 2023. The line consists of future point forecasts that almost levels out since the beginning of the forecast period. The fluctuations of the forecast values are within 0.01. The shaded areas represent 80% and 95% confidence intervals. Compared to the stableness of the point forecasts, these interval forecasts offer relatively large fluctuations. The range of 80%

Table 5. Point Forecast and confidence intervals from the seasonal ARIMA model

week	Point Value of Forecasting	Low 80	High 80	Low 95	High 95
1	1.059740	1.047155	1.072325	1.040492	1.078988
2	1.060432	1.040459	1.080404	1.029887	1.090977
3	1.060169	1.035637	1.084702	1.022650	1.097689
4	1.060272	1.031625	1.088919	1.016461	1.104083
5	1.060167	1.028035	1.092300	1.011025	1.109310
6	1.060233	1.024916	1.095551	1.006219	1.114247
7	1.060273	1.022051	1.098495	1.001818	1.118728
8	1.060238	1.019311	1.101165	0.997645	1.122830

confidence interval is 0.96 to 1.16. This can be interpreted as there is an 80% chance that the next year's Euro-to-USD exchange rate will fall in this interval. Similarly, it is 95% confident that the next year's Euro-to-USD exchange rate will be between 0.90 and 1.22.

4 Discussion

The ARIMA model suggests that the Euro-to-USD exchange rate will stay in the neighborhood of 1.06 in the following year from January 2023. It is not likely to bounce back continuously as in the past few months. However, it also reveals the unlikelihood that the exchange rate will continue to go down as the general trend of the past ten years. The exchange rate will maintain its current position with tiny fluctuations except for some sudden events that occur which is not included by the forecasting model.

Less precisely but more practically, the confidence intervals also provide useful information. The future exchange rate actually may take any value within these intervals with certain probabilities or even beyond these intervals. However, the range of the 95 % confidence interval is 1.00 to 1.12, the volatility of the exchange rate is predicted to be quite limited.

In addition, the unanticipated seasonal part of the ARIMA model is worth further discussion. The coefficient P of the seasonal model is 0.0046. However, its standard error is more than ten times at 0.048. This numerous standard error implies the seasonal part might not perfectly fit the time series although it is recommended by R after searching all potential models (stepwise = FALSE).

The original time series is revisited by Seasonal and Trend decomposition using Loess (STL) [11]. The seasonal part can be found in Fig. 6, however, the residuals tend to be several times the coefficient from the seasonal part. This coincides with the tenfold standard error for P in the SAR1 model.

As the seasonal part of the model might invite questioning, an ARIMA model without seasonality was also established to compare. The ARIMA (2,1,1) model became the most fitted model without seasonality. The new model issued also passed all the tests mentioned previously. The forecast plot is plotted in Fig. 7 and Table 6.

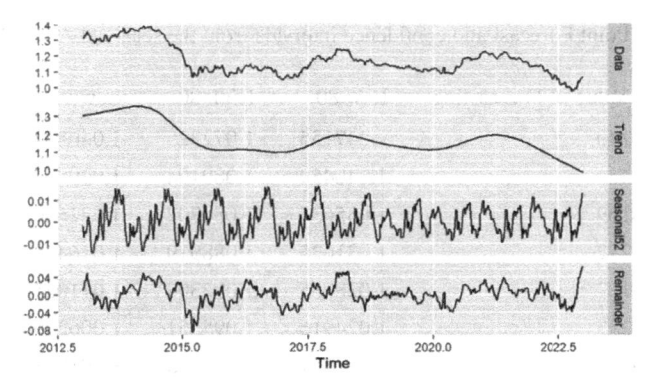

Fig. 6. STL decomposition of the Euro-to-USD exchange rate series

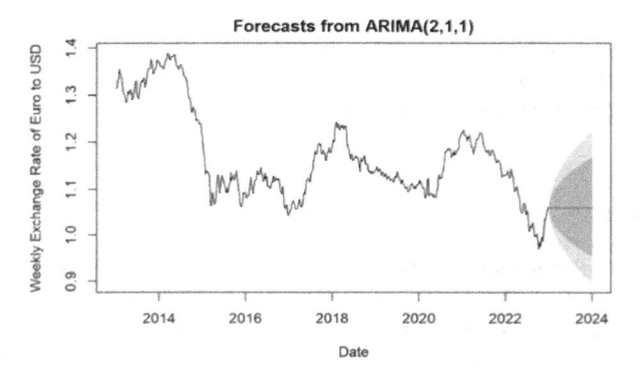

Fig. 7. Forecasts from the non-seasonal ARIMA model

Table 6. Point Forecast and confidence intervals from the non-seasonal ARIMA model

Week	Point Forecast	Lo 80	Hi 80	Lo 95	Hi 95
1	1.059754	1.047172	1.072337	1.0405107	1.078998
2	1.060508	1.040481	1.080535	1.0298795	1.091137
3	1.060096	1.035347	1.084845	1.0222459	1.097946
4	1.060318	1.031308	1.089328	1.0159511	1.104685
5	1.060198	1.027624	1.092773	1.0103799	1.110017
6	1.060263	1.024405	1.096120	1.0054238	1.115102
7	1.060228	1.021400	1.099056	1.0008456	1.119611
8	1.060247	1.018642	1.101852	0.9966171	1.123876

As Table 7 illustrates, the accuracy of these two models are comparable by examining the errors of them [12]. For example, the difference between RMSE of two models is smaller than 0.00001. And the forecast results are also quite similar. No significant contradictions can be discovered.

Table 7. Error terms in two models

Seasonal	ME	RMSE	MAE	MPE	MAPE	MASE	ACF1
Training set	0.0004	0.0098	0.0077	0.0381	0.6662	0.0918	0.0047
Non-seasonal	ME	RMSE	MAE	MPE	MAPE	MASE	ACF1
Training set	0.0004	0.0098	0.0077	0.0375	0.6660	0.0918	0.0006

Next, there are some real-life implications and suggestions providing the available forecasts. Firstly, Investors should be wary of the potential volatility of the exchange rate. No significant trend of rise or drop are expected in the following year. As a convention, portfolio diversification can effectively avoid the risk from the exchange rate market. Secondly, there are some advice for international traders from related countries. Companies can adjust their inventories orders and productions ahead to avoid potential loss from the exchange rate. Finally, the government can adjust potential policies in advance. Policy makers are recommended to focus on purchasing power parity, the control of national inflation, international trade balances, and speculations in the financial market. The ideal policies should handle problems from these four areas perfectly. The foreign exchange market and regulation of capital flows can be better handled with certain predictions, a better economic environment can be witnessed wishfully [13].

Back to the ARIMA model applied, the ARIMA model naturally possesses some advantages and disadvantages. On the one hand, the model is very simple, only endogenous variables namely the previous exchange rates are required for forecast, and no requirement for other exogenous variables. On the other hand, it requires the stationarity of the time series, as the first difference is taken in the ARIMA model in this paper. In essence, only linear relationships can be captured. For example, stock data is unstable and frequently fluctuates due to exogenous variables such as policies and news. ARIMA method fails to present such nonlinear changes. The ARIMA model applied to forecast the Euro-to-USD exchange rate also confronts such problems. Although the exchange rate is less volatile than stock price conventionally, it still exhibits certain fluctuations, especially under accidental events. Sometimes the potential plummet or rocket of the exchange rate cannot be predicted by the ARIMA model.

It might be meaningful to generalize the forecast model from the Euro-to-USD exchange rate to other exchange rates among nations. Panel data analysis might be used if the data source is reliable and the data is enough. In this way, the accuracy of the model can be better examined with more empirical data. In addition, other time series models such as ETS and GARCH models can also be established to do such forecasts on exchange rates. By comparing these models with different characteristics, there might be the most fitted models under varied scenarios.

5 Conclusion

In summary, this paper focused on the topic of Euro-to-USD exchange rate forecasting. Firstly, background information is given in the introduction. Historically, the Euro-to-USD exchange rate was above one since 2002. However, in 2022 it dropped below one due to both internal reasons such as central bank policies, and external reasons such as the Russia-Ukraine conflict and energy crisis. Pessimistic views were held by the public on the Euro. This research was aimed at predicting the future trends of the Euro-to-USD exchange rate to see whether it is likely to decrease, increase or remain stable. Then forecast results were interpreted with some suggestions.

Data from the Federal Reserve from the past ten years was extracted as the training data. Then ARIMA models were constructed by R through auto. ARIMA function with some adjustments to conduct forecasts. Examinations were made to ensure the correctness of these models. Following were the results derived from these two models with comparisons. Both seasonal and non-seasonal ARIMA models provided similar results; the Euro-to-USD exchange rate was predicted to stay around 1.06 for the next eight weeks with 80 % and 95 % confidence intervals. In addition, fluctuations of the rate were predicted to be within 0.1. Finally, a detailed discussion was carried out on various aspects. Traders, investors, and policymakers were suggested to adapt to the future potential exchange rate through pre-planned movements. The limitations of this project and the scope for future research were listed. ARIMA models focused on the mean level of future values, so the volatility of the exchange rate might not be manifested significantly. Different models such as GARCH can be used in the future, to provide more insights into exchange rate forecasting. Furthermore, the subjects of interest can be enlarged by choosing more countries to study or extending the time period of research. At the same time, in terms of depth of research, this article focuses on the study of linear relationships. In the future, this paper can try to analyze the nonlinear relationships of variables using the multivariate GARCH model to deeply analyze the change rules of variables.

References

1. Barbara, R.: Exchange rate predictability. J. Econ. Lit. **51**(4), 1063–1119 (2013)
2. Rogoff, K.S., Stavrakeva, V.: The continuing puzzle of short horizon exchange rate forecasting. National Bureau of Economic Research. No. w14071 (2008)
3. Daniela, F., Giancarlo, G.: The Euro/Dollar exchange rate: Chaotic or non-chaotic? A continuous time model with heterogeneous beliefs. J. Eco. Dynam. Control. Lit. **36**(4), 670–681 (2012)
4. Yemba, B.P., et al.: Nowcasting of the short-run euro-dollar exchange rate with economic fundamentals and time-varying parameters. Finance Research Letters. Lit. **52**, 103571 (2023)
5. Hajizadeh, E.: A new NN-PSO hybrid model for forecasting Euro/Dollar exchange rate volatility. Neu. Comp. Appl. Lit. **31**(7), 2063–2071 (2019)
6. Escudero, P., Alcocer, W., Paredes, J.: Recurrent neural networks and ARIMA models for euro/dollar exchange rate forecasting. Applied Sci. Lit. **11**(12), 5658 (2021)
7. Jamaleh, A.: Explaining and forecasting the euro/dollar exchange rate through a non-linear threshold model. Europ. J. Fina. Lit. **8**(4), 422–448 (2002)

8. Board of Governors of the Federal Reserve System (US): U.S. Dollars to Euro Spot Exchange Rate [DEXUSEU], retrieved from FRED, Federal Reserve Bank of St. Louis; URL: https://fred.stlouisfed.org/series/DEXUSEU. Last accessed 1 February 2023
9. Hyndman, R.J., Athanasopoulos, G.: Forecasting: Principles and Practice, 3rd edition (2022)
10. Hyndman, R.J., Khandakar, Y.: Automatic time series forecasting: the forecast package for R. J. Stati. Softw. Lit. **27**(1), 1–22 (2008)
11. Cleveland, R.B., et al.: STL: a seasonal-trend decomposition procedure based on loess. J. Offi. Stati. Lit. **6**(1), 3–33 (1990)
12. Hyndman, R.J., Koehler, A.B.: Another look at measures of forecast accuracy. Int. J. Forecas. Lit. **22**(4), 679–688 (2006)
13. Guzman, M., et al.: Real exchange rate policies for economic development. World Development. Lit. **110**, 51-62 (2018)

Analysis and Forecasting of Exchange Rate Between Yuan and Dollar

Sitian Yi[✉]

College of Arts and Science, Boston University, Boston, USA
sitiany@bu.edu

Abstract. Sino-US trade relations have been a hot topic in the economy in recent years, with the effects of the pandemic and the trade conflicts that have created a float between the Chinese and US economies. The U.S.-China exchange rate is an overall indicator that provides a good overview of various indicators of the economic relationship between the two countries. By forecasting the US-China exchange rate trend through the R studio, it is possible to identify the patterns in the economic float and the underlying trends and use this information to get a general idea of future economic trends. This information can help investors and consumers make long-term or short-term decisions to avoid economic distress. The data is obtained from FRED, and the ARIMA and KNN models are used for forecasting. The projections show a slight increase in the US-China exchange rate between 2023 and 2024. This predicts a further depreciation of the yuan and a recovery from the economic shock. This study will provide a scientific and objective data analysis and provide a reference for consumers and multinational investors.

Keywords: Exchange Rate · China · ARIMA · U.S

1 Introduction

Defining the strength of a country's ranking is a complex process that considers many aspects. According to the annual Best Countries ranking published by U.S. News and World Report in conjunction with the BAV Group and the Wharton School of the University of Pennsylvania in 2021, the United States and China are ranked first and second, respectively. The factors used to determine a country's power are divided into five categories: "military alliances, international alliances, political influence, economic influence, and leadership [1]. As the number one country, the United States had a GDP of $20.89 trillion in 2022, and China had a GDP of $14.72 trillion. Both countries have the same ranking in the world GDP ranking as the powerful countries ranking [2]. These two pieces of information prove that the overall ranking of countries is primarily related to the country's GDP. The economic development of the United States and China are quite different, and China is catching up or even surpassing the United States. To compare the data, in 1960, China's GDP was about 11% of that of the United States, but in 2019, this figure increased alarmingly to 67%. This proves that China's economic level is soaring to keep up with that of the United States at a much faster level [3]. According to a comparison of various data, it shows that the US lags behind China by 17.58% in agriculture as well as industry. This lag contributes to the reduction of the economic gap between the two countries [4].

Notably, the emergence of COVID-19 in 2019 dealt a massive blow to the economies of both countries. China's economy grew by only 3% in 2022, a very significant slowdown in growth that proves that the country has not yet recovered from the blow of the pandemic [5]. The U.S. was similarly hit by a strong economic slowdown, with GDP growth of 2.1% in 2022 [6]. This substantial slowdown in growth has had a powerful impact on the exchange rates of both countries and the world economy.

The economic relationship between China and the United States is very important. With the trade conflicts between China and the United States, China, and the United States began to impose additional tariffs on each other, which led to a decrease in trade between China and the United States and more negative effects. For producers in each country, huge profits or losses have been generated. For example, since China increased its tariffs on the U.S. in 2018, U.S. soybean exports to China have decreased dramatically, resulting in Brazilian soybean producers replacing Chinese soybean supplies thereby realizing increased profits, while U.S. soybean producers have suffered economic losses [7]. Thus, the effects of trade policy between the United States and China are extensive. The trade relationship between the two countries affects the global economy.

And the U.S.-China exchange rate changes with the U.S.-China economic relationship and holds great importance. When the yuan depreciates against the dollar, it causes U.S. purchases of Chinese goods to become cheaper, and therefore demand increases, and conversely, Chinese demand for U.S. goods falls because they are expensive, causing a trade deficit for the U.S. [8]. The decrease in net exports will cause a reduction in GDP. Thus, the exchange rate can have many consequences, including changes in trade decisions or changes in the interests of U.S. consumers and producers. Studying and predicting the exchange rate between the U.S. and China allows us to look forward to changes in the U.S. and China. For consumers, producers, and policymakers alike, such forecasting of future U.S.-China exchange rates can help prevent them from falling into significant losses.

In this paper, official data and reports, such as the International Monetary Fund, FRED Economic Data, and the US-China Business Council, are used for analysis. The literature provides an overview of the changes in the political, trade, and economic relations between the United States and China from 2018 to 2022. The selected literature provides an overview of the changes in political, business, and economic relations between China and the United States from 2018 to 2022. In addition, the literature chosen provides a timeline of U.S.-China trade policy. It provides detailed data sets and graphs to identify all trends related to the U.S.-China exchange rate, which provides a good theoretical and background information base for this study.

This research will mainly use the ARIMA and KNN models in R studio to forecast and analyze the trends of the US-China exchange rate. This paper will first visualize the raw data in R studio and then analyze the presented data, including whether there are intuitive trends, patterns, etc. After that, there will be a hypothesis about the final prediction with real background information. After the completion of the hypothesis, the central part of the prediction will be carried out, using the ARIMA and KNN models to analyze and predict the same group of data, respectively. The two sets of prediction results will then be compared to determine the final predicted data by comparing the degree of model matching. Finally, the predicted data will be compared and analyzed with the original assumption to further elaborate on the reasons for the differences between them.

2 Method

2.1 Data Visualize and Analyse

First, this article starts with an explanation of the selection of data. The data used for analysis and forecasting in this side of the paper are monthly data on the U.S.-China exchange rate between 1895 and 2022. The reasons for selecting monthly data are twofold. First, in the data provided by the FRED Economic Data website (https://fred.stlouisfed.org/series/EXCHUS), the monthly data for the US-China exchange rate goes back to 1981, but the daily data can only start from 2018 [9]. Since monthly data will contain more information and patterns. Second, the monthly data are smoother compared to the daily data, which reduces the effect of random noise. In the daily data, the ups and downs of the US and China exchange rates are affected by many subtle random policy and trade changes, which could be more conducive to long-term forecasting. The monthly data are minus these subtle time-dependent influences. Thirdly, why the data from 1985 to 2022 was chosen. It is because the leading foreign exchange regime in China started in 1988 [10]. The choice of data beginning in January 1985 ensures that all data have a full one-year rotation and include data from the period immediately before and after the reform event.

Next, the raw data can be analyzed using the R studio's visual presentation code. By looking at the time series plot of the exchange rate between the yuan and the dollar, several conclusions can be drawn. First, the overall trend of the plot is increasing and then gradually downward fluctuation, and there is a huge increase between 1990 and 1995, with the exchange rate rising from about 3.5 to about 8.7. This may be related to China's reform to embrace a "socialist market economy" in 1994. After that, starting in 2005, the exchange rate began to decline gradually and continued to fluctuate [10]. On 21st July 2005, the Chines Central Bank made a small revaluation to revalue the yuan from 8.27 to 8.11, and they announced that "the yuan will be no longer pegged to the US dollar" [11]. At last, during the COVID-19, the exchange rate between the yuan and the dollar was unstable and seemed to have an increasing trend.

Based on the seasonal plot of the exchange rate, the lines for each year are flat and have small fluctuations, and there are no apparent patterns between lines for each year's exchange rate (Fig. 1). Therefore, this paper can conclude that the raw data for the US-China exchange rate is not seasonal. To confirm this, using the seasonality and trend functions in R language yields that this data set has a strong trend (0.9952215) but no seasonality (-0.003964942), the results are show in Fig. 2.

2.2 Assumption

China's economy is rebounding from the trauma of the pandemic as the country recovers from the outbreak. But the dollar is experiencing a recent depreciation. In January,

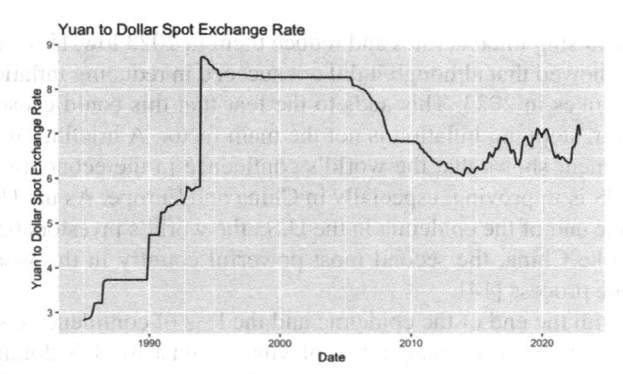

Fig. 1. Chinese yuan renminbi to U.S. dollar spot exchange rate.

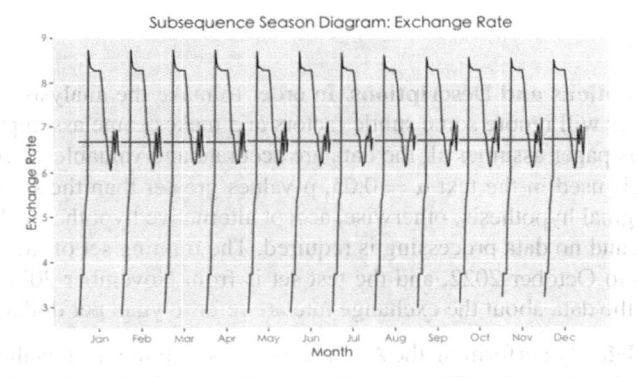

Fig. 2. Subsequence season diagram of yuan to dollar spot exchange rate.

the spot rate of the yuan once rose to an intraday high of 6.69 against the dollar, an 8.6 percent. Meanwhile, the yuan's central parity rate has appreciated by 2.93 percent against the US dollar in January [12]. In other words, the value of the yuan experienced a sustained rise from November 2022 to January 2023. This rise is still very likely to continue as China stabilizes its economy even more. Moreover, China's confidence in the Yuan's value growth and stability is evident through its support for real estate, its accommodative lending lines, and "the volume of overseas capital inflows to purchase yuan-denominated assets" [12]. The Chinese government has confidence in the value growth and stability of the yuan and has started implementing more new policies to promote economic development.

In a trend analysis of the dollar, the dollar could enter a cyclical period of depreciation in mid-2023. However, the general trend for the dollar is stronger with the addition of rising interest rates in 2022. Through the analysts at Wells Fargo, there are reasons to believe that the value of the dollar will gradually decline as the Fed's monetary tightening cycle comes to an end and a gradual economic downturn is generated [13]. Expectations are also a factor in the dollar's movement, as inflation has peaked with the significant strength of 2022, leading investors to make predictions about the Fed's policy, which is to stop raising interest rates and reduce them in 2023 low. However, Fed Chair Jerome Powell showed that although it did not succeed in reducing inflation, it will still implement rate hikes in 2023. This adds to the fear that this could cause the dollar to decline. However, stopping inflation is not the main factor. A briefing from JP Morgan Wealth Management shows that the world's confidence in the economies of countries other than the US is improving, especially in China and Europe. As the U.S. dollar saw a sharp rise at the end of the epidemic in the U.S., the world's investors began to expect that a country like China, the second most powerful country in the world, would go through the same process [14].

Therefore, with the end of the epidemic and the loss of confidence due to the Fed's policy, it is likely that the exchange rate of yuan against the US dollar will decline between 2023 and 2024, representing an expected increase in the value of the yuan and a depreciation of the US dollar.

2.3 Forecast

Model Assumptions and Descriptions. In order to make the analysis process convenient, this paper will ignore some subtle factors and makes some assumptions:

Firstly, this paper assumes all the data are accurate and valuable. Secondly, all significance levels used in the text $\alpha = 0.05$, p-values greater than the significance level accept the original hypothesis; otherwise, accept alternative hypothesis. Third, the data are complete, and no data processing is required. The training set of the model is from January 1985 to October 2022, and the test set is from November 2022 to December 2022. Lastly, the data about the exchange rate are refer to yuan per dollar.

ARIMA Model. By performing the Augmented Dickey-Fuller test on the original time series, the p-value is 0.5624. Therefore, cannot reject the initial hypothesis, which is that this time series is non-stationary. Therefore, this time series is not stationary and there is a need to differential the data and perform the stationarity test again after differencing. After first-order differencing, rerun the Augmented Dickey-Fuller test and get a p-value less than 0.01, which is less than the significance level of 0.05. Therefore, the time series is smooth after first-order differencing. Also, none of the bars in the ACF and PACF plots after first-order differencing exceeded the boundaries, proving that the data are white noise and not autocorrelated.

Next, the auto arima. function in R studio is used to fit the ARIMA model and make predictions on the data. The fitted ARIMA model is ARIMA (1, 2, 1). Figure 3 below shows the forecast of the exchange rate for the next year using ARIMA (1, 2, 1). The light blue part represents the 95% confidence interval, and the dark blue region represents the 80% confidence interval. The forecast results largely align with reality, as the exchange rate underwent a small fluctuation in the previous period. Therefore, the forecast results indicate that the exchange rate will be between 5.5 and 8.5 from 2023 to 2024.

After fitting the ARIMA model, a residual test is needed to determine that the model has captured the correlation of all the data. An excellent residual series should show white noise, i.e., no autocorrelation. By analyzing the residuals in Fig. 4 below, the residuals are basically normally distributed, and there are no significant fluctuations in the ACF picture, nor are there any bars crossing the boundaries.

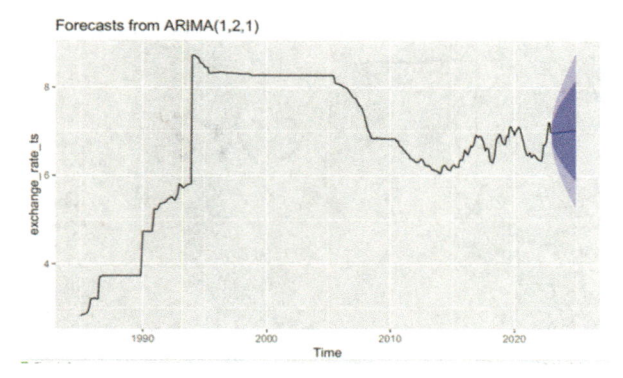

Fig. 3. Forecast with ARIMA (1,2,1) model.

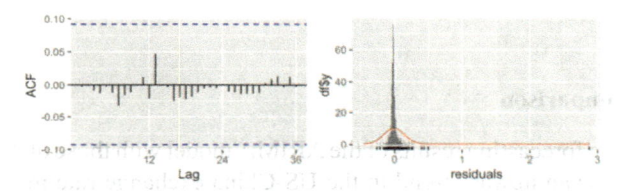

Fig. 4. ACF Plot of residuals and distribution diagram of residuals.

Using the Ljung-Box test to distinguish whether the residuals are white noise or not, obtain a p-value of 1, which is greater than the significant level 0.05, so this paper cannot reject the original hypothesis, which is that autocorrelation is different from 0. Therefore, the residuals are white noise distribution, and this model is an appropriate prediction model.

KNN Model. Another model that can be used to forecast time series is the KNN model. The KNN model consists of instances, features, and targets.

The time series instance is used as a reference vector to find the closest feature vector. The Euclidean Distance Formula is used to calculate the distance metric. K nearest neighbors are the number of K feature vectors with closest instances determined using the Euclidean Distance Formula. Targets are the time series data immediately after the nearest neighbors, and the targets of the nearest neighbors are averaged to predict the following data.

Figure 5 below shows the time series predicted using the KNN model. From the image, there is some overlap of features, targets, and instances, which occurs in some specific uptrends. The red part is the predicted data for the period 2023 to 2024. The forecasted rates show an upward trend.

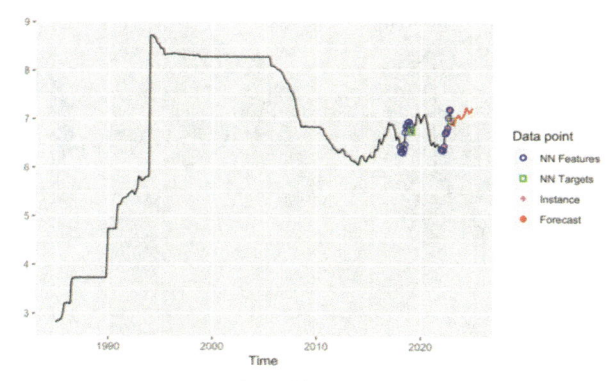

Fig. 5. Forecast with KNN model.

3 Result

3.1 Result Comparison

By comparing the forecasting results of the ARIMA model with those of the KNN model, both models show an upward trend in the US-China exchange rate in 2023 and 2024. However, the forecast images given by the two models are different. The forecast graph given by ARIMA is a wide range of forecast intervals, which lacks the volatility of time series. The slope of the solid line in the middle of the forecast range is not as large as that of the KNN model. The ARIMA model favors conservative estimation, unlike the KNN model gives an accurate forecast line.

3.2 Model Accuracy Comparison

It is impossible to tell which model has the most accurate prediction by looking at the prediction images, so the accuracy of the two models needs to be compared. By testing the accuracy of the ARIMA model, the following results in Table 1 were obtained:

Table 1 ARIMA model accuracy

	RMSE	MAE	MAPE
Training set	0.1485264	0.04351538	0.6796622
Test set	0.1724997	0.13438238	1.9220536

Using the rolling origin function to evaluate the accuracy of the KNN model based on the rolling origin, the test must be a constant vector, so the function set the rolling to FALSE. Then the accuracy test result for KNN model is shown in Table 2.

Based on the comparison of RMSE and MAPE, it can be concluded that the prediction accuracy of ARIMA model is better than the prediction accuracy of the KNN model.

Table 2 KNN model accuracy

RMSE	MAE	MAPE
0.3336461	0.2130950	3.0940903

Therefore, the final forecast results should be based on the ARIMA model's forecast. The US-China exchange rate will show an increase from 2023 to 2024, and the last range of fluctuation is likely to be between 5.5 and 8.5.

4 Discussion

Both the ARIMA model and the KNN model predict exchange rate movements that are contrary to the assumptions made before the construction of the model. The pre-model assumption is that the U.S.-China exchange rate will start falling next because China is recovering economically. However, the model proves that the most likely trend is a sustained upward. Thus, the resulting assumptions may not take an objective macro perspective on the entire topic, as seen in the article "China's economic growth fell to 3% in 2022 but slowly reviving" in the context of COVID-19 policy and real estate. The piece "China's economic growth fell to 3% in 2022 but slowly reviving" shows that China's economic growth fell to 3% in 2022 from 8.1% in 2021 during the COVID-19 policy and real estate downturn. And as China's aging population increases, the working age group's share of China's population falls to 62% from 70% a decade ago. While China's economy is now slowly recovering from the blow, the economic disruption caused by COVID-19 policies and strict foreign policy has also hit China's trading partners. Therefore, it is unlikely that the Chinese economy will fully emerge from the shadow of COVID-19 in two years. Nevertheless, there is reason to believe in the model's predicted upside figures.

Therefore, in the face of a potentially rising exchange rate, China should maintain a friendly diplomatic strategy and strengthen its support for various industries. Meanwhile, efforts should be made to increase the economic growth rate while maintaining the current economic recovery.

5 Conclusion

Based on the influence of the U.S. and Chinese economies on the world economy, both countries have made a series of economic policy changes with trade conflicts, pandemics, and various political situations. Understanding and analyzing the economic trends between the two countries is a valuable way for consumers and investors alike to avoid risk. The exchange rate is a good indicator of the difference in economic levels between the two countries and the results of all economic policies. Hence, a detailed forecast of the exchange rate between the U.S. and China is a good way to keep track of the economic trends between the two countries and make favorable financial decisions for consumers and investors in the future, considering current events.

This paper presents a forecast of the US-China exchange rate based on historical data. The ARIMA and KNN models are used to forecast the US-China exchange rate for 2023 and 2024 in a range based on the trend of past data. The forecasts prove that the US-China exchange rate will likely rise slightly from 2023 to 2024 based solely on the exchange rate data, accompanied by a certain increase range. This represents a possible tendency for the RMB to continue to depreciate.

This study has some limitations. ARIMA model is not necessarily the most suitable model for predicting this topic because of the limited academic resources and capabilities. ARIMA model is a single data forecasting model. It can only predict the trend based on a single data structure and cannot combine multiple factors for analysis. There are many elements that affect the exchange rate between the US and China, and they may be correlated with each other. The ARIMA model cannot capture the interaction between the exchange rate and other factors. Moreover, the ARIMA model can only focus on future trend. It does not capture the fluctuations in the data, resulting in broad forecasting results.

In further research, models such as multiple regression and factor analysis are expected to correlate multiple data. The single exchange rate data will be broken down into several data sets of the most significant factors, and a more detailed analysis of individual factors and integration analysis will be performed. Such an approach would allow for a more credible forecast of the overall exchange rate, considering trends in multiple data sources and covering various influences.

References

1. World Population Review: Most Powerful. Countries 2023. URL: https://worldpopulationreview.com/country-rankings/most-powerful-countries, last accessed 25 March 2023
2. Global PEO Services: Top 15 countries by GDP in 2022.URL: https://globalpeoservices.com/top-15-countries-by-gdp-in-2022/, last accessed 25 March 2023
3. International Monetary Fund: World Economic Outlook Database. URL: https://www.imf.org/en/Publications/WEO/weo-database/2021/April/weo-report?c=924%2C&s=NGDPD%2CPPPGDP%2C&sy=2020&ey=2025&ssm=0&scsm=0&scc=0&ssd=1&ssc=0&sic=0&sort=country&ds=.&br=1, last accessed 25 March 2023
4. Statistics Times: Comparing United States and China by economy. URL: https://statisticstimes.com/economy/united-states-vs-china-economy.php, last accessed 25 March 2023
5. The New York Times: China's economy stumbled last year with Covid lockdowns hobbling growth. URL: https://www.nytimes.com/2023/01/16/business/china-gdp-fourth-quarter-2022.html, last accessed 25 March 2023
6. U.S. Bureau of Economic Analysis: Gross Domestic Product, Fourth Quarter and Year 2022 (Advance Estimate). URL: https://www.bea.gov/news/2023/gross-domestic-product-fourth-quarter-and-year-2022-advance-estimate, last accessed 17 March 2023
7. Cerutti, E., Gopinath, G., Mohammed, A.: The impact of US-China Trade Tensions. International Monetary Review **82** (2014)
8. Bai, S., Koong, K.S.: Oil prices, stock returns, and exchange rates: Empirical evidence from China and the United States. The North American Journal of Economics and Finance **44**, 12–33 (2018)
9. FRED: Chinese yuan renminbi to U.S. dollar spot exchange rate. URL: https://fred.stlouisfed.org/series/EXCHUS, last accessed 10 March 2023

10. Reuters: Timeline: China's reforms of yuan exchange rate. URL: https://www.reuters.com/article/us-china-yuan-timeline-idUSBRE83D03820120414, last accessed 25 March 2023
11. Goujon, M., Guérineau, S.: The modification of the Chinese Exchange Rate Policy. China Perspectives **2006**, 64 (2006)
12. Global Times: Yuan gains value against US dollar, appreciating nearly 3% in January alone. URL: https://www.globaltimes.cn/page/202302/1284606.shtml, last accessed 22 March 2023
13. FXStreet: US dollar to weaken starting in mid-2023-Wells Fargo. URL: https://www.fxstreet.com/news/us-dollar-to-weaken-starting-in-mid-2023-wells-fargo-202212081631, last accessed 25 March 2023
14. Morningstar: What will happen to the dollar in 2023? URL: https://www.morningstar.com/articles/1129782/what-will-happen-to-the-dollar-in-2023, last accessed 25 March 2023

Forecast of China's Real Estate Industry Development Situation Based on ARIMA Model: Taking Vanke as an Example

Xiangyu Li(✉)

School of Architecture and Urban Planning, Huazhong University of Science and Technology, Wuhan 430074, Hubei Province, China
u201915306@hust.edu.cn

Abstract. In recent years, under the influence of various factors such as the COVID-19, the economic situation is not optimistic around the world. Among them, China's real estate industry has experienced particularly large fluctuations during this period. The future development of Chinese real estate market is also one of the economic topics that people pay close attention to. This study adopts the principle of time series analysis and forecasting, selects the stock price data of Vanke Group, a representative enterprise in China's real estate industry, from 2018 to 2023 as the analysis object. Using the ARIMA model to analyse and predict the data in order to forecast the future development of Vanke and even the entire Chinese real estate market. The research found that the stock price will continue to show a downward trend in the remaining 2023 and it will start to rise slowly on the eve of 2024, which means that Chinese real estate will usher in a certain recovery after a period of continuous trough in the future.

Keywords: Real Estate Industry · China · ARIMA

1 Introduction

In recent years, China's real estate situation has declined seriously, which has aroused widespread concern from all kinds of people. What's more, owing to the slump in the real estate industry, the entire construction industry closely related to it in China has been greatly affected, resulting in a large number of company bankruptcy, employee unemployment and project failure. Therefore, the analysis and forecast of the outlook for China's real estate sector has strong practical significance. In the aspect of national policy, the main tone of industrial policy remains unchanged. The 2021 Politburo meeting put forward that it is crucial to improve the construction of affordable housing, support the commercial housing market to better meet the reasonable housing needs of consumers. Promoting the healthy future of the real estate market and a virtuous circle. In the same year, the Central Economic Work Conference clearly pointed out: positioning must be adhered to that houses are for living, not for speculation. From the above, it can be seen that the main policy tone of China's real estate sector remains unchanged [1].

In the existing research, the analysis of relevant policies and development status about Chinese real estate industry are relatively comprehensive. The future strategy of China's real estate economy mainly includes five aspects: focusing on macro adjustment, solving housing problems, improving the market system, strengthening management and innovating related products. The future of the real estate economy will continue to develop toward a more mature market, more diverse policies, more reasonable prices, more novel patterns and more improved needs [2]. Meanwhile, the evolution trend and future development path of China's real estate financialization are analysed, which pointed out that in order to achieve sustainable development and progress, the real estate industry must learn to develop new financing methods and models, break through the traditional financing pattern and enhance the relationship with the real estate melting rate [3]. There are also quantitative studies related to China's real estate industry. Combining big data with traditional real estate industries and focusing on real estate disciplines can guide researchers and practitioners to use data-centric methods, conducting analysis from application and theoretical perspectives [4]. Some studies focus on real estate prices, which is predicted by the ARIMA time series model and the conclusion shows that the real estate price is related to the industrial development cycle [5]. The ARIMA model is also used for stocks forecasting research, which shows that stock price forecast with ARIMA model is very useful and as an efficient tool for stock market investors [6]. Focusing on the imperfection of ARIAM model in forecasting stock prices with comparatively complicated fluctuation trends, proposing a more polished ARIMA approach (BMA-ARIMA) based on model averaging and B-spline basis expansion [7]. Although the existing research covers a wide range, it lacks the special analysis and prediction of the stock price data of the real estate industry using the ARIMA model, and further forecasts the development of the industry. In this study, the ARIMA model is used in the research of real estate stock prices, which has a certain degree of innovation. The quantitative forecast of the development of the real estate market is of great significance for solving related industry problems and guiding the healthy development of the industry.

Based on the stock price data of Vanke from January 2018 to March 2023, the research uses time series theories and ARIMA model to analyse and predict the future changes of it, which can also be used to forecast the future development of Chinese real estate sector. To better understand the data, this study carries out multiple analysis of moving averages, returns and seasonality on the raw data prior to the forecasting work. An augmented Dickey-Fuller Test (ADF) will be used for testing whether the data is stationary and the differences should be computed until the data series has become stationary. If the time series data looks like a white noise series and has no autocorrelations, the ARIMA model will be formally used to analyse and predict the data. The research uses seasonal models and non-seasonal models at the same time, then selects the most suitable model for forecast analysis by comparing multiple results. Finally draw the definite conclusion of this research.

2 Model for Closing Stock Price Forecast

2.1 Time Series Analysis

Time series include stationary models of autoregressive models (AR), moving average models (MA), autoregressive moving average models (ARMA) and nonstationary models of differential ARIMA.

Time series models play a pivotal role in time series analysis and can represent the peculiarities of time series. The numerical value of each time indicates the observation of the phenomenon at that time, where the time interval of adjacent points can be different. If there is a time series, there is Eq. (1):

$$X = \{(t_1, x_1), \ldots, (t_i, x_i), \ldots, (t_n, x_n)\}, t_i < t_{i+1} (i = 1, \ldots n - 1) \tag{1}$$

where t_i represents time, x_i represents the observation, and (t_i, x_i) indicates that the observation at time t_i is x_i.

2.2 ARIMA

When ARIMA model performing d-order differential processing on a nonstationary time series. Firstly makes it a stationary series and enters the data into the ARMA model for fitting, abbreviated as ARIMA (p,d,q), there is Eq. (2):

$$X_t = \varphi_1 x_{t-1} + L + \varphi_p x_{t-p} + \varepsilon_t + \theta_1 \varepsilon_{t-1} + L + \theta_q \varepsilon_{t-q} \tag{2}$$

where $\varphi_1, \varphi_2, \ldots, \varphi_p$ are autoregressive coefficients, $\theta_1, \theta_2, \ldots, \theta_q$ are moving averages coefficients, q is the moving average order, p is the autoregressive order, and ε_t is the white noise process.

The modeling steps for ARIMA are shown in Fig. 1. Firstly, determine whether the time series data is stationary. If not, differential operations need to be performed on it to get the stationary data. Moreover, after determining whether the data is stationary, white noise detection is required and white noise detection is to make the data meet the model fitting requirements. Finally, the appropriate ARIMA model is fitted to the data detected by white noise [8].

3 Data Source and Analysis

3.1 Reasons for Data Selecting

The closing stock price Vanke Group, one of the most representative benchmark real estate enterprises in China, will be selected as the data analysis object. This is because stock price is one of the data that best reflects the market value. The company's stock price can reflect the fundamentals of the company, i.e., those financial data related to the company's financial strength and operating conditions. With these data, researchers can not only review the past historical financial data, but also look forward to the future expected financial data. Therefore, stock data is of vital significance for analyzing and forecasting the company's environment and industry prospects in China.

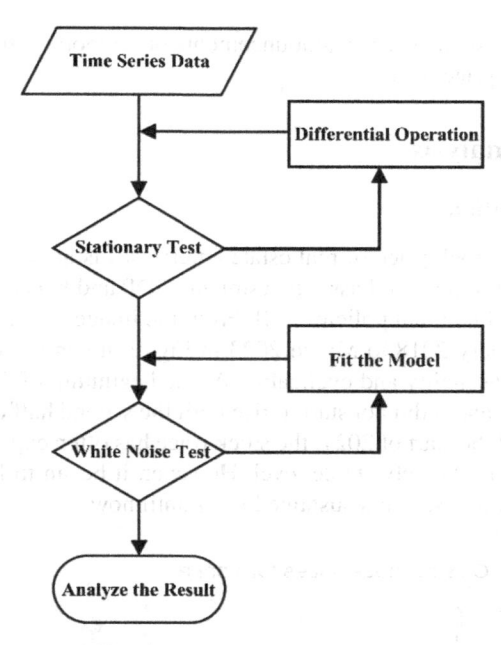

Fig. 1. ARIMA modeling steps.

3.2 Data Source

The time range of the selected stock price data is from January 2018 to March 2023, so as to fully understand the influence of the pandemic on the housing industry represented by Vanke and the development situation in the post-epidemic era. The source of stock price data is Wind Financial Terminal, which provides a complete set of Chinese financial market data and information [9]. It is a widely used authoritative information channel and can ensures that the data is comprehensive and accurate.

3.3 Data Frequency

The frequency of data simulated in this research varied at different stages, using daily data in data analysis phase and monthly data in the forecast phase and the reasons are as follows.

As the analysis of raw data, the daily closing stock prices are used as they provide a detailed picture of the price movements of the stocks on a day-to-day basis. This level of granularity allows the identify trends, patterns, and anomalies in the data that may be relevant to further analysis. However, when it comes to forecasting, monthly closing prices are used because they can provide a smoother, less noisy view of the data. By aggregating the daily prices into monthly closing stock prices, the research can reduce the impact of short-term fluctuations and focus on the long-run trends and patterns that are more relevant for forecasting purposes. It can also help reduce the effects of random noise and increase the accuracy of forecasts because the monthly prices are less susceptible to short-term events, such as news announcements or temporary market shocks, which can distort the daily price data.

4 Raw Data Analysis

4.1 Data Visualization

It's obvious that the stock price of real estate enterprises is affected by factors such as the stock market, inflation, fixed asset investment, GDP and benchmark money supply, urban population and national policies [10]. From the image of the closing stock prices for Vanke from January 2018 to March 2023 in Fig. 2, it can be seen that the data do not have obvious seasonality and cyclicality. At the beginning of 2018, the stock price began to fall sharply and it did not start to rise until the second half of the year. Between the start of 2019 and the start of 2021, the stock price has often experienced fluctuations but has maintained a relatively stable level. However, it began to fall sharply again in the first half of 2021 and still at a sustained level until now.

Fig. 2. Stock prices' chart for Vanke from 2018 to 2023.

The decline in the stock price in 2018 may be due to the fierce equity dispute at that time and the effect of important changes in the company's personnel, while the decline in 2021 may be due to the signal of "housing is not speculation" and the impact of the "three red lines" national policy. It is worth mentioning that Vanke's stock price has not changed much during the outbreak of the COVID-19 and is still relatively stable. This may be due to the fact that the period of home isolation has triggered people's thinking and demand for the spaciousness and comfort of living space, so the epidemic has not only not suppressed the purchase of houses, but might stimulate people's needs to buy houses. The Moving Averages in Fig. 3 tries to explore the data more deeply.

Based on the Eq. (3), using the line of prices and moving averages with different colors. For calculating two moving averages for the stock prices series, one with ten days window and the other with 30 days [11].

$$MA_t^q = \frac{1}{q} \sum_{i=0}^{q-1} x_{t-1} \qquad (3)$$

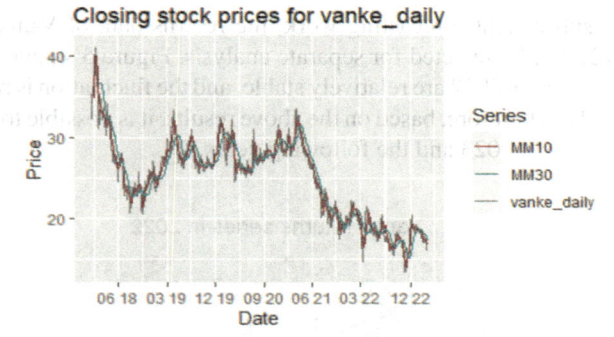

Fig. 3. The plot of moving averages for Vanke's stock prices.

An existing theory in Technical Analysis is the one that when two MAs of the short and long-term intersect with each other, there is an indication of buying or selling the stock. There's a buy signal when the short-term MA crosses the long-term upwards. Instead, there's a sell signal. This pattern can be observed clearly in the stock charts of Vanke and the trends can be found in the series of the same graphs about prices.

4.2 Returns

After seeing how the stock price has changed over time, the research will verify how the stock return has behaved in the same period. Then, logarithm properties will be used to calculate the log return of the stock. As the Eq. (4) as follows.

$$r_t = ln(1 + R_t) = ln(\frac{P_t}{P_{t-1}}) = ln(P_t) - ln(P_{t-1}) \approx R_t \qquad (4)$$

Figure 4 shown below are related to returns and observing how they fluctuate over time. With a brief analysis of the graphs, it is clear that for Vanke, the overall data is relatively stable.

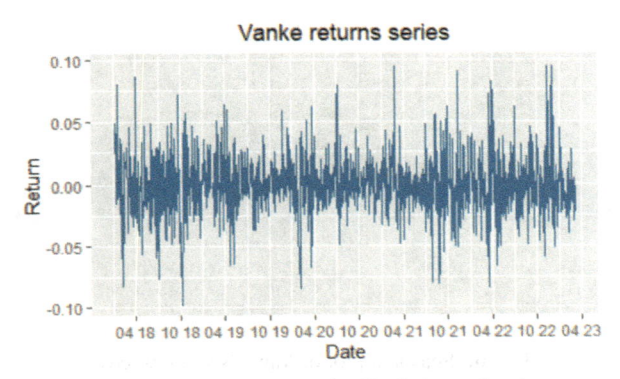

Fig. 4. The plot of returns for Vanke's stock prices.

To facilitate subsequent forecasting work, the returns data of Vanke for the most recent year, 2022, will be selected for separate analysis. Figure 5 shown below that the returns of the company in 2022 are relatively stable, and the fluctuation is roughly regular between -0.10–0.10. Therefore, based on the above results, it is possible to expect a fairly steady rate of returns in 2023 and the following years.

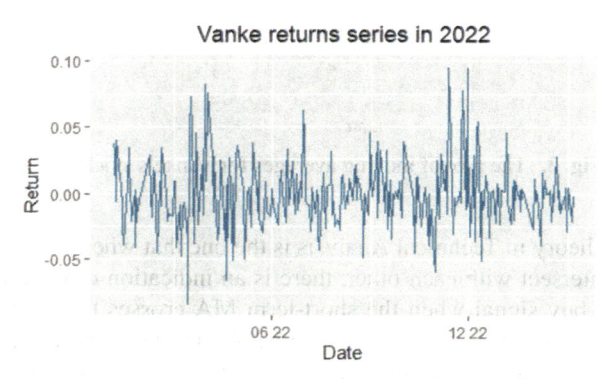

Fig. 5. The plot of returns for Vanke's stock prices in 2022.

4.3 Seasonality

Different from the analysis above, the monthly closing stock price will be used to investigate the seasonality of the dataset. This is because monthly data can lead to a clear and stable results when testing the seasonality. As shown in the seasonal plots from Fig. 6 and Fig. 7, although the trends are similar in some periods, most regions are generally overlapped, suggesting that the seasonality of these the dataset is weak.

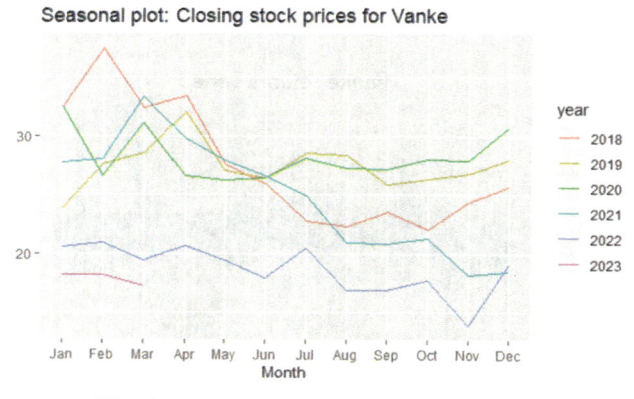

Fig. 6. Seasonal plot of Vanke's stock prices.

Polar seasonal plot: Closing stock prices for Vanke

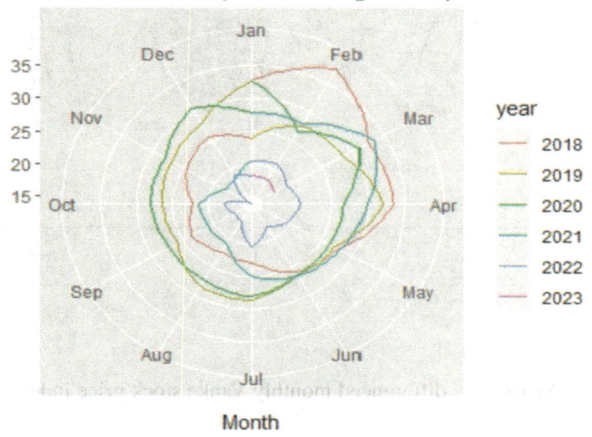

Fig. 7. Polar seasonal plot of Vanke's stock prices.

5 Data Forecast

To forecast the monthly closing stock price of Vanke, an augmented Dickey-Fuller Test will be used to test whether the stock price data is stationary. For this test, the null hypothesis in the time series is non-stationary. Through the results of the trial in Table 1, the p-value of the test about the monthly closing stock price for Vanke Company is 0.3548, which is larger than 0.05. On the other hand, the time plots show that the monthly closing stock prices for Vanke are non-stationary because some significant fluctuation exists. Following that, the differences should be computed between the consecutive observations to make the time series stationary.

Table 1. Results from Dickey-Fuller Test.

Dickey-Fuller	Lag order	p-value
−2.5437	3	0.3548

Figure 8 shows that the ACF and PACF plot of the differenced monthly Vanke stock price looks like white noise series since most of values are within the blue dotted line. The monthly change in the Vanke closing stock price is essentially a random amount, which is no association with the previous date.

There are no autocorrelations exceeding the 95% limits, and the p-value of the Ljung-Box test (0.2842) in Table 2 also proves this.

Firstly, the auto.arima() function in R will be used to automatically select a suited ARIMA model. And this is an ARIMA (1,1,0) model as Table 3 shows.

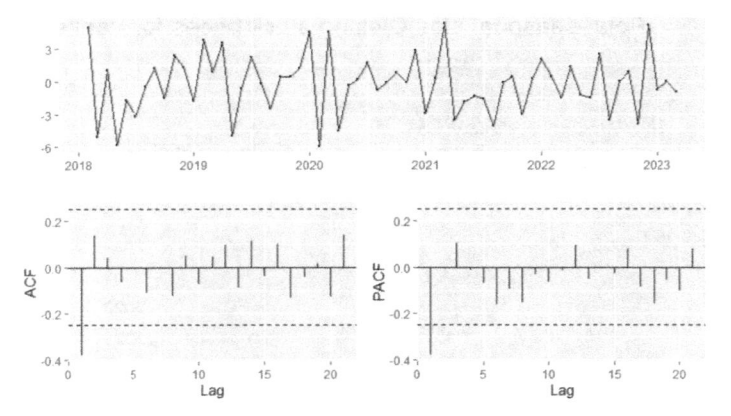

Fig. 8. Seasonally differenced monthly Vanke stock price index.

Table 2. Results from Ljung-Box test.

X-squared	df	p-value
14.263	12	0.2842

Table 3. Results from the auto.arima() function.

Model	AIC	AICc	BIC
ARIMA (1,1,0)	293.03	293.23	297.28

The ACF plot of the residuals from the ARIMA (1,1,0) model in Fig. 9 indicates that all autocorrelations are within the blue dotted line, which means that the residuals seem to be white noise.

A portmanteau test in Table 4 returns a large p-value(0.8367), also indicating that the residuals are white noise [12].

Forecasts from the ARIMA(1,1,0) model are shown in Fig. 10. However, the results forecasted by the model are approximately a fixed value and it is difficult to explain the true trend of the stock price of real estate companies. Therefore, consider adding some seasonal factors and using the seasonal ARIMA model to forecast the data again.

By observing the ACF plot and PACF plot of the data and comparing several models for multiple rounds, it is found that the $ARIMA(1,1,0)(0,1,1)^{12}$ model has a small ACF value and the forecasting result are the most suitable.

The ACF plot of the residuals from the $ARIMA(1,1,0)(0,1,1)^{12}$ model in Fig. 11 returns that all autocorrelations are within the blue dotted line, meaning that the residuals seem to be white noise.

A portmanteau test in Table 5 shows a large p-value (0.8392), also indicating that the residuals are white noise [12].

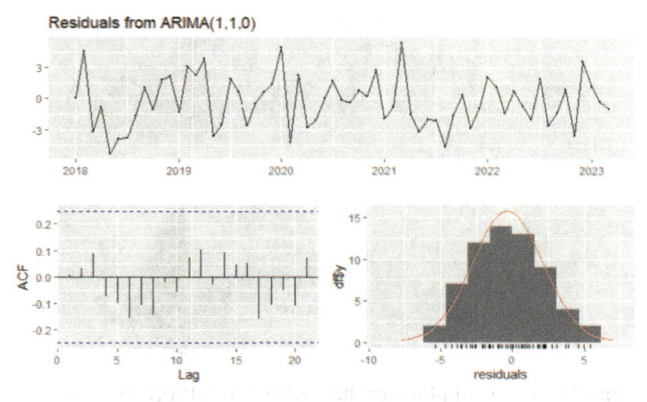

Fig. 9. Residual plots for the ARIMA(1,1,0) model.

Table 4. Results from the portmanteau test.

Q*	df	p-value
7.3064	12	0.8367

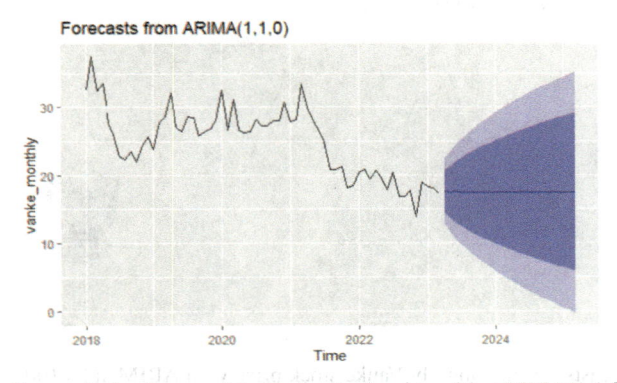

Fig. 10. Forecasts for the monthly Vanke stock price with ARIMA(1,1,0) model.

Forecasts from the ARIMA$(1,1,0)(0,1,1)^{12}$ model are shown in Fig. 12 and the result looks more appropriate, which indicates that Vanke's stock price will continue to decline in 2023 with a trend similar to that in 2022, and the stock price will begin to recover when 2024 is approaching.

6 Discussion

The outlook for Chinese real estate sector is greatly affected by policies, which have always regulated the benign and stable development of the housing market, so that it will neither be too hot nor continue to slump and has a certain period. The results of this

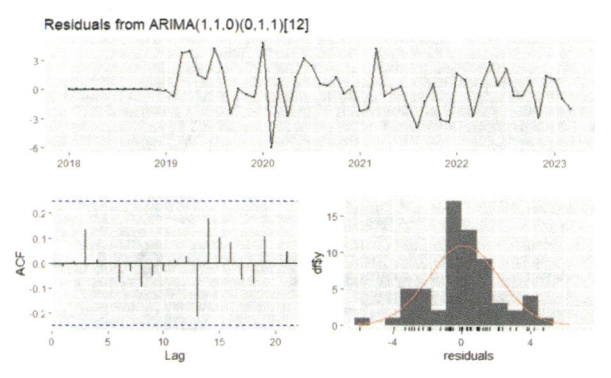

Fig. 11. Residual plots for the ARIMA(1,1,0)(0,1,1)^{12} model.

Table 5. Results from the portmanteau test.

Q*	df	p-value
6.4846	11	0.8392

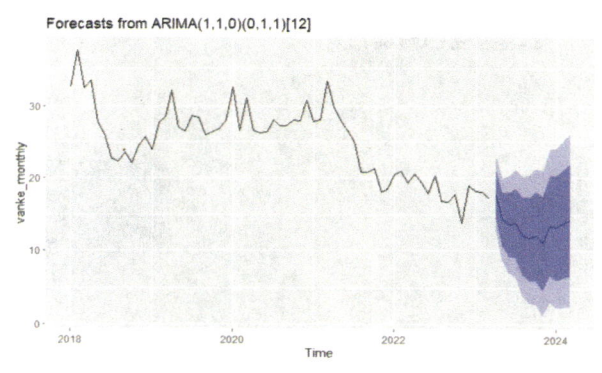

Fig. 12. Forecasts for the monthly Vanke stock price with ARIMA(1,1,0)(0,1,1)^{12} model.

research also confirm this feature. For example, at the end of 2022, China proposed a number of policies that are very beneficial for the real estate industry. As shown in the forecasting result, the continuous decline in Vanke's stock price in 2023 may be due to the fact that these rescue policies have not been fully popularized and efficiently applied. On the other hand, the recovery of stock prices in 2024 may be that these policies have matured and played a very positive role in the future of the real estate market.

Overall, investors and decision-makers should carefully consider the factors that affect the stock price of real estate companies, especially in a complex situation like the population, inflation, fixed asset investment and political changes in China. For the aspect of forecasting models, the auto-generated non-seasonal model in R did not work as well as the manually selected seasonal model, which can also show that Vanke Group's stock price and even the development of the housing market have certain seasonal factors.

7 Conclusion

Through the comparative analysis in the research process, it is found that the seasonal model is more suitable for the model prediction work. The experimental results show that Vanke's stock price will continue to decline for nearly a year, but then gradually recover, which can be inferred that Chinese real estate will gradually recover after a period of trough. This also reflects the cyclical characteristics of the housing market. The national policy has always maintained the benign process of the real estate industry, appropriately suppressed when it is hot to maintain its stability and extended a helping hand to support the market when it is at a low point. The results can also show that although the industry has been sluggish in the past few years, there are still opportunities and hopes in the future. In consequence, industry practitioners should also be confident in the future, believing that spring after the cold winter is coming. At the same time, for investors, it is also necessary to comprehensively consider the various factors affecting the situation of nation's real estate market and invest prudently and rationally.

In addition to conventional macro analysis of policy aspects, this research combines ARIMA model predictions with Chinese real estate stock price data. Quantitative analysis based on specific data has been introduced and the prediction effect of seasonal models and non-seasonal models have been compared to select the most reasonable research method. Therefore, this research idea is conducive to relevant practitioners to obtain a clearer understanding of the industry, and also provides reference for the future prediction research of the real estate industry and even other industries.

However, there are also some limitations of models exist. For example, the ARIMA model only considers the relationship between a single variable's past and future values. It cannot capture the relationship between multiple variables, but in practice, when we forecast the stock, we need to consider many covariates that affect the fluctuation of stock prices. In view of this shortcoming, future research can use more comprehensive model prediction methods. Multiple factors affecting stock prices can be considered in the data analysis and prediction of the models, so as to draw more accurate experimental conclusions.

References

1. Xie, L.: Discussion on the development trend of real estate industry under the new situation. Real Estate World **374**(18), 5–8 (2022)
2. Zhang, L.P.: Analysis of the Current Situation and Future Development Trend of Real Estate Economy Development in China. Housing and Real Estate **638+641**(Z1), 62–66 (2022)
3. Zhang, A.M.: Analysis of the evolution trend of china's real estate financialization and prospect of future development path. Times Economics and Trade **506**(09), 10–11 (2020)
4. Kimberly, W.G., Andy, K., Clifford, A.L., Nick, E.: Real Estate Analysis in the Information Age: Techniques for Big Data and Statistical Modeling, pp. 16–17. CRC Press, Boca Raton (2017)

5. Meng, Y.Z., Sun, S.N.: Real estate price forecast based on ARIMA time series model——taking shenyang as an example. Neijiang Science and Technology **42**(05), 65+74 (2021)
6. Khan, S., Alghulaiakh, H.: ARIMA model for accurate time series stocks forecasting. IJACSA **11**, 07 (2020)
7. Gao, M.S., Feng, C.Y.: An improved ARIMA stock price forecasting method based on B-spline expansion and model averaging. Acad. J. Comp. Info. Sci. **05**, 10 (2022)
8. Xu, H.B., Shi, D.H.: Prediction of construction safety accidents based on ARIMA and LSTM models. Software Engineering **26**(03), 9–14 (2023)
9. Wind Financial Terminal: URL: https://www.wind.com.cn/mobile/WFT/zh.html, last accessed 21 March 2023
10. Qian, Y.L.: Analysis of Factors Influencing Vanke's Stock Price——Based on the Empirical Analysis of Listed Companies in the Real Estate Industry. Taxation **13**(05), 166–167+169 (2019)
11. LAMFO: Introduction to Stock Analysis. URL: https://lamfo-unb.github.io/2017/07/22/intro-stock-analysis-1/, last accessed 21 March 2023
12. Hyndman, R.J., Athanasopoulos, G.: Forecast: Principles and Practice. Monash University, Melbourne (2018)

US Trade Balance Analysis on Imports and Exports Based on ETS and ARIMA Models

Shiqi Fan(✉)

Fu Foundation School of Engineering and Applied Science, Columbia University,
New York 10025, USA
`snf2125@columbia.edu`

Abstract. There are concerns over keeping the U.S. trade deficit at a high level for long since trade deficit can potentially lead to a financial crisis. Different studies hold different opinions in terms of the future U.S. trade balance, and this study intends to forecast its near future value from the time series analysis perspective. Two classic time series models based on the imports and exports series are being used, respectively ETS and ARIMA models. The results show that the future trade balance have a higher chance to be fluctuate at the current level than to be deteriorate. However, the circumstance is unlikely to be mitigated based on the model predictions. This prediction of non-decreasing trade deficit can be a hidden threat towards the U.S. economy.

Keywords: Trade · ETS · ARIMA · Imports and Exports

1 Introduction

Many theoretical analysis and historical evidence indicate that financial crisis is likely to happen preceded by current account deficit [1, 2]. Statistic shows that the U.S. trade deficit persists at a high level for decades, which raises concerns about instability of the U.S. economy [2]. Some researchers suggest this trade imbalance will be forced narrowing by economic naturally [3]. However, others treat the U.S. a special case and its trade deficit will not be improved [4]. Therefore, this research intends to study the U.S. trade balance by analyzing its time series patterns from the statistical perspective, and to forecast its near future value.

As is known to all, the definition of the trade balance is subtracting the imports from the exports. This means that there are two approaches to forecast the trade balance by collecting both imports and exports time series data. The first approach is to train trade balance model directly by using the exports data minus imports data, and the second approach is to subtract the imports model from the exports model.

This research also uses two classic time series models ETS and ARIMA for fitting both imports and exports series, for which are tested to be non-stationary. On the one hand, ETS models are non-stationary, and thus, it is sufficient to pass the raw data in. On the other hand, ARIMA models are stationary. This research then explores different ways of data transformations to make the series stable. It turns out that Box-Cox transformation followed by 1st order differencing can do this work. Finally, four different ways to forecast the U.S. trade balance are being conducted. More details in the following sections.

2 Method

2.1 Data Processing

Data Collection and Visualization. Both the U.S. imports and exports data are collected from the Federal Reserve Bank of St. Louis with a quarterly frequency from 1960 to 2022 [5, 6]. Top two graphs in Fig. 1 show the time series plots from the data set collected, and the bottom graph is the plot of trade balance computed from subtracting two data sets. Plots for both imports and exports data show a trend of exponentially increasing, a cyclical pattern for around 10 years, and a clear seasonal pattern. However, the trade balance series only exhibits a rapidly declining trend together with a strong seasonal pattern. There is no obvious cyclical pattern in the balance of trade.

Also, the magnitude between adjacent sample points for all three series become larger over time, which means the variance of data increases with the level and series. This increasing variance indicates a non-stationary time series characteristic, which the ARIMA model cannot handle well. Since one of the models being used in this research is the ARIMA, undertaking data transformation is needed.

Box-Cox Transformation. Box-Cox transformation is a desirable technique for stabilizing and normalizing the variable [7]. Before applying the transformation through Eq. 1, an optimal lambda needs to be selected to maximally converge the variable towards normality [8].

$$y_i^\lambda = \begin{cases} \frac{y_i^\lambda - 1}{\lambda} & \text{if } \lambda \neq 0, \\ \ln y_i & \text{if } \lambda = 0, \end{cases} \qquad (1)$$

Many existing packages support computing the optimal lambda automatically. This research utilizes the forecast package, which is one of the most popular forecasting packages for time series data in R. It can be seen from Fig. 2 that the variables for both imports and exports data are much more stable after performing Box-Cox transformation, but it does not improve much for the trade balance.

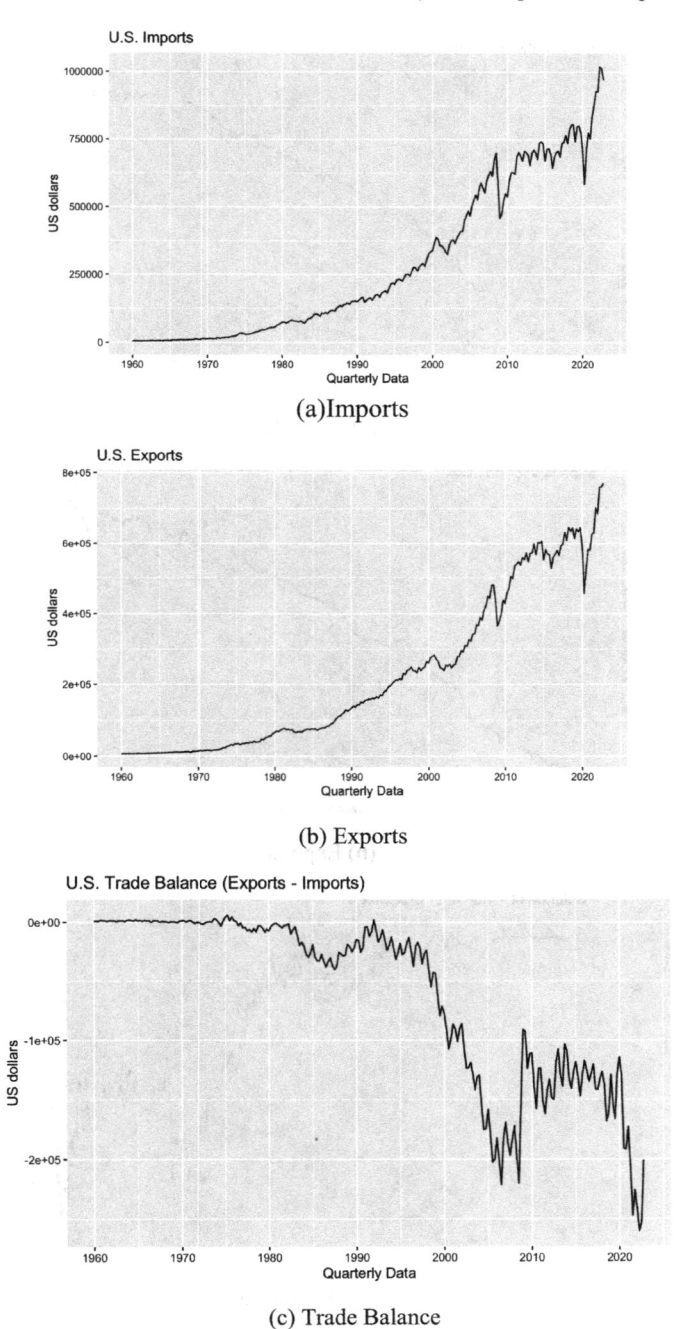

Fig. 1. Time series plots for the U.S. imports (a), exports (b), and balance of trade (c) in dollars from 1960 to 2022 every quarter

(a) Imports

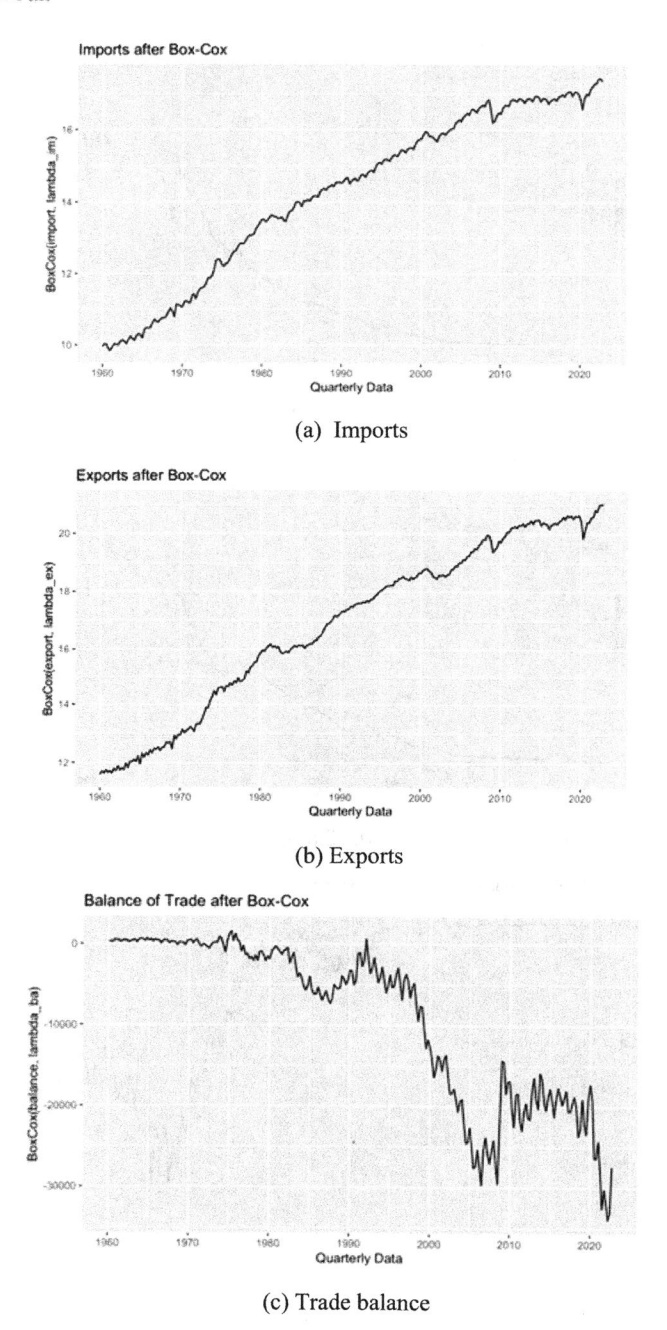

(b) Exports

(c) Trade balance

Fig. 2. Top two plots are imports (a) and exports (b) data with Box-Cox transformation; bottom one (c) is the balance of trade with Box-Cox transformation

This research further testifies the sufficiency of only applying the Box-Cox transformation through KPSS tests, a hypothesis test that examines the stationarity of the target series [9]. Unfortunately, KPSS test results from two R packages, urca and tseries, on all transformed series show that they are non-stationary. This is because the test statistics exceed the critical value for 95 percent confidence interval and p-values are smaller than 0.05 (Table 1). Therefore, further transformation is needed, for example differencing the time series data [10].

Table 1. KPSS test results for imports, exports, trade balance with Box-Cox transformation

Time series data	urca: critical value for 5pct	urca: test statistic	tseries: p-value
imports	0.463	4.176	< 0.01
exports	0.463	4.2104	< 0.01
trade balance	0.463	3.6977	< 0.01

Differencing. By using the ndiffs() function provided in the R forecast package, the optimal number of differencing to transform data can be computed. The results show that 1st order differencing can stabilize all three series with box-cox transformation. Still, the KPSS test is conducted again on data with box-cox and differencing to testify their stationarity. Table 2 shows that all test statistics are smaller than critical value and p-values are larger than 0.05, suggesting null hypothesis cannot be rejected. In short, all three series are stationary eventually.

Table 2. KPSS test results for imports, exports, trade balance with Box-Cox transformation and 1st order differencing.

time series data	urca: critical value for 5pct	urca: test statistic	tseries: p-value
imports	0.463	0.3915	> 0.0808
exports	0.463	0.2325	> 0.1
trade balance	0.463	0.0808	> 0.1

2.2 Models

ETS. The ETS models are common approaches to forecast time series, where E stands for error, T stands for trend, and S stands for seasonality [11]. This model focuses on these three components as well as combining these components through additive methods, multiplicative methods, or excluding specific features [11]. Since the U.S. Imports and exports series both show an apparent trend of increasing and obvious seasonality, the ETS model is an intuitive method to start with.

One advantage of these models is that they are non-stationary models which do not require the input time series data to be stationary. Therefore, this research will simply pass the raw data without any transformation as input of the ETS models.

ARIMA. The AutoRegressive Integrated Moving Average (ARIMA) models are another widely used approach to conduct time series forecasting [12]. This model concentrated on the effect of past values and past errors [12]. There are three parameters p, q, and d in ARIMA models, respectively the lag for auto regression, the error for moving average, and the non-seasonal differencing for integrated.

However, AR and MA processes require stationary data, so this research will pass the transformed data, first performing Box-Cox transformation and then conducting 1st order differencing, as discussed in the previous Data Processing section as input.

Comparative Analysis of ETS and ARIMA. ETS models focus on the exponential smoothing by analyzing error, trend, and seasonality data points. On the other hand, ARIMA models focus on the autocorrelation of past data and past error in the sample data. These two models provide different points of view for analyzing the data, and thus, it is worth comparing their results together.

3 Results

This research uses the built-in function in the R forecast library to automatically select the best fitting parameters for each model. This is applicable for both ETS and ARIMA models. Then, forecasting the balance of trade value for next two years based on the model selected.

3.1 ETS

Balance of Trade Model. Firstly, this research trains the model by using the exports data minus imports data as direct input. The optimal ETS model selected is ETS (A, N, A) with more details in Table 3. In other words, this model emphasizes the error and seasonality terms, but the trend is being ignored. Also, more weight is being given to the error than seasonality suggesting that values of recent data points are critical. The forecasted trade balance fluctuated around the value of last observation, which is consistent with a model having seasonality but no trend.

Table 3. ETS model parameters for balance of trade.

	error	trend	seasonal
method	additive	/	additive
coefficient	0.8702	/	0.1298

However, this ETS model cannot interpret all the features in trade balance data. This is because of the residual check result shown in Fig. 3. It is worth noting from the ACF plot that there is a strong autocorrelation with the lag 1, which indicates a correlation between residual and original series. In other words, the residuals from fitting ETS models are not white noise indicating this model might not be a good fit.

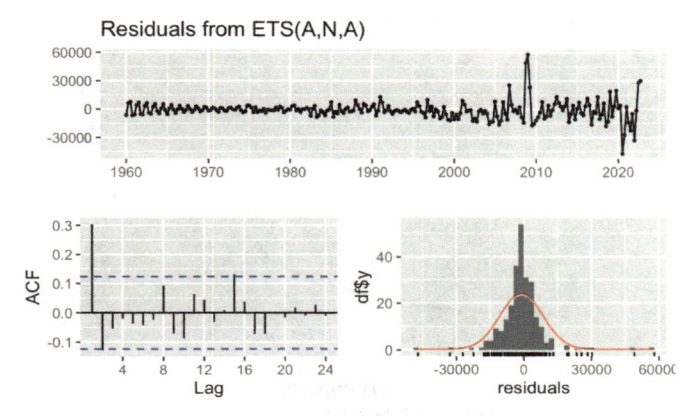

Fig. 3. ETS model residual for balance of trade.

Subtracting Imports Models from Exports Models. Secondly, this research finds the optimal ETS model for both imports and exports data, and then subtract these two models to get the balance of trade forecast. Table 4 shows that the auto-computed models for both series are ETS (M, A, M) with a majority of weight being given to recent data points. This is as expected since both raw data looks exponential growth, multiplicative methods can better model the rapid increasing pattern.

Table 4. ETS model parameters for imports and exports.

	Imports			Exports		
	error	trend	seasonal	error	trend	seasonal
method	multiplicative	additive	multiplicative	multiplicative	additive	multiplicative
coefficient	0.9453	0.0494	0.0547	0.8846	0.0503	0.1033

Moreover, both models capture the feature of trends although their weight is not significant, and thus, the future prediction for imports and exports are gradually increasing (Fig. 4).

Forecasts from ETS(M,A,M)

(a) Imports

Forecasts from ETS(M,A,M)

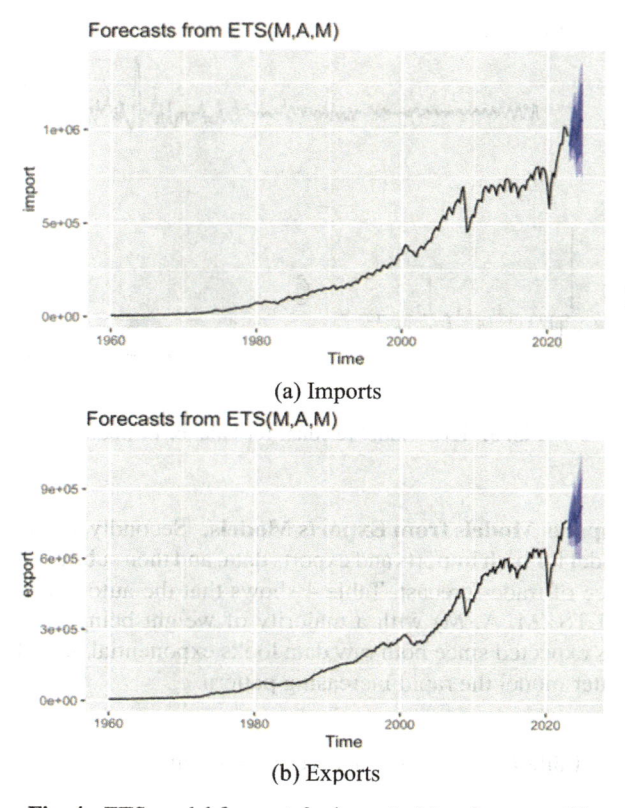

(b) Exports

Fig. 4. ETS model forecast for imports (a) and exports (b).

Validity checks are again performed on these two models by evaluating the residuals. Figure 5 shows that the residual plots look like white noise and approximately normally distributed. Only one or two lags slightly exceeding the 95% confidence interval, which is a tolerable result for a model fitting.

Both historical and prediction values of trade balance are computed by directly subtracting the imports and exports for the corresponding time periods.

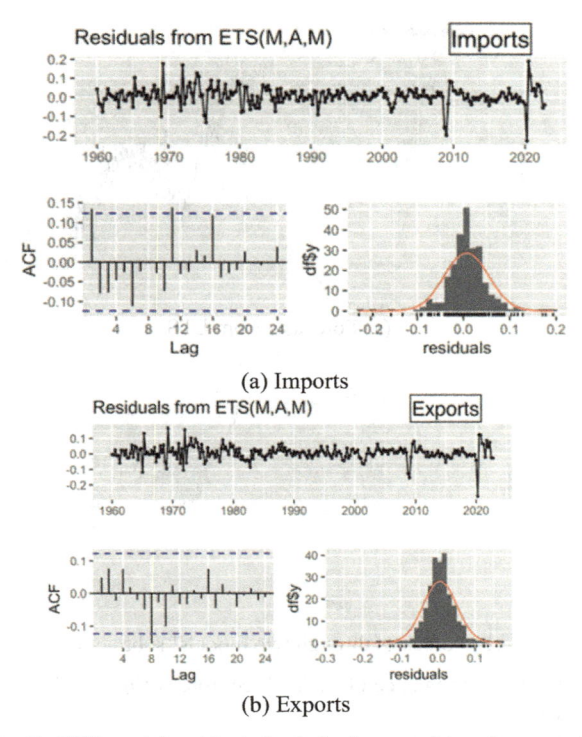

Fig. 5. ETS model residual check for imports (a) and exports (b).

Comparison of Forecasts from Two Approaches. Figure 6 shows the U.S. Trade balance forecast by using two approaches discussed above. Both predictions present a strong seasonality feature. Interestingly, there is a clear trend of decreasing when using two model subtraction methods, which is absent from direct modeling trade balance. One more difference is that the confidence intervals computed through the subtraction method are wider, which indicates the instability of prediction.

3.2 ARIMA

As discussed in the Data Processing section, this research uses Box-Cox transformation and 1st order differencing as inputs to the ARIMA models. After finishing the forecast, inverse transformation is conducted to make the result compatible with the original value.

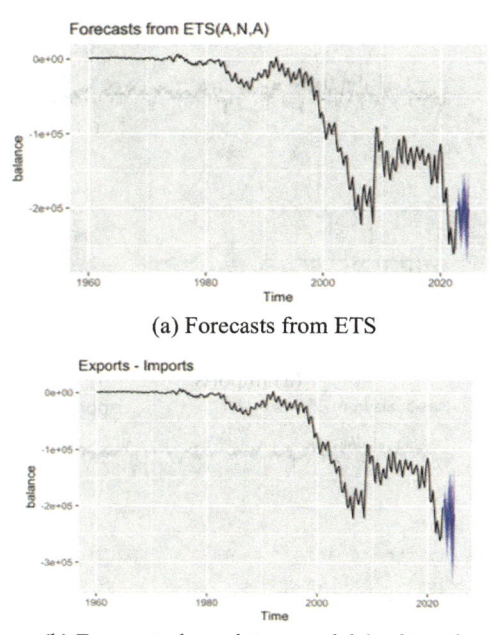

Fig. 6. ETS model forecast for balance of trade, direct forecasting (a); forecasting through two models' subtraction (b).

Balance of Trade Model. ARIMA (0, 0, 2) (0, 1, 1) is the auto-selected best fitting ARIMA model for the trade balance (Table 5). It only has MA terms and Seasonal MA terms indicating that this model only focuses on the error and discards the past sample data. A positive MA1(0.2672) suggests the last error has a positive influence on the prediction while a negative MA2(-0.1071) suggests the second-to-last error negatively influences the forecast. Also, the magnitude of SMA1(-0.8043) is larger than MA1 and MA2, meaning that the error from last season negatively affects the next value to a great extent.

Table 5. ARIMA model parameters for balance of trade.

	ma1	ma2	sma1
coefficient	0.2672	−0.1071	−0.8043
s.e.	0.0670	0.0628	0.0471

Although the residual plot looks like the variance is increasing (Fig. 7), the Ljung-Box hypothesis test suggests the null hypothesis of residuals are white noise cannot be rejected. This is because the p-value in the hypothesis test equals 0.1401, which is larger than 0.05. In other words, this model fits the trade balance series well.

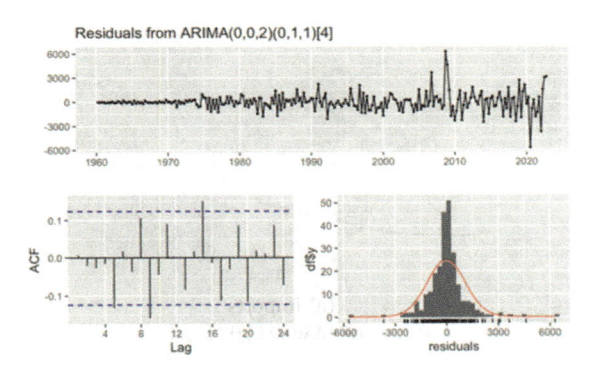

Fig. 7. ARIMA model residual for balance of trade.

Subtracting Imports Models from Exports Models. The best fitted ARIMA model for both U.S. imports and exports data are shown in Table 6. The imports model put emphasis on the last three data values, last two data errors, and last seasonal error. In addition, the exports model only takes the seasonal error from the previous two seasons into account.

Table 6. ARIMA model parameters for imports and exports.

	Imports							Exports	
term	ar1	ar2	ar3	ma1	ma2	sma1	drift	sma1	sma2
coefficient	0.0477	0.7444	−0.1750	0.1042	−0.8590	−0.8448	−1e-04	−0.7699	−0.1087
s.e.	0.1083	0.0968	0.0664	0.0905	0.0898	0.0598	1e-04	0.0707	0.0712

Plots for both models are shown in Fig. 8 for clarity.

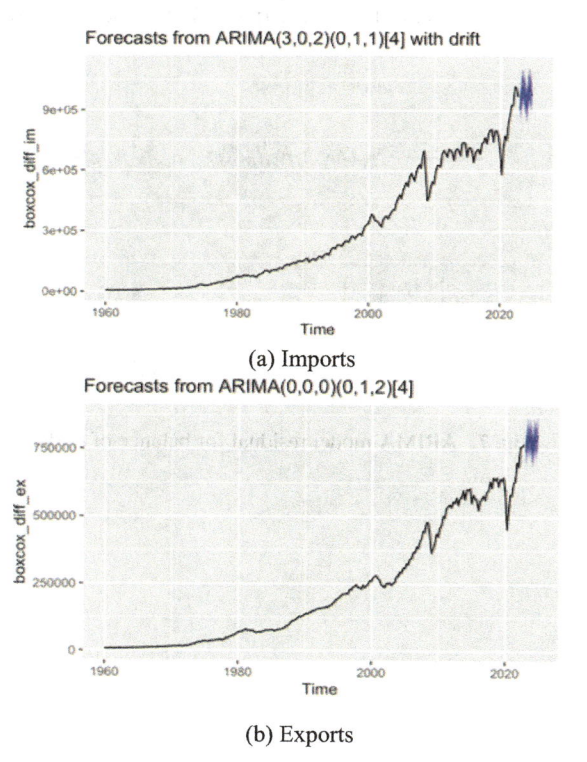

(a) Imports

(b) Exports

Fig. 8. ARIMA model forecast for imports (a) and exports (b).

These two models both fit the data well according to the residual checks. It is obvious that the residual is consistent with white noise since the residual plots look random and residuals are normally distributed in both cases (Fig. 9). Again, subtractions on both series are computed to get the trade balance results. More details discussed in the next section.

Residuals from ARIMA(3,0,2)(0,1,1)[4] with drift

(a) Imports

Residuals from ARIMA(0,0,0)(0,1,2)[4]

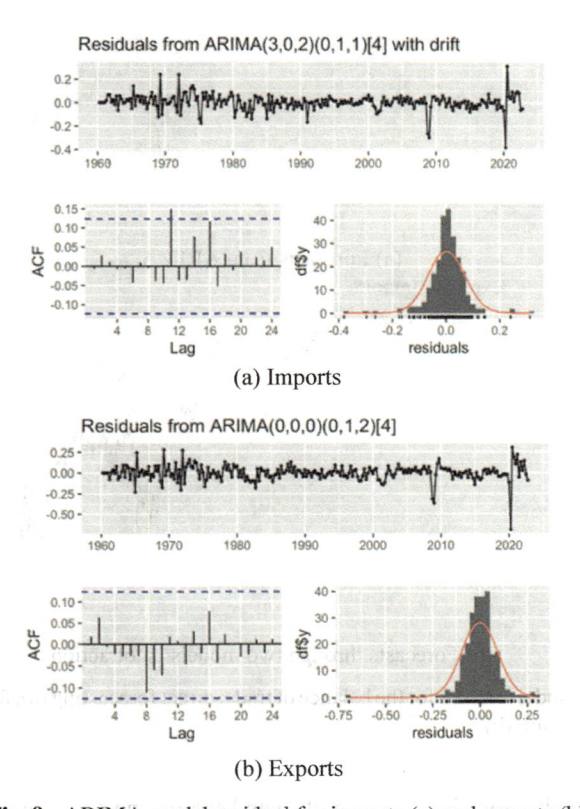

(b) Exports

Fig. 9. ARIMA model residual for imports (a) and exports (b).

Comparison of Forecasts from Two Approaches. Putting two methods of forecasting the trade balance via ARIMA models together, their results are similar (Fig. 10). The only difference is that the first forecasted value is larger when subtracting two models, but it is not significant.

4 Discussion

Forecasts of the U.S. trade balance by using four different methods provide some interesting insights. All predictions show a feature of strong seasonality, which is in line with the historical data. The forecast from ETS models' subtraction approach show a downward trend and this is consistent with the entire time series plot. However, the other three methods are just fluctuated around the last observation without any trend pattern.

Forecasts from ARIMA(0,0,2)(0,1,1)[4]

(a) Forecasts from ARIMA

Exports - Imports

(b) Forecasts through two models' subtraction

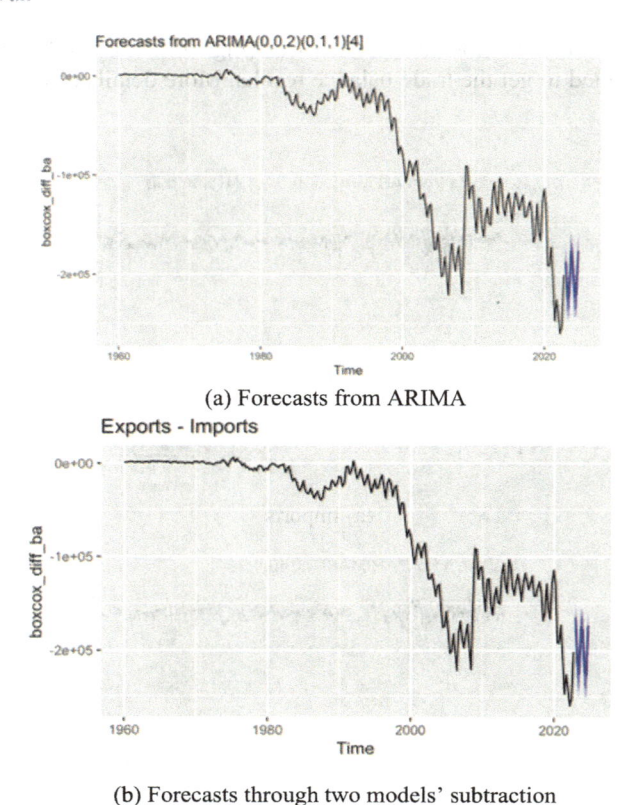

Fig. 10. ARIMA model forecast for the balance of trade, direct forecasting (a); forecasting through two models' subtraction (b).

Since they all weight more for the recent data and errors, one possible reason is that they capture the ten-year stable period feature starting from 2010 and reflect it in the results. None of the models give an upward prediction. In summary, the U.S. trade deficit is highly unlikely to be mitigated based on these forecasted results.

5 Conclusion

The research aims to analyze and forecast the U.S. balance of trade from the time series analysis perspective. Two classic models are being used in this study, respectively ETS and ARIMA models. Each models forecast the U.S. balance of trade by using two approaches, subtracting imports value from exports before fitting the models as well as subtracting them after getting imports model and exports model. Therefore, all together four different forecasts are given in this research.

Among these four forecasted trade balances, three of them indicate a future stable trade balance maintaining at a low level but one prediction suggests the trade balance will continuously decrease. This implies the future U.S. trade deficit will not be mitigated, which is not an optimistic tendency. It also suggests that the economic is unlikely to narrow the trade deficit automatically, and thus, more attention should be paid.

One limitation for this research is that it only uses ETS and ARIMA models. These two models are the most intuitive start points for time series data. Therefore, future research can be conducted on other different models such as GARCH, Neural Network, etc.

References

1. Claessens, M.S., Kose, M.A.: Financial crises explanations, types, and implications (2013)
2. The US Trade Deficit: Causes, Consequences, and Recommendations for Action, The Commission (2000)
3. Mann, C.L.: Is the US trade deficit sustainable? Peterson Institute (1999)
4. Krugman, P.R., Baldwin, R.E., Bosworth, B., Hooper, P.: The persistence of the US trade deficit. Brook. Pap. Econ. Act. **1**, 55 (1987)
5. International Trade: Imports: Value (goods): Total for the United States, https://fred.stlouisfed.org/series/USAXTIMVA01CXMLM, last accessed 13 March 2023
6. International Trade: Exports: Value (goods): Total for the United States, https://fred.stlouisfed.org/series/USAXTEXVA01CXMLM, last accessed 13 March 2023
7. Osborne, J.: Improving your data transformations: Applying the Box-Cox transformation. Pract. Assess. Res. Eval. **15**, 1 (2010)
8. Box, G.E., Jenkins, G.M., Reinsel, G.C., Ljung, G.M.: Time series analysis: forecasting and control. John Wiley & Sons (2015)
9. Hobijn, B., Franses, P.H., Ooms, M.: Generalizations of the KPSS-test for stationarity. Stat. Neerl. **58**, 4 (2004)
10. Dickey, D.A., Pantula, S.G.: Determining the order of differencing in autoregressive processes. J. Bus. Eco. Stati. **5**, 4 (1987)
11. Gardner, E.S., Jr.: Exponential smoothing: The state of the art—Part II. Int. J. Forecast. **22**, 4 (2006)
12. Box, G.E., Pierce, D.A.: Distribution of residual autocorrelations in autoregressive-integrated moving average time series models. J. Am. Stat. Assoc. **65**, 332 (1970)

Research on the Factors Affecting Mobility Rate Across States in the United States

Xinyu Shi[✉]

Faculty of Business and Economics, The University of Melbourne, Victoria, Australia
xinyus1@stu.qhnu.edu.cn

Abstract. Mobility rates contribute to social stability and development, so it is meaningful to study the factors that influence mobility rates. This paper uses data from the United States from 2011 to 2021 across different states, first, finding that people who have the characteristics of being single, highly educated, or renting to live have relatively higher mobility rates. Regression models were then used to analyze the impact on mobility rates from various factors, including demographics, economics, weather, education, and geographic factors. These results can be instructive for local governments aiming to improve mobility rates and provide some ideas for those who want to research mobility rates in depth.

Keywords: Mobility Rate · United States · Education

1 Introduction

The population mobility rate is the proportion of the population that moves from one area to another over a given period of time. The study of migration rates is important for understanding and analyzing economic, social, and geopolitical changes [1]. For example, a high mobility rate usually indicates a booming economy because people usually look for better jobs and a better quality of life. On the other hand, low mobility rates usually indicate a depressed economy or limited resources because people cannot easily leave their original locations [2]. Population mobility rates can also provide information about social change. Societies with high mobility rates may experience social pluralism and cultural integration as different population groups come together [3]. Information on geopolitical changes can also be revealed by population mobility rates. Unusual mobility rates may imply political instability or resource competition in border areas. In addition, political conflicts or disasters may lead to large population movements, which can also be analyzed by mobility rates [4]. Researchers analyze these patterns and trends in population movements, including destination, origin, volume, and size of migration. These studies can provide important information for policymakers to develop more effective migration policies. In recent reaches, with the advance of digitalization, new technologies such as mobile-phone-based travel big data are being applied to the study of population mobility. These technologies can help researchers more accurately identify and analyze patterns and trends in population mobility [5]. More precisely, many literatures examining population mobility during COVID-19 have used these mobile phone data to obtain more accurate and real-time data [6].

In the United States, as a nation of immigrants, population mobility has always been a significant research area. The study of population mobility rates between different states in the United States can help to gain insights into the trends and causes of population flow in different regions and provide valuable information for policy-making and social development [7]. Analyzing the data from various sources, including census data, tax data, and population migration surveys, researchers have identified significant migration patterns, factors that influence mobility preference, and changes in migration trends over time. For example, young people and highly educated populations tend to migrate from cities to suburbs and from wealthy states to poor states. These research results indicate that population mobility is influenced by various factors, including economic development, employment opportunities, housing affordability, and lifestyles [8]. At the same time, some literature point out the relationship between climate change and migration rate, the unfavored climate and the associated decrease in agricultural productivity would induce the adult population to leave rural counties [9]. In addition, other researchers found that during the last decades, the long-distance movement had significantly decreased because one of the main reasons for long-distance migration is that job-related moves declined substantially since the 1980s [10].

This paper aims to provide a comprehensive overview of the research on population mobility rates across different states in the U.S. This paper first investigates the differences in population mobility among different population segments using statistical analysis. Then construct the regression estimation to explore the trends and drivers of population mobility across different states in the U.S., highlighting the factors that influence population mobility and interpreting the results. Finally, the paper will discuss the implications of the findings for policy-making and future studies.

2 Data

All the data used in this paper is collected from the U.S. census bureau, which is an official website of the U.S. government, thus that is confident in their accuracy. This paper focuses on mobility within the country across different states, so the primary data is the percentage of residents who moved from other states in 1 year. In addition to the overall population data, this paper also collects data on different marital statuses, educational levels, and housing statuses. The data is collected for the years 2011–2021 and include the individual data for the 51 states in the U.S. except for Puerto Rico because it is not a state, also the District of Columbia and Washington are separated into two different areas according to the census bureau data.

Table 1 provides the descriptive statistics of the mobility for different characteristics of the population. In the subgroup of different marital statuses, never married people have the highest migration rate of an average of 4.61% and have a huge gap with other marital status people, and more than double the difference with widowed people. The second highest group is divorced or separated people, as expected, single people are more convenient and can move for less money, while married or widowed people are more likely to live with their families and therefore do not tend to move. In the subgroup of different education levels, there is a clear trend that people with higher education will more likely to move around. People with higher levels of education may be more likely to adapt to different environments and cultures and have better possibilities to seek new challenges and opportunities. These factors may lead them to be more willing to move around. In the subgroup of different housing statuses, the people living in the renter-occupied house have average mobility of 5.33% which is almost 4 times that of people living in the owner-occupied house. People who live in the ranting houses will have less difference to rent a house in other states, they will have fewer opportunity costs to move around.

Table 1. Descriptive statistics for different groups of mobility.

Marital Statuses Subgroup			
	Average	Max	Min
Never married	3.36%	3.50%	3.30%
Now married, except separated	1.85%	2.00%	1.70%
Divorced or separated	2.27%	2.40%	2.10%
Widowed	1.40%	1.50%	1.30%
	Max: 3.36% (Never married) Min: 1.40% (Widowed)		
Education Level Subgroup			
	Average	Max	Min
Less than high school graduate	1.22%	1.30%	1.10%
High school graduate	1.51%	1.60%	1.50%
college or associate degree	1.97%	2.10%	1.90%
Bachelor's degree	2.71%	2.80%	2.60%
Graduate or professional degree	3.15%	3.30%	3.00%
	Max: 3.15% (Graduate or professional degree) Min: 1.22% (Less than high school graduate)		
Housing Statuses Subgroup			
	Average	Max	Min
Owner-occupied	1.21%	1.50%	1.00%
Renter-occupied	3.95%	4.20%	3.70%
	Max: 3.95% (Owner-occupied) Min: 1.32% (Renter-occupied)		

Table 2 shows the maximum and minimum mobility across different states. District of Columbia has the highest migration rate which is 8.24% on average. As the capital of the U.S., it has a highly developed transportation and business center, as well as a large number of governmental and cultural institutions. These characteristics may be the reason that DC has higher population mobility than other states. The lowest migration rate is in California with an average of 1.27%. California's relatively high housing prices and tax burden may cause some people to choose not to move to California for financial reasons. It is also relatively far away from the East and Central regions, which may cause some people to choose not to move to California because of the distance. These are just a few possible factors; the reality can be more complex. The decision to move is often influenced by a variety of factors, including demographics, economics, weather, education, and geographic location. So, this paper collects data for some of these factors in order to get a better understanding of how they influence people's migration preferences. For demographic factors, this paper includes the population of the states, the percentage of other races(except white), and the percentage of elders(age above 65); for economic factors, includes median income, median housing price, and unemployment rate; includes the higher education rate(percentage of population enrolled in college or graduate school) for the educational factors; and for geographical factors, this paper uses region dummies to indicate different regions: the Northeast, South, Midwest, and West. All these data are collected for each state from 2011–2021, the log transformation is used for the data with large numbers to avoid heteroskedasticity caused by large differences in the values of variables.

Table 2. Mobility across different states.

Mobility			
	Average	Max	Min
51 states	2.99%	8.24%	1.27%
	Max: District of Columbia Min: California		

3 Empirical Results

To further understand how different factors influence the propensity for population mobility, this paper constructs a FE model using the data from 51 different states across the U.S. from 2011 to 2021. This paper constructs both random effect model and fixed effect model in order to control the omitted variable bias from unobserved heterogeneity (states' individual-specific effect in this case). And by using the Hausman test, the result suggests that the fixed effect model will be more appropriate. The fixed effect model is specified as follows:

$$POP_{it} = constant + \beta_1 population_{it} + \beta_2 POR_{it} + \beta_3 POE_{it} + \beta_4 MedianIncome_{it} + \beta_5 MHP_{it} + \beta_6 unemployment_{it} + \beta_7 HER_{it} + \beta_8 northeast_i + \beta_9 south_i + \beta_{10} midwest_i + \beta_{11} west_i (omitted) + \varepsilon_{it}$$

(1)

Definitions of variables are shown in Table 3.

Table 3. The definition of variables.

POP	population mobility rate
POR	percentage of other races
POE	percentage of elders
MHP	Median Housing Price
HER	higher education rate

Population mobility rate is the explanatory variable, and the independent variables with coefficients β1 to β11 are factors that be expected to affect mobility rates, which have already been explained in the Data part. The variables population, median income, and median housing price are taken as the log values in the estimation. The result is shown in Table 4.

Table 4. Results of RE and FE model.

Population Mobility	RE	FE
Population	−0.0066133***	0.0063636***
Percentage of Other Races	0.0040763	0.0072068**
Percentage of Elders	−0.011972	−0.0151288
Median Income	0.0142765***	0.0152901***
Median Housing Price	−0.0060317***	−0.008924***
Unemployment Rate	−0.0491462***	0.0811642***
Higher Education Rate	0.1276732***	0.1375108***
Northeast	−0.0165631***	0.0170627***
South	−0.0068612***	0.0082059***
Midwest	−0.0132207***	0.0148406***
West	omitted	Omitted
Constant	0.0191574	0.0394251

Note: Significance level: * $p < 0.01$, ** $p < 0.05$, *** $p < 0.01$. Using robust standard error.

The results obtained from Table 4 agree with expectations, most of the coefficients are significant at 5% level except for the percentage of elders. This suggests the percentage of elders is not a directly correlated factor to mobility rate. Focus on those significant results, starting with the demographic factors, the size of the population negatively correlated with mobility, but the percentage of other races have a positive impact. States with large populations have relatively higher costs of living and more competition, so moving to such places may incur more opportunity costs and thus be less desirable. The higher percentage of other races indicates the state is more ethnically diverse and has a more egalitarian social environment, maybe more inclusive of migrants and more attractive to people of all races. In economic terms, higher wages will attract migrants while higher housing prices and higher unemployment rates will not be favored migrants. It is worth noting that the magnitude of coefficients on house prices is much lower than income, a 100% increase in wage will associate with a 0.015% increase in mobility rate, but a 100% increase in house price will only correlate with a 0.009% decrease in mobility rate. So, the combination of higher wages and higher house prices has a positive effect on mobility rates when they both increase proportionally. And together with the impact of unemployment, overall a better economic environment will attract migrants because it means a better quality of life, more jobs, and investment opportunities. For the educational factor, the result shows a 1% increase in high education rate will associate with a 0.1375% increase in the mobility rate. Its coefficient is the largest of all, and although all variables have different bases and cannot be compared, this still shows that education has a significant impact on people moving decisions. This also correlates with the results in the data section: people with higher education will more likely to move around; the states with higher education rates are more attractive to this group of people. Education is also the basis for other developments, so people consider the state's education to a large extent when choosing where to migrate. In the geographical part, the West region is omitted because of perfect collinearity, so this region will be used as the comparison group. All other regions have lower migration rates than the West, in order of popularity, the West is the most popular, followed by the South and Midwest, with the Northeast having the lowest rate of migration.

Several factors may have contributed to this sorting; first, the weather is different in these regions. The climate in the West is typically warm and dry, making it a popular choice for retirees and those who enjoy outdoor activities. The South and Midwest also have relatively warm climates, especially in the winter. In contrast, the Northeast has cold, wet winters and hot summers, which are less comfortable for people to live [11]. Second, different job opportunities across regions, the West is loaded with emerging cities and technology centers, such as the San Francisco Bay Area and Seattle, which offer a large number of high-paying jobs and have attracted many people to move to these locations. The South and Midwest also have many industrial and service sector jobs. However, the job market in the Northeast is relatively small, especially in manufacturing and traditional industries, which may be another reason for the low migration rate.

4 Conclusion

This paper investigates the population mobility rate in the United States. The population was first divided into different category groups and the mobility rates of the different types of population in the groups were compared. It was found that people who have the characteristics of being single, highly educated, or renting to live have relatively higher mobility rates. This paper then constructs a FE model using a more detailed 51-state mobility rate. From the estimation results, a more inclusive environment, a better economy, lower housing costs, and higher education rates are all important factors in attracting people to migrate. And geographically, the West, with its more favorable climate and better job opportunities, is favored by migrants. The results obtained in this paper are instructive and can provide some ideas for the local government to develop policies to attract migrants. For example, combining the conclusion that highly educated people prefer to migrate and that a high education rate attracts migrants, then developing policies that can attract highly educated people will also increase the education rate and attract more migrants to form a virtuous circle. For instance, combining this idea with the impact of housing prices on migration, giving subsidies to highly educated people to rent or buy a house could be a strategy to attract migrants. This paper only provides a preliminary analysis of the factors that influence mobility rates, and further research could be conducted in more subtle areas, such as economic, political, or educational aspects. Alternatively, it may be possible to examine how changes in mobility rates in return affect unemployment, housing prices, and wages, which were the original independent variables.

References

1. Brown, T.A.: Migration and politics: the impact of population mobility on American voting behavior. UNC Press Books (2018)
2. Güell, M., Pellizzari, M., Pica, G.: Econ. J. **128**(612), F353–F403 (2018)
3. Martín-Cano, M.C., Sampedro-Palacios, C.B., Ricoy-Cano, A.J.: JERPH **17**(18), 6460 (2020)
4. Cummings, C., Pacitto, J., Lauro, D.: Why people move: understanding the drivers and trends of migration to Europe. ODI London (2015)
5. Yang, Z., Gao, W., Zhao, X.: Sustain. Sci. **12**(10), 4012 (2020)
6. Zhou, Y., Xu, R., Hu, D.: Lancet Digit. Health **2**(8), e417–e424 (2020)
7. Liu, X., Andris, C., Desmarais, B.A.: PloS one **14**(11), e0225405 (2019)
8. Jia, N., Molloy, R., Smith, C.: JEL **61**(1), 144–180 (2023)
9. Feng, S., Oppenheimer, M., Schlenker, W.: Climate change, crop yields, and internal migration in the United States. NBER (2012)
10. Molloy, R., Smith, C.: US internal migration: Recent patterns and outstanding puzzles, Federal Reserve Bank of Boston's 63rd Economic Conference. A House Divided: Geographical Disparities in Twenty-First Century America (2019)
11. National Centers for Environmental Information: Regional Climate Centers. URL: https://www.ncei.noaa.gov/regional/regional-climate-centers, Last accessed 13 March 2023

Exploring the Risks of Blockchain to the Financial Market and Its Countermeasures

Yujiang Duan[1], Fengfan Ge[2], and Zhixing Wen[3(✉)]

[1] Sichuan University, Chengdu Sichuan 610064, China
[2] Soochow University, Suzhou Jiangsu 215500, China
[3] Hebei University of Technology, Tianjin 300401, China
202958@stu.hebut.edu.cn

Abstract. Blockchain technology, which has emerged as a distributed ledger technology, has been widely applied in different sectors because of the advancement of Internet technology. However, the use of Blockchain technology also poses numerous risks that need to be addressed. To better understand and manage these risks, the paper, by referring to relevant literature and materials and refining them, finally classified them into three major categories: technical risk, operational risk, and legal risk. Technical risk involves the reliability, scalability, and security of Blockchain systems, while operational risk pertains to the potential for user error, and malicious attacks. Legal risk includes legal deficiencies and regulatory failures. Based on these categories, the paper proposes suggestions and solutions in order to reduce the risks associated with Blockchain technology. These solutions include measures such as the application of new technologies, optimization of algorithms, specification, and training of personnel, and construction of laws and regulations. Finally, several suggestions are proposed to address the research direction of Blockchain risk. In the future, we may continue to conduct in-depth research on strengthening financial regulation and central bank digital currency.

Keywords: Blockchain · Risk · Countermeasures · Financial Supervision · CBDC

1 Introduction

Blockchain is a technology that has gained a lot of attention in recent years. The Blockchain is a digital ledger that allows users to monitor transactions and share documents without the need for centralized record keeping, such as the registrar's office in the case of diplomas and transcripts. On the Blockchain, each transaction is referred to as a "block" [1]. At their most basic, they allow a community of users to record transactions in a shared ledger within that community, so that no transaction can be altered once published under normal operation of the Blockchain network. As a result, it is primarily used in the financial sector for conducting transactions and keeping records.

Y. Duan, F. Ge and Z. Wen—These authors contributed equally.

Although Blockchain has numerous advantages such as decentralization, anonymity, and auditability, there is a diverse range of Blockchain applications spanning from cryptocurrency, financial services, risk management, internet of things (IoT), and public and social services [2]. Like any other technology, Blockchain also has some inherent risks associated with it [3]. However, there have been some recent studies on Blockchain security, but few of them conduct a systematic examination of the risks to Blockchain and the associated countermeasures [2].

Under the guidance of the Blockchain Committee of the China Information Association, SAFEIS Security Research Institute released the 2022 Blockchain Security White Paper. According to the report, the total amount of money involved in Blockchain security incidents in 2022 exceeded $75.3 billion, including major crashes of more than $60 billion. What's more, there are 204 Blockchain security incidents involving more than $100,000 in 2022 such as 59 vulnerability attacks. Readers can have an intuitive feeling through the following two pie charts (Fig. 1 and Fig. 2).

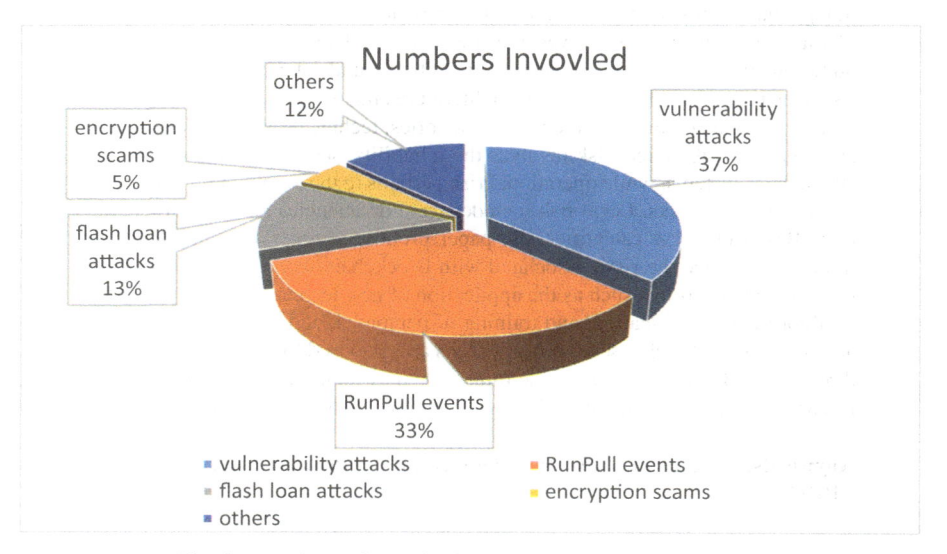

Fig. 1. Numbers of security incidents of Blockchain in 2022.

Moving to February 2023, according to the data statistics by SAFEIS, Blockchain ecological security events in February resulted in losses of more than $57.8 million. It can be seen that the risk response measures must be accelerated. Under the circumstances, this literature review aims to explore the existing risks associated with Blockchain technology and the solutions proposed to mitigate them. Previous studies focused more on the security problems formed by Blockchain and the leakage of property and privacy, but few articles broke down why such a crisis occurred. After sorting and summarizing, this paper described and summarized the causes of Blockchain risks and their solutions from the operational and legal levels respectively, examined the underlying logic and implementation methods of Blockchain technology from a technical standpoint, and proposed a technical optimization scheme.

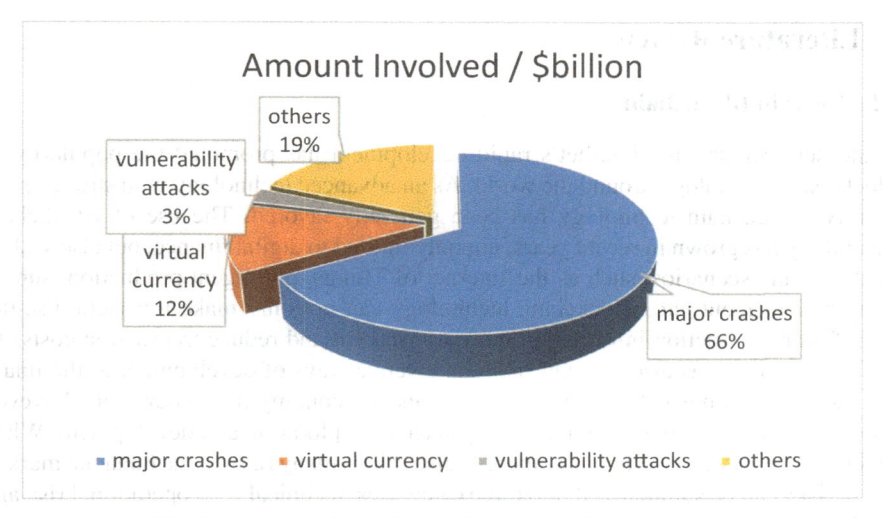

Fig. 2. Amount of security incidents of Blockchain in 2022.

This paper contributes to the field in several ways. First, our paper is distinct from similar studies looking at the risk problems in Blockchain. This paper have synthesized the definitions of Blockchain risk in many relevant papers and summarized them, and then proposed a new classification of Blockchain risk. Second, this paper have basically given their countermeasures to the various risks mentioned, and have got a perfect solution system, which is not done in other papers. Finally, through reading a large number of relevant documents, this paper find that there is still a big gap in the financial supervision of Blockchain, especially the need to propose more complete and detailed internationally applicable laws for Blockchain.

This paper will begin by providing a brief overview of Blockchain technology, its working, and its applications in different industries. It will then delve into the potential risks associated with Blockchain technology, including technical, operational and legal risks. The review will analyze the different types of attacks that can be carried out on Blockchain networks and the vulnerabilities that can be exploited. Subsequently, this paper will combine the most cutting-edge research today to sort and summarize, and describe our effective solutions from the aspects of technical risks, operational risks, and legal risks, and propose our Blockchain optimization plan from the algorithm level, explore the existing solutions proposed to mitigate these risks. This will include a discussion of techniques such as consensus mechanisms, smart contracts, and cryptographic protocols that can be used to enhance Blockchain network security and speed. Additionally, the review will analyze the regulatory frameworks and best practices developed by different countries and organizations to ensure compliance and reduce legal risks associated with Blockchain technology.

Overall, this literature review will provide a comprehensive analysis of the risks associated with Blockchain technology and the solutions proposed to mitigate them. It aims to serve as a valuable resource for researchers, practitioners, and policymakers working in the field of Blockchain technology.

2 Literature Review

2.1 Risks in Blockchain

In the new century, the internet's rapid development has promoted the popularity of Blockchain technology around the world. As an advanced technology with strong applicability, Blockchain technology has been generally favored. The use of Blockchain technology has grown in recent years, not only limited to digital finance, but also widely used in many scenarios, such as the Internet of Things, intelligent production, supply chain management, etc. Blockchain technology can not only make transaction settlement faster, transaction information more transparent and reduce transaction costs. At the same time, it has also brought many innovative ways of development to the financial industry and pushed the Internet and financial economy into a new era. However, Blockchain technology is still in the early stage of exploration and development. When Blockchain innovates financial business, it also brings many risks to the financial market. These risks can be summarized into three categories: technical risk, operational risk and legal risk.

Technical Risk. Blockchain technology is not yet mature and is still in the development and testing stage. First, there are risks in key security. In Blockchain technology, the key is generated by asymmetric encryption technology and has uniqueness. But the keys can be compromised by viruses and malware. If the key is sent via unencrypted channels such as email and text messages, or is kept in unencrypted files, the key may be lost or leaked, thus leaking the customer's personal information [4]. Second, the security and computing power of the Blockchain system are difficult to balance. The more nodes the Blockchain system participates in, the more difficult it is to crack, and the more secure the data is. However, due to the weak foundation of technology, with the increase of the number of nodes, the computing power of the database also needs to be increased accordingly. When computing capacity falls short of the requirements, trading efficiency suffers [5]. Third, there are application risks in smart contracts. Smart contracts have the characteristics of enforcement and real-time settlement, and once there are loopholes in the program code, they may cause irreparable losses. Zachariadis et al. discovered that if the subject's governance and confidence are completely dependent on the code base, an attacker can abuse the smart contract's implementation vulnerability to obtain illegal gains within the code permission [6]. Nitin argued that when smart contracts are being implemented and executed in Blockchain, users may cause losses due to insufficient legal understanding and coverage awareness of smart contracts [7]. Fourth, the underlying mechanism of Blockchain is security risk. The bottom layer of the Blockchain is primarily concerned with data storage and transmission. In 2014, due to the technical loopholes at the bottom of the Blockchain, some users used the loopholes to repeatedly withdraw cash, resulting in the loss of about 850,000 bitcoins in this incident, and finally declared bankruptcy [8].

Operational Risk. Luo asserted that operational risk refers to problems in the Blockchain caused by incorrect operations when operators trade or manage the Blockchain in the Blockchain [5]. On the one hand, the Blockchain cannot be fully reviewed by managers, and there may be improper configuration of procedures and internal controls and failure to repair technical vulnerabilities. Criminals may use loopholes to tamper with transaction data and personal information to obtain illegal gains, such as illegal fund-raising, community funding, and money laundering. Simultaneously, due to data and information tampering, financial security regulators' controllability to the Blockchain database will be reduced, and these illegal and criminal acts endangering financial security will be unable to be located, tracked, and investigated through the information in the Blockchain system, implying that financial security cannot be further guaranteed. On the other hand, in the application process of Blockchain finance, if the staff have not received professional training and assessment, and lack of understanding of the specific implementation methods and key points of business, operational errors may occur due to lack of experience and strong subjective initiative, resulting in serious losses [9].

Legal Risk. The supervision of Blockchain banking primarily reflects legal risks. When faced with the issue of Blockchain risk, regulators find it difficult to correctly capture all of the risks posed by new technologies to market infrastructure, users, and society as a whole. Supervision is mainly facing two major difficulties. First, the lack of relevant laws and regulations. Blockchain adopts distributed bookkeeping, which is cross regional and cross-border. There are great differences in the law enforcement of Blockchain finance in different countries and regions, and even there are rules gaps in the supervision of Blockchain in some countries. Therefore, the lack of law hinders the supervision of Blockchain. Anderson believed that asset classes attract new participants and create new problems, namely money laundering, terrorist financing, tax evasion and fraud, due to the use of Blockchain or decentralized ledgers to promote decentralized value exchanges among market participants [10]. Legal recognition here refers to the recognition of some legal effect and effectiveness of the use of decentralized ledgers. If it is not approved by relevant laws, it will lack legal stability for users of decentralized accounts. Second, the decentralization of Blockchain is inconsistent with the regulatory system. Blockchain has certain characteristics of avoiding financial supervision, which needs to be further reconciled with the current supervision mode. Zeng believed that the development of financial science and technology, especially the entry of Blockchain, leads to the further expansion of existing financial market risks, while the decentralized mechanism makes supervision weak, and the information protection of financial consumers will be more difficult than before [11]. Cui believed that Blockchain finance is facing a series of risks derived from the early application of Blockchain in the financial field due to the existence of technical loopholes. At the same time, the unique decentralization mechanism of Blockchain will make Blockchain finance face regulatory difficulties and alienation risks [12].

2.2 Risks Countermeasures

Countermeasures for Technical Risk. To address the risk of loss and leakage of the key, Blockchain researchers can strengthen the encryption of private keys. Anita mentioned that dynamic password generation can be used for authentication. In this case, the user even if one device is attacked, other devices are protected from the attack because of the presence of dynamic keys [13]. Aydar and his team built an efficient encryption and recovery system by applying biometric techniques such as fingerprint recognition. Users can use their biometrics to encrypt and decrypt keys more securely [14]. Therefore, the Blockchain key can enhance its stability and security by referring to other fields of cryptography to guarantee the security of users' information.

And for the problem of security and computing power of Blockchain, it can be solved from three aspects. The first aspect optimizes the consensus algorithm of the Blockchain. Consensus algorithms are the basis of Blockchain security and they have been developed with different advantages and disadvantages. Choosing the right algorithm or developing a new one will help to reduce the computational power required by the Blockchain while maintaining its security. For example, Yang proposed an effective consensus algorithm named Delegated Proof of Stake with Downgrade (DDPoS) by combining the advantages of Proof of Work (PoW) and Delegated Proof of Stake (DPoS), which can reduce computational energy consumption and improve operational efficiency while enhancing the security of the Blockchain [15]. Another aspect can be improving the computational efficiency of the Blockchain by improving the hardware. For example, the use of high-end hardware such as Application Specific Integrated Circuits (ASICs) can increase computational power while reducing the required energy consumption. The last aspect can be found in designing the network architecture of the Blockchain. The network architecture is critical to Blockchain security. The network should be designed to be able to handle high traffic without slowing down or crashing. The most effective solution to the risk of smart contracts due to vulnerabilities is that an efficient vulnerability detection system should be established.

The most effective solution to the risk of vulnerabilities in smart contracts is to establish an efficient vulnerability detection system. Some experts have developed many types of vulnerability detection tools. Jiang introduced a detection tool called ContractFuzzer to test the security vulnerability of the Ethereum smart contract [16]. While Feng's team applied deep learning to automatically detect vulnerabilities in smart contracts on the Blockchain using the VSCL framework [17]. Researchers can develop or optimize vulnerability detection tools to avoid malicious exploitation of smart contracts through the use of new technologies and real-world practices. Finally, for the hazards caused by the underlying mechanism, administrators need to maintain the stability of data storage and transmission by regular security testing in addition to encrypting data and maintaining firewalls.

Countermeasures for Operational Risk. For information leakage and malicious attacks, Blockchain needs to adopt and strengthen privacy protection techniques. Hassan introduced a perturbation technique called differential privacy, which is able to address the information leakage problem of Blockchain more effectively [18]. Zhuang believed that Shamir secret sharing (SSS), a technology that can share secret information into multiple participants and recover original information only with the consent of more than a certain number of participants, is combined with Blockchain to ensure the protection of privacy and traceability of real identity information [19]. Kiktenko and his team, on the other hand, developed a new Blockchain platform with the ability to resist quantum computer attacks by invoking quantum key distribution (QKD) technology and redefining the protocol [20]. However, almost all encryption and protection technologies have their own flaws and application limitations. Researchers need to develop or adopt technologies for privacy protection in the context of specific application scenarios of Blockchain. Meanwhile, these technologies need to be continuously updated and patched to cope with the advances in cracking and attack techniques. Another regulatory risk of Blockchain that can easily cause social impact. Because of the anonymity and decentralized nature of the Blockchain, Blockchain could drive criminals into illegal activities, such as money laundering or drug trafficking. On the other hand, in response to the risks caused by operational errors, organizations that use Blockchain technology need to develop a training program on how to properly use Blockchain technology to improve the technical skills of their employees. In addition, a special supervisory department should be established to monitor the use of Blockchain to further avoid risks caused by human factors.

Countermeasures for Legal Risk. Regarding the risks caused by the lack of regulation of Blockchain, first of all, each country should cooperate to propose a set of international effective laws and regulations for the application of Blockchain. The regulations in the law set international standards for Blockchain regulation, thus guiding the financial regulatory organizations of each country to effectively supervise and control the use of Blockchain. Simultaneously, the international community should establish an international law enforcement organization with the above-mentioned law as a platform for action. This international organization needs to be able to enjoy certain law enforcement powers in most regions and internationally in order to stop transnational crimes through the use of Blockchain. Besides, financial regulatory organizations need to adjust their regulatory models to cope with the decentralized mechanism of Blockchain. The first approach is to promote the innovation of regulatory technology. Financial regulatory organizations can actively explore and promote innovation in regulatory technology to adapt to the decentralized nature of Blockchain systems. For example, regulators can study how to use Blockchain technology itself to regulate Blockchain transactions, or how to use technological tools such as smart contracts to automate regulation. The second approach is developing new regulatory policies and regulations. Financial regulatory organizations can develop new regulatory policies and regulations to address the decentralized nature of Blockchain technology. For example, regulators could require Blockchain transaction participants to comply with specific rules and standards, or develop new transaction reporting and disclosure requirements. A final approach is to work with the Blockchain industry. They can actively work with the Blockchain industry to understand the latest developments and trends in Blockchain technology so that it can better understand how Blockchain systems work and develop appropriate regulatory policies and regulations.

3 Conclusions

As an emerging technology, the use of Blockchain technology has spread to financial technology, digital asset trading, the Internet of things and Internet applications, supply chain management, government public management and social governance, energy management, intelligent manufacturing, and other fields, potentially sparking a new wave of technological innovation and industrial change. The advantages of Blockchain technology include: wide application; Transparency of trading data; Transaction settlement is more convenient; No intermediaries are needed to reduce transaction costs. However, while Blockchain technology has a positive effect on the financial industry, there are risks associated with it. By summarizing and refining the relevant literature, this paper divides the Blockchain risk into three categories: technical risk, operational risk and legal risk. Technical risks involve the security of keys, smart contracts and underlying mechanisms, and the coordination of security and computing power. Operational risk involves the wrong operation of managers and malicious attacks by criminals. The supervision of Blockchain primarily reflects legal risks: on the one hand, there is a lack of relevant laws and regulations, on the other hand, there is a contradiction between the decentralization of Blockchain and the regulatory system. In view of these risks, this paper also puts forward their corresponding countermeasures, including establishing vulnerability detection system, optimizing algorithms, strengthening the training of operators, accelerating the introduction of relevant laws and regulations and so on.

Although the risks of Blockchain and their responses discussed in this article may not be detailed or comprehensive, this article provides a general introduction to the risks and responses posed by Blockchain technology for users. Blockchain technology is not yet mature and is still in its early stages of development, and its full effect is unknown. However, the further application of Blockchain is an inevitable trend of scientific and technological development. In the process of use, users should carefully consider the risks and challenges of Blockchain, strengthen the attention to risk prevention and control, take effective preventive measures in combination with the actual situation, give full play to the financial benefits of Blockchain, and effectively prevent and resolve financial risks.

The lack of financial supervision is a major obstacle to the application of Blockchain in the financial field. In the future, the financial supervision of Blockchain should be deeply studied. Traditional financial regulation requires innovative changes, and a dedicated Blockchain financial regulatory system needs to be established. Simultaneously, it is necessary to give full play to the advantages of Blockchain technology and improve the ability to prevent and respond to Blockchain risks, thereby promoting the development of the financial industry. In addition, Central bank digital currencies (CBDC) based on Blockchain system architecture is a new starting point for Blockchain technology research. CBDC based on Blockchain can solve the inefficiencies and vulnerabilities of existing central bank infrastructure, ensuring the security, availability, accessibility, and transparency of transactions. The promotion of CBDC will lead to a more standardized development of Blockchain. This new technology promotes the reform of national digital finance, reducing costs and improving efficiency through digital currency to promote the development of the national economy.

References

1. Hope, J.: What is blockchain and how does it work? The Department Chair **29**(4), 11–11 (2019)
2. Li, X., Jiang, P., Chen, T., et al.: A survey on the security of blockchain systems. Future generation computer systems **107**, 841–853 (2020)
3. Monrat, A.A., Schelén, O., Andersson, K.: A survey of blockchain from the perspectives of applications, challenges, and opportunities. IEEE **7**, 117134–117151 (2019)

4. White, B.S., King, C.G., Holladay, J.: Blockchain security risk assessment and the auditor. J. Corp. Acc. Fin. **31**(2), 47–53 (2020)
5. Luo, K.: Blockchain financial regulatory risks and prevention considerations. Hebei Enterprise **2**(379), 99–100 (2021)
6. Zachariadis, M., Hileman, G., Scott, S.V.: Governance and control in distributed ledgers: understanding the challenges facing blockchain technology in financial services. LSE Research Online Documents on Economics **29**(2), 105–117 (2019)
7. Upadhyay, N.: Demystifying blockchain: A critical analysis of challenges, applications and opportunities. Int. J. Info. Manage. **54**(12), 1–26 (2020)
8. Yli-Huumo, J., et al.: Where is current research on blockchain technology? - A systematic review. PLoS One **11**(10) (2016)
9. Zhi, M., Wang, H.: Risk prevention of internet finance under blockchain technology. Modern Business **652**(27), 103–105 (2022)
10. Anderson, B.: Regulating the future of finance and money: an integrated regulatory approach to maximizing the value of cryptocurrencies and blockchain systems. The Asian Business Lawyer **21**(9), 115–157 (2018)
11. Zeng, F.: The regulatory path for the development of financial technology - An analysis from the perspective of blockchain technology. Special Economic Zone **367**(08), 92–97 (2019)
12. Cui, Z.: Blockchain finance: innovation, risk, and legal regulation. Oriental Law **3**, 87–98 (2019)
13. Anita, N., Vijayalakshmi, M.: Blockchain security attack: a brief survey. In: 10th International Conference on Computing, Communication and Networking Technologies 2019, pp. 1–6. ICCCNT, Kanpur (2019)
14. Aydar, M., et al.: Private key encryption and recovery in blockchain (2019)
15. Yang, F., et al.: Delegated proof of stake with downgrade: A secure and efficient blockchain consensus algorithm with downgrade mechanism. IEEE **7**, 118541–118555 (2019)
16. Jiang, B., Liu, Y., Chan, W.: ContractFuzzer: fuzzing smart contracts for vulnerability detection. In: Proceedings of the 33rd ACM/IEEE International Conference on Automated Software Engineering, pp. 3–7. ASE, Montperllier (2018)
17. Mi, F., et al.: VSCL: automating vulnerability detection in smart contracts with deep learning. In: IEEE International Conference on Blockchain and Cryptocurrency 2021, pp. 1–9. IEEE, Sydney (2021)
18. Hassan, M.U., Rehmani, M.H., Chen, J.: Differential privacy in blockchain technology: a futuristic approach. J. Paral. Distri. Comp. **145**, 50–74 (2020)
19. Zhuang, C., Dai, Q., Zhang, Y.: Bcppt: a blockchain-based privacy-preserving and traceability identity management scheme for intellectual property. Peer-to-Peer Networking and Applications **15**(1), 724–738 (2022)
20. Duplinskiy, A.V., Kiktenko, E.O., Pozhar, N.O., et al.: Quantum-Secured data transmission in urban fiber-optics communication lines. J. Russian Laser Res. **3**(3), 113–119 (2018)

To a Decentralized Future: Benefits that Blockchain Could Endow the Financing World

Yiping Li[1], Yuqing Liu[2], Ruixuan Sun[3], and Zihui Xu[4(✉)]

[1] Zhongnan University of Economics and Law, Wuhan 430073, Hubei, China
[2] Nankai University, Tianjin 300350, China
[3] Henan University of Economics and Law, Zhengzhou 450016, Henan, China
[4] Beijing Institute of Technology, Beijing 100081, China
zihui.xu@bit.edu.cn

Abstract. The initial appearance of blockchain technology has brought about profound changes in the financial area. Researchers have discovered that the advantages of blockchain can be used to address the drawbacks of traditional centralized financial systems. Existing papers focus on three main aspects: the technology introduced by blockchain, such as DLTs and Smart Contracts; the unique advantages of blockchain, such as trustworthiness, security, and efficiency; finance-oriented potential applications of blockchain, including both current applications and future challenges. To gain a comprehensive understanding of blockchain's application in finance, the document conducts a systematic review of existing papers on the advantages, risks, and applications of blockchain. The document firstly shows the prominent superiority of blockchain from three aspects including trustworthiness, efficiency and cost reduction. Then the document discusses the main obstacles to the application of blockchain which mainly exists in scalability and permission protocol changes. At last, the document briefly describe the road for blockchain to implementation from both present and future perspectives. In summary, while there are both advantages and challenges in the application of blockchain in finance, continuous efforts are being made in blockchain research.

Keywords: Blockchain · Finance · Distributed Ledger Technology · Bitcoin

1 Introduction

The disrupting blockchain technology has been given close attention to for years thanks to its irreplaceable practicability. Blockchain helps build and safeguard a reliable and unchangeable public database in a decentralized way, utilizing multiple advanced technologies like cryptography and peer-to-peer network synthetically. The blockchain technology gets rid of the inherent credible central party in traditional financial system where

---

Y. Li, Y. Liu, R. Sun, and Z. Xu Contributed equally.

users' private information is stored and allows all middle procedures to take place in a distributed manner [1]. The cutting-edge technology can be a big step forward towards evolution of global financial infrastructure [2]. New decentralized business models implementing blockchain technology can be the next stage in the whole progress in which business systems evolve to remove the conventional central agencies and intermediaries [3].

There will be no more need for participants to know or trust business partners, for digital signature technology can accomplish necessary authentication tasks. Bitcoin is the first instance of blockchain application that acquires great success in practice. Additionally, Blockchain acts as the crucial underlying technology for Bitcoin, and finally gets into the public scene since Bitcoin' remarkable performance [4]. Blockchain has several impressive and unique characteristics, for it's decentralized, open, self-governing, trust-needless and anonymous. With high security and information transparency, blockchain is starting a revolution sweeping diverse fields.

Some pressing challenges for blockchain include its scalability, vulnerability to attacks and high privacy leakage risks [5]. The blockchain technology is still far from mature and bothers regulators a lot despite its superior nature and great potential. Systems based on blockchain can be fragile when faces invasion coming in specific modes [1]. Besides, the anonymous mechanism does not always come with high security. On the contrary, high transparency can be accompanied by high risks of information disclosure in numerous cases.

To review the valuable characteristics of this fast-growing technology and present promising outlooks for it, this paper combines many authoritative perspectives together to promote accuracy and comprehensiveness. It reviews lots of literature about blockchain and aims to provide a systemic summary about blockchain's general situation as well as current implementation, presenting how blockchain can overcome urgent temporary problems to change the existing business system into more thorough future versions. At the same time, this paper talks about the technology's extraordinary versatility, trying to discuss how blockchain will modify the existing centralized financial patterns. The document first presented certain aspect of blockchain's prominent superiority from three aspects respectively and provide corresponding highlighted implementation examples. Then the document exhibits main obstacles to blockchain's wide adoption. At last, the document provided particular representative applications taking use of blockchain technology and places prospect for them and concluded the paper.

2 A Decentralized Nature to Bring Trust and Security

2.1 The Cost of Trust

The decentralized nature has endowed the blockchain technology with some very unique and much-needed properties in comparison of today's centralized system of finance. Conventional transactions can be tedious and expensive due to the need of anti-fraud, compliance regulation and reconciliation, for trust is crucial for transactions between traders over any centralized financial institution. Investors trust in external auditors of a company for their information disclosed to take actions accordingly; traders trust the institution for their transparency and fairness to both sides of the transaction; as well as depositors must trust their banks for the safety of their asset. All the trust above has been maintained by a set of costly procedures and strict legislations. The breakdown of trust can lead to severe consequences, as Sapienza and Zingales concluded in their paper surveying the breakdown of trust between investors and institutions during the 2008 financial crisis [6]. In their words, a crucial asset has been lost at that time is trust, and with its absence, economic backwardness took place in a violent manner. Blockchain carries the power of mitigating the cost and risk of trust for both traders and institutions, and have the potential to simplify all traditional controlling and compliance procedures mentioned above.

Utilizing the power of blockchain to lower the cost of trust, Distributed Ledger Technologies (DLTs) are being researched by institutions and investors. DLT's name speaks of itself: the distribution of ledgers across the entire network greatly improves the transparency and irrevocability of transactions, as Harish et al. addressed DLT's advantage of greater transparency and easier auditability [7]. The existence of absolute transparency ensures that no one can break the rules under broad sunlight, and everyone act as both the regulator and participant of transactions.

Although DLTs are still in its breaking-in period with institutions and investors, matured solutions and conceptual frameworks are widely discussed and are even more ready to be implemented than ever before.

2.2 Resiliency and Security

It was well proved that blockchain is a resilient technology, for both individuals, companies and the economy itself. Bitcoin is already a resilient mechanism that have already gone through years of operation and has not failed its purpose [8]. The Proof-of-Work (PoW) consensus is used within Bitcoin's blockchain to grant miners additional bitcoins and to ensure the security of transactions. Similarly, blockchains in a finance system can adopt more compatible consensus algorisms such as the well-researched Proof-of-Authority (PoA) and Practical Byzantine Fault Tolerance algorisms (PBFT), which both have their own expertise facing the conflicting need between data integrity and performance in different scenarios [9].

What is worth mentioning is that there are already a number of well conducted research on the implementation of blockchain aiming towards reinforcements on resiliency. It was proved that blockchain is an effective risk management and security boosting tool, if correctly implemented, in certain scenarios regarding power grids and supply chains [10, 11]. Although the demand of data integrity and resiliency in a financial scenario far exceeds the simple scenario of power grids and supply chains, the future of blockchain in finance is deemed promising as such basic implementation was proved to be successful.

3 Blockchain as an Automated Tool for Efficiency

In a sense, resource allocation, production process and transaction in society are determined by coordination form. As a new technology, blockchain is expected to bring a new coordination form, thus it can coordinate traditional markets, reduce market friction and improve transaction efficiency.

3.1 Coordination Form

In the past few years, academic research mainly focuses on the effect of coordination on economic transactions. Markets and hierarchies are the two common approaches to coordination [12]. When the ideally market coordination cannot meet the demand of the economic transaction, to compete and maximize benefits, individuals are also actively choosing different approaches of coordination, the most important form of which is coordination through the hierarchy. Within a hierarchy, people reduce costs and increase efficiency by coordinating activities and allocating resources. However, as the company expands in size, it will face more obvious problems of information quality and behavioral biases, which will directly lead to the decline of coordination efficiency [13].

To sum up, there are inevitable problems in the traditional way of coordination. Therefore, people are now looking for new coordination ways as blockchain emerges in due time. It is generally believed that the effective coordination there are now facing three challenges: imperfect information, asymmetric information and behavioral biases [13].

Blockchain has brought some special tools such as cryptography; hashes and distributive consensus, through these tools, blockchain can represent and verify data while protecting anonymity, thus the market frictions brought by falsification, double-spending, and anonymity may be systematically reduced.

Through the above tools, blockchain was thought to bring a reformation in hierarchies. For example, if a company incorporates the control right to cash flow into the smart contract, the traditional financial basis such as bank account and stock may be no longer necessary [14]. In addition, people can build up a blockchain protocols instead of traditional firm, the contributors of the "firm" are spread across the globe, they are anonymous and don't need to know about each other. In general, blockchain makes it possible to create a firm without assets. Therefore, the blockchain firms do not have to face the problem of increasing costs and decreasing management efficiency caused by diseconomies of scale. Thus, the economic transaction can approach effective coordination.

3.2 Smart Contract

Smart contracts are simple applications hosted on a blockchain, and has certain control of an account that could be interacted with. In the most successful blockchain application, the Ethereum, smart contracts work like vending machines, reacting to requests from the blockchain in a preset manner decided by codes. In short, smart contracts appear as bot-controlled accounts that can automatically process transactions.

Although a smart contract-based financial market is still currently a niche market, the concept is appealing to larger organizations that wants to participate in a decentralized finance system, giving them a platform to host an automatic account for mass and timely transactions. Settling transactions automatically with predetermined rules, smart contracts do not require manual control or the existence of controllers, which are the reason for slowing down the execution speed of transactions in the real world. The smart contract records every part of the transaction, reduces the communication and paper contracts required, which can be efficient, transparent, secure and versatile with no need of continuous operation [15].

By inheriting the efficiency and secure characteristic brought by the decentralized nature of blockchain, a smart contract can become a powerful tool in experienced hands. However, flawless smart contract requires skills to tackle with bugs and security breaches, and even demand know-hows of operational technology and law making. Along with the lack of proper development tool-chain and an acknowledged general way of securing the code [16], the smart contract is still in its early days of development and implementation.

4 Operational Cost Reduction

Blockchain technologies show huge potential for continuously driving cost savings in various ways, such as cutting costs of transactions between companies and optimizing global financial infrastructure.

Costs can come from different aspects of the daily operation and management, like fees paid for inefficient intermediaries, fraud risk left by antiquated global financial system and friction created through unnecessary and endless paperwork [17]. Blockchain is certain to bring huge changes to the current economic pattern and profoundly enhance efficiency in financial transactions and processing all over the world.

Blockchain implementations affect business model by removing inefficient manual processes and reducing IT infrastructure costs, which help save negotiation and search costs as well as expenses of intermediaries [18, 19]. The peer-to-peer mass collaboration model which blockchain supports promotes economic vitality to a great extent and can vastly simplify or even replace some of existing redundant organizational structures. In addition, blockchain technologies largely reduce resources wasted in authorization holds. Fewer manual steps create opportunities for firms to chase for higher efficiency and revenue, which can all be allowed to become reality thanks to blockchain technology adoption. Besides, high transaction speed makes it possible for firms to reduce the time spent on pecuniary exchange, allowing them to cut down opportunity costs. Similar changes can also take place in capital market and insurance sector. In practical operation of insurance companies, blockchain technologies can help check claims and screen out the valid ones, as well as assessing fraud, reducing labor cost in a way [20].

Implementations of blockchain in banking industry and global financial system are also accompanied by significant opportunities and challenges. If blockchain applications such as the Bitcoin system successfully solve their main problems, which mainly is the high demand for computational power, it would be undoubted that they will thoroughly rebuild current financial infrastructure, accelerate the sustainable development of worldwide low-cost green economy and reduce resources and energy consumption [21]. According to scientific calculations, banks may cut infrastructure costs by up to 30% via the use of blockchain, which is equal to approximately 8–12 billion dollars per year [22]. Blockchain adoption is rebuilding global financial system step by step and irreversibly.

5 Difficulties and Risks Before the Dawn of a Decentralized Future

5.1 Scalability Challenges

Large quantity of transactions is expected to take place every day on the blockchain, bringing outstanding problems lead by latency and storage problems, along with limited bandwidth and read-performance drops [23]. Generally, we conclude such problem induced by scale as scalability challenges. Scalability could easily be the biggest barrier to the wide adoption of blockchain at present, for instance it is proved that scalability is a threat to bitcoin, a truly representative cryptocurrency which relies on the blockchain technology [24].

Traditional finance systems rely on centralized servers to host large capacity of traders, processing their everyday activities and use certain protocol to interact with other centralized networks. The blockchain, on the other hand, is not designed to run a powerful server, thus effective and sophisticated design is needed to host the same amount of activity. Meanwhile, one of the common goals for a decentralized finance system is its inclusiveness, allowing free entry and trade between all participants. This means that any blockchain based financial system, if not designed to be enclosed, should be ready to accept new users anytime anywhere, or shall we say, preserve a scalability in any circumstances.

5.2 Permission Protocol Changes

Blockchain technology is still far from practical commercial use in the market, as most finance-oriented blockchain is still under development. Thus, most operating DLTs or blockchains in the world may only consists of few or even one running node under laboratory environment, often controlled by the original creator.

This means that blockchain in today's shape is far from decentralized, as the mass usage of blockchain to finance was only an outlook compared to the current situation. It is reasonable for owners to establish a downscaled permissive blockchain to test its capability, while simplifying the security, privacy and safety problems. A small, permissive blockchain indeed mitigates the scalability problem, but rather than fixing this problem, permissions are just pushing it away, manually control the scale before the blockchain hits the scalability bottleneck.

Meanwhile, the permission granted to verified nodes in the blockchain still needs a centralized verification process before the nodes can trade within the blockchain without problem. In other words, permissive blockchain still bases on trust into one or few organizations and parties, still bringing up the "cost of trust" problem. Anyway, it can't be denied that a permissive blockchain can be the gamechanger in easily trusted scenarios such as cross-border payments or trading between recognized institutions, where the blockchain can reduce friction while not hitting the scalability bottleneck [25].

Blockchain will still be valuable even if we only reach for these low-hanging fruits, but there is more potential to be unleashed if one day the progress of technology finally breaks through the scalability problem.

5.3 Sharding

Sharding is a technological method to overcome the current scalability problem, by splitting the whole blockchain into different shards, each node will be required with less computation and storage power. The original blockchain require each individual node to process and store all transactions that took place on the blockchain, requiring massive amount of communication between nodes because of the distributed consensus protocol, which brings up the latency. Hence, sharding technology was used by researchers within the forefront to explore the possibility of improving their transaction efficiency at scale.

Allowing different shards to run parallel in a blockchain, sharding can impact the capacity of a blockchain in a multiplier effect without giving up much of its advantages. Compared to the way of simply gatekeeping the blockchain with permissions granted by organizations that requires your trust, sharding provides true improvements to the internal logic of blockchain in order to push back the scalability problem.

However, sharding technology is still not perfect even in today. It is hard to maintain stability and integrity of a complex system such as a sharded blockchain, and it is even harder to balance between the performance gain and error tolerances or failure rates. Inherent drawbacks such as high failure probability and deployment difficulties still affect some of the current methods, while performance or latency problems are neither completely solved. But still, new proposals of novel ways on blockchain sharding continuously emerge as the technology evolves in time, achieving better fault resiliency and eventually unlocking the full potential of sharding via fully parallel sharding technology [26].

6 The Road to Implementation

6.1 The Versatility of Blockchain

Diverse applications of blockchain spanning numerous domains and industries are mushrooming around the world, giving a tremendous boost to production and operation activities. Blockchain by itself is a simple concept yet a versatile tool that has little limitation, leading to a wide range of use, form the most basic of production and logistics to more complex usage of management and finance. Despite the well-known use on cryptocurrency, blockchain also help solve urgent problems of banking industry by starting a revolution in its underlying financial infrastructure, achieving asset digitization as well as point-to-point transfer of value. Additionally, blockchain can settle the friction trouble caused by low mutual trust and reduce intermediary expenses by setting up new mechanisms acting on credit issues and payment clearing respectively. Innovations include the use of encryption technology and supply chain enhancements [27].

6.2 The Application of Blockchain and DLTs

Blockchain had been investigated and used by investors or large companies interested in the field of economy and finance. To begin with, in the financial area, blockchain is considered of huge potential values. The most common application that could be in our daily life is the digital currency (DIGICCY). Bitcoin, on the behalf of blockchain, is the first yet the most successful concept to be widely used. Besides it is worth mentioning that the central bank digital currencies (CBDC), which is a generic term for all the central bank developed digital currencies in the world, is already under heavy development by the government in many countries. CBDCs are visioned to accomplish most peer-to-peer transactions in the near future [28]. In addition, under the stress of interest rate liberalization and profit recession, the government is asked to improve the banking efficiency by new technologies like blockchain, which would accelerate a "multi-center, weakly intermediated" form of finance markets [27].

Blockchains could also be useful in public service, as the technology of block chains is closely bound up production and living. Because of the security, privacy and reliability that the technology can provide, institutions can ensure the data and information wouldn't be falsified. Blockchains can be considered as a highly traceable system, which can be further used to ensure the quality and safety of production in food supply [29].

At the same time, blockchain can also be applied within the government system as an effective way to streamline processes. The traits such like transparent, traceable and immutable can fulfill the duties of governance, improve their work efficiency or even play the part of a useful assistant in management [30].

6.3 Overcoming the Inertia of a Traditional System

The current finance system has been operated continuously for decades, constantly being refined and updated. Basic assumptions build up a common sense for participants, that the current finance system is built all around agents and banks, in which agents coalesce the banking system and the market of public trading market. To transfer money from whom deposits to whom needs money, or the surplus units to the deficit units, agents sprout form this special need as a trusted third-party. Agents with large numbers of customers and a clean background tend to be selected by more and more traders, naturally creating an economy of scale as the agents become powerful organizations and eventually monopolize the industry [31].

The traditional finance system has a tendency to be centralized, but blockchain, on the otherwise, is a fundamentally decentralized tool. Rather than putting trust in a private controlled entity, blockchain proposes a possibility of putting trust in a flawless consensus embedded in the system and complied by everyone. Accompanied by advancements in encryption technology, the last hesitate about confidentiality in certain scenarios can also be assured.

The implementation of blockchain could be aggressive and radical to the current finance system. Most concerns about the transformation into a blockchain based finance system is not anything regarding theoretical incompatibility or deficiencies, but rather interest conflicts and the distrust of a newborn technology. A centralized system provides advantages to large agencies, even under strict legislation and controlling procedures. Timely information of the market can be easily exploited in many ways to gain benefits in realms where any regulation is less than jurisdiction. Agencies with the true power of raising a revolution in the finance market would like to thoroughly inspect the blockchain technology and analyze its advantages and disadvantages to themselves before adopting it.

It should be noted that large cross border organizations represented by the SWIFT has already begun looking into the possibility of blockchain implementation [32]. In the position paper, SWIFT concludes that DLTs should be joint developed by the whole industry to form a universal accepted standard. It is a good sign for leading organizations to recognize the value of the blockchain technology, as they are the only entities that could lead the vanguard of a blockchain revolution.

7 Conclusion

The document investigates into the possibilities that blockchain can bring if proper implemented in contrast to the traditional finance system. The document has concluded the result of various literatures in each frontier of the blockchain technology and investigated into new concept or examples of the implementation of blockchain in the finance area. With a relative comprehensive grasp of the usage and advantages of the blockchain technology, the document then presented its possible benefits to the banking world in different vectors. The document found that blockchain bears the potential to reduce the cost of trust in everyday financial activities; increase the system's overall resiliency and security; reduce friction and improve efficiency; also lower the cost of opportunity. While there are also outstanding challenges such as scalability issues and the inertia of the current system, novel technologies and joint development proposals has emerged to tackle these issues. Under a mature concept, blockchain will continue to evolve in the foreseeable future as more and more technologies emerge to enhance its basic framework to add more functions and boost its performance. It is now the time for blockchain to enter a rapid yet steady period of continuous development, along with more and more jointed discussion to establish a public recognized standard.

References

1. Zheng, Z., Xie, S., Dai, H.-N., Chen, X., Wang, H.: Blockchain challenges and opportunities: a survey. Int. J. Web Grid Serv. **14**, 352–375 (2018)
2. Davidson, S., De Filippi, P., Potts, J.: Blockchains and the economic institutions of capitalism. J. Inst. Econ. **14**, 639–658 (2018)
3. Chen, Y., Bellavitis, C.: Blockchain disruption and decentralized finance: the rise of decentralized business models. J. Bus. Ventur. Insights **13**, e00151 (2020)
4. Beck, R., Müller-Bloch, C.: Blockchain as radical innovation: a framework for engaging with distributed ledgers as incumbent organization. In: Hawaii International Conference on System Sciences (2017)
5. Chang, V., Baudier, P., Zhang, H., Xu, Q., Zhang, J., Arami, M.: How Blockchain can impact financial services–the overview, challenges and recommendations from expert interviewees. Technol. Forecast. Soc. Chang. **158**, 120166 (2020)
6. Sapienza, P., Zingales, L.: A trust crisis. Int. Rev. Financ. **12**, 123–131 (2012)
7. Natarajan, H., Krause, S., Gradstein, H.: Distributed Ledger Technology and Blockchain. World Bank, Washington, DC (2017)
8. Nakamoto, S., Bitcoin, A.: A peer-to-peer electronic cash system. Bitcoin.–URL: https://bitcoin.org/bitcoin.pdf 4 (2008)
9. De Angelis, S., Aniello, L., Baldoni, R., Lombardi, F., Margheri, A., Sassone, V.: PBFT vs Proof-of-authority: Applying the CAP Theorem to Permissioned Blockchain (2018)

10. Mylrea, M., Gourisetti, S.N.G.: Blockchain: a path to grid modernization and cyber resiliency. In: 2017 North American Power Symposium (NAPS), pp. 1–5. IEEE (2017)
11. Min, H.: Blockchain technology for enhancing supply chain resilience. Bus. Horiz. **62**, 35–45 (2019)
12. Coase, R.H.: The Nature of the Firm. Springer, London (1995)
13. An, J., Rau, R.: Finance, technology and disruption. Eur. J. Financ. **27**, 334–345 (2021)
14. Yermack, D.: Corporate governance and blockchains. Rev. Financ. **21**, 7–31 (2017)
15. Schär, F.: Decentralized finance: on blockchain-and smart contract-based financial markets. FRB of St. Louis Rev. **103**(2):153–174 (2021)
16. Zou, W., et al.: Smart contract development: challenges and opportunities. IEEE Trans. Software Eng. **47**, 2084–2106 (2019)
17. Tapscott, A., Tapscott, D.: How blockchain is changing finance. Harv. Bus. Rev. **1**, 2–5 (2017)
18. Morkunas, V.J., Paschen, J., Boon, E.: How blockchain technologies impact your business model. Bus. Horiz. **62**, 295–306 (2019)
19. Osterwalder, A., Pigneur, Y.: Business Model Generation: A Handbook for Visionaries, Game Changers, and Challengers. John Wiley & Sons (2010)
20. Gregorio, M.: Blockchain: A New Tool to Cut Costs. PricewaterhouseCoopers (2017)
21. Cocco, L., Pinna, A., Marchesi, M.: Banking on blockchain: costs savings thanks to the blockchain technology. Future Internet **9**, 25 (2017)
22. Garcia, A.: IBM's blockchain app store wants to help banks cut costs (2018)
23. Sanka, A.I., Cheung, R.C.: A systematic review of blockchain scalability: issues, solutions, analysis and future research. J. Netw. Comput. Appl. **195**, 103232 (2021)
24. Karame, G.: On the security and scalability of bitcoin's blockchain. In: Proceedings of the 2016 ACM SIGSAC Conference on Computer and Communications Security, pp. 1861–1862 (2016)
25. Casey, M., Crane, J., Gensler, G., Johnson, S., Narula, N.: The Impact of Blockchain Technology on Finance: A Catalyst for Change. CEPR Press, Paris (2018)
26. Zamani, M., Movahedi, M., Raykova, M.: Rapidchain: Scaling blockchain via full sharding. In: Proceedings of the 2018 ACM SIGSAC Conference on Computer and Communications Security, pp. 931–948 (2018)
27. Guo, Y., Liang, C.: Blockchain application and outlook in the banking industry. Financ. Innov. **2**, 1–12 (2016)
28. Sethaput, V., Innet, S.: Blockchain application for central bank digital currencies (CBDC). Cluster Comput. **26**:1–15 (2023)
29. Tse, D., Zhang, B., Yang, Y., Cheng, C., Mu, H.: Blockchain application in food supply information security. In: 2017 IEEE international conference on industrial engineering and engineering management (IEEM), pp. 1357–1361. IEEE (2017)
30. Hou, H.: The application of blockchain technology in E-government in China. In: 2017 26th International Conference on Computer Communication and Networks (ICCCN), pp. 1–4. IEEE (2017)
31. Boot, A.W., Thakor, A.V.: Financial system architecture. Rev. Financ. Stud. **10**, 693–733 (1997)
32. SWIFT: https://www.swift.com/node/22221. Last accessed 10 Mar 2023

Relevance Between ESG Scores and Annual Turnover: Evidence from 453 Industrial Hong Kong Stocks

Nanqi Liu[1(✉)], Changyou Qi[2], and Junjie Zhuge[3]

[1] Brunel London School, North China University of Technology, Beijing 100144, China
2053796@brunel.ac.uk
[2] School of Information Management, Shanghai Lixin University of Accounting and Finance, Shanghai 201620, China
[3] School of Information Engineering, Guangdong University of Technology, Guangzhou 510006, China

Abstract. The international ESG score system has grown quickly in recent years. ESG is a generally accepted value investing standard as well as a responsible investment concept that considers the advantages of the economy, environment, society, and corporate governance. The relationship between ESG scores and stock annual turnover is examined in this study. This research selected 453 industrial Hong Kong stocks with information for 2022 and their most recent ESG scores on March 16, 2023, which could illustrate the performance over the preceding three years. For statistical data description, correlation analysis, and logistic regression, the research employed the R programming language. According to the study's findings, there is a positive association between industrial stocks' annual turnover on the Hong Kong Exchange and their ESG scores. Turnover, which is determined by multiplying volume by the stock price, refers to the total number of shares that were traded. When there is a shortage of stock, market participants will trade more actively, more money will be bought and sold, and turnover will subsequently rise. In contrast, when stocks are abundant, participants will trade less actively, less money will be bought and sold, and turnover will fall. In other words, the more active the trading, the higher the ESG score of the stock, and the securities supervisory agency should step up its oversight of this stock's trading.

Keywords: ESG · Corporate Financial Performance · Annual Turnover · Logistic Regression

1 Introduction

1.1 Research Background

As a pioneer in boosting the "double carbon" goal and green development, the Guangdong-Hong Kong-Macao Greater Bay Area is charged with the important mission of sustainable financial innovation and development, and ESG assessment is a key step

---

N. Liu, C. Qiu, and J. Zhuge Contributed equally.

in implementing the long-term value investment concept in the capital market. Corporate social responsibility (CSR) is becoming more and more significant for institutional and personal investors. Organizations may benefit from the environmental, social, and governance (ESG) aspects of CSR performance [1]. For the past ten years, global investors have used ESG, or the integration of environmental, social, and governance factors into the investment process, as a key technique to manage portfolio risks. ESG performance, a multidimensional alternative data, plays an increasingly crucial part in financial decision-making in the present day. The ESG grading organization's client companies greatly enhance their output of green innovation by 3.9% [2].

Fig. 1. ESG Introduction. (Source: https://marketbusinessnews.com/financial-glossary/esg-definition-meaning/)

Figure 1 shows that three recognized dimensions of ESG performance are: Environmental standards, which look at how an organization manages to preserve the environment. Social criteria, which consider how the business handles its customers. Governance criterion, which looks at how an organization manages its internal affairs, or how it is governed.

According to Sanoran's study, corporate sustainability contributes considerably to positive sustained development for businesses engaged in the manufacturing and construction industries [3]. As a result, industrial area has a relatively great impact on the environment and must prioritize sustainable development. Companies with large carbon footprints are more susceptible to investor sentiment. However, if the companies have better ESG performance, the unfavorable reaction lessens [4]. In addition, the study carried out by Bai verifies that ESG investment is preferred particularly by institutional investors, and these preferences are especially notable for publicly traded companies that are private-owned or belong to secondary and tertiary industries [5]. The majority of China's industrial companies are listed in Hong Kong, such as China Railway Group and Air China. The research, therefore, chooses 453 industrial corporate stocks with information for 2022 in the trading market of Hong Kong and their latest ESG score based on Wind Platform on March 2023, which can illustrate the performance over the preceding three years.

The corporate ESG performance could greatly affect the price of the stock for the reason that it is representative of credit rating, social responsibility, management efficiency, and sustainable development. The team of Gao discovered that the better the ESG performance, the lower the likelihood of a stock price crash [6]. Unlike most of the traditional financial data, ESG performance exposes significantly more potential value of medium- and long-term investment. According to the China ESG Development Report 2021, only 66 quoted companies in the A-share market released outright ESG reports in 2021 [7]. As a result, in contrast to previous studies, what the research going to research is the relationship between industrial corporate ESG performance and investor behavior which is reflected by corresponding stock annual turnover in the Hong Kong market by logistic regression.

1.2 Research Hypothesis

In terms of our research hypothesis and variable selection, at present, there is no relevant literature to study the relationship between ESG and annual turnover. Therefore, we have carried out the derivation of some financial risk indicators. For investors, ESG has an impact on the enterprise value through the internal mechanism. ESG can improve the profitability and dividend rate of listed companies, thus affecting the stock price. In the Discounted Cashflow Model (DCF), the stock price is equal to the discount value of future cash flow, which is determined by the cash flow (CF) and discount rate (R) received by investors in each period, where the CF of each period is the dividend received by investors. On the other hand, The R is related to the risk level of stocks. If the risk level of listed companies is high, the discount rate will also be at a high level [8, 9]. Through the influence transmission of these two mechanisms, we can see the impact of ESG score on the stock valuation level, thus affecting the annual turnover.

So we assume that ESG scores are positively correlated with annual turnover of industrial stocks in the Hong Kong market. We employed the R programming language for statistical data description, correlation analysis, and logistic regression, to verify the hypothesis.

In the following sections, we'll start by reviewing the pertinent literature, focusing on the empirical approach and data analysis technique which are used to investigate the impact of ESG on financial performance and stock information. Next, we will discuss the research design and data used in this paper, focusing primarily on the regression model and correlation analysis that we utilize to draw findings. In the part of the conclusion, we present the research summary, limitations, and future potential research orientation.

2 Literature Review

In the first place, the team of Tian conducted a survey that unravelled the relevance between ESG scores and Corporate Financial Performance (CFP), which was verified by the logistic regression model. This research is our key paper and the most relevant research. They investigated 377 China A-share companies covered by both agencies and found that ESG rating is instrumental in predicting the trend of corporate financial performance. They also discovered that adding ESG grades to the dataset increased forecasting accuracy when evaluating the tendency of upcoming financial results [10]. Secondly, to investigate the relevance between ESG rating and financial performance in the energy power business, the team of Zhao examined the power-producing groups listed in China by panel regression model. According to the findings, ideal ESG performance boosts profitability, which has important implications for investment and regulation [11]. Additionally, Engelhardt analyzed the relationship between ESG performance and stock returns using the Ordinary Least Squares (OLS) model. They discovered that during the pandemic outbreak, the better environmental and social scores are, the larger anomalous stock gains the companies had [12]. Since the majority of relevant studies adopt regression models, this paper also adopts regression analysis.

In terms of corporate financial performance and stock returns, we have also found relevant research evidence. ESG scores do have an impact on corporate financial performance and individual stock information. The findings of Friede's study demonstrated how analytically robust the business case for ESG investment was. In around 90% of research, the ESG-CFP relationship was non-negative. Significantly, most research presented positive results. They emphasized that the positive ESG effect on CFP was consistent throughout time [13]. After adjusting for the five Fama-French criteria, the study by Liu employing the ESG scores of China's stocks from 2009 to 2020 demonstrates that purchasing high-ESG shares and selling low-ESG stocks generates considerable profits [14]. According to the portfolio research, in the post-2016 scenario, good ESG portfolios generate noticeably greater anomalous profits than poor ESG portfolios. Besides, the stock research demonstrates that high ESG profiles, on average post-2016, forecast larger abnormal returns. Strong ESG returns are greatly driven by the equity cost advantage, except for improved profitability [15]. In conclusion, it is reasonable to believe that regression analysis can be used to study the relevance between ESG performance and the annual turnover of industrial stock in the Hong Kong market.

3 Data and Method

3.1 Data Description

The data used in this study is the ESG data of some industrial companies in Hong Kong and some data on the companies stocks. According to the above-mentioned, the paper obtained the ESG score from the Wind scoring system on 16th March 2023. First of all, we simply screened the data according to the quantity and quality of the data. A large amount of data was needed to build the model, but due to the lack of ESG information disclosure, we chose the industrial industry with a large amount of data and thus controlled the influence of the industry on the ESG score. And according to the preliminary observation of the data, we believe that ESG may have some linear relationship with the following variables and descriptive statistical analysis is made (Table 1), and finally chose to use the stock results in 2022 and delete all the missing data. Considering the information already disclosed, ESG captured its performance and properly handled this part of the missing data. After data cleaning, the paper obtained a total of 453 companies' ESG score data, focusing on 6 relevant stock indicators.

Table 1. Metadata Descriptive Statistics.

Variable	Description	Quantity	Mean	Min.	Max.	Standard Deviation
S1	ESG score	453	6.025	3.100	8.930	1.412
S2	Average annual price	453	3.583	0.013	201.468	14.806
S3	Annual rise and fall	453	−0.411	−20.461	28.188	2.524
S4	Annual increase and decrease	453	−12.265	−93.775	868.750	61.415
S5	Annual turnover rate	453	40.911	0.021	1246.407	101.567
S6	Annual average turnover rate	453	0.189	0.001	5.067	0.418
S7	Annual turnover	453	2.443e+09	1.660e+05	1.185e+11	9133398162

According to descriptive statistical analysis (Table 1), S1 and S2 may be negatively correlated, and S1 may be positively correlated with other variables.

Table 2. Metadata Correlation Analysis.

Variable	S1	S2	S3	S4	S5	S6	S7
S1							
S2	0.13**						
S3	−0.042	0.023					
S4	−0.064	0.031	0.024***				
S5	0.032	0.026	−0.049	−0.029			
S6	0.011	0.02	−0.068	−0.032	0.099***		
S7	0.21***	0.50***	−0.081*	0.027	0.22***	0.20***	

Asterisks mean correlation, "*" means weak correlation, "***" means strong correlation, and "**" the correlation is somewhere in between.

It can be seen from the data (Table 2) that there is a weak correlation between S1 and S2 in the financial sense and there is a strong correlation between S1 (ESG score) and S7 (annual turnover). So we think that there is a positive correlation between the two. By R calculation, we get the correlation coefficient is 1.363e+09.

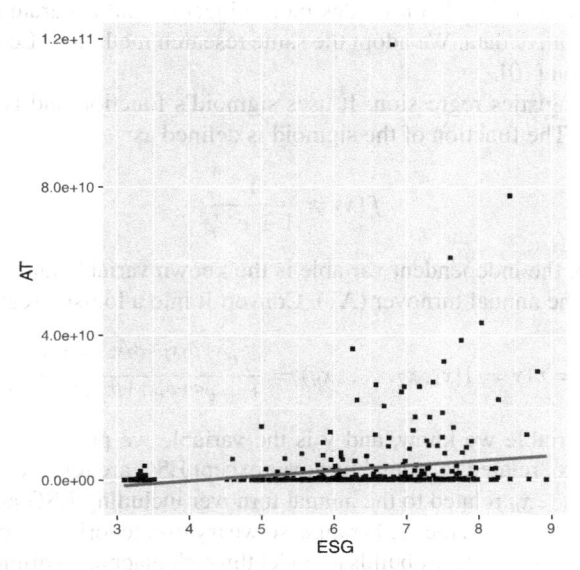

Fig. 2. ESG Score and annual transaction data distribution.

Therefore, we try to find a deep relationship between ESG and annual turnover. First, we calculated the correlation coefficient between the annual turnover and other variables to prepare for the subsequent establishment of the model. The following results are obtained (Table 3).

Table 3. Annual turnover correlation description.

Name	Description	AT	ESG	AAP	ARF	ATR	AAR
AT	Annual turnover						
ESG	ESG score	0.26***					
AAP	Average annual price	0.71***	0.34***				
ARF	Annual rise and fall	−0.15***	−0.042	−0.18***			
ATR	Annual turnover rate	0.77***	0.1**	0.27***	−0.081*		
AAR	Annual average turnover rate	0.66***	0.063	0.19***	−0.088*	0.96***	

According to the results of the above correlation analysis (Table 3), we further establish the following model.

3.2 Logistic Regression Model

We believe that this is an important investment indicator for stock investors and can help them benefit from it. ESG also provides more objective and accurate advice on stock selection as alternative data. We adopt the same research method as Lewis Tian and use logistics regression [10].

Principle of logistics regression: It uses sigmoid's function and is predicted to be between 0 and 1. The function of the sigmoid is defined as:

$$f(x) = \frac{1}{1+e^{-x}} \tag{1}$$

Among them, the independent variable is the known variable and f is the predicted variable, that is, the annual turnover (AT). Convert it into a logistic regression formula:

$$p = p(y=1|x_1, x_2, \ldots, x_n) = \frac{e^{a+\beta_1 x_1+\beta_2 x_2+\ldots+\beta_n x_n}}{1+e^{a+\beta_1 x_1+\beta_2 x_2+\ldots+\beta_n x_n}} \tag{2}$$

where x is the variable we know, and y is the variable we predict. In Model 1, variables $x_1, x_2, \ldots, x_n$ related to annual turnover except ESG are represented. In Model 2, variables $x_1, x_2, \ldots, x_n$ related to the annual turnover including ESG are represented.

Because y needs to be in the (0, 1) range, so we try to categorize them. And we divide the data into two parts. One part builds a model through machine learning, and the other part we use to test the accuracy of the model. We randomly select 75% of the 434 data for learning, and the remaining 25% is used to test whether our linear hypothesis is valid. We looked to see if the prediction became more accurate with the addition of ESG variables. If so, it shows that ESG plays an important role in predicting annual turnover. The two models are represented as follows:

$$Model\ 1: AT = \beta_1 AAP + \beta_2 APF + \beta_3 ATR + \beta_4 AAR \tag{3}$$

$$Model\ 2: AT = \beta_1 ESG + \beta_2 AAP + \beta_3 APF + \beta_4 ATR + \beta_5 AAR \tag{4}$$

We established the whole process through R language and finally demonstrated it through graphics to compare and observe whether ESG plays an important role in predicting the annual turnover.

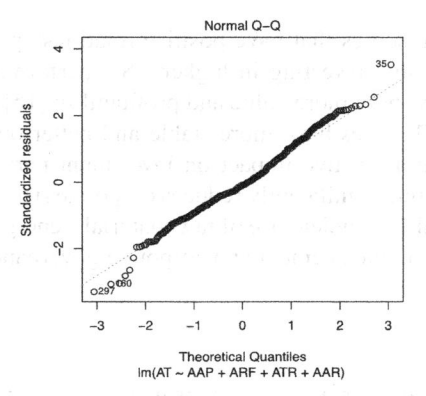

Fig. 3. Model 1 logistic learning result.

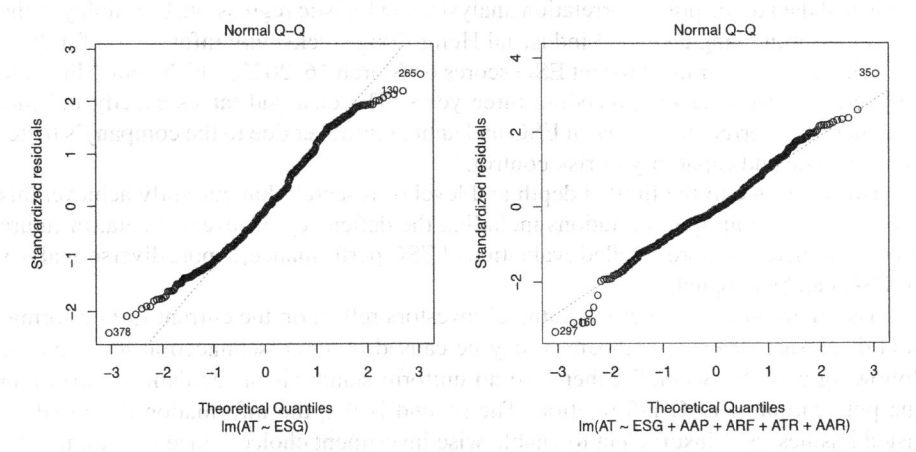

Fig. 4. Model 2 logistic learning result. The picture on the left shows the prediction effect after the ESG variable is added to Model 1, and the picture on the right shows the prediction effect of ESG on the annual turnover alone.

4 Result and Discussion

The results (Fig. 2) show that there is an obvious linear relationship between ESG and an annual turnover (coefficient 1.363e+09 and intercept −5.704e+09). However, although most of the data can be predicted accurately, there are still some obvious deviations compared with Model 1 and Model 2 (Fig. 3 and Fig. 4). Therefore, we believe that although ESG can serve as a reference for the annual turnover, it is still not enough to replace other variables for a more accurate prediction.

The data and tables (Table 2) indicate that there is a strong correlation between the S1 (ESG score) and the S7 (annual turnover). That is probably due to companies with higher ESG scores having better profitability, cheaper valuation, lower volatility, and lower capital costs. Aydoğmuş's team finds that the overall ESG combined score is a positive and strong correlation with firm value. ESG is a kind of score related to Environment,

Social, and Governance scores that have positive relationships with firm profitability. These findings suggest that investing in higher ESG performance promises financial return for the firm means both more value and profitability [16]. As a result, companies that own excellent ESG scores have more stable and better operating performance in the long term and have a positive impact on investment performance. Also, as He's research shows, ESG rating significantly reduces corporate risk-taking [17], these above advantages come from their efficient use of raw materials, energy, and human resources, as well as their better risk management and corporate governance capabilities.

5 Conclusion

The main research question of this paper is if there are positive correlations between ESG scores and the annual turnover of industrial stocks in the Hong Kong Market. For statistical data description, correlation analysis, and logistic regression, by employed the R programming language. 453 industrial Hong Kong stocks with information for 2022 are selected and their most recent ESG scores on March 16, 2023, which could illustrate the performance over the preceding three years. The data and tables exactly indicate that there is a correlation between ESG and annual turnover due to the company's better performance and capability of risk control.

However, due to the limited depth and level of research that currently achieve, this article still has multiple limitations including the deficiency of revealed data. In future studies, if there is a more detailed evaluation of ESG performance, a more diverse analysis of ESG can be adopted.

The main limitation that institutional investors reflect on the current ESG information disclosure of listed companies may be caused by the disconnection focus on the following aspects: Secondly, there are no uniform standards or regulations governing the publication of ESG information. The second is that the information disclosed by listed businesses is insufficient to enable wise investment choices since it is not timely, accurate, objective, non-standard, or of low quality and reliability. It also contains more qualitative than quantitative descriptions. Finally, it is challenging to assess and evaluate the ESG performance of listed firms since there isn't a single, impartial evaluation standard or indicator system. Fourth, there aren't many independent information disclosure audits of publicly traded businesses, and outside services like ESG ratings aren't always accurate.

In the future, in terms of data gathering, this paper only chooses one ESG evaluation method for its investigation of correlations with annual trade volume. After the research by third-party rating agencies become more abundant and detailed, this research can be extended to all listed companies in the A-share market in China and further study the correlation between factors and stock prices from the perspective of the ESG system. With rich and detailed data, relevant research conclusions will be more convincing. Further reference can be made to the continuously supplemented literature promoting relevant research, including more quantitative indicator methods and reasonable control factors, to rationalize and expand the study on the effect of ESG on the yearly trading volume of firm stocks.

References

1. Sila, I., Cek, K.: The impact of environmental, social and governance dimensions of corporate social responsibility on economic performance: Australian evidence. Procedia Comput. Sci. **120**, 797–804 (2017)
2. Juxian Wang, F., Mengdi Ma, S., Tianyi Dong, T., Zheyuan Zhang, F.: Do ESG ratings promote corporate green innovation? A quasi-natural experiment based on SynTao green Finance's ESG ratings. Int. Rev. Financ. Anal. **87**, 102623 (2023)
3. Kanyarat (Lek) Sanoran, F.: Corporate sustainability and sustainable growth: the role of industry sensitivity. Finance Res. Lett. **53**, 103596 (2022)
4. Jiazhen Wang, F., Xiaolu Hu, S., Angel Zhong, T.: Stock market reaction to mandatory ESG disclosure. Finance Res. Lett. 103402 (2022)
5. Xiong Bai, F., Jinmian Han, S., Yuanzhi Ma, T., Wenrui Zhang, F.: ESG performance, institutional investors' preference and financing constraints: empirical evidence from China. In: Borsa Istanb. Rev., Environmental, Social and Governance (ESG) and Sustainable Finance, vol. 22, S157–S168 (2022)
6. Jieying Gao, F., Dongxiao Chu, S., Jun Zheng, T., Tao Ye, F.: Environmental, social and governance performance: can it be a stock price stabilizer? J. Clean. Prod. **379**, 134705 (2022)
7. Dadi Wang, F., Zhongjuan Sun, S., Kai Wang, T., Han Zhang, F.: China ESG Development Report 2021, 1st edn. Economy & Management Publishing House, Beijing (2022)
8. Oikonomou, I., Brooks, C., Pavelin, S.: The interactive financial effects between corporate social responsibility and irresponsibility. ICMA Centre Discussion Papers in Finance (2012)
9. Godfrey, P.C., Merrill, C.B., Hansen, J.M.: The relationship between corporate social responsibility and shareholder value: an empirical test of the risk management hypothesis. Strateg. Manag. J. **30**(4), 425–445 (2009)
10. Lewis Tian, F.: Unraveling the relationship between ESG and corporate financial performance – logistic regression model with evidence from China. SSRN Electron. J. https://doi.org/10.2139/ssrn.3897207 (2021)
11. Changhong Zhao, F., et al.: ESG and corporate financial performance: empirical evidence from China's listed power generation companies. Sustainability **10**, 2607 (2018)
12. Nils Engelhardt, F., Jens Ekkenga, S., Peter Posch, T.: ESG ratings and stock performance during the COVID-19 Crisis. Sustainability **13**, 7133 (2021)
13. Gunnar Friede, F., Timo Busch, S., Alexander Bassen, T.: ESG and financial performance: aggregated evidence from more than 2000 empirical studies. J. Sustain. Finance Invest. **5**, 210–233 (2015)
14. Xufeng Liu, F., Die Wan, S.: Retail investor trading and ESG pricing in China. Res. Int. Bus. Finance **65**, 101911 (2023)
15. Xiaoke Zhang, F., Xuankai Zhao, S., Linsha Qu, T.: Do green policies catalyze green investment? Evidence from ESG investing developments in China. Econ. Lett. **207**, 110028 (2021)
16. Mahmut Aydoğmuş, F., Güzhan Gülay, S., Korkmaz Ergun, T.: Impact of ESG performance on firm value and profitability. In: Borsa Istanb. Rev., Environmental, Social and Governance (ESG) and Sustainable Finance, vol. 22, S119–S127 (2022)
17. Feng He, F., Cong Ding, S., Wei Yue, T., Guanchun Liu, F.: ESG performance and corporate risk-taking: Evidence from China. Int. Rev. Financ. Anal. **87**, 102550 (2023)

How Does Years Since Immigration to the U.S.A. Affect Hourly Wage?

Shizhe Lyu(✉)

Boston University, Boston, MA 02215, USA
`shizhel@bu.edu`

Abstract. The United States is the country that attracts most of the world's immigration population. This paper serves as a foundation to fulfill the gap from existing studies by exploring the relationship between immigration year and the earnings of immigrants, measured by hourly wage in US dollars. The paper analyzes cross-sectional data from the Current Population Survey (CPS). It concludes with a quadratic empirical model that the relationship between immigration duration and hourly wage is positive but non-linear, with diminishing marginal returns over time. These finding sheds light on the importance of the relationship between the duration of residency in the United States and the earnings of immigrants and provides guidance for future social policy reforms by taking consideration of the race, educational attainment, and gender of the immigrants.

Keywords: Immigration · Labor Market · Race · Quadratic Empirical Model

1 Introduction

Globalization led to an increase in immigration in recent years [1]. This study is dedicated to examining the relationship between an individual's duration of immigration to the United States and earnings. The United States has 14.6% of its residents classified as immigrants [2], which raised the question of how one's immigration status impacts income in the U.S. labor market.

Most previous studies on immigration in the United States emphasize how immigration impacts the U.S. economy and the labor market; less attention and research have been dedicated to focusing on how one's immigration status affects earnings on the personal level [3]. In *Immigration and the Wage Distribution in the United States* [4], researchers investigate the effect of immigration on local Americans' wage distribution and conclude that highly educated and skilled local workers would indeed benefit from immigrants regardless of the skill level of the immigrants, while immigrants would only marginally impact low-wage local workers; and the degree and direction of the effetcs depend on the education and skill levels of the immigrants. In addition, Lin's study suggests that education is a crucial factor in analyzing the relationship between immigration and hourly wage since skill level is closely related to education. Thus, education is included as a control variable, and an interaction term is included to study the impact of immigration duration on hourly wage. Regardless of the divergent research focus and distinct intuition of previous academic research papers, prior studies still shed light and provide valuable insights into this paper.

After careful consideration, it is reasonable to hypothesize that the relationship between years of immigration and an individual's hourly wage would be positive, but perhaps with a diminishing trend, which means that the longer one has stayed and becomes a legal citizen in the United States, the higher his hourly wage would be, and this positive relationship may fade away as the year of residence increases; due to factors such as an increase in experience and skills, tenures, and improvements in the social network. To enhance the precision of predictions and address the potential problem of omitted variable bias, the model includes supplementary control variables such as educational attainment, race, and gender in addition to the main independent and dependent variables.The inclusion of additional control variables serves to enhance the model's capacity to accurately capture the effect of the main variables, as well as control for potential confounding factors besides immigration duration.

The result from the regression result table shows that there is indeed a non-linear, positive but diminishing quadratic relationship between the years one individual immigrates to the United States and his hourly wage, and the immigrants' race, gender, and education do not make significant impact on this relationship.

2 Descriptive Data

2.1 Data Collection

To achieve a thorough investigation into the impact of the duration since immigration on hourly wage, cross-sectional data is collected from IPUMS-CPS (the Current Population Survey) in 2019. In this research paper, immigrants are those who have obtained US citizenship or residence and are legal to embark on a professional career in the US. To eliminate the impact of the recent Covid-19 pandemic on the U.S. economy and immigration policies, the year 2019 is selected as a benchmark for data collection in this study, and no data beyond 2019 is discussed in this paper. Therefore, if an individual immigrated to the U.S. in 1999, it would have a 20 for immigration year variable, indicating the person has immigrated to the U.S. for 20 years.

The data is collected for each observation concerning their immigration year, hourly wage, gender, education level, and race. The main independent variable for this paper is the year of immigration, and the dependent variable is one's hourly wage.

In order to conduct the analysis and gain a more holistic study of the relationship, the educational attainment variable is distinctly categorized into two groups, individuals with high school degrees or above and those without a high school diploma. The scope of this study encompasses three racial groups: white, black, and Asian immigrants. Observations outside of these three race groups are dropped from the analysis, and the remaining 1,106 observations are utilized to successfully conduct empirical research on the relationship between one's immigration year and hourly wage.

2.2 Data Description

Hourly Wage. It represents the hourly wage of an individual, measured in US dollars in 2019.

Year of Immigration. It represents the number of years the individual has immigrated to the US before year 2019, measured in years in 2019.

Education. It is a binary variable for representing the highest education level one has obtained in 2019, $= 1$ if one has obtained high school degree and above; 0 otherwise.

Race. It is a categorical variable for representing three major races, $= 0$ if race is white (baseline); $= 1$ if race is black; $= 2$ if race is Asian only.

Female. It is a binary variable for gender female, $= 1$ if gender is female; 0 otherwise.

3 Econometric Model

$$\begin{aligned} log(hourwage)_i = {} & \beta_0 + \beta_1 immig\_yr_i + \beta_2 educ\_group_i \\ & + \beta_3 female_i + \beta_4 race\_category_i + \beta_5 immig\_yr_i * edu\_group_i \\ & + \beta_6 immig\_yr_i^{\wedge}2 + u_i \end{aligned}$$

Above is the regression model believed to be most plausible to explain the relationship between immigration duration and hourly wage from the collected cross-sectional data in 2019. The chosen regression model involves a multivariable regression with a logged dependent variable on hourly wage and an interaction term between years since immigration and levels of education, as well as a quadratic model on years since immigration. The dependent variable *hourly wage* is a quantitative and continuous variable measured in dollars. The main independent variable is $immig_{yr}$, refers to the number of years one person has immigrated to the United States, with year 2019 as a reference point. The intuitive and initial hypothesis for the relationship between the dependent and independent variable $immig_{yr_i}$ and *hourly wage* is that β_1 is positive; one additional years of immigration would be associated with a higher percentage increase in one's expected hourly wage when holding constant other variables.

The coefficient of $educ\_group_i$ is β_2, and the initial hypothesis is that this coefficient would be positive, meaning that immigrants whose education attainment is high school and above would receive an hourly wage higher than groups of immigrants who did not complete high school, when holding all other variables constant.

An interaction term between the binary education level and immigration duration was created and included in this empirical model to test if the relationship between the dependent and independent variables is non-linear and depends on some other factors, such as education. It is rational to hypothesize that the effect of how many years one has immigrated to the United States on hourly wage depends on the level of education attainment of that immigrant. Furthermore, it is logical to assume that the coefficient of the interaction term β_4 would be negative, indicating that with a higher education level, the impact of one more year since immigration on hourly wage would be less prominent and substantial.

Lastly, a quadratic term is also included to test whether the relationship between years since immigration on hourly wage is diminishing and if the relationship gets stronger or weaker the longer one stays in the United States. By hypothesis, this β_6 coefficient would be negative, indicating that the relationship between years since immigration on hourly wage diminishes.

4 Empirical Analysis

Table 1. Regression results.

Variables	(1)	(2)	(3)	(4)	(5)
	Hourly Wage	loghourly_wage	Hourly Wage	Hourly Wage	Hourly Wage
Years Since Immigration	0.113***	0.00597***	0.113***	0.0772***	0.244***
	(0.0228)	(0.000961)	(0.0227)	(0.0182)	(0.0594)
High School Degree or above			5.106***	4.233***	5.217***
			(0.482)	(0.780)	(0.489)
Female			−3.013***	-3.039***	−3.035***
			(0.618)	(0.619)	(0.617)
White			−1.004	−1.007	−0.959
			(0.667)	(0.666)	(0.665)
Black			3.868***	3.892***	3.800***
			(1.105)	(1.108)	(1.100)
immigyr_educ				0.0452	
				(0.0330)	
c.immig_yr#c.immig_yr					−0.00267**
					(0.00122)
Constant	15.69***	2.646***	12.72***	13.42***	11.58***
	(0.516)	(0.0231)	(0.608)	(0.523)	(0.739)
Observations	1,106	1,106	1,106	1,106	1,106
Adj. R-squared	0.018	0.028	0.105	0.105	0.107

Robust standard errors in parentheses
*** $p < 0.01$, ** $p < 0.05$, * $p < 0.1$.

In model (1), the coefficient on main independent variable $immig\_yr_i$ is 0.113, which points out that there is a positive relationship between immigration duration and one's hourly wage; one additional year one individual has immigrated to the United States is associated with a $0.113 increase in expected hourly wage. The coefficient is statistically significant at 1% significance level, as indicated by the regression result table (Table 1).

In model (2), logged hourly wage variable is introduced as it is hypothesized that it would be reasonable to talk about changes in hourly wage in terms of percentage change instead of unit changes. The coefficient of the independent variable on the dependent variable is 0.00597, which can be interpreted as one additional year in immigration is associated with a 0.58% increase in expected hourly wage, and this relationship is statistically significant at a 1% significance level.

In order to determine whether the simple linear regression or the logged simple regression would be a better fit, a 10-step process is carried out to compare the R-squared of the log-y model (2) and the linear-y model (1). After a few steps on Stata, it turns out that the regular simple linear regression model (1) would be a better model for this data with a higher R-squared of 0.0192, as comparing to the log-y model (2) where the R-squared is only 0.01844164. As a result, future regression models would only be using the regular dependent variable, instead of log(y).

Moreover, in order to eliminate potential omitted variable bias, three more control variables education level, gender, and race are based on model (1). However, the coefficient of the model (3) is once again 0.113, and this is significant at 1% significance level. This result suggests that perhaps education level, gender, and race do not cause bias on the dependent variable. Although the educational attainment, gender and race variables may not cause omitted variable bias, it would still be wise to keep them in the regression because the coefficient on these variables are still statistically significant at 1% significance level, indicating that they are still correlated and have impacts on the dependent variable.

The study introduced the interaction term in model (4) and the interaction term between immigration year and education level is statistically insignificant at the 10% significance level. With the insignificant result I observed, I decided to test this further with a graphical representation below (Fig. 1).

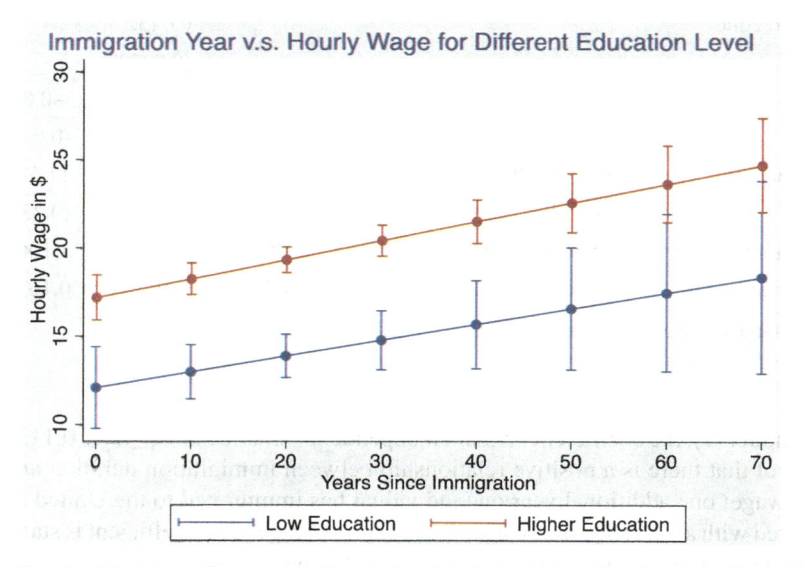

Fig. 1. Graph of the interaction term on the relationship between immigration duration and hourly wage.

After generating a scatterplot for this model, the regression lines turned out to be approximately parallel and the gap between the two scatterplots is approximately the same. Noticeably and intuitively, the immigrants with a low education level appeared to have a lower hourly wage, as illustrated by the lower y-intercept, when comparing to groups of immigrants with higher education level as demonstrated by the red regression line. Despite that the two regression lines have different starting point, they appear to have the same or similar slopes, which corresponding to the coefficient β_5 in our empirical model, indicating that perhaps that the coefficient on the interaction term is insignificant and there is no statistically difference for relationship between years since immigration on hourly wage between immigrants without high school degree and immigrants with high school degree or further education, put differently, the return of being immigrants would be the same for both low education and high education immigrants. Therefore, including an interaction term in the empirical model may not bring any significant changes to the regression model and this finding corresponds well with the insignificant result of the interaction term from the regression result table. Lastly, the overlap of confidence interval for higher levels of years since immigration such as the 60 and 70 group may be due to limited simple size in these two categories.

Model (5) is a quadratic model intended to test if the relationship between immigration duration on hourly wage depends on immigration duration. The coefficient β_1 on independent variable is 0.244 and this is positive and statistically significant at 1% significance level. The coefficient β_6 is −0.00267 and statistically significant at 5%. The interpretation of the coefficients is that the effect of years since immigration on hourly wage is positive but diminishing and there will be a turning point at age of approximately 46 years old; also holding constant the immigrants' education level, race and gender, one more year of immigration duration is associated with a $0.244 increase in expected hourly wage, however, with as the immigrates get one year older, this effect will reduce by $0.00267 each year. The adjusted R-squared in model (5) suggests that 10.7% of the variance in hourly wage is explained by number of years since immigration based on my data and model. By conclusion, model (5) would be the best model for our data and analysis (Fig. 2).

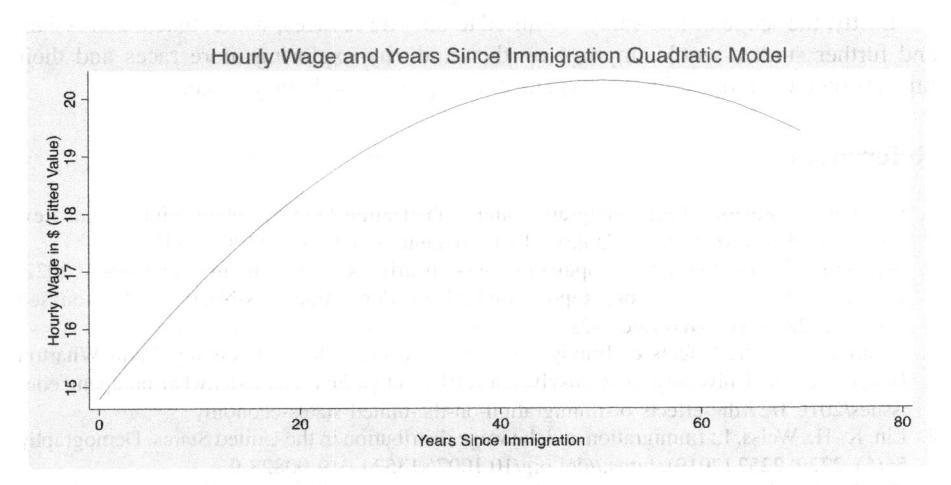

Fig. 2. Graph of quadratic relationship between years since immigration and hourly wage.

5 Conclusion

This paper primarily investigates the relationship between immigration duration on hourly wage, and after constructive data analysis, it is concluded that there is indeed a significant positive but diminishing non-linear relationship between these two variables, and factors such as the immigrant's gender, race and educational attainment correlated with the dependent variable hourly wage. In addition, it is also unexpected that there is no significant difference for people with low levels of education and people who are highly educated, since the return of immigrate one year to the United States longer would be the same for people regardless of their educational attainment.

The study findings reveal a positive yet declining association between the length of time spent in immigration and hourly wage. Furthermore, the relationship remains unchanged regardless of the level of education attained by immigrants. The results suggest that individuals considering a long-term career and permanent settlement in the United States may benefit more from allocating their financial resources towards earlier migration, as opposed to investing heavily in higher education such as obtaining a college degree or higher.

Since the scope of this study is limited to datasets prior to 2019 and restricted to only immigrants to the United States, researchers would find it worthwhile to expand on this study by looking at datasets and similar issues in other countries that rely heavily on the immigrant communities, such as Canada and Australia [5]. In addition, in recent years, with the incessant disruption to society brought by the pandemic, there have been some tight controls regarding immigration policies, such as border controls and reduction on international flights. Future research could further investigate the impact of the pandemic on the immigrant group with a difference-in-difference model for times before and after the pandemic or policy changes about Covid-19. In addition, researchers interested in this topic of study would collect and utilize panel data to further investigate the relationship between immigration duration and hourly wage.

Lastly, the scope of this study is limited to only three races, white, black, and Asian, and further studies would improve on this study by exploring more races and their impacts on the relationship of years since immigration on hourly wage.

References

1. Leblang, D., Peters, M.E.: Immigration and globalization (and deglobalization). Ann. Rev. Polit. Sci. 25(1) (2022). https://doi.org/10.1146/annurev-polisci-051120-105059
2. McHugh, P.: Foreign-born population hits nearly 48 million in September 2022. CIS.org (2022). https://cis.org/Report/ForeignBorn-Population-Hits-Nearly-48-Million-September-2022. Accessed 6 Dec 2022
3. Wharton PPI. The Effects of Immigration on the United States' Economy. Penn Wharton Budget Model; University of Pennsylvania (2016). https://budgetmodel.wharton.upenn.edu/issues/2016/1/27/the-effects-of-immigration-on-the-united-states-economy
4. Lin, K.-H., Weiss, I.: Immigration and the wage distribution in the United States. Demography 56(6), 2229–2252 (2019). https://doi.org/10.1007/s13524-019-00828-9
5. The Top Sending Countries of Immigrants in Australia, Canada, and the United States (2018). Migrationpolicy.org. https://www.migrationpolicy.org/programs/data-hub/top-sending-countries-immigrants-australia-canada-and-united-states

A Controversy in Sustainable Development: How Does Gender Diversity Affect the ESG Disclosure?

Bolin Fu[1(✉)], Keqing Wang[2], and Tianxin Zhou[3]

[1] School of Social Science, University of California Irvine, Irvine 92612, USA
fubolinzzz@gmail.com
[2] School of Economics, University of Xi'an Finance and Economics, Xi'an 710038, China
[3] School of International College Beijing, China Agricultural University, Beijing 100080, China

Abstract. As sustainable development is valued by more and more companies, the Environment, Society, and Governance (ESG) have become the standard for companies, investors, and policymakers to examine their strategies and investments. Recently, there has been increasing evidence that a company's women employees can bring a powerful impact on a company's strategies and development. This article combines the topics of both gender diversity and ESG disclosure and explores the relationship between them in a deeper insight. To this end, this research uses the regression model to use samples collected from A-share listed companies in the Shanghai and Shenzhen Stock Exchanges to discover the relationship between the present or proportion of women in Top Management Teams (TMT as follows) and the disclosure of ESG performance. This model shows that the presence of women and the proportion of women in TMT can positively affect ESG disclosure scores. This result provides valuable insight for companies, investors, and policymakers into the relationship between gender diversity in TMT and ESG disclosure, emphasizing the implicit values laying under women leaders in sustainable development and proposing another strategy for the century's goal of human sustainable development.

Keywords: ESG · Top Management Team · Gender Diversity · Women · Upper Echelon Theory

1 Introduction

Human beings' excessive deprivation of the natural environment and resources has made sustainable development and environmental protection the most significant challenge human development faces in the 21st century. The pandemic sweeping the world has also forced human society to pay more attention to future development and blueprints. Global warming, natural disasters, and more human problems make our society urgently require more changes and adjustments. Because of this, Environment, Society, and Governance

---

B. Fu, K. Wang and T. Zhou—These authors contributed equally to this work and should be considered co-first authors.

(ESG) has gradually become the vane of more enterprises and companies and have attracted the attention of many investors and government departments. ESG factors help companies and investors assess the non-financial risks and opportunities of an investment or business, including issues related to climate change, human rights, and other social and environmental issues. Some companies are also looking for ways to improve the disclosure of ESG performance in the composition of the TMT. Although there is extensive analysis examines firm characteristics and financial performance, little attention has been paid to how the gender distribution at the top management teams of companies affects ESG performance. Gender diversity and women proportion is one of the leading indicators to characterize top management group and has a dominant influence on the company's decision-making and development direction. This article is dedicated to studying the relationship between the proportion of female members in the TMT and ESG disclosure.

The research results can offer companies, investors, and policymakers a better implication or reference when appointing top member groups and help achieve better ESG disclosure performance by controlling the ratio of top management men and women as they seek to improve sustainability, diversity, and corporate governance practices. In the context of the increasing pursuit of gender equality in society, more and more companies recruit more female employees and female top management members. The value of female members to firms and the impact they have on firm decision-making and planning of companies have been the focus of recent research. The majority of research has discovered that the leadership styles of women tend to be more collaborative and goal-oriented. They achieve this by fostering participation and knowledge exchange among team members and by establishing and sustaining clear channels of communication with those they manage [1], which, we hypothesized, is favorable for enhancing ESG performance. By examining the relationship between TMT gender diversity and ESG disclosure, we can better understand how gender diversity and sustainability practices interact and influence each other.

This paper is organized into five following sections: the first section is the introduction of the study that demonstrates the basic background information, research questions, and the significance behind the result. The second section is the literature review and hypothesis. The third section is the methodology, which displays the data sources, variables, regression model, descriptive statistics, and correlation analysis. The fourth section is the results of operating the models, which summarizes the overall data association and evaluates the hypothesis. The fifth section is the conclusion which summarizes the results, findings, and research expectations of the final study.

2 Literature Review and Hypothesis Development

ESG, as a new concept being valued and put forward in recent years, brings many benefits to enterprises. ESG is comprehensive, clear, extensible to the classification system, and widely applicable to all industries. Moreover, it considers the universality and specificity of evaluation, affecting the long-term value of the business. Some studies have found that limited partners are motivated to include ESG because they believe ESG use is more relevant to financial performance [2]. ESG also has a long-term value impact on enterprises: ESG issues should substantially impact the financial performance or investment value of enterprises. This impact must be in the long-term, laying the foundation for sustainable development of the enterprise and marking an important starting point for building all ESG issues. Take the "governance (G)" level issue of "financial information disclosure" as an example. If short-term accounting manipulation is used instead of prudent management to improve financial performance, companies may exhibit higher market capitalization in secondary market transactions. However, in the long run, the market will someday reveal the unfair value of companies. The opacity of financial information disclosure can damage the enterprise's value and even stop operations. The reasons ESG can bring new competitive advantages to enterprise investments are varying and diverse. Firstly, it breaks through the boundary of traditional ownership advantage and forms a new asset advantage. Secondly and more importantly, it improves the legitimacy of investment because the distinctive feature of ESG is its legitimacy [3]. The ESG is a UN compact organization that puts forward a relatively clear classification principle for "sustainable development" related issues. Better ESG disclosure indicates healthier firms can be and hence can trade at higher prices. Therefore, improving ESG disclosure can boost the worth of the company and the profit of their investment, bringing many benefits to the company [4].

There are many ways to push companies to strengthen ESG disclosure. Digital finance can help to improve corporations' ESG performance by reducing their financial constraints [5]. Enterprises in sensitive industries generally have superior environmental performance compared to other enterprises [6]. The ESG perceptions of companies' executives have a very important role in improving corporate green innovation [7]. Through creating the ESG criteria, companies will gain more awareness to strengthen their ESG ratings to attract investment funds and financing [8]. Overall, there are many different factors that affect the disclosure of ESG.

There are several articles discussing the impact of gender diversity on ESG disclosure and performance. For example, Shakil studied the moderating effect of ESG controversy and gender diversity on the board and he found that the ESG controversy and gender diversity on the board significantly moderated the relationship between ESG and financial risk [9]. Furthermore, he also found that gender diversity on the board significantly impacts ESG performance. However, the impact of gender equality in top management teams on ESG disclosure needs to be explored and tested, which is what we want to study.

Top-level theory suggests that, among other factors, the characteristics of senior executives influence a company's strategic decisions. Thus, even if all other conditions are equal in decision-making, the outcome may vary from company to company [10]. When there are more women at the leadership level, companies' performance may improve. Moreover, start-ups led by women are more likely to be successful, and innovative companies with a higher proportion of women in the top management team may have higher profits. There is a comprehensive analysis of 95 studies on gender differences showing that women are more competent in leadership skills, although men are usually more confident.

In a study, Rosener found that female leaders prefer interactions and their leadership styles are more instrumental, so they encourage the input and sharing of information between people and always create open communication channels with subordinates [1]. Other researchers showed that women are more willing to be collaborative than men in organizational settings [11]. In the United States today, women tend to be more pragmatic. In addition, existing research suggests that women are more risk-averse [12], better monitored [13], and more focused on the long term when developing strategies [14]. These behaviors, called feminine management styles, promote critical information sharing and efficient operation of the business [15]. Some studies said that women on the board and in the top management team can bring positive influences to business performance [16]; and female leadership is seen as a corporate performance driver.

The leadership styles of women are quite different from the traditional leadership of men [17, 18], and women have their own advantages. Women are generally more prosocial than men. In an experiment exploring whether gender differences in prosocial behavior are found in some economic games, Kamas and Preston discovered that women have a more significant prosocial response than men because of women's higher level of empathy, which means that women tend to make more prosocial behaviors or decisions in the face of social events such as charity donation [19].

To sum up, we propose the following two hypotheses:

Hypothesis 1: Having women in the TMT can enhance the disclosure of ESG performance;
Hypothesis 2: The more significant the proportion of women in the TMT, the stronger the disclosure of ESG will be.

3 Methodology

3.1 Data Sources

We chose samples from A-share listed companies in the Shanghai and Shenzhen Stock Exchanges between 2007 and 2020. Our original data is from CSMAR and WIND which are two authoritative databases in China. The data we use is panel data. We chose the Bloomberg ESG disclosure score as our dependent variable. We deleted the companies in the monetary financial service industry and only kept those normally listed companies. To avoid the effect from extreme values, we minorize the main continuous variables at the 1% level. After processing data, we finally obtained 9912 observations. The data processing software we use is Stata15.

3.2 Variables

Dependent Variable. The Bloomberg ESG disclosure score reflects the quantity of ESG information a company discloses to the public. The higher the ESG disclosure score, the more non-financial information is disclosed [20]. And we name our dependent variable as *ESG1*.

Independent Variables. Because we want to analyze the impact of gender equality on the corporate ESG disclosure, we choose two measurements as our independent variables, including whether there are women in the TMT (named as *vTMTfemdummy*, No-0, Yes-1) and the percentage of women in the TMT (named as *vTMTfemper*).

Control Variables. Refer to existing research [20, 21], we chose the following variables as our control variables: *roa* (return on assets, ratio of net profit to shareholders' equity), *lnTA* (the logarithm of total assets), *leverage* (total liabilities divide total assets), *bodysize* (the size of the board, the logarithm of the number of people in the board), *insholdper* (proportion of shares held by institutional investors), *age* (duration of company listing, current year minus list year), *tang* (asset structure = (net fixed assets + net amount of inventory)/total assets), and *ppe* (fixed assets ratio = total non-current assets/total assets). In order to control the influence of industry and time, we set an industry dummy variable *industry1* according to the industry classification standard in 2012 of China Securities Regulatory Commission, and also set a time dummy variable *year*.

The main variables and their measurement methods are shown in Table 1.

Table 1. The main variables and their measurement methods.

Dependent Variable	ESG1	ESG disclosure score from Bloomberg
Independent variables	vTMTfemdummy	whether there are women in TMT, No-0, Yes-1
	vTMTfemper	the percentage of women in TMT
Control variables	roa	return on assets, the ratio of net profit to shareholders' equity
	lnTA	the logarithm of total assets
	leverage	total liabilities divide total assets
	bodsize	the size of the board, the logarithm of the number of people in the board
	insholdper	proportion of shares held by institutional investors
	age	duration of company listing, current year minus list year
	tang	asset structure = (net fixed assets + net amount of inventory)/total assets
	ppe	fixed assets ratio = total non-current assets/total assets
	industry1	industry dummy variable
	year	time dummy variable

3.3 Regression Model

To test our hypothesis, we use the following model:

$$ESG1 = \beta 0 + \beta 1 fem + \beta 2 roa + \beta 3 leverage + \beta 4 lnTA + \beta 5 age$$
$$+ \beta 6 bodsize + \beta 7 tang + \beta 8 ppe + \beta 9 insholdper + u$$

We select two measurements to analyze the impact of gender equality on corporate ESG disclosure, including whether there are women in TMT and the percentage of women in TMT. The *vTMTfemdummy* is used for testing hypothesis 1 and the *vTMTfemper* is used for testing hypothesis 2.

3.4 Descriptive Statistics

Table 2 shows the descriptive statistics for all variables. The average ESG disclosure score of all observations is about 20.71, showing that these companies have relatively low ESG disclosure score. About 61% companies have women in their top management teams. And on average, the percentage of women in top management teams of these companies is less than 15%, which is a small number.

Table 2. The descriptive statistics for all variables.

Variable	Obs	Mean	Std.Dev.	Min	Max
ESG1	9,912	20.71	7.012	1.240	64.11
vTMTfemdummy	9,912	0.610	0.488	0	1
vTMTfemper	9,912	0.147	0.157	0	1
roa	9,912	0.0529	1.094	−3.164	108.4
leverage	9,912	0.478	0.215	−0.195	7.034
lnTA	9,912	23.11	1.367	16.16	28.64
age	9,912	13.18	6.738	−1	30
bodsize	9,912	2.179	0.204	1.099	2.890
tang	9,912	0.385	0.187	1.48e-05	0.971
ppe	9,912	0.465	0.221	0.000442	0.983
insholdper	9,912	0.532	0.228	6.00e-06	1.011

3.5 Correlation Analysis

The Pearson correlation analysis results of all variables are shown in Table 3. We can see that besides our two independent variables, there is no strong correlation between other variables. And we will put these two independent variables into two regression equations to do the test independently.

Table 3. The Pearson correlation analysis results of all variables.

	ESG1	vTMTfemdummy	vTMTfemper	roa	leverage	lnTA	age
ESG1	1						
vTMTfemdummy	−0.0198	1					
vTMTfemper	−0.0680	0.748	1				
roa	−0.0189	−0.00960	−0.00610	1			
leverage	0.128	−0.0966	−0.138	−0.0626	1		
lnTA	0.444	−0.0769	−0.147	−0.0549	0.482	1	
age	0.227	−0.0320	−0.0553	0.000300	0.246	0.307	1
bodsize	0.0978	−0.0731	−0.132	−0.0120	0.114	0.209	0.0981
tang	0.0799	−0.117	−0.142	−0.0305	0.304	0.158	0.136
ppe	0.139	−0.0647	−0.0609	−0.0294	−0.00710	0.121	0.144
insholdper	0.244	−0.0798	−0.122	−0.00500	0.186	0.454	0.206
	bodsize	tang	ppe	insholdper			
bodsize	1						
tang	0.124	1					
ppe	0.137	0.223	1				
insholdper	0.208	0.135	0.0828	1			

4 Results

The regression results of hypothesis testing are shown in Table 4.

The first column tests the impact of whether or not there are women in top management teams on companies' ESG disclosure score. The *vTMTfemdummy* is statistically significant at 1% level (p < 0.001) and it is positively associated with *ESG1* ($\beta 1 = 0.587$). It shows that if there are women in a TMT, the ESG disclosure of a company will be higher than without women. Our hypothesis 1 has been tested.

The second column tests the effects of the percentage of women in TMT on companies' ESG disclosure score. The *vTMTfemper* is statistically significant at 1% level (p < 0.01) and it is also positively associated with *ESG1* ($\beta 1 = 1.046$). It shows that the higher the percentage of women in a TMT is, the higher the ESG disclosure of a company is. Our hypothesis 2 has been tested.

Table 4. The regression results of hypothesis testing.

	(1)	(2)
vTMTfemdummy	0.587***	
	(4.63)	
roa	0.0129	0.0111
	(0.23)	(0.20)
leverage	−2.526***	−2.564***
	(−7.16)	(−7.26)
lnTA	2.159***	2.166***
	(35.76)	(35.79)
age	0.0841***	0.0838***
	(7.99)	(7.95)
bodsize	0.252	0.270
	(0.81)	(0.86)
tang	1.446***	1.389***
	(3.71)	(3.56)
ppe	0.537	0.550
	(1.49)	(1.52)
insholdper	2.054***	2.053***
	(6.54)	(6.53)
vTMTfemper		1.046**
		(2.61)
_cons	−31.88***	−31.84***
	(−23.68)	(−23.45)
N	9912	9912
industry1	Yes	Yes
year	Yes	Yes

t statistics in parentheses.
* $p < 0.05$, ** $p < 0.01$, *** $p < 0.001$.

5 Conclusion

As a result, this research shows the relationship between gender diversity in TMT and ESG disclosure. We use a regression model focusing on the impacts of women's presence and percentage in TMT on ESG disclosure scores. Research findings strongly indicate that the presence and higher percentage of women in TMT are positively associated with higher ESG disclosure scores, providing statistically important associations to support our previous hypothesis.

The research's results offer companies, investors, and policymakers a better implication or reference when appointing top management team members, and help achieve better ESG disclosure performance by hiring more female leaders in the management teams as they seek to improve sustainability, diversity, and corporate governance practices. Companies with diverse leadership teams that include women or a high proportion of women are more likely to prioritize ESG issues and disclose their ESG practices, which can help improve their reputation and long-term financial performance. More companies, who are more likely to improve their reputation and long-term financial performance through better ESG disclosures, are expected to recruit more female executives, according to the results of this experiment. Our conclusions serve as evidence to provide a clearer direction for two social dilemmas of sustainable development and gender equality. The importance and value of women are recognized to a higher degree, and the wage level and employment rate of women are increased. At the same time, it helps the company to make more environmentally friendly decisions to improve the company's ESG disclosure and increase the social value and investment profits brought by the company. It points out another direction for the century's goal of human sustainable development.

Overall, this research provides valuable insight into the relationship between gender diversity in TMT and ESG performance, emphasizing the need for more diversity and sustainability practices in business leadership. By promoting gender diversity to enhance ESG performance, companies and investors can create long-term value for all stakeholders and contribute to more sustainable future development.

References

1. Rosener, J.B.: America's Competitive Secret: Utilizing Women as a Management Strategy. Oxford University Press, New York (1995)
2. McCahery, J., Pudschedl, P., Steindl, M.: Institutional investors, alternative asset managers and ESG preferences. Eur. Bus. Organ. Law Rev. **23**(4), 821–868 (2022). https://doi.org/10.1007/s40804-022-00264-0
3. Xie, H., Lyu, X.: Responsible Multinational Investment: ESG and Chinese OFDI (2022)
4. Mercereau, B., Melin, L., Lugo, M.M.: Creating shareholder value through ESG engagement. J. Asset Manag. **23**, 550–566 (2022). https://doi.org/10.1057/s41260-022-00270-4
5. Mu, W., Liu, K., Tao, Y., Ye, Y.: Digital finance and corporate ESG. Financ. Res. Lett. **51**, 103426 (2023). https://doi.org/10.1016/j.frl.2022.103426
6. Garcia, A.S., Mendes-Da-Silva, W., Orsato, R.J.: Sensitive industries produce better ESG performance: evidence from emerging markets. J. Clean. Prod. **150**, 135–147 (2017). https://doi.org/10.1016/j.jclepro.2017.02.180
7. Wang, D., Luo, Y., Hu, S., Yang, Q.: Executives' ESG cognition and enterprise green innovation: evidence based on executives' personal microblogs. Front. Psychol. **13**, 1053105 (2022). https://doi.org/10.3389/fpsyg.2022.1053105
8. Passas, I., Ragazou, K., Zafeiriou, E., Garefalakis, A., Zopounidis, C.: ESG controversies: a quantitative and qualitative analysis for the sociopolitical determinants in EU firms. Sustainability **14**, 12879 (2022). https://doi.org/10.3390/su141912879
9. Shakil, M.H.: Environmental, social and governance performance and financial risk: moderating role of ESG controversies and board gender diversity. Resour. Policy **72**, 102144 (2021). https://doi.org/10.1016/j.resourpol.2021.102144

10. Kind, F.L., Zeppenfeld, J., Lueg, R.: The impact of chief executive officer narcissism on environmental, social, and governance reporting. Bus. Strategy Environ. 1–19 (2023). https://doi.org/10.1002/bse.3375
11. Ravasi, D., Schultz, M.: Responding to organizational identity threats: exploring the role of organizational culture. Acad. Manag. J. **49**(3), 433–458 (2006)
12. Palvia, A., Vähämaa, E., Vähämaa, S.: Are female CEOs and chairwomen more conservative and risk averse? Evidence from the banking industry during the financial crisis. J. Bus. Ethics **131**(3), 1–18 (2014)
13. Adams, R., Ferreira, D.: Women in the boardroom and their impact on governance and performance. J. Financ. Econ. **94**(2), 291–309 (2009)
14. Reguera-Alvarado, N., de Fuentes, P., Laffarga, J.: Does board gender diversity influence financial performance? Evidence from Spain. J. Bus. Ethics **141**(2), 337–350 (2015)
15. Van Knippenberg, D., De Dreu, C.K.W., Homan, A.C.: Work group diversity and group performance: an integrative model and research agenda. J. Appl. Psychol. **89**(6), 1008–1022 (2004)
16. Moreno-Gómez, J., Lafuente, E., Vaillant, Y.: Gender diversity in the board, women's leadership and business performance. Gender Manag. Int. J. (2018). https://doi.org/10.1108/GM-05-2017-0058
17. Pegues, D.A., Cunningham, C.J.L.: Diversity in leadership: where's the love for racioethnic minorities? Bus. J. Hisp. Res. **4**, 12–17 (2010)
18. Mc kinsey and company. Women matter 2: female leadership, a competitive edge for the future. In: Company, m. K (2008)
19. Kamas, L., Preston, A.: Empathy, gender, and prosocial behavior. J. Behav. Exp. Econ. **92**, 101654 (2021). https://doi.org/10.1016/j.socec.2020.101654
20. Yu, E.P., Luu, B.V.: International variations in ESG disclosure – do cross-listed companies care more? Int. Rev. Financ. Anal. **75**, 101731 (2021). https://doi.org/10.1016/j.irfa.2021.101731
21. Dong, J., Deng, H., Zhao, G.: CEO Overpayment and Strategic Change: From the Perspective of Behavioral Agency Theory (2020)

Controlling Shareholders' Equity Pledges, Environmental Regulations and Corporate Green Performance—Based on Data from Listed Companies in Highly Polluting Industries

Mingfei Chen(✉)

Accounting, Zhongnan University of Economics and Law, Wuhan 430073, China
chenmingfei@stu.zuel.edu.cn

Abstract. The proposal of "Carbon Neutral" in the 14th Five-Year Plan highlights China's deep involvement in global environmental governance and re-emphasises the importance of green and low-carbon transformation in the new development pattern. As an emerging financial product, equity pledge not only provides sufficient cash flow, but also provides a convenient new channel for commercial loans supported by the financial market. Therefore, the ways in which controlling shareholders choose equity pledge are increasing. But actually, as a common financing practice for controlling shareholders in China, equity pledging has increased the risks borne by enterprises while providing financing facilities for shareholders. This study uses the Tobit model to investigate the impact of controlling shareholders' equity pledges on corporate green innovation, to investigate the mediating and regulating effects, to explore the role of internal corporate governance and external environmental regulation in the impact mechanism. This study will provide a new perspective on the economic consequences of shareholders' equity pledging behaviour and provide new ideas for promoting the green development of highly polluting enterprises.

Keywords: Equity Pledges · Environmental Regulation · Green Performance · Tobit Model

1 Introduction

1.1 Background

In order to deal with the increasing occurrence of major environmental pollution incidents, green R&D institutions need to be vigorously promoted to provide technical support for an effective response to environmental pollution problems. Yang Dong and Chai Huimin [1] consider green technology innovation as an exploratory innovation of new knowledge and technological routes compared to previous innovation activities, and is expected by companies to achieve win-win goals in terms of environmental and economic benefits. Zhang et al. [2] explain that companies should take into account the wishes of stakeholders other than shareholders and implement green technology innovation to obtain more resources to improve their business conditions. When environmental stakeholders are dissatisfied with the company, the implementation of environmental responsibility can fully resolve the conflicts with stakeholders, deepen the cooperation and communication with stakeholders, and correctly handle the stakeholder relationship in economic, legal and ethical factors, thus helping the company to carry out green innovation activities [3]. Research by Wang Yun et al. [4] suggests that the news media is an important information intermediary that can help companies change their development paths according to the demands of their stakeholders. Zhao et al. [5] and Yang et al. [6] argue that the media plays an important role in the management of firms as an extra-legal monitoring mechanism that can force the correction of irregularities and thus improve the innovative behavior of firms. Chen Hong et al. [7], Chen et al. [8] state that effective control activities can improve management's risk tolerance or reduce unnecessary corporate risk through activities such as segregation of duties and operational performance evaluation, which in turn promote innovative output. Wang et al. [9] and Tang Hua et al. [10] found that high quality internal controls can enhance innovation performance. Lee [11] identified buyer influence, government involvement and green supply chain maturity as the main factors driving firms to engage in green behaviors. According to Demirel et al. [12], the motivation for companies to adopt green innovation is directly influenced by environmental regulation and cost-cutting strategies. According to Eiadat et al. [13], market tools can encourage green innovation and assist businesses in creating incentives for a circular economy. Chang [14] conducted an empirical study of Taiwan's manufacturing sector and came to the conclusion that business environmental ethics support the development of green products and foster long-term competitive advantage. Wang et al. [15] showed that local government quality can positively moderate the impact of environmental regulations on firms' green product and process innovation. Song et al. [16] found that green technology innovation in China is influenced by domestic independent R&D and international technology spillover.

1.2 Significance

Through reading a large amount of literature, the current paper summarizes the relevant literature on equity pledges, surplus management and the relationship between the two. In terms of equity pledges, controlling shareholders pledge their equity for the purpose of financing, increasing control and encroaching on the interests of small and medium-sized shareholders, which can have a negative impact on the company. According to existing international research findings, the pledge of controlling shareholders' equity is positively correlated with surplus management. Firstly, the research objects are not targeted. Almost no scholars have previously studied the connection between controlling shareholders' equity pledges, environmental regulation, and corporate green innovation. Secondly, the moderating role of other factors has not been considered. Green innovation is a systematic and complex process, and the current research framework on the mechanism affecting green innovation is rather vague. Thirdly, in the past, when studying the impact of policies, a single policy was usually chosen, which is a one-sided issue and may lead to biased findings. Fourth, there is a certain lack of research perspective. Therefore, this study selects A-share listed companies in high-pollution industries as the research object, and uses the Tobit model to explore the influence mechanism of controlling shareholders' equity pledges on corporate green innovation, and to investigate its mediating and regulating effects, and to explore the role of internal corporate governance and external government environmental regulation in the influence mechanism. This study will provide a new perspective on the economic consequences of shareholders' equity pledging behavior, and provide new ideas for promoting the green development of highly polluting enterprises.

2 Theoretical Analysis and Research Hypothesis

There are currently two theories explaining how equity commitments made by controlling shareholders of heavily polluting companies affect corporate green performance.

On the one hand, equity pledges in highly polluting companies are beneficial to improving corporate green performance. In a time of increasingly stringent environmental regulation, government environmental authorities are constantly increasing their efforts to regulate and punish environmental violations. Companies face increasing costs for environmental violations. Secondly, from the standpoint of media external governance, with China's ardent promotion of ecological civilization, media coverage of business environmental protection activities has increased over the past few years. Once a company's environmental violations are reported, there is a high risk that the market value will be reduced. In addition, from a public governance perspective, environmental protection is becoming more and more of a public concern and with the internet becoming more and more developed, media reports of corporate violations will quickly spread and leave a negative impact on the public mind. For all three reasons, a reduction in the level of environmental governance during the period of equity pledging could lead to a fall in the share price of the company, which could lead to a transfer of shareholder control and damage the rights of shareholders. Therefore, even though companies face greater earnings pressure and financing constraints during the equity pledge period, shareholders will still maintain a high level of corporate green performance compared to the risk of a transfer of control.

On the other hand, equity pledges of highly polluting firms will inhibit the improvement of corporate green performance established research suggests that equity pledges can create high financing constraints, lower levels of corporate financing and reduced risk-taking capacity, which can lead to more short-sighted levels of investment. At this point, firms are more inclined to forego projects that will increase their long-term value and instead invest in those that have obvious short-term benefits. Investment in environmental protection is difficult to obtain in the short term and has a large externality, so lower environmental expenditure occurs and inhibits green performance.

In summary, the mechanism of the impact of controlling shareholders' equity pledges on the green performance of highly polluting enterprises can be summarized as shown in Fig. 1.

In summary, this project proposes the following competing hypotheses.

H1a: Controlling shareholder equity pledges have a negative impact on corporate green performance.

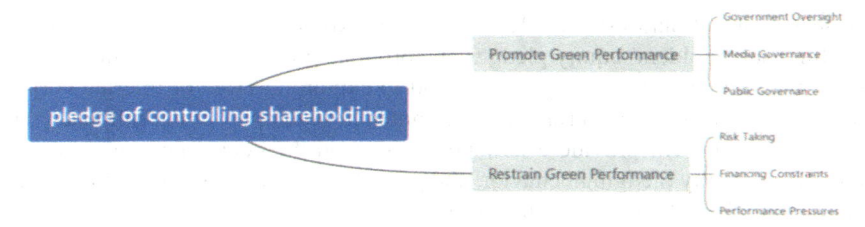

Fig. 1. Impact of controlling shareholders' equity pledges on corporate green performance of highly polluting firms.

H1b: Controlling shareholder equity pledges have a positive impact on corporate green performance.

This project focuses on the role of command-and-control environmental regulation. It is mainly measured by regional pollution emissions. When the intensity of environmental regulation is relatively high, enterprises face greater costs of environmental violations, which bring greater risks to enterprises. During equity pledges, on the other hand, enterprises' risk-taking capacity is reduced. Therefore, stricter environmental regulation measures may lead to higher levels of corporate green performance when the equity of highly polluting firms is pledged. Accordingly, we propose Hypothesis 2.

H2: Firms in regions with higher intensity of environmental regulations have better green performance when controlling shareholder equity pledges occur in highly polluting firms.

3 Main Research Design

3.1 Sample Selection

The article selected Shanghai and Shenzhen main board listed companies in highly polluting industries from 2000–2019 as the research sample. Based on the Guidelines on Industry Classification of Listed Companies revised by the China Securities Regulatory Commission in 2012, heavily polluting industries mainly include coal, mining textile, tannery, paper, petrochemical, pharmaceutical, chemical, metallurgical, thermal power and other 16 industries.

3.2 Data Sources

Data on controlling shareholders' shareholding pledges were mainly obtained from the RESET database and outliers were processed.

The data on environmental regulations were mainly obtained from the China Urban Statistical Yearbook to obtain three categories of pollutants, namely wastewater, SO2 and soot, in order to calculate a comprehensive index of environmental regulations. In addition, we obtained corporate financial data from the Guotaian database.

3.3 Basic Data Processing

The samples of listed companies in the financial sector, ST, *ST and PT were excluded, and the continuous variables were subjected to a 1% upper and lower tail reduction in order to exclude the effect of outliers on the regression results.

3.4 Variable Definitions

Explained Variable. Level of environmental governance: By searching for construction in progress, other payables, and management expenses in the notes of listed firms' financial statements using keywords connected to environmental investment, the pertinent environmental investment data was found. However, as construction in progress, management expenses and other payables belong to both sides of the balance sheet debit and credit, direct summation may involve double counting, therefore, only two items, construction in progress and management expenses, are selected for screening.

Explanatory Variables. Whether the controlling shareholder's shareholding was pledged during the year, with a value of 1 if there was a pledge during the year and 0 otherwise.

Moderating Variables. Environmental regulation intensity: The emissions per unit of pollutant for each city are linearly normalised through the emission data of the three wastes, and the detailed calculation process is as follows.

P1: Each city's unit pollution emissions are linearly standardised. In this article, we primarily calculate three different forms of pollutants: SO2, soot, and wastewater.

$$UE_{ij}^s = [UE_{ij} - \min(UE_j)]/[\max(UE_j - \min(UE_j))] \tag{1}$$

UE_{ij}, Pollution j's output value for pollutant j's per unit emissions in city i.

max (UE_j) and min (UE_j), Maximum and minimum values for each indicator in all cities.

UE_{ij}^s, Standardised values for indicators.

P2: An adjustment factor is employed to approximation the differences in pollutant characteristics because the share of pollutant emissions varies significantly between cities and the intensity of emissions of different pollutants also varies significantly. The adjustment factor is calculated by the formula:

$$W_j = UE_{ij}/\overline{UE_{ij}} \tag{2}$$

$\overline{UE_{ij}}$, Emissions for pollutant j per unit of output in the city during the sample period

P3: Calculating the intensity of command-based environmental regulation in each city.

$$ER_i = \frac{1}{3}\sum_{j=1}^{3} W_j UE_{ij}^s \tag{3}$$

ERi, The intensity of command-based environmental regulation in city i.

Control Variables. Control variables are as follows (see Fig. 2).

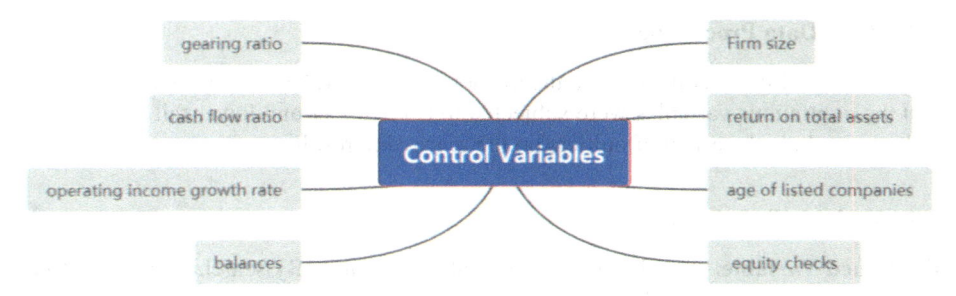

Fig. 2. Control variables.

3.5 Descriptive Statistics

Descriptive statistics are shown in Table 1:

Table 1. Descriptive statistics for key variables.

Variable Name	Mean	Median	Minimum	Maximum	Variance	N
ENVI	15.99	16.44	0	21.82	3.644	4438
Pledge_dum	0.429	0	0	1	0.495	3945
ER	0.135	0.0380	0	2.210	0.303	4438
Size	22.49	22.31	20.12	26.27	1.319	4438
ROA	0.0410	0.0350	−0.157	0.226	0.0570	4438
Lev	0.477	0.489	0.0730	0.911	0.199	4438
CF	0.0630	0.0620	−0.670	0.600	0.0710	4438
Growth	0.168	0.116	−0.418	1.821	0.323	4280
Age	2.198	2.398	0	3.332	0.784	4438
Balance	0.576	0.394	0.0130	2.483	0.562	4438

3.6 Model Construction

Main Regression Equation

$$ENVI = \alpha_0 + \alpha_1 Pledge\_dum + \alpha_2 Size + \alpha_3 ROA + \alpha_4 Age + \alpha_5 Lev + \alpha_6 CF$$
$$+ \alpha_7 Growth + \alpha_8 Balance + Year + Industry \quad (4)$$

Test for Moderating Effects

$$ENVI = \mu_0 + \mu_1 Pledge\_dum + \mu_2 ER + \mu_3 Pledge\_dum * ER + \sum Controls$$
$$+ Year + Industry \quad (5)$$

4 Further Research

4.1 Analysis of Differences in the Impact of Different Types of Environmental Expenditures Affected by Equity Pledges

In the main regression design, the level of environmental governance is measured by all environmental protection related expenditures. This topic will further analyse whether there will be differences in the impact of equity pledges on expensed and capitalised environmental protection expenditures, as shown in Fig. 3.

Fig. 3. Classification of environmental expenditure.

4.2 Analyzing the Impact of Heterogeneous Environmental Regulation

In the main regression equation, we focus on the moderating role of command-and-control environmental regulation, and furthermore we analyse the differences in the role of different types of environmental regulation.

Command-and-control environmental regulation: The number of penalties imposed in environmental cases, with the main data collected manually (crawlers) from legal databases.

Market-incentivised environmental regulation: Measured by emission fees and environmental protection taxes (in 2018 environmental fees will be changed to taxes, after 2018 they will be measured by environmental taxes), data from the RESET database.

Public participation-based environmental regulation: Measured mainly by the number of environmental proposals. The specific measurement criteria are shown in Table 2.

Table 2. Heterogeneous environmental regulation metrics.

Types of environmental regulation	Metrics	Symbols
Command-and-control environmental regulation	Number of penalties for environmental cases	ER1
Market-inspired environmental regulation	Sewage charges and environmental protection taxes	ER2
Public participation in environmental regulation	Number of environmental proposals from CPPCC and NPC	ER3

4.3 Change the Measure of Green Performance

The number of green patent applications of listed companies was obtained through the China Research Data Service Platform. Since there is a path-dependent effect of technological innovation and the effect of environmental regulation may lag behind, a dynamic panel data model with a one-period lag was established to reflect the impact of the accumulated technological innovation and environmental regulation measures on the current period, and a systematic GMM method was used for estimation. The measures of green patent-related variables are as shown in Table 3.

Table 3. Green patents as a measure of green performance.

Variable name	Variable definitions	Variable symbols
Green inventions	GI	ln(Number of corporate green invention applications + 1)
Green Utility Models	GU	ln(Number of corporate green utility model applications + 1)
Green Innovation	CGI	ln(Number of corporate green invention applications + Number of corporate green utility model applications + 1)

An invention patent emphases breakthrough, originality and novelty, and is a groundbreaking upgrade or creation of a technical solution. A utility model patent is generally a new technical solution to the shape, construction or combination of a product, which is at a lower level in terms of technological breakthrough and technology, but has practical utility value. Due to the differences in the way the two types of patents are defined and the application criteria, this topic will further examine the impact of controlling shareholders' equity pledges on both.

5 Robustness Tests

5.1 Endogeneity Tests

The major findings of this study could also be explained by the fact that companies with effective corporate environmental governance are more likely to have equity pledges from large shareholders, have reduced environmental risk, and are less inclined to unwind their positions as a result of a crash. Thus, there may be a serious endogeneity between large shareholder equity pledges and corporate environmental governance.

For this reason, we use the following two methods to mitigate possible bias in the regression results caused by the endogeneity problem.

PSM Test. To screen out the control group with similar characteristics to the treatment group by using companies whose majority shareholders have pledged their shares as the treatment group and companies whose majority shareholders have not pledged their shares as the control group, and re-run the regression, we employ the technique. Specifically, we matched the control group to the treatment group based on all the characteristics variables in the model using a 1:1 non-relaxation with a caliper value set at 0.03. After matching was completed, the regression was repeated according to the model.

Instrumental Variables Approach. To mitigate the endogeneity problem due to reverse causality, we conducted regressions using the instrumental variables approach. Since whether a firm's equity is pledged by a major shareholder is influenced by the regional "pledge culture" [10]. In this project, we refer to the existing literature [10]; Tang Wei et al. [15] and select the average level of pledging (PLEDGE_PROV) in the province where the company is located in the current year as the instrumental variable for whether the company's equity is pledged by the majority shareholder (PLEDGE), using a two-stage regression (2SLS) to test the instrumental variable.

5.2 Replacement of the Measurement of the Explanatory Variables

In the previous regressions, the continuous variable corporate environmental protection investment was used as the explanatory variable. In order to make the results more robust, firstly, we used whether the firm invested in environmental protection (ENVI1), corporate environmental protection expenditure divided by total assets (ENVI2) and corporate environmental protection expenditure divided by operating income (ENVI3) as proxy variables for the explanatory variables to be tested, as shown in Table 4.

Table 4. Alternative measures of the explanatory variables.

Name of the explanatory variable	Symbols	Definition
Environmental expenditure levels	ENVI1	Whether to make environmental related expenditures Yes is assigned a value of 1, no is assigned a value of 0
	ENVI2	Environmental expenditure/total assets
	ENVI3	Environmental expenditure/operating income

5.3 Replacement of the Measurement of Explanatory Variables

This project will employ the percentage of stock pledged by large shareholders as an explanatory variable for robustness testing in order to increase the reliability of the conclusions of this study. As shown in Fig. 4, we calculate Pledge_rate1 and Pledge_rate2 as proxy variables for whether there is equity pledge of controlling shareholders, and refer to the model in the previous section for regression

$$ENVI = \beta_0 + \beta_1 Pledge\_rate_i + \beta_2 Size + \beta_3 ROA + \beta_4 Age + \beta_5 Lev + \beta_6 CF$$
$$+ \beta_7 Growth + \beta_8 Balance + Year + Industry \tag{6}$$

Fig. 4. Alternative measures of explanatory variables.

Pledge rate:
- Pledge_rate1: Number of shares pledged by shareholders of controlling shareholders at the end of the year / Number of shares of listed companies held by controlling shareholders
- Pledge_rate2: Number of shares pledged by shareholders of controlling shareholders at the end of the year / Number of shares of listed companies held by controlling shareholders; Number of shares pledged by shareholders of controlling shareholders at the end of the year / Total number of shares issued and outstanding of all listed companies

6 Conclusion

The findings of the empirical analysis demonstrate that the degree of environmental management is adversely impacted and that substantially polluting enterprises considerably reduce their investment in environmental protection after pledging the stock of their controlling shareholders. This finding remains valid after a series of robustness checks. Additional investigation revealed that the environmental governance of the company can be less affected by equity pledges if there are environmental control mechanisms in place where the company is located. By analysing how equity pledges affect various environmental investments, we also discovered that during the pledge period, businesses increase their expenditures on things like sewage, cleaning, and greening fees in an effort to lower the risk of environmental violations. This is in contrast to the positive impact that pledges have on the level of environmental governance. Also, based on the heterogeneity of enterprises, it is found that the negative impact of controlling shareholder pledges on environmental investments is mainly found in non-state enterprises, and that the negative impact of controlling shareholder pledges on the level of environmental governance is mitigated by the receipt of government subsidies.

The main contributions of the empirical results of this project are: firstly, to further the study of the financial effects of managing shareholder promises. Studies that have already been conducted on the subject of pledging controlling shareholders' shares have generally concentrated on the consequences of corporate operations, such as financing constraints, information asymmetry and the risk of share price collapse. Existing research on corporate environmental governance has focused on government regulation, policy implementation, media governance and executive characteristics, but few papers have looked at controlling shareholders' shareholding pledges to provide evidence from the capital market on the factors influencing corporate environmental governance.

Based on our findings, we propose two main recommendations: Firstly, due to different factors like financial limitations and performance pressure, a controlling shareholder of a highly polluting firm may not make enough current investments in environmental protection. As a result, there will be less chance of environmental infractions during equity commitments, and company value and social value will be more closely aligned.

Secondly, for the government, the level of environmental governance is significantly reduced when the controlling shareholder's equity is pledged. In order to ensure the continued promotion and implementation of environmental governance in China, the relevant authorities should adopt stricter regulations for companies with special circumstances such as equity pledges. The findings of this study demonstrate that an effective system of environmental regulation and government subsidies can reduce the detrimental effects of regulating shareholder commitments on the level of environmental management of firms. Therefore, local governments should adopt the right environmental regulation measures according to the actual situation in each region, and should also provide appropriate government subsidies to reduce the financial pressure of enterprises in environmental management.

References

1. Yang, D., Chai, H.: A review of the drivers of corporate green technology innovation and its performance impact. China Popul. Resourc. Env. **25**(S2), 132–136 (2015)
2. Zhang, Z., Zhang, C., Pei, X.: A study on environmental management system certification and corporate environmental performance. J. Manag. **17**(07), 1043–1051 (2020)
3. Castillo, M.: From corporate social responsibility to global conscious innovation with Mandalah. Glob. Bus. Organ. Excell. **34**(4), 42–49 (2015)
4. Wang, Y., Li, Y., Ma, Z., et al.: Media concerns, environmental regulation and corporate environmental investment. Nankai Manag. Rev. **20**(06), 83–94 (2017)
5. Zhao, L., Zhang, L.: The impact of media attention on firms' green technology innovation: the moderating role of the level of marketization. Manage. Rev. **32**(09), 132–141 (2020)
6. Yang, D., Chen, H., Liu, Q.: Media pressure and corporate innovation. Econ. Res. **52**(08), 125–139 (2017)
7. Chen, H., Na, C., Yutian, M., et al.: A study on internal control and R&D subsidy performance. Manage. World **34**(12), 149–164 (2018)
8. Chen, J., Shu, W.: The impact of management risk appetite on technological innovation - the moderating role of internal control-based. Soft Sci. **35**(03), 76–82 (2021)
9. Wang, Y., Dai, W.: Do internal controls inhibit or promote corporate innovation? – The logic of China. Audit Econ. Res. **34**(06), 19–32 (2019)
10. Tang, H., Wang, L., Cheng, H.: Internal control effectiveness, R&D expenditure and corporate innovation performance - based on empirical data of high-tech firms. Friends Account. **2021**(08), 136–141 (2021)
11. Lee, S.Y.: Drivers for the participation of small and medium-sized suppliers in green supply chain initiatives. Supply Chain Manag. Int. J. **13**(3), 185–198 (2008)
12. Demirel, P., Kesidou, E.: Stimulating different types of eco-innovation in the UK: government policies and firm motivations. Ecol. Econ. **70**(8), 1546–1557 (2011)
13. Eiadat, Y., Kelly, A., Roche, F., et al.: Green and competitive? An empirical test of the mediating role of environmental innovation strategy. J. World Bus. **43**(2), 131–145 (2007)
14. Chang, C.: The influence of corporate environmental ethics on competitive advantage: the mediation role of green innovation. J. Bus. Ethics **104**(3), 1–10 (2011)
15. Wang, F., Jiang, T., Guo, X.: Government quality, environmental regulation and corporate green technology innovation. Sci. Res. Manag. **39**(01), 26–33 (2018)
16. Song, W., Lin, H.: Autonomous R&D, technology spillover and green technology innovation in China. Res. Financ. Econ. **2017**(08), 98–105 (2017)

9789819705221VOL01